the chapters in Part I with the reading selections in Part II and the added reading materials in Part III.

4. Use a workshop approach. Just as students benefit from varied exercises, they profit from varied approaches to a skill. One way to cover a skill is to work through a chapter page by page, alternating between putting some of the material on the board and explaining or reading some of it aloud. When you get to a practice in a chapter, give students a couple of minutes to do the practice. When a majority of the class has finished the practice, call on someone to read the first question and answer it. If the answer is right, say "Good job," and call on someone else to read the next question. If the answer is wrong, say something like "Does anyone have a different answer?" This can lead to a discussion where you can see if students are catching on, and you can find a way to move them in the right direction.

You should feel confident about having students read a sentence or so out loud. Even if they have limited reading skills, a sentence or two will not cause them undue anxiety or embarrassment. On the other hand, reading an entire paragraph may be too much for some students. It is best to call on volunteers for paragraphs or to read them aloud yourself. Or, if there are time constraints, have students read the paragraph silently and then ask them to read aloud the questions that follow the paragraph.

5. Use a small group approach at times. When you get to a review test, you may want to divide the class into groups of four and ask them to work together to do the answers for the test. Tell them that when they are done and everyone in the group agrees on the answers, a representative from the group should go to the board and write down the group's answers. Say, "Let's see which group is first to answer all the questions correctly."

Put a grid such as this one on the board:

	1	2	3	4	5
Kim's Group					
Robert's Group					
Nelson's Group					
Nina's Group					

Students will enjoy the competition, and peer pressure will keep everyone attentive and involved. When all of the groups have finished, you and the class can look at the board together to see just where the groups agree and disagree. You can then focus discussion on answers where there is disagreement.

6. Use a pairs approach at times. Having two students work together on questions is another way to energize students and help them teach one another. When an exercise has been completed by the majority of the class, one way to go over the material is to have one student in each pair read a question and the other student read the answer.

7. Use a one-on-one approach at times. If your class is small, have students work on their own on a given chapter, reading the explanations and doing the activities. Call students up to your desk individually to check their answers and to confer on the skill. Make the conference short—five minutes per student is enough time. Students really benefit from the individualized, personal contact.

8. Evaluate frequently. Students have been conditioned to work hard on tests. Take advantage of this conditioning by giving a lot of tests. The mastery tests in Part I and the combined-skills tests in Part III will give students a chance to see that they are learning the material and will show them that they are capable of success. The tests are also clear signals to students who are not learning the skills. Note that there are over seventy tear-out mastery tests in the book as well as over forty more tests in the *Instructor's Manual and Test Bank* that can be easily duplicated.

When you grade a test, try to include some praise or encouragement for each student. A personal comment such as "Good job, Elena" or "Well done, Hakim" can do wonders for a student's self-esteem.

9. For variety, make some tests count and some not. When it is time to do a test, have students put their names on it and tell them that you may or may not count the test. The fact that you may count the test will ensure that students give their full effort. At times, don't collect the test, but simply go over it in class. Doing so will help to provide immediate feedback to students. Afterwards, you can give another mastery test that will count as a grade.

When tests do count, have students exchange papers. The best way to do this is to collect the papers and distribute them to students in other parts of the room. (Some students resist marking an answer as wrong on a paper that belongs to the person sitting right next to them.) Have class members read and answer the questions as well as grade the papers.

10. Require some writing at the end of each class. To help students integrate what they have learned in a given class, have them do a writing assignment in the last part of the class. One good summarizing activity is to have students write a "Dear _____" letter to a missing classmate, telling him or her what was learned in the class that day. Have students give you the letters before they leave, and explain you will read the letters and then pass them on to the missing student.

Another exercise is to have students write about a reading selection discussed in class. Part III provides three writing assignments for each of the twenty readings in the book. Ask students to choose one of the three and to turn in a paper to you before they leave. In some cases, you may want to make the paper an overnight assignment instead.

These activities will help make your classroom alive and will turn learning into an active process. I think you will find them rewarding, and I encourage you to try them out. I wish you luck!

John Langan

TEN STEPS TO IMPROVING COLLEGE READING SKILLS

THIRD EDITION

JOHN LANGAN

ATLANTIC COMMUNITY COLLEGE

TOWNSEND PRESS   Marlton, NJ 08053

Books in the Townsend Press Reading Series:

GROUNDWORK FOR COLLEGE READING
KEYS TO BETTER COLLEGE READING
TEN STEPS TO BUILDING COLLEGE READING SKILLS, FORM A
TEN STEPS TO BUILDING COLLEGE READING SKILLS, FORM B
TEN STEPS TO IMPROVING COLLEGE READING SKILLS
IMPROVING READING COMPREHENSION SKILLS
TEN STEPS TO ADVANCING COLLEGE READING SKILLS

Books in the Townsend Press Vocabulary Series:

VOCABULARY BASICS
GROUNDWORK FOR A BETTER VOCABULARY
BUILDING VOCABULARY SKILLS
IMPROVING VOCABULARY SKILLS
ADVANCING VOCABULARY SKILLS
BUILDING VOCABULARY SKILLS, SHORT VERSION
IMPROVING VOCABULARY SKILLS, SHORT VERSION
ADVANCING VOCABULARY SKILLS, SHORT VERSION

Supplements Available for Most Books:

Instructor's Edition
Instructor's Manual, Test Bank and Computer Guide

Send book orders and requests for desk copies or supplements to:
Townsend Press
1038 Industrial Drive
West Berlin, New Jersey 08091

For even faster service, call us at our toll-free number:
1-800-772-6410

Or FAX your request to:
1-609-753-0649

ISBN 0-944210-73-2

Contents

Preface
to the Instructor

We all know that many students entering college today do not have the reading skills needed to do effective work in their courses. A related problem, apparent even in class discussions, is that students often lack the skills required to think in a clear and logical way.

The purpose of *Ten Steps to Improving College Reading Skills,* Third Edition, is to develop effective reading and clear thinking. To do so, **Part I** presents a sequence of ten reading skills that are widely recognized as essential for basic and advanced comprehension. The first six skills concern the more literal levels of comprehension:

- Using vocabulary in context
- Recognizing main ideas
- Identifying supporting details
- Recognizing implied main ideas and the central point
- Understanding relationships that involve addition and time
- Understanding relationships that involve examples, comparison or contrast, and cause and effect

The remaining skills cover the more advanced, critical levels of comprehension:

- Distinguishing between facts and opinions
- Making inferences
- Understanding purpose and tone
- Evaluating arguments

In every chapter in Part I, the key aspects of a skill are explained and illustrated clearly and simply. Explanations are accompanied by a series of practices, and each chapter ends with four review tests. The last review test consists of a reading selection so that students can apply the skill just learned to real-world reading materials, including newspaper and magazine articles and textbook selections. Together, the ten chapters provide students with the skills needed for basic and more advanced reading comprehension.

Following each chapter in Part I are six mastery tests for the skill in question. The tests progress in difficulty, giving students the additional practice and challenge they may need for the solid learning of each skill. While designed for quick grading, the tests also require students to think carefully before answering each question.

Part II is made up of ten additional readings that will improve both reading and thinking skills. Each reading is followed by *Basic Skill Questions* and *Advanced Skill Questions* so that students can practice all of the ten skills presented in Part I. In addition, an *Outlining, Mapping,* or *Summarizing* activity after each reading helps students think carefully about the basic content and organization of a selection. *Discussion Questions* then afford instructors a final opportunity to engage students in a variety of reading and thinking skills and deepen their understanding of a selection.

Part III serves a variety of purposes. A personal essay, "Reading for Pleasure and Power," encourages students to become regular readers and suggests practical ways to achieve this goal. Twelve combined-skills passages and tests review the skills in Part I and help students prepare for the standardized reading tests that are often a requirement at the end of a semester. A section on propaganda techniques (one of the ten reading skills in the second edition of the book) offers instruction and practice in a reading skill that some but probably not all instructors will have time to address. There is also a section on logical fallacies that can be covered, depending on student needs and course requirements. Finally, writing assignments for all twenty readings in the text help reinforce reading and thinking skills by asking students to do some writing as well.

Important Features of the Book

- **Focus on the basics.** The book is designed to explain in a clear, step-by-step way the essential elements of each skill. Many examples are provided to ensure that students understand each point. In general, the focus is on teaching the skills—not just on explaining or testing them.

- **Frequent practice and feedback.** Because it is largely through abundant practice and careful feedback that progress is made, this book includes numerous activities. Students can get immediate feedback on the practice exercises in Part I by turning to the limited answer key at the back. The answers to the review and mastery tests in Part I, the reading questions in Part II, and the combined-skills tests in Part III are in the *Instructor's Manual.*

The limited answer key increases the active role that students take in their own learning. They are likely to use the answer key in an honest and positive way if they know they will be tested on the many activities and selections for which answers are not provided. (Answers not in the book can be easily copied from the *Instructor's Edition* or the *Instructor's Manual* and passed out at the teacher's discretion.)

- **High interest level.** Dull and unvaried readings and exercises work against learning. Students need to experience genuine interest and enjoyment in what they read. Teachers as well should be able to take pleasure in the selections, for their own good feeling can carry over favorably into class work. The readings in the book, then, have been chosen not only for the appropriateness of their reading level but also for their compelling content. They should engage teachers and students alike.

- **Ease of use.** The logical sequence in each chapter—from explanation to example to practice to review test to mastery test—helps make the skills easy to teach. The book's organization into distinct parts also makes for ease of use. Within a single class, for instance, teachers can work on a new skill in Part I, review other skills with one or more mastery tests, and provide variety by having students read one of the selections in Part II. The limited answer key at the back of the text also makes for versatility: it means that the teacher can assign some chapters for self-teaching. Finally, the mastery tests and the combined-skills tests—each on its own tear-out page—make it a simple matter for teachers to test and evaluate student progress.

- **Integration of skills.** Students do more than learn the skills individually in Part I. They also learn to apply the skills together through the reading selections in Parts I and II as well as the combined-skills tests in Part III. They become effective readers and thinkers by means of a good deal of practice in applying a combination of skills.

- **Thinking activities.** Thinking activities in the form of outlining, mapping, and summarizing are a distinctive feature of the book. While educators agree that such organizational abilities are important, they are all too seldom taught. From a practical standpoint, it is almost impossible for a teacher to respond in detail to entire collections of class outlines or summaries. This book then, presents activities that truly involve students in outlining, mapping, and summarizing—in other words, that truly make students *think*—and yet that enable a teacher to give feedback. Again, it is through continued practice *and* feedback on challenging material that a student becomes a more effective reader and thinker.

- **Supplementary materials.** The three helpful supplements listed below are available at no charge to instructors using the text. Any or all can be obtained quickly by writing or calling Townsend Press (Pavilions at Greentree—408, Marlton, New Jersey 08053; 1-800-772-6410).

  1 An *Instructor's Edition*—chances are that you are holding it in your hand—is identical to the student book except that it also provides hints for teachers (see the front of the book), answers to all the practices and tests, and comments on selected items. (The only answers not provided are for activities immediately explained in the text.)

  2 A combined *Instructor's Manual and Test Bank* includes suggestions for teaching the course, a model syllabus, and readability levels. The test bank contains four additional mastery tests for each of the ten skills and four additional combined-skills tests—all on letter-sized sheets so they can be copied easily for use with students.

  3 A set of *computer disks* (in IBM and Macintosh formats) provides two additional mastery tests for each of the ten skill chapters in the book. The disks contain a number of user- and instructor-friendly features: brief explanations of answers, a sound option, frequent mention of the user's first name, a running score, and a record-keeping score file.

- **One of a sequence of books.** This is the intermediate text in a series that includes three other books. *Ten Steps to Building College Reading Skills*, Forms A and B, are the basic books in the series, and *Ten Steps to Advancing College Reading Skills* is an advanced text.

  The *Building* books are suited for a first college reading course. The two forms of the book allow teachers to easily alternate texts from one semester to the next. The *Improving* book is appropriate for the core developmental reading course offered at most colleges. The *Advancing* book is a slightly higher developmental text than the *Improving* book. It can be used as the core book for a more advanced class, as a sequel to the intermediate book, or as a second-semester alternative to it.

  A companion set of vocabulary books, listed on page iv, has been designed to go with the *Ten Steps* books. Recommended to accompany this book is *Improving Vocabulary Skills* or *Improving Vocabulary Skills, Short Version*.

  Together, the books and all their supplements form a sequence that should be ideal for any college reading program.

To summarize, *Ten Steps to Improving College Reading Skills*, Third Edition, provides ten key reading skills to help developmental college students become independent readers and thinkers. Through an appealing collection of readings and a carefully designed series of activities and tests, students receive extensive guided practice in the skills. The result is an integrated approach to learning that will, by the end of a course, produce better readers and stronger thinkers.

Changes in the Third Edition

I am grateful for the helpful comments of reviewers as well as the instructors who have either written or spoken to me about the book over the last several years. Based on their suggestions and my own use of the text, I have made some major changes:

- **More emphasis on main ideas.** In response to many requests for added material on main ideas, I have created a new chapter devoted exclusively to implied main ideas and the main idea, or central point, of an entire selection. I have also expanded the original "Main Ideas" chapter.

- **Fresh materials.** Four of the twenty readings in the book are new, as are about 30 percent of the practice materials. In choosing new material, the questions repeatedly asked have been "Is it truly interesting?" and "Does it clearly teach the skill or skills in question?"

- **Major chapter revisions.** The chapter on vocabulary in context, for example, has been enlarged, and all of the mastery tests are new. The treatment of main ideas is spread over two chapters. The chapter on supporting details now includes information on outlining, mapping, and summarizing. The chapters on relationships make it much easier for students to see the connection between transitions and patterns of organization. The chapter on argument has integrated into the text the two most common errors in reasoning (changing the subject and hasty generalization) and moved other logical fallacies to Part III. In general, it will be apparent to past users that changes and improvements appear on almost every page of the text.

- **Integration of transitions with patterns of organization.** The previous edition of the book presented transitions and patterns of organization in separate chapters. The chapters now emphasize relationships and help students understand that just as transitions show the relationships between ideas in sentences, so patterns of organization show the relationships between supporting ideas in paragraphs or longer passages. Specifically, in "Relationships I," students learn how transitions and patterns of organization show relationships that involve addition and time. In "Relationships II," students learn how transitions and patterns of organization show relationships that involve examples, comparison or contrast, and cause and effect.

- **Relocation of the mastery tests.** For greater ease of use, the six mastery tests for each skill now immediately follow the chapter on that skill.

- **Additional combined-skills tests.** In this edition, there are twelve short reading passages that gradually progress in difficulty. Each passage is followed by questions that review many of the reading comprehension skills in Part I.

- **New design elements.** To increase readability, a typeface slightly larger than the one in the previous edition has been used for the reading selections, as well as a two-column format.

- **Expanded discussion questions and the addition of writing assignments.** All twenty readings in the book are now followed by discussion questions, and a new section in Part III presents three writing assignments for each selection. Reading and writing are closely connected skills, so practicing one helps the other. By asking students to write about some of the selections, the instructor can improve their ability to read closely and to think carefully.

- **Promotion of the habit of reading.** New to the book is a motivational essay titled "Reading for Pleasure and Power" that details my own experience in becoming a regular reader and suggests practical guidelines for developing the reading habit. Also included as an incentive for students is a free book offer.

Acknowledgments

I am grateful for the many helpful suggestions provided by the following reviewers: Gwendolyne Bunch, Midlands Technical College; Belinda C. Hauenstein, Burlington County College; Ellen Kaiden, Ramapo College; Miriam Kinard, Trident Technical College; Jerre J. Kennedy, Brevard Community College; Jackie Lumsden, Greenville Technical College; Vashti Muse, Hinds Community College; Eileen Suruda, Essex Community College; and José Rafael Trevino, Laredo Community College. I also thank Dot Carroll, Eliza Comodromos, Sue Gamer, Greg Giuffrida, Beth Johnson, Paul Langan, and Judy Nadell for the help they provided along the way.

I owe special thanks to two of my colleagues at Townsend Press. Because of Janet Goldstein's extraordinary design and editing skills, the book enjoys an even more clear and "user-friendly" format than the previous edition. Her work also made possible the creation of the *Instructor's Edition*, complete with answers and marginal comments, that accompanies the book. I value equally Carole Mohr's exceptional editorial role. Thanks to her many insights into the nature of each skill and her unfailing sensitivity to the needs of students, the text is significantly better than it would have been otherwise. It has been a special pleasure to work with colleagues who aspire toward excellence. With them, I have been able to create a much better book than I could have managed on my own.

John Langan

How to Become a Better Reader and Thinker

The chances are that you are not as good a reader as you should be to do well in college. If so, it's not surprising. You live in a culture where people watch an average of *over seven hours of television every day!!!* All that passive viewing does not allow much time for reading. Reading is a skill that must be actively practiced. The simple fact is that people who do not read very often are not likely to be strong readers.

- How much TV do you guess you watch on an average day? _____

Another reason besides TV for not reading much is that you may have a lot of responsibilities. You may be going to school and working at the same time, and you may have a lot of family duties as well. Given a hectic schedule, you're not going to have much time to read. When you have free time, you're exhausted, and it's easier to turn on the TV than to open up a book.

- Do you do any regular reading (for example, a daily newspaper, weekly magazines, occasional novels)? _____
- When are you most likely to do your reading? _____

A third reason for not reading is that school may have caused you to associate reading with worksheets and drills and book reports and test scores. Experts agree that many schools have not done a good job of helping students discover the pleasures and rewards of reading. If reading was an unpleasant experience in school, you may have concluded that reading in general is not for you.

- Do you think that school made you dislike reading, rather than enjoy it?

Here are three final questions to ask yourself:

- Do you feel that perhaps you don't need a reading course, since you "already know how to read"? _____
- If you had a choice, would you be taking a reading course? (It's okay to be honest.) _____
- Do you think that a bit of speed reading may be all you need? _____

Chances are that you don't need to read *faster* as much as you need to read *smarter.* And it's a safe bet that if you don't read much, you can benefit enormously from the reading course in which you are using this book.

One goal of the book is to help you become a better reader. You will learn and practice ten key reading comprehension skills. As a result, you'll be better able to read and understand the many materials in your other college courses. The skills in this book have direct and practical value: they can help you perform better and more quickly—giving you an edge for success—in all of your college work.

The book is also concerned with helping you become a stronger thinker, a person able not just to understand what is read but to analyze and evaluate it as well. In fact, reading and thinking are closely related skills, and practice in thoughtful reading will also strengthen your ability to think clearly and logically. To find out just how the book will help you achieve these goals, read the next several pages and do the brief activities as well. The activities are easily completed and will give you a quick, helpful overview of the book.

HOW THE BOOK IS ORGANIZED

The book is organized into three parts:

Part I: Ten Steps to Improving College Reading Skills (pages 7–354)

To help you become a more effective reader and thinker, this book presents a series of ten key reading skills. They are listed in the table of contents on page v. Turn to that page to fill in the skills missing below:

   1 Vocabulary in Context
   2 *Main Ideas* _____
   3 *Supporting Details* _____
   4 Implied Main Ideas and the Central Point
   5 Relationships I
   6 Relationships II
   7 *Fact and Opinion* _____
   8 Inferences
   9 *Purpose and Tone* _____
  10 Argument

Each chapter is developed in the same way.

First of all, clear explanations and examples help you *understand* each skill. Practices then give you the "hands-on" experience needed to *learn* the skill.

- How many practices are there for the second chapter, "Main Ideas" (pages 39–78)? ___*Six*___

Closing each chapter are four review tests. The first review test provides a check of the information presented in the chapter.

- On which page is the first review test for "Main Ideas"? ___57___

The second and third review tests consist of activities that help you practice the skill learned in the chapter.

- On which pages are Review Tests 2 and 3 for "Main Ideas"? ___58–61___

The fourth review test consists of a story, essay, or textbook selection that both gets you reading and gives you practice in the skill learned in the chapter as well as skills learned in previous chapters.

- What is the title of the reading selection in the "Main Ideas" chapter?
  "Here's to Your Health"

Following each chapter are six mastery tests which gradually increase in difficulty.

- On what pages are the mastery tests for the "Main Ideas" chapter? ___67–78___

The tests are on tear-out pages and so can be easily removed and handed in to your instructor. So that you can track your progress, there is a score box at the top of each test. Your score can also be entered into the "Reading Performance Chart" on the inside back cover of the book.

Part II: Ten Reading Selections (pages 355–452)

The ten reading selections that make up Part II are followed by activities that give you practice in all of the skills studied in Part I. Each reading begins in the same way. Look, for example, at "The Yellow Ribbon," which starts on page 357. What are the headings of the two sections that come before the reading itself?

- ___*Preview*___
- ___*Words to Watch*___

Note that the vocabulary words in "Words to Watch" are followed by the numbers of the paragraphs in which the words appear. Look at the first page of "The Yellow Ribbon" and explain how each vocabulary word is marked in the reading itself.

- ___*It has a small circle after it.*___

Activities Following Each Reading Selection

After each selection, there are four kinds of activities to improve the reading and thinking skills you learned in Part I of the book.

1 The first activity consists of **basic skill questions**—questions involving vocabulary in context, main ideas (including implied main ideas and the central point), supporting details, and relationships.

  • Look at the basic skill questions for "The Yellow Ribbon" on pages 359–360. Note that the questions are labeled so you know what skill you are practicing in each case. How many questions deal with understanding vocabulary in context? _____*Two*_____

2 The second activity is made up of **advanced skill questions**—ones involving fact and opinion, inferences, purpose and tone, and argument.

  • Look at the advanced skill questions on pages 361–362. How many questions deal with making inferences? _____*Four*_____

3 The third activity involves **outlining**, **mapping**, or **summarizing**. Each of these activities will sharpen your ability to get to the heart of a piece and to think logically and clearly about what you read.

  • What kind of activity is provided for "The Yellow Ribbon" on page 363? _____*Summarizing*_____

  • What kind of activity is provided for the reading titled "Urban Legends" on page 372? _____*Mapping*_____

  Note that a **map**, or diagram, is a highly visual way of organizing material. Like an outline, it shows at a glance the main parts of a selection.

4 The fourth activity consists of **discussion questions**. These questions provide a chance for you to deepen your understanding of each selection.

  • How many discussion questions are there for "Urban Legends" (page 373)—and indeed for every other reading? _____*Four*_____

Part III: For Further Study (pages 453–536)

This part of the book contains additional materials that can help improve your reading.

1 The first section, "Reading for Pleasure and Power," is a personal essay that describes my own experiences in becoming a reader and suggests ways for you to develop the reading habit.

- How many suggestions are provided on pages 459–460? _____Five_____
- What book are you invited to write for? _____*Everyday Heroes*_____

2 The second section, "Combined-Skills Tests," on pages 462–486 is made up of short passages that give you practice in all ten of the skills in the book.

- How many such tests are there in all? _____*Twelve*_____

3 The third section, "Propaganda," discusses techniques that your instructor may choose to cover, depending on the needs of the class.

- How many kinds of propaganda techniques are explained? _____*Seven*_____

4 The fourth section, "More About Argument: Logical Fallacies," explains a number of common errors in reasoning.

- How many fallacies are treated on pages 511–523? _____*Six*_____

5 The fifth section, "Writing Assignments," presents writing assignments for all twenty of the reading selections in the book. Reading and writing are closely connected skills, and writing practice will improve your ability to read closely and to think carefully.

- How many assignments are offered for each reading? _____*Three*_____

HELPFUL FEATURES OF THE BOOK

1 The book centers on *what you really need to know* to become a better reader and thinker. It presents ten key comprehension skills and explains the most important points about each one.

2 The book gives you *lots of practice.* We seldom learn a skill only by hearing or reading about it; we make it part of us by repeated practice. There are, then, numerous activities in the text. They are not "busywork" but carefully designed materials that should help you truly learn each skill.

   Notice that after you learn each skill in Part I, you progress to review tests and mastery tests that enable you to apply the skill. And as you move from one skill to the next, the reading selections help you practice and reinforce the skills already learned.

3 The selections throughout the book are *lively and appealing.* Dull and unvaried readings work against learning, so subjects have been carefully chosen for their high interest level. Almost all of the selections here are good examples of how what we read can capture our attention. For instance, begin "The Yellow Ribbon," which is about a repentent man just released from prison who is wondering if his wife will allow him to return home—and try to stop reading. Or look at the textbook selection on pages 425–427, which considers the question of whether Lizzie Borden really was an ax-murderer.

Or read the textbook selection "Preindustrial Cities," which, despite its unexciting title, is full of fascinating details about city life before modern food distribution and sanitary facilities.

4 The readings include *eight selections from college textbooks.* Therefore, you will be practicing on materials very much like the ones in your other courses. Doing so will increase your chances of transferring what you learn in your reading class to your other college courses.

HOW TO USE THE BOOK

1 A good way to proceed is to read and review the explanations and examples in a given chapter in Part I until you feel you understand the ideas presented. Then carefully work through the practices. As you finish each one, check your answers with the "Limited Answer Key" that starts on page 537.

For your own sake, *don't just copy in the answers without trying to do the practices!* The only way to learn a skill is to practice it first and then use the answer key to give yourself feedback. Also, take whatever time is needed to figure out just why you got some answers wrong. By using the answer key to help teach yourself the skills, you will prepare yourself for the review and mastery tests at the end of each chapter as well as the other reading tests in the book. Your instructor can supply you with answers to those tests.

If you have trouble catching on to a particular skill, stick with it. In time, you will learn each of the ten skills.

2 Read the selections first with the intent of simply enjoying them. There will be time afterward for rereading each selection and using it to develop your comprehension skills.

3 Keep track of your progress. Fill in the charts at the end of each chapter in Part I and each reading in Part II. And in the "Reading Performance Chart" on the inside back cover, enter your scores for all of the review and mastery tests as well as the reading selections. These scores can give you a good view of your overall performance as you work through the book.

In summary, *Ten Steps to Improving College Reading Skills* has been designed to interest and benefit you as much as possible. Its format is straightforward, its explanations are clear, its readings are appealing, and its many practices will help you learn through doing. *It is a book that has been created to reward effort*, and if you provide that effort, you will make yourself a better reader and a stronger thinker. I wish you success.

John Langan

Part I

TEN STEPS TO IMPROVING COLLEGE READING SKILLS

1

Vocabulary in Context

If you were asked to define the words *torrid*, *ascertain*, and *euphoria*, you might have some difficulty. On the other hand, if you saw these words in sentences, chances are you could come up with fairly accurate definitions. For example, see if you can define the words in italics in the three sentences below. Circle the letter of each meaning you think is correct.

To avoid the burning sun in *torrid* climates such as deserts, many animals come out only at night.

Torrid means
a. familiar.   b. extremely hot and dry.   c. humid.

The officer tried to *ascertain* the truth about the accident by questioning each witness separately.

Ascertain means
a. create.   b. avoid.   c. find out.

In their *euphoria*, the fans of the winning team danced in the stadium aisles and chanted victory songs, until their intense joy was dampened by a sudden downpour.

Euphoria means
a. intense joy.   b. hurry.   c. disappointment.

In each sentence above, the **context**—the words surrounding the unfamiliar word—provides clues to the word's meaning. You may have guessed from the context that a *torrid* climate is an extremely hot and dry one, that *ascertain* means "find out," and that *euphoria* is "intense joy."

Using context clues to understand the meaning of unfamiliar words will help you in several ways:

- It will save you time when reading. You will not have to stop to look up words in the dictionary. (Of course, you won't always be able to understand a word from its context, so you should always have a dictionary nearby as you read.)

- After you figure out the meaning of the same word more than once through its context, it may become a part of your working vocabulary. You will therefore add to your vocabulary simply by reading thoughtfully.

- You will get a good sense of how a word is actually used, including its shades of meaning.

TYPES OF CONTEXT CLUES

There are four common types of context clues:

1 Examples

2 Synonyms

3 Antonyms

4 General Sense of the Sentence or Passage

In the following sections, you will read about and practice using each type. The practices will sharpen your skills in recognizing and using context clues. They will also help you add new words to your vocabulary.

1   Examples

Examples may suggest the meaning of an unknown word. To understand how this type of clue works, read the sentences below. An *italicized* word in each sentence is followed by examples that serve as context clues for that word. These examples, in **boldfaced** type, will help you figure out the meaning of each word. Circle the letter of each meaning you think is correct.

Note that examples are often introduced with signal words and phrases like *including* and *such as*.

1. *Nocturnal* creatures, such as **bats and owls,** have highly developed senses that enable them to function in the dark.

   Nocturnal means
   a. feathery.   b. living.   c. active at night.

2. The *adverse* effects of this drug, including **dizziness, nausea, and headaches,** have caused it to be withdrawn from the market.

   Adverse means
   a. deadly.   b. harmful.   c. expensive.

3. Common *euphemisms* include **"final resting place"** (for *grave*), **"intoxicated"** (for *drunk*), and **"comfort station"** (for *toilet*).

Euphemisms means
a. unpleasant reactions.   b. answers.   c. substitutes for offensive terms.

In the first sentence, the examples given of nocturnal creatures—bats and owls—may have helped you to guess that nocturnal creatures are those that are active at night, since bats and owls do come out at night. In the second sentence, the unpleasant side effects mentioned are clues to the meaning of *adverse*, which is "harmful." Finally, as the examples in sentence three indicate, *euphemisms* means "substitutes for offensive terms." (By the way, remember that you can turn to your dictionary whenever you want to learn to pronounce an unfamiliar word.)

➤ *Practice 1*

For each item below, underline the examples that suggest the meaning of the italicized term. Then circle the letter of the meaning of that term. Note that the last five sentences have been taken from college textbooks.

1. Today was a day of *turmoil* at work—the phones were constantly ringing, people were running back and forth, and several offices were being painted.

   Turmoil means
   a. discussion.   (b.) confusion.   c. harmony.

2. Some mentally ill people have *bizarre* ideas. For example, they may think that the TV is talking to them or that others can steal their thoughts.

   Bizarre means
   (a.) very strange.   b. realistic.   c. creative.

3. There are several common *gambits* used in singles bars, such as "What sign are you?" "How do you like this place?" and "You remind me of someone."

   Gambits means
   a. questions.   (b.) conversation starters.   c. steps.

4. Since my grandfather retired, he has developed several new *avocations*. For instance, he now enjoys gardening and long-distance bike riding.

   Avocations means
   (a.) hobbies.   b. vacations.   c. jobs.

5. In biology class today, the instructor discussed such *anomalies* as creatures with two heads or webbed toes.

   Anomalies means
   a. groups.   b. illnesses.   (c.) abnormalities.

6. Each day, the neglected boy received one *meager* meal, often only a spoonful of rice and a few beans.

   Meager means
   (a.) small.　　　　　b. sweet.　　　　　c. filling.

7. The Chinese government provides *incentives* for married couples to have only one child. For example, couples with one child get financial help and free medical care.

   Incentives means
   a. warnings.　　　　b. penalties.　　　　(c.) encouragements.

8. Changes in such abilities as learning, reasoning, thinking, and language are aspects of *cognitive* development.

   Cognitive means
   a. physical.　　　　(b.) mental.　　　　c. spiritual.

9. Researchers have proven that negative gestures, including folded arms and lack of eye contact, are *impediments* to open communication.

   Impediments means
   (a.) obstacles.　　　　b. aids.　　　　c. additions.

10. *White-collar crime*—for example, accepting a bribe from a customer or stealing from an employer—is more costly than "common" crime.

    White-collar crime means crime committed by
    a. gang members.　　b. strangers.　　(c.) people in the
    　　　　　　　　　　　　　　　　　　　　course of their work.

2　Synonyms

A context clue is often available in the form of a **synonym**: a word that means the same or almost the same as the unknown word. A synonym may appear anywhere in a passage to provide the same meaning as the unknown word.

In each of the following items, the word to be defined is italicized. Underline the synonym for the italicized word in each sentence.

1. Are you *averse* to exercise? You would not be so opposed to it if you had a partner to work out with you.

2. If we *assess* ourselves favorably, our self-esteem will be high, but if we judge ourselves negatively, it will suffer.

3. Although the salesperson tried to *assuage* the angry customer, there was no way to soothe her.

You should have underlined "opposed" as a synonym for *averse*, "judge" as a synonym for *assess*, and "soothe" as a synonym for *assuage*.

➤ *Practice 2*

Each item below includes a word that is a synonym of the italicized word. Write the synonym of the italicized word in the space provided. Note that the last five sentences have been taken from college textbooks.

___embarrasses___ 1. Speaking in front of a group *disconcerts* Alan. Even answering a question in class embarrasses him.

___examine___ 2. Because my friends had advised me to *scrutinize* the lease, I took time to examine all the fine print.

___practical___ 3. The presidential candidate vowed to discuss *pragmatic* solutions. He said the American people want practical answers, not empty theory.

___begged___ 4. Rita successfully begged her father for five dollars and then *implored* her mother for another five.

___mercy killing___ 5. The lawyer decided to lecture on *euthanasia* to the Nurses' Association because there is a great deal of interest in mercy killing these days.

___carried___ 6. To reach Venice, a city of islands, food first had to be carried by wagon to the water's edge and then *conveyed* by barge to the islands.

___opponents___ 7. Managers should beware of having *adversaries* work together; opponents often do not cooperate well.

___arrival___ 8. In the same way that the arrival of mechanical equipment meant fewer farm jobs, the *advent* of the computer has led to fewer manufacturing jobs.

___customary___ 9. Throughout history, the *prevalent* authority pattern in families has been patriarchy, in which males are in control. In only a few societies has matriarchy been the customary authority pattern.

___custom___ 10. *Convention* limits the acceptance of something new to a culture. If it were not for existing custom, for example, we might all be wearing wild fashions unlike anything seen before.

3   Antonyms

An **antonym**—a word that means the opposite of another word—is also a useful context clue. Antonyms are often signaled by words and phrases such as *however, but, yet, on the other hand*, and *in contrast*.

In each sentence below, underline the word that means the opposite of the italicized word. Then circle the letter of the meaning of the italicized word.

1. Trying to control everything your teens do can *impede* their growth. To advance their development, allow them to make some decisions on their own.

   Impede means
   a. block.   b. predict.   c. improve.

2. Religions in America are not *static*, but changing, especially in this period of shifting values.

   Static means
   a. unchanging.   b. unknown.   c. shifting.

3. Many people have pointed out the harmful effects that a working mother may have on the family, yet there are many *salutary* effects as well.

   Salutary means
   a. well-known.   b. beneficial.   c. hurtful.

In the first sentence, *impede* is the opposite of "advance"; *impede* means "block." In the second sentence, the opposite of *static* is "changing"; *static* means "unchanging." Last, salutary effects are the opposite of "harmful effects"; *salutary* means "beneficial."

Note that the three antonyms above are indicated by signal words: *instead, but*, and *yet*.

➤ *Practice 3*

Each item below includes a word that is an antonym of the italicized word. Underline the antonym of each italicized word. Then circle the letter of the meaning of the italicized word. Note that the last five sentences have been taken from college textbooks.

1. He was born to a family that possessed great wealth, but he died in *indigence*.

   Indigence means
   a. a hospital.   b. an accident.   c. poverty.

2. Many politicians do not give *succinct* answers. They prefer long ones that help them avoid the point.

Succinct means
a. brief.　　　　　　　b. accurate.　　　　　　c. complete.

3. "I've seen students *surreptitiously* check answer sheets during exams," said the professor. "However, until today I never saw one openly lay out a cheat sheet on his desk."

   Surreptitiously means
   a. legally.　　　　　　b. secretly.　　　　　　c. loudly.

4. While Irma's house is decorated plainly, her clothing is very *flamboyant*.

   Flamboyant means
   a. inexpensive.　　　　b. flashy.　　　　　　c. washable.

5. To keep healthy, older people need to stay active. Remaining *stagnant* results in loss of strength and health.

   Stagnant means
   a. inactive.　　　　　b. lively.　　　　　　c. unhealthy.

6. In formal communication, be sure to avoid *ambiguous* language. Clear language prevents misinterpretation.

   Ambiguous means
   a. wordy.　　　　　　b. ineffective.　　　　c. unclear.

7. Being raised with conflicting values can be a *detriment* to boys' and girls' relationships with each other. In contrast, shared values can be a benefit.

   Detriment means
   a. improvement.　　　　b. harm.　　　　　　c. relationship.

8. While houses and antiques often increase in value, most things, such as cars and TV's, *depreciate*.

   Depreciate means
   a. remain useful.　　　　b. lose value.　　　　c. break.

9. Reliable scientific theories are based not upon careless work, but rather upon *meticulous* research and experimentation.

   Meticulous means
   a. hasty.　　　　　　b. expensive.　　　　c. careful.

10. In the early days of automobile manufacturing, *stringent* laws controlled motorists' speed. In contrast, the laws designed to protect consumers from faulty products were extremely weak.

    Stringent means
    a. informal.　　　　　b. not effective.　　　　c. strict.

4   General Sense of the Sentence or Passage

Sometimes it takes a bit more detective work to puzzle out the meaning of an unfamiliar word. In such cases, you must draw conclusions based on the information given with the word. Asking yourself questions about the passage may help you make a fairly accurate guess about the meaning of the unfamiliar word.

Each of the sentences below is followed by a question. Think about each question; then circle the letter of the answer you think is the correct meaning of the italicized word.

1. A former employee, *irate* over having been fired, broke into the plant and deliberately wrecked several machines.
   (What would be the employee's state of mind?)

   Irate means
   a. relieved.   b. very angry.   c. undecided.

2. Despite the *proximity* of Ron's house to his sister's, he rarely sees her.
   (What about Ron's house would make it surprising that he didn't see his sister more often?)

   Proximity means
   a. similarity.   b. nearness.   c. superiority.

3. The car wash we organized to raise funds was a *fiasco*—it rained all day.
   (How successful would a car wash be on a rainy day?)

   Fiasco means
   a. great financial success.   b. welcome surprise.   c. complete disaster.

The first sentence provides enough evidence for you to guess that *irate* means "very angry." *Proximity* in the second sentence means "nearness." And a *fiasco* is a complete disaster. (You may not hit on the exact dictionary definition of a word by using context clues, but you will often be accurate enough to make good sense of what you are reading.)

➤ *Practice 4*

Try to answer the question that follows each item below. Then use the logic of each answer to help you circle the letter of the meaning you think is correct. Note that the last five sentences have been taken from college textbooks.

1. Jamal didn't want to tell Tina the entire plot of the movie, so he just gave her the *gist* of the story.
   (What kind of information would Jamal give Tina?)

   Gist means
   a. ending.   b. title.   c. main idea.

2. The lizard was so *lethargic* that I wasn't sure if it was alive or dead. It didn't even blink.
(How active is this lizard?)

   Lethargic means
   a. green.   (b.) inactive.   c. big.

3. After the accident, I was angered when the other driver told the police officer a complete *fabrication* about what happened. He made it seem that I was the only person at fault.
(How truthful was the other driver's information?)

   Fabrication means
   (a.) lie.   b. description.   c. confession.

4. The public knows very little about the *covert* activities of CIA spies.
(What kind of activities would the CIA spies be involved in that the public wouldn't know much about?)

   Covert means
   a. public.   (b.) secret.   c. family.

5. Whether or not there is life in outer space is an *enigma*. We may never know for sure until we are capable of space travel or aliens actually land on our planet.
(What would we call something to which we have no answer?)

   Enigma means
   a. reason.   b. certainty.   (c.) mystery.

6. Suicide rates tend to *fluctuate* with the seasons, with much higher rates in the winter than in the summer.
(What happens to the suicide rate from season to season?)

   Fluctuate means
   (a.) go up and down.   b. disappear.   c. stay the same.

7. Human beings are *resilient* creatures—they can often bounce back from negative experiences and adjust well to life.
(What point is the author making about the nature of human beings?)

   Resilient means
   a. not flexible.   b. living.   (c.) able to recover.

8. A major accomplishment of sociology is *dispelling* the myths and prejudices that groups of people have about each other.
(What would a profession do to "myths and prejudices" that could be considered a "major accomplishment"?)

   Dispelling means
   a. ignoring.   (b.) making vanish.   c. creating again.

9. Ten years of research *culminated* in a report explaining the mysterious behavior of the praying mantis, a large green or brownish insect.
(What would be the relationship of the report to the research?)

Culminated means
a. failed.   b. began.   (c.) concluded.

10. Despite complaints from parents, educators, and government officials, violence and sex on television seem to go on *unabated*.
(What happens despite the complaints from parents, educators, and government officials?)

Unabated means
a. more slowly.   (b.) with no decrease.   c. at great expense.

A NOTE ON TEXTBOOK DEFINITIONS

You don't always have to use context clues or the dictionary to find definitions. Very often, textbook authors provide definitions of important terms. Also, after giving a definition, authors usually follow it with one or more examples to ensure that you understand the word being defined. Here is a short textbook passage that includes a definition and an example:

> People do not always satisfy their needs directly; sometimes they use a substitute object. Use of a substitute is known as ***displacement***. This is the process that takes place, for instance, when you control your impulse to yell at your boss and then go home and yell at the first member of your family who is unlucky enough to cross your path.

Textbook authors, then, often do more than provide context clues: they define a word and provide examples as well. When they take the time to define and illustrate a word, you should assume that the term is important enough to learn.

More about textbook definitions and examples appears on pages 185–186.

➤ *Review Test 1*

To review what you've learned in this chapter, answer the following questions.

1. Often, a reader can figure out the meaning of a new word without using the dictionary—by paying attention to the word's _____*context*_____.

2. In the sentence below, which type of context clue is used for the italicized word?
   - (a.) example
   - b. antonym
   - c. synonym

   You can't take certain courses unless you've taken a *prerequisite*; for instance, you can't take Spanish Literature I unless you've taken Spanish III.

3. In the sentence below, which type of context clue is used for the italicized word?
   - a. example
   - (b.) antonym
   - c. synonym

   There are thick pine forests at the foot of the mountain, but higher up, the trees become *sparse*.

4. In the sentences below, which type of context clue is used for the italicized word?
   - a. example
   - b. antonym
   - (c.) synonym

   Talent may take years to surface. When Beethoven was a young child, his great *aptitude* in music was not at all apparent to his teachers.

5. Often when textbook authors introduce a new word, they provide you with a _____*definition*_____ and follow it with _____*examples*_____ that help make the meaning of the word clear.

➤ *Review Test 2*

A. Using context clues for help, circle the letter of the best meaning for each italicized word.

1. *Nepotism* is commonplace where I work: the boss's daughter is vice-president of the company, her husband runs the order department, and their son has just started working in the warehouse.
   - a. good managerial practice
   - (b.) favoritism to relatives
   - c. arguments among employees
   - d. confusion among management

2. Although the professor's explanation was *nebulous*, none of the students asked him to make himself clear.
   - (a.) vague
   - b. boring
   - c. fascinating
   - d. brief

   Comments: Item 1—Examples of *nepotism.* Item 2—Antonym of *nebulous* ("clear").

3. The bank robber was apparently *nondescript*—none of the witnesses could think of any special characteristics that might identify him.
   a. poorly disguised
   (b.) lacking distinctive qualities
   c. memorable
   d. cruel

4. The lake water was so *murky* that my hand seemed to vanish when I dipped it only a few inches below the surface.
   a. cold
   b. dangerous
   (c.) dark
   d. inviting

5. During the Revolutionary War, the English paid German *mercenaries* to help fight the Americans.
   (a.) hired soldiers
   b. traitors
   c. rebels
   d. recent immigrants

B. Using context clues for help, write the definition for each word in italics. Choose from the definitions in the box below. Each definition will be used once.

provided	doubtful	discouraged
overjoyed	nag	

6. I would not be just glad if I won the lottery; I'd be *ecstatic*.

   Ecstatic means _____overjoyed_____.

7. Nature has *endowed* hummingbirds with the ability to fly backward.

   Endowed means _____provided_____.

8. Opponents of the death penalty say it has never actually *deterred* anyone from committing murder.

   Deterred means _____discouraged_____.

9. Around the age of two or three, small children like to *badger* their parents with endless questions beginning with the word "why."

   Badger means _____nag_____.

10. While four-year-old Mattie claimed she was going to stay up until midnight on New Year's Eve, her parents were *dubious* of her ability to remain awake that late.

    Dubious means _____doubtful_____.

Comments: Item 3—Antonym-like clue for *nondescript* ("special characteristics").

Items 4–10: General sense of the sentence. For example, to find the meaning of *murky* in item 4, one could ask, "What would be a characteristic of water that makes a hand seem to vanish?"

➤ *Review Test 3*   *Answers may vary.*

A. Use context clues to figure out the meaning of the italicized word in each of the following sentences, and write your definition in the space provided.

1. When people are broke, they find that many things which seem *indispensable* are not so necessary after all.

   Indispensable means _____*necessary*_____

2. It's amazing that my neighbors always appear *immaculate*, yet their apartment is often quite dirty.

   Immaculate means _____*clean*_____

3. Rose thought selling cosmetics door-to-door would be a *lucrative* part-time job, but in her first month she earned only twenty-nine dollars.

   Lucrative means _____*profitable*_____

4. Doctors should *alleviate* the pain of terminally ill patients so that their final days are as comfortable as possible.

   Alleviate means _____*relieve*_____

5. Working as a team, a coyote and a badger may *simultaneously* attack an area crowded with squirrels. The attack panics the squirrels, making them easier to catch.

   Simultaneously means _____*at the same time*_____

B. Use context clues to figure out the meaning of the italicized words in each of the following textbook passages, and write your definition in the space provided.

   Although mysteries and science fiction may seem like very different kinds of writing, the two forms share some basic similarities. First of all, both are action-directed, emphasizing plot at the expense of character development. Possibly for this reason, both types of literature have been *scorned* by critics as being "merely entertainment" rather than "literature." But this attack is unjustified, for both mysteries and science fiction share a concern with moral issues. Science fiction often raises the question of whether or not scientific advances are of benefit to humanity. And a mystery story rarely ends without the *culpable* person being brought to justice.

6. *Scorned* means _____*looked down upon*_____

7. *Culpable* means _____*guilty*_____

Comments: Context clues: Item 1—synonym of *indispensable* ("necessary").

Item 2—antonym of *immaculate* ("dirty").

Items 3–10: General sense of the sentence. To find the meaning of *alleviate* in item 4, for example, one could ask, "What would a doctor do to pain to make patients comfortable?"

Why did people begin to live in cities? To answer this question, we must start by looking back some ten thousand years ago. In certain parts of the world (probably those where the natural food supply was fairly unreliable), people *endeavored* to tame nature for their own purposes. They began weeding and watering groups of edible plants, adding organic matter to help fertilize the soil, and saving the seeds from the strongest, most desirable plants to sow the next spring. At the same time, they began protecting herds of small wild animals that are often hunted by larger animals. They would move them to more plentiful pastures during the dry months of summer. During the harshest periods of winter, they would *supplement* whatever fresh food was available with stored food. These changes, *coupled* with a few simple techniques for storing grain and meat, enabled people to abandon a wandering lifestyle in favor of settlement in small villages. These villages were the basic form of human social organization for the next several thousand years.

8. *Endeavored* means _____tried_____

9. *Supplement* means _____add to_____

10. *Coupled* means _____joined_____

➤ *Review Test 4*

Here is a chance to apply the skill of understanding vocabulary in context to a full-length selection. Read the story below, a version of which appeared in *Reader's Digest*, and then answer the questions that follow.

Words to Watch

Below are some words in the reading that do not have strong context support. Each word is followed by the number of the paragraph in which it appears and its meaning there. These words are indicated in the article by a small circle (°).

smudged (2): dirty with streaks or stains
boondocks (3): a rural region
maneuvers (3): military exercises

NIGHT WATCH

Roy Popkin

1   The story began on a downtown Brooklyn street corner. An elderly man had collapsed while crossing the street, and an ambulance rushed him to Kings County Hospital. There, during his few returns to consciousness, the man repeatedly called for his son.

2   From a smudged°, oft-read letter, an emergency-room nurse learned that the son was a Marine stationed in North Carolina. Apparently, there were no other relatives.

3   Someone at the hospital called the Red Cross office in Brooklyn, and a request for the boy to rush to Brooklyn was relayed to the Red Cross director of the North Carolina Marine Corps camp. Because time was short—the patient was dying—the Red Cross man and an officer set out in a jeep. They located the sought-after young man wading through marshy boondocks° on maneuvers°. He was rushed to the airport in time to catch the one plane that might enable him to reach his dying father.

4   It was mid-evening when the young Marine walked into the entrance lobby of Kings County Hospital. A nurse took the tired, anxious serviceman to the bedside.

5   "Your son is here," she said to the old man. She had to repeat the words several times before the patient's eyes opened. Heavily sedated because of the pain of his heart attack, he dimly saw the young man in the Marine Corps uniform standing outside the oxygen tent. He reached out his hand. The Marine wrapped his toughened fingers around the old man's limp ones, squeezing a message of love and encouragement. The nurse brought a chair, so the Marine could sit alongside the bed.

6   Nights are long in hospitals, but all through the night the young Marine sat there in the poorly lighted ward, holding the old man's hand and offering words of hope and strength. Occasionally, the nurse suggested that the Marine move away and rest a while. He refused.

7   Whenever the nurse came into the ward, the Marine was there. His full attention was on the dying man, and he was oblivious of her and of the night noises of the hospital—the clanking of an oxygen tank, the laughter of night-staff members exchanging greetings, the cries and moans and snores of other patients. Now and then she heard him say a few gentle words. The dying man said nothing, only held tightly to his son through most of the night.

8   Along toward dawn, the patient died. The Marine placed on the bed the lifeless hand he had been holding, and went to tell the nurse. While she did what she had to do, he relaxed—for the first time since he got to the hospital.

9   Finally, she returned to the nurse's station, where he was waiting. She started to offer words of condolence for his loss, but the Marine interrupted her. "Who was that man?" he asked.

10 "He was your father," she answered, startled.

11 "No, he wasn't," the Marine replied. "I never saw him before in my life."

12 "Why didn't you say something when I took you to him?" the nurse asked.

13 "I knew right off there'd been a mistake, but I also knew he needed his son, and his son just wasn't here. When I realized he was too sick to tell whether or not I was his son, I figured he really needed me. So I stayed."

14   With that, the Marine turned and left the hospital. Two days later a routine message came in from the North Carolina Marine Corps base informing the Brooklyn Red Cross that the real son was on his way to Brooklyn for his father's funeral. It turned out there had been two Marines with the same name and similar serial numbers in the camp. Someone in the personnel office had pulled out the wrong record.

15   But the wrong Marine had become the right son at the right time. And he proved, in a uniquely human way, that there are people who care what happens to their fellow human beings.

Vocabulary Questions

Use context clues to help you decide on the best definition for each italicized word. Then circle the letter of each choice.

1. In the sentence below, the word *relayed* means
   a. hidden.
   b. passed along.
   c. made a gift.
   d. ignored.

   To find the meaning of *relayed,* one might ask, "What could be done with a request to get it from one person to another?"

   "Someone at the hospital called the Red Cross office in Brooklyn, and a request for the boy to rush to Brooklyn was relayed to the Red Cross director of the North Carolina Marine Corps camp." (Paragraph 3)

2. In the sentence below, the words *enable him* mean
   a. stop him.
   b. encourage him.
   c. know him.
   d. make him able.

   "He was rushed to the airport in time to catch the one plane that might enable him to reach his dying father." (Paragraph 3)

3. In the excerpt below, the word *sedated* means
   a. spoken loudly.
   b. wide awake.
   c. armed.
   d. drugged with a pain reliever.

   "'Your son is here,' she said to the old man. She had to repeat the words several times before the patient's eyes opened. Heavily sedated because of the pain of his heart attack, he dimly saw the young man . . . "(Paragraph 5)

Comment: Most of the context clues here are general-sense-of-the-passage clues.

4. In the excerpt below, the word *dimly* means
   a. clearly.
   b. unclearly.
   c. rarely.
   d. often.

   "She had to repeat the words several times before the patient's eyes opened. Heavily sedated because of the pain of his heart attack, he dimly saw the young man . . . " (Paragraph 5)

5. In the sentence below, the word *limp* means
   a. lacking firmness and strength.
   b. equally tough.
   c. long.
   d. bleeding.

   "The Marine wrapped his toughened fingers around the old man's limp ones, squeezing a message of love and encouragement." (Paragraph 5)

6. A clue to the meaning of *limp* in the sentence above is the antonym
   _____ toughened _____.

7. In the excerpt below, the word *oblivious* means
   a. mindful.
   b. bothered.
   c. unaware.
   d. informed.

   "Whenever the nurse came into the ward, the Marine was there. His full attention was on the dying man, and he was oblivious of her and of the night noises of the hospital . . . " (Paragraph 7)

8. In the excerpt below, the word *condolence* means
   a. excuse.
   b. bitterness.
   c. surprise.
   d. sympathy.

   "She started to offer words of condolence for his loss . . . " (Paragraph 9)

9. In the excerpt below, the word *startled* means
   a. very pleased.
   b. with admiration.
   c. angry.
   d. surprised.

   "'Who was that man?' he asked. 'He was your father,' she answered, startled." (Paragraphs 9–10)

10. In the sentence below, the words *uniquely human* mean
    a. impossible for humans.
    b. scary to humans.
    c. done only by humans.
    d. sudden by human standards.

    "And he proved, in a uniquely human way, that there are people who care what happens to their fellow human beings." (Paragraph 15)

Discussion Questions

1. When do you think the Marine realized that calling him to the hospital was a mistake? Was it when he first saw the old man or before? What parts of the reading support your conclusion?

2. How do you think the dead man's real son felt about the other Marine being with his dying father? How would you feel?

3. By going out of his way for a stranger, the Marine showed "in a uniquely human way that there are people who care what happens to others." Have you or someone you know ever gone out of your way to help a stranger? Tell what the situation was and what happened.

4. The incident in the reading took place because of some surprising coincidences. What were they? Has a surprising or interesting coincidence ever taken place in your life? If so, what was it and how did it affect you?

Check Your Performance		VOCABULARY IN CONTEXT	
Activity	*Number Right*	*Points*	*Score*
Review Test 1 (5 items)	_____	x 2 =	_____
Review Test 2 (10 items)	_____	x 3 =	_____
Review Test 3 (10 items)	_____	x 3 =	_____
Review Test 4 (10 items)	_____	x 3 =	_____
		TOTAL SCORE =	_____ %

Enter your total score into the **Reading Performance Chart: Review Tests** on the inside back cover.

VOCABULARY IN CONTEXT: Test 1

A. For each item below, underline the **examples** that suggest the meaning of the italicized term. Then circle the letter of the meaning of that term.

1. When I finally get around to cleaning out my refrigerator, I always find something *vile* at the back of a shelf, such as <u>moldy fruit</u> or <u>a container of old smelly beans</u>.
   a. tempting   c. false
   b. recent   (d.) disgusting

2. The Easter egg hunt featured *cryptic* clues such as, <u>"You'll find a prize somewhere narrow"</u> and <u>"Look for the pink."</u>
   a. rhyming   c. clear
   (b.) puzzling   d. overused

3. *Verbose* writing can be hard to follow. For instance, <u>"At this point in time, we have an urgently felt need for more and greater financial resources"</u> is less clear than "We now need money urgently."
   a. realistic   (c.) wordy
   b. informal   d. ungrammatical

B. Each item below includes a word or words that are a **synonym** of the italicized word. Write the synonym of the italicized word in the space provided.

_____*risk*_____ 4. "I'll try any ride in this amusement park except the Twister," said Nick. "I'll *venture* getting sick to my stomach, but I won't risk my life."

_____*search*_____ 5. In the past three hundred years, several people have gone on a *quest* for Noah's Ark. The search has taken some to northeastern Turkey, on Mount Ararat, thousands of feet above sea level.

_____*false name*_____ 6. Samuel Langhorne Clemens wasn't the first author to use the *pseudonym* Mark Twain. A newspaper writer of the time used the same false name.

(Continues on next page)

C. Each item below includes a word that is an **antonym** of the italicized word. Underline the antonym of each italicized word. Then circle the letter of the meaning of the italicized word.

7. Computer manuals are often very hard to understand, so I was surprised to discover how *lucid* this one is.
   a. long
   b. expensive
   c. clear
   d. new

8. When my sister first got her job at the recording studio, she was excited to go to work each day. Now after ten years, she's *blasé* about her work and wants to change jobs.
   a. tardy
   b. bored
   c. thrilled
   d. curious

D. Use the general sense of each sentence to figure out the meaning of each italicized word. Then circle the letter of the meaning of the italicized word.

9. A person can be very intelligent and yet be *deficient* in common sense.
   a. lacking
   b. well supplied
   c. overqualified
   d. lucky

10. The store detective faced the *dilemma* of either having an elderly, needy man arrested or ignoring store rules about shoplifters.
   a. memory
   b. difficult choice
   c. proof
   d. reason

VOCABULARY IN CONTEXT: Test 2

A. For each textbook item below, underline the **examples** that suggest the meaning of the italicized term. Then circle the letter of the meaning of that term.

1. Every *habitat* in the world, from volcano tops to icebergs, can support some sort of life.

   a. country
   (b.) environment
   c. food source
   d. practice

2. Common *redundant* phrases include "cooperate together" (instead of simply "cooperate") and "postponed until later" (instead of "postponed").

   (a.) repetitious
   b. descriptive
   c. difficult
   d. useful

B. Each textbook item below includes a word that is a **synonym** of the italicized word. Write the synonym of the italicized word in the space provided.

_____*plain*_____ 3. The Amish people prefer *austere* styles—their clothing and homes are plain.

_____*conduct*_____ 4. Airport security guards must observe people's *demeanor* so as to notice any suspicious conduct.

_____*modest*_____ 5. In business, it can be harmful to be too *unassuming*. If you're overly modest about your achievements, for example, you may be passed up for a promotion.

C. Each textbook item below includes a word or words that are an *antonym* of the italicized word. Underline the antonym of each italicized word. Then circle the letter of the meaning of the italicized word.

6. Even when textbooks are *standardized* throughout a school system, methods of teaching with them may be greatly varied.

   a. different
   b. expensive
   (c.) made the same
   d. lacking

7. During the Middle Ages, everyone—from the rich landowner down to the most *impoverished* peasant—had a clear place in society.

   a. weak
   b. common
   (c.) poor
   d. decent

(Continues on next page)

D. Use the general sense of each sentence to figure out the meaning of each italicized word. Then circle the letter of the meaning of the italicized word.

8. America has often been called a "melting pot" into which people of many different cultures *assimilate*.
   a. learn
   b. leave
   c. avoid each other
   (d.) blend

9. During the 1960s and 1970s, many American folk singers used anti-war lyrics to *espouse* an end to the Vietnam War.
   a. recognize
   b. remember
   c. reject
   (d.) argue for

10. It is widely believed that Columbus sailed westward to *validate* the theory that the world is round. In fact, it was already well known at that time that the world is round.
    a. think up
    (b.) prove
    c. contradict
    d. foresee

VOCABULARY IN CONTEXT: Test 3

Using context clues for help, circle the letter of the best meaning for each italicized word or words.

1. It's a good idea for married couples to discuss their plans in case of each other's *demise.* For example, do they wish to be buried or cremated?
   a. death
   b. success
   c. desire to divorce
   d. concern

2. The press *assailed* the company responsible for the oil spill until it increased its efforts to clean up the mess.
   a. searched for
   b. paid
   c. attacked
   d. fined

3. One *tenet* of Islam is that its followers should not drink alcohol.
   a. answer
   b. prediction
   c. teaching
   d. guarantee

4. Toddlers are naturally *inquisitive.* It is because they are so curious about their surroundings that they are so eager to explore everything.
   a. unreliable
   b. clumsy
   c. curious
   d. tired

5. After x-rays were discovered in 1895, there were some *preposterous* reactions. For example, London merchants sold x-ray-proof underwear.
   a. logical
   b. ridiculous
   c. dangerous
   d. delayed

6. The foolish defendent *waived* his right to an attorney and instead spoke for himself in court.
   a. depended upon
   b. greeted
   c. wrote
   d. gave up

7. Sexual standards in England during the 1800s were so strict that it was considered *sordid* for women to reveal their legs in public.
   a. proper
   b. impossible
   c. popular
   d. indecent

8. Young children believe their parents are perfect, until they become teenagers, when their parents suddenly become quite *fallible.*
   a. unhealthy
   b. dangerous
   c. imperfect
   d. skilled

(Continues on next page)

9. At the company where Gerry works, people who are laid off during a brief *recession* are often rehired when there's a business upturn.
   - (a.) business decline
   - b. bankruptcy
   - c. holiday
   - d. war

10. The Englishman John Merrick's illness gave him such a *grotesque* appearance that he was called "The Elephant Man." Despite people's reactions to his misshapen head and body, Merrick remained affectionate and gentle.
    - a. strong
    - (b.) deformed
    - c. gray
    - d. childlike

Comments: Context clues:

Item 1—Examples revealing the meaning of *demise*: "buried" and "cremated."

Item 2—General sense of the sentence. One could determine the meaning of *assailed* by asking, "What would the press do to cause the company to increase its cleanup efforts?"

Item 3—Example of a *tenet* of Islam: "followers should not drink alcohol."

Item 4—Synonym of *inquisitive*: "curious."

Item 5—Example of a *preposterous* reaction: selling "x-ray-proof underwear."

Item 6—General sense of the sentence.

Item 7—General sense of the sentence.

Item 8—Antonym of *fallible*: "perfect."

Item 9—Opposite of *recession*: "a business upturn."

Item 10—Examples revealing the meaning of *grotesque*: "misshapen head and body."

VOCABULARY IN CONTEXT: Test 4

Using context clues for help, circle the letter of the best meaning for each italicized word or words. Note that all of the sentences have been taken from college textbooks.

1. After the Civil War, trolleys and streetcars greatly expanded workers' *mobility*, permitting them to move beyond walking distance from factories.
   a. pay
   c. ability to move
   b. skills
   d. interests

2. What people say may not reflect accurately what they are actually feeling. It is sometimes necessary to *resort to* clues other than their spoken words to understand them fully.
   a. remove from
   c. make use of
   b. make light of
   d. ignore

3. Individual political organizations often join together to form *coalitions* to increase the support for their issues.
   a. partnerships
   c. contests
   b. lines
   d. questions

4. Surveys about people's sexual habits are often inaccurate because people may lie, and there is no way to *corroborate* what they say.
   a. forget
   c. change
   b. prove the truth of
   d. recall

5. Burning the flag and damaging a church are outrageous acts that *blatantly* violate American norms.
   a. secretly
   c. barely
   b. accidentally
   d. obviously

6. Following the English principle that voters had to have a *stake* in the community, the colonies generally required citizens to own a certain minimum amount of land in order to vote.
   a. job
   c. investment
   b. relative
   d. employee

7. William Henry Harrison's 1840 campaign brought many *innovations* to the art of electioneering. For example, for the first time, a presidential candidate spoke out on his own behalf.
   a. new things
   c. crimes
   b. people
   d. financial skills

(Continues on next page)

8. To fully *assess* patients in order to place them in appropriate programs, mental health professionals need information on emotional adjustment and physical health.
   a. find
   b. recognize
   c. hide
   d. evaluate

9. In the eating disorder bulimia nervosa, a person will go on huge eating binges and then will try to *nullify* the outrageous food intake by purposely vomiting or strictly dieting.
   a. increase
   b. undo
   c. forget
   d. delay

10. Adults who have both elderly parents and children need to balance their commitments: while they are responsible for their own family, they also should *allocate* time and energy to caring for their parents.
    a. recall
    b. pay for
    c. set aside
    d. view

Comments: Items with general-sense-of-the-sentence context clues: 1, 2, 3, 4, 8, 10. To determine the meaning of *mobility* in sentence 1, for example, one could ask, "What would trolleys and streetcars expand for workers that would permit them to move beyond walking distance from factories?"

Items with examples for context clues:

Item 5—Examples of "acts that *blatantly* violate American norms": "burning the flag," "damaging a church."

Item 6—Example of having "a *stake* in the community": owning "a certain minimum amount of land."

Item 7—Example of an *innovation* "to the art of electioneering": "for the first time, a presidential candidate spoke out on his own behalf."

Item 9—Examples of ways "to nullify the outrageous food intake": "vomiting or strictly dieting."

VOCABULARY IN CONTEXT: Test 5

A. Using context clues for help, circle the letter of the best meaning for each italicized word. Note that all of the sentences have been taken from college textbooks.

1. The possibility of developing a top seller is so *alluring* that American companies spend billions of dollars a year trying to create new products or improve old ones.
   a. dangerous
   b. final
   c. attractive
   d. unreasonable

2. Using sign language, chimpanzees can *convey* such ideas as "Candy sweet" and "Give me hug."
   a. reject
   b. accept
   c. think of
   d. communicate

3. Smoking or chewing tobacco, wrote King James I, was "*loathsome* to the eye, hateful to the nose, harmful to the brain, and dangerous to the lungs."
   a. appealing
   b. hidden
   c. disgusting
   d. healthy

4. The death of a spouse can cause *profound* depression that, in some cases, can even lead to the death of the partner.
   a. deep
   b. accidental
   c. occasional
   d. mild

5. The healthiest type of parents are those who guide and instruct their children, but also grant them a degree of *autonomy*, encouraging the children to make their own decisions and form their own opinions.
   a. financing
   b. knowledge
   c. independence
   d. guidance

B. Use context clues to figure out the meaning of the italicized word in each of the following items. Then write your definition in the space provided.

6. A person giving first aid needs to make sure a body part that has been completely *severed* is sent to the hospital with the victim. Surgeons can often reattach the body part with microsurgery.   *Wording of answers may vary.*

   Severed means _____ *cut off* _____

7. Tabloid newspapers often *distort* the news by reporting rumors as if they were true.

   Distort means _____ *give a false account of; misrepresent* _____

(Continues on next page)

8. It's not always necessary for adults to *intervene* in children's fights; sometimes it's best to let children handle quarrels themselves.

   Intervene means _____ *come between in order to influence an action* _____

9. Many companies once had retirement policies that made it *mandatory* for people to quit working as soon as they turned a certain age.

   Mandatory means _____ *required* _____

10. After a heavy public relations campaign against the union, the hospital finally *relented* and allowed its workers to join.

   Relented means _____ *became more forgiving* _____

Comments: Item 7—Example of distorting the news: "reporting rumors as if they were true."

The rest of the items have general-sense-of-the-sentence clues. To determine the meaning of *alluring* in item 1, for example, one could ask, "How would American companies view the possibility of developing a top seller?"

VOCABULARY IN CONTEXT: Test 6

A. Five words are italicized in the textbook passage below. Write the definition for each italicized word, choosing from the definitions in the box. Read the entire passage before making your choices. Note that five definitions will be left over.

colorful	delayed	disappeared	increased
passed	most common	pray	punished
stir up interest	uncontrolled		

¹Back in the "bad old days" before the turn of the century, the *prevailing* view among industrialists was that business had only one responsibility: to make a profit. ²By and large those were not good times to be a low-level worker or an incautious consumer. ³People worked sixty-hour weeks under harsh conditions for a dollar or two a day. ⁴The few people who tried to fight the system faced violence and unemployment. ⁵Consumers were not much better off. ⁶If you bought a product, you paid the price and took the consequences. ⁷There were no consumer groups or government agencies to come to your defense if the product was defective or caused harm. ⁸If you tried to sue the company, chances were you would lose.

⁹These conditions caught the attention of a few crusading journalists and novelists known as muckrakers. ¹⁰They used the power of the pen to create public anger and *agitate* for reform. ¹¹Largely through their efforts, a number of laws were passed to limit the power of monopolies and to establish safety standards for food and drugs.

¹²Despite these reforms, business continued to pursue profits above all else until the Great Depression. ¹³When the economic system collapsed in 1929 and 25 percent of the work force was unemployed, people lost their faith in *unbridled* capitalism. ¹⁴Pressure *mounted* for government to fix the system.

¹⁵At the urging of President Franklin Roosevelt, Congress voted in laws to protect workers, consumers, and investors. ¹⁶The Social Security system was set up, employees were given the right to join unions and bargain collectively, the minimum wage was established, and the length of the workweek was limited. ¹⁷Legislation was also *enacted* to prevent unfair competition and false advertising.

1. In sentence 1, *prevailing* means _____ *most common* _____.

2. In sentence 10, *agitate* means _____ *stir up interest* _____.

3. In sentence 13, *unbridled* means _____ *uncontrolled* _____.

4. In sentence 14, *mounted* means _____ *increased* _____.

5. In sentence 17, *enacted* means _____ *passed* _____.

(Continues on next page)

B. Five words are italicized in the textbook passage below. Write the definition for each italicized word, choosing from the definitions in the box. Read the entire passage before making your choices. Note that five definitions will be left over.

causing	deadly	delay	die
enjoyable	give credit for	helpful	reducing
pay for	put through		

[1]In the early days of medicine, there were few drugs or treatments that gave any real physical benefit. [2]As a result, patients were treated in a variety of strange, largely ineffective ways. [3]For instance, Egyptian patients were medicated with "lizard's blood, crocodile dung, the teeth of a swine, the hoof of an ass, rotten meat, and fly specks." [4]If the disease itself didn't cause the patient to *succumb*, he or she had a good chance of dying instead from the treatment. [5]Medical treatments of the Middle Ages were somewhat less *lethal*, but not much more effective. [6]And as late as the eighteenth century, patients were *subjected to* bloodletting, freezing, and repeatedly induced vomiting to bring about a cure.

[7]Amazingly, people often seemed to get relief from such treatments. [8]Physicians have, for centuries, been objects of great respect, and this was no less true when few remedies were actually effective. [9]To what can one *attribute* the fair level of success that these treatments provided and the widespread faith in the effectiveness of physicians? [10]The most likely answer is that these are examples of the tremendous power of the placebo effect—"any medical procedure that produces an effect in a patient because of its therapeutic intent and not its specific nature, whether chemical or physical." [11]Even today, the role of placebos in *curtailing* pain and discomfort is substantial. [12]Many patients who swallow useless substances or who undergo useless procedures find that, as a result, their symptoms disappear and their health improves.

6. In sentence 4, *succumb* means _____ *die* _____.

7. In sentence 5, *lethal* means _____ *deadly* _____.

8. In sentence 6, *subjected to* means _____ *put through* _____.

9. In sentence 9, *attribute* means _____ *give credit for* _____.

10. In sentence 11, *curtailing* means _____ *reducing* _____.

Comment: All items have general-sense-of-the-passage clues.

2

Main Ideas

More than any other skill, the key to good comprehension is recognizing main ideas. The basic question you must ask about any selection that you read is, "What is the main point the author is trying to make?" For instance, read the following paragraph:

> Spanking is a poor way to shape a child's behavior. For one thing, the spanking will result in feelings of anger and frustration. The child, then, will not learn anything positive from the punishment. In addition, the spanking may actually lead to more bad behavior. Having learned that hitting is okay, the child may attack smaller children. Finally, the spanking teaches children to hide certain actions from their parents. Once out of their parents' sight, children may feel they can get away with the bad behavior.

What is the main point of this paragraph? To find the main idea, it is often useful first to determine what topic is being discussed. In the above paragraph, the topic is spanking. The main idea about the topic of spanking is that it "is a poor way to shape a child's behavior." The rest of the paragraph then supports that idea by providing the author's reasons.

Think of the **main idea** as an "umbrella" idea. It is the author's primary point about a topic, under which fits all the other material of the paragraph. That other material is supporting details in the form of examples, reasons, facts, and other evidence. The diagram below shows the relationship.

SPANKING IS A POOR WAY TO
SHAPE A CHILD'S BEHAVIOR

Results in feelings of anger and frustration.
May lead to more bad behavior.
Teaches children to hide actions from their parents.

THE TOPIC SENTENCE

In a paragraph, authors often present the main idea to readers in a single sentence called the **topic sentence**. For example, look again at the paragraph above on spanking. As we have already seen, the topic of this paragraph is spanking, and the primary point about spanking is that it "is a poor way to shape a child's behavior." Both the topic and the point about the topic are expressed in the opening sentence, which is therefore the topic sentence. All the sentences that follow provide details about the negative effects of spanking. The parts of the paragraph can be shown in outline form:

Topic: Spanking

Main idea (as expressed in the topic sentence): Spanking is a poor way to shape a child's behavior.

Supporting details:
1. Results in feelings of anger and frustration.
2. May lead to more bad behavior.
3. Teaches children to hide actions from their parents.

This chapter will sharpen your sense of the three basic parts in everything you read: 1) the topic, 2) the main idea about the topic, expressed in a topic sentence, and 3) the supporting details that develop the main idea. The chapter will also give you practice at finding main ideas at different locations within a paragraph. The next chapter, Chapter 3, will deepen your understanding of supporting details. You will then go in Chapter 4 to two more advanced skills: finding implied main ideas as well as central points, which are the main ideas of longer selections.

Using the Topic to Find the Main Idea

The **topic** is the subject of a selection. It can often be expressed in a few words. Textbooks typically give the overall topic of each chapter in the title of the chapter. They also provide many topics and subtopics in boldfaced headings within the chapter. Many magazine and journal articles, as well, give you the topic in the title of the piece.

To find the topic of a selection for which there is no helpful title, ask this simple question:

Who or what is the selection about?

Ask this question as you read carefully the paragraph that follows. Then, on the line below, write what you think is the topic.

Topic: _____

[1]Extrasensory perception, or ESP, is an area that fascinates people. [2]However, ESP is not documented by any convincing evidence. [3]For instance, it would seem that ESP would be an excellent way of winning at games of chance, such as are played at gambling casinos. [4]But casino owners in Las Vegas and Atlantic City report no problem with "psychics" winning great sums of money. [5]For another thing, although great publicity is generated when a psychic seems to help police solve a crime, the value of such help has never been scientifically proven. [6]Psychics' tips are usually worthless, and a case is solved through traditional police work. [7]And while audiences may be amazed at the feats of "mind readers," the fact is that mind readers use simple psychological tricks to exploit their audiences' willingness to believe.

Explanation:

The first sentence suggests that the topic of this paragraph is extrasensory perception. And as you read the paragraph, you see that, in fact, everything does have to do with ESP. Thus your first impression in this case was correct—the topic is ESP.

Once you have the topic, your next step is to ask the question:

What is the author's primary point about the topic?

The answer will be the main idea of the paragraph. Read the paragraph again, and then write in the space below the number of the sentence that expresses the author's main point about the topic of ESP.

Topic sentence: _____

Explanation:

The main idea about the topic, ESP, is that it "is not documented by any convincing evidence," so if you said the second sentence was the topic sentence, you were right. Here as in other paragraphs, the main idea is a general idea that summarizes what the entire paragraph is about. In other words, the main idea is an "umbrella" statement under which the other material in the paragraph fits. In this case, the other material is in the form of several examples that back up the main idea. The parts of the paragraph can be shown as follows:

Topic: ESP

Main idea: ESP is not documented by any convincing evidence.

Supporting details:
1. There have been no reports of "psychics" winning great sums at casinos.
2. Crimes are solved by police work, not psychics' tips.
3. Mind readers use simple psychological tricks, not psychic ability.

Finding the Topic

As the ESP paragraph shows, recognizing the topic of a selection can help you find the main idea. Remember that to find the topic, you should ask, "Who or what is the selection about?" Your choice for a topic should then be a subject that is neither too broad nor too narrow. Consider, for example, the following paragraph:

> In response to customers' bitter complaints about long lines, banks are trying new ways to shorten the wait or at least to make it more pleasant. One bank provides coffee and cookies so customers can munch while they wait. Other banks show action movies on a large video screen. One daring bank in California will pay a customer five dollars if he or she must wait more than five minutes for service. Still other banks offer the most obvious solution of all—they simply hire more bank tellers.

Now circle the letter of the item that you think is the topic of the paragraph. Then read the explanation below.

a. Waiting in line
b. Waiting in bank lines
c. Hiring more bank tellers

Explanation:

"Waiting in line" is too broad—it covers all types of lines, not just bank lines. "Hiring more bank tellers" is too narrow—it covers only one of the ways mentioned in the paragraph in which banks deal with long lines. There are other ways banks use that this item obviously does not cover. The topic of this paragraph is *b*, "Waiting in bank lines."

Now try to find the topic of the paragraph below. One of the three subjects shown is too broad to be the topic. In other words, it includes too much—it covers much more than what the paragraph covers. One is too narrow to be the topic. That is, it is not inclusive enough—it covers only a part of the paragraph, not all or most of it. A third subject is neither too narrow nor too broad—it is the topic of the paragraph.

Put a **B** by the subject that is too broad, an **N** by the topic that is too narrow, and a **T** by the subject that is the topic of the paragraph. Then read the explanation that follows.

> Desert plants have various features that make them highly tolerant of long dry spells. Many have waxy leaves, stems, or branches to reduce water loss. Others have very small leaves or no leaves at all, thereby reducing the surfaces from which they can evaporate. Also, the roots of some species often extend to great depths in order to tap the moisture found there. In

contrast, other desert plants produce a shallow but widespread root system that enables them to absorb great amounts of moisture quickly from the infrequent desert downpours. Often the stems of these plants are thickened by a spongy tissue that can store enough water for the plant until the next rainfall comes.

_____ Plants

_____ Deep root systems of desert plants

_____ Desert plants

Explanation:

The paragraph discusses only one type of plant, not all plants. Therefore "Plants" is too broad to be the topic. The one type of plant discussed in the paragraph is the topic: "Desert plants." "Deep root systems of desert plants" is too narrow to be the topic—it is only one of the several features of desert plants discussed in the paragraph.

In summary, to decide if a particular subject is the topic of a passage, ask yourself these questions:

1 Does this subject include much more than what the passage is about? (If so, the subject is too broad to be the topic.)

2 Is there important information in the passage that isn't covered by this subject? (If so, the subject is too narrow to be the topic.)

➤ *Practice 1*

After each paragraph are three subjects. One is the topic, another is too broad to be the topic, and a third is too narrow to be the topic. Label each subject with one of the following:

T — for the **topic** of the paragraph
B — for the subject that is too **broad** to be the topic
N — for the subject that is too **narrow** to be the topic

1. Before clocks were made, people kept track of time by other means. In ancient Egypt, people used a water clock. Water dripped slowly from one clay pot into another. People measured time according to how long it took one pot to empty and the other one to fill. Candle clocks were common during the Middle Ages. As such a candle burned, marks on its side showed about how much time had passed. A final ancient way to measure time was the sundial, which used the movement of the sun across the sky. The shadows moving across the face of the sundial showed what time it was.

      ___N___   Water clocks

      ___T___   Measuring time before clocks

      ___B___   Ancient inventions

2.   Have you ever wondered why the food in television advertisements often looks more mouth-watering than the same food at home? The reason is that TV advertisers use imaginative techniques to make food in ads look very appealing. According to one TV food stylist, Elmer's glue is often added to milk in television ads to make it look white and delightful. Similarly, the steaming roasted chickens in many fast-food commercials rely on spray paint, not seasonings, to get that rich brown color. Likewise, Ivory Soap is used to give coffee a fresh-brewed look.

      ___N___   Milk in TV ads

      ___T___   Food in TV ads

      ___B___   Television

3.   To reduce absenteeism, some businesses are using inventive techniques. One manufacturing company had each present worker pick a playing card each day. In each department, the employee with the best poker hand at the end of the week won twenty dollars. Attendance improved by 18 percent and remained high as long as poker hands were dealt. Another manufacturing plant distributed daily bingo numbers. When their bingo cards were filled, workers could spin a wheel and win from five to twenty-five dollars. This program was effective in reducing absenteeism and tardiness.

      ___B___   Business problems

      ___N___   Using bingo to reduce absenteeism

      ___T___   Reducing absenteeism

4.   For most of human history, societies were very small, usually having only about fifty members. Based on how they made their living, there were several kinds of simple societies. The majority were hunting and gathering societies. Rather than living in a fixed spot, they moved in search of game and edible plants. Slightly more advanced simple societies lived by herding animals. They, too, moved about as their animals required new grazing areas. Other simple societies mastered elementary gardening and thus tended to be less nomadic than the herders or the hunter-gatherers were. Nevertheless, they tended to stay in one spot just long enough to grow one crop and then moved on.

      ___B___   Human history

      ___T___   Early societies

      ___N___   Hunting societies

Finding the Topic Sentence

As you have seen, finding the topic of a paragraph prepares you to find the main idea. Once you have found the topic, you should ask yourself this question:

What is the author's main point about the topic?

For example, look again at the paragraph on bank lines.

> [1]In response to customers' bitter complaints about long lines, banks are trying new ways to shorten the wait or at least to make it more pleasant. [2]One bank provides coffee and cookies so customers can munch while they wait. [3]Other banks show action movies on a large video screen. [4]One daring bank in California will pay a customer five dollars if he or she must wait more than five minutes for service. [5]Still other banks offer the most obvious solution of all—they simply hire more bank tellers.

As you learned earlier, the topic of this paragraph is "waiting in bank lines." But what is the chief point the author is trying to make about that topic? Notice that sentences 2–5 discuss specific ways that banks try to make the wait more pleasant or shorter. The first sentence, however, is more general—it states that banks are responding to customers' complaints about long lines. It is supported by the specific details in the rest of the paragraph. Therefore sentence 1 is the topic sentence of the paragraph. The specific details provide examples of the main idea.

Below is the paragraph about desert plants that you have already read. You probably remember that the topic of this paragraph is desert plants. Now try to find the topic sentence, the sentence that states the main idea about that topic. Test a statement that you think is the main idea by asking, "Is this statement supported by all or most of the other material in the paragraph?" Write the number of the sentence you choose in the space provided. Then read the explanation that follows.

Topic sentence: _____

> [1]Desert plants have various features that make them highly tolerant of long dry spells. [2]Many have waxy leaves, stems, or branches to reduce water loss. [3]Others have very small leaves or no leaves at all, thereby reducing the surfaces from which they can evaporate. [4]Also, the roots of some species often extend to great depths in order to tap the moisture found there. [5]In contrast, other desert plants produce a shallow but widespread root system that enables them to absorb great amounts of moisture quickly from the infrequent desert downpours. [6]Often the stems of these plants are thickened by a spongy tissue that can store enough water for the plant until the next rainfall comes.

Explanation:

The first sentence makes a point about desert plants, the topic of the paragraph. After thinking about the paragraph, you may have decided that sentence is the topic sentence. If so, you should have checked yourself by asking, "Does the other material in the paragraph support the idea that 'Desert plants have various features that make them highly tolerant of long dry spells'?" In fact, the rest of the paragraph does describe characteristics that make plants tolerant of dry spells. The specific details about features that reduce water loss, that reach moisture, and that store water all develop the general idea expressed in the first sentence. By asking and answering a basic question, you have made it clear that the first sentence is indeed the topic sentence.

The important hint given above for finding the topic sentence is worth repeating: Always test yourself on an idea you think is the main idea by asking, "Is this statement supported by all or most of the other material in the paragraph?"

The following practices will sharpen your sense of the difference between the topic and the topic sentence of a paragraph.

➤ Practice 2

This exercise will give you more practice in distinguishing between a topic (the general subject), a main idea (the primary point being made about the subject), and the specific ideas that support and develop the main idea. Each group of statements below includes one topic, one main idea (expressed in a topic sentence), and two supporting ideas. In the space provided, label each item with one of the following:

T — for the **topic**
MI — for the **main idea**
SD — for the **supporting details**

Group 1

_SD_ a. Staying in the sun too long can cause sunstroke.

_SD_ b. People develop skin cancer after years of working on their suntans.

_T_ c. Time in the sun.

_MI_ d. Spending time in the sun can be dangerous.

Group 2

_SD_ a. The creakings of a house settling may sound like a monster coming out of a grave.

_MI_ b. Nighttime noises can be frightening to children.

_SD_ c. Gusts of wind rattling a bedroom window can sound like invaders about to break in.

_T_ d. Noises at night.

Group 3

_T_ a. How vitamin C can cause scurvy.

_SD_ b. When a person takes large doses of vitamin C, the body speeds up its process of eliminating the excess.

_MI_ c. Taking large amounts of vitamin C and quitting suddenly can cause scurvy, a vitamin-deficiency disease.

_SD_ d. The body continues to rid itself of the vitamin for some time even after the large dose is discontinued, and a shortage results.

Group 4

_MI_ a. Love at first sight is a poor basis for a happy marriage, according to a study of one thousand married and divorced couples.

_SD_ b. Couples who knew each other only slightly but fell instantly in love found that their feelings for each other grew weaker instead of stronger.

_T_ c. Love at first sight.

_SD_ d. The couples who considered themselves happily married reported that they were not powerfully attracted to their partners when they first met, but that they gradually found each other more attractive as they grew to know and understand each other.

➤ *Practice 3*

Circle the letter of the correct topic of each paragraph. (To find the topic, remember to ask yourself, "Who or what is the paragraph about?") Then circle the letter of the topic sentence—the author's main point about the topic.

1.   Some people believe that if you spill salt, you must toss a pinch of salt over your left shoulder "into the Devil's face" in order to avoid bad luck. There are many such superstitions that cover everyday events. Others are the beliefs that umbrellas should not be opened indoors and that people should leave a friend's house by the same door they entered. And there are those who believe in knocking on wood when talking about good luck.

Topic:
a. Spilling salt
b. Umbrellas
c. Superstitions
d. Knocking on wood

Main idea:
a. "Some people believe that if you spill salt, you must toss a pinch of salt over your left shoulder 'into the Devil's face' in order to avoid bad luck."
b. "There are many such superstitions that cover everyday events."
c. "[Other superstitions] are the beliefs that umbrellas should not be opened indoors and that people should leave a friend's house by the same door they entered."
d. "And there are those who believe in knocking on wood when talking about good luck."

2.   According to one scientist who has studied aging, there are ways to remain healthy in old age. The key, he believes, is to continue to find mental and physical challenges. In addition, he recommends that people stick to a balanced, low-cholesterol diet and a reasonable exercise program throughout their lives. He also cautions people about the dangers of smoking.

Topic:
a. Science
b. Mental and physical challenges
c. Health in old age
d. Dangers of smoking

Main idea:
a. "According to one scientist who has studied aging, there are ways to remain healthy in old age."
b. "The key, he believes, is to continue to find mental and physical challenges."
c. "He recommends that people stick to a balanced, low-cholesterol diet and a reasonable exercise program throughout their lives."
d. "He also cautions people about the dangers of smoking."

3. One common example of instinct is the spider's spinning of its intricate web. No one teaches a spider how to spin; its inborn instinct allows it to accomplish the task. Another example of instinctive behavior is the salmon's struggle to swim upstream to lay its eggs. It would be much easier for the salmon to follow the current downstream, but instinct overrides all other considerations. Instinct is clearly a strong influence on animal behavior.

    Topic:
    a. Instinct
    b. Spiders
    c. The salmon's upstream struggle
    d. The spider's intricate web

    Main idea:
    a. "One common example of instinct is the spider's spinning of its intricate web."
    b. "Another example of instinctive behavior is the salmon's struggle to swim upstream to lay its eggs."
    c. "It would be much easier for the salmon to follow the current downstream, but instinct overrides all other considerations."
    d. "Instinct is clearly a strong influence on animal behavior."

4. Coal has been used for centuries. Yet it is far from being a desirable fuel. Mining it is dangerous and usually leaves large areas of land unfit for further use. Also, the air pollution due to burning coal damages the health of millions of people. Acid rain from the same source harms plant and animal life on a large scale. Most estimates put the number of deaths in the United States from cancer and respiratory diseases caused by burning coal at over ten thousand per year. Coal-burning power plants expose the people living around them to more radioactivity, from traces of uranium, thorium, and radon in their smoke, than do normally operating nuclear plants.

    Topic:
    a. Fuels
    b. Mining
    c. Effects of acid rain
    d. Coal

    Main idea:
    a. "Coal has been used for centuries."
    b. "Yet [coal] is far from being a desirable fuel."
    c. "Acid rain from the same source harms plant and animal life on a large scale."
    d. "Most estimates put the number of deaths in the United States from cancer and respiratory diseases caused by burning coal at over ten thousand per year."

LOCATIONS OF THE TOPIC SENTENCE

A topic sentence may appear at any point within a paragraph. Very commonly, it shows up at the beginning, as either the first or the second sentence. However, topic sentences may also appear further within a paragraph or even at the very end. They may even appear twice—at the beginning and the end. Following are explanations and examples of the various locations of topic sentences.

Topic Sentences at the Beginning

Topic Sentence
Supporting Detail
Supporting Detail
Supporting Detail
Supporting Detail

Introductory Detail
Topic Sentence
Supporting Detail
Supporting Detail
Supporting Detail

In textbooks, it is very common for the topic sentence to be either the first or the second sentence. As you may remember, the topic sentence of the paragraph about spanking is in the first sentence:

> **Spanking is a poor way to shape a child's behavior.** For one thing, the spanking will result in feelings of anger and frustration. The child, then, will not learn anything positive from the punishment. In addition, the spanking may actually lead to more bad behavior. Having learned that hitting is okay, the child may attack smaller children. Finally, the spanking teaches children to hide certain actions from their parents. Once out of their parents' sight, however, children may feel they can get away with the bad behavior.

When the topic sentence is the second sentence, the first sentence may have any of various functions. It may provide a transition from the previous paragraph, arouse the reader's interest, or provide important background for the main idea. It may introduce the topic of the paragraph or even present a supporting detail. The topic sentence of the ESP paragraph is the second sentence. The first sentence introduces the subject of ESP and leads the reader into the main idea.

> Extrasensory perception, or ESP, is an area that fascinates people. **However, ESP is not documented by any convincing evidence.** For instance, it would seem that ESP would be an excellent way of winning at games of chance, such as are played at gambling casinos. But casino owners in Las Vegas and Atlantic City report no problem with "psychics" winning great sums of money. For another thing, although great publicity is generated when a psychic seems to help police solve a crime, the value of such help has never been scientifically proven. Psychics' tips are usually worthless, and a case is solved through traditional police work. And while audiences may be

amazed at the feats of "mind readers," the fact is that mind readers use simple psychological tricks to exploit their audiences' willingness to believe.

➤ *Practice 4*

You have already found the topics of the following paragraphs in Practice 1. For this practice, try to find the sentence that expresses the main idea about each of those topics. Write the number of each topic sentence in the space provided. In each case, the main idea is expressed in either the first or the second sentence.

1. ^{1}Before clocks were made, people kept track of time by other means. ^{2}In ancient Egypt, people used a water clock. ^{3}Water dripped slowly from one clay pot into another. ^{4}People measured time according to how long it took one pot to empty and the other one to fill. ^{5}Candle clocks were common during the Middle Ages. ^{6}As such a candle burned, marks on its side showed about how much time had passed. ^{7}A final ancient way to measure time was the sundial, which used the movement of the sun across the sky. ^{8}The shadows moving across the face of the sundial showed what time it was.

    Topic sentence: __1__

2. ^{1}Have you ever wondered why the food in television advertisements often looks more mouth-watering than the same food at home? ^{3}The reason is that TV advertisers use imaginative techniques to make food in ads look very appealing. ^{3}According to one TV food stylist, Elmer's glue is often added to milk in television ads to make it look white and delightful. ^{4}Similarly, the steaming roasted chickens in many fast-food commercials rely on spray paint, not seasonings, to get that rich brown color. ^{5}Likewise, Ivory Soap is used to give coffee a fresh-brewed look.

    Topic sentence: __2__

3. ^{1}To reduce absenteeism, some businesses are using inventive techniques. ^{2}One manufacturing company had each present worker pick a playing card each day. ^{3}In each department, the employee with the best poker hand at the end of the week won twenty dollars. ^{4}Attendance improved by 18 percent and remained high as long as poker hands were dealt. ^{5}Another manufacturing plant distributed daily bingo numbers. ^{6}When their bingo cards were filled, workers could spin a wheel and win from five to twenty-five dollars. ^{7}This program was effective in reducing absenteeism and tardiness.

    Topic sentence: __1__

4. ^{1}For most of human history, societies were very small, usually having only about fifty members. ^{2}Based on how they made their living, there were several kinds of simple societies. ^{3}The majority were hunting and gathering

societies. [4]Rather than living in a fixed spot, they moved in search of game and edible plants. [5]Slightly more advanced simple societes lived by herding animals. [6]They, too, moved about as their animals required new grazing areas. [7]Other simple societies mastered elementary gardening and thus tended to be less nomadic than the herders or the hunter-gatherers were. [8]Nevertheless, they tended to stay in one spot just long enough to grow one crop and then moved on.

Topic sentence: ___2___

Topic Sentences Within a Paragraph

Introductory Detail
Introductory Detail
Topic Sentence
Supporting Detail
Supporting Detail

When the topic sentence appears somewhere within a paragraph, it is preceded by introductory sentences that may have any of the same functions as a single introductory sentence. They may relate the main idea to the previous paragraph, arouse the reader's interest, or give background for the main idea. They may introduce the topic of the paragraph or present one or more supporting details.

Here is an example of a paragraph in which the topic sentence is somewhere in the middle. Try to find it, and then write its number in the space provided. Then read the explanation that follows.

Topic sentence: _____

[1]Many of us are annoyed by telephone solicitors who call us day and night, trying to sell us everything from magazine subscriptions to vacation homes. [2]These electronic intruders don't seem to care how much they are inconveniencing us and refuse to take "no" for an answer. [3]However, these nuisance callers can be stopped if we take charge of the conversation. [4]As soon as one of them asks if we are Mr. or Ms. X, we should respond, "Yes, and are you a telephone solicitor?" [5]This technique puts them on the defensive. [6]We then have an opening to say that we don't accept solicitations over the phone, only through the mail. [7]This puts a quick end to the conversation.

If you thought the third sentence gives the main idea, you were correct. The two sentences before the topic sentence introduce the topic: the problem of annoying telephone solicitors. The topic sentence then gives the writer's main idea, which is that we can stop annoying telephone solicitors from going on by taking charge of the conversation. The rest of the paragraph develops that idea.

End of a Paragraph

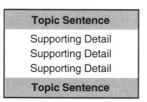

When the topic sentence is at the end of a paragraph, the previous sentences build up to the main idea. Here is an example of a paragraph in which the topic sentence comes last.

A study at one prison showed that owning a pet can change a hardened prison inmate into a more caring person. Another study discovered that senior citizens, both those living alone and those in nursing homes, became more interested in life when they were given pets to care for. Even emotionally disturbed children have been observed to smile and react with interest if there is a cuddly kitten or puppy to hold. **Animals, then, can be a means of therapy for many kinds of individuals.**

Beginning and End of a Paragraph

Even though a paragraph has only one main idea, it may include two topic sentences, with each providing the main idea in different words. The author may choose to state the main idea near the start of the paragraph and then emphasize it by restating it in other words later in the paragraph. In such cases, the topic sentences are often at the very beginning and the end. Such is the case in the following paragraph.

We are on our way to becoming a cashless, checkless society, a trend that began with the credit card. Now some banks are offering "debit cards" instead of credit cards. The costs of purchases made with these cards are deducted from the holder's bank account instead of being added to a monthly bill. And checking accounts, which are mainly used for paying bills, are going electronic. Now some people can make computer transactions over their push-button phones to pay bills by transferring money from their account to the account of whomever they owe. **Soon we may be able to conduct most of our business without signing a check or actually seeing the money we earn and spend.**

Note that the main idea in the first sentence of this paragraph—that "we are on our way to becoming a cashless, checkless society"—is restated in other words in the final sentence.

➤ *Practice 5*

The topic sentences of the following paragraphs appear at different locations—the beginning, somewhere in the middle, at the end, or at both the beginning and the end. Identify each topic sentence by filling in its sentence number in the space provided. *In the one case where the paragraph has a topic sentence at both the beginning and the end, write in both sentence numbers.*

1. ¹Serious depression, as opposed to the fleeting kind we all feel at times, has several warning signs. ²One symptom of depression is a change in sleep patterns—either sleeplessness or sleeping too much. ³Another sign is abnormal eating patterns; a person either may begin to eat a great deal or may almost stop eating. ⁴Finally, a general feeling of hopelessness may signal depression. ⁵People then feel indifferent to their families and jobs and may begin to think that life is not worth living.

    Topic sentence(s): ___1___

2. ¹School officials complain about vandalism that leaves classrooms wrecked and damages expensive equipment. ²Teachers complain about the low salaries they get for their difficult and important jobs. ³And parents complain that their children's test scores are dropping, that their children can't read or do math. ⁴The problems within our school systems are varied and affect almost everyone involved.

    Topic sentence(s): ___4___

3. ¹Every thirty-seven seconds, a car is stolen somewhere in the United States. ²Although this statistic is frightening, it is possible for drivers to prevent car theft if they take a few simple precautions. ³When they leave their cars, they should lock all valuables in the trunk or glove compartment to avoid tempting a thief to break in. ⁴Parking in the middle of the block on a busy, well-lighted street will deter would-be thieves. ⁵The most obvious precaution, of course, is always to lock the car and take the keys—even if the driver is stopping for just a minute. ⁶One out of every five stolen cars was left unlocked with the keys in the ignition.

    Topic sentence(s): ___2___

4. ¹One of the most significant factors in selling a product is how it is packaged. ²When Stuart Hall Company, which manufactures notebooks and paper

products for students, realized its sales were declining because fewer children were being born, it decided to change its products' appearance. ³So, beginning in 1968, the company replaced its plain tablets with colored paper and decorated the covers of its notebooks with the Pink Panther and other cartoon characters. ⁴Students loved the new designs, and sales soared. ⁵Packaging, therefore, can be a method of solving marketing problems.

Topic sentence(s): ___1, 5___

5.   ¹Effective punishment can help eliminate an undesirable behavior. ²However, if punishment is not chosen carefully, it can encourage—not discourage— bad behavior. ³A teacher may believe she is punishing a six-year-old boy when she shouts, "Mike, don't tell me you are out of your seat again. ⁴You never sit still!" ⁵In reality, Mike is gaining the attention he is seeking. ⁶Classmates turn and notice him, and the teacher becomes totally preoccupied with his problem. ⁷What she thought was a punishment turns out to be positive reinforcement. ⁸The next time Mike feels a need for attention, he will know that getting out of his seat and walking around the classroom will win the notice he wants. ⁹Similarly, a hockey player put in the penalty box for a clash and fight often gets cheers from the crowd. ¹⁰His rowdy behavior may well increase because of the attention of the crowd.

Topic sentence(s): ___2___

Topic Sentences That Cover More Than One Paragraph

At times you will find that a topic sentence provides the main idea for more than one paragraph. This occurs when an author wishes to break up the development of a main idea for some reason. For instance, the supporting details may seem too lengthy for one paragraph. He or she then breaks up the material into two or more paragraphs to make it easier to read.

See if you can find the topic sentence for the paragraphs below. Then write its number in the space provided. The paragraphs are taken from an essay on factors involved in highway accidents.

Topic sentence: _____

¹Like poor highway and automobile design, poor attitudes about driving contribute to the high rate of traffic accidents and their brutal effects. ²Some people persist in believing that they can drink and be alert drivers. ³Yet alcohol is estimated to be a factor in at least half of all fatal highway accidents. ⁴Refusing to wear safety belts is another way to increase fatalities. ⁵Statistics show that the chances of being seriously hurt or dying in a car accident are greater when a seat belt is not worn.

⁶Also potentially deadly is the view that the best driving is fast driving. ⁷Again, statistics contradict this attitude—fast driving is more likely to be deadly driving. ⁸After the speed limit was lowered in 1973 to fifty-five miles per hour, traffic fatalities fell significantly. ⁹Evidence on speed limits in other countries is just as telling. ¹⁰Where high-speed driving is permitted, a higher rate of accidents occurs.

Explanation:

After you read the first paragraph, it may have become clear that sentence 1 is the topic sentence. The main idea is that "poor attitudes about driving contribute to the high rate of traffic accidents and their brutal effects." Sentences 2 and 3 deal with the attitude of those who feel that drinking does not interfere with driving. Sentences 4 and 5 deal with not wearing seat belts.

By beginning with the words "also potentially deadly," the first sentence of the next paragraph tells us that it will continue to develop the topic sentence of the previous paragraph. The author has simply chosen to break the subject down into two smaller paragraphs rather than include all the information in one long paragraph. The relationship between the two paragraphs can be seen clearly in the following outline:

Main idea: Some attitudes about driving contribute to traffic accidents.
1. Drinking does not interfere with driving.
2. Wearing seat belts is not important.
3. Good driving is fast driving.

➤ *Practice 6*

Below are two examples of topic sentences that cover more than one paragraph. Fill in the number of the topic sentence in each case.

1.   ¹People often think of shame as a strong form of embarrassment. ²A psychological study of 104 persons, however, suggests that shame and embarrassment are quite different experiences. ³In general, embarrassment results from a relatively minor event that occurs while others are around. ⁴It is more likely to cause a person to blush. ⁵Also, an embarrassing event is likely to include an element of surprise and to be remembered with smiles or jokes. ⁶Embarrassment generally does not lead to a feeling that one must correct a situation.

⁷Shame is felt when people reveal a personal flaw to themselves and perhaps to others. ⁸Unlike embarrassment, it is likely to make one feel that a situation needs repairing. ⁹In addition, while embarassment is strongly related to how we believe others view us, shame is often felt when one is alone. ¹⁰And it is not generally looked upon later as humorous.

Topic sentence: ___2___   The two paragraphs are not about shame as a form of embarrassment, so sentence 1 cannot be the topic sentence. The paragraphs are about the differences alluded to in sentence 2.

2.   ¹A controversial free-speech issue of recent years has been whether the First Amendment protects the right to burn or disfigure an American flag. ²In 1989 the Supreme Court, by a 5-to-4 vote, declared unconstitutional a Texas law against violating the flag. ³Soon after, Congress enacted a law that made it a federal crime to burn or deface the American flag. ⁴In June 1990 the Court, again by a 5-to-4 vote, made this law invalid. ⁵In both cases the Court found that the government was engaged in illegal content regulation. ⁶It was singling out certain ideas for prohibition while allowing other ideas to be expressed.

⁷Opponents of the Court's ruling, with the support of President George Bush, placed pressure on Congress to initiate a constitutional amendment. ⁸This amendment would have given both Congress and the states the "power to prohibit the physical desecration of the Flag of the United States." ⁹However, the proposed amendment failed to get the required two-thirds vote in the House of Representatives.

Topic sentence: ___1___   Sentences 2–9 illustrate the controversy referred to in Sentence 1.

➤ Review Test 1

To review what you've learned in this chapter, complete each of the following sentences about main ideas.

1. The umbrella statement that covers all of the material in a paragraph is its

   (topic, topic sentence, supporting detail) _____*topic sentence*_____.

2. To locate the main idea of a selection, you may find it helpful to first decide

   on its *(topic, location)* _____*topic*_____.

3. An idea that is *(too broad, too narrow)* _____*too broad*_____ to be

   the topic of a paragraph will include much more than the paragraph covers.

4. While a topic sentence many appear anywhere within a paragraph, in

   textbooks it very commonly appears at the _____*beginning*_____.

5. To help you decide if a certain sentence is the topic sentence, ask yourself,

   "Is this statement supported by all or most of the _____

   _____*material in the paragraph*_____?"

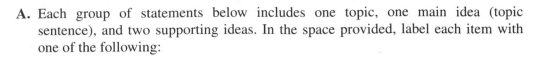

➤ *Review Test 2*

A. Each group of statements below includes one topic, one main idea (topic sentence), and two supporting ideas. In the space provided, label each item with one of the following:

> **T** — for the **topic**
> **MI** — for the **main idea**
> **SD** — for the **supporting details**

Group 1

_T_   a. Stretching exercises.

_SD_   b. Limbering up after strenuous exertion reduces the risk of stiffness, soreness, and injury.

_SD_   c. Slow, simple stretching before exercising make muscles more pliable so that vigorous activity becomes easier.

_MI_   d. Stretching is important both before and after strenuous exercise.

Group 2

_SD_   a. Rubbing one's nose and eyes transfers viruses to the hands, which then contaminate whatever they touch, such as a table top or telephone.

_SD_   b. Because the dried cold virus can live as long as three hours, you can pick it up long after the person with a cold is gone.

_T_   c. The most likely way of catching a cold.

_MI_   d. The most likely way to catch a cold is by touching an object that someone suffering from a cold has handled.

Group 3

_MI_   a. Beethoven continued to compose even when he was completely deaf.

_SD_   b. Sometimes he tried out passages at the piano to make sure they could be played, but his playing was agonizing to hear.

_SD_   c. Every day at dawn, Beethoven began working at his desk, writing down the music he heard in his head.

_T_   d. Beethoven.

Group 4

  _SD_ a. Antibiotics have helped cure children of certain infectious diseases.

  _T_ b. Childhood diseases that used to be fatal.

  _SD_ c. Better hygiene has helped to stop infectious diseases from spreading.

  _MI_ d. Many childhood diseases that used to be fatal are now under control.

B. Circle the letter of the correct topic of each paragraph. (To find the topic, remember to ask yourself, "Who or what is the paragraph about?") Then circle the letter of the topic sentence. Remember that the topic sentence will be the author's main idea about the topic. It will cover all or most of the details of the paragraph.

1. One of the gravest charges against the human race is that only humans make war. The German writer Hans Magnus Enzensberger began his recent book on European civil war by saying, "Animals fight, but they do not wage war." Despite the common belief that only humans engage in warfare, some animals do wage war. Ant wars are the best known, but insects are sufficiently unlike us that people seldom take that to heart. In recent years, it has become clear that animals as closely related to us as chimpanzees can go to war. The famous chimps of Gombe not only patrol the borders of other bands, but make raids with deadly intent. [7]They may kill and eat one another.

    Topic:
    (a.) Animals and war   c. Hans Magnus Enzensberger
    b. Ants and war   d. The chimps of Gombe

    Main idea:
    a. "One of the gravest charges against the human race is that only humans make war."
    (b.) "Despite the common belief that only humans engage in warfare, some animals do wage war."
    c. "Ant wars are the best known, but insects are sufficiently dissimilar to us that people seldom take that to heart."
    d. "The famous chimps of Gombe not only patrol the borders of other bands, but make raids with deadly intent."

2. Men, we are reminded over and over, are the stronger sex. Yet in terms of health, males are more vulnerable than females at every age. More males than females are miscarried, are stillborn, or die in their first year of life. In all societies, men die earlier than women do. American men are more likely than women to die from heart disease, lung disease, and cirrhosis of the liver. They are more likely to suffer from stress-related diseases, such as hypertension, ulcers, and asthma. They are hospitalized for mental illness

more frequently. Women attempt suicide more often than men, but men succeed in killing themselves three times as often (largely because they use violent means—guns rather than sleeping pills).

Topic:

a. Men's and women's health   c. Men and heart disease
b. Men and women   d. Suicide among men and women

Main idea:

a. "Men, we are reminded over and over, are the stronger sex."
b. "Yet in terms of health, males are more vulnerable than females at every age."
c. "More males than females are miscarried, are stillborn, or die in their first year of life."
d. "American men are more likely than women to die from heart disease, lung disease, and cirrhosis of the liver."

➤ Review Test 3

The topic sentence (main idea) appears at various places in the following paragraphs. Write the number of each topic sentence in the space provided. *Fill in two numbers for the one paragraph in which the main idea appears at both the beginning and the end.*

1. ¹Some interior designers seem to think plastic plants are superior to real ones. ²Real plants, however, can do much that even the most realistic plastic ones can't. ³Plants, for instance, improve the quality of the air by giving off oxygen and absorbing certain air pollutants. ⁴Also, they cool the air as water evaporates from their leaves. ⁵Large plants—trees and shrubs—can even muffle the otherwise harsh sounds of construction work and street traffic.

   Topic sentence(s): ___2___

2. ¹New technology often creates unanticipated problems. ²Automobiles, for example, provide numerous benefits, but they also pollute the air and kill about fifty thousand Americans each year. ³It is difficult to imagine life without electricity, but the generation of electricity pollutes the air or causes the thermal pollution of rivers. ⁴Insecticides and chemical fertilizers have performed miracles in agriculture but have polluted food and streams (and even "killed" some lakes). ⁵Obviously, the slogan of the Du Pont Corporation—"Better living through chemistry"—is not entirely correct. ⁶Jet planes, while helping us in many ways, cause air pollution (one jet taking off emits the same amount of hydrocarbon as the exhausts from ten thousand automobiles) and noise pollution near busy airports.

   Topic sentence(s): ___1___

3.   ¹For many couples, the first vacation they take together can either make or break their relationship. ²If they both have careers, the daily pressures of work and home responsibilities may have covered up sources of disagreement. ³However, without these distractions, the disagreements can surface. ⁴In addition, if one wants to splurge and the other prefers a no-frills camping trip, or if one is a neat packer and the other is disorganized, conflicts will certainly result. ⁵Unless both partners communicate, are willing to compromise, and remain flexible during the vacation, their first trip together may be their last.

Topic sentence(s): _1, 5_

4.   ¹Queen Isabella of Spain, who died in 1504, boasted that she'd had only two baths in her life—at birth and before her marriage. ²In colonial America, leaders frowned on bathing, because it involved nudity, which, they feared, could lead to loose morals. ³Indeed, laws in Virginia and Pennsylvania either limited or outright banned bathing—and for a time in Philadelphia, anyone who bathed more than once a month faced jail. ⁴Furthermore, some of the early Christian churches discouraged sudsing up because of its association with the immorality common in the Roman baths. ⁵Clearly, the notion that cleanliness is next to godliness has not always been a popular one.

Topic sentence(s): _5_

5.   ¹Criticism is a valuable means of helping ourselves and others achieve personal growth. ²However, because it is often done carelessly or cruelly, criticism has a bad reputation. ³Here are some guidelines for offering criticism constructively. ⁴First, wait until the person asks for feedback on his or her performance or actions. ⁵Unasked-for criticism is not usually valuable. ⁶Second, describe the person's behavior as specifically as possible before you criticize it. ⁷Instead of just saying, "You were awful," tell the person exactly what you observed. ⁸And finally, try to balance your criticism with positive statements. ⁹Look for significant points in the other person's performance that you can honestly praise.

Topic sentence(s): _3_

Comments: Paragraph 1—Sentences 3–5 present some things plants can do that plastic plants cannot.
Paragraph 2—Sentences 2–6 present some of the unanticipated problems that are mentioned in the topic sentence.
Paragraph 3—Sentences 2–4 are about the challenges of vacationing together referred to in sentences 1 and 5.
Paragraph 4—Sentences 1–4 are about low standards of cleanliness of previous times.
Paragraph 5—Sentences 1 and 2 introduce the topic of giving criticism. Sentences 4–9 provide the guidelines mentioned in sentence 3.

➤ *Review Test 4*

Here is a chance to apply your understanding of main ideas to a full-length selection. Read the article below, and then answer the questions that follow on main ideas. There are also vocabulary questions to help you continue practicing the skill of understanding vocabulary in context.

Words to Watch

Below are some words in the reading that do not have strong context support. Each word is followed by the number of the paragraph in which it appears and its meaning there. These words are indicated in the article by a small circle (°).

tequila (1): a strong liquor made from a Mexican plant
myth (3): a false belief
illusion (8): false impression
irony (12): a meaning that is the opposite of what is actually said

HERE'S TO YOUR HEALTH

Joan Dunayer

1   As the only freshman on his high school's varsity wrestling team, Tod was anxious to fit in with his older teammates. One night after a match, he was offered a tequila° bottle on the ride home. Tod felt he had to accept, or he would seem like a sissy. He took a swallow, and every time the bottle was passed back to him, he took another swallow. After seven swallows, he passed out. His terrified teammates carried him into his home, and his mother then rushed him to the hospital. After his stomach was pumped, Tod learned that his blood alcohol level had been so high that he was lucky not to be in a coma or dead.

2   Unfortunately, drinking is not unusual among high-school students or, for that matter, in any other segment of our society. And that's no accident. There are numerous influences in our society urging people to drink, not the least of which is advertising.

Who can recall a televised baseball or basketball game without a beer commercial? Furthermore, alcohol ads appear with pounding frequency in magazines, on billboards, and in college newspapers. According to industry estimates, brewers spend more than $600 million a year on radio and TV commercials and another $90 million on print ads. In addition, the liquor industry spends about $230 million a year on print advertising. And recently, Joseph E. Seagram & Sons, Inc. decided to defy the liquor industry's voluntary ban on radio and TV ads for hard liquor. The company began running commercials for its Crown Royal Canadian Whiskey on a Texas TV station.

3   To top it all off, this aggressive advertising of alcohol promotes a harmful myth about drinking.

4   Part of the myth° is that liquor signals professional success. In a slick

men's magazine, one full-page ad for Scotch whiskey shows two men seated in an elegant restaurant. Both are in their thirties, perfectly groomed, and wearing expensive-looking gray suits. The windows are draped with velvet, the table with spotless white linen. Each place-setting consists of a long-stemmed water goblet, silver utensils, and thick silver plates. On each plate is a half-empty cocktail glass. The two men are grinning and shaking hands, as if they've just concluded a business deal. The caption reads, "The taste of success."

5   Contrary to what the liquor company would have us believe, drinking is more closely related to lack of success than to achievement. Among students, the heaviest drinkers have the lowest grades. In the work force, alcoholics are frequently late or absent, tend to perform poorly, and often get fired. Although alcohol abuse occurs in all economic classes, it remains most prevalent among the poor.

6   Another part of the alcohol myth is that drinking makes you more attractive to the opposite sex. "Hot, hot, hot," one commercial's soundtrack begins, as the camera scans a crowd of college-age beachgoers. Next it follows the curve of a woman's leg up to her bare hip and lingers there. She is young, beautiful, wearing a bikini. A young guy, carrying an ice chest, positions himself near to where she sits. He is tan, muscular. She doesn't show much interest—until he opens the chest and takes out a beer. Now she smiles over at him. He raises his eyebrows and, invitingly, holds up another can. She joins him. This beer, the song concludes, "attracts like no other."

7   Beer doesn't make anyone sexier. Like all alcohol, it lowers the levels of male hormones in men and of female hormones in women—even when taken in small amounts. In substantial amounts, alcohol can cause infertility in women and impotence in men. Some alcoholic men even develop enlarged breasts, from their increased female hormones.

8   The alcohol myth also creates the illusion° that beer and athletics are a perfect combination. One billboard features three high-action images: a basketball player running at top speed, a surfer riding a wave, and a basketball player leaping to make a dunk shot. A particular light beer, the billboard promises, "won't slow you down."

9   "Slow you down" is exactly what alcohol does. Drinking plays a role in over six million injuries each year—not counting automobile accidents. Even in small amounts, alcohol dulls the brain, reducing muscle coordination and slowing reaction time. It also interferes with the ability to focus the eyes and adjust to a sudden change in brightness — such as the flash of a car's headlights. Drinking and driving, responsible for over half of all automobile deaths, is the leading cause of death among teenagers. Continued alcohol abuse can physically change the brain, permanently impairing learning and memory. Long-term drinking is related to malnutrition, weakening of the bones, and ulcers. It increases the risk of liver failure, heart disease, and stomach cancer.

10   Finally, according to the myth, alcohol generates a warm glow of happiness that unifies the family. In one popular film, the only food visible at a wedding reception is an untouched wedding cake, but beer, whiskey, and vodka flow freely. Most of the guests are drunk. After shouting into the microphone

to get everyone's attention, the band leader asks the bride and groom to come forward. They are presented with two wine-filled silver drinking cups branching out from a single stem. "If you can drink your cups without spilling any wine," the band leader tells them, "you will have good luck for the rest of your lives." The couple drain their cups without taking a breath, and the crowd cheers.

11   A marriage, however, is unlikely to be "lucky" if alcohol plays a major role in it. Nearly two-thirds of domestic violence involves drinking. Alcohol abuse by parents is strongly tied to child neglect and juvenile delinquency. Drinking during pregnancy can lead to miscarriage and is a major cause of such birth defects

as deformed limbs and mental retardation. Those who depend on alcohol are far from happy: over a fourth of the patients in state and county mental institutions have alcohol problems; more than half of all violent crimes are alcohol-related; the rate of suicide among alcoholics is fifteen times higher than among the general population.

Advertisers would have us believe   12 the myth that alcohol is part of being successful, sexy, healthy, and happy; but those who have suffered from it— directly or indirectly—know otherwise. For alcohol's victims, "Here's to your health" rings with a terrible irony° when it is accompanied by the clink of liquor glasses.

Reading Comprehension Questions

Vocabulary in Context

1. In the excerpt below, the word *caption* means
   a. man.
   b. menu.
   c. contract that seals the business deal.
   d. words accompanying the picture.

   "In a slick men's magazine, one full-page ad for Scotch whiskey shows two men seated in an elegant restaurant. . . . The caption reads 'The taste of success.'" (Paragraph 4)

2. In the sentence below, the word *prevalent* means
   a. weak.
   b. colorful.
   c. widespread.
   d. inexpensive.

   "Although alcohol abuse occurs in all economic classes, it remains most prevalent among the poor." (Paragraph 5)

3. In the excerpt below, the word *substantial* means
   (a.) large.
   b. reasonable.
   c. weak.
   d. pleasing.

The word *small* is an antonym clue.

   "Beer . . . lowers the levels of male hormones in men and of female hormones in women—even when taken in small amounts. In substantial amounts, alcohol can cause infertility in women and impotence in men." (Paragraph 7)

4. In the sentence below, the word *impairing* means
   (a.) damaging.
   b. doubling.
   c. postponing.
   d. teaching.

   "Continued alcohol abuse can physically alter the brain, permanently impairing learning and memory." (Paragraph 9)

5. In the sentence below, the word *generates* means
   a. removes.
   b. hides.
   (c.) produces.
   d. follows.

Comment: Items 1, 2, 4, and 5 have general-sense-of-the-sentence context clues.

   "Finally, according to the myth, alcohol generates a warm glow of happiness that unifies the family." (Paragraph 10)

Main Ideas

6. The topic sentence of paragraph 2 is its
   a. first sentence.
   b. second sentence.
   (c.) third sentence.
   d. last sentence.

7. The topic sentence of paragraph 4 is its
   (a.) first sentence.
   b. second sentence.
   c. third sentence.
   d. last sentence.

The main idea is supported by one extended example.

8. The topic of paragraph 5 is
   a. drinking and grades.
   b. drinking and work.
   c. drinking and the poor.
   (d.) drinking and lack of success.

9. The topic sentence of paragraph 5 is its
   (a.) first sentence.
   b. second sentence.
   c. third sentence.
   d. fourth sentence.

10. The topic sentence of paragraph 10 is its
    (a.) first sentence.
    b. second sentence.
    c. next-to-the-last sentence.
    d. last sentence.

Discussion Questions

1. Unfortunately, Tod's experience with alcohol is not so rare. Do you know anyone who has had a negative experience because of drinking or because of drinking and driving? Where was that person drinking, and how much did he or she have? Explain what eventually happened.

2. If it's true that "beer doesn't make anyone sexier," why do you think so many young people drink so much beer in social situations?

3. Think about a wine, liquor, or beer ad you have seen in a magazine, in a newspaper, or on television. What part of the alcohol myth described in "Here's to Your Health" does that ad promote? What details of the ad contribute to that element of the myth?

4. Cigarette advertising is no longer allowed on television. Do you think beer ads should also be outlawed on TV? In college newspapers? Explain your answers.

Check Your Performance   **MAIN IDEAS**

Activity	Number Right	Points	Score
Review Test 1 (5 items)	_____	x 2 =	_____
Review Test 2 (20 items)	_____	x 1.5 =	_____
Review Test 3 (5 items)	_____	x 6 =	_____
Review Test 4 (10 items)	_____	x 3 =	_____
		TOTAL SCORE =	_____%

Enter your total score into the **Reading Performance Chart: Review Tests** on the inside back cover.

MAIN IDEAS: Test 1

Each of the following groups of statements includes one topic, one main idea (topic sentence), and two supporting ideas. Identify each item in the space provided as either the topic (**T**), the main idea (**MI**), or a supporting detail (**SD**).

Group 1

_MI_ a. A drive-in church in Daytona Beach, Florida, has unusual services.

_SD_ b. The church's members, nearly 1,800, come to services dressed in shorts.

_T_ c. Unusual church services.

_SD_ d. Members stay in their cars during services, which take place in a former drive-in movie.

Group 2

_SD_ a. It is said that the antidote to walking under a ladder is to quickly make a wish or cross your fingers.

_SD_ b. If a black cat crosses your path, go back home.

_MI_ c. For the superstitious, there are remedies for worrisome accidents.

_T_ d. Remedies for the superstitious.

Group 3

_SD_ a. Since powerwalkers always have one foot on the ground, they feel only half as much impact when they touch down.

_MI_ b. For the city dweller, powerwalking—or walking briskly—has advantages over jogging.

_T_ c. Powerwalking and jogging.

_SD_ d. The hard surfaces in our cities are kinder to the bodies of walkers than those of joggers.

(Continues on next page)

Group 4

_MI_   a. Driving is less safe at night than in the daytime.

_T_   b. Driving after dark.

_SD_   c. In 1996, for example, 58 percent of all traffic deaths took place at night.

_SD_   d. The chances of being in a fatal accident are much greater at night than during the day.

Group 5

_T_   a. Growth factors.

_SD_   b. Growth factors have healed eye wounds that previously would have required surgery.

_MI_   c. Scientists have discovered human substances called growth factors, chemicals that may revolutionize medicine.

_SD_   d. Researchers feel that growth factors may turn out to cure sterility in men and Alzheimer's disease.

MAIN IDEAS: Test 2

Circle the letter of the correct topic of each paragraph. (To find the topic, remember to ask yourself, "Who or what is the paragraph about?") Then circle the letter of the topic sentence—the author's main point about the topic.

1. People interested in physical fitness need not spend hundreds of dollars on fancy exercise equipment or health club memberships. Anyone can get into good shape simply by climbing stairs. Stair-climbing helps in weight loss; just walking up and down two flights of stairs a day instead of riding an elevator will take off six pounds a year. Climbing stairs is also good for the heart and can prevent heart attacks. And frequent stair-climbing strengthens the muscles of the legs and buttocks.

   Topic: a. Exercise equipment   c. Weight loss
               (b.) Stair-climbing   d. Health club memberships

   Main idea: a. "People interested in physical fitness need not spend hundreds of dollars on fancy exercise equipment or health club memberships."
               (b.) "Anyone can get into good shape simply by climbing stairs."
               c. "Stair-climbing helps in weight loss; just walking up and down two flights of stairs a day instead of riding an elevator will take off six pounds a year."
               d. "Climbing stairs is also good for the heart and can prevent heart attacks."

2. Why do people get married? According to pollster Louis Harris, there are three popular reasons for getting married. The most popular reason is for love, cited by 83 percent of both men and women as good grounds for getting married. The next most popular reason for getting married is "to be with a particular person," which was stated by 55 percent of the population. Finally, according to 44 percent, "to have children" is another compelling reason to get married.

   Topic: a. Love   (c.) Getting married
               b. Desire to be with a particular person   d. Having children

   Main idea: (a.) "According to pollster Louis Harris, there are three popular reasons for getting married."
               b. "The most popular reason is for love, cited by 83 percent of both men and women as good grounds for getting married."
               c. "The next most popular reason for getting married is 'to be with a particular person,' which was stated by 55 percent of the population."
               d. "Finally, according to 44 percent, 'to have children' is another compelling reason to get married."

(Continues on next page)

3.   Hospices are a special type of health-care institution. Hospices differ from hospitals and nursing homes in several ways. First of all, they treat patients suffering from incurable diseases who are not expected to live for more than a year. Hospitals, however, aim to help patients recover from disease, and nursing homes provide long-term care for the handicapped and elderly. Also, the hospice's purpose is to help the dying and their families. In contrast, hospitals and nursing homes have limited resources for helping patients' families.

Topic: a. Patients   c. Long-term care
              (b.) Hospices   d. Incurable diseases

Main idea: a. "Hospices are a special type of health-care institution."
              (b.) "Hospices differ from hospitals and nursing homes in several ways."
              c. "Hospitals, however, aim to help patients recover from disease, and nursing homes provide long-term care for the handicapped and elderly."
              d. "Also, the hospice's purpose is to help the dying and their families."

4.   Because the achieving of adulthood is a significant time in a young person's life, many traditional cultures mark the event in some ceremonial way. In some cultures, the ceremony is primarily a religious one. Jewish 13-year-olds are welcomed into the adult community through a bar or bat mitzvah, in which they read from the Torah during a synagogue service. Other ceremonies emphasize the taking on of adult characteristics. When a Northern Shoshone Indian girl begins menstruating for the first time, she is isolated and kept very busy so that she will become an industrious woman. And some ceremonies involve a painful coming-of-age rite. A boy of the Andaman Islands is welcomed to manhood by having sixty or more cuts made in his back with a sharpened arrowhead.

Topic: a. Young people   c. Painful coming-of-age ceremonies
              b. Religious ceremonies   (d.) The achieving of adulthood

Main idea: a. To young people, the achieving of adulthood is a significant time.
              b. Religious ceremonies vary from culture to culture.
              c. Painful coming-of-age ceremonies include cutting the back of a boy of the Andaman Islands with a sharpened arrowhead.
              (d.) The achieving of adulthood is marked in traditional cultures in ceremonial ways.

MAIN IDEAS: Test 3

The five paragraphs that follow are on a first level of difficulty. Each has a topic sentence (main idea) that may appear at any place within the paragraph. Write the number of each topic sentence in the space provided.

1.   [1]Creatures that are very sensitive to the changes in air before a storm can "predict" a change in the weather. [2]Birds, for example, sense the pressure change and fly lower. [3]Low-flying birds, then, indicate that rain is coming. [4]Similarly, houseflies detect this change and move indoors to avoid the downpour. [5]And cats are known to groom themselves just before a storm. [6]In doing so, they are reacting to the static electricity that enters the air before a thunderstorm. [7]The electricity separates their fur and makes them feel dirty, so they lick themselves to make the fur smooth and "clean" again.

Topic sentence: _____1_____

2.   [1]How does one decide on a career? [2]According to one researcher, the process of choosing a career begins in childhood and goes through three stages. [3]During the fantasy period, before adolescence, children choose careers that seem exciting to them; they are unaware that there are any limits on what they can do. [4]In adolescence they enter an uncertain period during which they begin to consider their interests and abilities and try to match them with various career opportunities. [5]In late adolescence and young adulthood, they enter the realistic choice period. [6]This period involves active exploration of various kinds of work, a further narrowing of alternatives, and finally a more or less permanent commitment to a career.

Topic sentence: _____2_____

3.   [1]The eruption of volcanoes has caused death and misery throughout the centuries. [2]Yet in parts of Italy, Iceland, Chile, and Bolivia, volcanic steam is used to run heat and power plants. [3]Pumice, which is made from volcanic lava, is used as a grinder and polisher. [4]Sulfur produced by volcanoes is useful to the chemical industry. [5]Hawaiian farmers grow crops on land made rich by decayed volcanic material. [6]Clearly, in spite of all the damage they cause, volcanoes do benefit us in various ways.

Topic sentence: _____6_____

(Continues on next page)

4.   [1]Adult children who move back home can avoid family conflicts by following some helpful tips. [2]First, they should contribute what they can—and it doesn't necessarily have to be in terms of money. [3]Being productive family members will help them earn their keep. [4]This can involve tutoring or coaching younger sisters or brothers, or helping Mom and Dad with household chores and errands. [5]Second, grown children at home should not expect their parents to rescue them from difficulties. [6]As adults, they are responsible for getting out of their own scrapes—and for trying to avoid scrapes in the first place. [7]Last, they must respect their parents' lifestyles and own needs for independence. [8]It is unrealistic to expect parents' lives to revolve around the needs of a grown child, as they may have when the child was younger.

Topic sentence: _____1_____

5.   [1]Police estimate that only 1 to 2 percent of hitchhiking crimes are reported, so there are no accurate statistics on such events. [2]But frequent horror stories indicate that hitchhiking can be dangerous to both hitchhiker and driver. [3]There was the nineteen-year old woman who accepted a lift from three young men in New Jersey, expecting a ride across the bridge to New York City. [4]Instead they drove to a motel, where they repeatedly raped her. [5]Luckily, she escaped with her life. [6]Less fortunate was the eighteen-year-old woman student who disappeared from campus after accepting a ride with a stranger and whose decomposed body was found in a suburban sewage plant two years later. [7]Male hitchhikers are less open to assault, but a number of incidents show that they are far from immune. [8]Hitchhikers also face the hazards of riding with an intoxicated or stoned driver, not the least of which is an accident. [9]They also risk assault or robbery by other hitchhikers and being stranded in out-of-the-way places. [10]Drivers, too, are subject to assault and robbery. [11]And they risk accident by stopping on a busy highway, or arrest if their passengers happen to be carrying drugs. [12]Some male drivers have picked up young girls who threatened to call the police and cry rape unless the men handed over all their money.

Topic sentence: _____2_____

Comments: Paragraph 1—Sentences 2–7 provide and explain examples of the main idea.

Paragraph 2—The first sentence cannot be the topic sentence because a question cannot be the main idea. Sentences 3–6 explain the "three stages" mentioned in sentence 2.

Paragraph 3—The first sentence cannot be the topic sentence, since if it were, the paragraph would have to be about the death and misery caused by the eruption of volcanoes. Instead, the paragraph lists the ways in which volcanoes benefit us.

Paragraph 4—Sentences 2–7 provides the tips mentioned in the topic sentence.

Paragraph 5—Sentence 1 introduces the topic of hitchhiking. Sentence 2 then mentions the "horror stories" about hitchhiking that are illustrated by the rest of the paragraph.

MAIN IDEAS: Test 4

The five paragraphs that follow are on a second level of difficulty. Each has a topic sentence (main idea) that may appear at any place within the paragraph. Write the number of each topic sentence in the space provided. For the one case in which there are two topic sentences, write in both numbers.

1. [1]Meditation provides several physical benefits. [2]For example, it has been found to change the brain-wave patterns of the meditator. [3]Specifically, it increases the occurrence of "alpha waves," which are associated with relaxation. [4]During meditation, a person usually consumes less oxygen than normal. [5]Decreased oxygen use indicates a very deep state of relaxation. [6]In some cases meditation has even been shown to lower high blood pressure. [7]The effects of meditation show that it can contribute to good health.

    Topic sentence(s): ___1, 7___

2. [1]By the end of the first series of Sherlock Holmes stories, the author, Sir Arthur Conan Doyle, had become tired of writing detective stories. [2]So at the end of his second book of Holmes stories, he decided to have the detective die. [3]The book ends with Holmes and his archenemy, Moriarty, plunging to their deaths from a high cliff overlooking a waterfall. [4]After that, hundreds of letters poured in to Conan Doyle, begging him to bring Holmes back. [5]Also, magazines offered him huge sums of money for additional Sherlock Holmes adventures. [6]Finally, after nine years, Conan Doyle wrote a new story in which Holmes reappears and tells Dr. Watson that he did not die after all. [7]Sometimes it is the reader, not the author, who determines how long fictional heroes will live.

    Topic sentence(s): ___7___

3. [1]The stages of life, from birth to death, may seem controlled by biology. [2]However, the way we think about life's stages is shaped by society. [3]During the Middle Ages, for example, children dressed—and were expected to act— just like little adults. [4]Adolescence became a distinct stage of life only fairly recently, when a separate teenage subculture began to appear. [5]Until then, young people were "children" until about age 16. [6]Then they went to work, married, and had their own children. [7]Today, "young adulthood" has become a new stage of life, stretching from about age 20 to 30. [8]As life expectancy becomes longer and people spend years in active retirement, older adulthood has also become a distinct life stage.

    Topic sentence(s): ___2___

(Continues on next page)

4.   ¹Fire extended humans' geographical boundaries by allowing them to travel into regions that were previously too cold to explore. ²It also kept predators away, allowing early humans to sleep securely. ³Fire, in fact, has been a significant factor in human development and progress in many ways. ⁴Other obvious benefits of fire are its uses in cooking and in hunting. ⁵Probably even more important, however, is that learning to control fire allowed people to change the very rhythm of their lives. ⁶Before fire, the human daily cycle coincided with the rising and setting of the sun. ⁷With fire, though, humans gained time to think and talk about the day's events and to prepare strategies for coping with tomorrow.

Topic sentence(s): _____3_____

5.   ¹With so many young, single people having babies, the question arises as to how happy they are being young parents. ²A national survey of young, single mothers and fathers reveals that most were happier before they became parents. ³Sixty-seven percent of the nine thousand new parents who responded to the survey said having a baby presented more problems than they envisioned. ⁴Fifty-six percent of the respondents said they had to drop out of school, despite their hopes that they could manage schoolwork plus rearing a baby. ⁵A majority (73 percent) said they were forced to seek financial help from family, friends and/or government agencies, and 37 percent said they accepted low-paying, unsatisfying jobs out of necessity. ⁶Also, 70 percent said they missed the "good times" with friends that they enjoyed before their babies were born.

Topic sentence(s): _____2_____

Comments: Paragraph 1—The first and last sentences are saying essentially the same thing: The "physical benefits" mentioned in sentence 1 are the "good health" referred to in sentence 7.

Paragraph 2—The main idea is a general conclusion illustrated by the anecdote about Sherlock Holmes.

Paragraph 3—The first sentence introduces the topic of the stages of life.

Paragraph 4—Some of the "many ways" referred to in sentence 3 are listed in the other sentences.

Paragraph 5—The supporting details are about the fact that young single parents "were happier before they became parents."

MAIN IDEAS: Test 5

The five paragraphs that follow, all taken from college textbooks, are on a third level of difficulty. Each has a topic sentence (main idea) that may appear at any place within the paragraph. Write the number of each topic sentence in the space provided.

1. ¹An author doing research for a book asked thousands of Americans what made them happy. ²Among the popular responses she received were: eating ice-cream sandwiches and candy, being offered a football ticket, and visiting city parks. ³Other common responses included eating ravioli, feeling the cool underside of a pillow, and rereading old love letters. ⁴Almost no one gave the answer of owning flashy jewelry, showy cars, or other fancy things. ⁵The author concluded that most of the things that put a smile on our face are simple and free or inexpensive.

   Topic sentence: _____5_____

   Sentence 1 cannot be the topic sentence because it is about what the author asked, and the paragraph is about the answers.

2. ¹To erase or not to erase? ²That is the question in many students' minds after they've penciled in one of those small circles in multiple-choice tests. ³Folk wisdom has long held that when answering questions on such tests—or, indeed, on any test—you should trust your first instincts. ⁴However, a research instructor has found that students who change answers they're unsure of usually improve their scores. ⁵The instructor spent three years compiling and analyzing college students' tests, watching for telltale erasure marks, which would indicate that the student had, indeed, revised his or her answer. ⁶What the instructor found was that revised answers were two-and-a-half times as likely to go from wrong to right as vice-versa. ⁷This statistic held up even across such variables as sex, age, and race; the subject matter of the tests studied also proved not to be a factor.

   Topic sentence: _____4_____

3. ¹In both Canada and the United States, many people arrested for a crime never receive appropriate punishment. ²Prosecutors often drop charges because of flaws in the arrest procedures—officers didn't follow the rules with sufficient care or file their paperwork properly. ³In many other cases, the charges are dismissed at preliminary hearings because of problems of evidence, such as key witnesses failing to appear. ⁴Of cases surviving these barriers, many are resolved by a plea bargain. ⁵That is, the charges are reduced in exchange for a plea of guilty. ⁶This spares the government the expense of a trial, but it also makes punishment less severe. ⁷And of those

(Continues on next page)

who do go to prison, very few will serve their full sentence. ⁸Most will be out on parole long before their time is up. ⁹Moreover, time runs on a unique calendar in prison. ¹⁰In American prisons, three days equal four in the outside world. ¹¹So unless a prisoner gets into trouble, time off for good behavior equals 25 percent of one's sentence.

Topic sentence: _____1_____

Sentences 2–10 are about ways in which the author feels people receive too little punishment for their crimes.

4.   ¹Finding a good way to get rid of garbage is a problem that faces many municipalities today. ²It may be of some consolation for them to know that getting rid of garbage has almost always involved problems. ³When settlements were very small, garbage was simply thrown outdoors, where it eventually decomposed. ⁴But as communities grew, pigs and other animals helped clear away garbage by eating it; of course, the animals, in turn, recycled that garbage and thus created an even less appealing garbage problem. ⁵The first municipal effort to deal with garbage was begun in Philadelphia by Benjamin Franklin, whose solution was to have it dumped into the Delaware River. ⁶A century later, municipal incinerators, generally located in the most crowded part of town, burned garbage and produced the worst of odors as a by-product.

Topic sentence: _____2_____

Sentences 3–6 discuss the problems referred to in the topic sentence.

5.   ¹If we compressed the entire history of life on the planet into a single year, the first modern human would not appear until December 31 at about 11:53 p.m., and the first civilizations would emerge only about a minute before the end of the year. ²Yet humanity's achievements in its brief history on Earth have been remarkable. ³Some 15,000 years ago, our ancestors practiced religious rituals and painted superb pictures on the walls of their caves. ⁴Around 11,000 years ago, some human groups began to domesticate animals and plants, thereby freeing themselves from total dependence on hunting and gathering food. ⁵About 6,000 years ago, people began to live in cities, to specialize in different forms of labor, to divide into social classes, and to create distinct political and economic institutions. ⁶Within a few thousand years empires were created, linking isolated groups and bringing millions under centralized rule. ⁷Advanced agricultural practices improved farming, resulting in growing populations and the emergence of large nation-states. ⁸A mere 250 years ago the Industrial Revolution began, thrusting us into the modern world of factories and computers, jets and nuclear reactors, instantaneous global communications and terrifying military technologies.

Topic sentence: _____2_____

Sentences 3–8 are about the achievements mentioned in the topic sentence.

MAIN IDEAS: Test 6

The five paragraphs that follow, all taken from college textbooks, are on a fourth level of difficulty. Each has a topic sentence (main idea) that may appear at any place within the paragraph. Write the number of each topic sentence in the space provided. For the one case in which there are two topic sentences, write in both numbers.

1. ¹People may think that love and romantic feelings are enough of a basis for choosing a spouse. ²The chances of a marriage surviving, however, would improve if prospective marriage partners considered a few unromantic questions before deciding on matrimony. ³For example, do the two individuals involved share a common socioeconomic background? ⁴The more similar they are in their social, economic, religious, and cultural backgrounds, the more similar their expectations about married life will be. ⁵In addition, what are their goals? ⁶It's a big advantage to the marriage if they know and share one another's goals concerning career, lifestyle, and family. ⁷Finally, and maybe most important, how does the prospective spouse treat others in his or her life? ⁸During the courtship, the boyfriend or girlfriend may get special consideration, but in the long run, spouses will probably treat each other about the same way they treat their own family members.

    Topic sentence(s): ____2____

2. ¹There is a tendency in our society to turn important decisions over to groups. ²In the business world, most important decisions are made around a conference table rather than behind one person's desk. ³In politics, major policy decisions are seldom made by just one person. ⁴Groups of advisers, cabinet officers, committee members, or aides meet to deliberate and decide. ⁵In the courts, a defendant may request a trial by jury, and for some serious crimes, a jury trial is required by law. ⁶And of course, the U.S. Supreme Court renders group decisions on issues of major importance.

    Topic sentence(s): ____1____

3. ¹Propaganda is information that is methodically spread in order to persuade audiences to adopt a certain opinion. ²Advertising is an ever-present form of propaganda in our lives. ³Four common propaganda techniques are present in the advertising we see and hear every day. ⁴One technique, the testimonial, involves having a well-known person appear on behalf of the product being sold. ⁵Advertisers assume, for example, that if we admire a sports star, we'll want to eat the cereal he or she endorses. ⁶Another common propaganda technique, the bandwagon, makes us want to be "one of the gang." ⁷"Everybody's switching to . . . " "Don't be left out . . . " and "All across America, people are discovering . . . " are phrases that signal a bandwagon

(Continues on next page)

approach. [8]The plain-folks propaganda technique is especially popular on TV. [9]In plain-folks commercials, we see and hear "regular" consumers talk about their experience using a certain phone company, headache remedy, or brand of coffee. [10]The fourth common propaganda technique, the transfer, encourages us to link two unrelated objects in our mind. [11]When a powerful cougar prowls around a shiny new car, for example, advertisers hope we will transfer our sense of the wild cat's speed, strength, and beauty to our vision of their product. [12]On a daily basis, these four propaganda devices are put to work in ads on TV, on radio, and in newspapers and magazines.

Topic sentence(s): _____3, 12_____   The four techniques mentioned in sentence 3 are the same as the four devices mentioned in sentence 12.

4.   [1]The American ideal of a lush green lawn is borrowed from England, where the cool misty climate makes it easy to grow grass. [2]In America, however, lawns are an energy-intensive, wasteful, and nonproductive form of landscaping. [3]To begin with, achieving a picture-perfect lawn requires gallons of expensive fertilizer and hazardous pesticides that pollute groundwater and run off into lakes and rivers. [4]In addition, lawn owners often exterminate the insects, moles, and gophers that play a part in the balance of nature. [5]Equally destructive is the constant watering lawns require, often where water is a limited resource. [6]Finally, the lawn must be mowed on a regular basis to give it that green carpet effect, requiring endless output of human and mechanical energy. [7]After all the labor and expense, the final result is a flat carpet that lacks interesting features, wildlife, or edible produce.

Topic sentence(s): _____2_____

5.   [1]Stories of the mythical Camelot, the location in England of King Arthur's court, depict a world of dashing knights in shining armor and beautiful damsels in distress. [2]In actuality, that world probably consisted of smelly men in rusty tin suits and damsels in a certain kind of distress—the distress of being constantly pregnant and of having no rights in a male-dominated society. [3]Those same stories often glorified the brave men who fought to the death for king and country. [4]Actually, most battle fatalities resulted from medieval medicine. [5]Letting the "bad blood" out of a sick person was a common medical practice, and cleanliness was not. [6]Other stories of the fabled Camelot housed royalty in glittering palaces, clothed them in silks, and covered them in mystery and awe. [7]But what is awesome about living in a cold, stone, rat-infested fortress with poor ventilation? [8]As for silks, war-indebted kings could rarely afford such foreign commodities. [9]Wool from home usually did the trick. [10]And there's certainly nothing silky about the discomfort caused by coarse woolen undergarments. [11]Clearly, the harsh realities of life in the Middle Ages have become overlooked, and we have created our own fantastic and unrealistic images of history.

Topic sentence(s): _____11_____   Sentences 1–10 contrast the "fantastic and unrealistic images" and the "harsh realities" mentioned in the topic sentence.

3

Supporting Details

You know from the previous chapter that the main idea is the umbrella statement covering all of the other material in a paragraph—examples, reasons, facts, and other specific details. All of those specific details are also called **supporting details**—they are the information that backs up and explains the main idea.

This chapter describes supporting details and also three techniques that will help you take study notes on main ideas and their supporting details: outlining, mapping, and summarizing.

UNDERSTANDING MAJOR AND MINOR DETAILS

There are two kinds of supporting details—major and minor. The **major details** are the primary points that support the main idea. Paragraphs usually contain minor details as well. While the major details explain and develop the main idea, they, in turn, are expanded upon by the **minor details**.

Just as the main idea is more general than its supporting details, major details are more general than minor ones. An important reading skill is the ability to distinguish between the major and minor supporting details.

To get a better idea of the role of major and minor supporting details, consider the following main idea from a popular science article:

Main Idea

The sex lives of insects are marked by horrible events.

This sentence immediately brings to mind the question "Just what is meant by horrible events?" This is where supporting details come in: they clarify and explain a main idea. Following is the same main idea with a major supporting detail:

Main Idea and Major Detail

> The sex lives of insects are marked by horrible events. In many cases, only the female partner leaves a sexual encounter alive.

Now we have a better idea of what the main idea really means. Often, however, the major details themselves are further explained, and that's where the minor support comes in. A major detail introduces a new point, and minor details develop that point. Here is the same main idea with several minor details that provide more information about the major detail:

Main Idea, Major Detail, and Minor Details

> The sex lives of insects are marked by horrible events. In many cases, only the female partner leaves a sexual encounter alive. The female praying mantis, for example, occasionally bites her mate's head off during sex. In the case of a certain species of fly, the female follows mating by sucking the body content of the male out through his mouth. Yet another example is seen in the queen ant and her mate, both of whom have wings. When they have finished their encounter high in the air, the male's wings fall off and he drops dead.

The author of the above passage then went on to provide other major and minor details in support of the main idea.

See if you can separate major from minor support in the following paragraph. It begins with the main idea and continues with several major and minor details. (To round off the paragraph, the main idea is restated at the end.) Try to locate and put a check in front of the three details that give major supporting information about the main idea.

As you read, keep an eye out for certain words that show the writer is adding a new point. Examples of such addition words are *first, next, another, in addition,* and *finally.*

Service Stations No More

Gas stations still provide gas, but often they no longer provide service. For one thing, attendants at many stations no longer pump gas. Motorists pull up to a combination convenience store and gas island where the attendant with clean hands is comfortably enclosed in a glass booth with an opening for taking money. Drivers must get out of their cars to pay for and pump their own gas, which has the bonus of perfuming their hands and clothes with a hint of gas. In addition, even at stations with "pump jockeys," workers have completely forgotten other services that once went hand in hand with pumping gas. They no longer know how to ask, "Check your oil or water?" Drivers must plead with attendants to wash windshields. And the last attendant who checked tire pressure must have died at least ten years ago. Finally, many gas stations no longer have mechanics on the premises. Limping down the highway in a backfiring car for emergency help at the friendly service station is a thing of the past. Car owners cannot even assume that their neighborhood station offers simple maintenance services. The skillful mechanic who can replace a belt or fix a tire in a few minutes has been replaced by a bored teenager in a jumpsuit who doesn't know a carburetor from a charge card. Today's gas stations are fuel stops, but too often that is all they are.

Now see if you checked correctly the three major supporting details. You'll find them after the main idea in the following outline of the paragraph:

Main idea: Many gas stations no longer provide service.

Major supporting details:
1. Attendants at many stations no longer pump gas.
2. Even at stations with "pump jockeys," workers have forgotten other services.
3. Many gas stations no longer have mechanics on the premises.

A more complete outline, showing minor details as well, would be as follows:

Main idea: Many gas stations no longer provide service.

Major and minor supporting details:
1. Attendants at many stations no longer pump gas.
   a. Stations are often combined with convenience stores, at which attendants only take money.
   b. Drivers must get out of their cars to pay for and pump gas.

2. Even at stations with "pump jockeys," workers have forgotten other services.
   a. Attendants do not ask to check oil and water.
   b. Attendants do not wash windshields.
   c. Attendants do not check tire pressure.

3. Many gas stations no longer have mechanics on the premises.
   a. The neighborhood station can no longer be counted on to help in emergencies.
   b. Stations may not even offer simple maintenance services.
   c. Skillful mechanics have been replaced by attendants who are ignorant about cars.

Notice how the complete outline about gas stations goes from the general to the specific. The more general statements are clarified and developed by the points beneath them. At a glance, you can see that the major supporting details introduce new points and that the minor details expand on those points. The outline, by its very nature, divides the paragraph into main idea, major supporting details, and minor supporting details.

USING OUTLINES TO ORGANIZE MAIN IDEAS
AND SUPPORTING DETAILS

Outlining organizes main ideas and supporting details in a way that shows at a glance the relationships between different parts of the material. Most outlines start with a main idea (or a title that summarizes the main idea) followed by one or more levels of supporting details. When there's only one level of details, they will be the major details. A two-level outline includes major details and the minor details that explain them.

- How many levels of supporting details are used in the above outline on service stations? _____

If you said there are two levels of detail, you were right. The first level is made up of the three major details, numbered *1*, *2*, and *3*. The second level is made up of minor details, lettered *a*, *b*, and *c*.

When making an outline, put all supporting details of equal importance at the same distance from the margin. In the above outline, the three major supporting details are all indented at the same point on the margin. Likewise, all of the minor supporting details are indented at their own fixed point on the margin. You can therefore see at a glance the main idea, the major details, and the minor details.

- Put appropriate numbers (*1*, *2*, *3*) and letters (*a*, *b*) in front of the items in the following outline.

Main idea

___ Major detail

   ___ Minor detail

   ___ Minor detail

___ Major detail

   ___ Minor detail

   ___ Minor detail

___ Major detail

You should have put a *1*, *2*, and *3* in front of the major details and an *a* and *b* in front of the minor details. Note that an outline proceeds from the most general to the most specific, from main ideas to major details to minor details.

Outlining a Passage

Read the following passage and then complete the outline by filling in the four major supporting details.

[1]Several factors can interfere with having a good memory. [2]One such factor is a lack of motivation. [3]Without a real desire to learn or remember something, you probably won't. [4]Another cause is a lack of practice. [5]To stay sharp, memory skills, like any other skill, must be used on a regular basis. [6]Another factor that can hurt memory is self-doubt. [7]If you're convinced you won't remember something, you probably won't. [8]A person with a positive attitude will do much better on a test than someone who is sure he or she won't remember the material. [9]Finally, distraction can interfere with memory. [10]If you are being distracted by the sound of a television or a conversation nearby, try to find a quiet environment before you attempt to commit something to memory.

Main idea: Several factors can interfere with having a good memory.

1. _____

2. _____

3. _____

4. _____

Explanation:

You may have realized that the topic of this paragraph is having a good memory and the main idea is that several factors can interfere with having a good memory. To find the major details, it often helps to *turn the main idea into a question.* In this case, the obvious question you could ask is "*What* are the factors that interfere with memory?" The answers are the major supporting details of the paragraph: 1) lack of motivation, 2) lack of practice, 3) self-doubt, 4) distraction.

Notice that the four factors are introduced in sentences 2, 4, 6, and 9. The other sentences go on to develop the major details with minor supporting details. Minor supporting details may be important to a thorough understanding, but they can be eliminated without removing the author's major points. Note how the following version of the paragraph—without the minor details—still makes sense.

[1]Several factors can interfere with having a good memory. [2]One such factor is a lack of motivation. [4]Another cause is a lack of practice. [6]Another factor that can hurt memory is self-doubt. [9]Finally, distraction can interfere with memory.

At times you will want to include minor details in your notes; at other times, it may not be necessary.

➤ *Practice 1*

Read each passage, and then complete the outline that follows. Begin by completing each main idea, and then fill in the supporting details. The first outline requires only major details; the second calls for you to add minor details as well.

1. In a low-key way, parents can do several things to discourage TV watching and encourage reading. For one thing, have only one television set, and place it in the family room. Then if your child wants privacy, he or she will have to go elsewhere, away from the TV. Secondly, connect reading with eating. Put a bookcase rather than a television in the kitchen and make sure it is filled with comics, magazines, local newspapers, and so on. Explain that all snacks have to be eaten in the kitchen. Given the fact that most kids can go only a short time without putting food in their mouth, your kids should get a lot of reading done while they're snacking. Last of all, don't even dream of putting a television set in a child's bedroom. You want your kids to fall asleep over books, not glued to a flickering screen.

Main idea: Parents can do several things to ___*discourage TV watching and*___

___*encourage reading*_____.

1. ___*Have only one TV set, and place it in the family room.*___

2. ___*Connect reading with eating.*___

3. ___*Don't put a TV set in a child's bedroom.*___

2. The microbes that cause infection are transmitted to people in one of three ways. Direct transmission involves bodily contact with an infected person, such as handshaking, kissing, or sexual relations. For example, a cold may be passed along through a kiss, and herpes is transmitted through sexual contact. Second, indirect transmission occurs when microbes are passed from an infected person to an individual via airborne particles, dust, water, food, or anything else the infected person touches. For example, someone might catch the flu by drinking from a glass that has been used by a person with the flu. Or a person can catch a cold by breathing air into which someone with a cold has sneezed. Third, animals and insects can transmit microbes. Yellow fever, for instance, is spread through the bite of certain tropical mosquitoes. Flies carry harmful microbes on their feet, which they can transmit to people by landing on their food.

Comments: Paragraph 1—The three major supporting details are introduced with the addition words *for one thing*, *secondly*, and *last of all*.

Paragraph 2—The second and third major details are introduced with the addition words *second* and *third*.

Main idea: Microbes that cause infection *are transmitted to people in*

one of three ways:

1. *Direct transmission through bodily contact with an infected person*

    a. Example: *Passing a cold along through a kiss*

    b. Example: *Transmitting herpes through sexual contact*

2. *Indirect transmission through air, dust, water, food, or anything else*

    touched by an infected person

    a. Example: *Catching flu by drinking from a glass used by someone who*

       has the flu

    b. Example: *Catching a cold by breathing air into which someone with a*

       cold has sneezed

3. *Transmission by animals and insects*

    a. Example: *Spread of yellow fever through mosquito bite*

    b. Example: *Transmission of microbes to people by flies landing on food*

USING MAPS TO ORGANIZE MAIN IDEAS AND SUPPORTING DETAILS

Students sometimes find it helpful to use mapping rather than outlining. In **mapping**, or diagramming, you create a visual outline using circles, boxes, and other shapes to show the relationships between main ideas and supporting details. Each major detail is connected to the main idea, often presented in title form. If minor details are included, each is connected to the major detail it explains.

A map of the paragraph on page 83 about factors that interfere with a good memory might look like this:

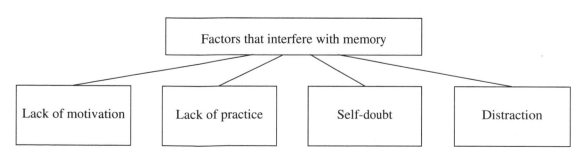

Mapping a Passage

Read the following passage and then complete the map by filling in the two major supporting details.

Many bosses share two weaknesses. First, they are often poor communicators. They tell people what to do and how and when to do it, without explaining the reasons for their rules, and they do not welcome feedback or questions. In addition, many bosses are workaholics. Their jobs tend to be their lives, and they expect everybody who works for them to think and act the way they do. These bosses frown upon hearing that a family matter will keep an employee from working late, and they come out of their offices looking irritated if there is too much talk or laughter during a coffee break.

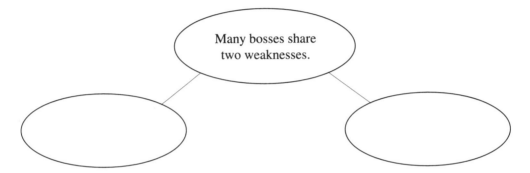

Many bosses share two weaknesses.

Explanation:

The map sets off the major details in a very visual way. You see at a glance the two major weaknesses of many bosses: they are poor communicators, and they are workaholics.

(If you were in doubt about what the major details are, you could have asked yourself a question based on the main idea: "What are the two weakness that many bosses share?")

➤ *Practice 2*

Read each passage, and then complete the maps that follow. The main-idea headings are given to you so that you can focus on finding the supporting details. The first passage requires only major details; the second calls for you to add both major and minor details.

1. Many people become nearly tongue-tied when they want to meet other people. For those of us who find starting conversations with strangers difficult, the following four strategies many be useful. Notice that each is developed in question form, inviting the other person to respond. One approach is to introduce yourself, giving your name and asking the name of

the other person. "Hi, I'm Shelby. And who are you?" A second approach is to refer to the physical setting. You might, for example, make such a comment as "This is awful weather for a game, isn't it?" Another approach is to ask a question that compliments the other person. You might say, for instance, "Your braid looks great. Did it take long to do?" Finally, you can seek direct information from the other person. At a work gathering, you can ask such a question as, "Which department do you work in?" At a party, you might say, "Walt and Jan give a really nice party. How do you happen to know them?"

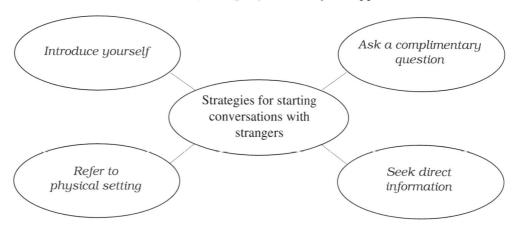

2. Companies are waking up to their ethical responsibilities and trying to do the right thing. First, many large companies have adopted a written code of ethics, which spells out the principles that should be used to guide decisions. Second, many companies run values programs which train employees in how to deal with ethical problems. Last, some companies screen potential employees for honesty. An interviewer, for example, may ask questions that help reveal the applicant's values. Also, a written "honesty" exam may help reveal a job candidate's principles.

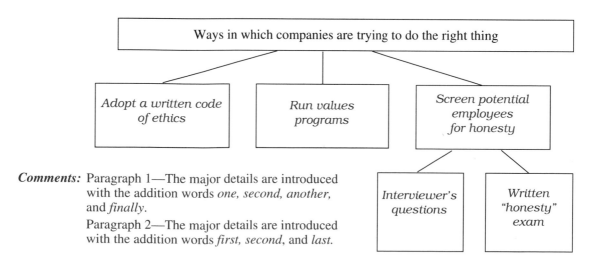

Comments: Paragraph 1—The major details are introduced with the addition words *one, second, another,* and *finally.*

Paragraph 2—The major details are introduced with the addition words *first, second,* and *last.*

SUMMARIZING

A **summary** is the reduction of a large amount of information to its most important points. The length and kind of summary will depend upon one's purpose as well as the material in question. Often, a summary will consist of a main idea and its major supporting details. As a general guideline, a paragraph might be reduced to a sentence or two, an article might be reduced to a paragraph, and a textbook chapter might be reduced to about three or so pages of notes.

One of the most common types of summarizing occurs when you are taking study notes on textbook material. Very often you will find it helpful to summarize examples of key terms. For instance, look at the following textbook passage and the summary that follows:

> In some circumstances, the most effective way of coping with stress is **withdrawal**—avoiding the situation. A person at an amusement park who is overcome by anxiety when just looking at a roller coaster can walk on to a less threatening ride or even leave the park entirely. A woman whose promotion depends on temporarily relocating might simply quit her job and join another company. Or she might withdraw figuratively from the stressful situation by deciding that promotion no longer matters to her and that she has already advanced in her career as far as she wants to go.

Summary:

Withdrawal is coping with stress by avoiding the situation. For example, a person made anxious by being near a roller coaster may walk elsewhere.

Note that a textbook definition of a key term (such as *withdrawal*) should generally not be summarized, but should be worded in the language chosen by the author. On the other hand, it usually makes sense to summarize the supporting information. Summarizing often involves two steps:

1 *Select* one example from several that might be given. Which example you select is up to you, as long as it makes the term clear for you. In the summary above, the example about the roller coaster has been chosen to illustrate withdrawal.

2 *Condense* the example if it's not already very brief. Notice that the example about the roller coaster has been condensed from a very long sentence to a short one.

A definition of a key term followed by one condensed example is a very useful way to take notes—especially in introductory college courses, where many terms are defined and illustrated.

Summarizing a Passage

Read the textbook selection below. Then complete the study notes by circling the answer choice that best summarizes the example of the term being defined.

> Try going through the following set of twelve letters just once and see if you can repeat them: TJYFAVMCFKIB. How many letters were you able to recall? In all likelihood, not all twelve. But what if you had been asked to remember the following twelve letters instead: TV FBI JFK YMCA. Could you do it? Almost certainly the answer is yes. These are the same twelve letters as before but here grouped into four separate "words." This way of grouping and organizing information so that it fits into meaningful units is called **chunking**. The twelve letters have been chunked into four meaningful items that can readily be handled by our short-term memory.

> **Study notes:**
>
> Chunking is grouping and organizing information so that it fits into meaningful units.
>
> Ex.—
> a. For example, twelve random letters can be easily remembered if they are grouped in a meaningful way: TV FBI JFK YMCA.
> b. For example, you would have trouble remembering the letters TJYFAVMCFKIB if you heard them just once and tried to repeat them.
> c. For example, meaningful items can readily be handled by our short-term memory.

Explanation:

Useful study notes should clearly show how an example illustrates the new term. In the case of the paragraph above, the example in the notes should show how something hard to remember can be reduced to short, easily recalled items. Answer *a* includes both something hard to remember— "twelve random letters"—and a way it can be reorganized into meaningful units: a series of familiar abbreviations. So if you answered *a*, you made the best choice. Answer *b* is not such a good summary because it doesn't fully explain the example—it includes only the problem, not the solution. Answer *c* doesn't include any example at all—it is part of the definition of *chunking*.

➤ *Practice 3*

Read each textbook selection below. Then complete the study notes by circling the letter of the answer that best summarizes an example of the term being defined.

1. People deceive themselves in various ways to cope better with problems. One such way is **denial**, the unconscious refusal to recognize a painful or

threatening reality. One researcher cites the example of a woman who was near death from severe burns. At first, she was depressed and frightened, but after a few days she began to feel sure that she would soon be able to return home and care for her children, although all her medical indications were to the contrary. By denying the extent of her injuries, this woman was able to stay calm and cheerful. She was not merely putting on an act for her relatives and friends: She believed she would recover. In another situation, researchers interviewed the parents of children who were dying of leukemia. Some parents denied their children's condition; others accepted it. Physical examinations revealed that those who denied the illness did not have the physiological sympoms of stress, such as excessive stomach acid, found in those who accepted their children's illness.

Study notes: Neither answer *a* nor answer *b* includes the "refusal to recognize a painful or threatening reality."

Denial is the unconscious refusal to recognize a painful or threatening reality.

Ex.—

a. Being near death from extreme burns depressed and frightened a woman.

b. A woman near death from extreme burns began to feel sure she would return home and care for her children.

(c.) By refusing to believe her burn injuries were deadly, a woman near death was able to stay calm and cheerful.

2.   Imagine a ball lying on a level table. Left alone, the ball stays where it is. Given a gentle push, the ball rolls a short way and then comes to a stop. The smoother the ball and the table top, the farther the ball rolls before stopping. Suppose that we have a perfectly round ball and a perfectly smooth and level table top, and that no air is present to slow down the ball. If the table is infinitely long and we give the ball a push, will it ever stop rolling? In fact, we can reasonably expect that under ideal conditions the ball would keep rolling forever. This conclusion was first reached by Galileo and later stated by Newton as the first law of motion: An object will continue in its state of rest or of motion in a straight line at constant speed if the object does not interact with anything else.

Study notes:

Newton's first law of motion—an object will continue in its state of rest or of motion in a straight line at constant speed if the object does not interact with anything else.

Ex.—

a. If a ball lying on a level table is given a gentle push, it won't roll too far.

(b.) A perfectly round ball on an endless table won't move if left alone, but can roll forever if pushed.

c. Galileo first came to a conclusion which Newton later stated as his first law of motion.

➤ *Practice 4*

Read each textbook selection below. Then take study notes by (1) writing down the definition of the key term, (2) selecting an example that makes the definition clear, and (3) writing that example in your notes, condensing it if possible.

1. **Altruistic behavior** is acting out of concern for another person, with no expectation of reward. For example, a little girl responds to two fellow preschoolers' complaints that they do not have enough modeling clay—her favorite toy—by giving them half of hers. Other children reach out to comfort a crying friend or stop to help someone who has fallen while crossing a street.

    Study notes:

    Altruistic behavior — *acting out of concern for another person, without*

    expectation of reward

    Ex.— *A little girl shares half her modeling clay with two friends who say*

    they do not have enough.

2. **Passive listening** occurs when a listener tries to make sense out of a speaker's remarks without being able to interact with the speaker. Probably the most familiar example of passive listening would be students hearing an instructor's lecture without having the opportunity to ask questions or otherwise interact with the speaker. Passive listening also takes place in interpersonal settings, as when one person dominates a conversation while the others fall into the role of audience members, or when some parents lecture their children without allowing them to respond.

    Study notes:

    Passive listening — *trying to make sense out of a* .

    speaker's remarks without being able to interact with the speaker

    Ex.— *Students listen to an instructor's lecture without having the chance*

    to ask questions.

A Final Note

As you see by now, active reading involves paying close attention to supporting details as well as to main ideas. You will practice such careful reading in answering the questions that follow the longer selections in this book, which ask you about specific important details.

➤ Review Test 1

To review what you've learned in this chapter, answer each of these questions about supporting details.

1. *Fill in the blanks:* Major supporting details are more (*general, specific*) _____ *specific* _____ than main ideas. Minor supporting details are more (*general, specific*) _____ *specific* _____ than major details.

2. _*T*_ TRUE OR FALSE? Supporting details can be reasons, examples, facts, or other specific information.

3. Outlining is a way to show at a glance the relationship between a main idea and its _____ *supporting details* _____ .

4. In _____ *mapping* _____ , you create a visual outline using circles, boxes, and other shapes to set off main ideas and supporting details.

5. When taking notes on textbook material, you will often write out each definition in full and then select and _____ *condense* _____ one example of that definition.

➤ Review Test 2

A. (1–7.) Complete the outline of the following paragraph by completing the main idea and adding the missing major and minor details.

Several factors have been found to influence the justice system's treatment of criminals. For one thing, the sex of offenders affects the severity of sentences. A woman is less likely to receive the death penalty than a man. Also, the court is more reluctant to send a mother to prison than a father. Another factor in the treatment of offenders is their race. Nonwhites are awarded parole and probation less often. In addition, blacks are executed more often for capital crimes. Finally, the age of offenders is considered in sentencing. Young offenders are given special treatment. And the elderly are given more lenient sentences.

Main idea: Several factors _have been found to influence the justice system's_

treatment of criminals.

Major detail: **1.** _Sex of offender affects severity of sentence_

Minor details: a. Woman less likely to receive death penalty than a man

                    b. _Court more reluctant to send mother to prison than father_

Major detail: **2.** _Race is another factor_

Minor details: a. _Nonwhites awarded parole and probation less often_

                    b. _Blacks executed more often for capital crimes_

Major detail: **3.** Age of offenders considered in sentencing

Minor details: a. _Young offenders given special treatment_

                    b. More lenient sentences for the elderly

B. (8–10.) Answer the questions about supporting details that follow the passage. Note that the main idea is boldfaced.

Years ago, in the 1920s, thousands of people bought land in Florida from smooth-talking salesmen. They were so impressed by the colorful brochures the salesmen gave them that they never visited Florida to look at the land before buying it. Later, they found out that the land they bought was at the bottom of a swamp. A swindle that is still popular today is the chain-letter or "pyramid" scheme. Those who get the letter are supposed to send money to the top name on a list. Then they copy the letter, with the top name left off and their own name at the bottom, and send it to several friends. The letter promises that everyone will make money. The only sure winner, though, is the person who starts the letter in the first place. **If moneymaking offers or schemes sound too good to be true, they probably are not true.**

8. Which question would help you find the major supporting details of the paragraph?
   a. Why did so many people buy land in Florida without even seeing it?
   b. What are examples of chain-letter or "pyramid" schemes?
   c. Which moneymaking offers or schemes have sounded too good to be true?
   d. Why do some moneymaking offers or schemes sound too good to be true?

9. The major details of this paragraph are
   a. statistics.
   b. examples.
   c. steps.

10. Fill in the blank: The paragraph includes (*one, two, three, four*) ____two____
major supporting details.   *Comment:*   Items 8–10—Paragraph B provides two
examples of moneymaking offers or
schemes that sound too good to be true
and are not true.

➤ *Review Test 3*

A. (1–5.) Outline the following passage by completing the main idea and filling in
the major supporting details.

> Serious depression, as opposed to the fleeting kind we all feel at times,
> has definite warning signs. Some or all of these signs may be present within
> the affected individual. One symptom of depression is a change in sleep
> patterns—either sleeplessness or sleeping too much. Another sign is
> abnormal eating patterns, either eating too much or loss of appetite. A third
> sign is trouble in thinking or concentrating—even to the point of finding it
> difficult to read a magazine or newspaper. Finally, a general feeling of
> hopelessness may signal depression. People feel indifferent to their families
> and jobs and may begin to think that life is not worth living.

Main idea: Serious depression has   ____definite warning signs____ .

1. ____Change in sleep patterns____

2. ____Abnormal eating patterns____

3. ____Trouble in thinking or concentrating____

4. ____General feeling of hopelessness____

B. (6–9.) Map the following passage by filling in the main idea heading and the
major supporting details.

> Researchers have identified a series of conditions needed to make
> punishment work. Punishment should be swift. Children who misbehave
> should be punished right away so that they know that what they have done is
> wrong. If punishment comes too late, it may not be clear to children why they
> are being punished. In addition, punishment should be sufficient without being
> cruel. If a parent merely warns a child not to bully other children, the effect may
> be less than if the warning is accompanied by the threat of being "grounded" for
> a day. Third, punishment should be consistent. The common practice of
> making the punishment for each successive misdeed more severe than the last
> is not so effective as maintaining a constant level of punishment. The parent
> should try to punish the child each and every time he or she misbehaves.

Comments: Paragraph A—The four major details (the definite warning signs of serious depression)
are introduced with the addition words *one, another, third,* and *finally.*

Paragraph B—In maps, the major details are often summarized in a word or a few words.

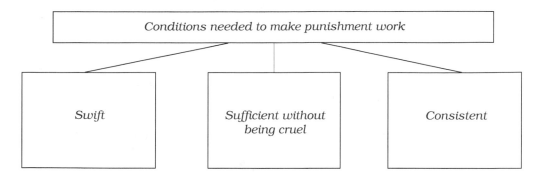

C. (10.) Read the textbook selection below. Then complete the study notes by circling the letter of the answer choice that best summarizes the example of the term being defined.

> **Cultural lag** refers to a situation where a practice or belief that once was functional persists even though it is no longer useful. You can see an example of cultural lag every time that you eat. Americans, after they cut their meat, put down the knife and switch the fork from the left hand to the right. Only then do they put the food in their mouths. This differs from the European practice of simply raising the food to the mouth with the fork in the left hand after cutting the meat. Why did Americans develop this habit? Some experts guess that in the old days of the American frontier, Americans needed to keep a hand free in case they had to grab a weapon to fight an intruder. Today the frontier is gone, and putting down the knife and switching the fork to the other hand is no longer of practical use. Americans continue to do it anyway, and to eat in the European style is considered to be "bad manners."

Study notes:

Cultural lag refers to a situation where a practice or belief that once was functional persists even though it is no longer useful.

Ex.—

a. Europeans eat with a fork in the left hand, but Americans put the knife down after cutting and switch the fork to the right hand.

b. Americans consider the European style of eating with a fork in the left hand to be bad manners even though that method is more practical than switching the fork to the right hand.

c. Americans consider it correct to switch the fork to the right hand after cutting even though the supposed purpose—keeping the left hand free for a weapon—no longer exists.

Comment: Item 10—Only answer *c* includes the idea in the definition of a practice continuing even after its original purpose is gone.

➤ *Review Test 4*

Here is a chance to apply your understanding of supporting details to a passage from a college textbook: *Psychology*, Second Edition, by Diane E. Papalia and Sally Wendkos Olds (McGraw-Hill). Read the passage and then answer the questions that follow.

To help you continue to strengthen your work on the skills taught in previous chapters, there are also questions on vocabulary in context and main ideas.

Words to Watch

Below are some words in the reading that do not have strong context support. Each word is followed by the number of the paragraph in which it appears and its meaning there. These words are indicated in the article by a small circle (°).

provocation (1): annoyance
loath (1): reluctant
temperament (1): emotional makeup
competence (2): skill
thrive (3): grow well
self-reliant (3): independent
assertive (3): positive and confident
detached (4): emotionally apart from others
withdrawn (4): shy

CHILD-REARING STYLES

Diane E. Papalia and Sally Wendkos Olds

1   What makes Mary burst into tears of frustration when she can't finish a jigsaw puzzle, while Gary will shrug and walk away from it, and Cary will sit with it for hours until he finishes? What makes Polly independent and Molly a clinger? What makes Tim ready to hit out at the slightest provocation° and Jim loath° to fight? One answer lies in the basic temperament° children are born with. A second very important influence on behavioral styles is the early emotional environment—how children are treated by their parents.

2   The psychologist Diana Baumrind set out to discover relationships between different styles of child rearing and the social competence° of children. She reviewed the research literature and conducted her own studies with ninety-five families of children in nursery school. Using a combination of long interviews, standardized testing, and observations at school and home, she identified three categories of parenting styles and linked them to children's behavior.

3   *Authoritative* parents exert firm control when necessary, but they explain

why they take a stand and encourage children to express their opinions. They feel confident in their ability to guide their children, while respecting the children's interests, opinions, and unique personalities. They combine firm control with encouragement and love. Their children know that they are expected to perform well, fulfill commitments, and carry out duties in the family. They know when they are meeting expectations and when it is worth risking their parents' displeasure to pursue some other goal. They seem to thrive° on their parents' reasonable expectations and realistic standards, and they are most self-reliant°, self-controlled, assertive°, exploratory, and content.

4   *Authoritarian* parents value unquestioning obedience and punish their children forcibly for not conforming to set and quite absolute standards. They are somewhat detached°, controlling, and distant. Their children tend to be discontented, withdrawn°, and distrustful of others.

5   *Permissive* parents make few demands on their children, set few rules, and hardly ever punish. As preschoolers, their children are immature—the least self-reliant, the least self-controlled, the least exploratory.

6   On the basis of her research, Baumrind has recommended that parents who want to raise competent, socially responsible, independent children should do several things:

- Teach by example, that is, behave the way you want your children to behave.
- Reward behaviors you want to encourage and punish behaviors you want to discourage, giving explanations in both cases.
- Show interest in children.
- Bestow approval only when the child has earned it.
- Demand achievement and the meeting of standards, while being open to hearing the child's point of view.
- Encourage original thinking.

7   Baumrind's work raises important issues about child-rearing practices, but before we conclude that parenting is all, we have to remember what children bring to the family. Through their own inborn temperaments, children influence their parents. It is possible, for example, that "easy" children will elicit an authoritative attitude from their parents, while "difficult" children may make tyrants out of theirs.

Reading Comprehension Questions

Vocabulary in Context

1. In the sentence below, the word *bestow* means
   a. deny.
   b. give.
   c. accept.   *Context clue:* Approval is given to someone.
   d. risk.

   "Bestow approval only when the child has earned it." (Paragraph 6)

2. In the excerpt below, the word *elicit* means
   a. draw out.
   b. dislike.   *Context clue:* A child might draw out
   c. imitate.   a particular attitude from parents.
   d. abuse.

   "Through their own inborn temperaments, children influence their parents. It is possible, for example, that 'easy' children will elicit an authoritative attitude from their parents, while 'difficult' children may make tyrants out of theirs." (Paragraph 7)

Main Ideas

3. The topic of paragraph 6 is
   a. the psychologist Diana Baumrind.
   b. ways in which Baumrind feels parents can teach by example.
   c. Baumrind's ideas about when to give approval to a child.
   d. things Baumrind feels parents can do to raise competent, socially responsible, independent children.

4. Which sentence best expresses the main idea of paragraph 6?
   a. "On the basis of her research, Baumrind has recommended that parents who want to raise competent, socially responsible, independent children should do several things:"
   b. "Teach by example, that is, behave the way you want your children to behave."
   c. "Reward behaviors you want to encourage and punish behaviors you want to discourage, giving explanations in both cases."
   d. "Demand achievement and the meeting of standards, while being open to hearing the child's point of view."

Supporting Details

5. *Complete the sentence:* To study the ninety-five families of children in nursery school, Baumrind used standardized tests, observations at school and at home, and _____*long interviews*_____.

6–10. Complete the following outline of parts of the reading by filling in the blanks.

A. Two influences on how a child behaves

1. *Basic temperament the child is born with* _____

2. *Early emotional environment* _____

B. Three parenting styles

1. *Authoritative* _____

2. *Authoritarian* _____

3. *Permissive* _____

Discussion Questions

1. What type of parenting style did you grow up with?

2. Why do you think Diana Baumrind feels that teaching by example is useful?

3. Baumrind encourages parents to show interest in children. What are some ways in which parents can show interest in children?

4. The authors feel that children are born with "their own inborn temperaments." Has your experience with children confirmed or contradicted their idea that children have different temperaments from the time they are born? Give some examples.

Comments: Item 5—See paragraph 2.
Items 6–10— A. The two minor details under A in the outline are stated in paragraph 1 of the selection.
B. Note how the authors' italics can be helpful in organizing a reading. The parts of the selection not represented in the outline are in paragraphs 6 and 7.

Check Your Performance   SUPPORTING DETAILS

Activity	Number Right	Points	Score
Review Test 1 (5 items)	_____	x 2 =	_____
Review Test 2 (10 items)	_____	x 3 =	_____
Review Test 3 (10 items)	_____	x 3 =	_____
Review Test 4 (10 items)	_____	x 3 =	_____
		TOTAL SCORE =	_____ %

Enter your total score into the **Reading Performance Chart: Review Tests** on the inside back cover.

SUPPORTING DETAILS: Test 1

A. (1–6.) Complete the outline of the following textbook passage by adding the main idea and the missing major or minor details.

Divorce has serious negative consequences. First, social adjustment after the divorce is a troublesome time. The former couple will find that starting to date again can be nerve-racking. Also, married friends may exclude singles from social plans. Secondly, emotional difficulties among the original family members are common. Feelings of guilt and resentment may persist between the former husband and wife. At the same time children may be confused and hurt; many also feel guilty, imagining that they were somehow to blame for the divorce. A third consequence is that financial adjustments are necessary. Alimony, child support, and property dispersal must be dealt with. Also, high lawyers' fees can be a burden.

Main idea: *Divorce has serious negative consequences.* _____.

Major detail: **1.** Social adjustment is troublesome.

Minor details: a. *Starting to date again can be nerve-racking.* _____

                b. Married friends may exclude singles from social plans.

Major detail: **2.** *Emotional difficulties among original family members* _____

                are common. _____

Minor details: a. *Husband and wife feel guilt and resentment.* _____

                b. Children may be confused and hurt and feel guilty.

Major detail: **3.** *Financial adjustments are necessary.* _____

Minor details: a. *Alimony, child support, and property disposal* _____

                must be dealt with. _____

                b. High lawyers' fees can be a burden.

Comment: In this test and the five supporting-details mastery tests that follow, the topic sentences are underlined in color in this *Instructor's Edition.*

The three major details in the passage above are introduced with the addition words *first,* *secondly,* and *third.*

(Continues on next page)

B. (7–10.) Answer the questions about supporting details that follow the passage.

When we call someone "pig" or "swine," we do not mean it as a compliment. But pigs do not deserve to be used as a symbol for an insult. They are probably not as dirty as they are made out to be. According to one pig keeper, swine are very clean when allowed to live in a clean environment. He feels pigs are usually dirty simply because their keepers don't clean their pens. In any case, no one has proven that the pig that wallows in mud prefers that to a cool bath. Furthermore, pigs are smarter than most people think. Many farmers, for example, have observed that pigs frequently undo complicated bolts on gates in search of adventure or romance. So the next time you call someone a pig, perhaps he or she ought to be someone you wish to praise.

7. In general, the major details of this passage are
   a. reasons why pigs are dirty.
   (b.) reasons why pigs should not be used as symbols for insults.
   c. ways to insult or compliment people.

8. Specifically, the major details are
   (a.) Pigs are probably not as dirty as people think; pigs are smarter than most people think.
   b. Pigs may be dirty because their pens are dirty; it hasn't been proved that pigs prefer mud to a cool bath; pigs have been seen undoing complicated bolts.
   c. People use "pig" and "swine" as insults; "pig" and "swine" should be considered praise.

9. One pig keeper feels that pigs will stay clean if they are
   a. given baths.
   b. praised.
   (c.) kept in a clean environment.

10. What example is used to show that pigs are smarter than they are often thought to be? _____ *They can undo complicated bolts on gates.* _____

_____

Comment: The first sentence introduces the topic of calling someone "pig" or "swine."

SUPPORTING DETAILS: Test 2

A. Answer the questions about supporting details that follow the textbook passage.

The climate becomes colder when the amount of dust at high altitudes in the atmosphere increases. There are several ways that dust may get into the atmosphere. Volcanic eruptions can add so much dust that sunlight is scattered back to outer space. Chimneys, especially industrial smokestacks, also throw large amounts of dust into the atmosphere. The burning of tropical forests to clear land for farming is another way the amount of airborne dust is increased. Finally, should a nuclear war ever occur, it might add so much dust to the atmosphere that it could cause a new ice age—a nuclear winter in which the climate becomes so cold that no new crops can be grown.

1. In general, the major details of this paragraph are
    a. reasons why dust in the atmosphere makes the climate colder.
    b. ways that dust may get into the atmosphere.
    c. natural causes of dust getting into the atmosphere.
    d. ways that industry puts dust into the atmosphere.

2. How many major details are in this paragraph?
    a. One
    b. Two
    c. Three
    d. Four

3. One source of dust in the atmosphere is
    a. sunlight.
    b. farming.
    c. chimneys.
    d. cold weather.

4. An enormous amount of dust in the atmosphere could lead to
    a. warmer weather.
    b. burning of tropical forests.
    c. volcanic eruptions.
    d. a new ice age.

5. The last major detail is introduced with the addition word
    a. *several.*
    b. *add.*
    c. *finally.*
    d. *another.*

(Continues on next page)

6. Which is the best outline of the paragraph?
   a. Ways the climate can become colder
      1. Dust getting into the atmosphere
      2. Scattering sunlight to outer space
      3. Clearing land for farming
      4. A nuclear winter

   (b.) Ways dust can get into the atmosphere and make climate colder
      1. Volcanic eruptions
      2. Chimneys
      3. Burning of tropical forests
      4. Nuclear war

B. (7–10.) Outline the following textbook passage by filling in the main idea and the major supporting details.

> Chimpanzees, skillful tool-users, use several objects found in their environment as tools. First of all, they use sticks. They have been seen inserting carefully trimmed sticks into termite mounds and then withdrawing the sticks and eating the termites that cling to them; they also are known to use sticks to steal honey from beehives. In addition, chimps use leaves in a variety of ingenious ways. For example, they have been seen rolling leaves into cones to use as drinking cups, dampening them and using them to clean their bodies, and chewing them until they can serve as sponges. Finally, chimpanzees have been observed using stones to crack open nuts.

Main idea: *Chimpanzees use objects in their environment as tools.*

_____.

1. *Sticks to catch termites and steal honey*

2. *Leaves as drinking cups, for cleaning, and as sponges*

3. *Stones to crack open nuts*

Comment: The three types of tools chimpanzees use are introduced with the addition words *first of all, in addition,* and *finally.*

SUPPORTING DETAILS: Test 3

A. Answer the questions about supporting details that follow the textbook passage.

[1]A **social dilemma** is a situation in which the most rewarding short-term choice for an individual will ultimately lead to negative outcomes for all concerned. [2]For example, as you hike along a beautiful mountain trail, you stop for a snack. [3]You are tempted to throw away your empty water containers and granola bar wrappers, knowing that your backpack will be lighter if you don't have to carry your trash to the top of the mountain and back. [4]But you hesitate, knowing that if all hikers litter the trail, it will soon be unpleasant for all who use it. [5]Or consider the situation of many communities in the Southwest that have suffered severe drought for years, so that water conservation is essential. [6]Individuals living in such drought-stricken areas face personal decisions. [7]For instance, should I forgo the pleasure of a long shower today so that there will be more water for all in the future?

1. The main idea is expressed in
   a. sentence 1.
   b. sentence 2.
   c. sentence 4.
   d. sentence 7.

2. In general, the major supporting details of this paragraph are
   a. rewarding short-term choices.
   b. examples of social dilemmas.
   c. examples of negative outcomes.
   d. common rewarding experiences.

3. How many major details are in this paragraph?
   a. Two
   b. Three
   c. Four
   d. Five

4. The second major detail of the paragraph begins in
   a. sentence 1
   b. sentence 2.
   c. sentence 4.
   d. sentence 5.

(Continues on next page)

5. In the Southwest, the desire to take a long shower presents a social dilemma because

   See sentence 7.

   a. cleanliness and neatness are important there.
   b. a pleasant long shower could mean less water for others.
   c. the water is polluted.
   d. water costs more there, so long showers are expensive.

6. Circle the letter of the summary that best completes the study notes of the paragraph.

   Social dilemma—a situation in which the most rewarding short-term choice for an individual will ultimately lead to negative outcomes for all concerned.

   Ex.—

   a. Littering a beautiful trail is tempting, but would soon make for an unpleasant trail for all.
   b. Littering a beautiful trail is convenient because then you wouldn't have to carry trash to the top of the mountain and back.
   c. To avoid littering when hiking in public places, carry empty containers and wrappers until you get to a trash can.

B. (7–10.) Complete the outline of the textbook passage by filling in the missing main idea and major details, including a brief explanation of each. One explanation has been done for you.

   The three types of human memory allow a person to remove or retain information, as needed. Everything that we notice—see, smell, hear, or touch—forms a brief mental impression called a sensory memory. Information is stored in this sensory memory for only a few tenths of a second before it disappears forever. Information that is retained for slightly longer enters what's called short-term memory. This form of memory can store about seven items for about thirty seconds—about enough information to dial a telephone number. In order to be remembered for a long period, information must pass into long-term memory. No one knows just how much information can be stored in a person's long-term memory, but the capacity seems enormous.

   Main idea: _Three types of human memory allow us to remove or keep information as needed._

   1. _Sensory memory_ —stores memory for a few tenths of a second.

   2. _Short-term memory—stores about 7 items for about 30 seconds._

   3. _Long-term memory—stores enormous number of items for a long period._

Comment: Item 6—Answer *a* includes both the rewarding short-term choice and the negative outcome mentioned in the definition.

SUPPORTING DETAILS: Test 4

A. (1–6.) Outline the following textbook passage by filling in the missing major and minor details.

> Certain significant differences exist between the House and the Senate. The most obvious difference, of course, is size—the Senate has 100 members and the House 435. This factor leads to differences in style. Perhaps, as one author has stated, "the most striking difference noticed by most visitors to the Capitol is the apparent formality and impersonality in the House chamber as contrasted to the relatively informal and friendly atmosphere in the Senate." Size also influences the procedures followed by the House and the Senate. Senate rules are short and relatively simple; House rules are many and complex. House rules, for example, sharply limit the time in which a member may speak during a debate, whereas senators are subject to few limits.
>
> Another difference between the two houses of Congress derives from the different terms of office of their members (two years in the House, six years in the Senate). This means that most representatives are campaigning almost all the time, whereas senators have more time before they must seek reelection. As a result, senators can pay more attention to aspects of legislation that do not directly affect their chances of winning or losing voters' support.
>
> A further major difference between the two houses of Congress is the political outlook of their members. Senators have statewide constituencies. As a result, they must keep in mind the interests of a variety of groups. Most representatives have smaller constituencies; each speaks for the residents of a particular district. The representative's concerns, therefore, are often limited to more local issues that are of interest to fewer groups.

Main idea: Significant differences exist between the House and the Senate.
1. Differences in size: 100 in Senate vs. 435 in House
   a. Style differences
      1) Formal style in the House
      2) *Relaxed in Senate*
   b. *Procedural differences*
      1) *Senate rules are short and simple*
      2) *House rules are many and complex*
2. Differences in terms of office: 2 years in House vs. 6 years in Senate
   a. Constant campaigning of representatives
   b. More time for senators to spend on legislation not affecting their campaigns

(Continues on next page)

3. *Political outlook of members*

    a. Statewide outlook of senators

    b. *Representatives concerned with local issues*

B. (7–10.) Complete the map of the following textbook passage by filling in the heading (the general idea of the map) and the missing major supporting details.

> To a greater or lesser extent, all of us have learned aggressive responses. We are each a potential aggressor. A number of conditions have been found to stimulate aggression. For one thing, pain—both mental and physical— heightens aggressiveness. Any decidedly hurtful event, whether a big disappointment, a personal insult, or a physical pain, can incite an emotional outburst. Environmental irritants can also stimulate aggression. The most-studied is heat. Studies have found that, compared with students who answered questionnaires in a room with a normal temperature, those who did so in an uncomfortably hot room (over 90° F) reported feeling more tired and aggressive and expressed more hostility toward a stranger they were asked to rate. A third condition, one that especially provokes aggression, is attacks by another. Experiments confirm that attacks bring counterattacks, especially when the victim perceives the attack as intentional. Finally, crowding—the feeling of not having enough space—can be stressful. The stress experienced by animals allowed to overpopulate a confined environment produces heightened aggressiveness. And it is undeniably true that dense urban areas suffer higher rates of crime and emotional distress.

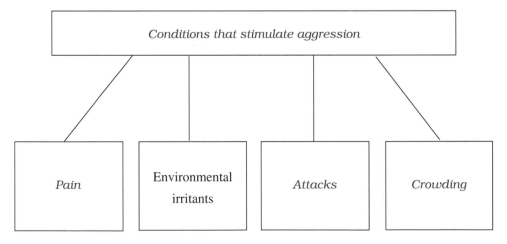

Comment: The conditions referred to in the topic sentence are introduced with the addition transitions *for one thing*, *also*, *third*, and *finally*.

SUPPORTING DETAILS: Test 5

A. (1–5.) Outline the following textbook passage by filling in the main idea and a brief statement of each major supporting detail.

> After studying all night for an important exam, most college students find themselves wishing for one thing after their big test: sleep. Although the exact reasons why people sleep are still being debated, researchers have created a number of theories to explain the functions of sleep. First of all, sleep is believed to give the body time to repair burned-out brain cells and make more of the special chemical that makes it possible for the brain to think. Another theory holds that sleep enables the body to save energy because when we sleep, the body temperature is lower, so less energy is needed to create heat. This method of energy conservation may have helped people survive thousands of years ago when food was hard to find. Sleep may also have helped humanity survive by keeping people out of trouble. In prehistoric times, when many large predators like the saber-toothed tiger hunted in darkness, the habit of sleeping at night helped prevent people from being an animal's dinner. Scientists also believe that sleep, in addition to being a survival tactic, is used to reduce memory. It allows the brain to forget or unlearn things that are not necessary. Otherwise, the mind would become cluttered and overwhelmed with unneeded information.

Main idea heading: _____*Functions of sleep*_____.

1. *Gives body time to repair brain cells and create chemical that makes*

   brain think

2. *Enables body to save energy*

3. *Keeps people out of trouble*

4. *Reduces memory*

B. (6.) Read the textbook excerpt below. Then complete the study notes on the next page by circling the letter of the best summary of the supporting details.

> Any change in one part of our economic system creates changes elsewhere. Such change is known as the multiplier effect. For example, if a university decides to build a new dormitory, some construction workers will have more income. If some of these workers decide to spend the extra income on new boats, boat-builders will have more income. The boat-builders, in turn, might spend this income in neighborhood restaurants, and the restaurant owners might spend it on cars. Money never stays in one place, and every market decision has an impact on other markets.

(Continues on next page)

Study notes:

Multiplier effect—Any change in one part of our economic system creates changes elsewhere.   Answer *c* shows how work for construction workers "creates changes elsewhere."

Ex.—

a. The decision to build a new university dormitory will lead to work for some construction workers.

b. Our economic system is very complicated.

c. Building a dorm allows construction workers to buy boats, giving boat-builders money for restaurants, and so on.

C. Answer the questions about supporting details that follow the textbook passage.

> [1]Studies done in the 1930s in New Guinea by the social scientist Margaret Mead show that not all cultures share our views of the differences between the sexes. [2]The mountain people called the Arapesh, for example, do not think men and women are different in temperament. [3]They expect both sexes to be equally gentle, home-loving, and what we would call "maternal" in their relations with others. [4]The neighboring Mundugumor people, by contrast, are as fierce as the Arapesh are gentle. [5]Men and women are equally "macho," paying less attention to their children than to plotting for power and position. [6]A third tribe, the Tchambuli, do believe the sexes are different in temperament, but their sex roles are the reverse of ours. [7]Tchambuli women are the practical, hard-headed providers, while the men of the tribe spend their days beautifying themselves and looking for approval from the women.

7. Sentence 1 provides
   a. the main idea.
   b. a major supporting detail.
   c. a minor supporting detail.

8. In general, the major supporting details of this paragraph are
   a. differences between the sexes.
   b. examples of differing cultural views of the sexes.
   c. studies of the Arapesh.
   d. a series of stereotypes about Western culture.

9. How many major details are in this paragraph?
   a. Two
   b. Three
   c. Four
   d. Five

10. The Arapesh do not think that men and women are
    a. equally gentle.
    b. "maternal."
    c. alike in temperament.
    d. different in temperament.

SUPPORTING DETAILS: Test 6

A. Answer the questions that follow the textbook passage.

[1]Suburbs arose out of a complex set of social factors. [2]One factor was the economic and technological developments that made it possible for people to live far from where they worked. [3]Early in this century, most people were limited in where they could live by the need to find transportation to work. [4]This meant that most had to live in the cities near where the jobs were. [5]Because there were relatively few automobiles and highways, people walked or used public transportation to get to work and go shopping. [6]This encouraged the concentration of population, and central cities served as the commercial and cultural core of urban areas. [7]By the 1940s and 1950s, the increasing prosperity of many Americans, along with the automobile, made it possible for them to live farther from work and opened up suburban life to middle-class Americans.

[8]In addition, government policy was also a factor contributing to suburbanization. [9]First of all, the government paid 80 percent of the cost of developing the interstate highway system. [10]With cars and high-speed highways, people can now live far from where they work and shop. [11]In sprawling cities such as Los Angeles, for example, it is common to live fifty or more miles from where you work. [12]Also, government agencies made available federally guaranteed mortgage loans for the purchase of new homes. [13]Because land outside of the cities was both inexpensive and available, this is where much of the construction took place.

1. In general, the major details of this passage are
   a. economic developments that led to the growth of suburbs.
   b. factors that contributed to suburbanization.
   c. ways the government helped suburbs to develop.
   d. early roles of our cities.

2. Specifically, the major details of the passage are
   a. suburbs; cities.
   b. central cities; federally guaranteed mortgage loans for new homes.
   c. where people live; where people work.
   d. economic and technological developments; government policy.

3. Sentence 1 provides
   a. the main idea of the passage.
   b. a major detail of the passage.
   c. a minor detail of the passage.

Comments: Item 2—Economic and technological developments are discussed in the first paragraph (and introduced in sentence 2). Government policy is discussed in the second paragraph (and introduced in sentence 8).

(Continues on next page)

    4. Sentence 8 provides
        a. the main idea of the passage.
        (b.) a major detail of the passage.
        c. a minor detail of the passage.

    5. Sentence 12 provides
        a. the main idea of the passage.
        b. a major detail of the passage.
        (c.) a minor detail of the passage.

B. (6–10.) Complete a map of the following textbook passage by filling in a main idea heading and the four major supporting details.

> Through the years, experts have suggested various purposes of imprisonment in our country. Prior to 1800 it was widely assumed that the punishment of those who don't follow society's rules is necessary if the community is to feel morally satisfied. In recent years there has been a renewed interest in punishment—not for the sake of vengeance, but to restore a sense of moral order. During the last century and a half, a second purpose of imprisonment has been rehabilitation. In this view, crime resembles "disease," something foreign and abnormal to most people. It is presumed that individuals are not to blame for the disease, and that we should focus on curing them. Another purpose of imprisonment has been to deter crime. Some studies suggest that the certainty of arrest and punishment does tend to lower crime rates. Last, some argue that neither rehabilitation nor deterrence really works, so that it is useless to send people to prison with these goals in mind. Instead, imprisonment should be used as selective confinement, reducing crime rates by keeping "hard-core" criminals off the streets. One study of young men in Philadelphia showed that 6 percent of the men were responsible for over half the crimes committed by the entire group.

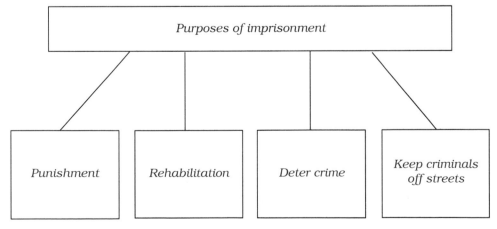

Comment: Paragraph B—The paragraph lists the "purposes of imprisonment" mentioned in the topic sentence.

4

Implied Main Ideas and the Central Point

In Chapters 2 and 3 you learned the basic parts of any piece of writing: A **main idea** is explained or developed by **supporting details**. If that main idea is stated in one sentence of a paragraph, the sentence is called the **topic sentence**.

This chapter goes on to give you practice with two more advanced ways of finding a main idea:

- **Figuring out implied main ideas.** Authors often imply, or suggest, a main idea without stating it clearly in one sentence. In such cases, the reader must figure out that main idea by considering the supporting details.

- **Finding central points.** A selection consisting of several paragraphs or more has an overall main idea called the **central point**, or **thesis**. The paragraphs that make up the selection provide the supporting points and details for that central point. As with the main idea of a paragraph, the central point may be either clearly stated or implied.

IMPLIED MAIN IDEAS

Sometimes a selection lacks a topic sentence, but that does not mean it lacks a main idea. The author has simply decided to let the details of the selection suggest the main idea. You must figure out what that implied main idea is by deciding upon the point of all the details. For example, read the following paragraph.

In ancient times, irrational behavior was seen as the result of demons and evil spirits taking possession of a person. Later, the Greeks explained irrational behavior as a physical problem, caused by an imbalance of body fluids called "humors" or by displacement of an organ. In the highly superstitious Middle Ages, the theory of possession by demons was revived. The idea of possession reached a high point again in the witch-hunts of eighteenth-century Europe and America. Only in the last one hundred years did true medical explanations of mental illness gain wide acceptance.

You can see that no sentence in the paragraph is a good "umbrella" statement that covers all of the other sentences. To decide on the main idea, we must first determine the topic by asking, "Who or what is this paragraph about?" Once we have the topic in mind, we can ask, "What is the main point the author is trying to make about that topic?" When we think we know the main point, we can test it out by asking, "Does all or most of the material in the paragraph support this idea?"

In the paragraph above, all of the details are about irrational behavior, or mental illness, so that must be the topic. And what is the general point that the author is trying to make about mental illness? The details reveal the point to be as follows: People have explained mental illness in different ways over the years. Although this idea is not stated, you can see that it is a broad enough summary to include all the other material in the paragraph—it is the main idea.

Recognizing Implied Main Ideas

The implied main idea of a paragraph will be a general statement that covers all or most of the specific ideas in a paragraph. It should not be too broad or too narrow. The following exercises will give you help and practice in finding implied main ideas. By the time you have finished working with implied main ideas in this chapter, you will be writing out full main ideas in your own words.

Begin by reading the following four statements. They are the supporting details for an implied main idea. Then circle the letter of the unstated main idea. Finally, read the explanation that follows.

1. When a left-hander uses a screwdriver, his or her elbow turns away from the body, lessening the power.
2. As lefties write, their hands move over what was just written, possibly smudging the writing.
3. Sports instruction manuals are usually worded to help righties, not lefties.
4. A hand weeder can be dangerous to a left-hander because the curved blade is stroked to the right—away from the body for a right-hander, but toward the body of a lefty.

Which statement best expresses the unstated main idea of these sentences?

a. Someone ought to invent a screwdriver for left-handed people.

b. It isn't easy to be a left-hander in our society.

c. Many lefties learn to play sports with their right hands.

d. Individual differences among people influence how they learn, work, and play.

Explanation:

a. Answer *a* is too narrow to be the implied main idea. It is based on only one of the four supporting details, statement 1.

b. In contrast to answer *a*, answer *b* is a general statement about being left-handed that is supported by all four of the supporting details. Each of the four original statements tells about one way in which life is made more difficult for left-handers in our society. So answer *b* is the main idea—it covers all of the statements in the group.

c. Like answer *a*, answer *c* relates to only one of the four supporting details— statement 3. So answer *c* is too narrow to be the main idea.

d. The words *individual differences* cover all types of differences between people, not just whether they are right- or left-handed. A paragraph in which answer *d* was the main idea would have to mention more differences than just handedness. Therefore answer *d* is too broad to be the main idea.

If you have trouble focusing in on an implied main idea, remember that finding the topic may help. For instance, you probably soon realized that the topic of the numbered statements above is left-handers. Then you could have asked yourself, "What are the supporting details saying about the topic of left-handers?" As you thought about the four statements, you would try to find a point about lefties that is general enough to cover all of the specific details.

Note that the general point can be worded in more than one way. For instance, the main idea about left-handers could also be stated as follows: Because our society is geared toward right-handers, left-handers have trouble with such things as tools and sports.

➤ Practice 1

Read each group of numbered sentences. The group provides the supporting details for an implied main idea. Circle the letter of the answer that best states each implied main idea.

Group 1

1. Teach your family that if their clothing catches on fire, they should immediately roll on the ground.

2. Keep the number of your fire department near your phone.
3. Install smoke detectors on each level of your home, and change their batteries at least once a year.
4. Practice a fire escape route from each room in your home, including keeping your eyes closed and feeling your way out.

Which statement best expresses the unstated main idea of these sentences?
a. A household fire can happen at any time.
b. Because of the smoke, you may need to escape from a fire with your eyes closed.
c. There are various ways to prepare your family to respond correctly to a fire.
d. Families should prepare themselves for a variety of household emergencies.

Hint: The topic of the first four statements is *fire*. What general point about fire do the four statements support?

Group 2

1. Social rules discourage people from directly expressing many of their emotions.
2. People are often fearful that revealing their emotions will hurt them in some way.
3. Social roles, such as salesperson and teacher, make it difficult for people to express most of their emotions.
4. A person who wishes to be seen as confident may not admit to being sorry or unsure.

Which statement best expresses the unstated main idea of these sentences?
a. Being a salesperson intereferes with one's ability to express emotions.
b. Social rules and roles often discourage people from expressing their emotions.
c. People may not show their affection for fear that others will interpret their feelings as being romantic when they are not.
d. There are many reasons people do not share their plans, feelings, and personal lives with fellow workers.

Group 3

1. Scientists count such animals as elephants, timber wolves, ducks, and whistling swans by flying over them and counting them.
2. Small animals such as field mice are counted by trapping every single one in a given area and then counting them.

3. Microscopic creatures are gathered in a sample and counted little by little under a microscope.
4. Songbirds are counted by people walking through every part of a certain area at the same time, with each person counting every single songbird seen in his or her assigned space.

Which statement best expresses the unstated main idea of these sentences?
a. There are various reasons for counting the population of certain types of animals.
b. The methods scientists use to count animals vary according to the species.
c. The microscope is one of the tools used by biologists in counting the populations of species.
d. Biologists face many difficult tasks in studying the large variety of animal life on Earth.   The four statements illustrate answer *b*.

Group 4

1. The first unions in the United States were craft unions, made up of skilled workers in a single craft or profession.
2. In 1792, a group of shoemakers met in Philadelphia and formed the first known union in the country.
3. In the 1930s, the second type of American union emerged—the industrial union, made up of skilled and unskilled workers from all phases of a certain industry.
4. Auto and steel manufacturing were the first industries to be organized in industrial unions.

Which statement best expresses the unstated main idea of these sentences?
a. The interests of American workers have been promoted by labor unions, laws, and progressive management.
b. The members of industrial unions are both skilled and unskilled workers from all phases of an industry.
c. The first known union in the United States was a craft union formed in 1792.
d. Two types of unions developed in the United States.

Recognizing Implied Main Ideas in Paragraphs

You have practiced finding implied main ideas of groups of statements. The next step is to work at finding unstated main ideas in paragraphs. Read the following paragraph and see if you can choose the statement that best expresses the main idea.

More and more commuters are forming car pools to save money on gas, tolls, and wear and tear on their cars. Also, the special (and often faster) lanes many expressways provide for cars with three or more passengers during the rush hours can make the commute shorter and more hassle-free. Finally, car-pooling can reduce the boredom of the daily drive back and forth to work. Members who are not driving can talk, eat breakfast, read the paper, or get a head start on the day's work.

    a. Car-pooling saves commuters money.
    b. Car-pooling can mean shorter, easier rides for commuters.
    c. Everyone should join a car pool.
    d. There are several reasons more commuters are forming car pools.

Explanation:

As we begin to read this paragraph, we might think the first sentence is the topic sentence. If that were the main idea, however, then the details in the paragraph would have to be about the savings in money. Such details would focus on how much money can be saved by buying less gas, sharing tolls, and saving on the wear and tear of cars. But as we continue to read, we find that the paragraph, instead, goes on to give more reasons for car-pooling, and so answer *a* is incorrect—it is too narrow to be the main idea.

Answer *b* is also too narrow to be the main idea—it also covers only a single reason for forming car pools.

Answer *c* is incorrect because the details of the paragraph do not include any judgment about what people *should* do. It discusses only what people *are* doing.

Answer *d* is a correct statement of the main idea. The phrase "several reasons more commuters are forming car pools" is a general reference to the three specific reasons listed in the paragraph: 1) Car-pooling saves money; 2) car-pooling can make for a shorter, easier ride; and 3) car-pool members who aren't driving can use the riding time to do something else.

➤ *Practice 2*

The following paragraphs have unstated main ideas, and each is followed by four sentences. In each case, circle the letter of the sentence that best expresses the unstated main idea.

Remember to consider carefully all of the details and ask yourself, "Who or what is the paragraph about?" Once you discover the topic of the paragraph, ask, "What is the author's main point about the topic?" Then test your answer by asking, "Does all or most of the material in the paragraph support this idea?"

1.   One myth about exercise is that if a woman lifts weights, she will develop muscles as large as a man's. Without male hormones, however, a woman cannot

increase her muscle bulk as much as a man's. Another misconception about exercise is that it increases the appetite. Actually, regular exercise stabilizes the blood-sugar level and prevents hunger pains. Some people also think that a few minutes of exercise a day or one session a week is enough, but at least three solid workouts a week are needed for muscular and cardiovascular fitness.

a. Women who lift weights cannot become as muscular as men.
b. There are several myths about exercise.   The passage lists three
c. Exercise is beneficial to everyone.   myths about exercise.
d. People use many different excuses to avoid exercising.

2.   The work homemakers do is essential to the economy. The estimated value of the cleaning, cooking, nursing, shopping, child care, home maintenance, money management, errands, entertaining, and other services homemakers perform has been estimated at equal to roughly one-fourth of the gross national product. In fact, the Commerce Department's Bureau of Economic Analysis has proposed a revision of the gross national product that would take into account the value of the homemaker's services. But homemaking is not formal employment that brings money or prestige. No financial compensation is associated with this position, and the Dictionary of Occupational Titles places mothering and homemaking skills in the lowest category of skills, lower than the occupation of "dog trainer."

a. We no longer value the work done by homemakers.
b. Housewives should receive salaries for their work.
c. Although homemaking is essential to the economy, it brings no money or prestige.
d. It's better to be a dog trainer than a homemaker.

3.   Earth is surrounded by a thick gaseous envelope called the atmosphere. The atmosphere provides the air that we breathe and protects us from the sun's intense heat and dangerous radiation. The energy exchanges that continually occur between the atmosphere and space produce the effects we call weather. If, like the moon, Earth had no atmosphere, our planet would be lifeless, and many of the processes and interactions that make the surface such an energetic place could not operate. Without weathering and friction, the face of our planet might more closely resemble the lunar surface, which has not changed much in nearly three billion years.

a. The atmosphere provides our air and protects us.
b. The moon, unlike Earth, has no atmosphere and has therefore not changed much in almost three billion years.
c. There are many influences on Earth's development.
d. The atmosphere is a key part of our environment and of Earth's processes.

4.   If you fear growing older, remember that Sigmund Freud published his first important work, on dream interpretation, at age 44; Henry Kissinger was appointed Secretary of State at 50; and Rachel Carson completed her classic book on environmental damage, *Silent Spring*, at 55. "If you continue reading, thinking and creating all of your life, your intelligence increases," says one medical researcher. The mental health of many people also tends to improve as they grow older. Young people often protect their feelings with such defenses as denial and impulsive actions. By middle age, we are more likely to use such constructive defenses as humor, altruism, and creativity. Finally, age will make you more "yourself," as new or previously unexplored aspects of your personality emerge. As the actress Candice Bergen wrote in her autobiography, "It takes a long time to become a person."

a. To keep your intelligence growing, continue reading, thinking, and creating all of your life.
b. As we get older, we get better in all ways.
c. In several important ways, people get better as they get older.
d. By middle age, people are less likely to protect their feelings with such defenses as denial and impulsive actions.

Putting Implied Main Ideas into Words

When you read, you often have to **infer**—figure out on your own—an author's unstated main idea. The implied main idea that you come up with should cover all or most of the details in the paragraph. See if you can find the unstated main idea in the following paragraph. Then read the explanation on the next page.

Some actors and rock stars are paid more than a hundred times as much per year as schoolteachers are. We enjoy such performers, but certainly they do not do work that is many times more important than those who teach and guide our nation's students. Indeed, the reverse is true. Also, professional athletes earn vastly more than firefighters. The first group may bring enjoyable diversion to our lives, but the latter literally saves lives. Again, there can be little doubt that the lower-paid group, firefighters, makes the more important, indeed essential, contribution to society. Similarly, most high-fashion designers, who can make up to $50,000 for a single gown, far outearn police officers. Now, we can easily live without sophisticated clothes (and probably about 99.9 percent of us do), but a society without law-enforcement officers would be unlivable for all of us.

What is the implied main idea of this paragraph? _____

_____

_____

Explanation:

To find an implied main idea, consider all of the supporting details. In this case, the supporting details are three comparisons between highly paid occupations in our society and lesser-paid, but more important occupations. The pairs of occupations are 1) rock stars and teachers, 2) professional athletes and firefighters, and 3) high-fashion designers and police officers. Therefore we can say that the topic of the paragraph is the relationship between the pay and importance of occupations. One way of wording the general idea about that topic is as follows: Workers in our society are not necessarily paid according to how important their work is.

➤ *Practice 3*   *Wording of answers will vary.*

Write the implied main ideas of the following paragraphs in your own words.

1.   Some people have opposed the death penalty for religious reasons. The Quakers, for instance, were the first to institute prison sentences in an effort to eliminate torture and execution. Others have opposed capital punishment on grounds of racism because African-Americans were executed more often than whites. Some have even argued that executions actually increase murders by brutalizing the public sense of the value of life. Still others point to social- science research that seems to show capital punishment does not deter murder. If that's true, they say, there is no good reason for risking the execution of an innocent person.

Implied main idea: _____ *People oppose capital punishment for different* _____
reasons.

Comment: Paragraph 1 lists reasons people oppose capital punishment.

2.   After a stressful day it's restful to just put your feet up and enjoy a favorite program. And, of course, TV is entertaining for all ages. Videotaped movies, video games, and special cable offerings, as well as regular network programming, provide a choice of amusements for the whole family. TV is deservedly famous for being our best source of up-to-the-minute news. When history is being made, we are often there, thanks to TV. Most importantly, television is a real educational tool. From *Sesame Street* to public television's nature programs, it teaches in a colorful and interesting fashion.

Implied main idea: _____ *There are benefits to watching television.* _____

Comment: Paragraph 2 lists benefits of watching TV.

3.   One mistaken idea is that sleepwalkers drift about in a ghost-like way, with arms extended. The fact is most sleepwalkers walk around quite normally, though their eyes are usually closed or glazed. It is also commonly believed that one should never wake a sleepwalker. But it is advisable to do so if the walker seems in immediate danger—for example, if he or she is going toward an open window or handling a sharp object. Another popular misconception is that sleepwalkers are not "really" sleeping or are only half-asleep. In fact, they are in a very deep state of sleep. A last commonly held belief is that sleepwalkers are easy to spot because they're in nighties or pajamas. Often this isn't true because sleepwalkers can do routine tasks, including getting completely dressed.

Implied main idea: _____ *Many commonly held beliefs about sleepwalking are*
not true.

Comment: Paragraph 3 lists and refutes commonly held beliefs about sleepwalking.

4.   Many people think that only children are lucky because of the material goods and attention they receive. But consider that only children have no privacy. Parents always feel entitled to know everything that's going on in an only child's life. Another drawback of being an only child is the lack of certain advantages that children with brothers and sisters have. An only child can never blame a sibling for something that goes wrong or ask for a privilege that an older brother or sister was given earlier. In addition, only children miss the companionship of siblings. Not only can they be lonely, but they may have trouble making friends later in life because they never learned to get along with a brother or sister.

Implied main idea: _____ *Being an only child is not as great a privilege as*
people think it is.

Comment: Paragraph 4 lists drawbacks to being an only child.

CENTRAL POINTS

Just as a paragraph has a main idea, so a longer selection has a **central idea** or **central point**, also known as a thesis. The longer selection may be in the form of an essay, an article, or even a section within a textbook chapter. The central point may be clearly stated, or it may be implied. You can find a central point in the same way that you find a main idea—by considering the supporting material. The paragraphs within the longer reading will provide supporting points and details for the central point.

In the following essay, the central point is stated. See if you can find it. Then write the point in the space provided.

Disappointment

Ben Franklin said that the only sure things in life are death and taxes. He left something out, however: disappointment. No one gets through life without experiencing many disappointments. But many people seem unprepared for disappointment and react to it with depression or escape, rather than using it as an opportunity for growth.

Depression is a common negative response to disappointment. Yvonne, for example, works hard for over a year in her department, trying to win a promotion. She is so sure she will get it, in fact, that she has already picked out the car she will buy when her salary increase comes through. However, the boss names one of her coworkers to the spot. The fact that all the other department employees tell Yvonne she really deserved the promotion doesn't help her deal with the crushing disappointment. Deeply depressed, Yvonne decides that all her goals are doomed to defeat. She loses her enthusiasm for her job and can barely force herself to show up every day. She tells herself that she is a failure and that doing a good job just isn't worth the work.

Another negative reaction to disappointment is escape. Kevin fails to get into the college his brother is attending, the college that was the focus of all his dreams, and reacts to his disappointment by escaping his circumstances. Why worry about college at all? Instead, he covers up his real feelings by giving up on on his schoolwork and getting completely involved with friends, parties, and "good times." Or Linda doesn't make the varsity basketball team—something she wanted very badly—and so refuses to play sports at all. She decides to hang around with a new set of friends who get high every day; then she won't have to confront her disappointment and learn to live with it.

The positive way to react to disappointment is to use it as a chance for growth. This isn't easy, but it's the only useful way to deal with an inevitable part of life. Yvonne, the woman who wasn't promoted, could have handled her disappointment by looking at other options. If her boss doesn't recognize talent and hard work, perhaps she could transfer to another department. Or she could ask the boss how to improve her performance so that she would be a shoo-in for the next promotion. Kevin, the young man who didn't get into the college of his choice, should look into other schools. Going to another college may encourage him to be his own person, step out of his brother's shadow, and realize that being turned down by one college isn't a final judgment on his abilities or potential. Rather than escape into drugs, Linda could improve her basketball skills for a year or pick up another sport, like swimming or tennis, that might turn out to be more useful to her as an adult.

Disappointments are unwelcome but regular visitors to everyone's   5
life. The best response is to step over the unwelcome visitor on the
doorstep and get on with life.

Central point: _____

_____

_____

Explanation:

The central point is a general statement that covers all or most of the details
in a reading. To select the central point of the essay above, look at its major
details. The first major detail, presented in paragraph 2, is about a negative
response to disappointment: depression. The second major detail, discussed
in paragraph 3, is about another negative response to disappointment: the
desire to escape. Paragraph 4 then explains a positive reaction to
disappointment—using it as a chance for growth.

The central point, then, will be a statement that covers the two negative
responses and the one positive response to disappointment. As is often the
case, the central point is stated near the start of the essay, in the first
paragraph. The *last* sentence in that paragraph mentions reacting to
disappointment with depression or escape, or using it as an opportunity for
growth, so that sentence is the central point.

➤ Practice 4

Read the following selection from a history textbook. See if you can find the
clearly stated central point that covers most of the supporting details. Then write
the point in the space provided.

Housewives in Nineteenth-Century America

For many people, the image of the woman in Western movies is a
gentle one of a mother quietly tending to her kitchen, shopping at the general
store, and raising her children. In fact, the days of a housewife in nineteenth-
century America were spent in harsh physical labor.

Preparing even a simple meal was a time- and energy-consuming chore.
Prior to the twentieth century, cooking was performed on a coal- or wood-
burning stove. Unlike an electric or a gas range, which can be turned on with

the flick of a single switch, cast-iron and steel stoves were especially difficult to use. Housewives would first have to clean out the ashes left from previous fires. Then, paper and kindling had to be set inside the stove, dampers and flues had to be carefully adjusted, and a fire had to be lit. Since there were no thermostats to regulate the stove's temperature, a woman had to keep an eye on the contraption all day long. Any time the fire slackened, she had to adjust a flue or add more fuel. All day long, the stove had to be fed with new supplies of coal or wood—an average of fifty pounds or more. At least twice a day, the ash box under the fire had to be emptied. All together, a housewife spent four hours every day rubbing the stove with thick black wax to keep it from rusting, lighting the fire, adjusting dampers, sifting ashes, and carrying wood or coal.

It was not enough for a housewife to know how to use a cast-iron stove. She also had to know how to prepare unprocessed foods for consumption. Prior to the 1890s, there were few factory-prepared foods. Shoppers bought poultry that was still alive and then had to kill and pluck the birds. Fish had to have scales removed. Green coffee had to be roasted and ground. Loaves of sugar had to be pounded, flour sifted, nuts shelled, and raisins seeded.

Cleaning was an even more arduous task than cooking. The soot and smoke from coal- and wood-burning stoves blackened walls and dirtied drapes and carpets. Gas and kerosene lamps left smelly deposits of black soot on furniture and curtains. Each day, the lamps' glass chimneys had to be wiped and the wicks trimmed or replaced. And periodically floors had to be scrubbed, rugs beaten, and windows washed.

Since indoor plumbing was available only to the wealthy, chores that involved the use of water were especially demanding. The mere job of bringing water into the house was a challenge. According to calculations made in 1886, a typical North Carolina housewife had to carry water from a pump or well or a spring eight to ten times each day. Washing, boiling, and rinsing a single load of laundry used about fifty gallons of water. Over the course of a year, she walked 148 miles toting over 36 tons of water! Homes without running water also lacked the simplest way to dispose of dirty water: sinks with drains. That meant that women had to remove dirty dishwater, kitchen slops, and, worst of all, the contents of chamber pots from their house by hand.

Central point: *In fact, the days of a housewife in nineteenth-century*

America were spent in harsh physical labor.

Comment: The passage describes the harsh labor done by a nineteenth-century housewife.

➤ *Practice 5*

Read the following selection from a sociology textbook. See if you can find the clearly stated central point that covers most of the supporting details. Then write the point in the space provided.

Living in Poverty

Although the causes of poverty are complex, its consequences are clear. In virtually every way imaginable, life is more difficult for poor people. They are ill more often, receive poorer and more limited medical care, and live shorter lives. They also have a higher rate of mental illness, particularly for the more serious illnesses such as depression, schizophrenia, and personality disorders. They also report lower levels of personal happiness than the nonpoor.

The children of the poor are at greater risk of dying in infancy, and if they survive, they have a greater risk than nonpoor children of getting into trouble with the law or becoming pregnant as teenagers. Their education is inferior to that of nonpoor children, and they are far less likely to complete high school. One study showed that in Chicago's public schools, where a large proportion of the students are from poverty-stricken families, fewer than half graduated on time, and of those who did graduate, only one out of three could read at a twelfth-grade level.

Poor people spend more of their income on food and housing than the nonpoor, but they are still worse fed and worse housed. A study of housing in southern Illinois revealed that poor people were several times as likely as the general public to live in overcrowded housing, yet 80 to 90 percent of these poor people were paying more than the government standard of 25 percent of their incomes for rent.

Poor people are more likely to commit street crimes and to be the victims of such crimes. Crime rates are highest in poor neighborhoods, for criminals tend to victimize those who are close by and available. As a result, a highly disproportionate number of victims of robbery, assault, and homicide are poor. So high is the incidence of crimes in some poor neighborhoods that poor people are afraid to venture outside their homes. Summer after summer in major cities, elderly poor people have died from heat-related illnesses because they could not afford air conditioning and were afraid to open their windows because of crime.

Central point: *In virtually every way imaginable, life is more difficult for poor people.*

Comment: The passage lists numerous ways in which life is more difficult for poor people.

➤ *Review Test 1*

To review what you've learned in this chapter, complete each of the following sentences.

1. When a paragraph has no topic sentence, we say that its main idea is (*central, broad, implied*) _____*implied*_____.

2. If you have trouble finding an implied main idea, it may help to first find the (*topic, topic sentence, central point*) _____*topic*_____ of the paragraph.

3. After you figure out what you think is the implied main idea of a paragraph, test yourself by asking, "Does all or most of the material in the paragraph _____*support*_____ this idea?"

4. The "main idea" of a selection that is longer than several paragraphs is called the (*topic, topic sentence, central point*) _____*central point*_____.

5. The central point is (*never, sometimes, always*) _____*sometimes*_____ implied.

➤ *Review Test 2*

A. Circle the letter of the sentence that best expresses the implied main idea of the following paragraphs.

1. An old "preventative" for baldness required dusting the head with powdered parsley seed several times a year. Another old potion used parsley to supposedly lighten or eliminate freckles. Additionally, parsley earned the reputation of being a breath sweetener when simply held in the mouth. Today, parsley has become the overwhelming choice for a decorative addition to almost any plate.

   a. Parsley has been thought to be able to affect people's looks in various ways.
   b. A variety of unusual uses have been found for herbs of all kinds.
   c. People have found various ways to use parsley other than as a food.
   d. Parsley is one of the more decorative herbs.

2. Lean against a tree almost anywhere, and the first creature that crawls on you will probably be an ant. Stroll down a suburban sidewalk with your eyes fixed on the ground, counting the different kinds of animals you see. The ants will win hands down—more precisely, fore tarsi down. The British entomologist C. B. Williams once calculated that the number of insects alive

on Earth at a given moment is one million trillion. If, to take a conservative figure, 1 percent of those insects are ants, their total population is ten thousand trillion. Individual workers weigh on average between one and five milligrams, according to the species. When combined, all ants in the world taken together weigh about as much as all human beings.

a. Ants are commonplace in the suburbs.
b. There are huge numbers of ants on Earth.
c. There are too many ants in the world.
d. C. B. Williams, the British entomologist, calculated the number of insects alive on Earth at any one time.

3.   When anti-smoking campaigns made teens aware of the risks of smoking, the percentage of teens smoking dropped from 28 to 20 percent over the last ten years. Additionally, in schools where students have access to health clinics which provide birth control information and devices, pregnancy rates have declined by 30 percent. Furthermore, another study demonstrated that students in schools with comprehensive health education were less likely to use alcohol, to try drugs, or to attempt suicide.

a. If more schools would conduct anti-smoking campaigns, the number of teens who smoke would greatly decline.
b. Evidence suggests that health education programs have a favorable effect on teenagers' behavior.
c. Health education clinics are a positive influence on how people of all ages take care of themselves.
d. One study found that students in schools with comprehensive health education were less likely to use drugs or to attempt suicide.

B. Write out the implied main idea of the following paragraphs.

4.   If you have trouble getting a good night's sleep, don't have an alcoholic drink before bedtime. While alcohol can certainly knock you out, it also damages the quality of sleep you'll get. That's because it chemically interferes with dreaming, an important part of restful sleep. Also, avoid beverages and foods that contain caffeine, such as coffee, most teas, colas, and chocolate. Caffeine can stimulate you, making sleep difficult or impossible. A better before-bed choice is milk, which contains a mild, sleep-inducing type of protein. Another piece of good advice is to exercise during the day; this can leave you tuckered out enough at night to fall promptly and soundly asleep. But do avoid exercise right before bedtime, as its immediate effects are more stimulating than relaxing. Last, try to get up at about the same time every day; this practice will help your body establish a solid sleep

and wake cycle. Varying your hours too much can confuse your body's "inner clock."

Implied main idea: <u>There are several ways to ensure getting a good</u>

<u>night's sleep.</u>

<u>The passage lists suggestions for getting a good night's sleep.</u>

5. Lower-class criminals are more likely to be caught than wealthy criminals. And once caught, they are less likely to be able to afford highly skilled legal representation. When they appear in court, their life history—which often includes quitting school, unemployment, divorce, and an apparent lack of responsibility when judged by middle-class standards—may work against them. As a result, lower-income criminals are likely to receive heavier penalties than higher-income criminals for the same crime. And because they often cannot afford bail, lower-income criminals often have to wait for trial in jail cells rather than in the comfort of their own homes.

Implied main idea: <u>Lower-class criminals tend to be treated more</u>

<u>harshly by the justice system than higher-class criminals.</u>

<u>The passage compares some ways that lower-class and higher-class criminals are treated.</u>

➤ *Review Test 3*

1. Reread "Night Watch," which begins on page 23. Then circle the letter of the sentence below that best expresses that selection's implied central point.
   a. Hospitals and the Red Cross can provide important help to people at times of great need.
   b. The Red Cross was unable to find the Marine who was the son of a dying man.
   c. By going to great trouble to comfort a dying stranger, a Marine showed there are people who care about their fellow human beings.
   d. Because of a dying man, it was discovered that there were two Marines with the same name and similar serial numbers in the same camp.

2. Reread "Here's to Your Health," which begins on page 62. The central point appears twice in this essay. Write the number of one of the two paragraphs that contain the sentence expressing the central point. In the second space below, write the first few words of that sentence.
   • The central point of "Here's to Your Health" is stated in paragraph <u>3 or 12</u>
   • The first few words of the sentence with the central point are

   <u>*To top it all off, this aggressive* . . . or *Advertisers would have us believe* . . .</u>

Comment: Item 2—In "Here's to Your Health," paragraphs 1 and 2 are the introduction. Paragraphs 3–11 discuss the four elements of the "myth about drinking" promoted by the media. Paragraph 12 is the conclusion.

3. Reread "Child-Rearing Styles," which begins on page 96. Then circle the letter of the sentence below that best expresses that selection's implied central point.

   a. Children are greatly influenced by how they are treated by all the adults in their lives.

   b. Permissive parents make fewer demands on their children than authoritative and authoritarian parents do.

   (c.) Both a child's natural temperament and parents' child-rearing styles influence the child's behavior.

   d. To raise competent, socially responsible, and independent children, parents should teach by example.

> In "Child-Rearing Styles," the last two sentences of paragraph 1 express the central point. Paragraphs 2–6 discuss "parents' child-rearing styles." Paragraph 7 discusses the "child's natural temperament."

➤ *Review Test 4*

Here is a chance to apply your understanding of implied and central ideas to a reading about childhood cruelty.

To help you continue to strengthen your skills, the reading is followed by questions not only on what you've learned in this chapter but also on what you've learned in previous chapters.

Words to Watch

Below are some words in the reading that do not have strong context support. Each word is followed by the number of the paragraph in which it appears and its meaning there. These words are indicated in the article by a small circle (°).

simulate (1): imitate
musty (3): stale or moldy in odor
trudge (5): walk in a heavy, tired way
brunt (6): greatest part
taunted (6): mocked and insulted
gait (7): manner of moving
sinister (7): evil
distracted (9): interested in something else
stoic (13): emotionless
vulnerable (25): defenseless

ROWING THE BUS
Paul Logan

1   When I was in elementary school, some older kids made me row the bus. Rowing meant that on the way to school I had to sit in the dirty bus aisle littered with paper, gum wads, and spitballs. Then I had to simulate° the motion of rowing while the kids around me laughed and chanted, "Row, row, row the bus." I was forced to do this by a group of bullies who spent most of their time picking on me.

2   I was the perfect target for them. I was small. I had no father. And my mother, though she worked hard to support me, was unable to afford clothes and sneakers that were "cool." Instead she dressed me in outfits that we got from "the bags"—hand-me-downs given as donations to a local church.

3   Each Wednesday, she'd bring several bags of clothes through to the house and pull out musty°, wrinkled shirts and worn bell-bottom pants that other families no longer wanted. I knew that people were kind to give things to us, but I hated wearing clothes that might have been donated by my classmates. Each time I wore something from the bags, I feared that the other kids might recognize something that was once theirs.

4   Besides my outdated clothes, I wore thick glasses, had crossed eyes, and spoke with a persistent lisp. For whatever reason, I had never learned to say the "s" sound properly, and I pronounced words that began with "th" as if they began with a "d." In addition, because of my severely crossed eyes, I lacked the hand and eye coordination necessary to hit or catch flying objects.

5   As a result, footballs, baseballs, soccer balls and basketballs became my enemies. I knew, before I stepped on the field or court, that I would do something clumsy or foolish and that everyone would laugh at me. I feared humiliation so much that I became skillful at feigning illnesses to get out of gym class. Eventually I learned how to give myself low-grade fevers so the nurse would write me an excuse. It worked for a while, until the gym teachers caught on. When I did have to play, I was always the last one chosen to be on any team. In fact, team captains did everything in their power to make their opponents get stuck with me. When the unlucky team captain was forced to call my name, I would trudge° over to the team, knowing that no one there liked or wanted me. For four years, from second through fifth grade, I prayed nightly for God to give me school days in which I would not be insulted, embarrassed, or made to feel ashamed.

6   I thought my prayers were answered when my mother decided to move during the summer before sixth grade. The move meant that I got to start sixth grade in a different school, a place where I had no reputation. Although the older kids laughed and snorted at me as soon as I got on my new bus—they couldn't miss my thick glasses and strange clothes—I soon discovered that there was another kid who received the brunt° of their insults. His name was George, and everyone made fun of him. The kids taunted° him because he was skinny; they belittled him because he had acne that pocked and blotched his face, and they teased him because his voice

was squeaky. During my first gym class at my new school, I wasn't the last one chosen for kickball; George was.

7   George tried hard to be friends with me, coming up to me in the cafeteria on the first day of school. "Hi. My name's George. Can I sit with you?" he asked with a peculiar squeakiness that made each word high-pitched and raspy. As I nodded for him to sit down, I noticed an uncomfortable silence in the cafeteria as many of the students who had mocked George's clumsy gait° during gym class began watching the two of us and whispering among themselves. By letting him sit with me, I had violated an unspoken law of school, a sinister° code of childhood that demands there must always be someone to pick on. I began to realize two things. If I befriended George, I would soon receive the same treatment that I had gotten at my old school. If I stayed away from him, I might actually have a chance to escape being at the bottom.

8   Within days, the kids started taunting us whenever we were together. "Who's your new little buddy, Georgie?" In the hallways, groups of students began mumbling about me just loud enough for me to hear, "Look, it's George's ugly boyfriend." On the bus rides to and from school, wads of paper and wet chewing gum were tossed at me by the bigger, older kids in the back of the bus.

9   It became clear that my friendship with George was going to cause me several more years of misery at my new school. I decided to stop being friends with George. In class and at lunch, I spent less and less time with him. Sometimes I told him I was too busy to talk; other times I acted distracted° and gave one-word responses to whatever he said. Our classmates, sensing that they

had created a rift between George and me, intensified their attacks on him. Each day, George grew more desperate as he realized that the one person who could prevent him from being completely isolated was closing him off. I knew that I shouldn't avoid him, that he was feeling the same way I felt for so long, but I was so afraid that my life would become the hell it had been in my old school that I continued to ignore him.

10   Then, at recess one day, the meanest kid in the school, Chris, decided he had had enough of George. He vowed that he was going to beat up George and anyone else who claimed to be his friend. A mob of kids formed and came after me. Chris led the way and cornered me near our school's swing sets. He grabbed me by my shirt and raised his fist over my head. A huge gathering of kids surrounded us, urging him to beat me up, chanting "Go, Chris, go!"

11   "You're Georgie's new little boyfriend, aren't you?" he yelled. The hot blast of his breath carried droplets of his spit into my face. In a complete betrayal of the only kid who was nice to me, I denied George's friendship.

12   "No, I'm not George's friend. I don't like him. He's stupid," I blurted out. Several kids snickered and mumbled under their breath. Chris stared at me for a few seconds and then threw me to the ground.

13   "Wimp. Where's George?" he demanded, standing over me. Someone pointed to George sitting alone on top of the monkey bars about thirty yards from where we were. He was watching me. Chris and his followers sprinted over to George and yanked him off the bars to the ground. Although the mob quickly encircled them, I could still see the two of them at the center of the crowd,

looking at each other. George seemed stoic°, staring straight through Chris. I heard the familiar chant of "Go, Chris, go!" and watched as his fists began slamming into George's head and body. His face bloodied and his nose broken, George crumpled to the ground and sobbed without even throwing a punch. The mob cheered with pleasure and darted off into the playground to avoid an approaching teacher.

14   Chris was suspended, and after a few days, George came back to school. I wanted to talk to him, to ask him how he was, to apologize for leaving him alone and for not trying to stop him from getting hurt. But I couldn't go near him. Filled with shame for denying George and angered by my own cowardice, I never spoke to him again.

15   Several months later, without telling any students, George transferred to another school. Once in a while, in those last weeks before he left, I caught him watching me as I sat with the rest of the kids in the cafeteria. He never yelled at me or expressed anger, disappoint-ment, or even sadness. Instead he just looked at me.

16   In the years that followed, George's silent stare remained with me. It was there in eighth grade when I saw a gang of popular kids beat up a sixth-grader because, they said, he was "ugly and stupid." It was there my first year in high school, when I saw a group of older kids steal another freshman's clothes and throw them into the showers. It was there a year later, when I watched several seniors press a wad of chewing gum into the hair of a new girl on the bus. Each time that I witnessed another awkward, uncomfortable, scared kid being tormented, I thought of George, and gradually his haunting stare began to speak to me. No longer silent, it told me that every child who is picked on and taunted deserves better, that no one—no matter how big, strong, attractive or popular—has the right to abuse another person.

17   Finally, in my junior year when a loudmouthed, pink-skinned bully named Donald began picking on two freshmen on the bus, I could no longer deny George. Donald was crumpling a large wad of paper and preparing to bounce it off the back of the head of one of the young students when I interrupted him.

18   "Leave them alone, Don," I said. By then I was six inches taller and, after two years of high-school wrestling, thirty pounds heavier than I had been in my freshman year. Though Donald was still two years older than me, he wasn't much bigger. He stopped what he was doing, squinted and stared at me.

19   "What's your problem, Paul?"

20   I felt the way I had many years earlier on the playground when I watched the mob of kids begin to surround George.

21   "Just leave them alone. They aren't bothering you," I responded quietly.

22   "What's it to you?" he challenged. A glimpse of my own past, of rowing the bus, of being mocked for my clothes, my lisp, my glasses, and my absent father flashed in my mind.

23   "Just don't mess with them. That's all I am saying, Don." My fingertips were tingling. The bus was silent. He got up from his seat and leaned over me, and I rose from my seat to face him. For a minute, both of us just stood there, without a word, staring.

24   "I'm just playing with them, Paul," he said, chuckling. "You don't have to go psycho on me or anything." Then he shook his head, slapped me firmly on the chest with the back of his hand, and sat

down. But he never threw that wad of paper. For the rest of the year, whenever I was on the bus, Don and the other troublemakers were noticeably quiet.

25   Although it has been years since my days on the playground and the school bus, George's look still haunts me. Today, I see it on the faces of a few scared kids at my sister's school—she is in fifth grade. Or once in a while I'll catch a glimpse of someone like George on the evening news, in a story about a child who brought a gun to school to stop the kids from picking on him, or in a feature about a teenager who killed herself because everyone teased her. In each school, in almost every classroom, there is a George with a stricken face, hoping that someone nearby will be strong enough to be kind—despite what the crowd says—and brave enough to stand up against people who attack, tease or hurt those who are vulnerable°.

If asked about their behavior, I'm   26 sure the bullies would say, "What's it to you? It's just a joke. It's nothing." But to George and me, and everyone else who has been humiliated or laughed at or spat on, it is everything. No one should have to row the bus.

Reading Comprehension Questions

Vocabulary in Context

1. In the sentence below, the word *feigning* means
   a. escaping.
   (b) faking.
   c. recognizing.
   d. curing.

   "I feared humiliation so much that I became skillful at feigning illnesses to get out of gym class." (Paragraph 5)

2. In the excerpt below, the word *rift* means
   a. friendship.
   b. agreement.
   (c) break.
   d. joke.

   "I decided to stop being friends with George. . . . Our classmates, sensing that they had created a rift between George and me, intensified their attacks on him." (Paragraph 9)

Main Ideas

3. Which sentence best expresses the main idea of paragraphs 2–4?
   (a) The first sentence of paragraph 2
   b. The first sentence of paragraph 3
   c. The first sentence of paragraph 4
   d. The first sentence of paragraph 5

   Paragraphs 3 and 4 discuss ways in which the author "was the perfect target." Paragraph 5 begins a new topic.

4. The topic sentence of paragraph 8 is its
   a. first sentence.
   b. second sentence.
   c. third sentence.
   d. final sentence.

Supporting Details

5. When Chris attacked George, George reacted by
   a. fighting back hard.
   b. shouting for Logan to help him.
   c. running away.
   d. accepting the beating.

6. Logan finally found the courage to stand up for abused students when he saw
   a. Donald throwing paper at a younger student.
   b. older kids throwing a freshman's clothes into the shower.
   c. seniors putting bubble gum in a new student's hair.
   d. a gang beating up a sixth-grader whom they disliked.

Central Point

7. Which sentence best expresses the central point of the selection?
   a. Although Paul Logan was a target of other students' abuse when he was a young boy, their attacks stopped as he grew taller and stronger.
   b. When Logan moved to a different school, he discovered that another student, George, was the target of more bullying than he was.
   c. Logan's experience of being bullied and his shame at how he treated George eventually made him speak up for someone else who was teased.
   d. Logan is ashamed that he did not stand up for George when George was being attacked by a bully on the playground.

Implied Main Ideas

8. Which sentence best expresses the implied main idea of paragraph 5?
   a. Because of Logan's clumsiness, gym was a miserable experience for him in elementary school.
   b. Because Logan hated gym so much, he made up excuses to avoid it.
   c. The gym teacher caught on to Logan's excuses.
   d. Logan knew that other students did not want him to be a member of their team when games were played.

9. Which sentence best expresses the implied main idea of paragraph 6?
   a. Logan's mother moved so that Logan could get a fresh start in a new school.
   b. Even at the new school, students laughed at Logan's appearance.
   c. Riding on the bus was the worst part of Logan's school experience.
   d. Logan realized that at his new school, another student, George, was more unpopular than he was.

Answer *d* summarizes the important parts of paragraph 6.

10. Which sentence best expresses the implied main idea of paragraph 16?
    a. Older kids were often cruel to younger students at Logan's schools.
    (b.) Because of what happened to George, Logan became increasingly bothered by students' picking on others.
    c. In Logan's first year in high school, some students threw a freshman's clothes into the showers.
    d. In school, Logan learned a great deal about how people behave in various situations throughout life.

    Answers *a* and *c* are too narrow. Answer *d* is too broad—the paragraph focuses only on bullying, not "various situations."

Discussion Questions

1. Paul Logan titled his selection "Rowing the Bus." Yet very little of the essay actually deals with the incident the title describes—only the first and last paragraphs. Why do you think Logan chose that title?

2. Logan wanted to be kind to George, but he wanted even more to be accepted by the other students. Have you ever found yourself in a similar situation—where you wanted to do the right thing but felt that it had too high a price? Explain what happened.

3. Logan refers to "a sinister code of childhood that demands there must always be someone to pick on." Why do children need someone to pick on?

4. The novelist Henry James once said, "Three things in human life are important. The first is to be kind. The second is to be kind. And the third is to be kind." What do you think schools or concerned adults could do to encourage young people to treat one another with kindness rather than cruelty?

Check Your Performance   **IMPLIED MAIN IDEAS / CENTRAL POINT**

Activity	Number Right	Points	Score
Review Test 1 (5 items)	_____	x 2 =	_____
Review Test 2 (5 items)	_____	x 6 =	_____
Review Test 3 (3 items)	_____	x 10 =	_____
Review Test 4 (10 items)	_____	x 3 =	_____
		TOTAL SCORE =	_____ %

Enter your total score into the **Reading Performance Chart: Review Tests** on the inside back cover.

IMPLIED MAIN IDEAS AND THE CENTRAL POINT: Test 1

A. Circle the letter of the sentence that best expresses the implied main idea of each of the following paragraphs.

1. Many people think there is no difference between an alligator and a crocodile. However, the alligator's snout is shorter and broader than that of a crocodile. A more dramatic difference between the two creatures lies in how dangerous they are to humans. There are very few documented instances in which alligators have killed a person. On the other hand, crocodiles, particularly those along the Nile River, are quite dangerous to humans. It is said, in fact, that as far as killing people is concerned, crocodiles are second only to poisonous snakes.

    a. Poisonous snakes are more dangerous to humans than crocodiles.
    b. Many people believe that alligators and crocodiles are the same.
    c. There are clear differences between alligators and crocodiles.
    d. Alligators aren't particularly dangerous to humans.

2. A chemistry professor wished to demonstrate the harmful effects of alcohol to her class. On the lab table, she set two beakers—one containing water and the other filled with grain alcohol. Then she dropped a worm into each. The worm in the alcohol beaker wriggled violently in a vain attempt to escape and quickly died. The other worm, in the water beaker, moved slowly and gracefully, seeming to enjoy its new environment. The professor smiled with satisfaction and looked at the roomful of students. Then she asked, "What lesson can be learned from this demonstration?" One student quickly answered, "If you drink alcohol, you'll never have worms."

    a. Teaching chemistry is extremely difficult.
    b. The professor should not have sacrificed a worm for her lesson.
    c. More schools should be teaching students about the harmful effects of alcohol.
    d. Although the professor meant to teach the dangers of alcohol, a student assumed something quite different.

3. The earliest humans probably used the lengthening and shortening of shadows on the ground to measure the passage of time. Later, the sundial was invented to tell time more precisely, but still by using the shadow principle. The hourglass, a slightly more recent invention, measured time by allowing grains of sand to fall from one container to another. In about the year 1300, a primitive clock was invented. It had only an hour hand, but it became the most exact way yet to tell the time. Since then, clocks have been so improved technically that today's clocks and watches can be depended upon to be quite precise.

Comments: Paragraph 1—Answers *a*, *b*, and *d* are too narrow.

Paragraph 2—a. The single event in the paragraph is too little evidence for this conclusion.
b. and c. Nothing in the paragraph supports these opinions.

(Continues on next page)

137

(a.) Throughout history, people have found better and better ways to measure the passing of time.

b. The hourglass is a slightly more recent invention than the sundial.

c. The first methods of measuring the passing of time took advantage of the changing shadows cast by the sun throughout a day.

d. A primitive clock invented in about 1300 was the most exact way to tell time up to that point.   Answers *b*, *c*, and *d* are all too narrow.

B. (4.) The author has stated the central point of the following textbook selection in one sentence. Find that sentence, and write it in the space provided.

An Endangered Way of Life

Small towns across America are in crisis, and the quality of life for their citizens is declining.

In 1950, about 36 percent of Americans lived in small towns and rural areas; by 1990, only 25 percent did. Young people (especially those with higher education) are moving away, often leaving their parents behind. As a result, rural America is aging.

Also, the economic life of rural America is discouraging. Because many small towns depend on a single employer, their economies are fragile. Moreoever, with more people than jobs, employers are able to pay just the minimum wage. The poverty rate for young people in rural areas has more than doubled in the past twenty years, and the unemployment rate is twice the national average.

Health care in rural America is deteriorating. Of the three hundred hospitals that closed in the 1980s, more than half were in small towns. The country doctor is also disappearing. Many small towns have only a part-time physician who serves several communities, and some have no doctor at all.

Small-town schools are also in trouble. With dwindling numbers of students, the cost of educating a single student often becomes prohibitive, and many small districts have been forced to merge. In consolidated school districts, students may be forced to ttravel fifty miles back and forth to school each day.

The crisis in rural America is taking its toll on the mental health of its residents. A recent study of Iowa farmers found that one in three suffered symptoms of depression. Another study, of rural adolescents, found that they are far more prone to depression and suicidal thoughts than are their urban counterparts.

Central point: Small towns across America are in crisis, and the quality of life for their citizens is declining.

IMPLIED MAIN IDEAS AND THE CENTRAL POINT: Test 2

A. Circle the letter of the sentence that best expresses the implied main idea of each of the following paragraphs.

1. Many people dream of being celebrities, but do they consider what celebrities' lives are really like? For one thing, celebrities have to look perfect all the time. There's always a photographer ready to take an unflattering picture of a famous person looking dumpy in old clothes. Celebrities also sacrifice their private lives. Their personal struggles, divorces, or family tragedies all end up as front-page news. Most frighteningly, celebrities are in constant danger of the wrong kind of attention. Threatening letters and even physical attacks from crazy fans are things the celebrity must contend with.

   a. Many people dream of being celebrities.
   (b.) Being a celebrity is often difficult.
   c. Being a celebrity means having to look good all the time.
   d. Celebrities face dangers.

2. Chocolate comes from the beans of cacao trees found in Africa, Brazil, and the West Indies. The cacao bean was used as currency by the ancient Aztecs. In 1528, Spanish explorers introduced chocolate to the court of King Charles V. Chocolate quickly became popular throughout Europe, often being called the "food of the gods." Thomas Jefferson brought it to North America in 1765, opening the first chocolate factory in the Massachusetts Bay Colony. Two decades later, Conrad Van Houten, a Dutch chemist, discovered the way to blend cocoa butter with sugar to yield a chocolate very similar to that which we enjoy today.

   a. Chocolate didn't become popular throughout Europe until the 1500s.
   (b.) Chocolate has a long and interesting history.
   c. Before 1765, North Americans had to do without chocolate.
   d. The Spanish explorers found many new foods as well as new lands.

3. As you speak with someone, you can easily gather clues about how much he or she understands or agrees with you and adjust your conversation accordingly. But when you write, you must try to anticipate the reader's reactions without such clues. You also have to provide stronger evidence in writing than in conversation. A friend may accept an unsupported statement such as "He's a lousy boss." But in writing, the reader expects you to back up such a statement with proof.

   a. There are special techniques to communicating verbally with others.
   b. Speaking and writing are both challenging ways of communicating.
   (c.) Communicating effectively in writing is more demanding than communicating verbally.
   d. When speaking, you get feedback about a person's reaction that helps you to make your conversation more effective.

(Continues on next page)

B. (4.) The author has stated the central point of the following psychology article in one sentence. Find that sentence, and write it in the space provided.

Missing Persons

Many of the world's girls and women are missing from schools. In sub-Saharan Africa, for every ten boys, only six girls are enrolled in secondary school, and in southern Asia, only four. In these regions, three-quarters of women aged 25 and over are still illiterate. A major reason why girls leave school is that they are married off, often to older men, and begin bearing children in their teens. Some are sold by their parents to prostitution rings, where young girls are in demand because they are considered less likely to carry the AIDS virus.

Women are missing from the paid labor force. Women work as hard as or harder than men (on average, thirteen more hours a week worldwide). But the work women do—caring for children; providing food and health care to their families; tending gardens and livestock; processing crops; gathering firewood and hauling water; weaving cloth, carpets, and baskets; and selling home-grown food and home-made crafts at local markets—is not considered "real" work. When women do work for wages, they are usually employed in clerical, sales, and service occupations, and they are excluded from higher-paying jobs in manufacturing, transportation, and management. Even when women do the same work as men, they earn—on average and worldwide—30 to 40 percent less.

Women are missing in the halls of power, policy, and decision making. Although women make up more than half the world's population, less than 5 percent of heads of state, heads of corporations, and directors of international organizations are female.

Women are missing from the battlefield, but tragically not from the ranks of the dead and wounded. In the many ethnic and civil wars in the world today, hostile groups are fighting for towns and cities, and civilians are caught in the crossfire. Hundreds of thousands of women and children have become widows, orphans, and refugees.

War or not, women the world over are regularly abused sexually, physically injured, and even killed simply because they are women. In 1987 in India, 1,786 "dowry deaths" (in which the husband and/or his family kill a woman because her dowry was insufficient) were recorded. In Thailand, more than 50 percent of married women living in Bangkok's largest squatter settlement said they were regularly beaten by their husbands. Not until 1991 did the Brazilian Supreme Court outlaw the "honor" defense, which excused a man who murdered an adulterous wife on the grounds that he was defending his honor.

Throughout the world, females are clearly second-class citizens, and worse.

Central point: _Throughout the world, females are clearly second-class citizens,_

and worse.

Comments: Part A, paragraph 2—Answers *a, c,* and *d* and too narrow. Answer *b* is general enough to summarize all of the historical details of the passage.

Part A, paragraph 3—The paragraph contrasts two ways of communicating: verbally and in writing.

IMPLIED MAIN IDEAS AND THE CENTRAL POINT: Test 3

A. Circle the letter of the sentence that best expresses the implied main idea of each of the following paragraphs.

1. People with normal vision can perceive an infinite number of colors. They can experience the color blue, for example, ranging from the palest robin's-egg color to the deepest midnight hue. It is estimated, however, that 5,000 people in the United States do not experience color at all; rather, they see the world only in shades of gray. Even more—about 1.5 million Americans—are affected by partial color blindness. While most of them are unable to distinguish red and green colors, others cannot see blues or yellows.

   a. Many Americans are affected by partial color blindness.
   b. People with normal vision can see a wide range of colors.
   c. Total or partial color blindness robs many Americans of the ability to perceive color.
   d. Numerous Americans have a physical handicap of some kind.

2. Are you one of the millions of people who are terrified of going to the dentist? If so, why not find a dentist who's sympathetic to your plight? Some dentists actually specialize in treating people who are very fearful of dental work. These dentists encourage patients to discuss their fears and will answer questions in an honest, understanding manner. Even if your dentist does not have such a specialty, you can arrange with him or her to use a signal, such as raising your right hand, if you experience too much pain. This will give you a feeling of control and the assurance that the pain—if any—will not go beyond what you can tolerate. You can also try the relaxation technique of breathing deeply, before and during appointments. A last good idea is to bring headphones and listen to your favorite music in the dental chair. It's hard for the brain to register pain when your favorite rap group, or classical musician, is filling your head.

   a. Millions of people are frightened of visits to the dentist.
   b. There are ways to make visits to the dentist less painful and frightening.
   c. There are dentists who specialize in treating patients who are very fearful of dental work.
   d. If you are frightened of going to the dentist, try the relaxation technique of breathing deeply before and during appointments.

3. Much of what falls to Earth from outer space is made up of tiny fragments of comets so light that they do not burn up as they float through the air. Sometimes pieces of comets are large enough to survive their passage through the air as shooting stars. These large meteorites can weigh as much as several tons. Also, at least one rock seems to have fallen to Earth from the moon. It is a greenish-brown stone the size of a golf ball which was found in Antarctica in 1982. It is

(Continues on next page)

141

identical in makeup to rocks brought back from the moon by the Apollo 15 astronauts. Other rocks have been found that are probably from Mars, although no positive identification can be made until astronauts bring rock samples back from Mars.

(a.) Various kinds of matter from outer space have landed on Earth.
b. A stone found in Antarctica is thought to have come from the moon.
c. Some pieces of comets that land on Earth weigh as much as several tons.
d. Earth contains a wide variety of rocks of various kinds.

B. (4.) The author has stated the central point of the following textbook selection in one sentence. Find that sentence, and write it in the space provided.

Learned Helplessness

A researcher at Johns Hopkins University has repeatedly done a simple experiment with two rats. He holds one rat firmly in hand so that no matter how much the rats struggles, he cannot escape. The rat will finally give up. The reseacher then throws that unmoving rat into a tank of warm water. The rat then sinks, not swims. He has "learned" that there is nothing he can do, that there is no point in struggling. The researcher then throws another rat into the water—one that doesn't "know" that his situation is hopeless and that he is therefore helpless. This rat will swim to safety.

Here is a comparable experiment involving people, conducted by Martin E. P. Seligman of the University of Pennsylvania. Two groups of college students are put in rooms where they are blasted with noise turned up to almost intolerable levels. In one room there is a button that turns off the noise. The students quickly notice it, push it, and are rewarded with blissful silence. In the other room, however, there is no turn-off button. The students look for one, find nothing, and finally give up. There is no way to escape the noise (except to leave the room before a previously agreed-upon time period has elapsed), so they simply endure.

Later, the same two groups are put in two other rooms. This time, both rooms contain a switch-off mechanism—though not a simple button this time and not as easy to find. Nevertheless, the group that found the button the first time succeeds in finding the "off" switch the second time, too. But the second group, already schooled in the hopelessness of their circumstances, doesn't even search. Its members just sit it out again.

Both experiments suggest that past failures can teach one to feel helpless and, as a result, to give up trying. Being aware of this possibility may give people the courage to persist despite previous disappointments.

Central point: *Both experiments suggest that past failures can teach one to feel*

helpless and, as a result, to give up trying.

Comment: Part B—The words "both experiments" in the last paragraph are a clue that the author is about to summarize what's said about the experiments in the first three paragraphs.

IMPLIED MAIN IDEAS AND THE CENTRAL POINT: Test 4

A. Circle the letter of the sentence that best expresses the implied main idea of each of the following paragraphs.

1. There is no doubt that businesses can improve their productivity. If every person and machine did things right the first time, the same number of people could handle much larger volumes of work. High costs of inspection could be channeled into productive activities, and managers could take all the time they spend checking and devote it to productive tasks. Wasted materials would become a thing of the past. In fact, it's been estimated that attention to quality can reduce the total cost of operations anywhere from 10 to 50 percent. As Philip Crosby said: "Quality is free. What costs money are the unquality things—all the actions that involve not doing jobs right the first time."

    a. Philip Crosby is an expert in quality in business.
    b. It is wasteful to spend so much money on plant inspections.
    c. Businesses can improve their sales in several ways.
    d. If quality is improved, productivity improves.

2. In 1882, a tax collector from the German provinces was tired of making his rounds through the dark forests under constant threat of attack by highwaymen. He decided to do something about the problem that would benefit other travelers as well. A part-time policeman and keeper of the dog pound in his spare time, he decided to develop a breed of dog that would be fearless, powerful, and aggressive in protecting people and property—the first guard dog. After experimenting with different combinations over the years, he hit on the perfect blend of Great Dane, Rottweiler, Weimaraner, Manchester terrier, and German pointer. Loyal, agile, and quick to learn, the breed he developed is now the most popular guard dog and the official mascot of the U.S. Marine Corps. In addition to developing and refining the breed, Louis Doberman also gave it his name.

    a. The popular guard dog the Doberman pinscher was developed by a nineteenth-century German tax collector for protection when making his rounds.
    b. In the late 1800s, traveling through forests in the German provinces was dangerous.
    c. The Doberman pinscher is a perfect blend of Great Dane, Rottweiler, Weimaraner, Manchester terrier, and German pointer.
    d. Louis Doberman, a tax collector, felt threatened by highwaymen when traveling as a tax collector through the dark German forests.

B. Write out the implied main idea of the following paragraph.

3. You don't have to scare your family with statistics about heart attacks. To get them to exercise more often, emphasize instead how good they'll feel and how

(Continues on next page)

much better they'll look if they do daily calisthenics. Another method that works is to set an example. If they see you walking to the convenience store instead of driving, they might be encouraged to do likewise the next time they have errands in the neighborhood. Finally, make exercise a family activity. Suggest that the whole family go swimming together, take up early morning jogging, or join the Y at the group rate.

Implied main idea: *There are several positive ways to encourage your family to*

exercise more often.

C. (4.) The author has stated the central point of the following textbook passage in one sentence. Find that sentence, and write it in the space provided.

Teenagers and Jobs

Today's world puts a lot of pressure on teenagers to work. By working, they gain more independence from their families, and they also get the spending money needed to keep up with their peers. Many people argue that working can be a valuable experience for the young.

However, schoolwork and the benefits of extracurricular activities tend to go by the wayside when adolescents work more than fifteen hours a week. Teachers are then faced with the problems of keeping the attention of tired pupils and of giving homework to students who simply don't have the time to do it. In addition, educators have noticed less involvement in the extracurricular events many consider healthy influences on young people. School bands and athletic teams are losing players to work, and sports events are poorly attended by working students. Those teenagers who try to do it all—homework, extracurricular activities, and work—may find themselves exhausted and prone to illness.

Another drawback of too much work is that it may promote materialism and an unrealistic lifestyle. Some parents say that work teaches adolescents the value of a dollar. Undoubtedly, it can, and it's true that some teenagers work to help out with the family budget or save for college. But surveys have showns that the majority of working teens use their earnings to buy luxuries—stereos, tape decks, clothing, even cars. These young people, some of whom earn $300 and more a month, don't worry about spending wisely—they can just about have it all. In many cases, experts point out, they are becoming accustomed to a lifestyle they won't be able to afford several years down the road, when they'll no longer have parents to pay for car insurance, food and lodging, and so on. At that point, they'll be hard pressed to pay for necessities as well as luxuries.

Teens can benefit from both work *and* school—and avoid the pitfalls of materialism—simply by working no more than fifteen hours a week. As is often the case, a moderate approach is likely to be the most healthy and rewarding one.

Central point: *Teens can benefit from both work and school—and avoid the*

pitfalls of materialism—simply by working no more than fifteen hours a week.

Comment: Paragraph 3—The phrase "to get them to exercise more often" is one clue to the main idea.

IMPLIED MAIN IDEAS AND THE CENTRAL POINT: Test 5

A. Circle the letter of the sentence that best expresses the implied main idea of each of the following paragraphs.

1.   Baby mammals are born nearly helpless. They cannot survive if they are not cared for, usually by older members of their species. Food and shelter are the most obvious needs of a baby animal. But scientists have also observed another, less obvious need of baby mammals. Monkeys who are raised alone, with no physical contact with other animals, develop strange habits such as constantly rocking or moving in circles. In addition, they cannot relate normally to other monkeys. The males can rarely breed with females. The females who do bear young ignore or abuse their babies. When monkeys who were raised alone are put in contact with friendly, "motherly" monkeys who touch and cuddle them, they eventually develop normal monkey behaviors.

   a. Baby mammals need to be given food and shelter.
   (b.) Studies suggest that touching, like food and shelter, is key to normal mammal development.
   c. All animals who are raised without physical contact with other animals develop strange habits.
   d. Scientists have done studies of monkeys raised without physical contact with other animals.

2.   Losing a mate is in some ways more difficult for older men to adjust to than for women. Men now in their sixties and seventies tend to be unfamiliar with cooking and household chores. They may experience physical decline due to skipped meals and poor nutrition. At the same time, however, remarriage is almost exclusively a male option. In 1981, there were only twenty-three unmarried men age 65 and older for every hundred unmarried women. In addition, men age 65 and older are eight times more likely to remarry than older women are. Further, for a woman, widowhood today usually brings a decline in standard of living. Many women now in their sixties and seventies were full-time housewives for most of their lives and are unlikely to have savings and income from pension plans. In many cases, the husband's pension did not include a provision for widows, so this source of income is cut off. Even if the woman worked most of her life, the chances are that she earned much less than her husband and so receives less in Social Security benefits and pension after this death.

   a. Many of today's widows do not receive money from their husband's pensions.
   b. Men and women have very different experiences throughout life.
   c. It is generally more difficult for a man to lose a mate than for a woman.
   (d.) The experience of widowhood is different for men and women.

B. Write out the implied main idea of the following paragraph.

3.   Study experts say that slow and steady preparation for exams is best. Cramming the night before is ineffective and stressful. Arriving early for the examination is another helpful way of dealing with exams, experts suggest. It's reassuring to have a few minutes to sit down in the classroom, collect one's thoughts, and find a pen.

(Continues on next page)

Once the test begins, according to experts, it's best to answer the easier questions first, then go back and tackle the hard ones. On essay questions, it's most productive to think a few minutes and make a brief outline before beginning to write.

Implied main idea: *Experts have suggested several techniques for doing well on* *exams.*

C. (4.) The author has stated the central point of the following essay in one sentence. Find that sentence, and write it in the space provided.

Alcohol Reform

In the nineteenth century, reformers wanted to persuade Americans to adopt more godly personal habits. They set up associations to battle profanity and Sabbath breaking, to place a Bible in every American home, and to provide religious education for the children of the poor. And beginning early in the 1800s, an extensive moral reform campaign was conducted against liquor.

At the start of the century, heavy drinking was an integral part of American life. Many people believed that downing a glass of whiskey before breakfast was healthful. Instead of taking coffee breaks, people took a dram of liquor at eleven and again at four o'clock as well as drinks after meals "to aid digestion" and a nightcap before going to sleep. Campaigning politicians offered voters generous amounts of liquor during campaigns and as rewards for "voting right" on election day. On the frontier, one evangelist noted, "A house could not be raised, a field of wheat cut down, nor could there be a log rolling, a husking, a quilting, a wedding, or a funeral without the aid of alcohol."

By 1820 the typical adult American consumed more than 7 gallons of absolute alcohol a year (compared with 2.6 gallons today). Consumption had risen markedly in two decades, fueled by the growing amounts of corn distilled by farmers into cheap whiskey, which could be transported more easily than bulk corn. In the 1820s, a gallon of whiskey cost just a quarter.

In their campaign, reformers identified liquor as the cause of a wide range of social, family, and personal problems. Alcohol was blamed for the abuse of wives and children and the squandering of family resources. Many businesspeople linked drinking with crime, poverty, and inefficient and unproductive employees.

The stage was clearly set for the appearance of an organized movement against liquor. In 1826 the nation's first formal national temperance organization was born: the American Society for the Promotion of Temperance. Led by socially prominent clergy and laypeople, the new organization called for total abstinence from distilled liquor. Within three years, 222 state and local antiliquor groups were laboring to spread this message.

By 1835, membership in temperance organizations had climbed to 1.5 million, and an estimated 2 million Americans had taken the "pledge" to abstain from hard liquor. Reformers helped reduce annual per capita consumption of alcohol from seven gallons in 1830 to just three gallons a decade later, forcing four thousand distilleries to close. Fewer employers provided workers with eleven o'clock or four o'clock drams, and some businesses began to fire employees who drank on the job.

Central point: *And beginning early in the 1800s, an extensive moral reform* *campaign was conducted against liquor.*

Comment: Part C—The introductory paragraph begins by discussing various reform movements, then narrows its focus to the reform movement discussed in the rest of the passage.

IMPLIED MAIN IDEAS AND THE CENTRAL POINT: Test 6

A. Circle the letter of the sentence that best expresses the implied main idea of each of the following paragraphs.

1.   Salespeople who want to increase their sales may make promises which the company's production and accounting departments find difficult to support. Production, for example, may not be able to meet the sales department's schedule because purchasing didn't get raw materials in time. While salespeople might like to have large inventories available, production and finance are likely to resist building up stocks because of the high cost of storing and/or owning unsold goods. Also, if production is in the middle of union negotiations, it is likely to feel they are more important than anything else. At the same time, however, salespeople may feel that nothing is more urgent than increasing sales.

   a. The demands of the sales department should be given priority in an organization.   a. Nothing in the paragraph supports this point.
   b. Union demands can slow up production.   b. Too narrow.
   c. Businesses tend to be disorganized because of lack of communication.
   (d.) Different parts of a business may have competing needs.   c. The problems discussed in the paragraph are not due to a lack of communication.

2.   A Senate committee estimates the loss of earnings of men ages 25 to 34 who have less than high school-level skills at $236 billion. Half of the heads of households classified below the federal poverty line cannot read an eighth-grade book. More than a third of mothers on welfare are also functionally illiterate. (Functional illiteracy is the inability to read and write well enough for everyday practical needs.) So are 60 percent of the adult prison population and 84 percent of juveniles who come before the courts. Businesses have difficulty filling such entry-level jobs as clerk, bank teller, and paralegal assistant. A major insurance firm reports that 70 percent of dictated letters must be retyped "at least once" because secretaries cannot spell and punctuate correctly. The military, too, pays a price for functional illiteracy. The navy has stated that 30 percent of new recruits are "a danger to themselves and costly to naval equipment" because they cannot read very well or understand simple instructions.

   a. Americans are among the most poorly educated people in the world.
   (b.) Functional illiteracy, widespread among Americans, is costly for individuals and society.
   c. Businesses must face the problem of poorly prepared workers.
   d. Our prisons and courts are filled with adults and juveniles who are functionally illiterate.

B. Write out the implied main idea of the following paragraph.

3.   There are plenty of jokes about the trials of being married. And we all know that being married doesn't necessarily mean living happily ever after. But did you know that married people live longer and suffer fewer chronic illnesses than single people do? In contrast, divorced people have a greater risk of dying early than people in any other category. Widowed people, too, tend to die younger than married folks. In

(Continues on next page)

addition, single men are much more likely than married men to experience serious emotional breakdowns.

Implied main idea: <u>Marriage is good for people's physical and mental health.</u>

C.   (4.) The author has stated the central point of the following textbook selection in one sentence. Find that sentence, and write it in the space provided.

Marriage Contracts

Every year, thousands of couples marry unwisely. Their decision to wed is based on the great rush of emotion that comes along with falling in love. "We love each other!" they proclaim. "Of course our marriage will work!" Unfortunately, the rosy glow that accompanies romantic love doesn't last forever. Couples who promise "Till death do us part" often regret that vow a few months or years later. They may feel that their decision was made hastily, that they didn't know each other well enough, that their ideas about marriage are too different. And then they are faced with two unhappy options. They can continue on in a disappointing marriage, or they can start proceedings for an unpleasant, expensive, time-consuming divorce.

Another approach is needed here: People who want to marry should sign renewable marriage contracts. Such a marriage contract could be valid for three years, at which time the partners would decide whether or not to renew the agreement. If they did not choose to stay together, no divorce would be necessary. They would simply file a paper stating that they would not be renewing their contract.

One advantage of the marriage contract system is that it would force couples to think in concrete terms about their marriages. They would have to talk ahead of time about some essential questions. How will our money be handled? How will work around the house be divided? Will we have children? How will they be raised? Will we have a religious life? How often will our in-laws visit? These are the kinds of questions that most couples who are wildly in love would otherwise never face.

It would not be surprising if many couples in the process of working on a contract decided that they shouldn't get married after all. And that would be a good thing. They are the couples whose marriages probably wouldn't survive the first clash with reality.

In addition, a contract would encourage couples to work harder at their marriages. They couldn't afford to let problems simmer under the surface, assuming that they had unlimited years to fix them. If they knew that their contract was coming up for renewal every few years, people would give as much attention to their marriages as they do to their careers or relationships with friends.

Finally, a renewable marriage contract would make ending a marriage far easier than it is today. No longer would both partners have to hire expensive lawyers and endure long waits in the divorce courts. Their marriage contract would spell out the terms of a split. It would say how property would be divided and how custody of children would be handled. Ending a marriage would require the simple filing of a paper in the courthouse. The man and woman would then go their own ways, sadder perhaps, but wiser about what it takes to make a marriage work.

Central point: <u>Another approach is needed here: People who want to marry</u>
<u>should sign renewable marriage contracts.</u>

5

Relationships I

Authors use two common methods to show relationships and make their ideas clear. The two methods—**transitions** and **patterns of organization**—are explained in turn in this chapter.

TRANSITIONS

Look at the following items and put a check by the one that is easier to read and understand:

____ One way to lose friends is to always talk and never listen. It is a mistake to borrow money and never pay it back.

____ One way to lose friends is to always talk and never listen. Another mistake is to borrow money and never pay it back.

You probably found the second item easier to understand. The word *another* makes it clear that the writer is going on to a second way to lose friends. **Transitions** are words or phrases (like *another*) that show the relationships between ideas. They are like signs on the road that guide travelers.

Two major types of transitions are words that show addition and words that show time.

Words That Show Addition

Once again, put a check beside the item that is easier to read and understand.

____ Many people rent videotaped movies because prices are lower than ever before. Videos are now available almost everywhere.

____ Many people rent videotaped movies because prices are lower than ever before. Also, videos are now available almost everywhere.

The word *also* in the second item makes the relationship between the sentences more clear. The author is providing reasons why renting videotaped movies is popular. The first reason is that the cost is lower than ever. A second reason is that the movies are so readily available. The word *also* makes it clear that a second reason is being given. *Also* is known as an addition word.

Addition words tell you that writers are *adding to* their thoughts. They are presenting one or more ideas that continue along the same line of thought as a previous idea. Like all transitions, addition words help writers organize their information and present it clearly to readers. Here are some common addition words:

Words That Show Addition

also	furthermore	second(ly)	next
in addition	first (of all)	third(ly)	final(ly)
moreover	for one thing	another	last (of all)

Examples:

The following examples contain addition words. Notice how these words introduce ideas that *add to* what has already been said.

My friend Ellen is so safety-conscious that she had the wooden front door of her apartment replaced with a steel one. *Moreover*, she had iron bars inserted on all her apartment windows.

By recycling, our township has saved thousands of dollars in landfill expenses. *Furthermore*, we have made money by selling recycled glass, paper, and metal.

There are several places you can enjoy with your family without spending much money. *First*, the hands-on science museum downtown asks only for a donation. *Second*, there is the zoo, which is free on Sundays.

➤ *Practice 1*   *Answers may vary.*

Complete each sentence with a suitable addition word from the box. Try to use a variety of transitions.

1. As soon as the weather turned warm, ants invaded our kitchen. A few
   _____ *also* _____ visited the bathrooms.

2. There are several ways to use old jeans. _____ *For one thing* _____, you can use them for patching other jeans.

3. One million stray dogs live in the New York City metropolitan area. _____*In addition*_____, there are more than 500,000 stray cats in the same area.

4. "_____*First of all*_____, and most important," said my adviser, "you've got to complete that term paper or you won't graduate on time."

5. Part-time workers have second-class status. For one thing, they are easily laid off. Second, they get no fringe benefits. _____*Finally*_____, they are often paid less than half the hourly rate of a full-timer.

Words That Show Time

Put a check beside the sentence that is easier to read and understand:

____ The two neighboring families got along well. They are not on speaking terms.

____ Previously, the two neighboring families got along well. Now they are not on speaking terms.

The words *previously* and *now* in the second item clarify the relationship between the sentences. *Before* the families got along well, and *now* they don't speak to each other. *Previously* and *now* and words like them are time words.

These transitions indicate a time relationship. **Time words** tell us *when* something happened in relation to when something else happened. Here are some common time words:

Words That Show Time

before	during	while	later
previously	now	next	eventually
first	as	soon	finally
then	when	after	

Examples:

The following examples contain time words. Notice how these words show us *when* something takes place.

First I skim the pages of the television guide to see what movies will be on. *Then* I circle the ones I want to record on the VCR.

As Chris got ready to go home, his boss asked him to sweep the stockroom floor.

During World War II, meat was rationed.

Helpful Points About Transitions

Here are two points to keep in mind about transitions.

1 Some transition words have the same meaning. For example, *also*, *moreover*, and *furthermore* all mean "in addition." Authors typically use a variety of transitions to avoid repetition.

2 In some cases the same word can serve as two different types of transitions, depending on how it is used. For example, the word *first* may be used as an addition word to show that the author is continuing a train of thought, as in the following sentence:

> My mother has some strange kitchen habits. *First*, she loves to cook with the radio on full blast. Moreover, ...

First may also may be used to signal a time sequence, as in this sentence:

> Our English class turned into a shambles this morning. *First*, the radiator began hissing. Then, ...

> ***Practice 2***   *Answers may vary.*

Complete each sentence with a suitable time word from the box on the previous page. Try to use a variety of transitions.

1. _____*After*_____ my cousin took a long shower, there was no hot water left for anyone else in the house.

2. To make chicken stock, begin by putting a pot of water on the stove to boil. _____*Then*_____ drop in a chicken and some diced celery and onions.

3. Dan waited impatiently all day for the Monday night football game to begin on TV, but _____*during*_____ the first half, he fell asleep.

4. Recent advances in medicine make it possible to treat babies even _____*before*_____ they are born.

5. Some students listen to their stereo, eat snacks, and talk on the phone _____*while*_____ doing their homework.

PATTERNS OF ORGANIZATION

Just as transitions can show the relationships between ideas in sentences, so **patterns of organization** can show the relationships between supporting ideas in paragraphs, essays, or textbook chapters. Such patterns of organization help authors present their supporting material in a clearly organized way. By recognizing the patterns of organization that authors use to arrange information, you will be better able to understand and remember what you read.

Two major patterns of organization are the list of items pattern and the time order pattern. As you will see below, addition words are often used in the list of items pattern, and time words are used in the time order pattern. Noting the transitions in a passage can help you become aware of the patterns of organization being used. They can also help you find the major supporting details.

The List of Items Pattern

Arrange the following group of sentences into an order that makes sense. Put a *1* in front of the sentence that should come first, a *2* in front of the sentence that comes next, a *3* in front of the third sentence, and a *4* in front of the sentence that should come last. The result will be a short paragraph.

____ In addition, check a puppy's personality by watching how it plays with other puppies.

____ There are some important points to keep in mind when choosing a puppy.

____ Last, since curiosity is a sign of intelligence, clap your hands to see if a puppy is curious and interested.

____ First of all, look for signs of good health, including clear, bright eyes and firm, pink gums.

This paragraph begins with the main idea: "There are some important points to keep in mind when choosing a puppy." The next three sentences go on to list three of those points, resulting in the pattern of organization known as a list of items. The transitions *first of all*, *in addition*, and *last* introduce the points being listed and indicate their order:

First of all, look for signs of good health, including clear, bright eyes and firm, pink gums. In addition, check a puppy's personality by watching how it plays with other puppies. Last, since curiosity is a sign of intelligence, clap your hands to see if a puppy is curious and interested.

A **list of items** refers to a series of reasons, examples, or other points that support an idea. The items are listed in the order the author prefers. Addition words are often used in a list of items to tell us that another supporting point is being added to one or more points already mentioned. Textbook authors frequently organize material into lists of items, such as a list of types of economic systems, symptoms of heart disease, or reasons for teenage drinking.

A List of Items Paragraph

The paragraph below is organized as a list of items. Complete the outline of the list by, first, filling in the missing part of the main idea heading—the heading tells what is being listed in the paragraph. Then add the missing items to the outline.

To help you find the items (the major details of the paragraph), you may find it helpful to underline the addition words and number (*1, 2, . . .*) the items in the author's list.

> Like all social institutions, sports serve various purposes. First, they provide society with a vast number of vigorous leisure-time activities. Such activities have become increasingly necessary in a society in which the great majority of jobs provide little or no physical activity. Second, sports provide an outlet for energies that might otherwise strain the social order. Emotions such as anger and frustration can be expressed in ways that are acceptable to society—through both participation in sports and watching sports. Finally, sports can provide society with role models. At their best, athletes at all levels, but especially famous athletes, can supply examples of dedication, hard work, and conduct for others to imitate.

Main idea heading: Purposes of _____

1. _____

2. _____

3. _____

Explanation:

The heading of the outline should tell what is being listed in the paragraph: purposes of sports. (Note that the heading is called the main idea heading because it summarizes the main idea: that sports serve various purposes. Outlines can begin with either a main idea sentence or a main idea heading.) Following are the three purposes you should have filled into the outline:

1. They provide society with a vast number of vigorous leisure-time activities. (This point is signaled with the addition transition *first*.)

2. They provide an outlet for energies that might otherwise strain the social order. (This point is signaled with the addition transition *second*.)
3. They can provide society with role models. (This point is signaled with the addition transition *finally*.)

Comments: The topic sentences in Practices 3–5 are underlined in color in this *Instructor's Edition.*

➤ *Practice 3*   Note the helpful transitions in the paragraphs below. (Paragraph A: *first of all, second, finally*; Paragraph B: *third, finally*.)

A. The following passage uses a listing pattern. Outline the passage by filling in the main idea heading and the major details.

Hint: Include in the heading an *s* word—as in the heading of the paragraph on sports: Purpose**s** of sports.

There are several reasons why high schools should require students to wear uniforms. First of all, uniforms would save money for parents and children. It would be a big relief for families if they could simply buy two or three inexpensive uniforms, instead of constantly shelling out for designer jeans and other high-priced clothes. A second advantage of uniforms is that students would not have to spend time worrying about clothes, so they could concentrate more on schoolwork and less on making a fashion statement. Finally, uniforms would make the division between rich and poor students less obvious. If wealthy students didn't show off their expensive clothes, and students from modest backgrounds didn't feel second-rate because of their lower-cost wardrobes, everyone would get along better.

Main idea heading: *Reasons high schools should require uniforms*

1. *Saves money for both parents and children*

2. *Keeps students from having to spend time worrying about clothes*

3. *Makes divisions between rich and poor students less obvious*

B. The following passage uses a listing pattern. Finish the map of the passage by completing the main idea heading and filling in the missing major details.

Various theories explain the aging process. The most obvious is that our bodies simply wear out. Yet since many bodily systems are able to replace or repair their worn components (wounds heal, for example, and skin cells are constantly being generated), this version cannot be the whole story. A related theory is that as cells repeatedly divide, more and more contain genetic errors and stop working properly. A third theory holds that our body chemistry loses its delicate balance over the years. For example, our excretory system, after years of filtering pollutants from our bloodstream, becomes less efficient. The resulting change in our blood chemistry can produce a variety of other malfunctions. Finally, according to another theory, our bodies tend with age to reject some of their own tissues.

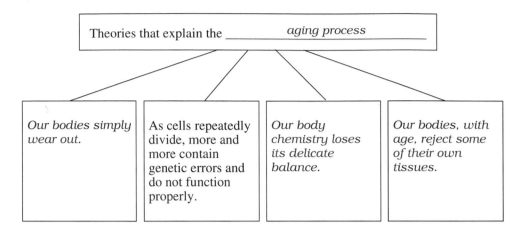

The Time Order Pattern

Arrange the following group of sentences into an order that makes sense. Put a *1* in front of the sentence that should come first, a *2* in front of the sentence that comes next, a *3* in front of the third sentence, and a *4* in front of the sentence that should come last. The result will be a short paragraph.

____ By 1960, the number of TV sets in the country had risen above 50 million.

____ After eight years, there were a million TV sets in the United States.

____ Interest in television grew rapidly when broadcasting began in 1941.

____ By 1994, there were over 211 million TV sets in American homes.

Authors usually present events in the order in which they happen, resulting in a pattern of organization known as **time order**. Clues to the pattern of the above sentences are dates and transitions (*after* and *when*) that show time. The sentences should read as follows:

> Interest in television grew rapidly when broadcasting began in 1941. After eight years, there were a million TV sets in the United States. By 1960, the number of TV sets in the country had risen above 50 million. By 1994, there were over 211 million TV sets in American homes.

As a student, you will see time order used frequently. Textbooks in all fields describe events and processes, such as the events leading to the Boston Tea Party, the important incidents in Abraham Lincoln's life, the steps involved for a bill to travel through Congress, the process involved in writing a paper, or the stages in the development of a cell.

In addition to the time transitions listed on page 151, signals for the time order pattern include dates, times, and such words as *stages*, *series*, *steps*, and *process*.

The two most common kinds of time order involve a series of events or stages and a series of steps (directions). Each is discussed below.

Series of Events or Stages

Following is a paragraph that is organized according to time order. Complete the outline of the paragraph by listing the missing stages in the order in which they happen. Refer as needed to the list of time transitions on page 151.

> Children master language in predictable stages. First, at about six months, babies start to repeat simple sounds, such as "ma-ma-me-me." About three or four months later, they can repeat sounds that others make and carry on little conversations. These interchanges are rich in emotional meaning, although the sounds themselves are meaningless. At the next stage, toddlers learn the meanings of many words, but they cannot yet talk. A toddler might understand a sentence such as "Bring me your sock" but be unable to say any of the words. Finally, the child begins to talk in single words and in two-word sentences.

Main idea: Children master language in predictable stages.

1. _____

   _____

2. Three or four months later, babies can repeat sounds and carry on little "conversations."

3. _____

   _____

4. _____

   _____

Explanation:

You should have added these points to the outline:

1. At about six months, babies begin to repeat simple sounds. (The author signals this stage with the time transition *first* and the mention of age: "at about six months.")
3. Toddlers understand many words but cannot talk. (The author signals this stage with the time word *next*: "At the next stage.")
4. Finally, a child talks in single words and two-word sentences. (The author signals this stage with the time word *finally*.)

As emphasized by the transitions used, the relationship between the points is one of time: The second stage happens *after* the first, and so on.

➤ *Practice 4*

The following passage describes a sequence of events. Outline the paragraph by filling in the main idea and major details. Note that the major details are signaled by time words and dates.

> The 1960s were a time of profound events in America. The first thunderclap occurred in 1963, with the bullets that assassinated President John Kennedy, depressing the spirit of the country. Then in 1965, urban riots brought to the foreground the simmering issue of racial equality. A minor summer incident involving police in Watts, a black section of Los Angeles, set off five days of looting and rioting that left thirty-four people dead. Over a hundred major urban riots, all centered in black ghettos in cities like Newark and Detroit, were to follow. And by 1968, anti-war protests against the increasing American presence in Vietnam began to spread across the country. They centered on college campuses, and soon almost every major campus in the United States was torn by rallies, teach-ins, and riots.

Main idea: *The 1960s in America contained significant events.*

1. *1963—the assassination of President Kennedy*

2. *1965—urban riots centered in black ghettos*

3. *1968—anti-war protests against the American presence in Vietnam*

Series of Steps (Directions)

Below is an example of a paragraph in which steps in a process are organized according to time order. Complete the outline of the paragraph that follows by listing the missing steps in the correct sequence. To help yourself identify each step, underline the time words.

> Here is a five-step technique that will help you relax quickly. First, lie down with your arms at your sides and your fingers open. When you are comfortable, close your eyes and put all distracting thoughts out of your mind. Next, tighten all the muscles of your body at once. Do this by pushing your toes together, tightening your buttocks and abdomen, clenching your fists, and squeezing your eyes shut. Then, let everything relax, and feel the tension flow out of your body. After that, take a deep breath through your mouth, hold it, and then let it out slowly, breathing slowly and easily, as you do when you are sleeping. Finally, think of a pleasant scene as you feel your whole body becoming calm and relaxed.

Main idea: Here is a five-step technique that will help you relax quickly.

1. _____

2. _____

3. Tighten all muscles, and then relax.

4. _____

5. _____

Explanation:

You should have added these steps to the outline:

1. Lie down, arms at your sides and fingers open. (The author signals this stage with the time word *first*.)
2. When you are comfortable, close your eyes and clear your mind. (The author signals this stage with the time word *when*.)
4. Take a deep breath through your mouth, hold it for twenty seconds, let it out, and breathe slowly and easily. (The author's signal is the time word *after*.)
5. Think of a pleasant scene as you feel yourself relax. (The author signals this last step with the time word *finally*.)

As indicated by the transitions used, the relationship between the steps is one of time: The second step happens *after* the first, and so on.

➤ *Practice 5*

The following passage gives directions involving several steps that must be done in order. Complete the map on the next page by filling in the heading in the top box and the three missing steps. To help yourself identify each step, you may want to underline the time words.

There are several steps to remembering your dreams. To begin with, you must make up your mind to do so, for consciously deciding that you want to remember increases the likelihood that it will happen. Then put a pen and a notebook near your bed, so that you can write down what you remember as soon as you wake up. When possible, turn off your alarm before you go to sleep so that you can wake up gradually; this will increase the likelihood of remembering your dreams. Finally, when you wake up in the morning and remember a dream, write it down immediately, even before getting out of bed.

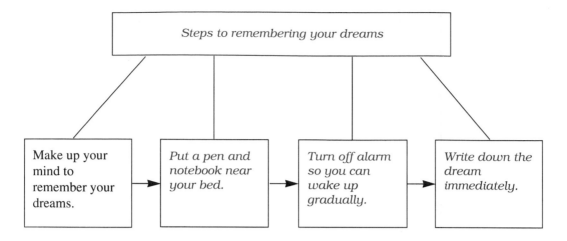

A Note on Topic Sentences and Patterns of Organization

A paragraph's topic sentence often indicates its pattern of organization. For example, here's the topic sentence of the paragraph you just read: "There are several steps to remembering your dreams." The words *several steps* suggest that this paragraph will be organized according to time order. Another good example is the topic sentence of the earlier paragraph on aging: "There are several theories about why we age." The words *several theories* suggest that this paragraph will be a list of items.

Paying close attention to the topic sentence, then, can give you a quick sense of a paragraph's pattern of organization. Try, for instance, to guess the pattern of the paragraph with this topic sentence:

> While there are thousands of self-help groups, they all fall into three basic categories.

The statement that self-help groups "fall into three basic categories" is a strong indication that the paragraph will list those categories. The topic sentence helps us guess that the paragraph will be a list of three items.

➤ *Practice 6*

Most of the topic sentences below have been taken from college textbooks. Circle the letter of the pattern of organization that each topic sentence suggests.

1. One rainy May morning in 1927, the plane *The Spirit of St. Louis* began its flight across the Atlantic Ocean.
   a. List of items   b. Time order

2. Bicycles should be equipped with several safety features.
   (a.) List of items   b. Time order

3. The process of digestion can be divided into four stages.
   a. List of items   (b.) Time order

4. A federal form of government has advantages and disadvantages.
   (a.) List of items   b. Time order

5. There are several cultural reasons why older people are discriminated against in American society.
   (a.) List of items   b. Time order

6. When we have a complex problem to solve, we can go through a series of helpful steps.
   a. List of items   (b.) Time order

7. Journalists have been taught that an event becomes news or newsworthy if it fulfills one or more of five basic criteria.
   (a.) List of items   b. Time order

8. Treating the allergic patient often involves a three-step process.
   a. List of items   (b.) Time order

9. Convenience products can be subdivided into four groups on the basis of how people buy them.
   (a.) List of items   b. Time order

10. Several key events led up to the firing on Fort Sumter, the first military action of the Civil War.
    a. List of items   (b.) Time order

Two Final Points

1   In a given paragraph or longer passage, an author may use both addition words and time words, depending on the relationships being expressed. Also, while a paragraph or passage may have just one pattern of organization, often the patterns are mixed. For example, you may find that part of a passage uses a list of items pattern, and another part of the same passage uses a time pattern.

2   Keep in mind that not all relationships between ideas are signaled by transitions. An author may present a list of items, for example, without using addition words. So as you read, watch for the relationships themselves, not just the transitions.

➤ Review Test 1

To review what you've learned in this chapter, fill in the blanks of the following items.

1. Transitions are words that signal *(parts of, relationships between, the importance of)* ___relationships between___ ideas.

2. A(n) *(addition, time)* ___addition___ transition means that the writer is adding to an idea or ideas already mentioned.

3. When a passage provides a series of directions or steps, or a series of events, it is likely to use *(addition, time)* ___time___ transitions.

4. __T__ TRUE OR FALSE? A topic sentence often suggests a paragraph's pattern of organization.

5. A passage's pattern of organization is the pattern in which its *(supporting details, main ideas, causes and effects)* ___supporting details___ are organized.

➤ Review Test 2

A. Fill in each blank with one of the words in the box. Use each word once.

then	second	also
one	before	final

1. Rubber tires were invented in 1845, ___before___ cars existed. The tires were then meant for bicycles.

2. The average square inch of human skin includes 19 million cells. It ___also___ includes 625 sweat glands and 60 hairs.

3. There are two main kinds of fats: ___one___ is saturated fats; the other is unsaturated fats.

4. Read the paragraph carefully and ___then___ answer the questions that follow.

5. First dig a hole and work peat moss into the soil. Then put the plant in and pile in enough dirt to refill the hole. The ___final___ step is to water the plant liberally.

6. The first type of small business is often called the "mom-and-pop operation." The majority of small businesses fall into this category. The _____*second*_____ type is the high-growth enterprise. This type of business aims to outgrow its small-business status as quickly as possible.

B. Read the textbook paragraph below, and then answer the questions that follow.

> [1]The first professional baseball team, the Cincinnati Red Stockings, was founded in 1869. [2]After only a short time, there were teams in all the major Eastern and Midwestern cities. [3]The ballpark brought together crowds of strangers who could experience a sense of community within the big city as they watched a baseball game. [4]Immigrants were able to shake loose their ethnic ties and become absorbed in the new national game. [5]The green fields and fresh air of the ballpark were a welcome change from the sea of bricks and stone that dominated the city scene. [6]Workers could temporarily escape the routine of their daily lives. [7]They loved indirectly participating in the competition and accomplishment that baseball games symbolized. [8]The ballpark also provided a means for spectators to release their frustrations against authority figures: [9]The umpire became a symbol of scorn, and frequent cries of "kill the umpire" were heard.

7. The relationship of sentence 2 to the sentence before it is one of
   a. addition.
   b. time.

8. The key transition word in sentence 2 is _____*after*_____.

9. Sentences 3–9 present
   a. a list of benefits people found in attending baseball games.
   b. a series of events in baseball's history.
   c. a series of stages in the history of baseball.

10. The relationship of sentence 8 to the sentences before it is signaled by the transition _____*also*_____.

Comment: Items 7–8—The events in sentences 1 and 2 occur in sequence.

➤ Review Test 3

A. Fill in each blank with the appropriate transition from the box. Use each transition once.

Then	Second	Finally	First

To read and study a textbook more effectively, follow a few helpful steps. (1) _____*First*_____, preview the reading, taking a couple of minutes to get a quick sense of what the selection is about. (2) _____*Second*_____, read and mark the selection, using a highlighter pen to set off important points. (3) _____*Then*_____ write up a set of study notes that summarize the most important ideas in the selection. (4) _____*Finally*_____, go over and over the ideas in your notes until you know the material.

5. The pattern of organization for the above selection is
   a. list of items.   The paragraph presents a series of steps in directions
   b.) time order.   for reading and studying a textbook more effectively.

B. Below are the beginnings of five passages. Label each one with the letter of its pattern of organization. (You may find it helpful to underline the transition or transitions in each item.)

a Time order
b List of items

_b_ 6. A good study space is well-lighted and well-supplied with paper, pens, and study aids. In addition, it is quiet and free from distractions such as television or stereo. . . .

_a_ 7. Childbirth, or labor, takes place in three overlapping phases. The first stage is the longest, lasting an average twelve to twenty-four hours for a woman having her first child. The second stage typically lasts about one and a half hours. . . .

_b_ 8. There are various ways to combat stress. One excellent way is exercise. Many people also find that meditation is another good way to minimize the effects of daily pressures. . . .

_b_ 9. Today's telephones offer various convenient features. Voice mail allows you to leave and receive messages and has taken the place of old-fashioned answering machines. Another popular feature is automatic dialing, which allows you to make calls by pressing just one or two buttons. . . .

_a_ 10. Even before he meets the three witches, Macbeth has dreamed of becoming king of Scotland. Then the witches predict he will be king and intensify his ambition. Finally, his wife persuades him to murder King Duncan and take over the country. . . .

➤ Review Test 4

Here is a chance to apply your understanding of addition and time relationships to a full-length reading—an article about stress in college. To help you continue to strengthen your skills, the reading is followed by questions not only on what you've learned in this chapter but also on what you've learned in previous chapters.

Words to Watch

Below are some words in the reading that do not have strong context support. Each word is followed by the number of the paragraph in which it appears and its meaning there. These words are indicated in the article by a small circle (°).

aptitude (4): natural ability
anorexia (6): an abnormal lack of appetite which can result in serious illness or death
bulimia (6): an abnormal craving for food that leads to heavy eating and then intentional vomiting
stability (9): steadiness
bombarded (9): attacked
devastating (9): very destructive
magnitude (11): great importance
meditation (13): a relaxation technique involving mental concentration
relevant (14): related to the issue at hand

STUDENTS IN SHOCK
John Kellmayer

1   If you feel overwhelmed by your college experiences, you are not alone—many of today's college students are suffering from a form of shock. Going to college has always had its ups and downs, but today the "downs" of the college experience are more numerous and difficult, a fact that the schools are responding to with increased support services.

2   Lisa is a good example of a student in shock. She is an attractive, intelligent twenty-year-old college junior at a state university. Having been a straight-A student in high school and a member of the basketball and softball teams there, she remembers her high school days with fondness. Lisa was popular then and had a steady boyfriend for the last two years of school.

3   Now, only three years later, Lisa is miserable. She has changed her major four times already and is forced to hold down two part-time jobs in order to pay her tuition. She suffers from sleeping and eating disorders and believes she has no close friends. Sometimes she bursts out crying for no apparent reason. On more than one occasion, she has considered taking her own life.

4   Dan, too, suffers from student shock. He is nineteen and a freshman at a local community college. He began college as an accounting major but hated that field. So he switched to computer programming because he heard the job prospects were excellent in that area. Unfortunately, he discovered that he had little aptitude° for programming and changed majors again, this time to psychology. He likes psychology but has heard horror stories about the difficulty of finding a job in that field without a graduate degree. Now he's considering switching majors again. To help pay for school, Dan works nights and weekends as a sales clerk at K-Mart. He doesn't get along with his boss, but since he needs the money, Dan feels he has no choice except to stay on the job. A few months ago, his girlfriend of a year and a half broke up with him.

5   Not surprisingly, Dan has started to suffer from depression and migraine headaches. He believes that in spite of all his hard work, he just isn't getting anywhere. He can't remember ever being this unhappy. A few times he considered talking to somebody in the college psychological counseling center. He rejected that idea, though, because he doesn't want people to think there's something wrong with him.

6   What is happening to Lisa and Dan happens to millions of college students each year. That means roughly one-quarter of the student population at any time will suffer from symptoms of student shock. Of that group, almost half will experience depression intense enough to warrant professional help. At schools across the country, psychological counselors are booked up months in advance. Stress-related problems such as anxiety, migraine headaches, insomnia, anorexia°, and bulimia° are epidemic on college campuses.

7   Suicide rates and self-inflicted injuries among college students are higher now than at any other time in history. The suicide rate among college youth is fifty percent higher than among nonstudents of the same age. It is estimated that each year more than 500 college students take their own lives.

8   College health officials believe that these reported problems represent only the tip of the iceberg. They fear that most students, like Lisa and Dan, suffer in silence.

9   There are three reasons today's college students are suffering more than those in earlier generations. First is a weakening family support structure. The transition from high school to college has always been difficult, but in the past there was more family support to help students get through it. Today, with divorce rates at a historical high and many parents experiencing their own psychological difficulties, the traditional family is not always available for guidance and support. And when students who do not find stability° at home are bombarded° with numerous new and stressful experiences, the results can be devastating°.

10   Another problem college students face is financial pressure. In the last decade tuition costs have skyrocketed— up about sixty-six percent at public

colleges and ninety percent at private schools. For students living away from home, costs range from eight thousand dollars to as much as twenty thousand a year and more. And at the same time that tuition costs have been rising dramatically, there has been a cutback in federal aid to students. College loans are now much harder to obtain and are available only at near-market interest rates. Consequently, most college students must work at least part-time. And for some students, the pressure to do well in school while holding down a job is too much to handle.

11   A final cause of student shock is the large selection of majors available. Because of the magnitude° and difficulty of choosing a major, college can prove a time of great indecision. Many students switch majors, some a number of times. As a result, it is becoming commonplace to take five or six years to get a degree. It can be depressing to students not only to have taken courses that don't count toward a degree but also to be faced with the added tuition costs. In some cases these costs become so high that they force students to drop out of college.

12   While there is no magic cure-all for student shock, colleges have begun to recognize the problem and are trying in a number of ways to help students cope with the pressures they face. For one thing, many colleges are upgrading their psychological counseling centers to handle the greater demand for services. Additional staff is being hired, and experts are doing research to learn more about the psychological problems of college students. Some schools even advertise these services in student newspapers and on campus radio stations. Also, juniors and seniors are being trained as peer counselors. These peer counselors may be able to act as a first line of defense in the battle for students' well-being by spotting and helping to solve problems before they become too big for students to handle.

13   In addition, stress-management workshops have become common on college campuses. At these workshops, instructors teach students various techniques they can use to deal with stress, including biofeedback, meditation°, and exercise.

14   Finally, many schools are improving their vocational counseling services. By giving students more relevant° information about possible majors and career choices, colleges can lessen the anxiety and indecision often associated with choosing a major.

15   If you ever feel that you're "in shock," remember that your experience is not unique. Try to put things in perspective. Certainly, the end of a romance or failing an exam is not an event to look forward to. But realize that rejection and failure happen to everyone sooner or later. And don't be reluctant to talk to somebody about your problems. The useful services available on campus won't help you if you don't take advantage of them.

Reading Comprehension Questions

Vocabulary in Context

1. In the sentence below, the word *prospects* means
   a. failures.
   (b.) possibilities.
   c. candidates.
   d. limitations.

   > "So he switched to computer programming because he heard the job prospects were excellent in that area." (Paragraph 4)

2. In the excerpt below, the word *warrant* means
   a. fight.
   b. have no need for.
   c. get degrees in.
   (d.) justify.

   > "Of that group, almost half will experience depressions intense enough to warrant professional help. At schools across the country, psychological counselors are booked up months in advance." (Paragraph 6)

Central Point and Main Ideas

3. Which sentence best expresses the central point of the selection?
   a. Going to college is a depressing experience for many students.
   (b.) College life has become more stressful, so schools are increasing support services.
   c. Lisa and Dan have experienced too much stress at school to enjoy college life.
   d. Colleges should increase their counseling services.

4. The main idea of paragraphs 2 and 3 is stated in the
   (a.) first sentence of paragraph 2.
   b. second sentence of paragraph 2.
   c. first sentence of paragraph 3.
   d. last sentence of paragraph 3.

5. The main idea of paragraphs 9, 10, and 11 is
   (a.) stated in the first sentence of paragraph 9.
   b. stated in the first sentence of paragraph 10.
   c. stated in the first sentence of paragraph 11.
   d. unstated.

Comments: Item 3—The central point is stated in Paragraph 1. Paragraphs 2–11 contain examples of, symptoms of, and reasons for increased numbers of students in shock. Paragraphs 12–14 present ways schools are trying to help students in shock.

Item 5—See item 7 on page 169.

Supporting Details

    6. According to the author, the large selection of majors now available
       a. makes for less stability in students' home lives.
       b. helps students get through school more quickly.
       c. makes many students' career choices more difficult.
       d. allows students to end up in careers for which they are especially well suited.

Transitions

    7. The first sentence of paragraph 9 states, "There are three reasons today's college students are suffering more than those in earlier generations." The reasons are then introduced in paragraphs 9, 10, and 11 by what three transitions?

       Transition introducing first reason for student shock: *first*

       Transition introducing the second reason for student shock: *another*

       Transition introducing the third reason for student shock: *final*

    8. The transitions that introduce the major details of paragraphs 9, 10, and 11 signal
       a. time.
       b. addition.

    9. The major details of paragraphs 12–14 are introduced with the transitions *for one thing, also, in addition*, and   *finally*   .

Patterns of Organization

    10. Paragraphs 12–14
       a. describe a series of school events in their order in time.
       b. list ways to help students cope.

Discussion Questions

    1. If you were a peer counselor for Lisa or Dan, what advice might you give her or him?

    2. What were—or are—the most stressful parts of college life for you? Explain why. What ways have you found for dealing with that stress?

    3. Kellmayer writes that "colleges . . . are trying in a number of ways to help students cope with the pressures they face." What resources does your college offer? Have you tried any? How do you think your school could improve the services it offers to help students deal with "student shock"?

    4. On the basis of your college experience so far, what one piece of advice would you give to an incoming freshman?

Check Your Performance   RELATIONSHIPS I

Activity	Number Right	Points		Score
Review Test 1 (5 items)	_____	x 2 =		_____
Review Test 2 (10 items)	_____	x 3 =		_____
Review Test 3 (10 items)	_____	x 3 =		_____
Review Test 4 (10 items)	_____	x 3 =		_____
		TOTAL SCORE =		_____%

Enter your total score into the **Reading Performance Chart: Review Tests** on the inside back cover.

RELATIONSHIPS I: Test 1

A. Fill in each blank with an appropriate transition word from the box. Use each transition once.

another	then	also
before	when	

1. I have a limited interest in people whose main topic of conversation is themselves and who never show any interest in what is happening to me. _____*Another*_____ group I avoid is people who never allow facts to interfere with their opinions.

2. To train a puppy, first buy some small dog biscuits or other small dog treats. Then teach the puppy one short command, such as "Sit!"—speaking the word loudly and firmly until he or she obeys. _____*When*_____ you get a correct response, give the dog a treat and praise him or her loudly.

3. For much of my life, I have been haunted by dreams of falling. In a typical dream, I have fallen off a tall building or over the edge of a cliff or out of a plane, and I am plunging at a breathtaking speed toward the ground. _____*Then*_____, just as I am about to crash into the ground, I wake up in a cold sweat, my heart racing.

4. Journalistic standards have changed. _____*Before*_____ the 1988 presidential election, journalists didn't generally report on politicians' sex lives. Now almost every aspect of a candidate's life is examined in the media.

5. The world of business is one area in which technology is isolating us. Many people now work alone at home, doing their jobs on display terminals that connect to a large central computer at a main office. Personal banking is _____*also*_____ becoming a detached process. To deposit or withdraw money from their accounts, customers often interact with machines rather than people.

(Continues on next page)

B. (6–9.) Fill in each blank with an appropriate transition word from the box. Use each transition once.

Before	While	Then	When

An incident happened yesterday that made me very angry. I got off the bus and started walking the four blocks to my friend's house. As I walked along, I noticed a group of boys gathered on the sidewalk about a block ahead of me. (6)_____*When*_____ they saw me, they stopped talking. Suddenly nervous, I thought about crossing the street to avoid them. But as I came nearer and heard them start to whistle, a different feeling came over me. Instead of being afraid, I was suddenly angry. Why should I have to worry about being hassled just because I was a woman? I stared straight at the boys and continued walking. (7)_____*Then*_____ the remarks started, with one boy making a rude comment about my pants. (8)_____*Before*_____ I knew what I was doing, I turned on him. "Do you have a mother? Or any sisters?" I demanded. He looked astonished and didn't answer me. I went on. "Is it OK with you if men speak to them like that? Doesn't it bother you that they can't walk down the street without some creep bothering them?" (9)_____*While*_____ I was speaking, the other boys backed away. The one I was facing gave a nervous-sounding laugh, then backed away too. I kept walking. An hour later, I was still shaking with anger.

10. The pattern of organization of the above selection is
    a. list of items.
    (b.) time order.

Comment: The paragraph narrates the *sequence of events* in the incident mentioned in the topic sentence (underlined in color in this *Instructor's Edition*).

RELATIONSHIPS I: Test 2

A. (1–5.) Fill in each blank with an appropriate transition word from the box. Use each transition once.

finally	moreover	next
first	when	

1. A good study space is well-lighted and well-supplied with paper, pens, and study aids. In addition, it is quiet and free from distractions such as television or stereo. _____*Finally*_____, it includes a comfortable chair and desk space.

2. Scotch tape is not wound up in the factory in the little rolls found in stores. During the manufacturing process, sheets of cellophane several feet wide are _____*first*_____ run through a machine that coats them with adhesive. After that, a machine winds the sticky film around tubes that are also several feet wide. Next, this wide roll of Scotch tape is fed through a slicing machine, a bar with various sizes of round knives. The knives cut through both the tape and the inner tube, resulting in the thin rolls of tape sold to consumers.

3. Many television ads proceed in three stages: the problem, the advice, and the resolution. For example, a mouthwash commerical will first establish the problem—that someone has bad breath. _____*Next*_____ it will suggest that the person try the advertised mouthwash. This is followed by an obvious resolution of the problem: the person's being chased by attractive members of the opposite sex.

4. After resting for 1,500 years, Italy's Mount Vesuvius woke up to do enormous damage. _____*When*_____ the volcano erupted in the early afternoon of August 24, A.D. 79, the residents of Pompeii, four miles away, could see and hear the explosion, which sent a black cloud into the sky. A second and greater explosion soon followed, and within a day Pompeii and its inhabitants were buried under thirty to fifty feet of stones and ash.

5. Most teenagers who smoke are familiar with the health hazards of smoking, yet for various reasons they drift into the habit anyway. A teenager with one parent who smokes is twice as likely to smoke as one with nonsmoking parents. _____*Moreover*_____, young people are more likely to smoke if their friends do. The chances are nine out of ten that a teenager whose best friend smokes will also start to smoke. In addition, teens who mature late are more likely to smoke than others, apparently because they hope that smoking will make them look more adult. *(Continues on next page)*

B. Read the passage and answer the question that follows.

Probably every child remembers digging a hole in his or her back yard and being told, "If you dig deep enough, you'll go to China." What would really happen if a man dug a hole through the center of the Earth and then jumped into it? The traveler entering the tunnel would first fall rapidly under the force of gravity. Eventually, as he approached the Earth's center, the jumper's weight would decrease. By the time he reached the center of the Earth, he would be weightless. An equal amount of the Earth's mass on all sides of him would cancel out the forces of gravity. Still, the traveler's original momentum would carry him past the center toward the opening on the far side of the world. After almost reaching that point, he would fall back down the hole toward his starting point. Back and forth he would then go, like a yo-yo, gradually slowing down until coming to a stop at the very center of the Earth.

6. The main pattern of organization of the passage is
   a. list of items.
   (b.) time order.   Paragraph B discusses a sequence of hypothetical *events*.

C. Fill in each blank with an appropriate transition word from the box. Use each transition once.

Also	Finally	First of all

Why does Japan have one of the world's lowest crime rates? Experts cite several factors. (7) _____First of all_____, Japan has a unified culture and racial population with fewer of the sharp differences between wealthy and poor found in the United States. (8) _____Also_____, Japan has had strict gun control for four hundred years. Only those in law enforcement can possess handguns. (9) _____Finally_____, Japan relies on some fifteen thousand small neighborhood police stations known as *koban*. Police officers and their families actually live in the koban. They are an integral part of the neighborhood, spending a good deal of time providing neighborhood services and helping prevent the growth of conditions that might lead to crime.

10. The pattern of organization of the above selection is
    (a.) list of items.   The paragraph *lists* several reasons for Japan's
    b. time order.   having one of the world's lowest crime rates.

RELATIONSHIPS I: Test 3

A. (1–5.) Arrange the scrambled sentences below into a logical paragraph by numbering them 1, 2, 3, 4, and 5 in an order that makes sense. Then circle the letter of the pattern of organization used.

     Note that transitions will help you by clarifying the relationships between sentences.

    __4__   A third reaction to danger used by opossums is to bluff their way out of a tight spot by hissing and baring their teeth.

    __1__   The opossum reacts to danger in one of several ways.

    __2__   First, some varieties of opossum can spray an unpleasant odor.

    __3__   Opossums are also very likely to run away from danger.

    __5__   Finally, the best-known of possum defenses is to "play dead" by entering into a coma-like state brought on by fear.

    6. The pattern of organization for the above selection is
       a. list of items.
       b. time order.

B. Read the passage and answer the question that follows. You may find it helpful to underline transitions as you read.

        In January of 1954, Ernest and Mary Hemingway left Nairobi on a vacation trip on which they flew over grazing elephants, hippos bathing in the lakes, and huge flocks of feeding flamingos. As they were circling a spectacular waterfall, a flock of ibises flew in front of the plane. When the pilot dived to avoid the birds, he struck an abandoned telegraph wire that crossed the gorge. In the crash that followed, Ernest sprained his shoulder; Mary was only slightly injured. Luckily, a boat came down the river the next morning, and its crew rescued them. By that evening, they were on board a small plane bound for Entebbe. The plane lifted from the plowed field that served as a runway, then crashed and burst into flames. Ernest escaped by breaking through a window with his head and injured shoulder, and Mary got out through another window. Twice in two days they had crashed and come out alive, but Ernest had injured his head, his backbone, and a kidney; after this, even writing a letter was difficult for him.

    7. The pattern of organization of the above selection is
       a. list of items.
       b. time order.

(Continues on next page)

C. (8–10.) Read the textbook passage below, and then answer the question and complete the outline.

> Prevention against injury involves a combination of two types of preventive measures. First is active prevention, which refers to methods that require people to do something to reduce the risk of being injured. Examples include the use of nonautomatic seat belts, the use of bicycle and motorcycle helmets, following drunk driving laws, and obeying gun laws. The second type of preventive measure is passive prevention. Passive prevention refers to methods requiring little or no action on the part of those being protected. These measures include seat belts that automatically engage when a person enters a car, automobile air bags, better street lighting, and built-in safety switches on power tools and electrical equipment.

8. The pattern of organization of the above selection is
   (a.) list of items.
   b. time order.

9–10. Complete the outline of the passage.

Main idea: _Prevention against injury involves a combination of two types_

of preventive measures.

Major supporting details:

1. Active prevention—methods that require people to do something to reduce the risk of injury.

2. _Passive prevention—methods requiring little or no action on the part of_

   those being protected.

Comment: Item 8—The paragraph *lists* the two types of preventive measures against injury mentioned in the topic sentence (underlined in color in this *Instructor's Edition*). Note the addition transitions that introduce those two major details: *first* and *second*.

RELATIONSHIPS I: Test 4

A. (1–4.) Arrange the scrambled sentences below into a logical paragraph by numbering them 1, 2, 3, and 4 in an order that makes sense. Then circle the letter of the pattern of organization used.

Note that transitions will help you by clarifying the relationships between sentences.

___4___ When you have chosen your apartment, have a lawyer or another person knowledgeable about leases examine your lease before you sign it.

___1___ When you're looking for an apartment, begin by making a list of promising openings. Check the classified ads and two or three real estate offices for apartments within your price range and desired locale.

___3___ As you inspect each apartment, make sure that faucets, toilets, stoves, and electrical wiring and outlets are functioning efficiently and safely.

___2___ After you have made a solid list, visit at least five of the most promising available apartments.

   5. The pattern of organization is
     a. list of items.
     (b.) time order.

B. Read the textbook passage and answer the question that follows.

Sociologists have identified several common reasons why people join religious cults. Many cult members come from homes filled with conflict; seeking to escape that conflict, they are drawn to the apparent security and acceptance offered by the cult. Another reason people join a cult is that they may be overwhelmed by the demands of adult life. The cult, with its strict rules and rigid discipline, relieves them from making many personal decisions. Finally, many cult members are highly idealistic persons—they are gratified by the feeling that by joining the cult, they are committing their lives to the establishment of a better world.

   6. The above selection
     a. lists religious cults.
     (b.) lists reasons for joining religious cults.
     c. describes stages in cult membership.
     d. describes a series of events in cult history.

Comment: Item 6—The paragraph *lists* three of the reasons mentioned in the topic sentence (underlined in color in this *Instructor's Edition*). The second and third reasons are introduced by the addition transitions *another* and *finally*.

(Continues on next page)

C. (7–10.) Complete the map of the following textbook passage.

Many people pass through three stages in reacting to their unemployment. At first they experience shock followed by relief. In many cases they had anticipated that they were about to lose their jobs, so when the dismissal comes, they may feel a sense of relief that at last the suspense is over. On the whole they remain confident and hopeful that they will find a new job when they are ready. During this time, they maintain normal relationships with their family and friends. The first stage lasts for about a month or two. The second stage centers on a strong effort to find a new job. If workers have been upset or angry about losing their jobs, the feeling tends to evaporate as they marshal their resources and concentrate on finding a new job. This stage may last for up to four months. But if another job is not found during this time, people move into a third stage, one of self-doubt and anxiety which lasts about six weeks. They must struggle to maintain their self-esteem as they question their own personal power and worth.

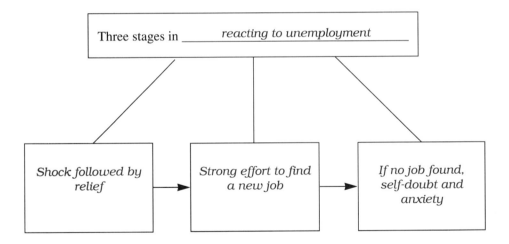

Comment: Note that the *time order* pattern is suggested by the words "three stages" in the topic sentence (underlined in color in this *Instructor's Edition*).

Name _____

Section _____ Date _____

SCORE: (Number correct) _____ x 10 = _____ %

RELATIONSHIPS I: Test 5

Read each textbook passage and answer the questions or follow the directions provided.

A. Many couples go through a predictable sequence of events moving toward greater commitment. Events that usually occur early in the development of a relationship include spending a whole day together and calling the partner by an affectionate name. At a later stage, partners start referring to each other as "boyfriend" and "girlfriend," and receive invitations to do things together as a couple. Eventually, the couple may begin to say "I love you" and to date each other exclusively. Common next steps are taking a vacation together and discussing living together and marriage. Events indicating great progress toward commitment include living together or becoming engaged.

1. The pattern of organization for the above selection is
   a. list of items.
   (b.) time order.

2. A transition that introduces one of the major details of the paragraph is

   _____*early* (or *later* or *eventually* or *next*)_____.

B. Many food products are stamped with dates that tell consumers when the product is still fresh. Products are dated in one of three ways. Some food products contain the date following the words "sell by." These foods remain fresh for about one week after the date on the label. Other foods list the date after the words "best if used by." Products with this label can still be used for a few weeks after the date on the label, but they might not have the same quality. _____, certain products, such as baby formulas, have an expiration date. These products should not be used after the date on the label.

3. The paragraph
   (a.) lists ways in which food products are dated.
   b. describes stages in dating food products.

4. The transition that would best fit the blank space is
   a. *After.*
   b. *Eventually.*
   (c.) *Third.*

Comment: Item 1—The *time order* pattern is suggested by the words "predictable sequence of events" in the topic sentence (underlined in color in this *Instructor's Edition*).

(Continues on next page)

C.   ¹Dr. Elisabeth Kübler-Ross has identified five stages in the reactions of dying patients. ²The first stage, she says, is denial. ³Patients will at first deny the seriousness of their illness, claiming that some error has been made. ⁴Then patients become angry. ⁵They ask, "Why me?" ⁶Their anger may be directed against God, fate, or even their doctors. ⁷Next comes depression. ⁸During this stage, patients feel hopeless and lose interest in life. ⁹After depression comes bargaining—patients try to bargain for their lives. ¹⁰They may promise God or their doctors that they'll be good, stop smoking, give up alcohol, or do whatever is necessary if only they can survive. ¹¹The fifth stage is that of acceptance. Patients finally resign themselves to the inevitable. ¹²They are not joyful, but they gain a sense of inner peace. ¹³While there has been some criticism of Kübler-Ross's stages, her work has contributed much to making death a more comfortable and better-understood subject.

5. The pattern of organization for the above selection is
   a. list of items.
   (b.) time order.

6–10. Complete the map of the paragraph.

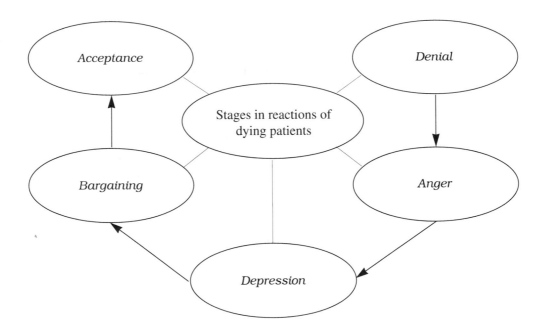

Comment: Item 5—The *time order* pattern is suggested by the words "five stages" in the topic sentence (underlined in color in this *Instructor's Edition*).

RELATIONSHIPS I: Test 6

Read each textbook passage and answer the questions or follow the directions provided.

A. According to the National Institute on Drug Abuse, thirty million Americans—one out of eight people—suffer from a drug or alcohol dependency. The development of an addiction typically unfolds in four stages. First, some stimulus—drugs, alcohol, sex, chocolate—holds out the promise of short-lived pleasure or excitement. Next, a person discovers that indulging in one of these activities temporarily satisfies some psychological need, making him or her feel good, if only for a short time. Third, certain recurring situations start to trigger the addictive behavior, and the pattern repeats itself. Finally, the habit takes control, and the individual loses self-control. Often by this stage a physical dependency will have been added to a psychological one, thereby making the addictive behavior pattern even more difficult to break.

1. The pattern of organization for the above selection is
   a. list of items.
   b. time order.

2–3. Two of the transitions that introduce the major details of the paragraph are
   _____ *Any two of the following: first, next, third, finally* _____.

B. After World War II began, women's roles changed. The most visible change was the sudden appearance of large numbers of women in uniform. The military organized them into auxiliary units with special uniforms, their own officers, and, amazingly, equal pay. Most either filled traditional women's roles, such as nursing, or replaced men in noncombat situations.

Women also substituted for men on the home front. During the war 6.3 million women entered the labor force, and for the first time in history married working women outnumbered single working women. The war challenged the public's image of proper female behavior, as "Rosie the Riveter" became the popular symbol of women who abandoned traditional jobs as domestic servants and store clerks to work in construction and heavy industry.

4. The pattern of organization for the above selection is
   a. list of items.
   b. time order.

5. The second major detail is signaled with the transition _____ *also* _____.

6. The total number of major details is
   a. two.
   b. three.
   c. four.

(Continues on next page)

C.   There are three main ways that children learn their sex roles. One is conditioning through rewards and punishments. For example, boys who play with model airplanes and girls who play with dolls will usually be encouraged by their parents. On the other hand, boys who prefer dolls and girls who prefer airplanes will often be criticized or even punished. Another element is imitation. Young children will usually imitate adults who they think are like themselves. This means that boys will usually imitate their fathers and girls their mothers. The third and perhaps the most important element is self-definition. Children quickly learn that all people are either male or female and define themselves as belonging to one sex rather than the other. They then use this self-definition to choose their future interests and to develop their personalities and social roles.

7. The pattern of organization for the above selection is
   (a.) list of items.
   b. time order.

8–10. Complete the outline of the paragraph.

Main idea: _Three ways in which children learn their sex roles_ _____

_____

Major supporting details:

1. Conditioning through rewards and punishments

2. _Imitation_ _____

3. _Self-definition_ _____

Comments: Item 1—The _time order_ pattern is suggested by the words "four stages" in the topic sentence (underlined in color in this _Instructor's Edition_).

Item 4—The statement that "women's roles changed" in the topic sentence suggests that the passage might _list_ the ways in which those roles changed.

Item 7—The _list of items_ pattern is suggested by the words "three main ways" mentioned in the topic sentence. Note that those three ways are introduced by the addition transitions _one_, _another_, and _third_.

6

Relationships II

In the previous chapter, you learned how authors use **transitions** and **patterns of organization** to show relationships and make their ideas clear. You also learned about two common types of relationships:

- Relationships that involve addition
- Relationships that involve time

In this chapter you will learn about three other types of relationships:

- Relationships that involve examples
- Relationships that involve comparison and/or contrast
- Relationships that involve cause and effect

1 EXAMPLES

Put a check beside the item that is easier to understand:

____ I've become very absent-minded. Last week I went to work on my day off.

____ I've become very absent-minded. Last week, for instance, I went to work on my day off.

The second item is easier to understand. The words *for instance* make it clear that what happened on that day off is just one example of the absent-mindedness. *For instance* and other words and phrases like it are example words.

Example words indicate that an author will provide one or more *examples* to develop and clarify a given idea. Here are some common example words:

Words That Show Examples

for example	for instance	to illustrate
including	such as	once

Examples:

The following items contain example words. Notice how these words signal that one or more examples are coming.

My grandmother doesn't hear well anymore. *For instance*, whenever I say, "Hi, Granny," she answers, "Fine, just fine."

There are various ways you can save money, *such as* bringing lunch to work and automatically putting aside a small portion of your check each week.

Rick will do anything on a dare. *Once* he showed up for a family dinner wearing only swimming trunks and a snorkeling mask.

➤ Practice 1

Answers may vary.

Complete each item with a suitable example word or phrase from the above box. Try to use a variety of transitions.

1. When a couple divorces, the partners often experience a wide range of emotions, _____*such as*_____ anger, regret, depression, and relief.

2. Animals were once tried for crimes. _____*For instance*_____, in 1740 a cow convicted of witchcraft was hanged by the neck until dead.

3. My mother believes in various superstitions, _____*including*_____ the idea that if you drop a fork, it means company's coming.

4. People have chosen to end their lives in a variety of unusual ways. _____*For example*_____, in ancient China, people committed suicide by eating a pound of salt.

5. Some soap opera fans take the shows too seriously. _____*To illustrate*_____, these viewers actually send threats to soap opera "villains."

Example words are common in all types of writing. In textbooks, they are used in the pattern of organization known as the definition and example pattern.

The Definition and Example Pattern

Arrange the following group of sentences into an order that makes sense. Put a *1* in front of the sentence that should come first, a *2* in front of the sentence that comes next, and a *3* in front of the sentence that should be last. The result will be a short paragraph.

____ You might, for instance, sit calmly through a friend's criticism and act as if it didn't bother you.

____ Apathy is an avoidance response in which a person acknowledges unpleasant information but pretends he or she does not care about it.

____ Another example is responding to the loss of a job by acting indifferent: "Who cares? It was a dumb job anyhow."

This paragraph begins with a definition: "Apathy is an avoidance response in which a person acknowledges unpleasant information but pretends he or she does not care about it." The second sentence makes clear the special meaning of *apathy* here with an example: "You might, for instance, sit calmly through a friend's criticism and act as if it didn't bother you." The third sentence then provides an added example: "Another example is responding to the loss of a job by acting indifferent: 'Who cares? It was a dumb job anyhow.'" The second and third sentences include the example words *for instance* and *example*. As you can see, the **definition and example pattern of organization** includes just what its name suggests: a definition and one or more examples.

An Important Note

Textbook authors want to help readers understand the important ideas and terms in a subject—whether it is psychology, sociology, business, biology, or any other specialized field. Authors often take time, then, to include definitions of important terms in their subject. And since definitions may be general and abstract, authors often present explanatory details and examples to help readers better understand each term.

When reading a textbook, you should mark off definitions and examples. Underline each definition and put *Ex* in the margin next to each example. If an author takes the time to define and illustrate a word, you can safely assume that the material is important enough to learn.

A Definition and Example Paragraph

The following paragraph defines a word, explains it a bit, and then gives an example of it. After reading the paragraph, see if you can answer the questions that follow.

¹Acrophobia is an intense, unreasonable fear of high places. ²People with acrophobia exhibit physical symptoms in response to being at great heights. ³For instance, one sufferer of extreme acrophobia, Sally Maxwell, is unable to go above the third floor of any building without feeling enormous anxiety. ⁴Her acrophobia began one evening when she was working alone in her office on the eighth floor of a large building. ⁵Suddenly she was struck with terror by the idea that she might jump or fall out the open window. ⁶She crouched behind a steel filing cabinet, trembling, unable to move. ⁷When she finally gathered her belongings and left the building, she was sweating, her breathing was rapid, and her heart was pounding. ⁸Yet she had no rational explanation for her fears.

What word is being defined? _____

What is the definition? _____

_____

Which sentence explains more about the word? _____

In which sentence does the example begin? _____

Explanation:

The word *acrophobia* is defined in the first sentence—"an intense, unreasonable fear of high places." The second sentence explains a bit more about acrophobia. The story about Sally Maxwell, which begins in the third sentence, provides an example of how acrophobia affects one sufferer. The example helps the author make the new term clear to the reader.

➤ Practice 2

Each of the following passages includes a definition and one or more examples, each marked by a transition. Underline the term being defined. Then, in the spaces provided, write the number of the definition sentence and the number of the sentence where each example begins.

A.   ¹A <u>boycott</u> is an organized refusal by a group of people to deal with another person or group to achieve a specific goal. ²An illustration is the famous boycott that began in 1955 when Mrs. Rosa Parks of Montgomery, Alabama, refused to obey a local ordinance requiring black people to sit at the back of city buses. ³Mrs. Parks was arrested, and that sparked off a boycott of the Montgomery bus system by blacks. ⁴The boycott was organized and led by

Comment: Note the helpful transitions in paragraphs A (*illustration*) and B (*for instance, example*).

Dr. Martin Luther King, Jr. ⁵Rather than continue to lose revenue needed to run the bus system, the city repealed the ordinance.

Definition _____1_____   *Example* _____2_____

B.   ¹Shaping is a way to teach a new behavior by encouraging a series of small bits of the whole behavior. ²This approach, for instance, was used to teach a disturbed little boy named Dickey to wear eyeglasses after cataract surgery. ³His physician feared that without glasses, his vision would deteriorate permanently. ⁴At the mere mention of eyeglasses, however, Dickey threw terrible temper tantrums. ⁵So researchers used shaping to ease him into the idea of wearing his glasses. ⁶Dickey was deprived of his breakfast so that food could be used as a reward. ⁷He received a bit of food each time he picked up some glass frames. ⁸Later in the procedure, he had to put glasses on in order to receive a reward. ⁹Within eighteen days, Dickey had learned through gradual steps to wear his glasses for twelve hours a day.

    ¹⁰Another example is teaching a circus tiger to jump through a flaming hoop. ¹¹The tiger might first be rewarded for jumping up on a pedestal and then for leaping from that pedestal to another. ¹²Eventually, the hoop would be set on fire, and the tiger would have to leap through the burning hoop to be rewarded.

Definition _____1_____   *Example 1* ____2____   *Example 2* ____10____

2   COMPARISON AND CONTRAST

Words That Show Comparison

Put a check beside the item that is easier to understand:

____ Driving a car is a skill that we learn through practice. Writing a paper is a skill that we learn through hands-on experience.

____ Driving a car is a skill that we learn through practice. Similarly, writing a paper is a skill that we learn through hands-on experience.

The first item makes us wonder, "What has learning to drive a car got to do with writing a paper?" The word *similarly* makes it clear that the author intends to compare learning to write a paper with learning to drive a car. *Similarly* and words like it are comparison words.

Comparison words signal that authors are pointing out similarities between subjects. A comparison word tells us that a second idea is *like* the first one in some way. Here are some common comparison words:

Words That Show Comparison

as	alike	in a similar manner
just as	in like manner	in the same way
just like	similar(ly)	resemble

Examples:

The sentences below contain comparison words. Notice how these words show that things are *alike* in some way.

> When buying milk, my mother always takes a bottle from the back of the shelf. *Similarly*, when my father buys a newspaper, he usually grabs one from the middle of the pile.

> If moviemakers have a big hit, they tend to repeat the winning idea in their next movie, *just like* certain authors who keep writing the same type of story over and over.

> Individuals are more likely to solve their problems if they communicate with one another. *In a similar way*, countries can best solve their problems through communication.

➤ Practice 3

Answers may vary.

Complete each sentence with a suitable comparison word or phrase from the above box. Try to use a variety of transitions.

1. Lighting a cigarette in a darkened theater will not win you any friends.
   _____*Similarly*_____, talking out loud with your movie partner will soon make people scowl in your direction.

2. There are so many gopher holes in our back yard that it looks
   _____*like*_____ a miniature golf course.

3. Spicy foods make me very thirsty. Believe it or not, ice cream affects me
   ____*in the same way*____.

4. Japanese women once blackened their teeth to improve their appearance.
   ____*In a similar manner*____, some Indian women stained their teeth red.

5. _____*Just as*_____ rats become hostile when they are made to live in a crowded cage, humans become more aggressive in crowded conditions.

Words That Show Contrast

Put a check beside the item that is easier to understand:

____ A roller coaster scares many kids. They love riding on it.

____ Even though a roller coaster scares many kids, they love riding on it.

In the first item, the two sentences seem to contradict each other. We want to ask, "Do kids like a roller coaster or don't they?" In the second item, the phrase *even though* makes clear the relationship between the two ideas: In spite of the fact that a roller coaster is scary, kids still love riding on it. *Even though* and other words and phrases like this are contrast words.

Contrast words show that things *differ* in one or more ways. Here are some common contrast words.

Words That Show Contrast

but	instead	still	even though
yet	in contrast	as opposed to	different
however	on the other hand	in spite of	differs from
although	on the contrary	despite	unlike
nevertheless	converse(ly)	rather than	while

Examples:

The sentences below contain contrast words. Notice how these words signal that one idea is different from another idea.

Some people think they have to exercise every day to stay in shape. *However*, three workouts a week are all they need.

Professional writers don't wait for inspiration. *On the contrary*, they stick to a strict writing schedule.

There are those who look upon eating as something to be done quickly so they can get on to better things. *In contrast*, other people think eating is one of the better things.

➤ Practice 4

Answers may vary.

Complete each sentence with a suitable contrast word or phrase from the above box. Try to use a variety of transitions.

1. _____*Although*_____ the diner was a pleasant place to eat, it still went out of business.

2. We use seventeen muscles when we smile; _____*in contrast*_____, we have to use forty-three muscles to frown.

3. At first we were planning on spending our vacation at a campground, _____*but*_____ now we've decided just to relax at home.

4. Paula was not satisfied with her paper _____*in spite of*_____ the fact that she had already written five drafts.

5. Keeping his independence is important to Michael. _____*However*_____, he likes to consult his parents before he makes certain decisions.

Comparison and contrast transitions often signal the pattern of organization called the comparison and/or contrast pattern.

The Comparison and/or Contrast Pattern

Arrange the following group of sentences into an order that makes sense. Put a *1* in front of the sentence that should come first, a *2* in front of the sentence that comes next, and a *3* in front of the sentence that should be last. The result will be a short paragraph.

____ Yet the large, hairy tarantula is relatively harmless, while the small brown recluse is dangerously poisonous.

____ The tarantula and the brown recluse are more different than they are similar.

____ It's true, both spiders are alike in inspiring a great deal of fear.

The first sentence of this paragraph is the general one, the one with the main idea: "The tarantula and the brown recluse are more different than they are similar." The words *similar* and *different* suggest a comparison and/or contrast pattern of organization. The comparison word *alike* and the contrast words *yet* and *while* in the other two sentences show that the spiders are indeed being compared and contrasted: "It's true, both spiders are alike in inspiring a great deal of fear. Yet the large, hairy tarantula is relatively harmless, while the small brown recluse is dangerously poisonous."

The **comparison-contrast pattern** shows how two things are alike or how they are different, or both. When things are compared, their similarities are pointed out; when they are contrasted, their differences are discussed. (The tarantula and the brown recluse spider are alike in the fear they inspire; they are different in the effects of their bites, as well as in their appearance.)

Authors frequently find it useful to compare and contrast. The author of a child-development textbook, for example, compares and contrasts the ways in which boys and girls develop. Although they are similar in experiencing a growth spurt at the beginning of adolescence, the spurt begins about a year or so earlier in girls. Also, while boys gain proportionately more muscle, girls gain proportionately more fat, giving them more of the look of an adult woman. The authors of a sociology text contrast American cities with those in underdeveloped nations. They point out, for instance, that although the populations of American cities are leveling off, the populations of most third-world cities are exploding.

A Comparison/Contrast Paragraph

In the following paragraph, the main idea is stated in the first sentence. As is often the case, the main idea suggests a paragraph's pattern of organization. Here the transition *differently* is a hint that the paragraph may be organized in a comparison-contrast pattern. Read the paragraph, and answer the questions below. Then read the explanation that follows.

> In middle age, men and women often view life very differently, especially if they are couples who have led traditional lives. By middle age, the husband is often comfortable in his position at work and has given up any dreams of advancing further. He may then become more family-oriented. In contrast, once the children are grown, the wife may find herself free to explore interests and develop abilities she has had no time for in the previous fifteen or twenty years. Unlike her husband, she may be more interested in non-family activities than ever.

1. Is this paragraph comparing, contrasting, or both? _____

2. What two things are being compared and/or contrasted? _____

   _____

3. Which three comparison or contrast transition words or phrases are used in the paragraph? _____

Explanation:

> This paragraph is only contrasting, not comparing—it discusses only differences, not similarities. The two things being contrasted are the views of traditional middle-aged men and women. The transition words or phrases that show contrast are *differently*, *in contrast*, and *unlike*.

➤ *Practice 5*

The following passages use the pattern of comparison or contrast. Read each passage and answer the questions which follow.

A.   Although mysteries and science fiction may seem like very different kinds of writing, the two forms share some basic similarities. First of all, both are action-directed, emphasizing plot at the expense of character development. Possibly for this reason, both types of literature have been scorned by critics as being "merely entertainment" rather than "literature." But this attack is unjustified, for both mysteries and science fiction are concerned with moral issues. Science fiction often raises the question of whether or not scientific advances are of benefit to humanity. And a mystery story rarely ends without the culpable person being brought to justice.

Check the pattern which is used in this paragraph:

   _✓_ Comparison

   ____ Contrast

What two things are being compared or contrasted?

   1. _____*mysteries*_____   2. _____*science fiction*_____

B.   The conflict over secrecy between the federal government and journalists arises from the different roles they play in society. The government has the job of conducting foreign policy. To do so effectively, government officials sometimes prefer to distort or withhold information. Journalists, however, see their role as digging up and giving information to the public. If they always sought government permission before publishing information, they would be able to print or broadcast only what the government wanted to appear in the media.

Check the pattern which is used in this paragraph:

   ____ Comparison

   _✓_ Contrast

What two things are being compared or contrasted?

   1. _____*federal government*_____   2. _____*journalists*_____

Comments: The topic sentences in Practice 5 are underlined in color in this *Instructor's Edition.*
   Paragraph A—The comparison relationship is signaled by the transition *similarities.*
   Paragraph B—The contrast relationship is signaled by the transitions *different* and *however.*

3   CAUSE AND EFFECT

Put a check beside the item that is easier to understand:

____   The varnish wore off the wooden patio table. Fungus has begun to grow on it.

____   Because the varnish wore off the wooden patio table, fungus has begun to grow on it.

In the first item, it seems the author is simply listing two things that have happened to the patio table. The word *because* in the second item makes clear the relationship between the two ideas—the protective varnish wore off, so the fungus was able to grow. *Because* and words like it are cause and effect words.

Cause and effect words signal that the author is explaining *the reason why* something happened or will happen. Here are some common cause and effect words:

Words That Show Cause and Effect

therefore	so	result	because (of)
thus	as a result	effect	reason
as a consequence	results in	cause	explanation
consequently	leads to	if . . . then	accordingly
due to	since	affect	

Examples:

The following examples contain cause and effect words. Notice how these words introduce a reason for something or the results of something.

My sister became a vegetarian *because* she doesn't want to eat anything that had a mother.

If the weather gets too humid, *then* our wooden doors swell up and become hard to open and shut.

My boss's correspondence had built up while he was on vacation. *As a result*, I've been typing letters for the last two days.

➤ *Practice 6*   *Answers may vary.*

Complete each sentence with a suitable cause and effect word or phrase from the above box. Try to use a variety of transitions.

1. _____*Because*_____ property taxes in the city have gone sky high, many corporations are moving to the suburbs.

2. Lisa's résumé is impressive; _____*as a result*_____, she has already had several job interviews.

3. _____*Since*_____ my family is full of great Italian cooks, canned ravioli tastes like cardboard to me.

4. Some zoo animals have not learned how to be good parents. _____*Consequently*_____, baby animals are sometimes brought up in zoo nurseries and even in private homes.

5. Car dealers like to sell a certain number of cars in any given month. They are _____*therefore*_____ more likely to hold sales near the end of a month.

Cause and effect transitions often signal the cause and effect pattern of organization.

The Cause and Effect Pattern

Arrange the following group of sentences into an order that makes sense. Put a *1* in front of the sentence that should come first, a *2* in front of the sentence that comes next, and a *3* in front of the sentence that should be last. The result will be a short paragraph.

____ The need for the specialized knowledge of industry leads to a system of formal education.

____ A society's change from an agricultural base to an industrial one results in the growth of formal education and a weaker family.

____ And because formal education replaces the instruction of older family members, the family's authority is weakened.

As the words *leads to*, *results in*, and *because* suggest, this paragraph is organized in a cause and effect pattern. The paragraph begins with the general idea: "A society's change from an agricultural base to an industrial one results in the growth of formal education and a weaker family." Next comes a more detailed explanation: "The need for the specialized knowledge of industry leads to a system of formal education. And because formal education replaces the instruction of older family members, the family's authority is weakened."

Information that falls into a cause-effect pattern addresses itself to the questions "Why does an event happen?" and "What are the results of an event?" In other words, this pattern answers the question "What are the causes and/or effects of an event?"

Authors usually don't just tell what happened; they try to tell about events in a way that explains both *what* happened and *why*. A textbook section on the sinking of the ship *Titanic*, for example, would be incomplete if it did not include the cause of the disaster—going at a high speed, the ship collided with an iceberg.

Or if the number of homeless families in the country increases, journalists will not simply report the fact of the increase. Stories would also explore the reasons *why* the number of homeless families has increased.

A Cause and Effect Paragraph

Read the paragraph below and see if you can answer the questions about cause and effect. Then read the explanation to see how you did.

> Even the best listeners are unable to listen carefully to everything that they hear. One reason for this inability is the overload of messages most of us encounter each day. Besides the numerous hours we spend hearing other people speak, we may spend several more hours listening to the radio or television. It just isn't possible to avoid having our attention wander at least part of all this time. Another cause of our not always listening carefully is a preoccupation with personal concerns. A romance gone sour or a good grade on a test may take prominence in our mind even as someone is speaking to us. In addition, the simple fact that we are at times surrounded by noise may result in poor listening. For example, many voices at a noisy party or the sound of traffic may make it difficult for us to hear everything that is being said.

1. What are the three *causes* described in this paragraph?

   a. _____

   b. _____

   c. _____

2. The three causes lead to what result or *effect*?

   _____

3. What three cause-effect signal words or phrases are used? _____

   _____

Explanation:

> The paragraph explains the reasons why we are unable to listen carefully to everything that we hear. It offers three reasons, or causes. The first is the overload of messages we hear each day. The second reason is our preoccupation with personal concerns. The third cause advanced is that we are at times surrounded by interfering noise. The effect is our inability to listen carefully to everything we hear. The cause-effect signals used are *reason*, *cause*, and *result in*.

➤ *Practice 7*

In the first paragraph below, label the one cause and the three effects. In the second paragraph, label the one effect and the four causes.

A.   Research over the last decade or so has shown that meditation can have positive effects on drug users and people with certain health problems. Studies have demonstrated that when people who take drugs become meditators, they either cut back on drug use or stop using drugs altogether. In one study of a group that practiced meditation, for example, the number of marijuana users fell from 78 percent to 12 percent after twenty-one months of meditation. Meditation has also been shown to lower blood pressure and regulate the heartbeat, both of which may be of considerable help to those with cardiovascular problems. And because meditation is a highly effective relaxation technique, it can also prove useful to those with stress-related diseases.

Meditation: _____ *cause* _____

Decrease or elimination of drug use: _____ *effect* _____

Cardiovascular improvements: _____ *effect* _____

Stress relief: _____ *effect* _____

B.   Why do people daydream? One cause of daydreaming is routine or boring jobs that are tolerable only when workers imagine themselves doing something else. Deprivation also leads to daydreaming. During World War II, conscientious objectors who volunteered to go on semistarvation diets for six months focused their daydreams on food. Some even hung enticing pictures of foods on their walls to give themselves something to daydream about. Another reason people daydream is to discharge hostile feelings. For example, if an angry student imagines dropping his instructor out of a classroom window, it might help him to laugh at and dismiss his annoyance with her. Some people also daydream as a way to plan for the future so that by the time they face the situations they imagine, they will know what to say and how to act.

Comments: Paragraph A—The paragraph lists the effects of meditation referred to in the topic sentence (underlined).

Daydreaming: _____ *effect* _____

Boring jobs: _____ *cause* _____

Deprivation: _____ *cause* _____

Note the cause-effect transitions in paragraphs A (*effects*) and B (*cause, leads to, reason, so*).

Discharge of hostile feelings: _____ *cause* _____

Way to plan for future: _____ *cause* _____

A Note on Topic Sentences and Patterns of Organization

As mentioned in the previous chapter, a paragraph's topic sentence often indicates its pattern of organization. For example, here is the topic sentence of a paragraph you worked on earlier: "In middle age, men and women often view life very differently, especially if they are couples who have led traditional lives." This sentence may have made you expect that the paragraph would go on to contrast the views of middle-aged men and women. If so, the paragraph would be organized according to the comparison and/or contrast pattern.

So finding the topic sentence of a paragraph may help you decide on its pattern of organization. Try, for instance, to guess the pattern of the paragraph with this topic sentence:

> Homeowners are not getting good results with their gardens because of the type of soil in the area.

The words *results* and *because* suggest that the paragraph will discuss the causes and effects of the type of soil in the area. This topic sentence helps us guess that the paragraph will probably have a cause and effect pattern.

➤ *Practice 8*

Most of the sentences below have been taken from college textbooks. Circle the letter of the pattern of organization that each topic sentence suggests.

1. Following are three reasons for the existence of stereotypes.
   a. Definition and example
   b. Comparison and/or contrast
   (c.) Cause and effect

2. College students in their thirties and forties face many of the same pressures as younger students, but they are often better equipped to withstand these pressures.
   a. Definition and example
   (b.) Comparison and/or contrast
   c. Cause and effect

3. The business practice known as dumping means charging less for certain goods sold abroad than at home.
   (a.) Definition and example
   b. Comparison and/or contrast
   c. Cause and effect

4. A growing concern with health has affected the way that many Americans eat.
   a. Definition and example
   b. Comparison and/or contrast
   (c.) Cause and effect

5. Vacillation is the tendency to be drawn first toward one possible resolution of a conflict and then toward another.
   (a.) Definition and example
   b. Comparison and/or contrast
   c. Cause and effect

6. Americans typically think of men as naturally better suited to perform the most strenuous physical labor, but not all peoples of the world hold the same view.
   a. Definition and example   (b.) Comparison and/or contrast   c. Cause and effect

7. Because of economic pressures, increasing numbers of people are seeking housing assistance.
   a. Definition and example   b. Comparison and/or contrast   (c.) Cause and effect

8. Constructive criticism is evaluation of behavior—usually negative evaluation—given to help a person identify or correct a fault.
   (a.) Definition and example   b. Comparison and/or contrast   c. Cause and effect

9. There are several possible explanations for why retail prices often end on certain numbers.
   a. Definition and example   b. Comparison and/or contrast   (c.) Cause and effect

10. First-year college students who expect to do well in school need to learn quickly the right and wrong ways of preparing for exams.
    a. Definition and example   (b.) Comparison and/or contrast   c. Cause and effect

A Final Point

Keep in mind that a paragraph or passage may often be made up of more than one pattern of organization. For instance, the paragraph in this chapter about acrophobia (the unreasonable fear of high places) uses the definition and example pattern. But the example itself—a series of events one evening in Sally Maxwell's life—uses a time order pattern.

Or consider the following passage:

Have you ever had the experience of recognizing someone's face but not being able to recall his or her name? The reason is that the information about that person is split up and stored in the two different sides of your brain, and each side has its own way of thinking and remembering. Recalling someone's face is the task of the right side of your brain, which understands whole things at once and is responsible for visualizing, recognizing similarities, and supplying intutions. This side of your brain provides insights that are hard to put into words. The left side of your brain deals with language and stores words themselves, including the person's name that you have temporarily forgotten. This is the side responsible for speaking, reading, writing, and listening.

The paragraph uses in part a cause-effect pattern, explaining the reason why we may recognize a face but not recall a name. It also uses a contrast pattern, explaining the different functions of the two sides of the brain.

➤ Review Test 1

To review what you've learned in this chapter, fill in the blanks or choose the best answer for the following items.

1. When textbook authors provide a definition of a term, they are also likely to provide one or more _____*examples*_____ to help make that definition clear.

2. A(n) _____*comparison*_____ transition signals that two things are alike in some way.

3. A(n) _____*contrast*_____ transition signals that two things are different in some way.

4. A cause and effect paragraph might be about
   a. results.   b. reasons.   (c.) *a* and/or *b.*

5. The pattern of organization of a paragraph may be suggested by
   a. the transitions it contains.   b. its topic sentence.   (c.) both *a* and *b.*

➤ Review Test 2

A. Fill each blank with one of the transitions in the box. Use each transition once.

because	effects	like	such as	yet

1. Strong emotions can have negative _____*effects*_____ on digestion.

2. Cleo's photos look _____*like*_____ abstract paintings.

3. _____*Because*_____ my closet is so crowded, I keep my shoes under my bed and some of my sweaters in the linen closet.

4. An adult elephant weighs about 12,000 pounds. _____*Yet*_____ its eyes are almost exactly the size of a human's.

5. For people who wish to work with children, there are many career choices, _____*such as*_____ teaching, school counseling, and working at a day-care center.

B. Below are the beginnings of five passages. Label each one with the letter of its pattern of organization. (You may find it helpful to underline the transition or transitions in each item.)

    a Definition and example
    b Comparison and/or contrast
    c Cause and effect

_c_ 6. Many drivers take to the roads in July and August, when families traditionally go on vacation. As a result, oil companies raise the price of gasoline during the summer months. . . .

_a_ 7. In a mystery story, the term "red herring" refers to a false or misleading clue inserted into the story to deceive the reader. One famous red herring is Sherlock Holmes's farewell note to Dr. Watson in "The Final Problem," which leads the reader to believe Holmes has fallen to his death. . . .

_b_ 8. Television news stories resemble newspaper articles in being timely and appealing to a wide audience. However, television news coverage tends to be more superficial, emphasizing the visual aspects of a story rather than important background issues. . . .

_a_ 9. A complementary relationship is one in which the distribution of power is unequal. One partner says, "Let's go to a movie tonight," and the other says, "Sure." The boss asks several employees to work overtime, and they all agree. . . .

_c_ 10. One type of hearing loss is caused by damage to the nerve cells in the inner ear. The damage may be the result of loud noises, allergic reactions to medicines, or a hard blow to the ear or skull. Certain diseases can also cause damage to the nerve cells of the inner ear. . . .

➤ *Review Test 3*

Read each paragraph and answer the questions that follow.

A. Alternate freezing and thawing is one of the most important processes of mechanical weathering. Water has the unique property of expanding about 9 percent as it freezes. This increase in volume occurs because as water solidifies, the water molecules arrange themselves into a very open crystalline structure. As a result, when water freezes it exerts a tremendous outward force. In nature, water works its way into cracks or voids in rock. When the water then freezes and expands, the effect is to break the rock into angular fragments.

1. The main pattern of organization of the selection is
   a. definition-example.
   b. cause-effect.
   c. comparison and/or contrast.
2. One transition that signals the pattern of organization is _____ *because* or *as a result* or *effect* _____.

B. In general, the similarities among siblings are inherited, while their differences come from their family experiences, which differ from child to child. Siblings often look alike, having a fifty-fifty chance of inheriting the same gene from their parents. And there are some personality traits that do run in families. However, despite the fact that they live together, siblings have very different experiences in the same household. Parents may treat their children quite differently, encouraging confidence in one and lack of confidence in another. And older children are often brought up more strictly than younger children.

3. The main pattern of organization of the selection is
   a. definition-example.
   b. cause-effect.
   c. comparison and/or contrast.
4. One transition that signals the pattern of organization is _while_ or _similarities_ or _differences_ or _differ_ or _alike_ or _however_ or _despite_ or _different_.

C. The use of fire by prehistoric people probably affected wildlife both intentionally and unintentionally. In all likelihood, early people used fire to drive game toward waiting hunters. Later, new plant growth in the burned areas would attract more wild animals. In addition, accidental fires must have occurred frequently. Because prehistoric people had trouble starting fires, they kept burning embers on hand. The result must have been widespread accidental fires, especially in dry areas. Certainly, these fires also would have greatly altered the habitat for wildlife.

5. The main pattern of organization of the paragraph is
   a. definition and example.
   b. contrast.
   c. cause and effect.
6. One transition that signals the pattern of organization is _____ *affected* or *because* or *result* _____.

D. The feeling of awe is similar to fear in some ways. With both, we have a sense of being overwhelmed, of confronting someone or something much more powerful than ourselves. But awe is a positive feeling, an expansive feeling. While fear makes us want to run away, awe makes us want to draw closer even as we hesitate to get too close. Instead of resenting our own smallness or weakness, we stand open-mouthed in appreciation of something greater than ourselves. To stand unsteadily at the edge of a steep cliff and look down is to experience fear. We want to get out of that situation as soon and quickly and safely as we can. To stand securely on a mountaintop and look around us is to feel awe. We could linger there forever.

7. The main pattern of organization of the paragraph is
    a. definition and example.
    (b.) comparison and contrast.
    c. cause and effect.

8. One transition that signals the pattern of organization is _____*similar*_____.

E. Are Nina and her exercise partner a group? Are the members of a fraternity or a sorority or of a board of directors a group? Group dynamics expert Marvin Shaw argues that all groups have one thing in common: Their members interact. He therefore defines a group as two or more people who interact and influence one another. Moreover, notes social psychologist John Turner, groups perceive themselves as "us" in contrast to "them." So Nina and her jogging companion are indeed an example of a group, as are members of social organizations and corporate decision-making bodies.

9. The main pattern of organization of the paragraph is
    (a.) definition and example.
    b. contrast.
    c. cause and effect.

10. One transition that signals the pattern of organization is _____*example*_____.

➤ *Review Test 4*

Here is a chance to apply your understanding of patterns of organization to a passage from a college textbook: *Sociology*, Fifth Edition, by Donald Light, Suzanne Keller, and Craig Calhoun (McGraw Hill). Whether you live in a small country town or a large city, you will probably find something familiar in this textbook passage about rural and urban areas.

To help you continue to strengthen your skills, the reading is followed by questions not only on what you've learned in this chapter but also on what you've learned in previous chapters.

Words to Watch

On the next page are some words in the reading that do not have strong context support. Each word is followed by the number of the paragraph in which it appears and its meaning there. These words are indicated in the article by a small circle (°).

pseudonym (2): fictitious name
decidedly (2): definitely
aloof (3): distant in personal relations
oriented (3): related
scrutiny (3): examination
indiscretions (3): unwise acts
spectrum (4): range
vestiges (4): traces; remaining bits
revitalization (5): a bringing back to life

COMMUNITIES AND CITIES

Donald Light
Suzanne Keller
Craig Calhoun

1   Main Street in Mineville starts to awaken at about 5 a.m. The cook at the restaurant arrives at this hour to start heating the stove and brewing the coffee. The postmaster makes an appearance at 5:30 to empty the one mailbox in this town of 1,400 people. All the out-of-town letters must be sorted and stamped in time to leave on the 6:30 train. Shortly before 6:30 the quiet is broken by the rumblings of the large dump truck that carries ore from the mine to the train station. Next, Reavley's cab pulls up at the depot to let off the few passengers who are taking the early train to Gold for shopping or business. By 7:00 the street is filled with miners on their way to work. They walk in groups, carrying their lunches; most of them have known each other since boyhood. At 8:30 a wave of children floods Main Street. Laughing, talking, running to catch up with friends, they head for the local school. The next big event is the arrival of the bus from Smelters, which delivers the daily papers. By 11:00 everyone is asking, "Is Julius [the bus driver] here yet?" With the papers in, attention turns to the arrival of the noontime mail train. For the rest of the day the post office is the busiest place in town. The people of Mineville go there not just to pick up their mail, but to chat with friends and neighbors and to catch up on town gossip.

2   New York City is 2,000 miles away from Mineville (a pseudonym° for a town in Montana), but considering its lifestyle the distance seems more like 200,000. On Manhattan's Upper West Side, for example, Columbus Avenue is the center of conspicuous consumption. Young urban professionals stroll through its stores on weekends, buying $400 sports jackets and $200 slacks, perfect for sitting in a fashionable café sipping Perrier at $5 a glass. On a typical Sunday thousands of people are part of this yuppie scene. One store owner reports that his new hardwood floor wore out from foot traffic in just two years! Some of these shoppers come from the suburbs, some from other sections of New York City, but a great many are Upper West Siders. They live in the same small area (five blocks wide by roughly twenty-

seven blocks long), and yet while browsing through a new shop, dining in a restaurant, or drinking at a bar, they usually do not know any of the people around them. The Upper West Side is decidedly° a "community" of strangers. Each resident is acquainted with only a tiny fraction of its 100,000 population.

3   Differences between Mineville and the Upper West Side of Manhattan could fill many pages. In Mineville the residents are involved in a continual round of community-centered activities, such as dances, club meetings, church programs, and projects sponsored by civic organizations. People are expected to participate, at least to some extent, in these activities. Those who do not are considered aloof° and antisocial. In contrast, on the Upper West Side most people's social lives are not at all neighborhood-oriented°. In fact, to be extremely neighborly tends to invite suspicion. Most Upper West Siders know almost nothing about the people who share their apartment building. It is common not even to know the tenant next door except as a name beneath a doorbell. Such anonymity is unheard of in Mineville. There, people know countless details about one another's lives. Sharing gossip about fellow residents is a favorite town pastime. Such close scrutiny° of everyone's activities helps to keep the people of Mineville from stepping very far out of line. Of course, sexual indiscretions°, incidents of drunkenness, and occasional teenage vandalism take place. But serious crime is so rare that the town council declared the office of police chief indefinitely vacant. Upper West Side residents would be horrified at the prospect of dismissing their police force. Muggings, robberies, rapes, and murders are a daily occurrence in New York City. Fear of crime drives many residents to install two, three, even four locks on their apartment door.

4   How can we sum up the differences between Mineville and the Upper West Side of Manhattan? What is the essence of the contrasts between them? Those contrasts are essentially differences of place, differences between a small town and a large city. Granted, Albert Blumenthal wrote his sociological description of Mineville in the early 1930s, a time when the United States was in many ways different than it is today. But small towns like Mineville still exist in our society. There are still places where, despite modern technology and mass communication, the basic features of small town life remain. According to sociologist Ernest Burgess, these features include "close acquaintanceship of everyone with everyone else, the dominance of personal relations, and subjection of the individual to continuous observation and control by the community." None of these features are found on the Upper West Side of Manhattan. In fact, the Upper West Side seems to present the opposite of the spectrum° in all three respects. Can we therefore conclude that the Upper West Side is nothing at all like Mineville? Probably not, because as you will see later in this chapter, some sociologists argue that vestiges° of traditional communities—and sometimes entirely new kinds of communities— thrive in even the most urbanized settings.

5   This chapter takes a sociological look at life in towns and cities. First, we examine the question of whether urbanization has destroyed community or simply given new form to the close, enduring relationships found in places like Mineville. Second, we consider the

historical process of urbanization. Where and when did cities first appear and why did they develop? Have the basic form and function of cities changed much over the centuries? What are the differences between, say, Venice, Italy, during the Renaissance and the sprawling metropolis of Los Angeles today? Third, we look more closely at the contemporary urban environment and evaluate several theories that attempt to explain its spatial organization. We conclude the chapter by returning to the relationship between community and urbanization and by considering two recent trends: revitalization° of inner-city neighborhoods and commercial districts, and the rapid growth of small towns where huge new industrial plants have been built.

Reading Comprehension Questions

Vocabulary in Context

1. In the excerpt below, the term *conspicuous consumption* means
   a. modest behavior.
   b. eating at expensive places.
   (c.) spending to impress.
   d. ordinary shopping.

   The context clues are the examples in the second sentence.

   > "Columbus Avenue is the center of conspicuous consumption. Young urban professionals stroll through its stores on weekends, buying $400 sports jackets and $200 slacks, perfect for sitting in a fashionable café sipping Perrier at $5 a glass." (Paragraph 2)

2. In the excerpt below, the word *anonymity* means a condition of
   (a.) not being personally known.
   b. fear and shame.
   c. real estate.
   d. wastefulness.

   > "Most Upper West Siders know almost nothing about the people who share their apartment building. . . . Such anonymity is unheard of in Mineville." (Paragraph 3)

Central Point and Main Ideas

3. Which sentence best expresses the central point of the first four paragraphs of the selection? (Note that the last paragraph is a more general introduction to the chapter.)

   Answers *a*, *c*, and *d* are all too narrow.
   a. People are more neighborly in small towns than in big cities.
   (b.) While small towns and large cities may share some characteristics, they are very different in important ways.
   c. Although the residents of the Upper West Side of New York live in a small area, they are strangers to each other.
   d. Mineville is the fictitious name of a real Montana town that was studied by a sociological researcher in the early 1930s.

4. Which sentence best expresses the main idea of paragraph 3?
    a. Sentence 1
    b. Sentence 2
    c. Next-to-the-last sentence
    d. Last sentence

Supporting Details

5. In general, the supporting details of paragraph 1 are
    a. events.
    b. reasons.
    c. statistics.
    d. quotations.

Transitions

6. The relationship of the second sentence below to the first is one of
    a. addition.
    b. contrast.
    c. cause and effect.
    d. example.

    "Of course, sexual indiscretions, incidents of drunkenness, and occasional teenage vandalism take place. But serious crime is so rare that the town council declared the office of police chief indefinitely vacant." (Paragraph 3)

7. In the final paragraph, what is the primary kind of transition that the authors use to organize their details?
    a. Contrast
    b. Addition
    c. Cause and effect
    d. Example

Patterns of Organization

8. The pattern of organization of paragraph 1 is
    a. time order.
    b. list of items.
    c. cause and effect.
    d. definition and example.

Comments: Item 7— The addition transitions used are *first, second, third,* and *we conclude* (which means the same here as *finally*).

Item 8— Since the paragraph lists a series of events (see item 5, above), the pattern of organization is naturally time order.

9. Paragraph 3
   a. lists various events of Mineville and the Upper West Side of Manhattan in a time order.
   (b.) contrasts life in Mineville with life on the Upper West Side of Manhattan.
   c. explains the causes and effects of social life and crime in Mineville and on the Upper West Side.
   d. defines and illustrates small town life.

10. Like paragraphs, longer selections have patterns of organization. Overall, "Communities and Cities" is organized according to a
    a. list of items pattern.
    b. time order pattern.
    (c.) comparison and contrast pattern.
    d. cause and effect pattern.

Discussion Questions

1. Do people in your neighborhood tend to know each other or not? What do you find to be the advantages or disadvantages of knowing and not knowing your neighbors?

2. The authors write that people go to the Mineville post office not only to get their mail, but "to chat with friends and neighbors and to catch up on town gossip." Is there any place you go to that serves a similar social function? If so, where is it, and what is it like there?

3. The authors state that on the Upper West Side of Manhattan, "to be extremely neighborly tends to invite suspicion." Why might this be?

4. Ernest Burgess states that the basic features of small towns include "subjection of the individual to continuous observation and control by the community." What does this mean, and how does its absence affect the people in a large city?

Comment: Item 10—See Item 3 to note how the central point reveals a pattern of comparison and contrast.

Check Your Performance   RELATIONSHIPS II

Activity	Number Right	Points		Score
Review Test 1 (5 items)	_____	x 2 =		_____
Review Test 2 (10 items)	_____	x 3 =		_____
Review Test 3 (10 items)	_____	x 3 =		_____
Review Test 4 (10 items)	_____	x 3 =		_____
		TOTAL SCORE =		_____ %

Enter your total score into the **Reading Performance Chart: Review Tests** on the inside back cover.

RELATIONSHIPS II: Test 1

A. Fill in each blank with an appropriate transition from the box. Use each transition once.

therefore	for example	just as
because	in contrast	

1. Some thieves read the newspapers to find out good times to rob houses. _____*For example*_____, after reading the obituaries, such thieves may "clean out" a home while the family is at a loved one's funeral.

2. Whenever something bad happens to me, my grandmother tries to help me through it. When I was depressed after breaking up with my boyfriend, she told me, "_____*Just as*_____ we must go through the storm before seeing the rainbow, we often must experience sorrow before joy."

3. Honeybees attack just to protect their hives. _____*Therefore*_____, if you run away from the hive when attacked, the bees will eventually lose interest in you.

4. _____*Because*_____ there are no clocks in gambling casinos, gamblers can easily lose all sense of time. That is clearly what the casino management wants to happen. The longer people stay at the tables or in front of the slot machines, the better.

5. Most birds are born in either of two very different states. Some are born weak, blind, and usually naked. About all they can do for themselves is open their mouths for food. _____*In contrast*_____, other newborn baby birds are born bright-eyed and covered with down. As soon as their down is dry, they are able to peck at things and run after their parents.

(Continues on next page)

B. Label each item with the letter of its main pattern of organization.

      a   Definition and example
      b   Comparison and/or contrast
      c   Cause and effect

_a_   6. Phobias are intense, irrational fears that are out of proportion to the actual danger in a situation. For example, people with the fear of open places (agoraphobia) are often reluctant to leave their homes.

_c_   7. Wives tend to see dirty dishes piled in the sink, unmade beds, and "dust bunnies" under the furniture as a reflection on them as women. As a result, they put more time into housework and pick up the wet towels if their husbands or children "forget."

_a_   8. Climate is the average weather experienced in a given geographic area. Areas fall into climate categories according to their year-round temperature and rainfall. An oppressively hot and humid region, for example, would be said to have a tropical climate.

_b_   9. In the 1890s, most Americans were struggling to reach a middle-class lifestyle. By the 1990s, in contrast, an overwhelming majority had achieved the middle class but were either losing it or struggling to hold on to it. In the 1890s, government responded to the prodding of reform-minded citizens and began to create a framework of rules to control the excesses of giant businesses and to protect the interests of the average citizen. But in the 1990s, on the other hand, that framework was being dismantled.

_c_ 10. Prison overcrowding is dangerous because it increases unrest among inmates and products a climate in which violence is more likely. Riots, escapes, and hostage taking become more of a problem. Prison overcrowding also makes it more difficult for correctional officers and prison administrators to manage the prison. The result is that prisons are more costly to run.

RELATIONSHIPS II: Test 2

Read each paragraph and answer the questions that follow.

A.   The incomes of middle- and working-class Americans stagnated during the 1980s. A major reason was deindustrialization, or a decline in the portion of the economy that is devoted to manufacturing goods as opposed to providing services. Most costly has been the transfer of manufacturing jobs (especially in the steel and auto industries) from the United States to Third World countries. Millions of blue-collar workers in the Midwest and Northeast were consequently stranded. The result was that they were forced into much lower-paying jobs with fewer benefits and opportunities for advancement.

   1. The main pattern of organization of the selection is
     a. definition-example.
     b. cause-effect.
     c. comparison and/or contrast.

   2. One transition that signals the pattern of organization is ___*reason* or *result*___.

B.   Boys who mature early physically have a decided advantage over their more slowly maturing peers. Early maturers become heroes in sports and leaders in both formal and informal activities. Other boys look up to them; girls have crushes on them. Even adults tend to trust them. They are more self-confident and independent than other boys. In contrast, their less mature male peers, with their high-pitched voices and underdeveloped physiques, feel inadequate. They are weaker at sports and more awkward with girls.

   3. The main pattern of organization of the selection is
     a. definition-example.
     b. cause-effect.
     c. comparison and/or contrast.

   4. The transition that signals the pattern of organization is ___*in contrast*___.

C.   Why does lightning make such a loud sound? The answer has to do with the electrical energy it gives off. A single bolt may produce as much as 3,750 million kilowatts of electrical energy. Most of this energy—75 percent—turns into heat, causing the temperature of the surrounding air to rise greatly. Since heated air expands, the sudden increase in temperature leads to a rapid expansion of the air around the lightning. And that air expansion causes sound waves—thunder—which can be heard up to eighteen miles away.

(Continues on next page)

5. The main pattern of organization of the selection is
   a. definition-example.
   (b.) cause-effect.
   c. comparison and/or contrast.

6. One transition that signals the pattern of organization is ___*leads to* or *causes*___.

   causing or *since* or

D. There are often more than two sides to a question, and offering only two choices when more actually exist is called an either-or fallacy. For example, the statement "Either you are with us or against us" assumes that there is no middle ground. Or consider the following conclusion: People opposed to total freedom of speech are really in favor of censorship. This argument ignores the fact that a person could believe in free speech as well as in laws that prohibit slander or that punish someone for falsely yelling "Fire!" in a crowded theater.

7. The main pattern of organization of the selection is
   (a.) definition-example.
   b. cause-effect.
   c. comparison and/or contrast.

8. The transition that signals the pattern of organization is ___*for example*___.

E. People are different from other primates, but not as different as they might like to think. It's true that that there are significant contrasts in size and proportion between humans and other primates. And, of course, humans are by far the more intelligent. Nevertheless, to use chimpanzees as an example, both they and humans have the same muscles and bones, located in almost the same places and working in nearly the same ways. The internal organs of both animals are also very much alike, as are their blood and other body fluids. Seen under a microscope, even their genes are strikingly similar.

9. The main pattern of organization of the selection is
   a. definition-example.
   b. cause-effect.
   (c.) comparison and/or contrast.

   different or
   contrasts or
   nevertheless or
   same or *alike* or

10. One transition that signals the pattern of organization is ___*similar*___.

Comments: Paragraph A discusses the *reasons* why the incomes of middle- and working-class Americans stagnated during the 1980s.

Paragraph B *contrasts* boys who physically mature early with their more slowly maturing peers.

Paragraph C discusses the *reasons* lightning makes such a loud sound.

Paragraph D *defines* and *illustrates* the either-or fallacy.

Paragraph E *compares* and *contrasts* people and other primates.

RELATIONSHIPS II: Test 3

A. (1–4.) Arrange the scrambled sentences below into a logical paragraph by numbering them *1*, *2*, *3*, and *4* in an order that makes sense. Then circle the letter of the primary pattern of organization used.

Note that transitions will help you by clarifying the relationships between sentences.

_3_ Also, high tuitions affect the amount of time available for studying; because loans and scholarships are hard to get, many students have to put in numerous hours at work in order to afford school.

_2_ For one thing, it undoubtedly prevents some students from attending college in the first place.

_4_ Finally, those who do manage to get loans know that they must begin their careers with large debts.

_1_ The high cost of college today causes problems for many students in more ways than one.

5. The primary pattern of organization is
    a. contrast.
    b. comparison.
    (c.) cause and effect.
    d. definition and example.

B. Men and women may interpret women's actions on a date very differently. One study found that acts such as speaking in a low voice or smiling were interpreted by men as indicating that the woman was interested in sex. Women, in contrast, tended to see the same behaviors as simply friendly. Drinking with a man, going to the man's apartment, or wearing sexy clothes were all seen by men as indicating a desire for sex, while women regarded these behaviors as appropriate or fashionable.

6. The main pattern of organization of the selection is
    a. definition-example.
    b. cause-effect.
    (c.) comparison and/or contrast.

7. One transition that signals the main pattern of organization is
    ___*differently* or *in contrast* or *while*___.

(Continues on next page)

C.   Mass hysteria is a type of group behavior that involves a widely held and contagious anxiety, usually as a result of a false belief. The reaction in part of the country to the radio broadcast of *The War of the Worlds* is one example. This dramatization of Martians landing on Earth was so realistic that people began to panic and flee before the realization set in that they were reacting to a radio play. The medieval witch-hunts are another good example of mass hysteria. They were based on the belief that witches were the cause of many problems in late medieval society, including natural disasters and illness. Those accused of being witches (mainly old women) were tortured until they confessed or they died. As many as 500,000 people were burned to death by the clergy between the fifteenth and seventeenth centuries.

8. The major supporting details of the selection are
   a. definitions.
   b. causes.
   c. comparisons.
   (d.) examples.

9. The main pattern of organization of the selection is
   (a.) definition-example.
   b. cause-effect.
   c. comparison and/or contrast.

10. The transition that signals the main pattern of organization is
    _____*example*_____ .

Comments: Paragraph A discusses the problems that *result from* the high cost of college.
Paragraph B *contrasts* men's and women's interpretations of women's actions on a date.
Paragraph C provides two *examples* of the term *defined*, "mass hysteria."

RELATIONSHIPS II: Test 4

A. (1–4.) Arrange the scrambled sentences below into a logical paragraph by numbering them *1, 2, 3,* and *4* in an order that makes sense. Then circle the letter of the primary pattern of organization used.

Note that transitions will help you by clarifying the relationships between sentences.

___4___ In contrast, the original Italian story is the gruesome tale of the Princess Talia, who falls into a deep magical sleep in the woods, where she is raped by a nobleman and, later on, gives birth to twins, whom the nobleman's wife tries to have killed and cooked for dinner.

___1___ It is often said that fairy tales, with their heavy doses of terror and violence, are too scary for young children.

___3___ Consider the story of Sleeping Beauty that today's children know, which involves a princess who is put to sleep by a wicked witch and then awakened by the kiss of her true love.

___2___ But today's versions of fairy tales are actually less frightening than the original stories.

5. The primary pattern of organization is
   a. list of items.
   b. comparison and/or contrast.
   c. cause and effect.
   d. definition and example.

B. Read each paragraph and answer the questions that follow.

A long sausage in a bun received the name "hot dog" in 1906 as the result of a cartoonist's poor spelling ability. A sausage vendor, Harry Stevens, sold what he called "dachshund sausages" (named after the short-legged dog) at New York City baseball games. During one of those games, newspaper cartoonist Tad Dorgan was in the audience. He sketched a cartoon of a live dachshund, smeared with mustard and folded into a bun. Not knowing how to spell "dachshund," however, he settled on "dog," giving the cartoon the caption "Get your hot dogs!" Once the cartoon was published in newspapers, readers began demanding their own "hot dogs."

6. The main idea is expressed in the
   a. first sentence.
   b. second sentence.
   c. last sentence.

(Continues on next page)

7. The selection mainly
   a. defines and illustrates the term "hot dog."
   (b.) gives the reason small sausages are now called hot dogs.
   c. contrasts "dachshund sausage" with "hot dog."

8. The transition that signals the main pattern of organization is
   _____*as the result*_____.

C. When a crowd is watching as someone threatens to jump from a building, its behavior seems affected by the time of day. In daylight, the crowd is usually quite quiet, but under the cover of darkness, many individual members will shout encouragement to the person to kill himself or herself. A similar reaction was seen when women college students took part in an experiment where they were asked to press a button to shock other volunteers. When the women pushing the buttons were visible to the victims, they administered only brief shocks. However, when they were allowed to wear gowns and masks that hid their identity, they shocked the volunteers twice as much. Clearly the feeling of being anonymous causes people to engage in antisocial behavior.

9–10. Two patterns of organization of the selection are *(circle two answers)*
   a. definition-example.
   (b.) cause-effect.
   (c.) comparison and/or contrast.

Comments: Paragraph A *contrasts* today's versions of fairy tales with the original stories.

Paragraph C discusses the *effects* of anonymity on people's behavior and *contrasts* the way people behave when they are not anonymous and when they are.

RELATIONSHIPS II: Test 5

A. Read the textbook paragraph below. Then answer the question and complete the outline that follows.

> There are several reasons why middle-aged adults are returning to school. Some want to learn to do their jobs better. College courses can help them improve their job skills and keep up in their fields. Others return to school because more credits may mean a raise or promotion. Teachers, for instance, get raises for reaching certain levels of education. Also, some adults return to the classroom because of interest in a new field, such as telecommunication or computer programming. Finally, others want to study subjects such as foreign languages, history, or literature for the sake of learning. Such classes help adults spend their time in more productive and interesting ways and deepen their understanding of themselves and their world.

1. The organizational patterns of the paragraph are list of items and
   a. definition-example.
   (b.) cause-effect.
   c. comparison and/or contrast.

2–5. Complete the outline of the paragraph by writing in the four major supporting details.

Main idea: There are several reasons why middle-aged adults are returning to school.

Major supporting details:

1. *Learn to do their jobs better* _____

2. *Get a raise or promotion* _____

3. *Interest in a new field* _____

4. *For the sake of learning* _____

Comment: Paragraph A *lists* the *reasons* why middle-aged adults are returning to school.

(Continues on next page)

B. Read the textbook paragraph below. Then answer the question and complete the map that follows.

> While management styles vary, there are certain factors that separate the good administrator from the poor one. A good manager anticipates problems and prepares for them, but a poor manager is often taken by surprise. The effective administrator makes changes to eliminate repeated problems; the less effective boss deals with one crisis at a time, never seeing patterns of problems. In addition, a good boss delegates work to others, while the poor one prefers to take on one extra task after another rather than train employees to do the work right. The effective administrator is also flexible enough to adapt to changing situations. In contrast, the poor one often clings to the old rules whether or not they apply.

6. The organizational patterns of the paragraph are list of items and
   a. definition-example.
   (b.) comparison and/or contrast.
   c. cause-effect.

7–10. Complete the map of the paragraph by writing in the missing supporting details.

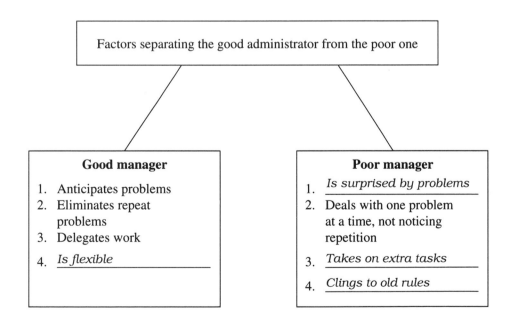

Factors separating the good administrator from the poor one

Good manager
1. Anticipates problems
2. Eliminates repeat problems
3. Delegates work
4. *Is flexible*

Poor manager
1. *Is surprised by problems*
2. Deals with one problem at a time, not noticing repetition
3. *Takes on extra tasks*
4. *Clings to old rules*

Comment: Paragraph B *lists* the *contrasting* factors that separate the good administrator from the poor one.

RELATIONSHIPS II: Test 6

A. Read the textbook paragraph below. Then answer the question and complete the outline that follows.

> One researcher has identified five basic causes of frustration above and beyond daily hassles. Delays are hard for us to accept because our culture stresses the value of time. Anyone who has been caught in a traffic jam is familiar with the frustration of delay. Lack of resources is especially frustrating to low-income Americans, who cannot afford the new cars or vacations that TV programs and magazine articles would have us believe everyone must have. Losses, such as the end of a love affair or a cherished friendship, are frustrating because they often make us feel helpless, unimportant, and worthless. Failure is a frequent source of frustration in our competitive society. The aspect of failure that is hardest to cope with is guilt. We imagine that if we had done certain things differently, we might have succeeded, and so we feel responsible for our own or someone else's pain and disappointment. Discrimination can also be a source of frustration. Being denied opportunities or recognition simply because of one's sex, age, religion, or skin color, regardless of one's personal qualifications or accomplishments, is immensely frustrating.

1. The organizational patterns of the paragraph are list of items and
   a. definition-example.
   b. comparison and/or contrast.
   (c.) cause-effect.

2–6. Complete the outline of the passage by writing in the five major supporting details.

Main idea: There are five causes of frustration above and beyond daily hassles.

Major supporting details:

1. _Delays_ _____

2. _Lack of resources_ _____

3. _Losses_ _____

4. _Failure_ _____

5. _Discrimination_ _____

Comment: Paragraph A *lists* five basic causes of frustration above and beyond daily hassles.

(Continues on next page)

B. Read the textbook paragraph below. Then answer the question and complete the map that follows.

Role conflict is a situation in which the different roles an individual is expected to play make incompatible demands. A working mother provides one example. In meeting the requirements of a full-time job, she automatically violates the expectation that a mother will put her children's needs before everything else. In meeting the cultural demands of motherhood (staying home if the child is sick, attending school plays) she automatically violates the requirements of a nine-to-five job. A priest provides another example. He is expected to treat confessions as strictly confidential. But a priest, like any other citizen, has responsibilities toward the community. What should he do if a parishioner confesses that he has commited several rapes and cannot control his behavior? In living up to one role expectation (confidentiality), the priest violates another (community responsibility). The key point here is that the difficulties the individuals in these positions experience—the feelings of conflict, inadequacy, and anguish—are not of their own making. They are built into their roles.

7. The main pattern of organization of the passage is
a. cause and effect.
(b.) definition and example.

8–10. Complete the map of the passage. In doing so, you will need to summarize the main idea and the two supporting details.

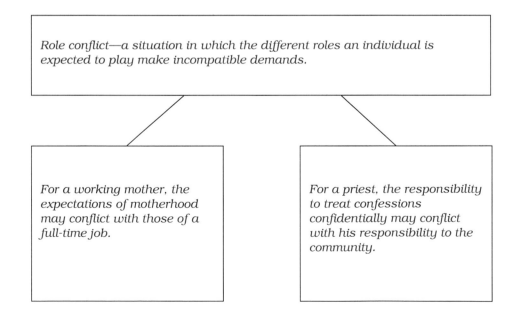

Role conflict—a situation in which the different roles an individual is expected to play make incompatible demands.

For a working mother, the expectations of motherhood may conflict with those of a full-time job.

For a priest, the responsibility to treat confessions confidentially may conflict with his responsibility to the community.

Comment: Paragraph B *defines* and *illustrates* the term "role conflict."

7
Fact and Opinion

On the television police drama *Dragnet*, whenever witnesses began to speak emotionally or to give their own theories, the hero, Sergeant Joe Friday, would ask for "just the facts." He wanted neutral, unbiased information—the kind that can be proven true or false—rather than a witness's interpretation of what happened.

The kind of information Sergeant Friday preferred, however, isn't easy to come by. When most speakers and writers communicate, they include their opinions of a subject. What they say is therefore at least partly biased.

While bias is often unavoidable, many writers do try to remain as objective as possible. News articles and scientific reports are examples of writing in which authors try to be as factual as they can. However, opinions are central to other types of materials, such as editorials, political speeches, and advertisements. Writers of these materials try to persuade readers who have different viewpoints to change their minds.

Both facts and opinions can be valuable to readers, but knowing the difference between the two is important in evaluating what is read. Thus, like Sgt. Friday, skilled readers must be able to distinguish fact from opinion.

Sorting out facts from opinions is something you do already, perhaps without even realizing it. For example, imagine a friend saying, "I saw a science-fiction movie last night about aliens invading Earth. The special effects were great; the aliens looked like reptiles—they had green skin and forked tongues. The acting was terrible, though." Hearing this description, you would probably realize that your friend's comments are a mixture of fact and opinion.

FACT

A **fact** is information that can be proved true through objective evidence. This evidence may be physical proof or the spoken or written testimony of witnesses. In the friend's comments about the movie, the facts are that it was about aliens invading Earth and that the aliens had green skin and forked tongues. If you wanted to, you could check the truth of these statements by questioning other witnesses or watching the movie yourself.

Following are some more facts—they can be checked for accuracy and thus proven true.

Fact: The Quad Tower is the tallest building in this city.

(A researcher could go out and, through inspection, confirm that the building is the tallest.)

Fact: Albert Einstein willed his violin to his grandson.

(This statement can be checked in historical publications or with Einstein's estate.)

Fact: The New York Yankees won the 1996 World Series in six games.

(Anyone can check sports records to confirm this.)

OPINION

An **opinion** is a belief, judgment, or conclusion that cannot be objectively proved true. As a result, it is open to question. Your friend, for instance, said that the movie's special effects were great and that the acting was terrible. These statements may be reasonable ones with which other people would agree, but they cannot be objectively proven. They are opinions. You might see the movie and reach very different conclusions.

Here are some more opinions:

Opinion: The Quad Tower is the ugliest building in the city.

(There's no way to prove this statement because two people can look at the same building and come to different conclusions about its beauty. "Ugly" is a **value word**, a word we use to express a value judgment. Value words are signals that an opinion is being expressed. By their very nature, these words represent opinions, not facts.)

Opinion: Einstein should have willed his violin to a museum.

(Who says? Not his grandson. This is an opinion.)

Opinion: The 1996 New York Yankees were the best team in the history of baseball.

(Whether something is "best" is always debatable. *Best* is another value word.)

Writing Facts and Opinions

To get a better sense of fact and opinion, take a few minutes to write three facts about yourself and then to write three of your opinions. Here, for example, are three facts about me and three of my opinions.

Three facts about me:

- I am six feet tall.
- I do my writing on a Macintosh computer.
- I have two sisters and one wife.

Three of my opinions:

- Schools should require students to do a great deal of reading.
- The education writer Jonathan Kozol is a true American hero.
- The most important issue our country faces today is helping people find decent jobs.

Now write your facts and opinions in the space below.

Three facts about you:

- _____
  _____
- _____
  _____
- _____
  _____

Three of your opinions:

- _____
  _____
- _____
  _____
- _____
  _____

FACT AND OPINION IN READING

To further sharpen your understanding of fact and opinion, read the following statements and decide whether each is fact or opinion. Put an **F** (for "fact") or an **O** (for "opinion") beside each statement. Put **F+O** beside the one statement that is a mixture of fact *and* opinion.

_____ 1. My brother Gary is very handsome.

_____ 2. Last night, a tree outside our house was struck by lightning.

_____ 3. Installing a new sink is an easy job for the do-it-yourselfer.

_____ 4. Richard Nixon was the worst president our country ever had.

_____ 5. Ostriches do not hide their heads in the sand.

_____ 6. It's a fact that the best of the fifty states to live in is Hawaii.

_____ 7. The Grimm brothers collected their fairy tales from other storytellers.

_____ 8. There is nothing like a bottle of Coca-Cola to satisfy thirst.

_____ 9. In the late 1890s, when Coke was first sold, it included a small amount of cocaine, which was then legal.

_____ 10. One of the most delicious of soft drinks, Coca-Cola was first intended to cure various ills, including headaches.

Explanations:

1. This is an opinion. You may like the way your brother looks (maybe because he looks so much like you), but other people might not find him so attractive. The word *handsome* is a value word.

2. This is a statement of fact. You and your family might have seen or heard the lightning strike, or you could go outside later and see the type of damage done to the tree.

3. This is an opinion. The word *easy* suggests that a judgment is being made. What might be an easy job for one person might be an impossible challenge for another.

4. This is an opinion. Not everyone would evaluate Richard Nixon's performance in this way. Here the value word *worst* shows us that a judgment is being expressed.

5. This is a fact (contrary to popular opinion) which can be checked through observation and reports of observations.

6. This is an opinion. Just saying that something is a fact doesn't make it so. Different people will judge locations very differently.

7. This is a fact. It can be confirmed through the Grimms' writings and through research on the background of their stories.

8. This is an opinion. Many people might prefer cold water or some other drink as a thirst-quencher.

9. All the details here are facts that can be looked up and confirmed in historical records.

10. The first part of the statement is an opinion—not everyone would consider Coke to be one of the most delicious of soft drinks. The second part of the statement is a fact that could be confirmed by researching historical records of the time.

➣ Practice 1

Some of the statements below are facts, and some are opinions. Label facts with an **F** and opinions with an **O**. Remember that facts can be proven, but opinions give personal views.

_F_ 1. Novels by Dean R. Koontz include *Watchers*, *Intensity*, and *The Bad Place*.

_O_ 2. *Watchers*, by Dean R. Koontz, is a terrifying story that is bound to keep you awake at night.

_F_ 3. A Colorado farmer wrote to the car maker Henry Ford asking to exchange six mounted moose heads for a new car.

_O_ 4. Henry Ford was wrong when he claimed that laziness and idleness cause most of the world's troubles.

_O_ 5. Touching other people is an important part of being human.

_F_ 6. Studies show that in the United States the amount of touching usually decreases with age. For example, parents touch their older children less often than their younger ones.

_O_ 7. There's no illness harder to cope with than depression.

_F_ 8. Depression is most common among persons between the ages of 25 and 44.

_F_ 9. More Bibles have been printed than any other book in history.

_O_ 10. The Roman Catholic concept of God is more correct than the Protestant or the Jewish view.

Other Points About Fact and Opinion

There are several added points to keep in mind when separating fact from opinion.

1　Statements of fact may be found to be untrue.

Suppose you went to the science-fiction movie your friend spoke of and discovered the aliens actually had blue rather than green skin. (Perhaps your friend is color-blind.) His statement would then be an error, not a fact. It is not unusual for evidence to show that a "fact" is not really true. It was once considered to be a fact that the world was flat, for example, but that "fact" turned out to be an error.

2　Opinions may be masked as facts.

People sometimes present their opinions as facts, as shown in sentence 6 on page 224. Here are two more examples:

In point of fact, neither candidate for the mayor's office is well-qualified.

The truth of the matter is that frozen foods taste as good as fresh foods.

Despite the words to the contrary, the above are not statements of fact but statements of opinion.

3　Remember that value words often represent opinions. Here are examples of value words:

Value Words

best	great	beautiful
worst	terrible	bad
better	lovely	good
worse	disgusting	wonderful

Value words often express judgments—they are generally subjective, not objective. While factual statements report on observed reality, subjective statements interpret reality. For example, the observation that it is raining outside is an objective one. The statement that the weather is bad, however, is subjective, an interpretation of reality. (Some people consider rain to be good weather.)

4　The words *should* and *ought to* often signal opinions. Those words introduce what people think should, or ought to, be done. Other people will think other things ought to be done.

Couples should definitely not live together before marriage.

Couples ought to live together before getting married to be sure they are compatible.

5   Finally, remember that much of what we read and hear is a mixture of fact and opinion.

Recognizing facts and opinions is important because much information that sounds factual is really opinion. A political candidate, for example, may say, "My record is outstanding." Voters would be wise to wonder what the value word *outstanding* means to this candidate. Or an advertisement may claim that a particular automobile is "the most economical car on the road today," a statement that at first seems factual. But what is meant by *economical*? If the car offers the most miles per gallon but the worst record for expensive repairs, you might not agree that it's economical.

➤ *Practice 2*

Some of the statements below are facts, and some are opinions; in addition, three include fact and opinion. Label facts with an **F**, opinions with an **O**, and statements of fact *and* opinion with an **F+O**.

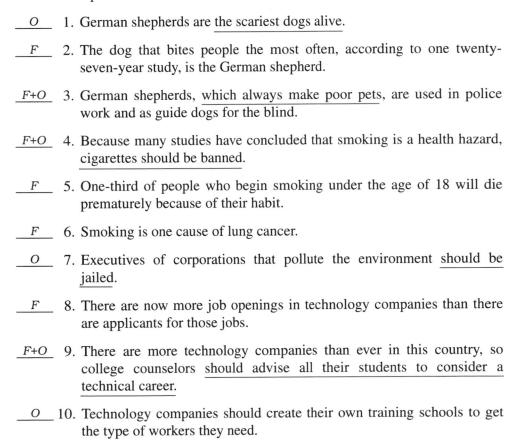

    O   1. German shepherds are the scariest dogs alive.

    F   2. The dog that bites people the most often, according to one twenty-seven-year study, is the German shepherd.

   F+O   3. German shepherds, which always make poor pets, are used in police work and as guide dogs for the blind.

   F+O   4. Because many studies have concluded that smoking is a health hazard, cigarettes should be banned.

    F   5. One-third of people who begin smoking under the age of 18 will die prematurely because of their habit.

    F   6. Smoking is one cause of lung cancer.

    O   7. Executives of corporations that pollute the environment should be jailed.

    F   8. There are now more job openings in technology companies than there are applicants for those jobs.

   F+O   9. There are more technology companies than ever in this country, so college counselors should advise all their students to consider a technical career.

    O   10. Technology companies should create their own training schools to get the type of workers they need.

Comment: The judgment words in the six items that contain opinions are underlined.

➤ *Practice 3*

A. Here are short descriptions taken from a restaurant guide. Some descriptions present only factual information; others contain opinions as well. Identify the three factual descriptions with an **F** and the two descriptions that include both fact *and* opinion with an **F+O**.

  F   1. **Dunkin Donuts.** 480 Hamilton Street. Coffee, donuts, soup, and more. Eat in or take out.

  F   2. **Country Club Diner.** Railroad Place and Exchange Street. Sandwiches to full meals. Soups and desserts made daily. Private room for small parties.

  F+O 3. **Fratelli's.** 107 Main Street. <u>Fine</u> Italian dining, with homemade pastas, veal, chicken, and seafood. <u>Tempting</u> desserts include ricotta cheesecake.

  F   4. **Wing Tai Oriental Restaurant.** 284 Bishop Street. Chinese cuisine. Full service restaurant and lunch buffet. Take-out also.

  F+O 5. **Mel's Bar and Grill.** Route 14 South. Popular menu features steak, lobster, pasta, veal, chicken, and brick-oven pizza. Free valet parking, live entertainment. <u>Upscale but affordable.</u> Selection of 35 <u>fine</u> wines.

B. Here are short reviews taken from a newspaper movie guide. Some reviews present only facts; others contain opinions about the movie as well. Identify the two factual reviews with an **F** and the three reviews that include both fact and the reviewer's opinion with an **F+O**.

  F   6. **Room Service, '38.** The Marx Brothers, Lucille Ball. A penniless theatrical producer and his aides fake the measles to keep from being kicked out of a hotel.

  F+O 7. **Born Free, '66.** Virginia McKenna, Bill Travers. <u>Touching</u> story of a pet lioness trained to live in the wilds of Kenya. <u>Good</u> family viewing.

  F+O 8. **Chinatown, '74.** Jack Nicholson, Faye Dunaway. One of the few <u>undisputed classics</u> of the '70s, a <u>near-perfect thriller</u>. Nicholson is great as the half-boiled private eye, Dunaway is <u>suitably mysterious</u> as "The Woman," and the score is <u>hypnotic</u>.

  F   9. **Cocoon, '85.** Don Ameche, Wilford Brimley. Residents of a Florida retirement home find a fountain of youth in an abandoned swimming pool supercharged with an alien life force.

  F+O 10. **Mother, '97.** Albert Brooks, Debbie Reynolds. A <u>moving</u> comedy about a twice-divorced writer who returns to his mother's home to figure out his problems with women. Reynolds plays the mother of all mothers in a performance <u>that you won't easily forget.</u>

Comment: The judgment words in the items that contain opinions are underlined.

Facts and Opinions in Passages

People tend to accept what they read as fact, but much of what is written is actually opinion. Keeping an eye out for opinion will help you to think for yourself and to question what you read.

Two sentences in the following passage are facts, two are opinions, and one combines fact and opinion. Read the passage, and identify facts with an **F**, opinions with an **O**, and the statement of fact *and* opinion with an **F+O**. Then read the explanation that follows.

[1]There were several queens of Egypt by the name of Cleopatra, including the one who ruled in the days of Antony and Caesar. [2]She is one of the most interesting figures in Egyptian history. [3]History records that she was born in 69 B.C. and killed herself almost forty years later. [4]The story of how she killed herself is very easy to believe. [5]Reports say she killed herself with an asp, the Egyptian cobra—a symbol of Egyptian royalty, so there could have been no better way for the queen to end her life.

1. _____   2. _____   3. _____   4. _____   5. _____

Explanation:

Sentence 1 contains facts set down in historical records. Sentence 2 expresses an opinion—some may feel Cleopatra is not one of the most interesting figures in Egyptian history. Sentence 3 contains more facts of history. Sentence 4 contains an opinion—how easy something is to believe will differ from person to person. The last sentence is a mixture of fact and opinion: The beginning parts of the sentence are facts, but what the best way would have been for Cleopatra to end her life is certainly a matter of opinion.

➤ *Practice 4*

A. The following passage contains five sentences. Two sentences are facts, two are opinions, and one combines fact and opinion. Identify the facts with an **F**, the opinions with an **O**, and the statement of fact *and* opinion with an **F+O**.

[1]Plants that people call weeds are often undeserving of such a negative name. [2]Ralph Waldo Emerson had the right idea—he once described a weed as "a plant whose virtues have not yet been discovered." [3]Clearly, weeds aren't always so bad. [4]For example, they can replenish depleted topsoil with minerals. [5]Also, some plants that are called weeds are edible and contain vitamins.

1. _O_   2. _F+O_   3. _O_   4. _F_   5. _F_

B. The following newspaper editorial contains five sentences. Three sentences are facts, and two combine fact and opinion. Identify the facts with an **F** and the statements of fact *and* opinion with an **F+O**.

[1]Currently, about half of all three- to five-year-olds in the United States are enrolled in preschool programs, including Head Start, school-based prekindergarten programs, nursery schools, and child care. [2]A task force of the Carnegie Corporation has now recommended that almost all children be enrolled in a preschool program at age 3 to improve their prospects for success in school. [3]The task force estimates that 75 percent of the funding for existing early-education services can be provided by families. [4]It is regrettable that the task force did not suggest who should pay the rest of the bill. [5]As a result, while the task force calls for immediate action, its proposal should be seen as a long-term goal that deserves serious study by policymakers and parents.

1. ___*F*___   2. ___*F*___   3. ___*F*___   4. ___*F+O*___   5. ___*F+O*___

➤ Practice 5

Here are excerpts from four book reviews. Identify the two factual descriptions with an **F** and the two descriptions that include both fact *and* the reviewer's opinion with an **F+O**.

___*F*___ 1. In *The Kindness of Strangers*, journalist Mike McIntyre describes his journey hitchiking across America without any money. Every city and every ride gave him stories. He ate dinner with a lady firefighter who used to be a man, shared self-defense tips with a biker-turned-minister, and ate soybeans with a guy who drove a white Cadillac. He traveled 4,223 miles, through 14 states, 82 rides, 78 meals, 5 loads of laundry, and one round of golf. People offered him money, food, hotel rooms, a tent. McIntyre noted that in most cases the poorest people were the ones who provided the most help.

___*F+O*___ 2. *Charlotte's Web*, one of the best-known books in children's literature, is loved by adults as well as children. This imaginative story by E. B.White centers on the barnyard life of a young pig who is to be butchered in the fall. The animals of the yard (especially a haughty gray spider named Charlotte) plan with the farmer's daughter to save the pig's life. While the author incorporates much humor into his story, he also skillfully blends a wise sadness into his themes of friendship and the cycle of life. This is a book that should not be missed.

___F___ 3. *Amazing Grace*, by Jonathan Kozol, is a book about children who grow up in the South Bronx—one of the poorest congressional districts in the United States. The children speak about the poverty and racial isolation that they experience. One fourth of the childbearing women in the neighborhoods where these children live test positive for HIV. Pediatric AIDS, deadly fires, and gang rivalries contribute to a high death rate. The book introduces us to Alice Washington, a mother of two in her late forties, separated from a husband who beat her and infected her with AIDS. We also meet her son, David, a high-school senior who cooks and cleans for his mother, who cares for her when she is ill, and who during the course of the book is admitted to college.

___F+O___ 4. In his book *Amazing Grace*, Jonathan Kozol brings us face to face with the daily lives and seemingly endless struggles of the people who live in Mott Haven, a desperately poor neighborhood in the South Bronx. The book reminds us that the residents, like those in poor communities throughout the country, are not a breed apart but human beings like the rest of us, with feelings and needs and hopes and dreams for their children. As human beings they have the right in this wealthy country to adequate shelter and food. They have the right to accessible health care and education that will enable them to survive in the twenty-first century. This is a painful and necessary book to read at an increasingly cold hour of our nation's history.

A Note on Informed Opinion

In much of what we read, the distinction between fact and opinion is not nearly as clear-cut as in the practice materials in this chapter. But the chapter has helped you to begin looking at information with the questioning eye necessary to being a critical reader.

As you question what you read, remember that just because something is an opinion doesn't mean it isn't valid. Opinions are fundamental to much of our lives (democracy is the best form of government, everyone should receive basic health care, etc.). However, look for realistic, meaningful support for opinions. Solid support is often made up of facts based on direct observation, expert opinion, and research. Textbook authors, in particular, work very hard to back up their opinions with such factual support.

The textbook passage on the next page is an example. One sentence represents an opinion. The rest of the passage is made up of facts used in support of that opinion. Somebody with an opposite view would choose very different information to support his or her opinion. Which sentence presents the author's opinion? Write its number in the space provided.

Sentence with the opinion: _____

> ¹Crime is probably one of the urban problems that the average citizen thinks most about. ²Although crime can be found in suburbs and rural areas, it is more common in cities. ³The rate of violent crime is eight times greater in our largest cities than it is in rural areas; the rate of property crimes is four times greater. ⁴The greatest disparity is for robbery, which is at least forty-five times greater in large cities than in rural areas! ⁵Also, the larger the city, the higher the crime rate. ⁶And suburban areas have lower crime rates than all but the smallest cities.

Explanation:

> Sentences 2–6 present facts that are based on statistics. The first sentence, however, represents the author's opinion (as suggested by the word *probably*). He assumes that since crime is common in cities, it is likely to be one of the urban problems that the average citizen thinks most about. You may agree with that opinion, or you may feel that the average citizen, while cautious about crime, tries not to think about it much.

➤ Review Test 1

To review what you've learned in this chapter, complete each of the following sentences about facts and opinions.

1. *(A fact, An opinion)* _____ *A fact* _____ can be proven true through objective evidence.

2. *(An editorial, A political speech, A news report)* _____ *A news report* _____ is likely to be totally factual.

3. Most of what we read is *(fact, opinion, a mixture of fact and opinion)* _____ *a mixture of fact and opinion* _____.

4. *(Facts, Opinions)* _____ *Opinions* _____ often include words that express judgments.

5. An example of a value word would be *(rectangular, objective, enjoyable, tall, wet, full, rounded)* _____ *enjoyable* _____.

➤ *Review Test 2*

A. Two of the statements below are facts, and two are opinions. Identify facts with an **F** and opinions with an **O**.

  _O_   1. A bouquet of red roses is the best possible Mother's Day gift.

  _F_   2. Roses have been found in dry bouquets in ancient Egyptian tombs.

  _F_   3. At the turn of the century, only one of ten married women held a paying job.

  _O_   4. For self-fulfillment, any mother in today's world should hold down an outside job as well as care for her children.

B. Here are short reviews taken from a movie guide. Identify the factual review with an **F** and the reviews that include both a factual report *and* an opinion with an **F+O**.

  _F_   5. **My Mom's a Werewolf, '89.** Susan Blakely, John Saxon. Bitten on the toe by a pet-shop owner, a woman turns into a werewolf.

  _F+O_   6. **Witness for the Prosecution, '58.** Tyrone Power, Marlene Dietrich. Agatha Christie's nail-biter about a London murder trial, directed by the matchless Billy Wilder. Superb acting by Power as the accused and Dietrich as his wife.

  _F+O_   7. **Braveheart, '95.** Mel Gibson. Big, booming epic tale of the thirteenth-century Scottish rebel warrior William Wallace. Manages to tell a gripping personal story that grows in scale through a series of eye-popping and bloody battle scenes. A powerful, passionate film.

  _F+O_   8. **101 Dalmatians, '96.** Glenn Close. It's supposed to be *about* dogs; it's not supposed to *be* a dog. Disappointing live-action remake of the Disney animated classic.

C. Here are excerpts from two book reviews. Identify the factual description with an **F** and the description that includes both fact *and* opinion with an **F+O**.

_F_ 9. Frank McCourt, who taught writing for many years in the public school system, waited more than forty years to tell the story of his childhood in his book *Angela's Ashes*. McCourt had a father who drank away the family's food money, and a mother who thus felt she had to beg to feed her family. The McCourts were too poor to afford sheets or blankets for their flea-infested bed, too poor to buy new shoes for the children, too poor to get milk for the new baby. By 11, Frank was the chief breadwinner for the family, stealing bread and milk so the family would have something to eat. By 15, he lost his first girlfriend to tuberculosis. By 19, he saved enough money to make his escape from Ireland to the United States.

_F+O_ 10. David Guterson's *Snow Falling on Cedars* is a murder mystery like no other, a haunting examination of the nature of prejudice, of forgiveness, and of the fierceness of pride. The story is set in the 1950s in an island community on Puget Sound. When one fisherman is found dead on his boat, another fisherman, a Japanese-American, is quickly blamed for the death. The accused man is so proud that he refuses to defend himself for a crime he says he did not commit. Convinced that the truth will speak for itself, he sits silent in his jail cell. Guterson builds the drama with gripping tension, and at the same time his story becomes a celebration of the mystery and wonder of the human heart.

➤ *Review Test 3*

A. Some of the statements below are facts, and some are opinions; in addition, two include both fact and opinion. Identify facts with an **F**, opinions with an **O**, and statements of fact *and* opinion with an **F+O**.

_F_ 1. My son once left half a sandwich under his bed for more than a week.

_O_ 2. My son is the most considerate person in our family.

_F+O_ 3. Although my son got a B in English this semester, he deserved an A.

_F_ 4. New York City is not the capital of New York State.

_F+O_ 5. New York City, where visitors can see Broadway plays, museums, and the Statue of Liberty, is the perfect place for a summer vacation.

_O_ 6. The Empire State Building is easily the most memorable of all the sights in New York.

_F_ 7. Elephants are the largest of all land animals.

_F_ 8. Researchers have found that elephants react nervously to rabbits and dachshunds, but not to mice.

_O_ 9. Maybe the lively scampering of the rabbits and dachshunds is what makes elephants nervous.

_F+O_ 10. Because they use their trunks both to clean themselves and to eat, elephants are the most fascinating animals in the zoo.

B. (11–20.) Each passage below contains five sentences. Two are facts, two are opinions, and one combines fact and opinion. Identify facts with an **F**, opinions with an **O**, and statements of fact *and* opinion with an **F+O**.

1. [1]There are few problems more annoying problems than hiccups, which can last for hours or even days. [2]According to one doctor who has studied them, hiccups are usually caused by eating or drinking too quickly. [3]People do some pretty strange things to remedy this ridiculous problem. [4]Some common remedies include holding your breath, eating a teaspoon of sugar, and putting a paper bag over your head. [5]Undoubtedly, that last one is the strangest one of all.

   1. _F+O_   2. _F_   3. _O_   4. _F_   5. _O_

2. [1]The Lincoln Memorial is surely America's best loved public monument. [2]Designed by Henry Beacon, it was dedicated on Memorial Day, 1922, more than fifty years after a memorial to Lincoln was first proposed. [3]Built to resemble a Greek temple, it contains a seated figure of Lincoln by sculptor Daniel Chester French. [4]Many people probably learn to admire the monument long before they visit it in person through seeing its picture, which is on the penny and the five-dollar bill. [5]All Americans must feel pride mingled with sorrow when they come to Washington in person and look up at the kindly, mournful face of Abraham Lincoln.

   1. _O_   2. _F_   3. _F_   4. _F+O_   5. _O_

➤ *Review Test 4*

Here is a chance to apply your understanding of facts and opinions to a full article. The selection will help you think about how much other people's expectations can influence your behavior.

To help you continue to strengthen your skills, the reading is followed by questions not only on what you've learned in this chapter but also on what you've learned in previous chapters.

Words to Watch

Below are some words in the reading that do not have strong context support. Each word is followed by the number of the paragraph in which it appears and its meaning there. These words are indicated in the article by a small circle (°).

randomly (7): without choosing in any particular way
incredibly (8): unbelievably
critical (12): of key importance; crucial
determinant (14): a factor that contributes to an effect

HOW PEOPLE RISE—AND FALL— TO EXPECTATIONS OF OTHERS

Darrell Sifford

1   I was at the seashore, listening to a radio station that plays big-band music, and I couldn't believe what I was hearing—not big-band music, but an announcement about a dance to which parents, it said, should be certain to direct their adolescents.

2   It was a fine idea for a dance, the announcer said, because it would bring peace of mind to the parents whose children attended. When everybody arrived, shortly after 7 on a Saturday night, the doors would be locked—yes, locked—and nobody would be permitted to leave until 10, when the dance would end and parents could pick up their children. There would be no need for parents to worry about liquor, drugs,

fights or undesirable people. Responsible adults would be there to supervise things, which would be safe and secure. Not to worry. Just bring your child and enjoy your Saturday night.

3   You understand—don't you?—why I couldn't believe what I heard. Can you imagine that, at this date, anybody still believes that it's prudent for parents to announce to their children that they don't trust them and that the only way they— the parents—can relax is to know that their children are locked up? Yes, safe and secure. Not to worry.

4   I wonder what the parents will do when their children go off to college.

5   It is so well established that it's beyond serious challenge, that people

tend to rise—or drop—to the expectations of others who are important in their lives.

6   Psychologist Kevin Leman has told me all about learning tracks. Children who are in the so-called Eagle reading class know that they're expected to do better, that they're considered brighter than everybody else—and, as a result, they consistently perform better. They're merely equaling what is expected of them. On the other hand, those in the Crow reading class know that they're expected to fumble and bumble, that they're considered somewhat slow in the head. And they don't disappoint those who have communicated their lack of high expectation.

7   There was an experiment that has become a legend in education—about a teacher who randomly° placed some students on a fast track and told them that they belonged there, and some students on a slow track and told them that they belonged there. The stated expectation carried more weight than the students' intelligence, because nearly all of them performed as they had been told they would—and should.

8   Psychiatrist Spurgeon English once told me during an interview that children tend to equal expectations in just about everything—not just educationally, but behaviorally. A child who constantly is told by parents that he is good and worthwhile acts that way. A child who constantly is told that he's no good acts that way, too. After that, things rapidly go downhill, and parents, incredibly°, scratch their heads and wonder what's wrong with the child.

9   To a great extent, it works the same way with adults, too. We tend to equal expectations, good or bad, high or low. During a football season when Mike Ditka was the head coach of the Chicago Bears, he announced at a news conference after a disappointing loss that his team was so inept that it probably wouldn't win another game all year. It would surprise him, said Ditka, if the players had enough inside them to win again.

10   True to Ditka's expectation, the rest of the season was a disaster. The Bears unquestionably were the most disappointing team in the National Football League. What happened? During an interview after the season had ended, the Bears' all-pro line-backer, Mike Singletary, explained it this way:

11   "We have a lot of young kids on this team, and if they're told often enough that they're not any good, they begin to believe it—and that's how they play."

12   Of course, it can work the other way, too. One of the many things I admired about Whitey Herzog, former manager of the St. Louis Cardinals baseball team, was how he handled many of his young players who had just been called up from the minor leagues. Time and time again he would throw them into critical° games—an inexperienced kid would be assigned to pitch in the heat of a pennant race—and time and time again, the inexperienced kid would deliver. Why? I like to think that it was because they wanted to equal Herzog's expectation that they were good enough to be Cardinals, that they belonged there.

13   Within marriage, expectations tend to be fulfilled, too. If you expect your spouse to treat you fairly—and if this is conveyed to the spouse—there is greater likelihood of your getting fair treatment. If you expect your spouse to cheat—and communicate this expectation through your actions—there is greater likelihood that your spouse will cheat.

14   At work, the boss who expects the people in his department to perform well consistently outshines the boss who expects his people to perform poorly. A few years ago, psychologist Alan Loy McGinnis, in his book *Bringing Out the Best in People*, listed expectation, clearly communicated to employees, as a key determinant° in how they performed.

15   Professional athletes, married people, workers—all of us, I am convinced—are captives of expectation. That's just the way people are.

16   I found myself thinking for days about the announcement of the lockup dance. Who—what youngster—would go to a lockup dance? I suspect that only those whose parents forced them to go—so they, the parents, could have a night off, free of worry. My guess is that someday, the parents might find that they had paid a high price for their nights off.

17   What do you think?

Reading Comprehension Questions

Vocabulary in Context

1. In the sentence below, the word *inept* means
   a. quiet.
   (b.) unskilled.
   c. underweight.
   d. unpopular.

   "Mike Ditka . . . announced . . . that his team was so inept that it probably wouldn't win another game all year." (Paragraph 9)

Central Point and Main Ideas

2. The central point of the article is stated in paragraph
   a. 1.
   b. 3.
   (c.) 5.
   d. 6.

3. The main idea of paragraph 13 is best expressed in its
   (a.) first sentence.
   b. second sentence.
   c. third sentence.

Supporting Details

4. According to Sifford, people are influenced by what is expected of them by
   a. spouses.
   b. bosses.
   c. both of the above.   See paragraphs 9–11, 12, 13, and 14.
   d. neither of the above.

Transitions

5. *Complete the sentence:* The contrast transition in paragraph 6 is
   _____*on the other hand*_____.

6. The relationship expressed in the sentence below is one of
   a. comparison.
   b. example.
   c. contrast.
   d. cause and effect.

   "If you expect your spouse to treat you fairly—and if this is conveyed to the spouse—there is greater likelihood of your getting fair treatment." (Paragraph 13)

Patterns of Organization

7. The article
   a. narrates a series of events in a time order.
   b. discusses a certain type of cause and effect.
   c. presents a definition with examples.

Fact and Opinion

8. The article is
   a. almost all fact.
   b. almost all opinion.
   c. a mix of fact and opinion.

9. Paragraph 7 is primarily
   a. fact.
   b. opinion.

10. In the last two sentences of paragraph 16, the author expresses
    a. facts about parents.
    b. his opinions.

Comments: Item 6—*Cause:* the communicated expectation of being treated fairly
Effect: greater likelihood of getting fair treatment
Item 7—*Cause:* expectations of people important in our lives
Effect: living up to those expectations

Discussion Questions

1. It is well known, writes Sifford, "that people tend to rise—or drop—to the expectations of others who are important in their lives." Whose high expectations of you have encouraged the best in you? In what ways? Do you know anyone (including yourself) who has been influenced by low expectations?

2. Sifford tells about the experiment in which a teacher randomly placed students of varying intelligence on the fast and slow tracks. Most students performed "as they had been told they would—and should." How can you explain the fact that students of ordinary intelligence were able to perform like superior students?

3. For various reasons, family and friends are sometimes unable or unwilling to expect the best in us. How can we have high expectations for ourselves even when there's nobody else around expecting much of us? Can you think of any good examples from your own or someone else's life?

4. Can you think of any way you can put the principle of high expectations to work positively in your life or the life of someone you know—at home, at work, or at school?

Check Your Performance   FACT AND OPINION

Activity	Number Right	Points		Score
Review Test 1 (5 items)	_____	x 2	=	_____
Review Test 2 (10 items)	_____	x 3	=	_____
Review Test 3 (20 items)	_____	x 1.5	=	_____
Review Test 4 (10 items)	_____	x 3	=	_____
		TOTAL SCORE	=	_____%

Enter your total score into the **Reading Performance Chart: Review Tests** on the inside back cover.

FACT AND OPINION: Test 1

A. Five of the statements below are facts, and five are opinions. Identify statements of fact with an **F** and statements of opinion with an **O**.

___F___ 1. In 1924, the Model T Ford could be purchased for $290.

___O___ 2. The Model T was the most significant invention of the first half of this century.

___O___ 3. By 2010, electric cars and small family helicopters will be in common use.

___F___ 4. The core of a pencil is made out of graphite and clay, not lead.

___O___ 5. It's good luck to find a double yolk in an egg.

___F___ 6. A hen in Russia once laid an egg that had nine double yolks.

___O___ 7. Masses of flowers all in one color are more attractive than plantings of two or more colors.

___F___ 8. Jay Leno became official host of *The Tonight Show* in 1992.

___O___ 9. Jay Leno is the greatest talk-show host of them all.

___F___ 10. Baltimore's traffic lights were designed with the color-blind in mind— green lights have a vertical shape, and red ones are horizontal.

B. Here are short reviews taken from a newspaper movie guide. Some reviews provide only factual reports; others contain opinions about the movie as well. Identify the factual reviews with an **F**; identify reviews that also contain the reviewer's opinion with an **F+O**.

___F+O___ 11. **Treasure Island, '50.** Bobby Driscoll, Robert Newton. Walt Disney changes the ending of Stevenson's novel, and everything is prettier, of course. Great fun, nonetheless, and Driscoll is terrific as young Jim Hawkins.

___F___ 12. **The Beautician and the Beast, '97.** Fran Drescher, Timothy Dalton. A beauty school teacher mistaken for a science instructor is brought to Slovetzia to teach the president's four children.

___F___ 13. **The Great White Hope, '70.** James Earl Jones, Jane Alexander. A film version of the play about Jack Johnson, the early black boxer who found skin color standing in the way of success.

(Continues on next page)

241

_F+O_ 14. **Norma Rae, '79.** Sally Field, Ron Leibman. Field is <u>great</u> in her Oscar-winning role as the simple, courageous textile worker who organizes a union.

_F+O_ 15. **Every Which Way But Loose, '78.** Clint Eastwood, Sondra Locke. A movie only an Eastwood fan could love. A yokel with a pet chimp falls in love with a bar-band crooner, who may or may not be married.

C. (16–20.) The passage below contains five sentences. Two sentences express facts, and two express opinions. In addition, one sentence combines fact and opinion. Identify facts with an **F**, opinions with an **O**, and combinations of fact *and* opinion with an **F+O**.

> [1]The first bathing suits for women were created in the mid-1800s. [2]Invented by a man, they were ridiculous-looking, high-necked costumes that included knee-length skirts, elbow-length sleeves, black stockings, and shoes. [3]Once such suits became wet, they could weigh as much as the bather, and they are actually thought to have caused drowning on more than one occasion. [4]It is incredible that women ever agreed to wear such clothing. [5]Only a man could have invented something quite so impractical for women.

1. _F_   2. _F+O_   3. _F_   4. _O_   5. _O_

Comment: In Part B, the value words that reflect an opinion are underlined. (Of course, not all opinions are marked by value words—for example, see item 4 in Part A and item 15 in Part B.)

FACT AND OPINION: Test 2

A. Five of the statements below are facts, and five are opinions. Identify statements of fact with an **F** and statements of opinion with an **O**.

_O_ 1. It would be nice to have more than 24 hours in a day.

_F_ 2. Earth makes a complete rotation on its axis every 23 hours, 56 minutes and 4.09 seconds.

_O_ 3. Persian cats are the most beautiful of all felines.

_F_ 4. A cat once fell from a building's twentieth floor and suffered only a pelvic fracture.

_O_ 5. Joining the armed forces is the best way to learn a job skill.

_O_ 6. Organ transplantation is the most important medical achievement of the twentieth century.

_F_ 7. Because of transplants, about three hundred people in the United States have a heart that once belonged to someone else.

_F_ 8. President and Mrs. George Washington once placed ads in the newspaper as they searched for a cook and a coachman.

_O_ 9. The globefish is one of nature's strangest creatures.

_F_ 10. The globefish keeps itself from being eaten by gulping so much water that it becomes too large to be swallowed by its enemies.

B. Here are five short book reviews. Identify a factual review with an **F**; identify a review that includes both facts about the book *and* the reviewer's opinion with an **F+O**.

_F_ 11. In his novel *The Old Man and the Sea*, Ernest Hemingway tells the story of an old fisherman and his battle with a giant marlin.

_F+O_ 12. Any reader who thrives on terror and suspense must read Mary Higgins Clark's novel *The Cradle Will Fall*. In it, a country prosecutor uncovers evidence that a famous doctor is killing women, not realizing that she herself is becoming his next target. Higgins squeezes every possible bit of tension into this story.

(Continues on next page)

_F_ 13. Beverly Donofrio writes about her life in *Riding in Cars with Boys*, which is subtitled "A Bad Girl Who Makes Good." As a teenager, Donofrio rode around in cars, drinking and smoking pot. She describes herself as one of those girls "who got pregnant in high school." Then, after a teenage marriage ended, she decided to take her son and go off to college.

_F_ 14. In *A Walk Across America*, Peter Jenkins tells about walking with his dog across America to find out more about his country. Among the stories he tells are those about the times he spent with a hermit mountain man, lived with an African-American family in North Carolina, worked in a Southern mill, and almost died on a mountaintop.

_F+O_ 15. *Me Me Me Me Me—Not a Novel* by M. E. Kerr is a charming, easy-to-read account of a young woman's growing up. The author provides a series of warm and witty stories that will be enjoyed by people of all ages.

C. (16–20.) The passage below contains five sentences. Identify each sentence with an **F** (for fact), an **O** (for opinion), or **F+O** (for a combination of fact *and* opinion). (One sentence combines fact and opinion.)

¹School administrators should either improve our children's unhealthy lunch menus or be replaced. ²There is little value in teaching academics to children only to hurt their minds and bodies with red meat and deep-fried foods at lunch time. ³A survey of schools throughout the country shows that school lunch menus include high-sodium, high-fat, and low-fiber foods. ⁴In addition, some school districts allow sugary and high-fat foods to be sold in vending machines; this proves that school administrators really care too little about our children. ⁵The first step toward improving our children's health should be to abolish vending machines from the schools.

1. _O_   2. _O_   3. _F_   4. _F+O_   5. _O_

FACT AND OPINION: Test 3

A. Some of the items below are facts, and some are opinions; in addition, three combine both fact and opinion. Identify facts with an **F**, opinions with an **O**, and combinations of fact *and* opinion with an **F+O**.

   F   1. Rice grows in a warm, wet climate.

   O   2. Rice is far better with stir-fried vegetables than noodles are.

   F   3. Brown rice provides more B vitamins than white rice does.

 F+O 4. White rice is the result of milling that removes much of the grain's nutrients; thus one should eat only brown rice.

   O   5. Comic strips are not suitable reading for adults.

   F   6. In 1907, the San Francisco Chronicle began publishing the first daily comic strip—"Mr. Mutt," later named "Mutt and Jeff."

 F+O 7. It's very amusing to note that before Popeye the Sailor became a children's cartoon, he was a freely swearing character in an adult comic strip.

   O   8. Boxing, an overly violent sport, should finally be outlawed.

   F   9. Basketball was invented in 1891 when a YMCA instructor created a game using two peach baskets and a soccer ball.

 F+O 10. Baseball players have been known to do some really ridiculous things; for example, some players break in a new glove by rubbing it with shaving cream.

B. Here are five short book reviews. Identify a factual review with an **F**; identify a review that includes both facts about the book *and* the reviewer's opinion with an **F+O**.

 F+O 11. Richard Adams's *Watership Down* is a wonderfully entertaining novel about rabbits who act a great deal like people. The plot may sound unlikely, but it will keep you on the edge of your seat.

   F   12. *The Silence of the Lambs*, a novel by Thomas Harris, is about an intelligent mentally ill killer who is on the loose. In trying to find him, the FBI relies upon the clues provided by the killer himself. This story was made into a movie.

(Continues on next page)

_F+O_ 13. In his inspiring book *Man's Search for Meaning*, Viktor Frankl answers the question "How do people go on when they have been stripped of everything, including human dignity?" In his short, moving book, the author describes his time in a concentration camp and what he learned there about survival.

_F_ 14. In *Cry of the Kalahari*, Mark and Delia Owens tell about going to Africa to study wildlife and to try saving some animals from destruction. This husband and wife team describe their encounters with hyenas, lions, and a predator they consider even more dangerous: man.

_F+O_ 15. *In Cold Blood* by Truman Capote is a frightening true story about the murder of a family and also an examination of what made their killers tick. Many books today tell gripping stories of real-life crimes. *In Cold Blood* was the first book of this type and may be the best.

C. (16–20.) The passage below contains five sentences. Identify each sentence with an **F** (for fact), an **O** (for opinion), or **F+O** (for a combination of fact *and* opinion). (One sentence combines fact and opinion.)

[1]Americans have become much too concerned about success and about owning things. [2]According to a recent study, as many as 80 percent of job résumés contain false or misleading information. [3]Also, studies show that Americans use as much as 50 percent of their paycheck to pay back consumer loans. [4]For their wardrobes alone, consumers each year pay out millions of dollars, dollars that should have ended up in such worthy projects as health research and in housing for the homeless. [5]It's time for Americans to become less selfish and to contribute more to the community.

1. _O_   2. _F_   3. _F_   4. _F+O_   5. _O_

FACT AND OPINION: Test 4

A. Some of the items below are facts, some are opinions, and three combine both fact and opinion. Identify facts with an **F**, opinions with an **O**, and combinations of fact *and* opinion with an **F+O**.

_O_ 1. Adults shouldn't consume dairy products.

_F+O_ 2. Goat's milk is more easily digested by some people who are allergic to cow's milk, and goat's milk tastes better, too.

_O_ 3. Watching sports events in person is better than watching them on TV.

_O_ 4. Children should not be allowed to watch more than one hour of television a day.

_F_ 5. In the Middle Ages it was commonly believed that the seat of human intelligence was the heart.

_F+O_ 6. The Middle Ages was the worst time to be alive; for example, in the mid-fourteenth century, bubonic plague killed millions of people.

_F_ 7. During the Middle Ages it was mainly the clergy that could read and write; most other people—including royalty—did not have these skills.

_F+O_ 8. Rubber is a wonderful elastic substance at first made only from the sap of certain tropical plants and now often made synthetically.

_F_ 9. Joseph Priestley, an eighteenth-century scientist, named the substance rubber because it could rub away pencil marks.

_F_ 10. Bessie Smith, known as the "empress of the blues," was killed in a car accident in 1937.

_F_ 11. A week after the stock-market crash of 1929, Columbia released Smith's recording of "Nobody Knows You When You're Down and Out."

_O_ 12. Nobody, not even Anita Baker, can sing that song better than Smith did.

(Continues on next page)

B. (13–17.) The passage below contains five sentences. Identify each sentence with an **F** (for fact), an **O** (for opinion), or **F+O** (for a combination of fact *and* opinion). (One sentence combines fact and opinion.)

> ¹A common definition of retirement includes the idea of leaving the labor force, but that notion of retirement is too narrow. ²After retiring, it is much better to remain involved in the work world part-time. ³Some companies have recently supported this type of involvement for the retired by hiring two or three older part-timers in place of one full-time employee. ⁴The Travelers Corporation, for example, has employed six hundred retired employees for three hundred shared jobs. ⁵Other retirees have continued to work part-time by volunteering for organizations such as hospitals and museums.

1. _F+O_   2. _O_   3. _F_   4. _F_   5. _F_

C. The following passage is from a newspaper editorial page. One of the excerpts listed below it is fact, one is opinion, and one combines fact and opinion. Identify the fact with an **F**, the opinion with an **O**, and the combination of fact *and* opinion with **F+O**.

> Even casual observers of school reform know that one of the most frequently heard topics revolves around the length of the school year. . . .
>
> We hear endlessly about the 240-plus days put in by Japanese students and, by implication, we assume that most of the rest of the world is a lot closer to their standard than to ours.
>
> Actually, the great majority of the world's countries are closer to our standard than to that of the Japanese. Almost all of them have more than our 180 days but most do not have many more. The international average is 190 days. Of some twenty-seven countries and provinces, only six exceed 200 days. . . .
>
> All of this suggests a couple of things. First, the length of the school day may be a bigger issue than the length of the school year, since students in other countries tend to spend more hours in the classroom than American students. Second, the broader issue of the quality of time in school is probably much more significant than the issue of the quantity of time.

_F_ 18. The international average is 190 days. Of some twenty-seven countries and provinces, only six exceed 200 days.

_F+O_ 19. First, the length of the school day may be a bigger issue than the length of the school year,` since students in other countries tend to spend more hours in the classroom than American students.

_O_ 20. Second, the broader issue of the quality of time in school is probably much more significant than the issue of the quantity of time.

FACT AND OPINION: Test 5

A. Read the following textbook excerpts, and identify facts with an **F**, opinions with an **O**, and combinations of fact *and* opinion with an **F+O**.

_O_ 1. Your attitude about college work is even more crucial than any reading or study skill.

_F_ 2. Most newborns sleep two-thirds of the time, on the average of sixteen hours a day.

_F+O_ 3. Some tycoons built their fortunes by ruthlessly destroying the competition. A classic example was John D. Rockefeller. He organized Standard Oil in 1870.

_O_ 4. Many instructors working with older adults are insensitive to their students' feelings of discouragement.

_F_ 5. Permanent precautions against frozen pipes include wrapping them in fiberglass insulation or heat tape.

_F_ 6. Amelia Bloomer (1818–1894) published the first newspaper issued expressly for women. She called it *The Lily*.

_F_ 7. Apple trees generally do not begin to bloom and bear fruit until they are five to eight years old.

_O_ 8. Farm life in the 1890s was harsh and dull.

_F_ 9. Surveys show that in the United States, the majority of children under eighteen years old live in a household with their mother and father.

_F+O_ 10. *The Kid* (1921), one of Charlie Chaplin's greatest films, starred Chaplin and a four-year-old named Jackie Coogan.

_O_ 11. As a general, Washington was not a brilliant strategist like Napoleon.

_F+O_ 12. Alfred Stieglitz published fifty-four volumes of *Camera Work* between 1903 and 1917, giving us the finest record ever made of the art of photography.

(Continues on next page)

B. (13–15.) The following paragraph contains three sentences. One expresses facts, one expresses an opinion, and one sentence combines fact and opinion. Identify the factual sentence with an **F**, the opinion with an **O**, and the combination of fact *and* opinion with an **F+O**.

> [1]The flashing of fireflies is one of the most delightful sights of a summer night. [2]These charming little insects blink their lights as part of their fascinating mating ritual. [3]Although many different varieties of firefly may be blinking in one area, males and females of the same type find one another through the pattern of flashes.

1. _*O*_   2. _*F+O*_   3. _*F*_

C. Read the following textbook passage, and then identify each of the listed excerpts from the passage as fact (**F**), opinion (**O**), or both fact *and* opinion (**F+O**). (Two of the excerpts are both fact and opinion.)

> Frederick Douglass, a former slave who had escaped from Maryland, was one of the most remarkable Americans of his generation. While a slave, he had received a full portion of beatings and other indignities. But he had been allowed to learn to read and write and to learn a trade. (Such opportunities were denied to the vast majority of slaves.) Settling in Boston, he became an agent of the Massachusetts Anti-Slavery Society and a featured speaker at its public meetings.
>
> Douglass was a majestically handsome man who radiated determination and indignation. In 1845 he published his *Narrative of the Life of Frederick Douglass*, one of the most gripping accounts of a slave's life ever written. Douglass insisted that emancipation alone would not provide the slaves with freedom. He demanded full equality, social and economic and well as political. Few white northerners accepted his reasoning. But fewer still who heard him or read his works could afterward maintain that all blacks were dull-witted or resigned to inferior status.

_*F+O*_ 16. Frederick Douglass, a former slave who had escaped from Maryland, was one of the most remarkable Americans of his generation.

_*F*_ 17. But he had been allowed to learn to read and write and to learn a trade.

_*F*_ 18. Settling in Boston, he became an agent of the Massachusetts Anti-Slavery Society and a featured speaker at its public meetings.

_*O*_ 19. Douglass was a majestically handsome man who radiated determination and indignation.

_*F+O*_ 20. In 1845 he published his *Narrative of the Life of Frederick Douglass*, one of the most gripping accounts of a slave's life ever written.

FACT AND OPINION: Test 6

A. Read the following textbook excerpts, and identify facts with an **F**, opinions with an **O**, and combinations of fact *and* opinion with an **F+O**.

_O_ 1. The selections throughout the book are lively and appealing.

_F_ 2. Alcohol was discovered and drunk during the Stone Age.

_O_ 3. The most difficult problem for single fathers is balancing the demands of work and child care.

_F+O_ 4. The Parthenon was built in Athens in the fifth century B.C. and dedicated to the goddess Athena. It remains an example of near-perfect architectural design.

_F_ 5. Infertility rates have been rising over the past twenty years: 10 to 15 percent of couples who want a baby cannot conceive.

_O_ 6. Beethoven came on the scene at a favorable moment in history.

_F_ 7. The maze is a tool sometimes used by psychologists as they measure animals' learning ability.

_F+O_ 8. By far the most important indirect effect of industrialization occurred in the South, which soon began to produce cotton for the new textile factories of Great Britain and New England.

B. (9–13.) The passage below contains five sentences. Identify each sentence with an **F** (for fact), an **O** (for opinion), or **F+O** (for a combination of fact *and* opinion). (One sentence combines fact and opinion.)

> [1]Legally, a check doesn't have to come from a checkbook; it can be written on any material. [2]For instance, a man in Iowa painted a check for $30 on a door and delivered it to a neighbor to whom he owed the money. [3]An Englishman named Albert Haddock paid his taxes in the strangest possible way: he painted a check on the side of a cow. [4]Although such unusual checks are legal, the law allows the persons being paid to refuse to accept them. [5]The government ought to outlaw such unconventional checks altogether.

1. _F_   2. _F_   3. _F+O_   4. _F_   5. _O_

C. Read the following textbook passages, and then identify each listed excerpt as either fact (**F**), opinion (**O**), or fact *and* opinion (**F+O**). (Only one of the excerpts combines fact and opinion.)

(Continues on next page)

The psychologist Neil Jacobson has developed a marital treatment plan that aims at teaching couples how to deal with conflict in more positive and constructive ways. That is, he teaches couples how to do less blaming and criticizing and how to be more supportive, cooperative, and resourceful. In the early part of the treatment, the couples practice discussing their problems, whatever these may be, during the treatment hour. As they talk, the therapist coaches and corrects them, showing them how to listen carefully, make clear criticisms, avoid name-calling, generate solutions, and so forth. Later the couples are assigned to engage in and tape two problem-solving sessions per week at home. The tapes are then analyzed by each couple and the therapist together during the treatment hour. . . .

This is a hopeful new approach, very appealing in terms of practicality.

_F_ 14. In the early part of the treatment, the couples practice discussing their problems, whatever these may be, during the treatment hour.

_F_ 15. Later, the couples are assigned to engage in and tape two problem-solving sessions per week at home.

_O_ 16. This is a hopeful new approach, very appealing in terms of practicality.

The Shawnee chief Tecumseh made a bold and imaginative effort to bind the tribes east of the Mississippi into a great confederation. Traveling from the Wisconsin country to the Floridas, he persuaded tribe after tribe to join him. "Let the white race perish," Tecumseh declared. "They seize your land; they corrupt your women. . . . Back whence they came, upon a trail of blood, they must be driven!"

Tecumseh was joined in his campaign by his brother Tenskwatawa, known as the Prophet. Instead of aping white customs, the Prophet said, Indians must give up all white ways. They must strengthen their own culture. Yielding lands to the whites must stop because the Great Spirit intended that the land be used by all.

The Prophet, a fanatic, saw visions and claimed to be able to control the movement of the heavenly bodies. Tecumseh, however, possessed true genius. A powerful speaker and a great organizer, he had deep insight into the needs of his people. General Harrison himself said of Tecumseh: "He is one of those uncommon geniuses which spring up occasionally to produce revolution and overturn the established order of things." The two brothers made an outstanding team—by 1811 thousands of Indians were organizing to drive the whites off their lands.

_F_ 17. Traveling from the Wisconsin country to the Floridas, he persuaded tribe after tribe to join him.

_F_ 18. Tecumseh was joined in his campaign by his brother Tenskwatawa, known as the Prophet.

_O_ 19. Tecumseh . . . possessed true genius.

_F+O_ 20. The two brothers made an outstanding team—by 1811 thousands of Indians were organizing to drive the whites off their lands.

8
Inferences

You have probably heard the expression "to read between the lines." When you "read between the lines," you pick up ideas that are not directly stated in what you are reading. These implied ideas are often important for a full understanding of what an author means. Discovering the ideas in writing that are not stated directly is called **making inferences**, or **drawing conclusions**.

INFERENCES IN EVERYDAY LIFE

Consider first how often you make inferences in everyday life. For example, suppose you are sitting in a coffee shop at lunchtime. A woman sits down at the next table. Here is what you observe:

- She is wearing an expensive-looking suit, a silk blouse, gold jewelry, and a gold band on the third finger of her left hand.
- The woman opens a briefcase and takes out some manila folders; she begins to study them.
- You notice that she also has a child's crayon drawing in the briefcase.

As you sit in the coffee shop, you may make several inferences about this woman:

- She's on her lunch break.
- She works in an office, perhaps as a lawyer or an executive.
- She is married and has a young child.

How did you arrive at these inferences? First of all, you used your experience and general knowledge of people. Secondly, you made informed guesses based on the facts you observed. Of course, your inferences might not all prove true. For example, the woman could run her own business, or the child's drawing might have been done by her nephew or niece. You cannot prove or disprove your guesses without asking the woman directly, but your inferences may well be correct.

Take a moment now and jot down what you might infer if you saw each of the following:

1. A high school has uniformed security guards patrolling the halls.

    Your inference: _____

2. A dog cringes when someone tries to pet him.

    Your inference: _____

The inferences you probably made are that, in the first situation, the high school has had some very disturbing problems with discipline or crime and, in the second situation, the dog has previously been mishandled.

Now look at the following *New Yorker* cartoon.

"Dad, can you read?"

Drawing by Peter Steiner; © 1990 The New Yorker Magazine, Inc.

Put a check (✓) by the two inferences that are most logically based on the information given in the cartoon. Then read the explanations that follow.

____ 1. The boy enjoys reading.

____ 2. The boy is doing his homework.

____ 3. The man must watch a great deal of television.

____ 4. The father cannot read.

____ 5. The father prefers a good novel to watching TV.

Explanations:

1. This inference is supported by the fact that the boy is reading instead of playing or watching TV.

2. This is not a logical inference. The cartoonist would have given us more clues if he wanted us to think that the boy was reading a schoolbook.

3. This is a logical inference. The boy's question and the father's activity in the picture lead us to believe that the boy never sees his father reading, only watching a great deal of TV.

4. This inference is not well supported. The father doesn't seem to read much, but that doesn't mean he cannot; in fact, the magazine on the television set suggests that he can read.

5. This is not a logical inference. The boy's question tells us that he never sees his father reading.

➤ *Practice 1*

Put a check (✓) by the inference most logically based on the information provided. Look first at the example.

Example

A student always sits in the back of the classroom.
____ a. The student dislikes the course.
____ b. The student is unprepared for class.
____ c. The student feels uncomfortable in the front of the room.
____ d. The student is farsighted.

The correct answer is *c*. On the basis of the information we are given, we can conclude only that the student—for some reason—does not like sitting in the front. We are not given enough information to know why the student feels this way.

1. A pencil has teeth marks on it.
____ a. The person who used the pencil was nervous.
____ b. The pencil was chewed up by a toddler or pet.
_✓_ c. Someone or something chewed the pencil.
____ d. The pencil belongs to someone who is trying to quit smoking.

2. People are crowding around the entrance to a department store, which won't open for another hour.

    ____ a. The store is the only department store in the entire region.

    ____ b. There is always a crowd like this an hour before opening.

    ____ c. The store has paid a crowd to show up.

    ✓ d. The store is having a big sale.

3. The street is all wet, but the sidewalks are dry.

    ____ a. An unusual rain fell only on the street.

    ____ b. It rained everywhere, but someone dried the sidewalks.

    ✓ c. A street-cleaning vehicle sprayed the street.

    ____ d. Children with water guns must have played on the street.

4. Inside of a car with an out-of-state license are several maps, suitcases, and bags of snacks.

    ____ a. The driver of the car is on vacation.

    ____ b. The driver of the car is on a business trip.

    ____ c. The driver of the car has children.

    ✓ d. The driver of the car is on a trip of some kind.

INFERENCES IN READING

In reading, too, we make logical leaps from the information given in a straightforward way to ideas that are not stated directly. As the scholar S. I. Hayakawa has said, inferences are "statements about the unknown made on the basis of the known." To draw inferences, we use all the clues provided by the writer, our own experience, and logic.

In this book, you have already practiced making inferences in Chapter 1, on vocabulary. There you had to use context clues within sentences to infer the meanings of words. Also, in Chapter 4, on implied and central ideas, you had to "read between the lines" in order to find implied main ideas. The intent of this chapter is to broaden your ability to make inferences about what you read.

Read the following passage and check (✓) the three inferences that can most logically be drawn from it. Then read the explanations that follow.

A famous psychology experiment conducted by Dr. John B. Watson demonstrates that people, like animals, can be conditioned—trained to respond in a particular way to certain stimulations. Watson gave an eleven-month-old baby named Albert a soft, furry white rat. Each time Albert tried to stroke the rat, Dr. Watson hit a metal bar with a hammer. Before long, Albert was afraid not only of white rats but also of white rabbits, white dogs, and white fur coats. He even screamed at the sight of a Santa Claus mask.

    1. Dr. Watson did not like small children.

    2. Before the experiment, Albert was not afraid of white rats.

    3. Albert had been familiar with rats before the experiment.

    4. If he had seen a black fur coat, Albert would have screamed.

    5. Albert connected the loud noise of the hammer striking the metal bar with the white rat.

    6. Albert was afraid of unexpected loud noises from the beginning.

Explanations:

1. This is not a logical inference. We might question the way the baby was used, but the passage doesn't give enough information for us logically to infer that Watson did not like small children.

2. This is a logical inference. Because Albert tried to pet the rat, it is fair to assume that he wasn't frightened of the animal.

3. This is not a logical inference. The passage gives no clues about Albert's having previous experience with rats.

4. This is not a logical inference. The passage makes no mention of Albert's response to any color but white.

5. This is a logical inference. Because the loud noise appears to have changed Albert's attitude toward the rat, we can assume he associated the noise with the rat.

6. This is a logical inference. Since the noise is what made Albert afraid of the rat, we have to infer that he was afraid of the noise. In addition, experience tells us that babies are likely to be frightened of unexpected loud noises.

Guidelines for Inferences in Reading

The exercises in this chapter provide practice in making careful inferences when you read. Here are three guidelines to that process:

1 Never lose sight of the available information. As much as possible, base your inferences on the facts. For instance, in the paragraph about Watson's experiment, we are told, "Albert tried to stroke the rat." On the basis of that fact, we can readily conclude that the baby had no fear of rats.

    It's also important to note when a conclusion lacks support. For instance, the idea that Albert would have screamed at the sight of a black fur coat has no support in the paragraph. We are told only that Albert was frightened by white furry things.

2 Use your background information and experience to help you in making inferences. Our understanding and experience with babies, for example, help us realize that Albert was frightened of unexpected loud noises.

The more background information people have, the more accurate their inferences are likely to be. So keep in mind that if your background information in a particular matter is weak, your inferences may be shaky. A doctor's inferences about your rash and fever are likely to be more helpful than those of your car mechanic.

3 Consider the alternatives. Considering alternative interpretations of the facts is one way to zero in on a likely interpretation. Don't simply accept the first inference that comes to mind. Instead, consider all of the facts of a case and all the possible explanations. For example, the doctor analyzing your rash and fever may first think of and then eliminate several possible diagnoses before seriously testing for one or two of the more likely ones.

➤ Practice 2

Read the following passages. Then circle the letter of the most logical answer to each question, based on the information given in the passage.

A.   My friends have no friends. They are men. They think they have friends, and if you ask them whether they have friends they will say yes, but they don't really. They think, for instance, that I'm their friend, but I'm not. It's OK. They're not my friends either.

The reason for that is that we are all men—and men, I have come to believe, cannot or will not have real friends. They have something else—companions, buddies, pals, chums, someone to drink with and someone to lunch with, but no one when it comes to saying how they feel—especially how they hurt.

Women know this. They talk about it among themselves. To women, this inability of men to say what they feel is a source of amazement and then anguish and then, finally, betrayal. Women will tell you all the time that they don't know the men they live with. They talk of long silences and of drifting off and of keeping feelings hidden and never letting on about troubles or bothers or whatever.

1. We can infer that the author of this passage
    a. believes "companions, buddies, pals, chums" are the same thing as real friends.
    b. has genuine friends himself.
    c. believes men have no need of genuine friends.
    d. feels something prevents men from having genuine friends.

2. We can infer that the author
   a. is proud he is able to share his feelings better than other men.
   (b.) believes women want the men in their lives to share their feelings.
   c. finds that men share their feelings with the women in their lives.
   d. believes men have more hurt feelings than women do.

3. We can infer that the author believes that women
   (a.) have genuine friends.
   b. prefer "strong, silent" men.
   c. keep their feelings to themselves.
   d. understand why men do not talk about their feelings.

4. We can conclude that the author thinks
   a. men realize that they don't have friends.
   (b.) men's relationships aren't deep enough to be genuine friendships.
   c. men generally have deeper friendships than women do.
   d. women should try to be more like men when it comes to friendship.

B. Parents bewildered by their teen alien can take comfort from one sign that Junior may be from the same species as they are: High school status ladders look just as they did when Corvettes were the hot cars of choice.

   A new study of social systems at eighteen high schools in various states reveals some familiar patterns, reports sociologist Murray Milner, Jr. Still tops in popularity: male athletes and attractive girls. Just beneath them stand well-dressed "preppies" who try to act indifferent to school and snag the "right" party invitations.

   "Nerds" cluster near the bottom. Their sin? Open preoccupation with academic success. But they're not lowest. The "dorks," Milner says, "were hopelessly inept" about clothes and social events. They often had low grades and poor athletic ability, too.

   Kids typically date only within their status level, which is set in stone by the first year and seldom can be upgraded. Downgrading is a danger, though. A girl dating a star athlete who later got injured and couldn't play found his status—and hers—suddenly declining. And being seen talking to classmates "beneath" one's status can pull students down very fast.

   "High school is a very scary place," Milner says.

   It often is, agrees San Diego psychiatrist Martin Greenberg. To take the pressure off at home, consider cutting teens some slack on minor disputes, he advises. "Try to be flexible because a lot of them are having a hard time. No matter how it looks," he says, "they're desperate for love."

5. From the beginning of the passage, we can conclude that a generation ago
   a. teens became popular for very different reasons than they do today.
   b. social status was not very important in high schools.

c. good-looking girls and athletic boys were the most popular kids.

d. only "dorks" drove Corvettes.

6. We can infer from the passage that
   a. teenagers generally don't care about their social status.
   b. the high-school years are stressful ones for many teens.
   c. most teens admire students who openly care about school.
   d. teens typically behave lovingly when they are home.

7. The passage suggests that in high school,
   a. boys are most valued for their athletic ability and girls for their appearance.
   b. female athletes are generally as popular as male athletes.
   c. a nonathletic boy can be very popular as long as he is a good student.
   d. athletes don't care about getting invited to parties.

8. The passage suggests that
   a. teenagers are independent thinkers who aren't bothered by other people's opinions.
   b. popular teens often make friends with less popular kids.
   c. outward appearance is an important factor in determining high schoolers' status.
   d. a teenager's social status often changes from year to year.

C. A corporate president recently made a visit to a nearby Native American reservation as part of his firm's public relations program. "We realize that we have not hired any Indians in the five years our company has been located in this area," he told the assembled tribespeople, "but we are looking into the matter very carefully." "Hora, hora," said some of the audience. "We would like to eventually hire 5 percent of our total work force from this reservation," he said. "Hora, hora," shouted more of the audience. Encouraged by their enthusiasm, the president closed his short address by telling them that he hoped his firm would be able to take some hiring action within the next couple of years. "Hora, hora, hora," cried the total group. With a feeling of satisfaction, the president left the hall and was taken on a tour of the reservation. Stopping in a field to admire some of the horses grazing there, the president asked if he could walk up closer to the animals. "Certainly," said his guide, "but be careful not to step in the hora."

9. To get the main point of this passage, the reader must infer
   a. the location of the reservation.
   b. what kind of company the president headed.
   c. the meaning of the word *hora*.

10. From the passage, we can infer that the audience
    a. believed the president's speech.
    b. did not believe the president's speech.
    c. was confused by the president's speech.

11. From the passage, we can infer that the president
    a. thought the Native Americans deserved to be hired.
    b. thought his company should not hire the Native Americans.
    c. misinterpreted the Native Americans' reaction to his speech.

12. From the passage, we can infer that the main reason the president spoke to the Native Americans about jobs was that
    a. they needed the jobs.
    b. he thought promising jobs to Native Americans would make his company look good.
    c. he thought hiring Native Americans would be good for his company.

D. During World War II, the troop ship *SS Dorchester* steamed out of New York harbor with 904 men headed for Greenland. Among those leaving anxious families behind were four chaplains, Methodist preacher George Fox, Rabbi Alexander Goode, Catholic priest John Washington, and Reformed Church minister Clark Poling. Some 150 miles from their destination, a Nazi submarine sighted the *Dorchester* in its cross hairs. Within moments of a torpedo's impact, reports a survivor, stunned men were pouring out from their bunks as the ship began tilting. With power cut off, the escort vessels, unaware of the unfolding tragedy, pushed on in the darkness. Onboard, chaos ruled as panicky men came up from the hold without life jackets and leaped into overcrowded lifeboats.

   When the four chaplains made it up to the steeply sloping deck, they began guiding the men to their boat stations. They opened a storage locker, distributed life jackets, and coaxed the men over the side. In the icy, oil-smeared water, Private William Bednar heard the chaplains preaching courage and found the strength to swim until he reached a life raft. Still onboard, Grady Clark watched in awe as the chaplains handed out the last life jackets, and then, with ultimate selflessness, gave away their own. As Clark slipped into the water he saw the chaplains standing—their arms linked—praying, in Latin, Hebrew, and English. Other men, now calm, joined them in a huddle as the *Dorchester* slid beneath the sea.

13. We can infer from this passage that
    a. the Nazis had been hunting for the *Dorchester* for a long time.
    b. the *Dorchester*'s passengers and their families knew that because the ship carried soldiers, it might be attacked.
    c. the Nazi submarine was eventually found and destroyed.

14. We can infer that the chaplains and others remaining on the boat didn't jump off because
    a. there was no more room in the lifeboats, and they knew they could not survive in the icy sea without a life jacket.
    b. they couldn't swim.
    c. they assumed a friendly ship would soon pass by and save them.

15. We can infer from the passage that Grady Clark
    a. was one of the men who died in the *Dorchester* tragedy.
    b. survived the attack and reported what the chaplains had done.
    c. alone survived the attack on the *Dorchester.*

16. The passage suggests that
    a. the chaplains had known each other for many years.
    b. religious faith may strengthen courage.
    c. the chaplains had no fear of death.

➤ *Practice 3*

Read the following textbook passages. Then put a check (✓) by the **three** inferences that are most logically based on the given facts in each passage.

A. The *Chicago Tribune* once wrote that Henry Ford, the founder of the Ford Motor Company, was an ignorant man. Ford sued, challenging the paper to "prove it." During the trial, Ford was asked dozens of simple, general information questions: "When was the Civil War?" "Name the presidents of the United States." And so on. Ford, who had little formal education, could answer very few. Finally, exasperated, he said, "I don't know the answers to those questions, but I could find a man in five minutes who does. I use my brain to think, not store up a lot of useless facts."

   ✓ 1. Henry Ford was probably angered by the article in the *Chicago Tribune*.

   ___ 2. Ford frequently sued people.

   ___ 3. The *Tribune* won the case in court.

   ✓ 4. Ford believed that knowing where to find a fact is good enough.

   ___ 5. Ford would have been even more successful in his career had he had a formal education.

   ✓ 6. Ford believed that knowing how to think is more important than knowing facts.

B. Most people would like to think that they choose their friends on the basis of personal characteristics. A classic study of a housing complex for married students at the Massachusetts Institute of Technology (MIT) suggests that proximity—nearness and availability—can be a decisive factor. Researchers asked couples to list their friends in the complex. They found that residents were far more likely to list the couple in the next apartment than one that lived two doors away, and more likely to visit with a couple two doors away than with one three or four doors away. A distance of thirty feet or a short elevator ride made the difference between friends and strangers! More recent studies have confirmed the importance of proximity. One possible explanation is that whenever people encounter strangers, they feel tense. The more they see a person, the more they come to think of that person as predictable and safe, and hence the more likely they are to strike up a conversation that leads to friendship. This would explain why the most popular couples in the MIT housing complex were those who lived at the bottom of the stairs near the garbage cans that everyone used.

✓ 1. Most people probably think their personal preferences determine whom they choose for friends.

___ 2. In fact, our personal preferences have no effect on who our friends are.

___ 3. A person who lives in a big country is more likely to be have more friends than someone who lives in a small country.

✓ 4. Someone living in an apartment house is likely to have more friends than someone who lives on a farm.

___ 5. A garbage collector is likely to have more friends than a mailperson.

✓ 6. Someone who works in a busy office is likely to have more friends than someone who works at home.

C. Most organizations and their managers realize the importance of maintaining good human relations. A climate of openness and trust can encourage performance and foster loyalty. According to one author, everyone at Walt Disney Productions—including the president—wears a name tag with first name only, and at IBM the chairman of the board personally answers employee complaints. This kind of atmosphere can only have a positive effect on human relations.

While many managers get a lift from knowing that they're treating their workers right, there are practical benefits as well. When workers are satisfied with the interpersonal aspect of their jobs, they are usually more productive.

✓ 1. The size of the paycheck is not the only thing that determines employee satisfaction.

___ 2. At Walt Disney Productions, employees don't have complaints.

✓ 3. Using first names on the job makes a company seem like a friendlier, more caring place.

___ 4. IBM is more productive than all of its competitors.

✓ 5. Workers who feel their employers do not care about them tend to be less productive.

___ 6. Walt Disney Productions was the first company to encourage employees and executives to use one another's first names.

D.   Of all the Western democracies, the United States has nearly the lowest voter turnout for elections. In recent decades, nations like Italy, Australia, and Canada have had turnouts of over 90, 80, and 70 percent respectively. During those years, the United States has managed about 60 percent in its presidential elections. In nonpresidential elections, voter turnout is even weaker. No such election since 1920 has drawn even 50 percent of voters. The voting rate in American elections is so low that the people who do not vote greatly outnumber the margin of victory for the winning candidates. For example, Richard Nixon defeated Hubert Humphrey by 510,635 votes in 1968. Nearly 62 million adult Americans did not vote that year! In one year's congressional elections, voter turnout was so low—a mere 37 percent— that one political cartoonist drew a picture of a cat wandering into a polling place and an election clerk asking it hopefully, "Are you registered?"

✓ 1. The results of elections in the United States might have been different if more people had voted.

___ 2. Voter turnout in American elections will continue to decline.

✓ 3. On the whole, citizens of Italy, Australia, and Canada take their responsibility to vote more seriously than do Americans.

___ 4. If more Americans had voted in 1968, Hubert Humphrey would certainly have defeated Richard Nixon.

___ 5. The cartoonist's point was that election clerks are not very smart.

✓ 6. The cartoonist's point was that election clerks were desperately hoping for more voters.

Inferences in Literature

Inference is very important in reading literature. While writers of factual material usually state directly much of what they mean, creative writers provide verbal pictures that *show* what they mean. It is up to the reader to infer the point of what the creative writer has said. For instance, a nonfiction writer might write the following:

Marian was angry at her father.

But a novelist might write this:

> Marian's eyes narrowed when her father spoke to her. She cut him off in mid-sentence, snarling, "I don't have time to argue with you."

The author has *shown* us the anger with vivid specific details rather than merely stating the fact of the anger. To understand imaginative writing, then, you must often use your inference skills—just as you do in everyday life.

Applying inference skills can increase your appreciation of literary forms—novels, short stories, plays, essays, autobiographies, and poetry. Poetry, especially, by its nature implies much of its meaning. Implications are often made through comparisons. For example, Emily Dickinson begins one of her poems like this:

> Hope is the thing with feathers
> That perches in the soul
> And sings the tune without the words,
> And never stops at all.

Here, Dickinson compares hope to a singing bird. This implies, among other things, that hope is a sweet and welcome thing.

Shown below is a well-known poem by the American poet Carl Sandburg. Read the poem and then choose the inferences which are most logically supported by the information given. Note that Sandburg refers in the poem to five battlefields where many died (Austerlitz, Waterloo, Gettysburg, Ypres, and Verdun).

Grass

Pile the bodies high at Austerlitz and Waterloo.
Shovel them under and let me work—
　　I am the grass; I cover all.
And pile them high at Gettysburg
And pile them high at Ypres and Verdun.
Shovel them under and let me work.
Two years, ten years, and passengers ask the conductor:
　　What place is this?
　　Where are we now?
I am the grass.
Let me work.

1. The poem refers to bodies of
   a. the living.
   b. all those who have died.
   c. those who have died in wars.

2. The poet suggests that
   a. the war dead were never found.
   b. there were numerous deaths during the wars.
   c. there were fewer deaths than one would suppose.

3. The supposed speaker of the poem is
   a. a train passenger.
   b. the grass.
   c. a conductor.

4. The poet implies that
   a. time passes too slowly.
   b. wars scar the land forever.
   c. even bloody battlefields can be cleansed by time and nature.

5. The poet implies that
   a. nature's work outlasts human works.
   b. humans and nature are equal partners.
   c. humans' work will outlast anything nature does.

Explanations:

1. The locations referred to are battlefields, and this fact clearly implies that the "bodies" are of people who were wartime casualties. Therefore answer *c* is correct.

2. The poet says of the bodies, "pile them high"; this tells us that there are many of them. Thus answer *b* is correct.

3. The imaginary speaker of the poem identifies itself in the third line: "I am the grass." Thus answer *b* is correct.

4. The passengers' questions ("What place is this? / Where are we now?") show that years after the wars ("two years, ten years"), the battlefields are no longer recognizable. Since the grass (an element of nature) says, "I cover all," we know it is nature that eventually hid the battlefields. So answer *c* is correct.

5. In implying that the grass has erased evidence of the battles, Sandburg suggests that human affairs are short-lived in the face of nature. Therefore, answer *a* is correct.

➤ *Practice 4*

Following is a passage from *A Hole in the World*, an autobiographical account by the Pulitzer Prize-winning author Richard Rhodes. Read the passage, and then check (✓) the **five** statements that can be logically inferred from the information given.

We played dodgeball at recess. Dodgeball was my sport. I was light and quick and often managed to escape being picked off until I was the last of my team inside the circle, the winner of the round. My friend was usually my competition. One day I kidded him too sharply when he lost and I won. He gathered a knot of classmates afterward, the girl I dreamed about among them. They strolled over and surrounded me. They were smiling and I thought they were friendly; it didn't occur to me to dodge. The boys grabbed me. My friend led them. "You stink," he told me happily. "We think you're dirty. We want to see." They jerked down the straps on my bib overalls, held my arms high, peeled off my ragged shirt. They exposed my filth, my black armpits, my dirty neck for everyone to see. The faces of those children, the girl well forward among them, filled with horror perverted with glee. I went the only way I could go, down, dropping to the asphalt of the playground. They formed a circle around me, laughing and pointing. I couldn't get away. I covered my head and drew up my knees. I knew how to make myself invisible. I'd learned to make myself invisible when my stepmother attacked. It worked because I couldn't see her even if she could still see me. I made myself invisible. They couldn't hear me crying.

  ✓   1. The event took place when the author was a schoolboy.

  ____   2. The event took place in the middle of winter.

  ____   3. The author was usually clean, but just happened to be dirty that day.

  ✓   4. The author's friend meant to embarrass him.

  ✓   5. The author probably wasn't very well cared for at home.

  ✓   6. The author's stepmother abused him.

  ____   7. Most stepmothers are cruel.

  ____   8. Despite his stepmother's attacks, the author was very fond of her.

  ✓   9. When the author made himself "invisible," he was really putting others out of sight.

  ____   10. The author never won at dodgeball again.

➤ Review Test 1

To review what you've learned in this chapter, answer each of the following questions about inferences.

1. An inference is an idea that is (*directly stated, suggested*) _____*suggested*_____ by the author.

2. When making inferences, it is (*a mistake, useful*) _____*useful*_____ to use our own experience as well as the author's clues.

3. When making inferences, it is (*a mistake, useful*) _____*useful*_____ to use our sense of logic as well as the author's clues.

4. __*T*__ TRUE OR FALSE? A reader must make inferences when finding the meaning of words through context and when finding implied main ideas.

5. Making inferences is a key skill in reading literature because writers of fiction do not so much (*tell, show*) _____*tell*_____ us what they mean as (*tell, show*) _____*show*_____ us with vivid specific details.

➤ Review Test 2

A. After reading each passage, put a check by the **two** inferences that are most firmly based on the given facts.

1. Pulling the collar of his ragged jacket up against the rain, the unshaven man headed for the shelter of a store doorway. He bit his lip as he thought about how wet everything would be tonight and wondered if he would need to pay for a dry bed.

    __✓__ a. The man is homeless.

    _____ b. He's thinking of stealing some money.

    __✓__ c. He sometimes sleeps outside at night.

2. The freak weather transformed the outdoors into a rigid fairyland. Young leaves hung stiffly, and the daffodils seemed buried alive under a glass-like coating.

    __✓__ a. The daffodils were encased in ice.

    _____ b. Such weather had never happened before.

    __✓__ c. Rain had turned to ice in spring.

Comment: Item 2—"Young leaves" and "daffodils" are signs of spring.

3. Shortly after the young woman sat down in the bus, she lit a cigarette. The man next to her waved some smoke away, nudged her, and pointed to the sign at the front of the bus.

    ___ a. The man had never smoked.

    ✓ b. The smoke was bothering the man.

    ✓ c. The man pointed to a no-smoking sign.

B. After reading each passage, put a check by the **two** inferences that are most firmly based on the given facts.

4. A man is talking to the Lord, trying to understand his eternal nature. "Lord," he asks, "what's a million years to you?" "A million years is but a second to me," the Lord explains. "And a million dollars?" "A penny," the Lord replies. The man feels bold and now proceeds to ask, "Lord, would you give me a million dollars?" "Sure," the Lord replies. "Just a second."

    ✓ a. In comparison with eternity, a million years is a short time.

    ✓ b. The man will not live long enough to collect his million dollars.

    ___ c. The Lord knows the man would just waste the money.

    ___ d. The man is poor.

5. George Washington's honesty is a trait that has been well publicized. The famous story of how little George chopped down his father's favorite cherry tree, then bravely admitted to the deed, has an honored place in American presidential history. The cherry tree story was first recorded in 1806 by Parson Mason Locke Weems, a Maryland preacher and storyteller. Unfortunately, Parson Weems was none too honest himself, and it appears that he invented the story of George and the cherry tree. There is no record of the cherry tree incident anywhere until it appears in Weems's book. The parson, it seems, thought it acceptable to teach the virtue of honesty through a made-up story. We can judge Weems's own truthfulness by the fact that he describes himself in the book as "formerly rector of Mount Vernon Parish." Such a parish never existed.

    ___ a. The passage suggests that George Washington was not so honest after all.

    ___ b. We can conclude that Parson Weems knew George Washington well.

    ✓ c. Widely accepted stories about history are not necessarily true.

    ✓ d. Parson Weems wrote about a virtue he didn't have himself.

Comments: Item 4—The underlined sentence is the key to the punchline at the end.
Item 5, answer *a*—The passage provides no new information on how honest George Washington was; it discusses only the truth of the famous story about the cherry tree.

➤ Review Test 3

A. Read the following textbook passage and then check the **five** statements that are most logically supported by the information given.

> Your sister has a new boyfriend. The first time you meet him, he corners you and talks to you for an hour about football, a subject in which you have no interest at all. You come away with the impression that he is an inconsiderate bore. The next two times you see him, however, he says not a word about football; instead, he participates in the general conversation and makes some witty and intelligent remarks. What is your impression of him now? Do you find him likable and interesting on the basis of the last two encounters? Do you average out the early minus and the later plus and come out with a neutral zero? Neither is likely—what is likely is that you still think of him as an inconsiderate bore. For psychological research suggests that first impressions, as our mothers and fathers told us, are quite lasting.

_____ 1. First impressions are usually negative.

_____ 2. It's a bad idea to discuss football when you first meet someone.

_✓_ 3. It is useful to make good first impressions.

_✓_ 4. To make a good impression, it helps to notice what interests the other person.

_____ 5. A "neutral zero" impression of someone would be negative.

_✓_ 6. A "neutral zero" impression of someone would be neither positive nor negative.

_____ 7. It's not so difficult to remain objective about others.

_✓_ 8. It's not so easy to be objective about others.

_____ 9. Second impressions can be even more powerful than first impressions.

_✓_ 10. We have to work to be objective in judging others.

Comments: Item 3—See the last sentence of the passage.

Item 4—See the second and third sentences.

Item 6—See the seventh sentence.

Items 8 and 10—To be objective, we must sometimes change our first impressions.

B. (11–20.) Shown below is a poem by Matthew Prior, who lived in England from 1664 to 1721. Read the poem and then check the **five** inferences most solidly based on it.

Note that the poem describes a scene where a man named Lubin lies dying; he is attended by his wife and by a minister named Parson Sly. The poem ends with a surprising twist in the last line.

Also note that the meaning of one word in the poem is given below.

affliction: a condition of pain, suffering, or anxiety

A Reasonable Affliction°

On his death-bed poor Lubin lies
   His spouse is in despair;
With frequent cries, and mutual sighs,
   They both express their care.

"A different cause," says Parson Sly,
   "The same effect may give:
Poor Lubin fears that he may die;
   His wife, that he may live."

   ✓   1. Lubin is deathly ill.

   ____ 2. His wife is also deathly ill.

   ____ 3. Lubin and his wife are very religious.

   ____ 4. The poet recognizes that most marriages are bad ones.

   ✓ 5. The poet recognizes that spouses aren't always devoted to each other.

   ✓ 6. The reader's view of Lubin and his wife changes greatly in the second stanza.

   ____ 7. Lubin is a poor man.

   ____ 8. Lubin's wife hopes to inherit his great wealth.

   ✓ 9. When Parson Sly speaks of "a different cause," he refers to the different reasons Lubin is crying and his wife is crying.

  ✓ 10. The word *affliction* (in the title) refers to two different problems, Lubin's and his wife's.

Comment: Items 9 and 10—See the last two lines of the poem.

➤ Review Test 4

Here is a chance to apply your understanding of inferences to a full-length article. The reading, from *Newsday Magazine*, is a firsthand account of what it was like for one boy to be the first black student in a midwestern school.

To help you continue to strengthen your skills, the reading is followed by questions not only on what you've learned in this chapter but also on what you've learned in previous chapters.

Words to Watch

Below are some words in the reading that do not have strong context support. Each word is followed by the number of the paragraph in which it appears and its meaning there. These words are indicated in the article by a small circle (°).

pristine (2): still pure
prevailing (2): common
deplored (4): disapproved of
incipient (6): in the first stage of existence
derivative (7): not original
tentatively (9): with uncertainty
groused (10): complained
ventured (10): dared
mortified (11): humiliated

I BECAME HER TARGET

Roger Wilkins

1   My favorite teacher's name was "Deadeye" Bean. Her real name was Dorothy. She taught American history to eighth graders in the junior high section of Creston, the high school that served the north end of Grand Rapids, Michigan. It was the fall of 1944. Franklin D. Roosevelt was president; American troops were battling their way across France; Joe DiMaggio was still in the service; the Montgomery bus boycott was more than a decade away, and I was a twelve-year-old black newcomer in a school that was otherwise all white.

2   My mother, who had been a widow in New York, had married my stepfather, a Grand Rapids physician, the year before, and he had bought the best house he could afford for his new family. The problem for our new neighbors was that their neighborhood had previously been pristine° (in their terms) and that they were ignorant about black people. The prevailing° wisdom in the neighborhood was that we were spoiling it and that we ought to go back where we belonged (or alternatively, ought not intrude where we were not wanted). There was a lot of angry talk among the adults, but nothing much came of it.

3   But some of the kids, those first few weeks, were quite nasty. They threw stones at me, chased me home when I was on foot, and spat on my bike seat while I was in class. For a time, I was a pretty lonely, friendless and sometimes frightened kid. I was just transplanted from Harlem, and here in Grand Rapids, the dominant culture was speaking to me insistently. I can see now that those youngsters were bullying and culturally disadvantaged. I knew then that they were bigoted, but the culture spoke to me more powerfully than my mind, and I felt ashamed for being different—a non-standard person.

4   I now know that Dorothy Bean understood most of that and deplored° it. So things began to change when I walked into her classroom. She was a pleasant-looking single woman, who looked old and wrinkled to me at the time, but who was probably about 40. Whereas my other teachers approached the problem of easing in their new black pupil by ignoring him for the first few weeks, Miss Bean went right at me. On the morning after having read our first assignment, she asked me the first question. I later came to know that in Grand Rapids, she was viewed as a very liberal person who believed, among other things, that Negroes were equal.

5   I gulped and answered her question and the follow-up. They weren't brilliant answers, but they did establish the facts that I had read the assignment and that I could speak English. Later in the hour, when one of my classmates had bungled an answer, Miss Bean came back to me with a question that required me to clean up the girl's mess and established me as a smart person.

6   Thus, the teacher began to give me human dimensions, though not perfect ones for an eighth grader. It was somewhat better to be an incipient° teacher's pet than merely a dark presence in the back of the room onto whose silent form my classmates could fit all the stereotypes they carried in their heads.

7   A few days later, Miss Bean became the first teacher ever to require me to think. She asked my opinion about something Jefferson had done. In those days, all my opinions were derivative°. I was for Roosevelt because my parents were and I was for the Yankees because my older buddy from Harlem was a Yankee fan. Besides, we didn't have opinions about historical figures like Jefferson. Like our high school building or old Mayor Welch, he just was.

8   After I had stared at her for a few seconds, she said: "Well, should he have bought Louisiana or not?"

9   "I guess so," I replied tentatively°.

10   Why! What kind of question was that, I groused° silently. But I ventured° an answer. Day after day, she kept doing that to me, and my answers became stronger and more confident. She was the first teacher to give me the sense that thinking was part of education and that I could form opinions that had some value.

11   Her final service to me came on a day when my mind was wandering and I was idly digging my pencil into the writing surface on the arm of my chair. Miss Bean impulsively threw a hunk of gum eraser at me. By amazing chance, it hit my hand and sent the pencil flying. She gasped, and I crept mortified° after my pencil as the class roared. That was the ice breaker. Afterward, kids came up to me to laugh about "Old Deadeye Bean." The incident became a legend, and I, a part of that story, became a person to talk to. So that's how I became just another kid in school and Dorothy Bean became "Old Dead-Eye."

274   INFERENCES

Reading Comprehension Questions

Vocabulary in Context

1. In the sentence below, the word *bungled* means
   a. improved.
   b. handled poorly.
   c. whispered.
   d. corrected.

   > "Later in the hour, when one of my classmates bungled an answer, Miss Bean came back to me with a question that required me to clean up the girl's mess and established me as a smart person." (Paragraph 5)

Central Point and Main Ideas

2. Which sentence best expresses the central point of the article?
   a. A boy used to Harlem schools had to go to a previously all-white school in Grand Rapids.
   b. The author was a lot smarter than the other kids thought he would be.
   c. A teacher helped the first black student in school to grow intellectually and to be welcomed as an individual.
   d. Teachers are the most important influences in a person's life.

3. Which sentence best expresses the main idea of paragraph 7?
   a. Miss Bean asked the author for his opinion about something Thomas Jefferson had done.
   b. Miss Bean was the first teacher to ask the author to have his own opinion about something.
   c. The author had been in favor of Franklin D. Roosevelt because his parents had been in favor of Roosevelt.
   d. It seemed odd to the author to have opinions about historical figures like Thomas Jefferson.

Supporting Details

4. At first, the teachers at the school other than Miss Bean
   a. ignored the author.
   b. challenged the author.
   c. praised the author.
   d. protected the author.

Transitions

5. The sentence below expresses a relationship of
   a. addition.
   b. contrast.

Comment: Item 3—The significant idea of paragraph 7 is in its first sentence.

    c. comparison.

    d. cause-effect.

> "They weren't brilliant answers, but they did establish the facts that I had read the assignment and that I could speak English." (Paragraph 5)

Patterns of Organization

  6. The patterns of organization of paragraph 11 are time order and

    a. list of items.

    b. comparison and contrast.

    c. definition and example.

    (d.) cause and effect.

Fact and Opinion

  7. The first paragraph is made up of

    (a.) facts.

    b. opinions.

    c. facts and opinions.

Inferences

  8. From the reading, we suspect that the author

    a. had been a poor student in Harlem.

    (b.) had never before attended a primarily white school.

    c. had begged not to move to Grand Rapids.

    d. moved away from Grand Rapids as soon as possible.

  9. In stating that "the teacher began to give me human dimensions" (paragraph 6), the author means that she

    a. made him physically stronger.

    (b.) helped the other students see him as a person, not a stereotype.

    c. described his size.

    d. helped him to become a better student and the teacher's pet.

  10. Wilkins must have considered Miss Bean's throwing the eraser at him to be a "service" to him because

    a. it helped him to return his thoughts to the learning activity going on in class.

    b. it showed him that she really cared about him.

    (c.) it made other students see his human side and gave them something to laugh about with him.

    d. it made Miss Bean gasp in front of all of the other students.

Comments: Item 6—The *cause* in the paragraph is the incident about the thrown eraser; the *effect* is given in the last sentence of the paragraph. The incident itself involves a series of events, told in the order in which they happened.

Item 10—See the last three sentences of paragraph 11.

Discussion Questions

1. Why do you suppose the incident in which Miss Bean threw an eraser at the author was such an "ice breaker"?

2. Have you ever experienced being in a school or class in which you were the only one of a certain group—the only student who was black, white, Spanish, or different in some other way? What was it like? Did things get better or worse? Why?

3. Did you have any teachers that required you to think on your own? How did they get you to do so?

4. "Deadeye" Bean is Wilkins's favorite teacher. Who was your favorite high school teacher, and why? Give an example of something special that teacher did.

Check Your Performance   **INFERENCES**

Activity	Number Right	Points		Score
Review Test 1 (5 items)	_____	x 2	=	_____
Review Test 2 (10 items)	_____	x 3	=	_____
Review Test 3 (10 items)	_____	x 3	=	_____
Review Test 4 (10 items)	_____	x 3	=	_____
		TOTAL SCORE	=	_____ %

Enter your total score into the **Reading Performance Chart: Review Tests** on the inside back cover.

INFERENCES: Test 1

A. Read each passage below. Then check the **two** statements after each passage which are most logically supported by the information given.

1. My day has not ended. When I get home I suddenly realize that I have between thirty and forty pounds of fish to clean—rockfish yet, all full of spines and pricklers and razor-sharp teeth. When I'm finished, I have so many holes in me I look like a composite of George Custer, Saint Sebastian, and Bonnie and Clyde, but my family comes out to view the catch and restore my faith in the whole enterprise.
    "Yuk," says my daughter.
    "That's a lot of rockfish for people who aren't all that into rockfish," says my wife.
    "I wouldn't eat that on a bet," says my son.

    ____ a. The family is on vacation.

    ✓ b. Rockfish are difficult to clean.

    ____ c. The author's family appreciates his hard work to feed them.

    ____ d. The man enjoys the challenge of cleaning rockfish.

    ✓ e. When he praises his family for restoring his faith, the author is being sarcastic.

2. I guess I did it because I hadn't studied very much. And it seemed so easy—everybody knows that Mr. Brown keeps his office door unlocked. It's just too bad things didn't work out for me. Now my classmates are mad at me because they must re-study for the new test Mr. Brown is making up. My parents have taken away my car keys. And even worse, I'll have to go to summer school for biology.

    ✓ a. The speaker stole a test.

    ____ b. The speaker had been failing the course.

    ✓ c. The class was a biology class.

    ____ d. The speaker regrets not studying more.

    ____ e. The speaker will never cheat again.

Comment: Passage 1— a. The author states that he got "home."
    b. Cleaning them caused "many holes" in the author.
    c. Their comments indicate otherwise.
    d. Since he "suddenly" realized he had "between thirty and forty pounds of fish to clean," we can conclude he hadn't looked forward to the challenge.
    e. Since the family's comments are not supportive, we must assume the author is being sarcastic. *(Continues on next page)*

B. Read the passage below, taken from an essay titled "Darkness at Noon" by Harold Krents, an attorney who was born blind. Then check the **six** statements which are most logically supported by the information given.

Note that the meanings of a few words in the passage are given below.

narcissistic: self-admiring
cum laude: with honor

Blind from birth, I have never had the opportunity to see myself and have been completely dependent on the image I create in the eye of the observer. To date it has not been narcissistic°.

There are those who assume that since I can't see, I obviously also cannot hear. Very often people will converse with me at the top of their lungs, enunciating each word very carefully. Conversely, people will also often whisper, assuming that since my eyes don't work, my ears don't either.

For example, when I go to the airport and ask the ticket agent for assistance to the plane, he or she will invariably pick up the phone, call a ground hostess and whisper: "Hi, Jane, we've got a 76 here." I have concluded that the word "blind" is not used for one of two reasons: Either they fear that if the dread word is spoken, the ticket agent's retina will immediately detach, or they are reluctant to inform me of my condition, of which I may not have been previously aware.

On the other hand, others know that of course I can hear but believe that I can't talk. Often, therefore, when my wife and I go out to dinner, a waiter or waitress will ask Kit if "he would like a drink," to which I respond that "indeed he would." . . .

The toughest misconception of all is the view that because I can't see, I can't work. I was turned down by over forty law firms because of my blindness, even though my qualifications included a *cum laude*° degree from Harvard College and a good ranking in my Harvard Law School class.

____ 1. It would offend Krents if people were to use the word "blind" in reference to him.

✓ 2. The airline's code for a blind passenger was "76."

____ 3. It is better to whisper to blind people than to speak to them loudly.

✓ 4. Krents prefers that people speak to him in a normal tone of voice.

✓ 5. Sighted persons are sometimes uncomfortable directing conversation toward a blind person.

✓ 6. Krents's wife is not blind.

____ 7. Blindness seems to harm a person's intelligence.

✓ 8. Some employers are biased against blind workers.

____ 9. Harvard is apparently biased against blind students.

✓ 10. Krents is outspoken about his blindness.

INFERENCES: Test 2

A. Read each passage below. Then check the **two** statements after each passage which are most logically supported by the information given.

1. Thinking his company had entirely too many rules, an office worker decided to do something about it. So he posted an official-looking notice next to the pencil sharpener. Next to that, he posted a log sheet. For each use of the sharpener, said the notice, everyone must write on the log the date, his or her name, and the number of pencils sharpened. After two weeks, seventeen people had signed the log. The worker who had thought it up had also signed it—twice. "Everyone else was doing it, so I thought I should sign it, too," he explained.

    ✓ a. Workers in that office were used to obeying orders.

    ___ b. This is the first of many times the writer of the notice would try to do something about office rules.

    ___ c. The writer of the notice rarely followed office rules.

    ✓ d. The writer of the notice did not want to appear different from the others.

    ___ e. The workers who did not sign the log were soon let go by the company.

2. Until the Industrial Revolution, the average person died by age 35, largely because of inadequate nutrition. Most people, even farmers, ate meager diets, deficient in vitamins and proteins. Most people ate meat, eggs, or dairy products very rarely, hardly ever ate fruit, and ate vegetables only in summer. They lived almost exclusively on bread and on mush and soup made from grain. As a result, their growth was stunted and their maturation delayed. Poor diet also made people more susceptible to illness and contagious diseases, the latter being most common among children.

    ___ a. Before the Industrial Revolution, fruits and vegetables were both easy to get.

    ✓ b. Before the Industrial Revolution, most people's diets were made up largely of grain.

    ___ c. In general, children do better on a poor diet than adults do.

    ___ d. Grains can provide a good deal of the vitamins and protein needed for good health.

    ✓ e. At the time of the Industrial Revolution, people's diets improved.

B. Ten statements follow the passage on the next page, taken from the essay "How to Say Nothing in 500 Words" by the American scholar Paul Roberts. Check the **six** statements which are most logically supported by the information given.

(Continues on next page)

It's Friday afternoon, and you have almost survived another week of classes. You are just looking forward dreamily to the weekend when the English instructor says: "For Monday you will turn in a five-hundred-word composition on college football."

Well, that puts a good big hole in the weekend. You don't have any strong views on college football one way or the other. You get rather excited during the season and go to all the home games and find it rather more fun than not. On the other hand, the class has been reading Robert Hutchins in the anthology and perhaps Shaw's "Eighty-Yard Run," and from the class discussion you have got the idea that the instructor thinks college football is for the birds. You are no fool, you. You can figure out what side to take.

After dinner you get out the portable typewriter that you got for high school graduation. You might as well get it over with and enjoy Saturday and Sunday. Five hundred words is about two double-spaced pages with normal margins. You put in a sheet of paper, think up a title, and you're off:

Why College Football Should Be Abolished

College football should be abolished because it's bad for the school and also bad for the players. The players are so busy practicing that they don't have any time for their studies.

This, you feel, is a mighty good start. The only trouble is that it's only thirty-two words. You still have four hundred and sixty-eight to go, and you've pretty well exhausted the subject. It comes to you that you do your best thinking in the morning, so you put away the typewriter and go to the movies. But the next morning you have to do your washing and some math problems, and in the afternoon you go to the game. The English instructor turns up too, and you wonder if you've taken the right side after all. Saturday night you have a date, and Sunday morning you have to go to church. (You shouldn't let English assignments interfere with your religion.) What with one thing and another, it's ten o'clock Sunday night before you get out the typewriter again.

✓ 1. The author is writing humorously about what he feels is a typical student.

___ 2. The student agrees with Robert Hutchins's views on football.

✓ 3. The student believes one gets a better grade by defending a point of view the instructor will agree with.

✓ 4. At first, it seemed to the student that his instructor was against college football.

___ 5. In class, the instructor has directly expressed his or her opinions on football.

___ 6. The student would probably choose church on Sunday instead of a desirable social event.

✓ 7. Writing essays probably does not come easily to the student.

✓ 8. The student is better at procrastinating than at writing compositions.

___ 9. The student is failing his English course.

✓ 10. The student will be doing homework until late into Sunday night.

INFERENCES: Test 3

A. Read the passage below, taken from the autobiographical book *Move On* by the television journalist Linda Ellerbee. Check the **five** statements which are most logically supported by the information given.

> Television changed my family forever. We stopped eating dinner at the dining-room table after my mother found out about TV trays. We kept the TV trays behind the kitchen door and served ourselves from pots on the stove. Setting and clearing the dining-room table used to be my job; now, setting and clearing meant unfolding and wiping our TV trays, then, when we'd finished, wiping and folding our TV trays. Dinner was served in time for one program and finished in time for another. During dinner we used to talk to one another. Now television talked to us. If you had something you absolutely had to say, you waited until the commercial, which is, I suspect, where I learned to speak in thirty-second bursts. As a future writer, it was good practice in editing my thoughts. As a little girl, it was lonely as hell. Once in a while, I'd pass our dining-room table and stop, thinking I heard our ghosts sitting around talking to one another, saying stuff.

✓ 1. Ellerbee preferred eating at the dining-room table to eating in front of the TV.

___ 2. Ellerbee must have been an only child.

___ 3. Families should watch more television together.

✓ 4. Watching television during dinner can interfere with family communication.

✓ 5. It's possible to feel lonely even when others are around.

___ 6. As a child, Ellerbee never enjoyed watching television.

✓ 7. Watching TV became more important at dinnertime than what a member of Ellerbee's family had to say.

___ 8. As a little girl, Ellerbee had few friends.

___ 9. Ellerbee's childhood home was haunted.

✓ 10. When Ellerbee imagined the ghosts, she was remembering better times.

Comments: Item 1—See the last two sentences of the passage.

Items 4 and 7—Ellerbee states, "If you had something you absolutely had to say, you waited until the commercial."

(Continues on next page)

B. Read the following textbook passage. Then check the **five** statements which are most logically supported by the information given, as well as your own knowledge.

> During the first half of this century, young people were encouraged to stay in school longer; this created adolescence. As twentieth-century America became increasingly industrialized and urbanized, positions for unskilled laborers became scarce. As a result, education was no longer a luxury—it was a necessity. So instead of being rushed into the adult world, young people were urged to finish high school or even college. During the Great Depression, staying in school was encouraged for another reason: It kept young people from crowding the shrinking job market. Indeed, between 1900 and 1956, the proportion of Americans graduating from high school rose from 6.3 to 62.5 percent.

_____ 1. After 1956, the percentage of Americans who finished high school fell sharply.

_____ 2. During the first half of the century, most young people who graduated from high school probably also went on to college.

✓ 3. In the 1800s, there was plenty of work for unskilled laborers.

_____ 4. Before the twentieth century, jobs for unskilled workers were hard to find.

✓ 5. In the 1800s, young people were considered adults at an earlier age than they are today.

✓ 6. During the Great Depression, young people who sought work competed with older people for jobs.

_____ 7. During the Great Depression, young people found jobs much more easily than older people.

✓ 8. In our society in general, adulthood is equated with leaving school and going to work.

_____ 9. The need for skilled laborers in the United States has greatly decreased since 1956.

✓ 10. Between 1900 and 1956, the number of high school teachers in the country must have greatly increased.

Comments: Item 3—The second sentence implies that there was no scarcity before America became very industrialized and urbanized.

Items 5 and 8—The passage contrasts the "adult world" with high school and college.

INFERENCES: Test 4

A. Following is Edward Arlington Robinson's well-known poem about a wealthy man named Richard Cory. Read the poem, and then check the **five** statements which are most logically supported by the information given.

Note that the meanings of a few words in the poem are given below.

Clean favored: clean-cut; wholesome-looking

imperially: in a superior way (since the rich had a superior, more healthy diet than the poor)

quietly arrayed: not dressed in a showy manner

Richard Cory

Whenever Richard Cory went down town,
We people on the pavement looked at him;
He was a gentleman from sole to crown,
Clean favored°, and imperially° slim.

And he was always quietly arrayed°,
And he was always human when he talked;
But still he fluttered pulses when he said
"Good-morning," and he glittered when he walked.

And he was rich—yes, richer than a king,
And admirably schooled in every grace;
In fine, we thought that he was everything
To make us wish that we were in his place.

So on we worked, and waited for the light,
And went without the meat, and cursed the bread;
And Richard Cory, one calm summer night,
Went home and put a bullet through his head.

____ 1. Richard Cory treated the poor disrespectfully.

____ 2. Richard Cory had many personal friends.

_✓_ 3. The speaker is poor.

_✓_ 4. Richard Cory was admired.

____ 5. Richard Cory was married.

_✓_ 6. The poor people in town thought Richard Cory was happy.

____ 7. Richard Cory had an unhappy love affair.

_✓_ 8. Richard Cory was not as fortunate as he seemed.

____ 9. The poor preferred bread to meat.

_✓_ 10. Money does not buy happiness.

(Continues on next page)

B. Read the following textbook passage. Then check the **five** statements which are most logically supported by the information given.

> Several years ago, smoldering cigarette butts caused almost 400,000 acres of the mighty Yellowstone National Park in Montana to go up in smoke. Its natural beauty was feared lost forever. But even as experts were declaring the blackened ground sterilized of any life, tiny shoots of grass were pushing up through the cinders. Within weeks, wind, rain, and the actions of birds seeded large areas of wildflowers that attracted colonies of insects. Following the insects were hungry birds, including the industrious nutcrackers, which carried in white-bark pine cones from far away to bury in the ground. The fire melted the lodgepole pine cones, scattering seeds for reforestation and providing food for squirrels and chipmunks. And treetop dwellers like the fish osprey found new nesting territory opened up by the burning of the forest canopy.

_____ 1. Most forest fires are caused by carelessness.

__✓__ 2. Experts can be wrong.

_____ 3. The fire was not at all destructive.

_____ 4. The blackened ground was sterilized of any life.

__✓__ 5. Nature has ways of seeding empty spaces.

__✓__ 6. Wildflowers provide food for insects.

__✓__ 7. Pine cones have more than one function in nature.

_____ 8. The fish osprey had never before lived in Yellowstone National Park.

_____ 9. Soon the parklands will look exactly as they used to.

__✓__ 10. The parkland's rebirth was due to the interaction of the fire, animals, plants, and weather.

Comments: Part A, item 3—See line 2 of the poem.
Part A, item 4—See lines 7 and 8.
Part A, item 6— See lines 11 and 12.

Part B, item 2—See the third sentence of the passage.
Part B, item 6—See the fourth sentence.
Part B, item 7—See the next-to-last sentence.

INFERENCES: Test 5

A. After reading the following textbook passage, circle the letter of the best answer to each question.

Note that the meanings of a few words in the passage are given below.

urban sprawl: the spreading out of cities
provincialism: narrowness in thought due to limited experience
unprecedented: new
exasperated: greatly irritated

By making automobiles available to the masses, the growing industry changed the face of America. The spreading web of paved roads fueled urban sprawl°, real-estate booms in California and Florida, and a new roadside culture. Thousands of "auto camps" opened to provide tourists with tents and crude toilets. "Auto clubs" like the Tin Can Tourists Association (named for the tin can tied to the radiator cap of a member's car) sprang up to aid travelers. Automobile travel broke down provincialism° and advanced standardized dialects and manners. By 1930 almost two farm families in three had cars. When asked why her family had bought a Model T when they had no indoor plumbing, a farm woman replied, "You can't go to town in a bathtub." Across the country the automobile gave the young unprecedented° freedom from parental authority. After hearing thirty cases of "sex crimes" (nineteen of which occurred in cars), an exasperated° juvenile court judge in Indiana declared that the automobile was "a house of prostitution on wheels."

1. Automobiles
   a. opened up opportunities for businesses that serve tourists.
   b. appealed more to farm families than to city families.
   c. made people less sociable.
   d. increased the number of farmers in the country.

2. The more interaction there is between different groups of people,
   a. the more a roadside culture is likely to form.
   b. the more alike their speech is likely to become.
   c. the more urban sprawl there will be.
   d. the less urban sprawl there will be.

3. The real estate booms in California and Florida must have been made possible by
   a. the profits from automobile sales.
   b. the widespread development of paved roads.
   c. a growing interest in farm life.
   d. standardized dialects.

(Continues on next page)

4. To the young, freedom from parental authority meant
   (a.) more sexual activity.
   b. better manners.
   c. joining an auto club.
   d. all of the above.

5. The automobile industry
   a. must have quickly become an important source of employment.
   b. brought consumers to a variety of businesses.
   c. in some cases weakened ties between immediate family members.
   (d.) all of the above.

B. Ten statements follow the textbook passage below. Check the **five** statements which are most logically supported by the information given.

> Suppose a man works six or seven days a week in a factory, trying to support his family, but never seems to be able to make ends meet. If he analyzed his situation rationally, he would probably blame the well-to-do generally and his employers specifically for failing to pay him an adequate wage. But these people have the power to cut off his income; to oppose them openly would be self-destructive. He could also blame himself for his financial problems, but this too makes him uncomfortable. Instead, he looks to the immigrants who have begun working in his factory. He doesn't really know them, but he suspects they're willing to work for low wages and that many other immigrants are eager to take his job. By a process of twisted logic, he blames these people for his poverty. Soon he is exchanging rumors about "them" with his cronies and supporting efforts to close the border. Hating immigrants makes the man and his friends feel a little better.

____ 1. Factory workers are not good at managing money.

____ 2. All factory workers are underpaid.

✓ 3. Some people are reluctant to oppose their bosses.

____ 4. Immigrants are eager to take other people's jobs.

____ 5. The immigrants don't do their jobs very well.

✓ 6. The author feels that the man in the example is underpaid.

✓ 7. Prejudice can be the result of wanting to blame someone for our problems.

____ 8. The man in the example would probably be violent against immigrants.

✓ 9. The man in the example would probably oppose hiring more immigrants.

✓ 10. Some people make themselves feel better by thinking less of others.

INFERENCES: Test 6

A. Read the following excerpt from a literary essay by the novelist Amy Tan. Then circle the letter of the best answer to each of the questions that follow.

Lately, I've been giving more thought to the kind of English my mother speaks. Like others, I have described it to people as "broken" or "fractured" English. But I wince when I say that. It has always bothered me that I can think of no way to describe it other than "broken," as if it were damaged and needed to be fixed, as if it lacked a certain wholeness and soundness. I've heard other terms used, "limited English," for example. But they seem just as bad, as if everything is limited, including people's perceptions of the limited English speaker.

I know this for a fact, because when I was growing up, my mother's "limited" English limited *my* perception of her. I was ashamed of her English. I believed that her English reflected the quality of what she had to say. That is, because she expressed them imperfectly her thoughts were imperfect. And I had plenty of evidence to support me: the fact that people in department stores, at banks, and at restaurants did not take her seriously, did not give her good service, pretended not to understand her, or even acted as if they did not hear her.

1. Which of the following statements is the implied main idea of the passage?
   a. People who speak "broken" English have limited ideas about life.
   b. Influenced by her mother, the author's English is also "broken."
   c. People who speak "broken" English are sometimes unfairly viewed as having defective ideas as well.
   d. The author feels that the word *broken* is a good description of the speech patterns of people who don't speak English correctly.

2. The author grew up believing that her mother had nothing important to say because
   a. her mother hardly ever spoke.
   b. other people treated her mother with disrespect.
   c. the author is far more intelligent than her mother.
   d. the author and her mother had very different interests.

3. The term *broken English* makes the author wince because
   a. she now sees that her mother's English really is in need of fixing.
   b. she dislikes it, but cannot come up with a better term.
   c. the term has been used to describe her own speech as well.
   d. she's not exactly sure what the term really means.

4. The author implies that
   a. even today she is ashamed of her mother's English.
   b. her mother has many valuable thoughts.

See the third and fourth sentences of paragraph 2.

(Continues on next page)

    c. people who speak well are usually treated well by others.
    d. people who speak "broken" English aren't very intelligent.

5. The author probably wishes that when she was growing up
    a. she had learned English better herself.
    b. she had helped her mother think more clearly.
    (c.) she had listened more to what her mother had to say than how she said it.
    d. people had used the term *limited English* rather than *broken English*.

B. Read the following textbook passage. Then check the **five** statements which are most logically supported by the information given.

> People interrupt for various reasons. One is believing that what they have to say is more important than what the other person is saying. Another reason people interrupt is that they believe they know what the other person is going to say and want the person to know that they already know. People may also interrupt when they are not paying close attention. The interruption communicates a lack of sensitivity, a superior attitude, or both. People need to be able to verbalize their ideas and feelings fully; inappropriate interruptions are bound to damage their self-concepts or make them hostile—and possibly both. Simply stated, whatever you have to say is seldom so important that it requires you to interrupt a person. When you do interrupt, you should realize that you may be perceived as putting a person down and are increasing the chances of a defensive reaction. The more frequent the interruptions, the greater the potential harm.

  _✓_ 1. People feel good if others listen carefully to their ideas.
  _____ 2. The author suggests that people who interrupt don't mind being interrupted themselves.
  _✓_ 3. One reason people who are not paying close attention may interrupt is that they don't realize that the speaker is in the middle of a point.
  _____ 4. The author feels it is okay to interrupt others if you feel you are superior to them.
  _____ 5. The author suggests that if you never interrupt others, you will never be interrupted.
  _✓_ 6. Interruptions can make people feel that their ideas are not worth listening to.
  _✓_ 7. We can conclude the author would say that a boss will gain more cooperation by not interrupting workers.
  _____ 8. We can conclude the author would say it is okay for a parent to interrupt a child.
  _✓_ 9. People who interrupt don't always realize how the other person will view the interruption.
  _____ 10. The author would consider anger to be an unlikely reaction to being interrupted.

9
Purpose and Tone

An important part of reading critically is realizing that behind everything you read is an author. This author is a person who has a reason for writing a given piece and who works from a personal point of view. To fully understand and evaluate what you read, you must recognize **purpose**—the reason why the author writes. You must also be aware of **tone**—the expression of the author's attitude and feeling.

PURPOSE

Authors write with a reason in mind, and you can better evaluate what is being said by determining what that reason is. The author's reason for writing is also called the purpose of a selection. Three common purposes are as follows:

- **To inform**—to give information about a subject. Authors with this purpose wish to provide facts that will explain or teach something to readers.

    For example, the author of an informative paragraph about baby-sitting might begin, "The would-be baby sitter should be aware that the job has both advantages and drawbacks."

- **To persuade**—to convince the reader to agree with the author's point of view on a subject. Authors with this purpose may give facts, but their main goal is to argue or prove a point to readers.

    The author of a persuasive paragraph about baby-sitting might begin, "Anyone who imagines that baby-sitting is an easy job is mistaken."

- **To entertain**—to amuse and delight; to appeal to the reader's senses and imagination. Authors with this purpose entertain in various ways, through fiction and nonfiction.

    The author of a humorous paragraph about baby-sitting might begin, "I once spent a wild and crazy night trying to survive as a baby sitter."

Read each of the three paragraphs below and decide whether the author's purpose is to inform, to persuade, or to entertain. Write in your answers, and then read the explanations that follow.

1. Using the present measurement system is as inefficient and old-fashioned as using Roman numerals. If more Americans realized how easy it is to convert milliliters to liters as opposed to converting tablespoons to quarts, the metric system would be adopted immediately.

    Purpose: _____

2. About 113 billion people have lived and died in the history of our planet, according to scientific estimates. Of all these people, the names of about 7 billion, or approximately 6 percent, are recorded in some way—on monuments or in books, manuscripts, and public records. The other 106 billion people are gone without a trace.

    Purpose: _____

3. Because of the contrast between his medium-size wardrobe and his extra-large-size body, my brother has made a commitment to only three meals a day. His definition of a meal, however, is as broad as his belly. If we spot a pretzel salesman or a hot-dog stand on our way to a restaurant, for example, he is not beyond suggesting that we stop. "It'll make a good appetizer," he says.

    Purpose: _____

Explanation:

In the first paragraph, the writer's purpose is to *persuade* the audience that Americans should change over to the metric system. That is clear because the author claims that our present system is "inefficient and old-fashioned," that conversions in the metric system are "easy," and that people would prefer the metric system. These are statements that are used to convince us rather than to inform us. The purpose of the second paragraph is to *inform*. The author is simply providing readers with information about the people who have lived and died on Earth. In paragraph three, the playful and exaggerated details tell us the author's main goal is to *entertain* with humor.

At times, writing may seem to blend two purposes. An informative article on losing weight, for example, may include comic touches, or a persuasive letter to the editor may contain factual information. Remember in such cases to focus on the author's primary purpose. Ask yourself, "What is the author's main idea?" That will help you determine his or her principal intention.

➤ *Practice 1*

Label each item according to its main purpose: to inform (**I**), to persuade (**P**), or to entertain (**E**).

_I_ 1. As Americans have grown more health-conscious, the menus in school cafeterias have begun to change.

_P_ 2. Nurses assigned to intensive care units should be given shorter shifts and higher pay because the work is unusually demanding and stressful.

_E_ 3. It's easy to quit smoking; I've done it hundreds of times.

_P_ 4. More women should get involved in local politics and support the growing number of female candidates for public office.

_I_ 5. The career of a professional athlete is usually quite short.

_I_ 6. An artificial odor is added to natural gas so that people can tell whether or not gas is leaking.

_E_ 7. Fred believes in a seafood diet: when he sees food, he eats it.

_P_ 8. Shoparama has low, low prices, an outstanding selection of health and beauty products, and a convenient location near you.

_E_ 9. The best approach to take when you feel the urge to exercise is to lie down quickly in a darkened room until the feeling goes away.

_I_ 10. In ancient Egypt, priests plucked all the hair from their bodies, including their eyebrows and eyelashes.

➤ *Practice 2*

Following are three passages, one each from a textbook, a humor book, and a collection of essays. Circle the letter of the best description of the purpose of each passage.

1. We have all heard the story of how the young, impoverished Abraham Lincoln trekked miles to borrow books from a neighbor and then read them by firelight. We know that nineteenth-century readers would rush to the wharf to greet the ship carrying the latest chapters of a Dickens novel. Today, reading seems less urgent and less exciting to many of us. Worse, few people impart a passion for books to their children. Instead, they leave the children in front of the television and hope, weakly, that too much watching won't be bad for them. But we cannot afford to stop reading. Books shed a light that

illuminates our problems and crises. They are also mirrors that reflect the truest image of ourselves.

The main purpose of this passage is to
a. explain something about Abraham Lincoln and Dickens to readers.
(b.) convince readers of the importance of books.
c. delight readers with entertaining material from books.

2. Most of what I know about carpentry, which is almost nothing, I learned in Shop. You should know that I took Shop during the Eisenhower administration, when boys took Shop and girls took Home Economics—a code name for "cooking." Schools are not allowed to separate boys and girls like that anymore. They're also not allowed to put students' heads in vises and tighten them, which is what our Shop teacher, Mr Schmidt, did to Ronnie Miller in the fifth grade when Ronnie used a chisel when he should have used a screwdriver. (Mr. Schmidt had strong feelings about how to use tools properly.) I guess he shouldn't have put Ronnie's head in the vise, but it (Ronnie's head) was no great prize to begin with, and you can bet Ronnie never confused chisels and screwdrivers in later life—assuming he made it to later life.

The main purpose of this passage is to
a. inform readers about the nature of shop classes.
b. argue that shop classes should be eliminated from public schools.
(c.) amuse readers with humorous details about shop classes.

3. Studies of job satisfaction indicate that the vast majority of workers are at least somewhat satisfied with their jobs and would continue to work even if they didn't have to. The meaning of work varies from person to person. To some, it is a source of self-respect and life purpose. For others, work is a means of passing time. To still others, it is primarily a source of financial independence. Among women, available work is often less satisfying than home management. Yet most women report increases in self-esteem when employed, especially if they experience support from their families.

The main purpose of this passage is to
(a.) report on what has been learned through studies of job satisfaction.
b. convince readers of the importance of job satisfaction.
c. entertain readers with rich, sensual descriptions of job satisfaction.

TONE

A writer's tone reveals the attitude he or she has toward a subject. Tone is expressed through the words and details the writer selects. Just as a speaker's voice can project a range of feelings, a writer's voice can project one or more tones, or feelings: anger, sympathy, hopefulness, sadness, respect, dislike, and so on. Understanding tone is, then, an important part of understanding what an author has written.

To appreciate the differences in tone that writers can employ, read the following versions of a murder confession:

"I just shot my husband five times in the chest with this .357 Magnum." (*Tone:* matter-of-fact, objective.)

"How could I ever have killed him? I just can't believe I did that!" (*Tone:* shocked, disbelieving.)

"Oh, my God. I've murdered my husband. How can I ever be forgiven for this dreadful deed?" (*Tone:* guilty, regretful)

"That dirty rat. He's had it coming for years. I'm glad I finally had the nerve to do it." (*Tone:* revengeful, well-satisfied.)

Words That Describe Tone

Below and on the next page is a list of words commonly used to describe tone. With the exception of the words *matter-of-fact* and *objective*, the words in the box reflect a feeling or judgment. The words on this page are more familiar ones. Brief meanings are given in parentheses for the words on the next page. Refer to these meanings as needed to learn any words you don't know yet.

Some Words That Describe Tone

admiring	curious	playful
affectionate	doubtful	praising
amused	encouraging	respectful
angry	excited	self-pitying
ashamed	forgiving	serious
calming	frightened	sorrowful
caring	grateful	sympathetic
cheerful	humorous	threatening
conceited	insulting	tragic
critical	joyous	warm
cruel	loving	worried

(Words continue on next page)

More Words That Describe Tone—with Their Meanings

ambivalent	*(uncertain about a choice)*
arrogant	*(full of self-importance; conceited)*
bewildered	*(confused; puzzled)*
bitter	*(angry; full of hate)*
compassionate	*(deeply sympathetic))*
depressed	*(very sad or discouraged)*
detached	*(emotionally uninvolved)*
disbelieving	*(unbelieving)*
distressed	*(suffering sorrow, misery, or pain)*
hypocritical	*(false)*
impassioned	*(filled with strong feeling)*
indignant	*(angry about something unfair or mean)*
instructive	*(teaching)*
ironic	*(meaning the opposite of what is expressed)*
lighthearted	*(happy and carefree)*
matter-of-fact	*(sticking to facts; unemotional)*
mocking	*(making fun of and/or looking down upon something)*
nostalgic	*(longing for something or someone in the past)*
objective	*(not influenced by feelings or personal prejudices)*
optimistic	*(looking on the bright side of things)*
pessimistic	*(looking on the gloomy, unfavorable side of things)*
pleading	*(begging)*
prideful	*(full of pride or exaggerated self-esteem)*
remorseful	*(guilty over a wrong one has done)*
revengeful	*(wanting to hurt someone in return for an injury)*
sarcastic	*(sharp or wounding; ironic)*
scheming	*(tricky)*
scornful	*(looking down on someone or something)*
self-mocking	*(making fun of or looking down on oneself)*
sentimental	*(showing tender feelings; romantic; overly emotional)*
solemn	*(involved with serious concerns)*
straightforward	*(direct and honest)*
superior	*(looking down on others)*
tolerant	*(respectful of other views and behavior; patient about problems)*
uncertain	*(doubting)*

More About Tone

Below are five statements expressing different attitudes about a shabby apartment. Five different tones are used:

optimistic	tolerant	humorous
bitter	sentimental	

Feel free to check the lists on pages 293–294 for the meaning of any unfamiliar tone words. Label each statement with the tone you think is present. Use each tone once. Then read the explanation that follows.

_____ 1. This place may be shabby, but since both of my children were born while we lived here, it has a special place in my heart.

_____ 2. This isn't the greatest apartment in the world, but it's not really that bad.

_____ 3. If only there were some decent jobs out there, I wouldn't be reduced to living in this miserable dump.

_____ 4. This place does need some repairs, but I expect the landlord to get around to them any day now.

_____ 5. When we move away, we're planning to release three hundred cockroaches and two mice so we can leave the place exactly as we found it.

Explanation:

The tone of item 1 is sentimental. "It has a special place in my heart" expresses tender emotions. In item 2, the words "not really that bad" show that the writer is tolerant, accepting the situation while recognizing that it could be better. We could describe the tone of item 3 as bitter. The writer resents a situation that forces him or her to live in a "miserable dump." Item 4 is optimistic since the writer is expecting the apartment to be improved soon. Finally, the tone of item 5 is humorous. Its writer claims to be planning a comic revenge on the landlord by returning the apartment to the terrible condition it was in when the tenants moved in.

A Note on Irony

One commonly used tone is irony. When writing has an **ironic** tone, it says one thing but means the opposite. Irony is found in everyday conversation as well as in writing. Following are a few examples; notice that the quotation in each says the opposite of what is meant.

If at the beginning of a semester you discover that one of your instructors is particularly demanding, you might comment, "This class is sure going to be a barrel of laughs!"

After seeing a terrible performance in a movie, someone might say about the actor involved, "Now there's a person with a great chance for an Oscar."

If a person is clumsy, someone might remark, "There goes an Olympic champion."

Irony also refers to situations in which what happens is the opposite of what we might expect. We would call it ironic, for example, if a young woman who failed English in high school went on to become a well-known writer, or if a young man who could not make his basketball team went on to become a professional basketball player. Here are a few more examples of this type of irony:

Helen won a lifetime supply of Marlboros a week after she quit smoking.

To get some needed cash, Elliot sold his stereo. For his birthday the next day, his girlfriend bought him the new Whitney Houston album.

A young man who adores basketball is five feet five inches tall. His brother, who plans on being a cartoonist and has no interest at all in sports, is six feet three.

Albert Einstein, one of the century's most brilliant scientists, did poorly in school.

When Beethoven wrote the *Ninth Symphony*, considered his greatest work, he was totally deaf.

➤ *Practice 3*

A. On the next page are five statements expressing different attitudes about a boss. Five different tones are used:

admiring	sympathetic	objective
ironic	critical	

For each statement, write the tone that you think is present. Use each tone once.

_____admiring_____ 1. Tony is an excellent manager—the best one I've ever had.

_____sympathetic_____ 2. I know Tony's daughter has been sick. Naturally it's hard for him to concentrate on work right now.

_____critical_____ 3. Tony's too ambitious for his own good. That ambition may yet destroy him and the company.

_____objective_____ 4. Since Tony Roberts became manager, sales in the appliance division have increased 30 per cent.

_____ironic_____ 5. Tony's wonderful, all right. He's gotten as far as he has without the slightest idea of how to manage a division.

B. The following conversation between a mother and son involves five of the tones shown in the box below. For each statement, write the tone that you think is present.

threatening	joyful	solemn	straightforward
sympathetic	pessimistic	self-pitying	sarcastic
nostalgic	disbelieving		

_____straightforward_____ 6. "Please take the garbage out on your way to school this morning."

_____sarcastic_____ 7. "Sure, Mom. I've been looking forward to that chore all morning."

_____threatening_____ 8. "Listen, young man, if you don't start fulfilling your responsibilities around this house, your father and I will start asking you to pay rent or find your own place."

_____self-pitying_____ 9. "Okay, I'll take the garbage out. But you know it's not easy going to school full-time and working twenty hours a week when I'm just getting over a bad case of the flu."

_____sympathetic_____ 10. "I know, honey, this semester has been an especially difficult one for you."

Comment: Part A, items 4 and 5—Statement 4 unemotionally expresses the facts. In statement 5, the speaker really means that Tony is *not* wonderful.

➤ *Practice 4*

Each passage illustrates one of the tones in the box below. In each space, put the letter of the tone that best applies. Don't use any letter more than once.

Remember that the tone of a selection reflects the author's attitude. To find the tone of a paragraph, ask yourself what attitude is revealed by its words and phrases.

a. superior	b. forgiving	c. tragic	d. supportive
e. self-mocking	f. affectionate	g. ambivalent	h. scornful

_____h_____ 1. Spam—that slimy canned pork product—is surprisingly still around after more than fifty years. Despite its high fat content (more than three and a half teaspoons per two-ounce serving) and high calorie count (171 calories per serving), more than four billion cans have been sold since 1937. Spam's greasy, rubbery consistency and salty flavor have made it the butt of many jokes—such as David Letterman's suggestion of Spam-on-a-rope for people who want to eat and shower at the same time. Shareholders in George Hormel and Company must be laughing all the way to the bank. More than three cans of the sorry excuse for a food are consumed every second, despite its high cost—pound for pound it costs about the same as strip steak.

_____d_____ 2. The mayor inherited a lot of problems when she came into the job. The city had a pile of bills it could not pay, morale among city employees was very poor, and members of the city council were fighting among themselves instead of working together. Those would be very tough situations for anyone to deal with. But she has done her very best. From early in the morning often until after midnight, the mayor is in her office. She has worked out agreements with many of the city's creditors. Her efforts at settling the arguments in city council are beginning to pay off. And people working for the city say they are feeling better about their jobs. She still has a lot of work to do, but I, for one, think she is doing a fine job.

_____e_____ 3. Puberty causes the changing of considerably more than your sheets. I remember that puberty inspired me to brush my hair so hard that I almost exposed the area where my brains should have been. The moment my glands kicked in, I began to brush my hair a hundred times a day so that not a single strand was out of place for the girls I now wanted to impress. I shined my own shoes, I cut the tiny hanging strings off the frayed parts of my collar, and, in a stunning blend of vanity and dopiness, I even began to flaunt my eyelashes, which were particularly long. Before puberty, I had actually trimmed these lashes because women had said I looked like a girl; but now I was grooming them with a toothbrush and wondering if girls would prefer them from the front or the side.

_f_ 4. My grandfather lived with my family as I grew up, and some of my warmest early memories revolve around him. He was a sweet man with simple tastes. He liked Western movies, and when I was a preschooler, he often took me along to see them. After the movies, we would go to a nearby Bridgeman's ice-cream shop. He would order a hot chocolate. It always came with a couple of sugar cookies, which he would give me to eat with my scoop of ice cream. Once I began school, he would go to the Westerns alone. But it wasn't unusual for me to come home from school and find those same sugar cookies waiting for me in a Bridgeman's napkin.

_g_ 5. The proposal has been made that students in our schools be required to wear uniforms. In some ways, this sounds good. It is true that shopping for fashionable clothing and deciding what to wear in the morning take up a lot of money and time. But kids need to learn to deal with social pressure about things like clothing, and school might be as good a place as any for that lesson. Also, the way people dress is one way they express themselves, and maybe students should have that avenue of expression open to them too. However, it is a shame if they constantly worry about their appearance and waste valuable class time by wishing they could have the name-brand shirt across the room. So uniforms might be helpful in keeping students' minds on their education. Uniforms could save students and their parents money, too, which is certainly a good thing. On the other hand, those uniforms are not cheap, and most students will want to have several sets, so the savings might not be all that significant. It's really hard to say whether uniforms are a good idea or not.

> *Practice 5*

Read the following letter to Ann Landers along with her response. Then answer the questions about purpose and tone that follow.

> **Dear Ann Landers:** When our daughter won a scholarship to a very fine university in the East last year, we were thrilled and proud of her.
>
> "Mary" does not drink or smoke and has high moral standards. We were not the least bit uneasy about her moving so far from home to go to school, and we didn't worry about peer pressure. She has always been a leader, not a follower.
>
> Mary's letters, however, are depressing. She says so many people who live in her dorm (it's mixed, both men and women) get drunk at least four nights a week, and they make so much noise she can't study. She also has spent several nights taking care of sick, hung-over friends. Her roommate, she says, often stays out until 3 or 4 in the morning, comes in dead drunk, and throws up. Mary resents having to clean up after her, but she has no choice.
>
> We did not anticipate this sort of thing when we sent our daughter away to college. We asked Mary if she would consider changing schools next year (we would be willing to forgo the scholarship and pay her tuition). She said, "No, an Ivy League school has always been my dream, and these problems exist all over."
>
> What on Earth is going on? Can you tell us?
>
> **Dear Parents:** You ask, "What's going on?" You just described it, according to the information I receive regularly from the National Clearinghouse for Alcohol and Drug Information. College students spend $5.5 billion a year on alcohol. Harvard School of Public Health researchers have reported that excessive use of alcohol on college campuses may be hazardous not only to the health of drinkers but to nondrinkers as well. Nondrinkers suffer from loss of sleep and study time, vandalism, physical assault, unwanted sexual advances, and rape.
>
> Dr. Henry Wechsler, director of college alcohol studies at the Harvard School of Public Health, was the lead author of a report that studied the drinking habits of 17,592 students from 140 colleges. The study found that alcohol on college campuses poses a serious hazard to the physical health and emotional well-being of students. One student said she was fed up with people urinating in the elevators, vomiting in the halls, wrecking the bathroom, and pounding holes in the walls.
>
> Wechsler's research revealed that nearly half the college students are binge drinkers who cause most of the trouble by depriving others of study time and sleep and attacking classmates. College security officers and administrators report that alcohol is involved in the majority of rapes and almost all violent incidents on campus.

Wechsler urges students who do not drink to speak up and demand their rights. *Time* magazine quoted Wechsler as saying, "If your roommate gets drunk every night, either insist on a new roommate or demand that you be moved." He urges people who are bothered by excessive drinking to complain. He said, "I want students to complain. I want parents to complain. That's the only way we will get change."

Although Wechsler does not beat the drum for total abstinence (he says it is not "realistic"), I disagree. If you don't drink at all, you will never have to worry about how much is too much.

1. The first paragraph of the parents' letter has a
   a. tragic tone.
   (b.) prideful tone.
   c. pleading tone.

2. In its third paragraph, the parents' letter takes on a
   (a.) distressed tone.
   b. revengeful tone.
   c. doubtful tone.

3. The parents' letter ends in a(n)
   a. instructive tone.
   (b.) bewildered tone.
   c. sentimental tone.

4. The purpose of much of the parents' letter is to
   (a.) inform Ann Landers of their daughter's situation.
   b. persuade Ann Landers to convince their daughter to leave her school.
   c. amuse Ann Landers with the ridiculous behavior of today's college students.

5. On the basis of the facts she has chosen to include and on her last paragraph, we can conclude that Landers's main purpose is
   a. simply to inform people about various views of alcohol.
   (b.) to persuade readers that it is best to drink little or no alcohol
   c. to entertain readers with colorful views about alcohol.

➤ Review Test 1

To review what you've learned in this chapter, fill in the blank(s) or circle the letter of the correct answer for each question.

1–3. What is the purpose of each of the types of writing below? Label each according to its usual main purpose: to inform, to persuade, or to entertain.

A news report: _____*inform*_____

A mystery novel: _____*entertain*_____

An editorial: _____*persuade*_____

4. The author's reason for writing something is also called the _____*purpose*_____ of a selection.

5. The tone of a selection reveals the author's _____*attitude*_____ toward his or her subject.

6. An ironic comment is one that means the _____*opposite*_____ of what is said.

7. Imagine a bad morning when everything goes wrong—there is no hot water for the shower, milk for the cereal is sour, a pool of oil is under the car, and so on. Which of the following would be an ironic comment on the situation?
   a. "What a lousy start to the day."
   b. "What a great day this is going to be."
   c. "Good grief. What did I do to deserve this?"

8. A (*forgiving, critical, matter-of-fact*) _____*matter-of-fact*_____ tone reveals no personal feeling.

9. An arrogant tone suggests that the speaker or writer
   a. is angry.
   b. looks on the unfavorable side of things.
   c. thinks a lot of himself or herself.

10. An objective tone indicates that the speaker or writer is telling something
    a. dishonestly.
    b. without personal prejudice.
    c. with a longing for something in the past.

➤ *Review Test 2: Purpose*

In the space provided, indicate whether the primary purpose of each passage is to inform (**I**), to persuade (**P**), or to entertain (**E**).

P   1. Americans love parks and wildlife refuges, but the crowding they find there is a national disgrace. Parking lots are packed, and roadways through parks and refuges are often so jammed that they might as well be the parking lots. Playing fields and barbecue grills are claimed early in the day, and even on remote trails voices can be heard from every direction. Americans badly need more land devoted to open space where nature walks, picnics, and camping can take place in uncrowded tranquility. Communities across the nation should establish parks and trails that provide free access to open space for everyone.

I   2. Sediment will sometimes accumulate in shower heads, causing the water to flow unevenly or completely clogging the shower head. Sometimes briskly opening and closing the adjustment mechanism a few times is enough to solve the problem. If this does not work, remove the shower head from the wall, holding onto the pipe while you unscrew the shower head so that you do not loosen the pipe inside the wall. Once you have removed the shower head, try cleaning it with a toothpick or wire. If necessary, take the shower head apart and soak it in water overnight to soften the mineral deposits.

E   3. An elderly woman in a Cadillac was preparing to back into a parking space. Suddenly a small red sports car appeared and pulled into the space. "That's what you can do when you're young and fast," the young man in the car yelled to the old woman. As he strolled away, laughing, he heard a terrible crunching sound. "What's that noise?" he asked. Turning around, he saw the old woman backing repeatedly into his small car and crushing it. "You can't do that, old lady!" he yelled.

"What do you mean, I can't?" she yelled back, as metal grated against metal. "This is what you can do when you're old and rich."

I   4. During the 1950s and 1960s, researchers discovered that monosodium glutamate (MSG), commonly used to flavor foods, caused brain damage in baby rats, mice, and monkeys. In 1970, a National Academy of Sciences committee concluded that MSG in food is unlikely to harm human infants, but the committee nevertheless recommended that MSG not be used in baby food. By then, however, the baby-food industry had already stopped using MSG because of public pressure.

___P___ 5. The practice of tipping goes back thousands of years, at least to the times of the ancient Romans. You would think that by now the public would have refused to cooperate with such an unfair and bothersome habit. Who else besides restaurant owners can get away with underpaying their employees and expect their customers to make up the difference? It has gotten so that waiters no longer look at a tip as a reward for superior service. Instead, it is an expected part of their day's pay, to the point that even a waiter who has provided lousy service will demand a tip if a customer does not offer one. Restaurant customers should band together and demand the elimination of this ridiculous custom.

➤ *Review Test 3: Tone*

Each of the following five passages illustrates one of the tones in the box below. In the space provided, put the letter of the tone that best applies to each passage. Don't use any letter more than once.

Remember that the tone of a selection reflects the author's attitude. To find the tone of a paragraph, ask yourself what attitude is revealed by its words and phrases.

a. tolerant	b. pessimistic	c. revengeful	d. ironic
e. indignant	f. sentimental	g. forgiving	h. surprised

___f___ 1. Emperor penguins are among the most adorable animals in the world. Like all penguins, they look like cute little people dressed in tuxedos. They flap their wings and waddle into the water in an utterly charming way. The most enchanting thing they do is care for their sweet little babies. The newborn chick squats on its father's feet, where it is warmed by his body and cared for affectionately until its mother returns from a trip to find food. Emperor penguins love their babies so much that they have been known to try to hatch blocks of ice if their own little ones die. This is a delightful testimony to the power of parental affection.

___e___ 2. Relentless greed and horrifying dishonesty characterized the treatment of Indians in the 1860s and 1870s, when massacres of Native Americans were commonplace. The massacre at Sand Creek in Colorado in 1864 was sadly typical. The territorial governor had persuaded the Indians to gather there and had promised them protection. Despite this pledge,

Comment: Paragraph 1 is characterized by an emotional view of penguins.

Colonel J. M. Chivington's militia attacked the defenseless Indian camp. They disregarded that sacred symbol, the American flag, and the white flag of truce that the Indians were flying at Sand Creek. Four hundred fifty peaceful Indians—men, women, and children—were slaughtered in what has been called "the foulest and most unjustified crime in the annals of America." This was only one of the heartless massacres of Native Americans recorded by history.

_b_   3. During my last physical, the doctor found a little lump in my throat. I'm going into the hospital tomorrow so they can check out what it is. The doctor said it was most likely a harmless cyst, but of course he would say that. What's he going to say: "Sorry—looks like cancer to me"? He also said that if it is cancer, it's probably of a kind that is easily treated. Right, I thought. He's trying to be nice, I know, but I also know how these things go. First he'll say it's nothing; then he'll say it's cancer but no big deal; and finally he'll tell me the truth. I'm done for.

_c_   4. Are you on my list? If you know me, you may well be. See, I keep a record of everyone who's ever crossed me—whether it's for making fun of my new dress or stealing my boyfriend. I believe in getting mad and getting even. It may take a while, but I settle the score with everyone on my list—the girl who made fun of my dress, for example. It took me a whole year to get back at her. Finally, one night a date took me to a party she gave. I took advantage of the opportunity and spilled red nail polish on the white rug in her powder room. That night, I took great satisfaction in crossing her name off my list.

_d_   5. Gregory Jenkins would make an ideal candidate for governor. A governor needs experience with a large organization, and in our state, there are fewer organizations bigger than the mob. Jenkins's connections statewide with that distinguished group of business people ensure him a plentiful supply of cash to support a long and difficult campaign. In addition, he is an inspiring speaker and civic activist. In a recent comment to the press, he noted, "Ain't no stronger supporter of our education system than me." And nobody has a more loving approach to his friends and colleagues than Jenkins. In fact, he's well known for loving his best pal's wife for several years.

Comment: Item 5—The examples in the paragraph tell us that the author means the opposite of what he or she is saying.

➤ *Review Test 4*

Here is a chance to apply your understanding of purpose and tone to a full-length selection. This reading is about one family's struggle over when to tell a child the truth about Santa Claus.

To help you continue to strengthen your skills, the reading is followed by questions not only on what you've learned in this chapter but also on what you've learned in previous chapters.

Words to Watch

Following are some words in the reading that do not have strong context support. Each word is followed by the number of the paragraph in which it appears and its meaning there. These words are indicated in the article by a small circle (°).

hedgy (2): avoiding a direct answer
pretentious (2): overly dignified
deceit (8): dishonesty
squiggliest (8): waviest
modicum (10): small amount
diplomatically (18): in a tactful way
reproachfully (32): in a disapproving way

COPING WITH SANTA CLAUS

Delia Ephron

1   Julie had turned 8 in October and as Christmas approached, Santa Claus was more and more on her mind. During the week before Christmas, every night she announced to her father, "I know who really brings the presents. You do!" Then, waiting a moment, she added, "Right?"

2   Jerry didn't answer. Neither he nor I, her stepmother, was sure she really wanted the truth. We suspected she did, but couldn't bring ourselves to admit it to her. And we both felt uncomfortable saying something hedgy°. Something pretentious°. Something like, "But Santa does exist dear, he exists in spirit—in the spirit of giving in all of us." That sounded like some other parents in some other house with some other child.

3   I actually resented Julie for putting us on the spot. Wasn't the truth about Santa something one learned from a classmate? The same classmate who knows a screwed-up version of the facts of life. Or else from a know-it-all older sister—as I did. Mine sneaked into my room on Christmas Eve, woke me and said, "Go into the hall and look. You'll see who really puts out the presents."

4   There was another problem. Jerry and I were reluctant to give up Santa Claus ourselves. We got to tell Julie and her younger brother, Adam, to put out the cookies in case Santa was hungry. We made a fuss about the fire being out in the fireplace so he wouldn't get burned. We issued a few threats about his list of good children and bad. It was all part of

the tension and thrill of Christmas Eve—
the night the fantasy comes true. And
that fantasy of a fat jolly man who flies
through the sky in a sleigh drawn by
reindeer and arrives via chimney with
presents—that single belief says everything about the innocence of children.
How unbearable to lose it. For them
and for us. So Jerry and I said nothing.
And the next night Julie announced it
again.

5   Christmas Eve Julie appeared with
a sheet of yellow lined paper. At the top
she had written, "If you are real, sign
here." It was, she said, a letter to Santa.
She insisted that on this letter each of
us—her father, Adam and I—write the
words "Santa Claus," so if Santa were to
sign it, she could compare our handwriting with his. Then she would know
she had not been tricked.

6   Jerry signed. I signed. Adam, who
was 5 and couldn't write, gave up after
the letter "S." Julie folded the paper into
quarters, wrote "Santa Claus" on the
outside and stuck it on a ledge inside the
chimney along with two Christmas
cookies.

7   After much fuss, Julie and Adam
were tucked into bed. Jerry and I put out
the presents. We were not sure what to do
about the letter.

8   After a short discussion, and
mostly because we couldn't resist, we
opted for deceit°. Jerry took the note and,
in the squiggliest° printing imaginable,
wrote "Merry Christmas, Santa Claus."
He put the note back in the fireplace and
ate the cookies.

9   The next morning, very early, about
six, we heard Julie and Adam tear down
the hall. Jerry and I, in bed, listened for
the first ecstatic reactions to the presents.
Suddenly, we heard a shriek. "He's real!
He's real! He's really real!!!!" The door
to our room flew open. "He's REAL!!!"

she shouted. Julie showed us the paper
with the squiggly writing.

Somehow, this was not what we   10
had bargained for. I had expected some
modicum° of disbelief—at least a "Dad,
is this for real?"

Julie clasped the note to her chest.   11
Then she dashed back to the presents.

That afternoon, our friend Deena   12
came over to exchange gifts. "Santa
Claus is real," said Julie.

"Oh," said Deena.   13

"I know for sure, for really, really   14
sure. Look!" And Julie produced the
proof.

Just then the phone rang. Knowing it   15
was a relative calling with Christmas
greetings, Julie rushed to answer it. "Santa
Claus is real," I heard her say to my sister
Nora, the same sister who had broken the
bad news about Santa Claus to me thirty
years ago. Julie handed me the phone.

"What is this about?" asked Nora.   16

I told her the story, trying to make it   17
as funny as possible, hoping she wouldn't
notice how badly Jerry and I had handled
what I was beginning to think of as "the
Santa issue." It didn't work.

"We may have made a mistake   18
here," said Nora, diplomatically° including herself in the mess.

"You're telling me!" I said. "Do   19
you think there's any chance Julie will
forget all this?" That was what I really
wanted, of course—for the whole thing
to go away.

"I doubt it," said Nora.   20

We had a wonderful day—good   21
food, good presents, lots of visitors. Then
it was bedtime.

"Dad?" said Julie, as he tucked her   22
in.

"What?"   23

"If Santa's real, then Rudolph must   24
be real, too."

"What!"   25

26   "If Santa's real—"

27   "I heard," said Jerry. He sat down on her bed and took a deep breath. "You know, Julie," and then he stopped. I could see he was trying to think of a way, any way, to explain our behavior so it wouldn't sound quite as deceptive, wrong and stupid as it was. But he was stumped.

28   "Yeah," said Julie.

29   "I wrote the note," said Jerry.

30   She burst into tears.

31   Jerry apologized. He apologized over and over while Julie sobbed into her pillow. He said he was wrong, that he shouldn't have tricked her, that he should have answered her questions about Santa Claus the week before.

32   Julie sat up in bed. "I thought he was real," she said reproachfully°. Then suddenly she leaned over the bed, pulled out a comic from underneath and sat up again. "Can I read for five minutes?" she said.

33   "Sure," said Jerry.

34   And that was it. One minute of grief at Santa's death, and life went on.

35   Jerry and I left Julie's room terribly relieved. I immediately got a craving for leftover turkey and headed for the kitchen. I was putting the bird back in the refrigerator when I heard Adam crying. I went down the hall. The door to his room was open and I heard Julie, very disgusted, say: "Oh, Adam, you don't have to cry! Only babies believe in Santa Claus."

Reading Comprehension Questions

Vocabulary in Context

1. In the excerpt below, the words *opted for* mean
   a. questioned.
   b. chose.
   c. decided against.
   d. admired.

   " . . . because we couldn't resist, we opted for deceit. Jerry took the note and, in the squiggliest printing imaginable, wrote 'Merry Christmas, Santa Claus.'" (Paragraph 8)

Central Point and Main Ideas

2. Which sentence best expresses the central point of this selection?
   a. Children should learn right away that Santa Claus does not exist.
   b. The author's experience suggests that when children seriously ask who brings the Christmas presents, it's time to tell them the truth.
   c. Jerry made a mistake in eventually telling Julie the truth.
   d. Parents should always tell their children the truth.

3. Which sentence best expresses the main idea of paragraph 4?
   a. The fantasy of Santa says everything about the innocence of children.
   b. Delia and Jerry were reluctant to tell Julie the truth not only so that she could hold on to the fantasy of Santa, but so that they could too.
   c. Delia and Jerry loved to tell the children to put out cookies on Christmas Eve in case Santa was hungry.

     d. The fantasy of Santa allowed Delia and Jerry to threaten the children using Santa's list of good and bad children.   Answers *a, c,* and *d* are too narrow.

Supporting Details

  4. Delia and Jerry
     a. felt Julie reacted in an immature way.
     b. never told Julie that the signature was a fake.
     (c.) realized that they had handled the problem poorly.   See paragraph 27.
     d. thought it was best that Adam also know the truth.

Transitions

  5. The relationship between the last sentence below and the sentences before it is one of
     a. time.
     b. comparison.
     c. contrast.
     (d.) cause and effect.

> "And that fantasy of a fat jolly man who flies through the sky. . . . How unbearable to lose it. For them and for us. So Jerry and I said nothing." (Paragraph 4)

Patterns of Organization

  6. The main pattern of organization of paragraphs 5 through 35 is
     (a.) time order.
     b. list of items.
     c. cause and effect.
     d. contrast.

Fact and Opinion

  7. Which of the following is mainly a statement of opinion?
     a. "We made a fuss about the fire being out in the fireplace so he wouldn't get burned."
     b. "We issued a few threats about his list of good children and bad."
     (c.) "And that fantasy of a fat jolly man who flies through the sky in a sleigh drawn by reindeer and arrives via chimney with presents—that single belief says everything about the innocence of children."
     d. "Christmas Eve Julie appeared with a sheet of yellow lined paper."

Inferences

  8. In paragraph 27, the author implies that Jerry
     (a.) finally knew he had to tell Julie the truth.
     b. is not a caring father.
     c. didn't feel they had misjudged how to deal with Julie.
     d. was angry at Julie.

Purpose and Tone

9. __T__ TRUE OR FALSE? One of the author's purposes in this narration is to persuade, through her own family's experiences, that it's better to tell children the truth about Santa when they seriously ask.   See item 2.

10. The author writes about her and her husband's mistakes mainly in a
    a. tone of great shame.
    b. bitter tone.
    c. tone of pride.
    d. straightforward tone.

Discussion Questions

1. How were your childhood fantasies—Santa Claus, the Easter Bunny, the Tooth Fairy, etc.—handled by adults? How did you react to learning the truth?

2. Why do you think the author feels she and her husband handled "the Santa issue" badly? Why didn't Jerry allow Julie to continue believing in the Christmas fantasy? Do you agree with his decision?

3. The author writes that she and her husband "were reluctant to give up Santa Claus" themselves. Why did they feel that way?

4. Have you ever believed something as an adult—about other people, about nature, about yourself, about school, or the like—and then found out it wasn't true? What was your belief, and how did you learn it was not true? What was your reaction?

Check Your Performance		**PURPOSE AND TONE**	
Activity	*Number Right*	*Points*	*Score*
Review Test 1 (10 items)	_____	x 1 =	_____
Review Test 2 (5 items)	_____	x 6 =	_____
Review Test 3 (5 items)	_____	x 6 =	_____
Review Test 4 (10 items)	_____	x 3 =	_____
		TOTAL SCORE =	_____ %

Enter your total score into the **Reading Performance Chart: Review Tests** on the inside back cover.

PURPOSE AND TONE: Test 1

A. In the space provided, indicate whether the primary purpose of each sentence is to inform (**I**), to persuade (**P**), or to entertain (**E**).

   I   1. The average dollar bill lasts about eighteen months.

   P   2. Federal taxes must be raised so that we can afford a national health program.

   E   3. Mac's idea of healthy eating is to have a double cheeseburger without putting any salt on it.

   P   4. Penalties against drunken drivers should be sharply increased.

   I   5. Among the Aztecs, a man could not get married until he'd graduated from school.

B. Each of the following passages illustrates one of the five different tones identified in the box below. In the space provided, put the letter of the tone that applies to each passage.

a. caring	b. critical	c. pessimistic
d. admiring	e. self-mocking	

   b   6. Whatever happened to the practice of saving up for what you want? It seems nobody has that kind of patience any more. Many Americans buy what they want when they want it and worry about paying for it later. The average American spends significantly more than he or she earns, much to the enjoyment of the credit-card companies. Apparently people need to reach a financial crisis before they realize that it's downright stupid to neglect to balance their budgets and to save for a rainy day.

   e   7. Machines are complete mysteries to me, and this has resulted in some embarrassing service calls at my home. For example, there was the time I called in a repairman because our refrigerator was too warm. Imagine my humiliation when he told me that the cause of the problem was a dirty filter, which I didn't know existed and therefore hadn't cleaned even once in the two years we owned the refrigerator. The best example of my brilliance with machines, however, has to be the time I

(Continues on next page)

called for someone to fix my washing machine. The repairman's solution was simply to put the plug back in the outlet, from which it had been jarred loose by the constant vibration of the washer.

_d_ 8. I think Tina Turner is a terrific role model for anyone who thinks he or she cannot overcome obstacles early in life. Turner grew up in poverty, survived an abusive marriage, and dealt with dishonest business associates early in her career. Many people might have just given in at any point along the way. But Turner had the determination and inner strength to go it alone. Doing it her way, she first became a superstar when she was in her 40s, when she finally received the money, the acclaim, and the respect she always deserved but had been deprived of. Not only is Turner talented and tough-minded; she has proved that beauty and sex appeal can be ageless. Way to go, Tina!

_c_ 9. Research on rats shows that when animals live in crowded conditions they live disorderly, violent lives. Humans are no different. Crowded inner cities are models of lawlessness; the crowded highways of Los Angeles encourage aggression by drivers, and even shootings. As our urban areas continue to grow in population density, these types of problems will surely also grow. That means more family violence and more fighting over available resources. The American dream will become just that—only a dream.

_a_ 10. Those addicted to drugs and alcohol probably feel terrible about themselves—even if they don't show it—and harsh judgments only worsen their self-image. What these people need are programs to help rid themselves of their addictions. It is also important that we all open our hearts and minds to these troubled people. Their addiction does not make them any less "children of God"; nor does it mean that they deserve to be stripped of the dignity that is the birthright of every human being. We must strive to create an environment of hope and help for those who so desperately need it.

Comments: Item 6—The author's attitude toward the average American's spending is critical.

Item 7—The author is mocking his or her total lack of insight into and skill with machines.

Item 8—The author admires Tina Turner.

Item 9—The author is pessimistic about the American dream.

Item 10—The author has a caring attitude toward addicts.

PURPOSE AND TONE: Test 2

A. In the space provided, indicate whether the primary purpose of each sentence is to inform (**I**), to persuade (**P**), or to entertain (**E**).

_*I*_ 1. The world's first ads were neither printed nor broadcast electronically; they were vocal, called out by street peddlers promoting their wares.

_*E*_ 2. Instead of nagging my father to lose weight, my mother bought him an extra-large T-shirt imprinted with the message "This space for rent."

_*P*_ 3. It is senseless to kill an animal just for a fur coat that is no warmer than the synthetic ones available today.

_*P*_ 4. People should be allowed to use their home computers to vote in elections.

_*E*_ 5. Rachel says she eats a balanced diet by choosing items from the four major food groups: chips, soda pop, candy, and pastries.

_*P*_ 6. The foundation of public education has always been reading, writing, and arithmetic—the three "R's." Yet the schools insist that students who have not mastered these fundamentals continue to take all the other subjects as well. What good does it do for young people to sit in on a history or science class if they can't read or calculate well? Schools ought to require students who are very far behind in the fundamentals to devote all their time to the three R's until they are at or near grade level.

_*I*_ 7. More and more elderly people are turning to shared housing as a way to live more economically, more securely, and with more companionship. There are dozens of such projects around the country, including group homes in California, communes in Baltimore, and "Share a Home" in Winter Park, Florida. While the last of these includes 125 participants, a shared-housing project may involve only a few members. Most shared housing projects have full- or part-time help, but members often share in such chores as shopping for food and cooking.

(Continues on next page)

B. Each of the following passages illustrates one of the tones identified in the box below. In each space provided, put the letter of the tone that applies to the passage. (Three tone choices will be left over.)

a. objective	b. amused	c. depressed
d. optimistic	e. critical	f. arrogant

___e___ 8. Parents who do not read to their children often excuse themselves by claiming a lack of time. But with few exceptions, their failure to read is a matter of priorities. Most parents find the time to put in a full workday, take a full complement of coffee breaks, eat lunch and dinner, read the newspaper, watch the nightly newscast or ball game, do the dishes, talk on the phone for thirty minutes (mostly about nothing), run to the store for a pack of cigarettes or a lottery ticket, drive to the mall, and never miss that favorite prime-time show. Somehow they find the time for those things—important or unimportant as they are—but can't find time to read to a child, which is much more important than all the other items on a leisure priority list.

___c___ 9. When I was younger I thought that by this age, I would be pretty well set for life. I imagined that I would have a nice house, be saving some money, and have a decent job. But things haven't worked out that way at all. I'm living a one-bedroom apartment with shabby furniture and a view of a parking lot. My office job is dull and unrewarding, and I bring home hardly enough to cover my rent and expenses, much less put anything away. My place is so unattractive that I don't want to invite anyone over, so I'm alone most of the time. Whatever dreams I had in my youth are pretty well gone now. Sometimes I think about going back to school and trying to prepare for a different career, but at my age there doesn't seem to be much point in doing that. I guess this is just what life had in store for me.

___a___ 10. Scientists say grilling meat creates cancer-causing substances that affect the meat in two ways. First, when fat drips onto the source of heat, the substances are formed and then carried up to the food by smoke. They are also formed when flames touch the meat. There are, however, a few ways that experts say will minimize the risk of grilling meat: l) Use low-fat meats and non-fat sauces. 2) Partially cook meat before grilling. 3) Cover the grill with foil; punch holes in the foil to let fat drip down. (4) Avoid fire flare-ups, which cause harmful smoke. 5) Scrape off blackened material on the surface of meat before eating it. 6) Don't cook out every day.

Comments: Item 8—The author is critical of parents who do not read to their children.

Item 9—The author is depressed about his or her prospects in life.

Item 10—The author presents the information in a straightforward manner.

PURPOSE AND TONE: Test 3

A. Eight quotations in the story below are preceded by a blank space. Identify the tone of each italicized quotation by writing in the letter of one of these tones. (Two tone choices will be left over.)

a. sympathetic	b. straightforward	c. pleading	d. angry
e. superior	f. excited	g. depressed	h. scheming
i. curious	j. frightened		

The television reporter knocked on the door of the small row home. A woman opened the door.

_b_ 1. *"My name is Tod Hunter,"* the reporter said. *"I'm with Action News, and I'd like to talk to the woman who lost her daughter in the school fire last night."*

"Oh, I'm sorry, but she's not much in the mood for visitors."

"I understand," the reporter said. "Please tell her that we only want a moment of her time."

While the woman was gone, the reporter turned to his crew.

_h_ 2. *"You could shoot from this angle,"* he whispered, *"but let's try to get inside. If she's at all responsive to my questions, let's gradually move in through the doorway."*

Children in the neighborhood crowded around the TV crew.

_f_ 3. *"Those are TV cameras!"* some shouted, laughing. *"Wow, real TV cameras!"*

_i_ 4. Pausing to look at the crew standing outside the house, passersby asked, *"What do you suppose happened there?"*

Then the mother of the fire victim appeared at the door, looking drawn and exhausted. "What do you want?"

_a_ 5. *"I'm really very sorry for your great loss, Ma'am."* Hunter continued, *"I'm here for Action News. Do you know what caused the terrible fire?"*

"Please, no interviews."

"Our viewers want to know about this awful fire."

_d_ 6. *"The people can go to blazes,"* she shouted. *"It's none of their business. It's none of your business, either, young man."*

_j_ 7. *"Run! She's mad!"* shouted the children as they raced away.

_c_ 8. *"All I want is two minutes,"* the reporter said. *"Please, just two minutes of your time."*

But the door had already slammed in his face.

"Let's get out of here," the frustrated reporter said to his crew. "I'm starved." *(Continues on next page)*

B. In the space provided, indicate whether the primary purpose of each passage is to inform (**I**), to persuade (**P**), or to entertain (**E**).

_____I_____ 9. Swollen glands can be uncomfortable, but they are a welcome sign that your body is working to defend itself. They are often associated with an illness such as mumps, German measles, a cold, or flu, but an insect bite or infected cut can also cause your glands to swell. A blocked duct in a salivary gland is another possible cause of a swollen gland. Still, if swollen glands last more than a few days, they can be a sign of a serious illness, such as Hodgkin's disease.

_____P_____ 10. Advertising aimed at children is not just annoying—it is destructive and should be controlled. Especially around the holiday season, children are hammered with media messages intended to make them want the latest toy, game, computer, sneakers, doll, music, and clothing on the market. While manufacturers are busy sucking money out of children and their families, they are contributing to a growing sense of dissatisfaction and greed. That serves the manufacturers' purpose—after all, if chidren were ever satisfied, they would not ask their parents to buy more merchandise. But the effect is to produce a nation of selfish men and women whose lives are ruled by the need to have more, more, more. It is frightening to see a generation growing up whose members have been trained from babyhood to be greedy consumers. What chance do they have to ever become contented adults whose values extend beyond a price tag?

Comments: Item 10—The word *should* (as in the first sentence) often indicates that the author is trying to persuade the reader.

PURPOSE AND TONE: Test 4

A. Eight quotations in the story below are preceded by a blank space. Identify the tone of each italicized quotation by writing in the letter of one of these tones. (Two tone choices will be left over.)

a. disgusted	b. ashamed	c. outraged	d. appreciative
e. cheerful	f. understanding	g. straightforward	h. sorrowful
i. joyous	j. vengeful		

The scene is a busy restaurant on a Saturday evening.

_e_ 1. *"Good evening!"* a young waitress chirped to a table of diners. *"It's so nice to see you here tonight! My name is Annette, and I'll be your server this evening."*

_a_ 2. Meanwhile, across the room, a man stared at his food as he pushed it around with his fork. *"Yuk! They call this 'ocean-fresh fish,' "* he said, *"but it sure doesn't smell all that fresh. It's making me gag!"*

_d_ 3. But at the next table, a young man said to his friend, *"This great spaghetti really hits the spot. I was starved."*

_i_ 4. Nearby, in a dimly lit corner of the restaurant, a young man and woman sat close together, smiling at the diamond ring on the woman's finger. *"Oh, darling,"* sighed the woman. *"This is the happiest night of my life. This restaurant will always be my favorite because this is where you asked me to marry you."*

_c_ 5. A conversation of a different sort was taking place at another table: *"I cannot believe you would do this!"* a woman hissed at her husband. *"What kind of man takes his wife into a public place to tell her he's having an affair with her best friend? What am I supposed to do now—order an appetizer?"*

_g_ 6. Back in the kitchen, the restaurant manager was instructing the staff. *"Annette, you cover tables one through four. Ben, you're responsible for five through eight. A party of sixteen people is coming in at eight o'clock; Lisa and Suzette will take care of them."*

"Well, we got passed over again, didn't we?" Ben remarked to Annette after the manager was gone. "Lisa and Suzette always get the big groups and the big tips. It makes me wonder why I try to do a good job here."

_f_ 7. *"Oh, I don't mind,"* Annette said. *"Lisa and Suzette do work a lot more hours than you or I do. I can see why the manager thinks they deserve the best assignments."* Then Annette walked out of the kitchen.

_j_ 8. *"Well, it's not okay with me,"* Ben muttered to himself. *"When I quit this lousy job, they're going to pay for the way they've treated me. I'll get back at them somehow."*

(Continues on next page)

317

B. This activity will give you practice in recognizing purpose and tone. Read the paragraph below. Then carefully consider the questions that follow it, and circle the best responses.

> There are certain types of people you should not trust. One type is people who tell you God told them to tell you to send them money. You know the guys I mean. They get on television and say: "God told me He wants you to send me some money, say $100, or even just $10, if that's all you can afford, but in all honesty I must point out that God is less likely to give you some horrible disease if your gift is in the $100 range." The theory here seems to be that God talks only to the guys on television. I always thought that if God needed money all that badly, He would get in touch with us directly.

9. The purpose of this paragraph is
   a. to persuade readers that they should not send money to television evangelists.
   b. to entertain readers by exaggerating points.
   c. both of the above.

10. The tone of this paragraph can be described as
    a. straightforward and serious.
    b. humorous and mocking.
    c. prayerful and respectful.
    d. sentimental and warm.

PURPOSE AND TONE: Test 5

This activity will give you practice in recognizing purpose and tone. Read each of the paragraphs below. Then carefully consider the questions that follow and circle the letters of the best responses.

A.   A successful doctor is scheduled to operate on a patient at 8 a.m., but it has snowed during the night, and driving is difficult. Do you think the doctor will stay home in bed? Not if he or she is professional. This attitude of professionalism is the key to being a successful college student, too. And it is within your reach, no matter how well or how poorly you have done in school up until now. You cannot undo the past, but you can adopt an attitude of professionalism from now on. All you have to do is intend to take school seriously, and the rest will follow. By attending classes, turning in assignments on time, and coming prepared for tests, you will gradually build your skills.

1. The primary purpose of this paragraph is to
    a. present facts on student behavior.
    b. encourage students to be conscientious.
    c. entertain students with a dramatic story about professionalism.

2. In general, the tone of this paragraph can be described as
    a. critical.
    b. pessimistic.
    c. encouraging.
    d. praising.

B.   According to memory experts, there are ways you can improve your chances of remembering the names of people you meet. One way is to make associations between a person's name and looks. For example, if you meet a man named Baker, you might picture him wearing a baker's hat. If the name is a difficult one, ask for the spelling and visualize the letters mentally. It's also useful to repeat the person's name as you converse, keeping your mental images in mind. And when your conversation ends, repeat the person's name as you say good-by.

3. The primary purpose of this paragraph is to
    a. inform.
    b. persuade.
    c. entertain.

4. The overall tone of this paragraph can be described as
    a. critical and angry.
    b. obviously humorous.
    c. doubtful.
    d. straightforward and instructive.

(Continues on next page)

C. I was sitting on a beach one summer day, watching two children, a boy and a girl, playing in the sand. They were hard at work building an elaborate sandcastle by the water's edge, with gates and towers and moats and internal passages. Just when they had nearly finished their project, a big wave came along and knocked it down, reducing it to a heap of wet sand. I expected the children to burst into tears, devastated by what had happened to all their hard work. But they surprised me. Instead, they ran up the shore away from the water, laughing and holding hands, and sat down to build another castle. I realized that they had taught me an important lesson. All the things in our lives, all the complicated structures we spend so much time and energy creating, are built on sand. Only our relationships with other people endure. Sooner or later, the wave will come along and knock down what we have worked so hard to build up. When that happens, only the person who has somebody's hand to hold will be able to laugh.

5. The primary purpose of this paragraph is to
    a. inform readers about how children behave.
    b. persuade readers of the importance of relationships.
    c. delight readers with a story of childhood playfulness.

6. The tone of this paragraph can be described as
    a. forgiving.
    b. humorous.
    c. self-pitying.
    d. instructive.

D. My best school report was in first grade from Mrs. Varulo. First, she told my parents about my amazing physical energy: "Lisa never tires of chasing and punching her classmates." Next, she praised my class participation and active, questioning mind: "After every instruction—even one as simple as 'Please take out your pencils'—Lisa asks 'Why?'" Mrs. Varulo was so impressed with my vocabulary that she commented, "I don't know where Lisa has picked up some of the words she uses—certainly not in my classroom." Somehow she even knew I would become a famous fiction writer. "More than any other student I have ever had," she wrote, "Lisa is a born liar."

7. The primary purpose of this paragraph is to
    a. inform.
    b. persuade.
    c. entertain.

8. The tone of this paragraph can best be described as
    a. enthusiastic and cheerful.
    b. annoyed and bitter.
    c. cheerful and nostalgic.
    d. ironic and humorous.

PURPOSE AND TONE: Test 6

This activity will give you practice in recognizing purpose and tone. Read each of the paragraphs below. Then carefully consider the questions that follow and circle the letters best responses.

A.   Throughout history, people have suffered from ailments that could have been easily avoided if they had only been understood. For instance, it used to be common for hat makers to be tortured by uncontrollable trembling, slurred speech, and mental confusion. The condition led to Lewis Carroll's creation of the Mad Hatter in his book *Alice's Adventures in Wonderland*. Sadly, the hatters did not know that the mercury they used in creating felt hats was poisoning them, leading to their strange symptoms. Similarly, many of the world's greatest artists suffered from terrible depression. Today we know that the lead in the paint they used probably affected their mental state. How tragic that so many lives were destroyed for want of a little knowledge.

1. The primary purpose of the passage is
   a. to tell readers about formerly misunderstood ailments.
   b. to persuade readers to protect themselves against easily avoidable ailments.
   c. both of the above.

2. The tone of the passage can be described as
   a. regretful.
   b. angry.
   c. alarmed.
   d. pessimistic.

B.   Al Smith, the Democratic candidate for President in 1928, was known for his ready wit and quick comebacks. Once he was heckled while making a campaign speech. "Tell 'em everything you know, Al," yelled the heckler. "It won't take very long."
   Al Smith answered with a grin, "I'll tell 'em everything we both know—it won't take any longer."

3. The primary purpose of this passage is to
   a. inform students about a humorous aspect of a historical figure.
   b. persuade people to support the Democrats.
   c. argue that Al Smith should have won the 1928 presidential campaign.

4. The tone of the paragraph can be described as
   a. forgiving.
   b. amused.
   c. bitter.
   d. disbelieving.

(Continues on next page)

C. Three people were killed because a man was angry that his girlfriend wanted to break up with him. Now the state is planning to kill him, and that's as it should be. Some may argue that taking a life is always wrong, that two wrongs don't make a right. But there is nothing right about making taxpayers give free room and board to a person who killed innocent people. And there's nothing right about putting such a dangerous person in prison, from which he will probably one day be released to again threaten society.

5. The primary purpose of this paragraph is to
   a. report on facts about the death penalty.
   b. persuade readers that the death penalty has merit.
   c. entertain readers with a description of an interesting problem.

6. The overall tone of this paragraph can be described as
   a. impassioned.
   b. insulting.
   c. compassionate and sentimental.
   d. excited and joyous.

D. When people are unemployed, two major sources of stress come into play. One is the loss of income, with all the financial hardships that this brings. Suddenly there is the issue of paying the monthly rent or mortgage, of making the car payment and paying credit card bills, of dealing with utility costs, and the fundamental matter of putting enough food to eat on the table. The other source of stress is the effect of the loss of income on workers' feelings about themselves. Workers who derive their identity from their work, men who define manhood as supporting a family, and people who define their worth in terms of their work's dollar value lose more than their paychecks when they lose their jobs. They lose a piece of themselves and their self-esteem.

7. The primary purpose of this paragraph is
   a. to inform readers about the major sources of stress for the unemployed.
   b. to persuade readers that unemployment should be eliminated.
   c. to amuse readers with observations about human nature.

8. The tone of this paragraph can be described as
   a. depressed and sorrowful.
   b. angry and desperate.
   c. surprised but optimistic.
   d. serious and sympathetic.

10

Argument

Many of us enjoy a good argument. A good argument is not an emotional experience in which people's feelings get out of control, leaving them ready to start throwing things. Instead, it is a rational discussion in which each person advances and supports a point of view about some matter. We might argue with a friend, for example, about where to eat or what movie to go to. We might argue about whether a boss or a parent or an instructor is acting in a fair or unfair manner. We might argue about whether certain performers or sports stars deserve to get paid as much as they do. In a good argument, the other person listens carefully as we state our case, waiting to see if we really have solid evidence to support our point of view.

Argumentation is, then, a part of our everyday dealings with other people. It is also an important part of much of what we read. Authors often try to convince us of their opinions and interpretations. Very often the most important things we must do as critical readers are

1　Recognize the point the author is making.
2　Decide if the author's support is relevant.
3　Decide if the author's support is adequate.

This chapter will give you practice in doing the above, first in everyday arguments and then in textbook material.

THE BASICS OF ARGUMENT: POINT AND SUPPORT

A good argument is one in which you make a point and then provide persuasive and logical evidence to back it up. Here is a point:

Point: The Beef and Burger Shop is a poor fast-food restaurant.

This statement hardly discourages us from visiting the Beef and Burger Shop. "Why do you say that?" we might legitimately say. "Give your reasons." Support is needed so we can decide for ourselves whether a valid point has been made. Suppose the point is followed by these three reasons:

1. The burgers are full of gristle.
2. The roast beef sandwiches have a chemical taste.
3. The fries are lukewarm and soggy.

Clearly, the details provide solid support for the point. They give us a basis for understanding and agreeing with the point. In light of these details, our mouths are not watering for lunch at the Beef and Burger Shop.

We see here, then, a small example of what clear thinking in an argument is about: making a point and providing support that truly backs up that point. A valid argument may also be described as stating a conclusion and providing logical reasons, facts, examples, and other evidence to support the conclusion.

Let's look at another example:

Point: My neighbors are inconsiderate.

We don't really yet know if the neighbors are inconsiderate. We might trust the opinion of the person who made the statement, but we don't know for sure until supporting details enable us to see and judge for ourselves. Here are details:

1. They play their stereo very loud late at night.
2. They let their children play on my front lawn.
3. They don't stop their dog from running into my back yard.

Again, the solid support convinces us that a logical point has been made.

The Point and Support of an Argument

In everyday life, of course, people don't simply say, "Here is my point" and "Here is my support." Nor do writers state their basic ideas so directly. Even so, the basic structure of point and support is still at work beneath the surface, and to evaluate an argument, you need to recognize that point.

To help you distinguish between a point and its support, do the following activity.

➤ *Practice 1*

In each group of statements, one statement is the point, and the other statement or statements are support for the point. Identify each point with a **P**, and identify each statement of support with an **S**.

Hint: If you can insert the word *because* in front of a sentence, you probably have a statement of support. For example, we could say, "*Because* the burgers are full of gristle, *because* the roast beef sandwiches have a chemical taste, and *because* the fries are lukewarm and soggy, I've come to the conclusion that the Beef and Burger Shop is a poor fast-food restaurant."

1. _S_ a. You are having trouble keeping your eyes open.

   _P_ b. You should take a nap.

2. _S_ a. A number of accidents have now occured at that intersection.

   _P_ b. A traffic light is needed at the intersection.

3. _S_ a. A television is always blaring in one corner of the lounge.

   _P_ b. The student lounge is an impossible place to try to study.

   _S_ c. There are always people there talking loudly to each other.

4. _S_ a. Department store salespeople are expected to dress conservatively.

   _S_ b. Cindy needs a job badly.

   _P_ c. Cindy should not go to the interview for a position as a department store salesperson in jeans and a T-shirt.

5. _P_ a. High schools need to teach personal finance skills.

   _S_ b. Many young couples do not know how to budget their money.

   _S_ c. More and more people are getting into serious credit-card debt.

6. _S_ a. The roaches seem to be taking over this apartment.

   _P_ b. We'd better look for another apartment.

   _S_ c. The landlord refuses to fix the leaky faucet.

   _S_ d. The people upstairs make a lot of noise.

7. _P_ a. The library should be kept open on Sundays and holidays.

   _S_ b. Many students save their studying for days when they do not have classes.

   _S_ c. Library facilities are overcrowded on weekdays.

   _S_ d. It's difficult to find research materials during the week; other students are often using the books.

8. _S_ a. Scientists have proved that acid rain harms trees and bodies of water.

   _P_ b. Laws should be passed to reduce acid rain.

   _S_ c. The damage done by acid rain is hard or impossible to undo.

9. _S_ a. Cats refuse to learn silly tricks just to amuse people.

   _P_ b. Cats are more sensible than dogs.

   _S_ c. Dogs will accept cruel mistreatment, but if a cat is mistreated, it will run away.

Comment: Hint—*Because* helps to clarify the relationship between a point and its support.
Example (Item 1): *Because* you are having trouble keeping your eyes open, you should take a nap.

10.   _S_   a. Now if workers go on strike, they may lose their jobs to replacement workers.

     _P_   b. Conditions in the workplace are tougher than they used to be.

     _S_   c. In many industries, workers have had to take wage cuts.

Relevant Support

Once you identify the point and support of an argument, you need to decide if each piece of evidence really applies to the point. The critical reader must ask, "Is this reason relevant support for the argument?" In their enthusiasm for making an argument, people often bring up irrelevant support. For example, in trying to persuade you to lend him some money this week, a friend might say, "You didn't lend me money last week when I needed it." But last week is beside the point; the question is whether or not you should lend him money this week.

An excellent way to develop your skill at evaluating the relevance of support is to work on point-support outlines of arguments. By isolating the items used to support an argument, such outlines help you think about whether each reason is really relevant.

Consider the following outline. The point is followed by six "reasons," only three of which are relevant support for the point. See if you can circle the numbers of the three relevant statements of support.

Point: My dog Otis is not very bright.

1. He's five years old and doesn't respond to his name yet.
2. He cries when I leave for work every day.
3. He always gets excited when visitors arrive.
4. He often attacks the back-yard hedge as if it's a hostile animal.
5. He gets along very well with my neighbor's cat.
6. I often have to put food in front of him because he can't find it by himself.

Now read the following comments on the six items to see which ones you should have circled and why.

Explanations:

1. Most dogs know their names, so Otis's unfamiliarity with his own name reveals a weak memory, one aspect of intelligence. You should have circled the number of this item.

2. Even an intelligent dog might be sad when its companions leave the house.

3. Both bright and not-so-bright dogs are happy to see old and new human friends.

4. The inability to distinguish between a bush and an animal—friendly or hostile—suggests a lack of analytical skills. Four is the second number you should have circled.

5. Dogs of all degrees of intelligence have been known to be friendly with cats.

6. Since most dogs recognize food much more often than their owners would like them to, Otis's inability to find food clearly indicates poor problem-solving skills. You should also have circled the number of this item.

➤ *Practice 2*

Each point is followed by three statements that provide relevant support and three that do not. In the spaces, write the letters of the three relevant statements of support.

1. **Point:** My neighbors are weird folks.

   a. Each family member, including the males, has purple fingernails.
   b. They call me if their dog gets loose.
   c. They have lived in the house for the past two years.
   d. They keep cows and goats inside the house.
   e. On nights with a full moon, they sit on lawn chairs placed on their roof.
   f. Each member of the family has his or her own car.

   Items that logically support the point: ___a___ ___d___ ___e___

2. **Point:** Yogurt is healthful.

   a. Yogurt contains natural antibiotics that can prevent certain kinds of infection.
   b. Yogurt is available in nearly all food stores.
   c. Yogurt kills the bacteria that can cause diarrhea.
   d. You can substitute yogurt in many recipes calling for milk or sour cream.
   e. Yogurt is a staple of the diet in many Middle Eastern countries.
   f. Eating yogurt has been shown to lower cholesterol levels.

   Items that logically support the point: ___a___ ___c___ ___f___

3. **Point:** Alcohol and tobacco are among the most dangerous drugs that Americans use.

   a. Cancer from cigarette smoking kills numerous Americans every year.
   b. During Prohibition, liquor bootleggers fought one another as drug dealers do today.
   c. About half of all fatal traffic accidents are due to drunk driving.
   d. Nothing is more annoying than trying to enjoy a restaurant meal when the people at nearby tables are smoking and drinking heavily.
   e. We often don't think of alcohol and tobacco as "drugs" because they are legal.
   f. Alcohol abuse causes many people to become more aggressive and violent.

   Items that logically support the point: ___a___ ___c___ ___f___

4. **Point:** Halloween should be abolished.

   a. The holiday encourages vandalism in older children.
   b. Summer would have been a better time for Halloween because it stays light longer then.
   c. Children who wear vision-obstructing masks and dark, hard-to-see costumes are in danger of being struck by cars.
   d. Thanksgiving is a lot more meaningful than Halloween.
   e. More and more incidents of poisoned treats are occurring.
   f. Some local business people overcharge for Halloween costumes and candy.

   *Items that logically support the point:*___*a*___   ___*c*___   ___*e*___

5. **Point:** There should be a limit on how much can be spent for political campaigns.

   a. The television networks profit greatly from the ads for local and national elections.
   b. Elected officials could spend more time on their jobs and less on raising money.
   c. Once and for all, candidates should stop using personal attacks in their campaigns.
   d. Candidates with less money would have a fairer chance of competing.
   e. Citizens must learn to evaluate political campaigns in a logical manner.
   f. Elected officials would be less likely to be influenced by rich contributors to their campaigns.

   *Items that logically support the point:*___*b*___   ___*d*___   ___*f*___

Relevant Support in Paragraphs

The point, or main idea, of the argument in the paragraph below is stated in the first sentence. One sentence is not relevant support for that point. Read the paragraph and see if you can find the statement that does *not* support the point of the argument.

> [1]Every high-school student should be required to take a class in parenting skills. [2]The absence of such classes shows how little our schools do for young people. [3]Far too many young people today are bearing children without having the least idea of how to be a good parent. [4]Many of them have grown up in families where poor parenting was the norm. [5]Well-planned parenting classes could give future parents at least an idea of what responsible parenting is all about. [6]The classes might then reduce future problems, including child abuse.

The number of the irrelevant sentence: _____

Explanation:

The point of this argument is stated in the first sentence: "Every high-school student should be required to take a class in parenting skills." Any statement that doesn't help prove this point is irrelevant. Sentences 3–6 support that argument: Sentences 5–6 tell the benefits of parenting classes. Sentences 3–4 explain why students need those benefits. Sentence 2, however, is about something else altogether—it complains about the little that is being done for young people by schools. Whether that is true or not doesn't change the point and support of the argument. Even if the schools did much for young people, parenting classes could still be useful. Thus sentence 2 is irrelevant to the argument.

➤ *Practice 3*

One sentence in each paragraph below does not support the point of the argument. Read the paragraph, and then decide which sentence is not relevant to the argument. To help you decide if a sentence is irrelevant or not, ask yourself, "Does this provide logical support for the point being argued?"

1. ¹Soon, the personal computer will be as useful to every American family as the telephone is today. ²Every family member will be able to use the computer in some way. ³Parents will find a computer of value for keeping family information such as tax records and recipe collections. ⁴Software programs now exist even for such annoying chores as balancing the family checkbook. ⁵Of course, some banks offer a computer service that balances customers' checkbooks right at the bank. ⁶In addition, children's grades will improve when they use a computer to master a subject or write an English paper. ⁷And everyone will enjoy taking a break with one of the popular computer games. ⁸Finally, with the widespread use of E-mail, the computer can actually take over some of the function of the telephone.

   Which of the following statements does not support the author's argument that soon the personal computer will be as useful in American homes as the telephone is?

   a. Sentence 3   c. Sentence 5
   b. Sentence 4   d. Sentence 6

2. ¹The proposed new highway linking Interstate 95 with the turnpike would be a disaster. ²The plans for this highway were drawn over thirty years ago, when the affected area was lightly settled. ³Now, a generation later, the area has become developed, and hundreds of families would lose their homes if the highway were built. ⁴There are already too many forces weakening the

American family structure these days. ⁵The environment will also be negatively affected by the construction of a new superhighway. ⁶Hundreds of thousands of birds and small animals, including several endangered species, will lose their natural habitats and may die out.

Which of the following does not support the author's argument that the proposed highway would be a disaster?

a. Sentence 2   (c.) Sentence 4
b. Sentence 3   d. Sentence 6

Adequate Support

A valid argument must include not only relevant support but also an adequate amount of support. For example, it would not be valid to argue "Abortion is wrong" if one's only support was "My sister had an abortion and has regretted it ever since." Such an important issue would require more support than the attitude and experience of a single relative. Arguing a point that doesn't have adequate support is called jumping to a conclusion.

In the argument below, three supporting reasons are given, followed by four possible points. The evidence (that is, the supporting reasons) adequately supports only one of the points; it is insufficient to support the other three. Choose the one point you think is adequately supported, and put a check mark beside it. Then read the explanation that follows.

Support:

- The first time I went to that beach, I got a bad case of sunburn.
- The second time I went to that beach, I couldn't go in the water because of the pollution.
- The third time I went to that beach, I stepped on a starfish and had to go to the emergency room to have the spikes removed from my foot.

Which point is adequately supported by the evidence above?

____ a. That beach is unsafe and should be closed.

____ b. I've had a string of bad experiences at that beach.

____ c. Beaches are not safe places.

____ d. We're never going to get this planet cleaned up.

Explanation:

The correct answer is *b*. Answer *a* is simply not supported by three isolated instances; we'd need many more reports of dangerous conditions before considering having the beach closed. Answer *c* is even more poorly supported.

We'd need many, many reports of dangerous conditions at beaches worldwide to come to the conclusion stated in *c*. Answer *d* is supported in part by the reference to pollution in the second statement of support, but the other two statements (about sunburn and starfish) are not examples of pollution.

➤ Practice 4

For each group, read the three items of support (the evidence). Then check (✓) the one point that is adequately supported by that evidence.

Group 1

Support:

- Unless you get to the video-rental store early, the best movies are all gone.
- Renting a movie requires two trips—picking up the movie and returning it.
- Many of the movies available for rent—and more—are eventually shown on cable TV.

Which point is adequately supported by the evidence above?

___ a. Rental movies simply cost too much.

___ b. Video rental stores are a fad and will go out of business within a few years.

___ c. The best movies can be seen only on cable TV.

✓ d. It's better to subscribe to cable TV than to rent movies.

Group 2

Support:

- Some people put off writing or calling a friend because they feel they do not have time to do it right, but a quick note or call is often better than nothing.
- Sometimes it makes sense to do a routine chore quickly rather than perfectly in order to save time for something more important.
- Even a desk and office need not be perfectly neat; sometimes cleaning them up is just an excuse for putting off more important work.

Which point is adequately supported by the evidence above?

✓ a. Perfection is not always a worthwhile goal.

___ b. People who aim for perfection never get around to important tasks.

___ c. You can be better organized if you plan each day more carefully.

___ d. Getting things done haphazardly is always better than not getting them done at all.

ARGUMENT IN TEXTBOOK WRITING

In most textbook writing, argument takes the form of well-developed ideas or theories presented with experiments, surveys, studies, reasons, examples, or other evidence of support. Textbook arguments generally have solid support, but recognizing the author's point and watching for relevant and adequate support will help you become a more involved and critical reader. Following are two exercises that will give you practice in thinking through the arguments in textbooks.

➤ Practice 5

One sentence in each textbook paragraph below does not support the point of the argument. Read each paragraph, and then decide which sentence is not relevant to the argument. To help you decide if a sentence is irrelevant or not, ask yourself, "Does this provide logical support for the point being argued?"

1. ¹Short-term goals encourage self-discipline better than distant aims. ²For instance, dieters lose more weight by attempting to shed two pounds a week than by worrying about a total of twenty pounds or more. ³Low-fat diets are another help for dieters. ⁴Also, students who try to increase study time by a half hour each day do better than those who think only about compiling straight A averages. ⁵And alcoholics and drug addicts achieve more lasting recovery when they deal with their problems one day at a time.

   Which sentence is not relevant support for the argument that short-term goals are better for will power than long-term goals?

   a. Sentence 2   c. Sentence 4
   b. Sentence 3   d. Sentence 5

2. ¹Sigmund Freud was one of the most important scientists of the twentieth century. ²A loving father, he had three sons and three daughters. ³He was among the first to study mental disorders, such as hysteria and neurosis, in a systematic way. ⁴He developed the theory of the unconscious and showed how people's behavior is greatly affected by forgotten childhood events. ⁵His discoveries are the basis of psychoanalysis, a method of treating mental illness that is still important today.

   Which sentence is not relevant support for the argument that Freud is one of the most important scientists of the twentieth century?

   a. Sentence 2   c. Sentence 4
   b. Sentence 3   d. Sentence 5

Comments: Item 1—The point is about short-term goals, not dieting.
   Item 2—Freud's family situation was no different from that of less important scientists.

➤ *Practice 6*

In each group, the support is from a study reported on in a textbook. Check (✓) the point in each case that is adequately supported by that evidence.

Group 1

Support:

- Some thieves who are sent to jail steal again as soon as they are released.
- A dog that has been hit for eating food off the table will often continue to gobble what it can find when the owner is not around.
- A teenage girl who is "grounded" because she sneaked out of the house may try to come up with a more creative plan to get out without being caught.

Which point is adequately supported by the evidence above?

____ a. Many studies have found advantages and problems with punishment.

_✓_ b. Punishment does not always have the intended effects.

____ c. Punishment is rarely effective.

____ d. Punishment can be effective in some cases.

Group 2

Support:

- Elderly nursing home patients who have little control over their activities tend to decline faster and die sooner than do those given more control over their activities.
- If two rats receive simultaneous shocks, but only one of them can turn a wheel to stop the shocks, the helpless rat becomes more vulnerable to ulcers and has lower immunity to disease.
- Given control over their work environments—by being able to adjust office furnishings and control interruptions and distractions—workers experience less stress.

Which point is adequately supported by the evidence above?

____ a. It is possible to gain full control over our lives.

____ b. Many negative life events are uncontrollable.

____ c. Loss of control is a major problem in our society.

_✓_ d. A loss of control is stressful and makes one more vulnerable to ill health.

A Final Note

This chapter has dealt with the basics of argument, including the need for relevant and adequate support. If time permits, you may want to turn to pages 511–522 to consider common errors in reasoning—also known as logical fallacies—that people may make when advancing an argument.

➤ *Review Test 1*

To review what you've learned in this chapter, complete each sentence or circle the letter of the correct answer.

1. The point of an argument can also be called its *(relevance, evidence, conclusion)* _____ *conclusion* _____.

2. The support for an argument can be referred to as the *(evidence, conclusion)* _____ *evidence* _____ that backs up the point.

3. Relevant support for an argument is information that *(enthusiastically, partially, logically)* _____ *logically* _____ supports the point.

4. If there is too little information to support a point, we say the support is *(dull, inadequate, irrelevant)* _____ *inadequate* _____.

5. Textbook authors may support their arguments with
   a. experiments.
   b. surveys.
   c. studies.
   d. all of the above and more.

➤ *Review Test 2*

A. In each group, one statement is the point, and the other statement or statements are support for that point. Circle the letter of the point of each group.

   Hint: If you can insert the word *because* in front of a sentence, you probably have a statement of support.

Group 1

   a. We'd better look for another preschool for our son.
   b. He says he hates his preschool teacher.
   c. Yesterday he hid under his bed when it was time to go to preschool.

Group 2

a. You're having trouble with math this quarter.
(b.) You should make an appointment to see a tutor.

Group 3

a. Chefs work on their feet most of the day.
(b.) A chef's job can be very difficult.
c. Some chefs put in long hours, as many as fifteen a day.
d. Even in restaurants with the best air-conditioning, the kitchen is uncomfortably hot.

Group 4

a. In recent years, the sun has been particularly active in producing harmful rays.
b. Air pollution has destroyed some of the ozone in the atmosphere, which protects against solar rays.
(c.) Wearing sun hats and using sun-protection lotion are important health habits.
d. Too much exposure to the sun can lead to skin cancer.

B. Each point is followed by three statements that provide relevant support and three that do not. In the spaces, write the letters of the three relevant statements of support.

5–7. **Point:** Drinking coffee can have unpleasant effects.
a. Some people don't like the taste of decaffeinated coffees.
b. Coffee in the evening can interfere with sleep at night.
c. As addictions go, coffee is less dangerous than tobacco.
d. Too much coffee can cause the hands to shake.
e. Drinking too much coffee can lead to a faster heartbeat and light-headedness.
f. Most coffees cost under five dollars a pound.

Items that logically support the point: ___b___ ___d___ ___e___

8–10. **Point:** Some people have very poor telephone manners.
a. They never identify themselves, but just begin the conversation.
b. They often make their calls on cordless phones.
c. They have an unlisted telephone number.
d. They conduct conversations with people around them at the same time they're talking on the phone.
e. Some people don't like to talk on the phone.
f. They often call around 6 p.m., which is most people's dinner hour.

Items that logically support the point: ___a___ ___d___ ___f___

➤ *Review Test 3*

A. Circle the letter of the irrelevant sentence in each paragraph—the sentence that changes the subject.

1.   [1]If the township would put street lights along Holly Drive, it would make life safer and easier for those of us who live along that street and our guests. [2]This township never seems to take the needs of the citizens into account. [3]It is so dark on Holly Drive that people have trouble seeing where they are going. [4]A few months ago, an elderly woman visiting a neighbor's home couldn't see a step and fell, breaking her hip. [5]And people who visit my home frequently complain about not being able to see our address, even though we have a light outside our front door.

Which sentence is not relevant to the argument that it would be safer and more convenient if the township put in street lights?

(a.) Sentence 2   c. Sentence 4
b. Sentence 3   d. Sentence 5

2.   [1]Children should be given an allowance as soon as they are old enough to want it. [2]Having to make decisions about what to do with their money is good training for the future. [3]They eventually learn to use their money on what they really want, instead of spending impulsively. [4]Furthermore, an allowance is one good way of telling a child that he or she is a responsible member of the family and that membership brings benefits as well as obligations. [5]That will make the expectation that they also have to do chores more reasonable. [6]Unfortunately, some people are reluctant to give young children an allowance.

Which sentence is not relevant to the argument that children benefit from being given an allowance?

a. Sentence 2   c. Sentence 5
b. Sentence 3   (d.) Sentence 6

3.   [1]Most people who have trouble with schoolwork don't lack intelligence—instead, they are tripped up by their own attitudes toward the work. [2]One attitude that gets in many students' way is the "I can't do it" syndrome. [3]Instead of making an honest effort to do the work, the "I can't do it" type gives up before he or she begins. [4]This type often also has trouble on the job. [5]Then there's the "I'm too tired" excuse. [6]Students with this problem give in to the temptation to nap whenever there is work to be done. [7]Another common excuse for low achievement is, "The instructor is boring." [8]These students expect every course to be highly entertaining and claim they can't be expected to learn anything otherwise.

Comment: Item 2—The fact that some people don't wish to give their children an allowance doesn't support the author's point that children *should* be given an allowance.

Which sentence does not support the argument that people who have trouble with school work are tripped up by their own attitudes rather than a lack of intelligence?

a. Sentence 2   (c.) Sentence 4
b. Sentence 3   d. Sentence 7

B. (4–5.) For each group, read the three items of support (the evidence). Then check (✓) the one point that is adequately supported by that evidence.

Remember that the point, or conclusion, should follow logically from the evidence. Do not jump to a conclusion that is not well supported.

Group 1

Support:

- Many day-care facilities have health and safety standards that are barely satisfactory.
- Long waiting lists exist at most good day-care centers.
- Day-care centers can't get enough qualified help.

4. Which point is adequately supported by the evidence above?

    ____ a. Day care is unreasonably expensive.

    ____ b. Mothers with young children should not work.

    ____ c. Our present birthrate must be drastically reduced.

    ✓ d. Our present day-care system is inadequate.

Group 2

Support:

- Last week, when I tried to take a copy of *Readings for Managers* out of the library, it wasn't on the shelf.
- Yesterday, I tried again, and it still wasn't there.
- Today, I asked the librarian, who said there was no record that anyone had borrowed that book.

5. Which point is adequately supported by the evidence above?

    ____ a. *Readings for Managers* has been stolen.

    ____ b. The librarian is careless.

    ____ c. The book has been misfiled.

    ✓ d. The book is not where it is supposed to be.

➤ Review Test 4

Can flunking be good for students? Here is a chance to apply your understanding of argument to an essay that addresses that question.

To help you continue to strengthen your skills, the reading is followed by questions not only on what you've learned in this chapter but also on what you've learned in previous chapters.

Words to Watch

Below are some words in the reading that do not have strong context support. Each word is followed by the number of the paragraph in which it appears and its meaning there. These words are indicated in the article by a small circle (°).

validity (1): soundness or worth
trump card (4): a tactic that gives one an advantage (like a trump suit in card games)
flustered (6): nervously confused
composure (6): calmness and self-control
radical (6): extreme
conspiracy (11): plot

IN PRAISE OF THE F WORD
Mary Sherry

1   Tens of thousands of eighteen-year-olds will graduate this year and be handed meaningless diplomas. These diplomas won't look any different from those awarded their luckier classmates. Their validity° will be questioned only when their employers discover that these graduates are semiliterate.

2   Eventually a fortunate few will find their way into educational-repair shops—adult-literacy programs, such as the one where I teach basic grammar and writing. There, high-school graduates and high-school dropouts pursuing graduate-equivalency certificates will learn the skills they should have learned in school. They will also discover they have been cheated by our educational system.

3   As I teach, I learn a lot about our schools. Early in each session I ask my students to write about an unpleasant experience they had in school. No writers' block here! "I wish someone would have had made me stop doing drugs and made me study." "I liked to party and no one seemed to care." "I was a good kid and didn't cause any trouble, so they just passed me along even though I didn't read well and couldn't write." And so on.

4   I am your basic do-gooder, and prior to teaching this class I blamed the poor academic skills our kids have today on drugs, divorce, and other impediments to concentration necessary for doing well in school. But, as I rediscover each time I walk into the classroom, before a teacher

can expect students to concentrate, he has to get their attention, no matter what distractions may be at hand. There are many ways to do this, and they have much to do with teaching style. However, if style alone won't do it, there is another way to show who holds the winning hand in the classroom. That is to reveal the trump card° of failure.

5   I will never forget a teacher who played that card to get the attention of one of my children. Our youngest, a world-class charmer, did little to develop his intellectual talents but always got by. Until Mrs. Stifter.

6   Our son was a high-school senior when he had her for English. "He sits in the back of the room talking to his friends," she told me. "Why don't you move him to the front row?" I urged, believing the embarrassment would get him to settle down. Mrs. Stifter looked at me steely-eyed over her glasses. "I don't move seniors," she said. "I flunk them." I was flustered°. Our son's academic life flashed before my eyes. No teacher had ever threatened him with that before. I regained my composure° and managed to say that I thought she was right. By the time I got home I was feeling pretty good about this. It was a radical° approach for these times, but, well, why not? "She's going to flunk you," I told my son. I did not discuss it any further. Suddenly English became a priority in his life. He finished out the semester with an A.

7   I know one example doesn't make a case, but at night I see a parade of students who are angry and resentful for having been passed along until they could no longer even pretend to keep up. Of average intelligence or better, they eventually quit school, concluding they were too dumb to finish. "I should have been held back," is a comment I hear frequently.

Even sadder are those students who are high-school graduates who say to me after a few weeks of class, "I don't know how I ever got a high-school diploma."

8   Passing students who have not mastered the work cheats them and the employers who expect graduates to have basic skills. We excuse this dishonest behavior by saying kids can't learn if they come from terrible environments. No one seems to stop to think that—no matter what environments they come from—most kids don't put school first on their list unless they perceive something is at stake. They'd rather be sailing.

9   Many students I see at night could give expert testimony on unemployment, chemical dependency, abusive relationships. In spite of these difficulties, they have decided to make education a priority. They are motivated by the desire for a better job or the need to hang on to the one they've got. They have a healthy fear of failure.

10   People of all ages can rise above their problems, but they need to have a reason to do so. Young people generally don't have the maturity to value education in the same way my adult students value it. But fear of failure, whether economic or academic, can motivate both.

11   Flunking as a regular policy has just as much merit today as it did two generations ago. We must review the threat of flunking and see it as it really is—a positive teaching tool. It is an expression of confidence by both teachers and parents that the students have the ability to learn the material presented to them. However, making it work again would take a dedicated, caring conspiracy° between teachers and parents. It would mean facing the tough reality that passing kids who haven't learned the material—while it might save them grief

for the short term—dooms them to long-term illiteracy. It would mean that teachers would have to follow through on their threats, and parents would have to stand behind them, knowing their children's best interests are indeed at stake. This means no more doing Scott's assignments for him because he might fail. No more passing Jodi because she's such a nice kid.

This is a policy that worked in the past and can work today. A wise teacher, with the support of his parents, gave our son the opportunity to succeed—or fail. It's time we return this choice to all students. 12

Reading Comprehension Questions

Vocabulary in Context

1. In the excerpt below, the word *impediments* means
   a. questions.
   b. skills.
   (c.) obstacles.
   d. paths.

   "I blamed the poor academic skills our kids have today on drugs, divorce and other impediments to concentration. . . . " (Paragraph 4)

Central Point and Main Ideas

2. Which sentence best expresses the central point of the selection?
   a. Before students will concentrate, the teacher must get their attention.
   b. Many adults cannot read or write well.
   c. English skills can be learned through adult literacy programs.
   (d.) The threat of failure should be returned to our classrooms.

3. Which sentence best expresses the main idea of paragraph 6?
   a. According to his teacher, Sherry's son sat at the back of the room, talking to his friends.
   b. Mrs. Stifter said that she didn't move seniors, she flunked them.
   (c.) The fear of flunking motivated Sherry's son to do well in English.
   d. Sherry was at first nervous and confused to learn that her son might be flunked by Mrs. Stifter.

   Statements *a, b,* and *d* are too narrow; they are specific details of the anecdote, the point of which is statement *c.*

Supporting Details

4. According to the author, many students who get "passed along"
   a. are lucky.
   b. don't get into trouble.
   (c.) eventually feel angry and resentful.
   d. will never learn basic grammar and writing skills.

   See the first sentence of paragraph 7.

Transitions

5. The relationship between the two sentences below is one of
   a. time.
   b. addition.
   c. comparison.
   (d.) contrast.

   > "Many students I see at night could give expert testimony on unemployment, chemical dependency, abusive relationships. In spite of these difficulties, they have decided to make education a priority." (Paragraph 9)

Patterns of Organization

6. The main pattern of organization of paragraph 6 is
   (a.) time order.
   b. list of items.
   c. definition and example.
   d. comparison.

Fact and Opinion

7. Paragraph 6 of the selection is primarily
   (a.) fact.
   b. opinion.

Inferences

8. The author implies that our present educational system is
   a. doing the best that it can.
   b. the best in the world.
   (c.) not demanding enough of students.
   d. very short of teachers.

Purpose

9. The author's primary purpose in this article is
   a. to inform.
   (b.) to persuade.
   c. to entertain.

   The author doesn't simply *explain* the advantages and disadvantages of failing students—she *supports* the practice. (See the statement of the central point in item 2.)

Argument

10. Label the point of the following argument from the reading with a **P**; label the two statements of support for the point with an **S**. Note that one statement should not be labeled—it is neither the point nor the support of the argument.

   _S_ a. Fear of failure motivated the author's son to do well in English.

   _P_ b. Fear of failure is a good motivator.

   ___ c. Some people learn skills after high school in adult literacy programs.

   _S_ d. Most kids won't put school first unless they know they might fail.

Discussion Questions

1. Do you know anyone who has flunked or almost flunked a course? What effect did the experience have on that person?

2. Most people think of flunking a course as a negative experience. Why then does Sherry consider the threat of flunking to be a positive teaching tool? Do you agree?

3. Besides the threat of flunking, what are some other ways that teachers can motivate students? What have teachers done to make you want to work harder for a class?

4. People often look back on their education and realize that some of the teachers they learned the most from were their strictest teachers. Who do you think you learned most from, strict teachers or lenient ones? Give examples to support your point.

Check Your Performance   **ARGUMENT**

Activity	*Number Right*	*Points*	*Score*
Review Test 1 (5 items)	_____	x 2 =	_____
Review Test 2 (10 items)	_____	x 3 =	_____
Review Test 3 (5 items)	_____	x 6 =	_____
Review Test 4 (10 items)	_____	x 3 =	_____
		TOTAL SCORE =	_____ %

Enter your total score into the **Reading Performance Chart: Review Tests** on the inside back cover.

ARGUMENT: Test 1

A. (1–4.) In each group, one statement is the point of an argument, and the other statements are support for that point. Circle the letter of the point of each group.

Group 1

    a. The anchors on Channel 1 spend more time on small talk than those on Channel 2.

    (b.) Channel 2's newscasts are better than Channel 1's.

    c. Channel 1 emphasizes sensational stories, such as local fires and highway accidents. Channel 2 features important local and world issues.

Group 2

    a. Often you'll wait half an hour for a Route 27 bus, and then three will show up at once.

    b. Sometimes Route 27 buses will roar right past you at a bus stop, even though they aren't full.

    c. Route 27 seems to be assigned the oldest buses, ones that rattle and have broken seats.

    (d.) It is wise to avoid the Route 27 bus whenever possible.

Group 3

    a. I feel dread every time I sit down to take our Friday math quiz.

    b. During the math midterm, I "froze" and didn't even try to answer most of the questions.

    (c.) I'm a good example of someone who has "math anxiety."

    d. I turned down a job as a salesclerk because I would have had to figure out how much change customers should get back.

Group 4

    (a.) Congress should enact a comprehensive highway program.

    b. Some of the numerous accidents, injuries, and fatalities on our nation's roads can are the result of poor highway design.

    c. There is an urgent need for bridge construction and maintenance throughout this country.

    d. This nation needs programs to alleviate traffic jams.

(Continues on next page)

343

B. Each point is followed by three statements that provide relevant support and three that do not. In the spaces, write the letters of the **three** relevant statements of support.

Point: My boss is a very unpleasant man to work for.

    a. He barks orders and never asks for an employee's opinion.
    b. His fashion-plate wife is said to be even nastier than he is.
    c. His office is decorated in dull browns and grays.
    d. Even when he invites employees out to lunch, he expects them to pick up their own checks.
    e. He changes his mind so often than an employee who pleased him on Friday can be in the doghouse by Monday.
    f. He once accumulated so many parking tickets that the police actually came to his home to arrest him.

5–7.   *Items that logically support the point:* ___*a*___   ___*d*___   ___*e*___

Point: Our old car is ready for the junkpile.

    a. The body has rusted through, and water trickles down on me if I drive it in the rain.
    b. The car is painted a particularly ugly shade of green.
    c. We've saved up enough to buy a much better car.
    d. Our mechanic says its engine is too worn to be repaired, and the car isn't worth the cost of a new one.
    e. I never really did like that car very much.
    f. Its brakes are shot.

8–10.   *Items that logically support the point:* ___*a*___   ___*d*___   ___*f*___

Comments: Items 5–7—Answers *b*, *c*, and *f* have nothing to do with the man's role as boss.
    Items 8–10— b.   This was true even when the car was in good shape.
                 c.   That doesn't mean that the old car can't be sold or traded in.
                  e.   The junkpile isn't the only option for cars we don't like.

ARGUMENT: Test 2

A. (1–3.) In each group, one statement is the point of an argument, and the other statements are support for that point. Circle the letter of the point of each group.

Group 1

    a. States that enforce the 55-miles-per-hour limit have lower highway death rates.

    b. Driving at 55 miles per hour saves fuel.

    (c.) The 55-miles-per-hour speed limit should be maintained.

    d. The chance of a fatal crash doubles when speeds go above 60 miles per hour.

Group 2

    a. Profits Unlimited has been the target of many complaints to the Better Business Bureau.

    b. The company's advertising tells you that you can learn the secrets of getting rich quickly by buying their guidebook and audio tapes for two hundred dollars.

    (c.) Profits Unlimited is very likely a dishonest business.

    d. The owner served time for fraud in state prison.

Group 3

    a. Most fur products are made from animals bred for that purpose, so few endangered species are threatened by the fur industry.

    (b.) Animal rights activists should not attack others for using animals for fur and medical experiments.

    c. Many treatments that save human lives were developed through animal testing programs.

    d. Animals bred for fur coats are generally well cared for because breeders want a healthy coat.

B. Each point on the next page is followed by three statements that provide relevant support and three that do not. In the spaces, write the letters of the **three** relevant statements of support.

(Continues on next page)

Point: Convenience stores live up to their name.

     a. Convenience stores are close to home.
     b. Small local businesses should be supported by the community.
     c. Some convenience store chains sell products under their own brand name.
     d. Convenience stores are open till late or all night.
     e. Parking is right outside the convenience store's door.
     f. The produce at most of our supermarkets is usually terrible.

4–6. *Items that logically support the point:*___*a*___ ___*d*___ ___*e*___

Point: Our town diner is an unsanitary health hazard and ought to be closed down.

     a. It serves the worst coffee in town.
     b. The last time I ate at the diner I got food poisoning and was sick for a week.
     c. For the prices the diner charges, the food ought to be better than it is.
     d. The city inspector found roaches in the diner's kitchen.
     e. Most of the customers at the diner are a shabby, untidy lot.
     f. The cook has been seen using the end of a mop to stir the soup.

7–9. *Items that logically support the point:*___*b*___ ___*d*___ ___*f*___

C. Read the following paragraph and then answer the question that follows.

    [1]Sexual harassment in the workplace must be recognized for the serious problem it is. [2]Too many people make light of the problem, believing sexual harassment to be nothing more than pleasant flirtation between coworkers. [3]However, many women, and even some men, have been driven to quit their jobs because of unwanted sexual attention from their supervisors. [4]An employer can more or less subtly pressure employees to grant sexual favors in order to keep their jobs. [5]Even employers who do not demand sex can make their employees miserable through unwelcome remarks about their bodies or dress. [6]Supervisors who sexually harass their employees must have a need to feel important or powerful. [7]All degrees of sexual harassment have the effect of creating a hostile and degrading atmosphere in the workplace. [8]To protect people from having to work in such an environment should be the aim of laws against sexual harassment.

10. Which sentence is not relevant to the argument that laws should protect people from unwanted sexual attention?

    a. Sentence 3
    b. Sentence 4
    c. Sentence 5
    (d.) Sentence 6

The seriousness of sexual harassment is a separate question from the supervisors' reason for sexually harassing employees.

ARGUMENT: Test 3

A. Circle the letter of the statement that is not logical support for the argument in each paragraph.

> [1]Proms are one traditional part of the high-school experience that should be discontinued. [2]For one thing, proms are just too expensive. [3]Between the girl's dress, the guy's tuxedo, flowers, tickets, and probably dinner in a restaurant, it's way too much money for an average high-school couple to spend. [4]Rich parents, however, are glad to show off their wealth by supporting such expensive occasions. [5]Secondly, proms encourage destructive forms of social competition. [6]Teenagers get caught up in worrying about who has the best-looking date, who spends most on a dress, or who arrives in a rented limousine. [7]And finally, proms often turn into excuses for underage drinking-and-driving excursions.

1. Which sentence is not relevant to the argument that high-school proms should be discontinued?
   a. Sentence 2
   b. Sentence 3
   (c.) Sentence 4
   d. Sentence 5

> [1]Renting a movie for a VCR makes much more sense these days than going to see a movie at a theater. [2]First of all, the large selection of video movies will always be many times greater than the available choices at all the neighborhood theaters. [3]The rental stores even offer cassettes of made-for-television movies, foreign films, and classics like the legendary comedies of Charlie Chaplin. [4]Also, the low cost of film rental is well below the price of admission to a movie these days. [5]And you won't have to put up with noisy patrons drowning out the sound track with their personal conversations or comments on the action on the screen. [6]These ill-mannered moviegoers should be ejected from a theater when they create a disturbance.

2. Which sentence is not relevant support for the argument that renting movies makes more sense than going to see movies at a theater?
   a. Sentence 3
   b. Sentence 4
   c. Sentence 5
   (d.) Sentence 6

> [1]Keeping up with the news is an important part of good citizenship. [2]First of all, it's only by watching the policies of our elected officials that we

(Continues on next page)

can make judgments about their performance. ³If we are not satisfied, we can then write them letters to try to influence them. ⁴We can also use what we learn about their performance to determine how we vote in the coming elections. ⁵Knowing about current events may also help us to impress instructors, bosses, and others. ⁶Finally, we can occasionally learn from the news about how we can be useful to our fellow citizens. ⁷Perhaps we can send a few dollars to a family on the news whose house burned down or volunteer at a shelter for the homeless that is featured on the news.

3. Which sentence is not relevant to the author's argument that keeping up with the news contributes to good citizenship?
   a. Sentence 4
   (b.) Sentence 5   Impressing teachers and bosses
   c. Sentence 6   is not part of good citizenship.
   d. Sentence 7

B. For each group, read the three items of support (the evidence). Then circle the letter of the point that is adequately supported by that evidence.

Group 1

Support:

- Corn is used to make glue, explosives, and lubricants.
- Cornstarches are used to manufacture disposable bags that decompose.
- Corn is a popular, nutritious, high-fiber vegetable.

4. Which point is adequately supported by the evidence above?
   a. Corn is our most important crop.
   (b.) Corn is a very important crop.
   c. Every farmer should grow at least some corn.
   d. Few vegetables are as nutritious as corn.

Group 2

Support:

- Dolphins appear to be able to talk to one another through a language of squeals and grunts.
- There have been reports of dolphins helping people who were lost at sea.
- Dolphins in captivity have learned to perform sophisticated tasks, such as fetching objects in a particular order.

5. Which point is adequately supported by the evidence above?
   a. There are no other animals as intelligent as dolphins.
   (b.) Dolphins appear to be highly intelligent animals.
   c. Dolphins are better off in captivity.
   d. Dolphins are good parents.

ARGUMENT: Test 4

A. Circle the letter of the statement that is not logical support for the argument in each paragraph.

[1]Much of America's drug problem could actually be eliminated by legalizing narcotics. [2]Harsh drug laws have not ended illegal drug use. [3]We already sell many drugs over the counter as cold and flu medicines. [4]If all drugs were legal, illegal street dealers would swiftly go out of business. [5]Actually, most drug-related crimes are not due to the drugs themselves, but to the need for money to buy drugs (which would be affordable if legal) or to turf battles between dealers. [6]Legalized drugs would also positively affect the problem of addiction because profits from drug sales could be taxed to support drug treatment and education programs.

1. Which sentence is not relevant to the the author's conclusion that drugs should be legalized?
   (a.) Sentence 3
   b. Sentence 4
   c. Sentence 5
   d. Sentence 6

[1]Statistics show that people travel more safely in airplanes than in cars. [2]For that reason, it seems foolish to be afraid of flying and not be concerned about safety in a car. [3]The figures are clear—planes are safer than cars, per passenger mile. [4]But statistics do not tell the whole story. [5]Automobile accidents usually involve only a few people per occurrence and kill or injure only some of the victims. [6]They involve situations which drivers believe they can avoid through skill or caution. [7]On the other hand, airplane accidents usually involve large numbers of people and high death rates. [8]One hundred percent is not uncommon. [9]Surviving an airplane accident requires luck, not skill or caution, and passengers are totally dependent upon their crew. [10]And to add insult to injury, passengers have paid unreasonably high amounts for tickets for this unsafe type of transportation. [11]There's no question about it: when driven by a safe and sober driver, a car is a safer bet than an airplane.

2. Which sentence is not relevant support for the argument that when a car is driven by a safe and sober driver, it is a safer bet than an airplane?
   a. Sentence 5
   b. Sentence 8
   c. Sentence 9
   (d.) Sentence 10

   Airplane accidents aren't caused by the high price of tickets.

(Continues on next page)

¹The level of personal service in the American marketplace is quite low. ²Catalog phone clerks have snapped at me in exasperation when I can't find the customer identification number on my catalog. ³Even worse, returning a catalog item is highly inconvenient—it must be rewrapped and mailed back to the company. ⁴Service in local stores is no better. ⁵Yesterday I waited for nearly five minutes at a cash register while two clerks complained bitterly to one another about how much they hated their jobs. ⁶I have heard workers in restaurants groan loudly when customers walked in too close to quitting time. ⁷Even when I ask for assistance in finding a product in a store, clerks sometimes shrug their shoulders and walk away.

3. Which sentence is not relevant support for the argument that the level of personal service in the American marketplace is low?
   a. Sentence 3
   b. Sentence 4
   c. Sentence 5
   d. Sentence 6

   Even if a catalog company's level of personal service is excellent, one would still have to rewrap and mail an item to return it.

B. For each group, read the three items of support (the evidence). Then circle the letter of the point that is adequately supported by that evidence.

Group 1

Support:

- Unprotected engine systems freeze at very low temperatures.
- Cold temperatures cause worn automobile belts and hoses to break.
- Weak batteries go dead in very cold weather.

4. Which point is adequately supported by the evidence above?
   a. One should buy new automotive belts and hoses every year or two.
   b. Improperly maintained cars are likely to break down in the winter.
   c. It's best to walk or take buses and taxis in very cold weather.
   d. Car mechanics take more advantage of consumers in winter than in summer.

Group 2

Support:

- Music is often quite effective in helping emotionally disturbed children communicate.
- Music can help relieve anxiety in patients about to undergo surgery.
- Music can help relieve persistent arthritis pain.

5. Which point is adequately supported by the evidence above?
   a. Everyone should listen to music each day.
   b. Music is one of our most effective medical tools.
   c. More people should enter the field of music therapy.
   d. Music is a useful treatment for physical and emotional ailments.

ARGUMENT: Test 5

A. Each point is followed by three statements that provide relevant support and three that do not. In the spaces, write the letters of the three relevant statements of support.

Point: Dolores spends money rather carelessly.

    a. When all her socks were dirty, she bought a few new pairs rather than do a load of laundry.

    b. She charges most of what she buys with her Visa or Master card.

    c. She bought a dress without trying it on, and when it didn't fit, she hung it in the back of her closet instead of returning it.

    d. Last year she bought an almost-new Toyota.

    e. Although she shops at a grocery store that will double the value of customers' coupons, she says it's too much bother to use coupons at all.

    f. She keeps a hundred-dollar bill in the top drawer of her bureau in case of an emergency.

1–3. *Items that logically support the point:*___*a*___ ___*c*___ ___*e*___

Point: Feeling guilty is not all bad.

    a. Some people feel guilty because they can't do everything others ask of them.

    b. Feelings of guilt can encourage a person to think about his or her behavior and act differently the next time.

    c. People who feel guilt are less likely to commit a crime than those who feel no guilt for their wrongdoings.

    d. People often feel guilty even when they have done nothing wrong.

    e. Parents often feel guilty when their children, even their adult children, do something wrong.

    f. People who feel guilt have more understanding and compassion for other people's imperfections.

4–6. *Items that logically support the point:*___*b*___ ___*c*___ ___*f*___

B. Read the following three items of support (the evidence). Then circle the letter of the point that is adequately supported by that evidence.

Support:

    • Under airline deregulation, one airline may have, for all practical purposes, a monopoly on air service to many cities.

    • Since the airlines were deregulated, airline fleets have become older and maintenance standards have slipped.

(Continues on next page)

- Airline deregulation has produced airline fares that are so confusing and complicated that even professional travel agents can't always figure them out.

7. Which point is adequately supported by the evidence above?
    a. Deregulation of an industry is always a bad idea.
    (b.) Airline deregulation was a bad idea.
    c. Flying is now extremely dangerous.
    d. Travel agents earn more money than they're worth.

C. Read the paragraphs below, and then answer the questions that follow.

> [1]In addition to highways and airlines, America should have a high-speed rail system. [2]Democrats and Republicans are equally to blame for our failure to develop such a system. [3]High-speed trains are good time-savers. [4]Over distances up to several hundred miles, they would actually get you there faster than jetliners, which have to fly to and from outlying airports. [5]In addition, trains, powered by electricity, produce less pollution than airplanes and also save oil. [6]Developing a high-speed rail system would also be a boost to American industry by providing a highly reliable, speedy method of transportation.

8. Which sentence is not relevant to the author's argument that the United States should build high-speed trains?
    (a.) Sentence 2
    b. Sentence 3
    c. Sentence 4
    d. Sentence 5

> [1]The death penalty is popular with voters, who are frightened of violent crime, but it is not very effective in reducing the murder rate. [2]In the 1960s and 1970s, when murder rates were lower than today, the death penalty was hardly ever used. [3]Even today, the states that use the death penalty most also often have the highest murder rates. [4]In addition, every death sentence costs taxpayers hundreds of thousands of dollars in appeals and lawyers' fees. [5]The number of executions that take place in a state doesn't seem to matter either. [6]There have actually been some years in which states that had many executions experienced higher homicide rates than states with fewer executions.

9. Which statement is the point of the argument?
    a. The death penalty is popular with voters, who are frightened of violent crime.
    (b.) The death penalty is not very effective in reducing the murder rate.
    c. The murder rate has gone up in this country since the 1960s and 1970s.
    d. Executions cost more than they are worth.

10. Which sentence is not relevant support for the point of the argument?
    a. Sentence 3   c. Sentence 5
    (b.) Sentence 4   d. Sentence 6

Comment: Item 10—Even if the death penalty were effective, it could still costs taxpayers a great deal of money in appeals and lawyers' fees.

ARGUMENT: Test 6

A. Each point is followed by three statements that provide relevant support and three that do not. In the spaces, write the letters of the three relevant statements of support.

Point: It makes sense to give alternative sentences, not jail, to some nonviolent offenders.

    a. Everyone is entitled to legal representation.
    b. Alternative sentences cost less than jail.
    c. The crime rate goes up every year.
    d. Prisons are overcrowded.
    e. The courts always have a backlog of cases.
    f. Evidence suggests that alternative sentences offer a better chance of rehabilitating the offender.

1–3. *Items that logically support the point:*___*b*___   ___*d*___   ___*f*___

Point: Religion is a powerful force in modern American life.

    a. The main religion in America is Christianity.
    b. Television evangelists can gather millions of dollars from contributors.
    c. Religious leaders are often influential voices on public issues in America.
    d. In America, there is no state religion.
    e. The Pilgrims came to America seeking religious freedom.
    f. Public opinion polls show that a majority of Americans consider religion personally important to them.

4–6. *Items that logically support the point:*___*b*___   ___*c*___   ___*f*___

B. Read the following three items of support (the evidence). Then circle the letter of the point that is adequately supported by that evidence.

Support:

- Vitamin C, unlike some other vitamins, is not stored in the body fat.
- Any vitamin C not used by the body is excreted within a few hours.
- In addition, vitamin C is an acid, and thus it's best not to take large doses of it on an empty stomach.

7. Which point is adequately supported by the evidence above?
    a. Everyone should take supplemental doses of vitamin C.
    b. For people who take vitamin C pills, it is more efficient to take one pill a day.
    c. People should spread their vitamin C intake throughout the day.
    d. It is not necessary to include vitamin C in one's diet if vitamin C pills are taken.

(Continues on next page)

C. Read the paragraphs below, and then answer the questions that follow.

[1]America's top corporate executives are often greatly overpaid. [2]They use their enormous incomes to support an overly lavish lifestyle. [3]Some corporate bosses make nearly a hundred million dollars a year—thousands of times more than what some of their employees are making. [4]Such wide discrepancies in pay lower the morale of employees, especially when the executives aren't performing well. [5]Some corporate executives have gotten multi-million-dollar bonuses even though their companies lost money.

8. Which sentence is not relevant to the the author's point that corporate executives are often overpaid?
   (a.) Sentence 2
   b. Sentence 3
   c. Sentence 4
   d. Sentence 5

[1]Despite what many parents say, video games aren't all that bad for children. [2]Educational psychologists believe that video games aid problem-solving skills by challenging children to reason out a solution. [3]Children must constantly use their thinking ability to respond to a rapidly changing game screen. [4]Many parents allow their children to watch Saturday morning cartoons, and those don't demand much thinking at all. [5]Another advantage to playing video games is that operating the keys and controls can increase a child's manual dexterity. [6]And many authorities feel that video games enable children to learn that they can master and control technology.

9. Which of the following is not relevant to the author's conclusion that there are benefits to having children play video games?
   a. Sentence 2
   b. Sentence 3
   (c.) Sentence 4
   d. Sentence 6

10. A point that is adequately supported by the passage is that children who play video games
    (a.) learn skills that they can transfer to real-life situations.
    b. also tend to read more books.
    c. forget to do their homework.
    d. don't watch much TV anymore.

Comments: Item 8—How the executives spend their money doesn't determine whether or not they are overpaid.

Item 9—The influence of Saturday morning cartoons on children has nothing to do with how good or bad video games are for them.

Part II

TEN READING SELECTIONS

1
The Yellow Ribbon
Pete Hamill

Preview

When is a yellow handkerchief like a pair of open arms? For the answer, read this selection, which first appeared in a *New York Post* newspaper column by Pete Hamill. The story became the inspiration for the popular song "Tie a Yellow Ribbon 'Round the Old Oak Tree." This moving article probably also suggests the origin of using yellow ribbons as a symbol of America's wish to see her troops return home safely.

Words to Watch

cocoon (2): protective covering
bluntness (13): abruptness
exaltation (22): joy

1 They were going to Fort Lauderdale, the girl remembered later. There were six of them, three boys and three girls, and they picked up the bus at the old terminal on 34th Street, carrying sandwiches and wine in paper bags, dreaming of golden beaches and the tides of the sea as the gray cold spring of New York vanished behind them. Vingo was on board from the beginning.

2 As the bus passed through Jersey and into Philly, they began to notice that Vingo never moved. He sat in front of the young people, his dusty face masking his age, dressed in a plain brown ill-fitting suit. His fingers were stained from cigarettes and he chewed the inside of his lip a lot, frozen into some personal cocoon° of silence.

3 Somewhere outside of Washington, deep into the night, the bus pulled into a Howard Johnson's, and everybody got off except Vingo. He sat rooted in his seat, and the young people began to

wonder about him, trying to imagine his life: Perhaps he was a sea captain, maybe he had run away from his wife, he could be an old soldier going home. When they went back to the bus, the girl sat beside him and introduced herself.

4 "We're going to Florida," the girl said brightly. "You going that far?"

5 "I don't know." Vingo said.

6 "I've never been there," she said. "I hear it's beautiful."

7 "It is," he said quietly, as if remembering something he had tried to forget.

8 "You live there?"

9 "I did some time there in the Navy. Jacksonville."

10 "Want some wine?" she said. He smiled and took the bottle of Chianti and took a swig. He thanked her and retreated again into his silence. After a while, she went back to the others, as Vingo nodded in sleep.

11 In the morning they awoke outside another Howard Johnson's, and this time Vingo went in. The girl insisted that he join them. He seemed very shy and ordered black coffee and smoked nervously, as the young people chattered about sleeping on the beaches. When they went back on the bus, the girl sat with Vingo again, and after a while, slowly and painfully and with great hesitation, he began to tell his story. He had been in jail in New York for the last four years, and now he was going home.

12 "Four years!" the girl said. "What did you do?"

13 "It doesn't matter," he said with quiet bluntness°. "I did it and I went to jail. If you can't do the time, don't do the crime. That's what they say and they're right."

14 "Are you married?"

15 "I don't know."

16 "You don't know?" she said.

17 "Well, when I was in the can I wrote to my wife," he said. "I told her, I said, Martha, I understand if you can't stay married to me. I told her that. I said I was gonna be away a long time, and that if she couldn't stand it, if the kids kept askin' questions, if it hurt her too much, well, she could just forget me. Get a new guy—she's a wonderful woman, really something—and forget about me. I told her she didn't have to write me or nothing. And she didn't. Not for three and a half years."

18 "And you're going home now, not knowing?"

19 "Yeah," he said shyly. "Well, last week, when I was sure the parole was coming through I wrote her. I told her that if she had a new guy, I understood. But if she didn't, if she would take me back, she should let me know. We used to live in this town, Brunswick, just before Jacksonville, and there's a great big oak tree just as you come into town, a very famous tree, huge. I told her if she would take me back, she should put a yellow handkerchief on the tree, and I would get off and come home. If she didn't want me, forget it, no handkerchief, and I'd keep going on through."

20 "Wow," the girl said. "Wow."

21 She told the others, and soon all of them were in it, caught up in the approach of Brunswick, looking at the pictures Vingo showed them of his wife and three children, the woman handsome in a plain way, the children still unformed in a cracked, much-handled snapshot. Now they were twenty miles from Brunswick and the young people took over window seats on the right side, waiting for the approach of the great oak tree. Vingo stopped looking, tightening his face into the ex-con's mask, as if fortifying himself against still another disappointment. Then it was ten miles,

and then five and the bus acquired a dark hushed mood, full of silence, of absence, of lost years, of the woman's plain face, of the sudden letter on the breakfast table, of the wonder of children, of the iron bars of solitude.

22   Then suddenly all of the young people were up out of their seats, screaming and shouting and crying, doing small dances, shaking clenched fists in triumph and exaltation°. All except Vingo.

Vingo sat there stunned, looking at 23 the oak tree. It was covered with yellow handkerchiefs, twenty of them, thirty of them, maybe hundreds, a tree that stood like a banner of welcome blowing and billowing in the wind, turned into a gorgeous yellow blur by the passing bus. As the young people shouted, the old con slowly rose from his seat, holding himself tightly, and made his way to the front of the bus to go home.

BASIC SKILL QUESTIONS

Vocabulary in Context

1. In the sentence below, the word *fortifying* means
   a. strengthening.
   b. watching.
   c. hurrying.
   d. losing.

   "Vingo stopped looking, tightening his face into the ex-con's mask, as if fortifying himself against still another disappointment." (Paragraph 21)

2. In the sentence below, the word *acquired* means
   a. needed.
   b. took on.
   c. stopped.
   d. lost.

   "Then it was ten miles, and then five and the bus acquired a dark hushed mood. . . ." (Paragraph 21)

Central Point and Main Ideas

Comment: Item 3—The main idea of a narrative will be a summary of the events.

3. Which sentence best expresses the main idea of this selection?
   a. Prison sentences can ruin marriages.
   b. If you commit a crime, you must pay for it.
   c. Vingo did not know what to expect.
   d. Vingo returned from prison to find that his wife still loved him.

4. Which sentence best expresses the main idea of paragraph 3?
   a. The bus stopped at a Howard Johnson's.   Too narrow.
   b. The young people began to be curious about Vingo.
   c. Vingo might have been a sea captain.   Too narrow.
   d. Everyone got off the bus except Vingo.   Too narrow.

Supporting Details

5. __F__ TRUE OR FALSE? Vingo felt he should not have been put in prison.

(See paragraph 13.)

Transitions

6. The relationship between the two sentences below is one of
   a. time.
   b. contrast.
   c. comparison.
   d. examples.

   Vingo is contrasting two possible reactions by his wife.

   ". . . I told her that if she had a new guy, I understood. But if she didn't, if she would take me back, she should let me know." (Paragraph 19)

7. The transition words *as, when, after, now,* and *then,* which Hamill uses throughout this selection, all signal
   a. cause and effect.
   b. examples.
   c. contrast.
   d. time.

   Because narratives tell about events in the order in which they happened, they use many time signals.

8. The relationship expressed in the phrase "a tree that stood like a banner of welcome" (paragraph 23) is one of
   a. contrast.
   b. comparison.
   c. cause and effect.
   d. time.

   The tree with handkerchiefs is being compared to a banner. Note the use of the transition *like.*

Patterns of Organization

9. The main pattern of organization of paragraph 2 is
   a. cause and effect.
   b. comparison and contrast.
   c. list of items.
   d. time order.

   The "items" listed are details that describe Vingo, so they can be presented in any order.

10. The main pattern of organization of the entire selection is
    a. cause and effect.
    b. comparison and contrast.
    c. list of items.
    d. time order.

    Narratives tell about events in a time order.

ADVANCED SKILL QUESTIONS

Fact and Opinion

11. In telling this narrative, Hamill
    a. stresses his own opinions.
    b. leaves out any of Vingo's opinions.
    c. reveals the bus driver's opinions.
    d. reveals through the young people's actions how they feel about Vingo.

    See paragraphs 20–22.

12. Judging by the first sentence of the selection, Hamill got some facts for this nonfiction narrative by
    a. observing everything as a passenger on the bus ride.
    b. only imagining what might have happened on such a ride.
    c. interviewing at least one passenger.
    d. using a tape recording of the bus ride.

    The words "the girl remembered later" (paragraph 1) suggest that Hamill got his information by interviewing one of the girls on the bus.

Inferences

13. We can infer that the young people were going to Florida
    a. on business.
    b. to visit relatives.
    c. on vacation.
    d. to get married.

    Hamill states that the young people were "dreaming of golden beaches and the tides of the sea" (paragraph 1).

14. The author implies that Vingo thought
    a. he would someday be in prison again.
    b. there might be no yellow handkerchief on the tree.
    c. his wife was wrong for not writing to him in prison.
    d. his wife was sure to want him back.

    Vingo's nervousness and the fact that his wife hadn't written imply the possibility that she might not want him back.

15. __T__ TRUE OR FALSE? The statement that Vingo "rose from his seat, holding himself tightly" (last paragraph) implies that Vingo was trying to contain his emotions.

    We can make this inference based on the "message" Vingo just received.

16. By telling us that the picture of Vingo's family was a "cracked, much-handled snapshot," the author implies that
    a. Vingo didn't know how to take good care of photos.
    b. the pictures were not really of Vingo's family.
    c. Vingo had looked at the snapshot a great deal while in jail.
    d. the photo was relatively new.

    For the four years that Vingo was in jail, the photo may have been his only concrete connection with his family.

Purpose and Tone

17. The main purpose of "The Yellow Ribbon" is to
    a. inform readers that a convict's life can be rebuilt after prison.
    b. persuade readers to avoid a life of crime.
    ⓒ entertain readers with a heartwarming story.

18. In paragraphs 17 through 21, the author's tone becomes increasingly
    a. bitter.
    b. amused.   The author chooses details that increase suspense
    ⓒ suspenseful.   over what the oak tree will look like.
    d. disbelieving.

Argument

19. Which of the following points is well supported by the evidence below?
    ⓐ Vingo was nervous about something.   Nothing in the
    b. Vingo was on the verge of a nervous breakdown.   sentence suggests
    c. Vingo had a hostile personality.   the points in *b*, *c*,
    d. Vingo disliked young people.   and *d*.

    "[Vingo's] fingers were stained from cigarettes and he chewed the inside
    of his lip a lot, frozen into some personal cocoon of silence." (Paragraph 2)

20. Which statement does *not* support the following point?

    Point: Vingo deserved the yellow handkerchiefs.

    a. He admitted his mistake.
    b. He paid for his crime by serving four years in jail.
    ⓒ He probably caused his wife and children a lot of pain and embarrassment.
    d. He seemed to regret causing his wife pain.

    Point *c* would be a reason for Vingo's family
    to reject him.

Comment: Item 17—If the author's *main* purpose had been to show that a convict's life can
be rebuilt after prison, he would have told us more about Vingo's life after the
bus ride. If *b* were his purpose, he would have focused more on Vingo's punishment.

SUMMARIZING

Following is an incomplete summary of "The Yellow Ribbon." Circle the letter (**a**, **b**, or **c**) of the item below that best completes the summary.

A man named Vingo had just been released from prison and was on a bus headed home. Some young people were also on the bus, and they got Vingo to tell his story. He said he had written to his wife when he went to prison to explain he would understand if she found another man. He hadn't heard from her since but still loved her very much. So he recently wrote to her, telling her to put a yellow handkerchief on a well-known oak tree in town if she wanted him to come home. If the handkerchief wasn't on the tree, he wouldn't get off the bus there. _____.

a. Vingo showed pictures of his wife and children to the young people, who got caught up in waiting to see the oak tree. As the bus got closer to Vingo's hometown, the bus became quiet and filled with suspense.

b. The young people got caught up in Vingo's situation. After a tense ride to his hometown, he and his fellow travelers finally got his wife's answer: not one, but scores of handkerchiefs fluttering on the tree.

c. Vingo would just continue on the bus to Florida, which is where the young people were going. He understood that while he was in prison, his wife might have started a new life for herself and their children.

DISCUSSION QUESTIONS

1. According to the information in the selection, what is Vingo's attitude toward his wife?

2. Has Vingo assumed responsibility for his crime, in your opinion?

3. While there is much we don't learn about Vingo in this very short narrative, Hamill does provide us with clues to some important aspects of his personality. What evidence is there that he is a decent man, a person who we could feel deserves a second chance?

4. Many people are thrilled, some even to tears, by this story. What makes "The Yellow Ribbon" have such a powerful effect on readers?

Check Your Performance   THE YELLOW RIBBON

Activity	Number Right	Points	Score
BASIC SKILL QUESTIONS			
Vocabulary in Context (2 items)	_____	x 4 =	_____
Central Point and Main Ideas (2 items)	_____	x 4 =	_____
Supporting Details (1 item)	_____	x 4 =	_____
Transitions (3 items)	_____	x 4 =	_____
Patterns of Organization (2 items)	_____	x 4 =	_____
ADVANCED SKILL QUESTIONS			
Fact and Opinion (2 items)	_____	x 4 =	_____
Inferences (4 items)	_____	x 4 =	_____
Purpose and Tone (2 items)	_____	x 4 =	_____
Argument (2 items)	_____	x 4 =	_____
SUMMARIZING (1 item)	_____	x 20 =	_____

TOTAL SCORE   =   _____ %

Enter your total score into the **Reading Performance Chart: Ten Reading Selections** on the inside back cover.

2

Urban Legends
Beth Johnson

Preview

Did you hear the one about a woman who was looking through some Asian carpets and was bitten by a poisonous snake? Or was the story that the woman tried on a coat from Mexico, put her hand in the pocket, and found the snake there? These are just two versions of what folklorists call an urban legend. This selection explains what urban legends are and gives more examples of them.

Words to Watch

homicidal (3): murderous
legend (8): a story that can't be proven true
sophisticated (9): knowledgeable about the world
mint (15): brand-new
agonizing (18): painful

1   A group of college freshmen were sitting around in a friend's dorm room one night, eating popcorn and comparing notes on classes. Eventually the talk drifted away from academics and into the area of spooky stories. Tales of haunted houses were being giggled and shivered over when a girl from a small town in Michigan broke in. "I know a scarier story than any of those!" she announced. "And the scariest thing is, this one is true. It happened to a girl my sister knew."

2   She began her story.

3   "This girl went to baby-sit at a house way out in the country one evening. It was a stormy night, and she was feeling a little nervous anyway when the phone rang. When she answered, a man said, 'Have you checked the children?' and laughed weirdly. She was scared to death and ran to check the kids. They were all right, but a few minutes later the guy called again and said again, 'Have you checked the children?' and

laughed like crazy. She called the operator to see if she could get the calls traced. A few minutes later, the operator called back to say, 'Get out of the house! He's in the house with you!' So she hurried and grabbed the kids and ran out into the rain just as the police pulled up. They found this escaped homicidal° maniac in the parents' upstairs bedroom. She was lucky to get out alive."

4 "Wow! What an awful story!" the girl's roommate exclaimed.

5 "But wait a minute!" called out another friend, this one from Iowa. "That didn't happen in Michigan. It happened near my home town, back when my mother was in high school. The guy had escaped from an asylum in Cedar Rapids."

6 "Well, it sounds an awful lot like something that happened a few years ago to a friend of my cousin's in Colorado," said another freshman. "Only the guy actually caught the babysitter."

7 What's going on here? How could the same event have happened to three different babysitters in three different parts of the country at three different times?

8 Urban legend° is what's going on.

9 Urban legend is the modern-day equivalent of the Paul Bunyan story. We're too sophisticated° these days to believe in Babe the blue ox or men who use pine trees to comb their beards. But we haven't quite given up our need for scary stories that are a little too good to be true. So we've developed our own type of slightly more believable tall tales. They're modern. They sound real. They include a humorous, unexpected, or frightening twist. And they probably never happened.

10 The deadly hairdo. Kentucky fried rats. The nude surprise party.

11 Do any of those ring a bell? Have you heard them told as true? Have you told them as true? If you've believed them, don't be embarrassed. You've got lots of company. And if you've helped spread them, well, you're just continuing a great American folk tradition.

12 Urban legends have come in for some serious attention in the last couple of decades. Their biggest fan is a University of Utah professor of English named Jan Harold Brunvand. Professor Brunvand has devoted years to collecting, researching, and analyzing urban legends all across the United States and even in other countries. He's written two books, *The Vanishing Hitchhiker* and *The Mexican Pet*. These books are jam-packed with the stories we love to tell and will swear are true—despite all evidence to the contrary.

13 Americans love their automobiles, and so some of the most familiar urban legends involve cars. One of the best-known is the classic story of teenagers parked late at night in a lovers' lane. The couple are listening to music on a car radio when a news bulletin comes on: a dangerous maniac has escaped from a nearby mental asylum. (Escaped mad-men are common characters in urban legends.) Frightened, the girl demands to be taken home. But when the boy tries to start the car, it won't run. The boy gets out, locks the girl in the car, and walks off to find help.

14 The girl huddles in the cold car, becoming more and more frightened as minutes and then hours go by with no sign of her boyfriend. Her fright turns to terror when she begins to hear a soft "click, click" noise on top of the car. Finally, just as dawn breaks, police cars arrive at the scene. Cops surround the car, help the girl out, and tell her, "Just walk to the police car and get in. Don't look back." Naturally, though, she does look

back. Her boyfriend's body, suspended from a rope, is hanging upside down from a tree. As he sways back and forth in the breeze, his class ring scrapes—"click, click"—against the roof of the car.

15 But not all "car" urban legends are so horrible. "The Playboy's Car" tells of a man who is in the market for a luxury sports car. He sees an ad in the newspaper for a nearly new Porsche for $29.95. He figures the price is a mistake but goes to check it out anyway. A woman greets him at the house, assures him that the price is correct, and invites him to test-drive the Porsche. He drives a few miles. The car is in mint° condition. Hardly believing his luck, he hurries back to the house to close the deal. As the ownership papers are changing hands, he blurts out, "I can't stand not knowing. Why are you selling this car so cheap?" The woman smiles and answers, "My husband left me and moved in with his secretary last week. He asked me to sell his Porsche and send him the money."

16 How do these stories spread from coast to coast—and sometimes beyond? They probably begin wherever people gather: slumber parties, bowling nights, breaks at the office water cooler, transcontinental airplane flights. Eventually, they make their way into our modern communications network: telephones, television, radio, and newspapers. They sometimes even slip into local and national publications as true events. The fact that the stories have shown up in the media convinces the public that they must be true. People clip the articles and send them to friends and family and also to columnists and radio and television talk-show hosts, who give them further publicity. And the more the stories travel, the more realistic-sounding details they pick up, and the more variations develop.

17 Another category of urban legends demonstrates, Brunvand believes, the great American concern with cleanliness and health. "The Spider in the Hairdo," popular in the 1950s and 1960s, told of the girl with a fashionable "beehive" hairdo. She rarely washed her highly teased and sprayed hair. So—wouldn't you know it—a black widow spider got in there, bit her, and she died. A subcategory of the "cleanliness" stories is the set of "dreadful contamination" stories. These include tales about people finding pieces of mice in their bottled soft drinks, or the poor girl who bit into an oddly shaped piece of restaurant chicken, only to discover that it was a batter-fried rat.

18 And then there are the stories concerning nudity. They sound familiar to any of us who've ever had the agonizing° dream of being at work or on stage with no clothes on. There's the man left naked by the roadside when his wife (not knowing he'd stepped out) drove off with their trailer. Or the crafty host who gave his female guests bathing suits that fell apart when they got wet. Or the poor woman who, feeling playful on her birthday, came downstairs naked to surprise her husband—and walked into her own birthday party.

19 What purpose do these stories serve? Why have they developed? They're part of a long tradition that includes Aesop's fables—remember the hare and the tortoise?—and the morality plays of the Middle Ages, where "Truth" and "Virtue" were actual characters. They are stories that touch some of our deepest fears and concerns. And they teach us lessons. Don't park on lonely lovers' lanes. Don't pick up strangers. Don't fool around on your spouse. Don't eat food you're not sure of. Bathe regularly. It's all

the same stuff your parents told you, but it's told in a far more entertaining way.

20   One more story? Well, have you heard about the cement-truck driver who stopped in to say hello to his wife during the day? When he got to his house, he found a brand-new Cadillac in his driveway. Becoming suspicious, he looked in the window and saw his wife and a strange man drinking coffee in the kitchen and laughing. Aha, he thought. So this is what she does all day. He could think of only one appropriate response. He backed his truck up to the Caddy, filled it full of cement, and then drove away.

21   When the truck driver got home that night, he found his wife hysterical. "Honey," she sobbed. "I've been saving my money for twenty years to buy you a wonderful present. It came today, and when the man that delivered it left the house—well, just go *look* at your car!"

BASIC SKILL QUESTIONS

Vocabulary in Context

1. In the sentence below, the word *equivalent* means
   a. explanation.
   b. cost.
   c. storyteller.
   (d.) equal.

   "Urban legend is the modern-day equivalent of the Paul Bunyan story." (Paragraph 9)

2. In the excerpt below, the word *contamination* means
   (a.) impurity.
   b. disease.
   c. restaurant.
   d. bottling.

   The context clues are examples.

   "'dreadful contamination' stories. . . . include tales about people finding pieces of mice in their bottled soft drinks, or the poor girl who bit into an oddly shaped piece of restaurant chicken, only to discover that it was a batter-fried rat." (Paragraph 17)

Central Point and Main Ideas

3. Which sentence best expresses the central point of the selection?
   a. Urban legends begin in unknown ways and then travel throughout the country.   Too narrow.
   b. Urban legends are scary stories based on old superstitions.   Incorrect.
   c. Urban legends are very interesting to scholars.   Too narrow.
   (d.) Urban legends are modern tales that touch upon deep fears and concerns and that teach lessons.

4. Which sentence best expresses the main idea of paragraph 16? Too narrow.
   a. Urban legends are believed because they sound so realistic. Too narrow.
   b. Urban legends are often published in newspapers.
   c. Urban legends spread in various ways, gaining more realism and variations.
   d. Because of our modern communications network, information of all kinds can be spread over a wide area relatively quickly. Too broad.

5. The main idea of paragraph 17 is best expressed in its
   a. first sentence.
   b. second sentence.
   c. third sentence.
   d. last sentence.

   The "cleanliness and health" referred to only generally in the first sentence is illustrated by the specific examples in the rest of the paragraph.

Supporting Details

6. According to the article, urban legends are
   a. always horrible and scary.
   b. very difficult to believe. See paragraph 9.
   c. usually started by college students.
   d. part of a long tradition of folktales.

7. The author specifically mentions urban legends that are concerned with
   a. cars.
   b. sports. See paragraph 13.
   c. twins.
   d. none of the above.

Transitions

8. The relationship of the second sentence below to the first is one of
   a. addition.
   b. time. One topic of conversation followed another.
   c. an example.
   d. cause and effect.

   "A group of college freshmen were sitting around in a friend's dorm room one night, eating popcorn and comparing notes on classes. Eventually the talk drifted away from academics and into the area of spooky stories." (Paragraph 1)

9. The relationship between the two parts of the sentence below is one of
   a. time.
   b. comparison. Urban legends contrast with "the stuff your parents told you" in how entertaining they are.
   c. contrast.
   d. examples.

   "It's all the same stuff your parents told you, but it's told in a far more entertaining way." (Paragraph 19)

Patterns of Organization

10. The main pattern of organization of the selection is a version of
    a. time order.
    b. comparison-contrast.
    c. cause and effect.
    (d.) definition and example.

    The reading defines, discusses, and gives examples of "urban legends."

11. The main pattern of organization of paragraph 3 is
    (a.) time order.
    b. comparison.
    c. cause and effect.
    d. examples.

    Anecdotes are mini-narratives.

ADVANCED SKILL QUESTIONS

Fact and Opinion

12. The word that makes the sentence below an opinion is
    (a.) *biggest.*
    b. *fan.*
    c. *Utah.*
    d. *named.*

    There's no way to *prove* who the biggest fan is.

    "Their biggest fan is a University of Utah professor of English named Jan Harold Brunvand." (Paragraph 12)

13. The statement below is
    (a.) fact.
    b. opinion.
    c. fact and opinion.

    The statement can be verified by checking programs and articles and by interviewing people.

    "[Urban legends] make their way into our modern communications network: telephones, television, radio, and newspapers." (Paragraph 16)

Inferences

14. The author implies that
    a. people should always check their food before eating.
    b. husbands should never be suspicious of their wives.
    (c.) throughout history people have told stories with morals.
    d. urban legends lack meaning and purpose.

    See paragraph 19.

15. From the selection we might conclude that urban legends are
    a. based upon European superstitions.
    (b.) worthy of serious study.
    c. not interesting to the average American.
    d. usually about true events.

    See paragraph 12.

16. We can infer that the lesson of the story about the cement-truck driver and the Cadillac is
    a. some cars cost too much.
    b. women should not have coffee with strange men.
    c. don't save money for something unimportant.
    (d.) don't jump to conclusions.

    The cement-truck driver jumped to the conclusion that his wife was having an affair (see paragraph 20).

Purpose and Tone

17. *Fill in the blank:* The author (*informs, persuades*) _____*informs*_____ the reader about urban legends and illustrates with entertaining examples.

18. *Fill in the blank:* In general, the author's tone is (*formal, conversational*) _____*conversational*_____.

    Examples of informal wording: "What's going on here?" (paragraph 7); "The deadly hairdo . . ." (10).

19. The tone of the urban legend about the baby sitter (paragraph 3) is
    a. playful.
    b. forgiving.
    (c.) threatening.
    d. mocking.

    The author emphasizes the sense of a growing threat to the baby sitter and the children.

Argument

20. Put a check by the statement that is the point of the following argument. The other statements are support for that point.

    ____ a. The baby-sitting legend relates to our desire for the safety of our children.
    ✓ b. Urban legends are about some of our deepest fears and concerns.
    ____ c. "The Spider in the Hairdo" story has to do with our interest in cleanliness and health.
    ____ d. Our fear of making fools of ourselves gives power to the legends about nudity.

    Answers *a*, *c*, and *d* are specific examples of "our deepest fears and concerns."

MAPPING

The map below divides the selection into three main parts. Complete the map by filling in the following four missing items.

- Gather more realistic details and variations as they travel
- The cement-truck driver's revenge
- What they are
- The playboy's car

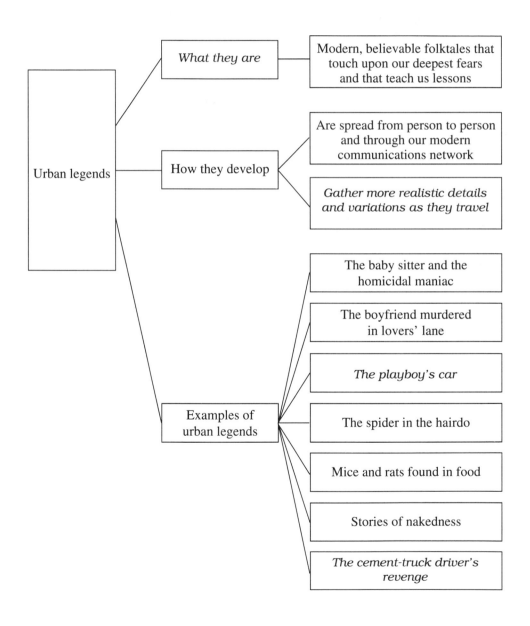

DISCUSSION QUESTIONS

1. Johnson writes that urban legends "teach us lessons." Which of the stories in the article do you think teaches the most effective lesson?

2. Have you ever heard any of the stories described, but in slightly different form? Or have you heard any story that is so dramatic that you wonder if it is true or not? Retell any such story you have heard, as best as you can remember it.

3. Johnson claims that "we haven't quite given up our need for scary stories that are a little too good to be true." In our culture, where else besides urban legends do we find such stories?

4. Why do you think people enjoy being scared so much?

Check Your Performance   **URBAN LEGENDS**

Activity	Number Right	Points	Score
BASIC SKILL QUESTIONS			
Vocabulary in Context (2 items)	_____	x 4 =	_____
Central Point and Main Ideas (3 items)	_____	x 4 =	_____
Supporting Details (2 items)	_____	x 4 =	_____
Transitions (2 items)	_____	x 4 =	_____
Patterns of Organization (2 items)	_____	x 4 =	_____
ADVANCED SKILL QUESTIONS			
Fact and Opinion (2 items)	_____	x 4 =	_____
Inferences (3 items)	_____	x 4 =	_____
Purpose and Tone (3 items)	_____	x 4 =	_____
Argument (1 item)	_____	x 4 =	_____
MAPPING (4 items)	_____	x 5 =	_____

TOTAL SCORE = _____ %

Enter your total score into the **Reading Performance Chart: Ten Reading Selections** on the inside back cover.

3
Shame
Dick Gregory

Preview

When we receive help, most of us feel grateful. But what if the help is given in an inconsiderate way? In this autobiographical piece, the comedian and social activist Dick Gregory shows that the good intentions of a giver are not enough if they don't take the recipient's pride into account.

Words to Watch

complected (1): complexioned
stoop (2): an outside stairway, porch, or platform at the entrance to a house
mackinaw (28): a short, plaid coat or jacket
googobs (29): Gregory's slang for *gobs*, a large amount

1   I never learned hate at home, or shame. I had to go to school for that. I was about seven years old when I got my first big lesson. I was in love with a little girl named Helene Tucker, a light-complected° little girl with pigtails and nice manners. She was always clean and she was smart in school. I think I went to school then mostly to look at her. I brushed my hair and even got me a little old handkerchief. It was a lady's handkerchief, but I didn't want Helene to see me wipe my nose on my hand. The pipes were frozen again, there was no water in the house, but I washed my socks and shirt every night. I'd get a pot, and go over to Mister Ben's grocery store, and stick my pot down into his soda machine. Scoop out some chopped ice. By evening the ice melted to water for washing. I got sick a lot that winter because the fire would go out at night before the clothes were dry. In the morning I'd put them on, wet or dry, because they were the only clothes I had.

2   Everybody's got a Helene Tucker, a symbol of everything you want. I loved her for her goodness, her cleanness, her

popularity. She'd walk down my street and my brothers and sisters would yell, "Here comes Helene," and I'd rub my tennis sneakers on the back of my pants and wish my hair wasn't so nappy and the white folks' shirt fit me better. I'd run out on the street. If I knew my place and didn't come too close, she'd wink at me and say hello. That was a good feeling. Sometimes I'd follow her all the way home, and shovel the snow off her walk and try to make friends with her Momma and her aunts. I'd drop money on her stoop° late at night on my way back from shining shoes in the taverns. And she had a Daddy, and he had a good job. He was a paper hanger.

3   I guess I would have gotten over Helene by summertime, but something happened in that classroom that made her face hang in front of me for the next twenty-two years. When I played the drums in high school it was for Helene and when I broke track records in college it was for Helene and when I started standing behind microphones and heard applause I wished Helene could hear it, too. It wasn't until I was twenty-nine years old and married and making money that I finally got her out of my system. Helene was sitting in that classroom when I learned to be ashamed of myself.

4   It was on a Thursday. I was sitting in the back of the room, in a seat with a chalk circle drawn around it. The idiot's seat, the troublemaker's seat.

5   The teacher thought I was stupid. Couldn't spell, couldn't read, couldn't do arithmetic. Just stupid. Teachers were never interested in finding out that you couldn't concentrate because you were so hungry, because you hadn't had any breakfast. All you could think about was noontime, would it ever come? Maybe you could sneak into the cloakroom and steal a bite of some kid's lunch out of a coat pocket. A bite of something. Paste. You can't really make a meal of paste, or put it on bread for a sandwich, but sometimes I'd scoop a few spoonfuls out of the big paste jar in the back of the room. Pregnant people get strange tastes. I was pregnant with poverty. Pregnant with dirt and pregnant with smells that made people turn away, pregnant with cold and pregnant with shoes that were never bought for me, pregnant with five other people in my bed and no Daddy in the next room, and pregnant with hunger. Paste doesn't taste too bad when you're hungry.

6   The teacher thought I was a troublemaker. All she saw from the front of the room was a little black boy who squirmed in his idiot's seat and made noises and poked the kids around him. I guess she couldn't see a kid who made noises because he wanted someone to know he was there.

7   It was on a Thursday, the day before the Negro payday. The eagle always flew on Friday. The teacher was asking each student how much his father would give to the Community Chest. On Friday night, each kid would get the money from his father, and on Monday he would bring it to the school. I decided I was going to buy a Daddy right then. I had money in my pocket from shining shoes and selling papers, and whatever Helene Tucker pledged for her Daddy I was going to top it. And I'd hand the money right in. I wasn't going to wait until Monday to buy me a Daddy.

8   I was shaking, scared to death. The teacher opened her book and started calling out names alphabetically.

9   "Helene Tucker?"

10   "My Daddy said he'd give two dollars and fifty cents."

11   "That's very nice, Helene. Very, very nice indeed."

12   That made me feel pretty good. It wouldn't take too much to top that. I had almost three dollars in dimes and quarters in my pocket. I stuck my hand in my pocket and held onto the money, waiting for her to call my name. But the teacher closed her book after she called everybody else in the class.

13   I stood up and raised my hand.

14   "What is it now?"

15   "You forgot me."

16   She turned toward the blackboard. "I don't have time to be playing with you, Richard."

17   "My Daddy said he'd . . . ."

18   "Sit down, Richard, you're disturbing the class."

19   "My Daddy said he'd give . . . fifteen dollars."

20   She turned around and looked mad. "We are collecting this money for you and your kind, Richard Gregory. If your Daddy can give fifteen dollars you have no business being on relief."

21   "I got it right now, I got it right now, my Daddy gave it to me to turn in today, my Daddy said . . . ."

22   "And furthermore," she said, looking right at me, her nostrils getting big and her lips getting thin and her eyes opening wide, "we know you don't have a Daddy."

23   Helene Tucker turned around, her eyes full of tears. She felt sorry for me. Then I couldn't see her too well because I was crying, too.

24   "Sit down, Richard."

25   And I always thought the teacher kind of liked me. She always picked me to wash the blackboard on Friday, after school. That was a big thrill, it made me feel important. If I didn't wash it, come Monday the school might not function right.

26   "Where are you going, Richard!"

27   I walked out of school that day, and for a long time I didn't go back very often. There was shame there.

28   Now there was shame everywhere. It seemed like the whole world had been inside that classroom, everyone had heard what the teacher had said, everyone had turned around and felt sorry for me. There was shame in going to the Worthy Boys Annual Christmas Dinner for you and your kind, because everybody knew what a worthy boy was. Why couldn't they just call it the Boys Annual Dinner, why'd they have to give it a name? There was shame in wearing the brown and orange and white plaid mackinaw° the welfare gave to three thousand boys. Why'd it have to be the same for everybody so when you walked down the street the people could see you were on relief? It was a nice warm mackinaw and it had a hood, and my Momma beat me and called me a little rat when she found out I stuffed it in the bottom of a pail full of garbage way over on Cottage Street. There was shame in running over to Mister Ben's at the end of the day and asking for his rotten peaches, there was shame in asking Mrs. Simmons for a spoonful of sugar, there was shame in running out to meet the relief truck. I hated that truck, full of food for you and your kind. I ran into the house and hid when it came. And then I started to sneak through alleys, to take the long way home so the people going into White's Eat Shop wouldn't see me. Yeah, the whole world heard the teacher that day, we all know you don't have a Daddy.

29   It lasted for a while, this kind of numbness. I spent a lot of time feeling sorry for myself. And then one day I met this wino in a restaurant. I'd been out hustling all day, shining shoes, selling

newspapers, and I had googobs° of money in my pocket. Bought me a bowl of chili for fifteen cents, and a cheeseburger for fifteen cents, and a Pepsi for five cents, and a piece of chocolate cake for ten cents. That was a good meal. I was eating when this old wino came in. I love winos because they never hurt anyone but themselves.

30   The old wino sat down at the counter and ordered twenty-six cents worth of food. He ate it like he really enjoyed it. When the owner, Mister Williams, asked him to pay the check, the old wino didn't lie or go through his pocket like he suddenly found a hole.

31   He just said: "Don't have no money."

32   The owner yelled: "Why in hell you come in here and eat my food if you don't have no money? That food cost me money."

33   Mister Williams jumped over the counter and knocked the wino off his stool and beat him over the head with a pop bottle. Then he stepped back and watched the wino bleed. Then he kicked him. And he kicked him again.

34   I looked at the wino with blood all over his face and I went over. "Leave him alone, Mister Williams. I'll pay the twenty-six cents."

35   The wino got up, slowly, pulling himself up to the stool, then up to the counter, holding on for a minute until his legs stopped shaking so bad. He looked at me with pure hate. "Keep your twenty-six cents. You don't have to pay, not now. I just finished paying for it."

36   He started to walk out, and as he passed me, he reached down and touched my shoulder. "Thanks, sonny, but it's too late now. Why didn't you pay it before?"

37   I was pretty sick about that. I waited too long to help another man.

BASIC SKILL QUESTIONS

Vocabulary in Context

1. In the excerpt below, the word *pledged* means
   a. repeated.
   b. studied.
   c. promised to give.
   d. brought home.

   Context clue: "The teacher was asking each student how much his father would give to the Community Chest."

   "I had money in my pocket . . . and whatever Helene Tucker pledged for her Daddy, I was going to top it." (Paragraph 7)

2. In the sentence below, the word *hustling* means
   a. complaining.
   b. relaxing.
   c. studying hard.
   d. working energetically.

   The context clues are the examples: "shining shoes" and "selling newspapers" [all day].

   "I'd been out hustling all day, shining shoes, selling newspapers, and I had googobs of money in my pocket." (Paragraph 29)

Central Point and Main Ideas

3. Which sentence best expresses the central point of this selection?
   a. Dick Gregory had a long-standing crush on a girl named Helene Tucker.
   b. The charity Gregory received was given in a way that labeled him as poor, which made him ashamed.
   (c.) As both a receiver and a giver, young Gregory learned that how something is given is as important as what is given.   Answers *a*, *b*, and
   d. Gregory grew up in a fatherless, poor family.   *d* are too narrow.

4. Which sentence best expresses the main idea of paragraph 2?
   (a.) The author adored Helene Tucker, a symbol of everything he wanted.
   b. Everybody has a symbol of everything he or she wants.
   c. Helene Tucker made the author feel ashamed of his looks.
   d. Unlike the author, Helene Tucker had a father.

5. Which sentence best expresses the main idea of paragraph 5?
   a. Gregory liked to eat paste.
   b. The teacher assumed that Gregory was stupid.
   c. The teacher never realized that Gregory was hungry all the time.
   (d.) The teacher assumed that Gregory was stupid and never realized that his poor work was the result of hunger.   Answers *a*, *b*, and *c* are too narrow.

Supporting Details

6. __T__ TRUE OR FALSE? Helene Tucker represented a way of life that Gregory wished he had.   See the first two sentences of paragraph 2.

7. After the teacher told him he was the type of person the Community Chest helped and that he was fatherless, Gregory
   a. never went back to school.   See the first two sentences of
   (b.) felt sorry for himself for a while.   paragraph 29.
   c. stopped working.
   d. felt that Helene Tucker did not feel sorry for him.

8. As support for his central point, the author uses several
   a. statistics.
   b. expert opinions.   Gregory relates his early
   (c.) personal experiences.   experiences in feeling shame.
   d. famous quotations.

Comments: Item 4—Answers *b*, *c*, and *d* are too narrow.

Transitions

9. The sentence below contains a(n)
   a. contrast signal.
   b. comparison signal.
   c. example signal.
   (d.) cause-effect signal.

   "I got sick a lot that winter because the fire would go out at night before the clothes were dry." (Paragraph 1)

10. The relationship of the second sentence below to the first is one of
    a. addition.
    b. comparison.   The teacher's action contrasted
    (c.) contrast.   with Gregory's expectation.
    d. an example.

    "I stuck my hand in my pocket and held onto the money, waiting for her to call my name. But the teacher closed her book after she called everybody else in the class." (Paragraph 12)

Patterns of Organization

11. The main pattern of organization of paragraph 28 is
    a. time order.   Gregory lists some of the places where he felt
    (b.) list of items.   shame. (The first sentence of paragraph 28 is
    c. definition and example.   the topic sentence.)
    d. contrast.

12. The pattern of organization used in paragraphs 30–36 is
    a. list of items.
    (b.) time order.   In these paragraphs, the author narrates a
    c. cause and effect.   series of events.
    d. comparison.

ADVANCED SKILL QUESTIONS

Fact and Opinion

13. Which of the following is a statement of opinion?
    a. "I was sitting in the back of the room, in a seat with a chalk circle drawn around it."
    (b.) "Paste doesn't taste too bad when you're hungry."   How something tastes
    c. "She turned toward the blackboard."   is a matter of opinion.
    d. "Helene Tucker turned around, her eyes full of tears."

Inferences

14. __F__   TRUE OR FALSE? In the classroom scene, the author implies that Helene is not sensitive.   See paragraph 23.

15. In paragraph 5, the author implies that
    a. he is stupid.
    b. teachers understood him well.
    c.) it was difficult for him to concentrate in school.
    d. the only way he ever got food was to steal it.

    Gregory writes that teachers "weren't interested in finding out that you couldn't concentrate because you were so hungry. . . ."

16. __T__   TRUE OR FALSE? The author implies that the wino taught him a valuable lesson.   Gregory implies this by including the wino story in his essay on shame and stating, in the last sentence, the lesson he learned.

Purpose and Tone

17. __T__   TRUE OR FALSE? One of the author's purposes is to inform readers of how he learned the meaning of shame.
                Gregory suggests this purpose in the first two sentences of the selection.

18. The word that best describes the tone of the last paragraph of the selection is
    a. angry.
    b. objective.
    c. sentimental.
    d.) ashamed.

    In the last two sentences, Gregory clearly expresses his sense of shame.

Argument

19. __T__   TRUE OR FALSE? The teacher's conclusion that Gregory was stupid did not take into account all the relevant evidence.   See paragraph 5.

20. Which evidence from the selection supports Gregory's statement that, after the school incident, he felt shame everywhere?
    a.) Gregory stuffed the plaid mackinaw into a garbage can.
    b. Gregory was always chosen to wash the blackboards on Fridays.
    c. Helene Tucker's eyes were full of tears.
    d. Gregory wanted to pay for the wino's dinner.   See paragraph 28.

OUTLINING

The following outline of "Shame" is missing two major supporting details and three minor supporting details. Complete the outline by filling in the missing details, which are listed after the outline.

Central point: Young Gregory learned both the shame of being let down by those who were supposed to help him and the shame of letting down another person.

1. *Becomes ashamed of his poverty*
    a. Intends to impress Helene Tucker by pledging to Community Chest
    b. *Is humiliated by teacher*
    c. *Leaves school and avoids it in the future*
2. *Becomes ashamed of his own failure to help another*
    a. Earns a lot of money one day and goes to a restaurant for a good meal
    b. Sees wino being beaten for not being able to pay for his meal
    c. *Offers to pay for meal, but too late*

Items Missing from the Outline

- Offers to pay for meal, but too late
- Becomes ashamed of his own failure to help another
- Is humiliated by teacher
- Becomes ashamed of his poverty
- Leaves school and avoids it in the future

DISCUSSION QUESTIONS

1. Why did Gregory include both the classroom and the restaurant anecdotes in one piece? What is the difference between the shame he felt in the first incident and the shame he felt in the second? What are the similarities between the two incidents?

2. What could Gregory mean by the sentence "The eagle always flew on Friday" (paragraph 7)? What does this fact reveal about his world?

3. One type of irony is an event or an effect that is the opposite of what might be expected. In what ways are the following parts of "Shame" ironic?

    - I never learned hate at home, or shame. I had to go to school for that.
    - If I knew my place and didn't come too close, she'd wink at me and say hello. That was a good feeling.
    - I looked at the wino with blood all over his face and I went over. "Leave him alone, Mister Williams. I'll pay the twenty-six cents."
      The wino got up. . . . He looked at me with pure hate.

4. Has anyone ever tried to help you in a way that didn't take all your needs into account? If so, how did you feel toward that person? In what ways might activities that are meant to help people also hurt them?

Check Your Performance   SHAME

Activity	Number Right	Points	Score
BASIC SKILL QUESTIONS			
Vocabulary in Context (2 items)	_____	x 4 =	_____
Central Point and Main Ideas (3 items)	_____	x 4 =	_____
Supporting Details (3 items)	_____	x 4 =	_____
Transitions (2 items)	_____	x 4 =	_____
Patterns of Organization (2 items)	_____	x 4 =	_____
ADVANCED SKILL QUESTIONS			
Fact and Opinion (1 item)	_____	x 4 =	_____
Inferences (3 items)	_____	x 4 =	_____
Purpose and Tone (2 items)	_____	x 4 =	_____
Argument (2 items)	_____	x 4 =	_____
OUTLINING (5 items)	_____	x 4 =	_____

TOTAL SCORE   =   _____ %

Enter your total score into the **Reading Performance Chart: Ten Reading Selections** on the inside back cover.

4

The Bystander Effect
Dorothy Barkin

Preview

A few years ago, thirty-eight people witnessed a brutal attack—and hardly raised a finger to stop it. That kind of unwillingness to get involved is the topic of this article by Dorothy Barkin, who analyzes the confusion and lack of responsibility bystanders often feel when witnessing a crime or medical emergency. She begins by describing four crisis situations—and placing you right there at the scene. How would you react?

Words to Watch

> *intervene* (2): interfere
> *phenomena* (4): facts
> *apathy* (23): indifference
> *diffusion* (32): spreading thin
> *paralysis* (32): inability to act

1   It is a pleasant fall afternoon. The sun is shining. You are heading toward the parking lot after your last class of the day. All of a sudden, you come across the following situations. What do you think you'd do in each case?

> *Situation One:* A man in his early twenties dressed in jeans and a T-shirt is using a coat hanger to pry open a door of a late-model Ford sedan. An overcoat and a camera are visible on the back seat of the car. You're the only one who sees this.

> *Situation Two:* A man and woman are wrestling with each other. The woman is in tears. Attempting to fight the man off, she screams, "Who are you? Get away from me!" You're the only one who witnesses this.

Situation Three: Imagine the same scenario as in Situation Two except that this time the woman screams, "Get away from me! I don't know why I ever married you!"

Situation Four: Again imagine Situation Three. This time, however, there are a few other people (strangers to you and each other) who also observe the incident.

2   Many people would choose not to get involved in situations like these. Bystanders are often reluctant to intervene° in criminal or medical emergencies for reasons they are well aware of. They fear possible danger to themselves or getting caught up in a situation that could lead to complicated and time-consuming legal proceedings.

3   There are, however, other, less obvious factors which influence the decision to get involved in emergency situations. Complex psychological factors, which many people are unaware of, play an important part in the behavior of bystanders; knowing about these factors can help people to act more responsibly when faced with emergencies.

4   To understand these psychological phenomena°, it is helpful to look at what researchers have learned about behavior in the situations mentioned at the beginning of this article.

Situation One: Research reveals a remarkably low rate of bystander intervention to protect property. In one study, more than 3,000 people walked past 214 staged car break-ins like the one described in this situation. The vast majority of passers-by completely ignored what appeared to be a crime in progress. Not one of the 3,000 bothered to report the incident to the police.

Situation Two: Another experiment involved staging scenarios like this and the next situation. In Situation Two, bystanders offered some sort of assistance to the young woman 65 percent of the time.

Situation Three: Here the rate of bystander assistance dropped down to 19 percent. This demonstrates that bystanders are more reluctant to help a woman when they believe she's fighting with her husband. Not only do they consider a wife in less need of help; they think interfering with a married couple may be more dangerous. The husband, unlike a stranger, will not flee the situation.

Situation Four: The important idea in this situation is being a member of a group of bystanders. In more than fifty studies involving many different conditions, one outcome has been consistent: bystanders are much less likely to get involved when other witnesses are present than when they are alone.

5   Thus, membership in a group of bystanders lowers the likelihood that each member of the group will become involved. This finding may seem surprising. You might think there would be safety in numbers and that being a member of a group would increase the likelihood of intervention. How can we explain this aspect of group behavior?

6   A flood of research has tried to answer this and other questions about bystanders in emergencies ever since the infamous case of the murder of Kitty Genovese.

7   In 1964 in the borough of Queens in New York City, Catherine "Kitty" Genovese, twenty-eight, was brutally

murdered in a shocking crime that outraged the nation.

8   The crime began at 3 a.m. Kitty Genovese was coming home from her job as manager of a bar. After parking her car in a parking lot, she began the hundred-foot walk to the entrance of her apartment. But she soon noticed a man in the lot and decided instead to walk toward a police call box. As she walked by a bookstore on her way there, the man grabbed her. She screamed.

9   Lights went on and windows opened in the ten-story apartment building.

10   Next, the attacker stabbed Genovese. She shrieked, "Oh, my God, he stabbed me! Please help me! Please help me!"

11   From an upper window in the apartment house, a man shouted, "Let that girl alone!"

12   The assailant, alarmed by the man's shout, started toward his car, which was parked nearby. However, the lights in the building soon went out, and the man returned. He found Genovese struggling to reach her apartment—and stabbed her again.

13   She screamed, "I'm dying! I'm dying!"

14   Once more lights went on and windows opened in the apartment building. The attacker then went to his car and drove off. Struggling, Genovese made her way inside the building.

15   But the assailant returned to attack Genovese yet a third time. He found her slumped on the floor at the foot of the stairs and stabbed her again, this time fatally.

16   The murder took over a half hour, and Kitty Genovese's desperate cries for help were heard by at least thirty-eight people. Not a single one of the thirty-eight who later admitted to having witnessed the murder bothered to pick up the phone during the attack and call the police. One man called after Genovese was dead.

17   Comments made by bystanders after this murder provide important insight into what group members think when they consider intervening in an emergency.

18   These are some of the comments:

19   "I didn't want my husband to get involved."

20   "Frankly, we were afraid."

21   "We thought it was a lovers' quarrel."

22   "I was tired."

23   The Genovese murder sparked a national debate on the questions of public apathy° and fear and became the basis for thousands of sermons, editorials, classroom discussions, and even a made-for-television movie. The same question was on everybody's mind—how could thirty-eight people have done so little?

24   Nine years later, another well-publicized incident provided additional information about the psychology of a group witnessing a crime.

25   On a summer afternoon in Trenton, New Jersey, a twenty-year-old woman was brutally raped in a parking lot in full view of twenty-five employees of a nearby roofing company. Though the workers witnessed the entire incident and the woman repeatedly screamed for help, no one came to her assistance.

26   Comments made by witnesses to the rape were remarkably similar to those made by the bystanders to the Genovese murder. For example, one witness said, "We thought, well, it might turn out to be her boyfriend or something like that."

27   It's not surprising to find similar excuses for not helping in cases

involving a group of bystanders. The same psychological principles apply to each. Research conducted since the Genovese murder indicates that the failure of bystanders to get involved can't be simply dismissed as a symptom of an uncaring society. Rather, the bystander effect, as it is called by social scientists, is the product of a complex set of psychological factors.

28   Two factors appear to be most important in understanding the reactions of bystanders to emergencies.

29   First is the level of ambiguity involved in the situation. Bystanders are afraid to endanger themselves or look foolish if they take the wrong action in a situation they're not sure how to interpret. A person lying face down on the floor of a subway train may have just suffered a heart attack and be in need of immediate medical assistance—or he may be a dangerous drunk.

30   Determining what is happening is especially difficult when a man is attacking a woman. Many times lovers do quarrel, sometimes violently. But they may strongly resent an outsider, no matter how well-meaning, intruding into their affairs.

31   When a group of bystanders is around, interpreting an event can be even more difficult than when one is alone. Bystanders look to others for cues as to what is happening. Frequently other witnesses, just as confused, try to look calm. Thus bystanders can mislead each other about the seriousness of an incident.

32   The second factor in determining the reactions of bystanders to emergencies is what psychologists call the principle of moral diffusion°. Moral diffusion is the lessening of a sense of individual responsibility when someone is a member of a group. Responsibility to act diffuses throughout the crowd. When a member of the group is able to escape the collective paralysis° and take action, others in the group tend to act as well. But the larger the crowd, the greater the diffusion of responsibility, and the less likely someone is to intervene.

33   The more social scientists are able to teach us about how bystanders react to an emergency, the better the chances that we will take appropriate action when faced with one. Knowing about moral diffusion, for example, makes it easier for us to escape it. If you find yourself witnessing an emergency with a group, remember that everybody is waiting for someone else to do something first. If you take action, others may also help.

34   Also realize that any one of us could at some time be in desperate need of help. Imagine what it feels like to need help and have a crowd watching you suffer and do nothing. Remember Kitty Genovese.

BASIC SKILL QUESTIONS

Vocabulary in Context

1. In the sentence below, the word *scenario* means
    a. fight.
    b. relationship.
    (c.) suggested scene.
    d. quotation.

    > "Imagine the same scenario as in Situation Two except that this time the woman screams, 'Get away from me! I don't know why I ever married you!'" (Paragraph 1)

2. In the excerpt below, the word *assailant* means
    a. observer.
    b. bystander.
    c. victim.
    (d.) attacker.

    Assailant is a synonym for *attacker*.

    > "Next, the attacker stabbed Genovese. . . . From an upper window in the apartment house, a man shouted, 'Let that girl alone!'
    >
    > "The assailant, alarmed by the man's shout, started toward his car . . . ." (Paragraphs 10–12)

3. In the excerpt below, the word *ambiguity* means
    a. argument.
    (b.) uncertainty.
    c. lack of interest.
    d. crowding.

    > "First is the level of ambiguity involved . . . . Bystanders are afraid to endanger themselves or look foolish . . . in a situation they're not sure how to interpret." (Paragraph 29)

Central Point and Main Ideas

4. Which sentence best expresses the central point of this selection?
    a. People don't want to get involved in emergencies.
    b. Kitty Genovese was murdered because no one helped enough.
    c. People don't care what happens to others.
    (d.) Understanding why bystanders react as they do in a crisis can help people act more responsibly.

    Answers *a* and *b* are too narrow; answer *c* is incorrect.

5. Which sentence best expresses the main idea of paragraph 27?
   a. Bystanders always have the same excuses for not helping.
   b. There has been research on bystanders since the Genovese murder.
   c. The "bystander effect" is a symptom of an uncaring society.
   d. Research shows that a number of psychological factors, not a simple lack
   of caring, keeps bystanders from getting involved.

   Answers a and b are too narrow; answer c is incorrect.

6. The sentence that makes up paragraph 28 states the main idea of
   a. paragraph 29.
   b. paragraphs 29–30.   *The two factors mentioned in paragraph 28 are intro-*
   c. paragraphs 29–31.   *duced by the addition transitions* first *and* second.
   d. paragraphs 29–32.

Supporting Details

7. Bystanders are most likely to help
   a. a woman being attacked by her husband.
   b. in any emergency when others are around.   *See "Situation Two" in*
   c. a woman being attacked by a stranger.   *paragraphs 1 and 2.*
   d. when property is being stolen.

8. According to the author, when there is a group of bystanders,
   a. everyone is more likely to help.
   b. it is easier to understand what is happening.
   c. they are not influenced at all by each other.   *See paragraph 32.*
   d. each is more likely to act after someone else takes action.

9. The author supports her statement that "bystanders are much less likely to
   get involved when other witnesses are present" with
   a. opinions.
   b. quotations from experts.   *The examples: The Genovese murder and the*
   c. research and examples.   *Trenton rape; the research-based information*
   d. no evidence.   *precedes and follows the examples.*

Transitions

10. In the excerpt below, *thus* serves as
    a. an addition signal.
    b. an example signal.   *The* cause: *confused witnesses try to look*
    c. a contrast signal.   *calm. The* effect: *bystanders mislead each*
    d. a cause-effect signal. *other about how serious an incident is.*

    Frequently other witnesses, just as confused, try to look calm. Thus
    bystanders can mislead each other about the seriousness of an incident.
    (Paragraph 31)

11. The relationship between the two parts of the sentence below is one of
    a. cause and effect.
    b. comparison.
    c. contrast.
    d. example.

    The *cause:* you take action.
    The *effect:* others may help.

    "If you take action, others may also help." (Paragraph 33)

Patterns of Organization

12. The pattern of organization of paragraphs 7–16 is
    a. comparison-contrast.
    b. list of items.
    c. definition and example.
    d. time order.

    A series of events is narrated in the order in which the events happened.

ADVANCED SKILL QUESTIONS

Fact and Opinion

13. Which sentence is a statement of opinion?
    a. "The crime began at 3 a.m."
    b. "From an upper window in the apartment house, a man shouted, 'Let that girl alone!'"
    c. "Though the workers witnessed the entire incident and the woman repeatedly screamed for help, no one came to her assistance."
    d. "Two factors appear to be most important in understanding the reactions of bystanders to emergencies."   The words "appear to be" tell us that the author feels it is not a proven fact that the two factors are the most important.

14. The following sentence is a statement of
    a. fact.
    b. opinion.
    c. fact and opinion.

    The number and outcome of the studies are factual.

    "In more than fifty studies involving many different conditions, one outcome has been consistent: bystanders are much less likely to get involved when other witnesses are present than when they are alone." (Paragraph 4)

Inferences

15. The reading suggests that people tend to believe
    a. theft is okay.
    b. loss of property is worse than bodily harm.
    c. bodily harm is worse than loss of property.
    d. rape is worse than murder.

    See "Situation One" and "Situation Two" in paragraph 4.

16. From the article, we can conclude that Kitty Genovese's killer
    a. knew his victim.
    b. was unaware of the witnesses.   *See paragraphs 12–15.*
    c. stabbed her too quickly for her to get help.
    (d.) kept attacking when he realized no one was coming to help her.

17. From the article, we can conclude that of the following situations, the bystander is most likely to get involved when
    a. a man passes a clothing store from which people are carrying away clothes.
    (b.) a college student sees a man collapsing on a street where no one else is present.
    c. a neighbor sees a father and son fighting in their yard.
    d. a softball team sees the coach angrily chasing his wife.

Purpose and Tone

18. The main purpose of this article is to
    a. inform readers about the bystander effect and the factors contributing to it.
    b. persuade people to be more helpful in emergency situations.
    (c.) both of the above.

19. The tone of the last paragraph of this article can be described as
    a. surprised.
    b. confused.
    (c.) pleading.
    d. lighthearted.

Argument

20. Put a check by the statement that is the point of the following argument. The other statements are support for that point.

    ____ a. When a member of the group is able to escape the collective paralysis and take action, others in the group tend to act as well."

    ✓ b. "If you take action [in an emergency], others may also help."

    ____ c. "Bystanders are afraid to endanger themselves or look foolish if they take the wrong action in a situation they're not sure how to interpret."

Comments: Item 17—The article suggests that bystanders tend not to help in cases of loss of property or family feuds, and when others are around.
Item 18—See paragraphs 33–34, in which the author appeals directly to readers.
Item 20—Statements *a* and *c* explain statement *b*.

SUMMARIZING

Wording of answers may vary.

Add the ideas needed to complete the following summary of "The Bystander Effect."

Witnesses to crisis situations are less likely to help when only property is at risk and when a woman is being attacked by a man who may be her husband. Numerous studies have shown that witnesses' resistance to helping is also increased when there are other _____*witnesses*_____ _____*present*_____. A famous example is the case of Kitty Genovese, who was stabbed to death at 3 a.m. while returning to her apartment. The attack went on for over half an hour. Thirty-eight people listened to her cries for help, but _____*no one called the police*_____ _____*during the attack*_____. In another example, employees of a roofing company ignored a rape taking place on a nearby parking lot. Two psychological factors seem to explain _____*the reactions*_____ _____*of bystanders to emergencies*_____. One is the level of uncertainty in the situation. If the bystanders don't know how to_____*interpret*_____ a situation, they don't want to take action. The other factor is the principle of moral diffusion. The larger the crowd that is watching, the less responsibility _____*is felt by*_____ _____*each member of the crowd*_____. Understanding these factors can help people be more useful in emergency situations.

DISCUSSION QUESTIONS

1. Have you ever been in a situation where the bystander effect played a part? Would your behavior be any different in light of what you have learned from this article?

2. The author states in paragraph 31, "Bystanders look to others for cues as to what is happening. Frequently other witnesses, just as confused, try to look calm." Why do you think witnesses would try to look calm during an emergency?

3. In paragraph 33, the author suggests that if you understand what causes "the bystander effect," you can act appropriately in an emergency: "If you take action, others may also help." If, say, you were in a group of onlookers while a fight was in progress, what could you do that would encourage others to intervene?

4. How does the conclusion of this article clarify the author's purpose for the reader? How does the article's beginning fit in with that purpose?

Check Your Performance   **THE BYSTANDER EFFECT**

Activity	*Number Right*	*Points*	*Score*
BASIC SKILL QUESTIONS			
Vocabulary in Context (3 items)	_____	x 4 =	_____
Central Point and Main Ideas (3 items)	_____	x 4 =	_____
Supporting Details (3 items)	_____	x 4 =	_____
Transitions (2 items)	_____	x 4 =	_____
Patterns of Organization (1 item)	_____	x 4 =	_____
ADVANCED SKILL QUESTIONS			
Fact and Opinion (2 items)	_____	x 4 =	_____
Inferences (3 items)	_____	x 4 =	_____
Purpose and Tone (2 items)	_____	x 4 =	_____
Argument (1 item)	_____	x 4 =	_____
SUMMARIZING (5 items)	_____	x 4 =	_____

TOTAL SCORE = _____%

Enter your total score into the **Reading Performance Chart: Ten Reading Selections** on the inside back cover.

5

Preview, Read, Write, Recite
Gayle Edwards

Preview

Do you sometimes wonder if others know something about studying that you don't? Do they seem to have a successful system that helps them deal with reading assignments? In fact, there are methods of study that can make you a more productive student. If you have never learned one of those methods, this selection is your opportunity to do so.

Words to Watch

randomly (9): in a here-and-there way
disclose (11): make known
decipher (12): interpret
seethe (12): feel greatly upset
perceived (13): seen
inconsequential (14): unimportant
detrimental (14): harmful
paralinguistic (15): related to language
attributable to (27): considered to be caused by

1   Your idea of studying a textbook assignment may be to simply read it once or twice. If so, you may be wondering why you have trouble understanding and remembering what you read. The PRWR system is an excellent way to boost your study power. By using it consistently, you'll become a better reader, you'll remember much more of what you read, and you'll be able to study effectively.

2   PRWR is an abbreviation of the system's four steps:

1. **P**review the reading.
2. **R**ead the material and mark important parts.
3. **W**rite notes to help you study the material.
4. **R**ecite the ideas in your notes.

3   You can put this system to work immediately. Each step is explained in detail below, and a textbook selection is included for you to practice on.

STEP 1: PREVIEW THE READING

4   When you go to a party, you might look the scene over to locate the buffet, check out the music, and see who's there. After getting an overview of what's happening, you'll be more at home and ready to get down to the business of serious partying. Similarly, a several-minute preview of a reading gives you a general overview of the selection before you begin a careful reading. By "breaking the ice" and providing a quick sense of the new material, the preview will help you get into the reading more easily. There are four parts to a good preview:

5   • **Consider the title.** The title is often a tiny summary of the selection. Use it to help you focus in on the central idea of the material. For instance, a selection titled "Theories of Personality" will tell you to expect a list of differing theories of personality.

6   • **Read over the first and last paragraphs of the selection.** The first paragraph or so of a reading is often written as an introduction. It may thus present the main ideas, giving you an overview of what's coming. The last paragraphs may be a summary of a reading and thus give you another general view of the main ideas.

• **Note headings and their relation-   7 ships.** Main headings tell you what sections are about. They are generally printed in darker or larger type; they may be written in all capital letters or in a different color. The main headings under the title "Theories of Personality," for example, would probably tell you which theories are being covered.

Subheadings fall under main   8 headings and help identify and organize the material under main heads. Subheads are printed in a way that makes them more prominent than the text but less prominent than the main headings. A selection may even contain sub-subheadings to label and organize material under the subheads. Here is how a series of heads might look:

MAIN HEAD (at the margin in larger type)

> **Subhead** (indented and in slightly smaller type)
>
>> *Sub-subhead* (further indented and in even smaller type)

Together, the headings may form a general outline of a selection. Note, for instance, the main heading and subheads in this article.

• **Sample the text randomly°.** Read a   9 few parts that seem likely to contain especially significant information—the first sentence of some paragraphs, words set off in italics or boldface, and visuals (pictures, diagrams, and graphs). Also, keep an eye out for prominent lists and definitions.

Does all this sound like a waste of   10 time to you? You may wonder if it wouldn't be better just to get on with reading the assignment. Well, don't reject previewing until you've tried it a few times. The few minutes spent on previewing will help you to better understand a selection once you do read it. To see how this works, take about three minutes to preview the following textbook selection, taken from a popular college textbook: *Communicate!* Sixth Edition, by Rudolph F. Verderber (Wadsworth).

DISCLOSING FEELINGS

An extremely important aspect of self-disclosure is the sharing of feelings. We all experience feelings such as happiness at receiving an unexpected gift, sadness about the breakup of a relationship, or anger when we believe we have been taken advantage of. The question is whether to disclose° such feelings, and if so, how. Self-disclosure of feelings usually will be most successful not when feelings are withheld or displayed but when they are described. Let's consider each of these forms of dealing with feelings.   11

Withholding Feelings

Withholding feelings—that is, keeping them inside and not giving any verbal or nonverbal cues to their existence—is generally an inappropriate means of dealing with feelings. Withholding feelings is best exemplified by the good poker player who develops a "poker face," a neutral look that is impossible to decipher°. The look is the same whether the player's cards are good or bad. Unfortunately, many people use poker faces in their relationships, so that no one knows whether they hurt inside, are extremely excited, and so on. For instance, Doris feels very nervous when Candy stands over her while Doris is working on her report. And when Candy says, "That first paragraph isn't very well written," Doris begins to seethe°, yet she says nothing —she withholds her feelings.   12

Psychologists believe that when people withhold feelings, they can develop physical problems such as ulcers, high blood pressure, and heart disease, as well as psychological problems such as stress-related neuroses and psychoses. Moreover, people who withhold feelings are often perceived° as cold, undemonstrative, and not much fun to be around.   13

Is withholding ever appropriate? When a situation is inconsequential°, you may well choose to withhold your feelings. For instance, a stranger's inconsiderate behavior at a party may bother you, but because you can move to another part of the room, withholding may not be detrimental°. In the example of Doris's seething at Candy's behavior, however, withholding could be costly to Doris.   14

Displaying Feelings

Displaying feelings means expressing those feelings through a facial reaction, body response, and/or paralinguistic° reaction. Cheering over a great play at a sporting event, booing the umpire at a perceived bad call, patting a person on the back when the person does something well, and saying, "What are you doing?" in a nasty tone of voice are all displays of feelings.   15

16   Displays are especially appropriate when the feelings you are experiencing are positive. For instance, when Gloria does something nice for you, and you experience a feeling of joy, giving her a big hug is appropriate; when Don gives you something you've wanted, and you experience a feeling of appreciation, a big smile or an "Oh, thank you, Don" is appropriate. In fact, many people need to be even more demonstrative of good feelings. You've probably seen the bumper sticker "Have you hugged your kid today?" It reinforces the point that you need to display love and affection constantly to show another person that you really care.

17   Displays become detrimental to communication when the feelings you are experiencing are negative—especially when the display of a negative feeling appears to be an overreaction. For instance, when Candy stands over Doris while she is working on her report and says, "That first paragraph isn't very well written," Doris may well experience resentment. If Doris lashes out at Candy by screaming, "Who the hell asked you for your opinion?" Doris's display no doubt will hurt Candy's feelings and short-circuit their communication. Although displays of negative feelings may be good for you psychologically, they are likely to be bad for you interpersonally.

Describing Feelings

18   **Describing feelings**—putting your feelings into words in a calm, nonjudgmental way—tends to be the best method of disclosing feelings. Describing feelings not only increases chances for positive communication and decreases chances for short-circuiting lines of communication, it also teaches people how to treat you. When you describe your feelings, people are made aware of the effect of their behavior. This knowledge gives them the information needed to determine whether they should continue or repeat that behavior. If you tell Paul that you really feel flattered when he visits you, such a statement should encourage Paul to visit you again; likewise, when you tell Cliff that you feel very angry when he borrows your jacket without asking, he is more likely to ask the next time he borrows a jacket. Describing your feelings allows you to exercise a measure of control over others' behavior toward you.

19   Describing and displaying feelings are not the same. Many times people think they are describing when in fact they are displaying feelings or evaluating.

20   If describing feelings is so important to communication effectiveness, why don't more people do it regularly? There seem to be at least four reasons why many people don't describe feelings.

21   1. *Many people have a poor vocabulary of words for describing the various feelings they are experiencing.* People can sense that they are angry; however, they may not know whether what they are feeling might best be described as annoyed, betrayed, cheated, crushed, disturbed, furious, outraged, or shocked. Each of these words describes a slightly different aspect of what many people lump together as anger.

22   2. *Many people believe that describing their true feelings reveals too much about themselves.* If you tell people when their behavior hurts you, you risk their using the information against you when they want to hurt you on purpose.

Even so, the potential benefits of describing your feelings far outweigh the risks. For instance, if Pete has a nickname for you that you don't like and you tell Pete that calling you by that nickname really makes you nervous and tense, Pete may use the nickname when he wants to hurt you, but he is more likely to stop calling you by that name. If, on the other hand, you don't describe your feelings to Pete, he is probably going to call you by that name all the time because he doesn't know any better. When you say nothing, you reinforce his behavior. The level of risk varies with each situation, but you will more often improve a relationship than be hurt by describing feelings.

3. *Many people believe that if they describe feelings, others will make them feel guilty about having such feelings.* At a very tender age we all learned about "tactful" behavior. Under the premise that "the truth sometimes hurts" we learned to avoid the truth by not saying anything or by telling "little" lies. Perhaps when you were young your mother said, "Don't forget to give Grandma a great big kiss." At that time you may have blurted out, "Ugh—it makes me feel yucky to kiss Grandma. She's got a mustache." If your mother responded, "That's terrible—your grandma loves you. Now you give her a kiss and never let me hear you talk like that again!" then you probably felt guilty for having this "wrong" feeling. But the point is that the thought of kissing your grandma made you feel "yucky" whether it should have or not. In this case what was at issue was the way you talked about the feelings—not your having the feelings. | 23

4. *Many people believe that describing feelings causes harm to others or to a relationship.* If it really bothers Max when his girlfriend, Dora, bites her fingernails, Max may believe that describing his feelings to Dora will hurt her so much that the knowledge will drive a wedge into their relationship. So it's better for Max to say nothing, right? Wrong! If Max says nothing, he's still going to be bothered by Dora's behavior. In fact, as time goes on, Max will probably lash out at Dora for other things because he can't bring himself to talk about the behavior that really bothers him. The net result is that not only will Dora be hurt by Max's behavior, but she won't understand the true source of his feelings. By not describing his feelings, Max may well drive a wedge into their relationship anyway. | 24

If Max does describe his feelings to Dora, she might quit or at least try to quit biting her nails; they might get into a discussion in which he finds out that she doesn't want to bite them but just can't seem to stop, and he can help her in her efforts to stop; or they might discuss the problem and Max may see that it is a small thing really and not let it bother him as much. The point is that in describing feelings the chances of a successful outcome are greater than they are in not describing them. | 25

To describe your feelings, first put the emotion you are feeling into words. Be specific. Second, state what triggered the feeling. Finally, make sure you indicate that the feeling is yours. For example, suppose your roommate borrows your jacket without asking. When he returns, you describe your feelings by saying, "Cliff, I [indication that | 26 the feeling is yours] get really angry [the feeling] when you borrow my jacket without asking [trigger]." Or suppose that Carl has just reminded you of the very first time he brought you a rose. You describe your feelings by saying, "Carl, I [indication that the feeling is yours] get really tickled [the feeling] when you remind me about that first time you brought me a rose [trigger]."

27   You may find it easiest to begin by describing positive feelings: "I really feel elated knowing that you were the one who nominated me for the position" or "I'm delighted that you offered to help me with the housework." As you gain success with positive descriptions, you can try negative feelings attributable to° environmental factors: "It's so cloudy; I feel gloomy" or "When the wind howls through the cracks, I really get jumpy." Finally, you can move to negative descriptions resulting from what people have said or done: "Your stepping in front of me like that really annoys me" or "The tone of your voice confuses me."

28   If you have previewed the above selection carefully, you already know a bit about it—without even having really read much. To confirm this to yourself, answer these questions:

- What is the selection about?

- Which are three ways of dealing with our feelings?

- What are four reasons why many people don't describe feelings?

STEP 2: READ THE MATERIAL AND MARK IMPORTANT PARTS

29   After previewing a selection, take the time to read it through from start to finish. Keep reading even if you run into some parts you don't understand. You can always come back to those parts. By reading straight through, you'll be in a better position to understand the difficult parts later.

30   As you read, mark points you feel are especially significant. This will make it easy for you to find them later when you take study notes. The goal is to mark the most important ideas of a selection.

They include:

- Definitions

- Helpful examples

- Major lists of items

- Points that receive the most space, development, and attention

Because you noted some of these ideas during the preview, identifying them as you read will be easier.

Ways to Mark

31   Here are some ways to mark off important ideas:

- Underline definitions and identify them by writing *DEF* in the margin.

- Identify helpful examples by writing *EX* in the margin.

- Number 1, 2, 3, etc. the items in lists.

- Underline obviously important ideas. You can further set off important points by writing *IMP* in the margin. If important material is several lines long, do not underline it all, or you will end up with a page crowded with lines.

Instead, draw a vertical line alongside the material, and perhaps underline a sentence or a key few words. If you're not yet sure if material merits marking, simply put a check by it; you can make your final decision later.

32   As you mark a selection, remember to be selective. Your markings should help you highlight the most significant parts of the reading; if everything is marked, you won't have separated out the most important ideas. Usually you won't know what the most important ideas are in a paragraph or a section until you've read all of it. So it's good to develop a habit of reading a bit and then going back to do the marking.

STEP 3: WRITE STUDY NOTES

33   After reading and marking a selection, you are ready to take study notes. *Notetaking is the key to successful learning.* In the very act of deciding what is important enough to write down, and of then writing it down, you begin to learn and master the material.

34   Here are some guidelines to use in writing study notes:

1. After you have previewed, read, and marked the selection, reread it. Then write out the important information on 8½- by 11-inch sheets of paper. Write on only one side of each page.

2. Write clearly. Then you won't waste valuable study time trying to decipher your handwriting.

3. Use a combination of the author's words and your own words. Using your own words at times forces you to think about and work at understanding the material.

4. Organize your notes into a rough outline that will show relationships between ideas. Do this as follows:

   a. Write the title of the selection at the top of the first sheet of notes.

   b. Write main headings at the margin of your notes. Indent subheads about half an inch away from the margin. Indent subsubheads even more.

   c. Number items in a list, just as you did when marking important items in a list in the text. Be sure each list has a heading in your notes.

35   Try preparing a sheet of study notes for the material on feelings. Here is a start for such a sheet of study notes:

   Three Ways of Dealing with Feelings

   A. *Withholding feelings—keeping them inside and not giving any verbal or nonverbal clues to their existence.*

      Ex.—poker player with a "poker face."

The activity of taking notes will help you see how useful it is to write out the important information in a selection.

STEP 4: RECITE THE IDEAS IN YOUR NOTES

36   After writing your study notes, go through them and write key words in the margin of your notes. The words will help you study the material. For example, here are the key words you might write in the margin of notes taken on the material about disclosing feelings.

3 ways of dealing with feelings

Def and ex of withholding feelings

Def and ex of displaying feelings

Def and ex of describing feelings

4 reasons many people don't describe feelings

3 steps to describing feelings

37   To study the material, turn the words in the margin into questions. First ask yourself, "What does *describing feelings* mean?" Then recite the answer until you can say it without looking at your notes. Then ask yourself, "What are the four reasons many people don't describe their feelings?" Then recite that answer until you can say it without looking at your notes.

38   Then—and this is a key point—go back and review your answer to the first question. Test yourself—see if you can say the answer without looking at it. Then test yourself on the second answer. *As you learn each new bit of information, go back and test yourself on the previous information.* Such repeated self-testing is the real key to effective learning.

39   In summary, then, this article describes a simple but extremely helpful study system that you can use to learn textbook material. On a regular basis, you should preview, read, write, and recite your college reading assignments. By doing so, and by reciting and learning your classroom notes as well, you will be well prepared to deal with college exams.

BASIC SKILL QUESTIONS

Vocabulary in Context

1. In the sentence below, the word *merits* means
   a. forbids.
   b. deserves.
   c. illustrates.
   d. provides.

   "If you're not yet sure if material merits marking, simply put a check by it; you can make your final decision later." (Paragraph 31)

2. In the excerpt below, the word *selective* means
   a. colorful in marking.
   b. neat.
   c. careful in choosing.
   d. quick in making choices.

   "As you mark a selection, remember to be selective. Your markings should help you highlight the most significant parts of the reading. . . . " (Paragraph 32)

Central Point and Main Ideas

3. Which sentence best expresses the central point of the selection?
    a. Some people have trouble understanding their textbooks.
    b.) PRWR is a four-step system that improves textbook study skills.
    c. There are systems that can improve study skills.
    d. The PRWR system begins with previewing the reading.

Answers *a* and *d* are too narrow; answer *c* is too broad.

4. The main idea of paragraph 31 is expressed in its
    a.) first line.
    b. second line.
    c. third line.
    d. last sentence.

The specific details in the rest of the paragraph are "ways to mark off important ideas."

Supporting Details

5. When previewing a selection, you should not
    a. look at the title.
    b. read the first and last paragraphs.
    c.) read every word.
    d. check the headings and their relationships.

See paragraph 5.
See paragraph 6.
See paragraph 9.
See paragraph 7.

6. __F__ TRUE OR FALSE? According to the author, as you read through a selection for the first time, you should stop to reread parts you don't understand.   See paragraph 29.

7. Study notes
    a.) focus your attention on the important parts of a reading.
    b. should be written on both side of the paper.
    c. should always be taken word for word from the text.
    d. should be written before the selection is marked.

Transitions

8. The relationship of the second sentence below to the first is one of
    a. time.
    b. addition.
    c. comparison.
    d.) example.

The words *for example* indicate that an example follows.

"Main headings tell you what sections are about. . . .The main headings under the title "Theories of Personality," for example, would probably tell you which theories are being covered." (Paragraph 7)

Patterns of Organization

9. *Fill in the blank:* Paragraph 4 (*compares, contrasts, defines and illustrates*)

_____*compares*_____ previewing a reading and getting an overview of a party.   The comparison is signaled with the transition *similarly.*

10. The main pattern of organization of paragraph 34 is
   a. definition and example.
   b. cause and effect.
   (c.) list of items.   The paragraph lists guidelines to use
   d. comparison.   in writing study notes.

11. The main pattern of organization of the PRWR system (and thus of the selection) is
   (a.) time order.
   b. comparison.   The selection presents steps in a
   c. cause and effect.   process of studying.
   d. contrast.

ADVANCED SKILL QUESTIONS

Fact and Opinion

12. The word that makes the statement below an opinion is
   a. *system.*
   (b.) *excellent.*   The value word *excellent* is central to the statement.
   c. *boost.*
   d. *power.*

   "The PRWR system is an excellent way to boost your study power."
   (Paragraph 1)

13. The statement below is
   (a.) a fact.   The statement is either true or not and can be
   b. an opinion.   verified by checking the article.
   c. both fact and opinion.

   "Each step [of PRWR] is explained in detail below, and a textbook selection is included for you to practice on." (Paragraph 3)

Inferences

14. __T__ TRUE OR FALSE? From the first paragraph, we can conclude that for study purposes, one or two readings are not enough.

Comment: Item 14—The author suggests that students who read an assignment only once or twice will "have trouble understanding and remembering" it.

15. From the selection, we can conclude that the PRWR system
    a. is used by all good students.
    b. is too difficult for some students.
    c. is a relatively new approach to study.
    (d.) can help you improve your grades.

Since the system will well prepare students for college exams (see the last sentence of the selection), we can assume it will help a student's grades.

Purpose and Tone

16. Which purpose or purposes best apply to this selection?
    (a.) To inform and persuade
    b. To inform and entertain
    c. To inform

The author wishes to inform readers about how to use the PRWR system and to encourage them to use it.

17. Which purpose best applies to the textbook selection "Disclosing Feelings"?
    (a.) To teach
    b. To convince
    c. To amuse

The author wishes to explain the differences between as well as the advantages and disadvantages of three ways of sharing feelings.

18. The tone of "Preview, Read, Write, Recite" is
    a. lighthearted.
    b. scolding.
    (c.) helpful.
    d. annoyed.

The author wants to benefit her readers by providing specific, helpful instructions.

Argument

19. Which item does *not* support the following point?

    Point: The PRWR system is probably a helpful study system:

    a. Repetition is known to help students remember information.
    b. The system provides for a thorough reading of assigned material.
    (c.) Too often, students do their schoolwork at the last minute.
    d. The system provides for carefully organized study notes.

20. Put a check by the statement that is the point of the following argument. The other statements are support for that point.

    ___ a. Study notes of a selection are easier to review than the entire selection itself.

    ✓ b. Writing study notes on a reading is a good study technique.

    ___ c. Writing study notes forces you to think about what is important in a reading.

    ___ d. You are more likely to remember a point when you take the time to write it in your study notes.

Comments: Item 19—The PRWR system requires *not* doing schoolwork at the last minute.
Item 20—Statements *a*, *c*, and *d* are reasons why writing study notes is a good study technique.

MAPPING

Wording of answers may vary.

Complete the following map of "Preview, Read, Write, Recite." You will find headings and lists in the selection helpful. Note that the map does not include the reading on disclosing feelings.

Central point: PRWR, a helpful textbook study system, involves four steps.

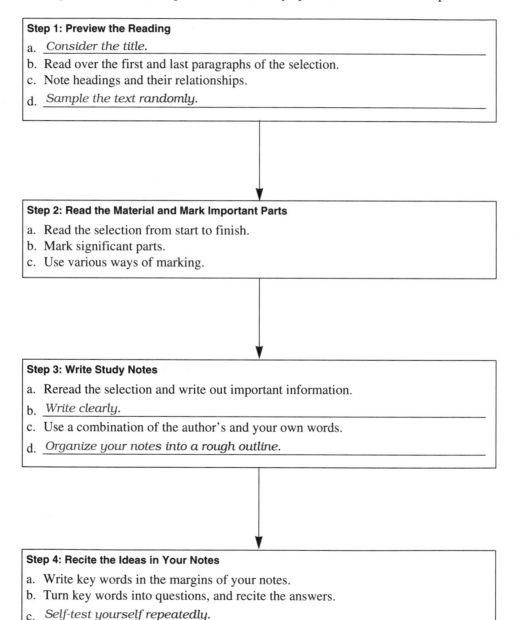

Step 1: Preview the Reading

a. *Consider the title.*
b. Read over the first and last paragraphs of the selection.
c. Note headings and their relationships.
d. *Sample the text randomly.*

Step 2: Read the Material and Mark Important Parts

a. Read the selection from start to finish.
b. Mark significant parts.
c. Use various ways of marking.

Step 3: Write Study Notes

a. Reread the selection and write out important information.
b. *Write clearly.*
c. Use a combination of the author's and your own words.
d. *Organize your notes into a rough outline.*

Step 4: Recite the Ideas in Your Notes

a. Write key words in the margins of your notes.
b. Turn key words into questions, and recite the answers.
c. *Self-test yourself repeatedly.*

DISCUSSION QUESTIONS

1. What study system or approach to study do you use? How does it compare or contrast with the PRWR approach?

2. Do you plan to use all or part of the PRWR system? (Be honest.) Why or why not?

3. In what ways has Edwards organized her article so that it can be studied with the PRWR system?

4. Why does Edwards write that "notetaking is the key to successful learning"? Why aren't merely reading and marking a selection enough?

Check Your Performance   **PREVIEW, READ, WRITE, RECITE**

Activity   *Number Right*   *Points*   *Score*

BASIC SKILL QUESTIONS

    Vocabulary in Context (2 items)   _____   x   4 =   _____

    Central Point and Main Ideas (2 items)   _____   x   4 =   _____

    Supporting Details (3 items)   _____   x   4 =   _____

    Transitions (1 item)   _____   x   4 =   _____

    Patterns of Organization (3 items)   _____   x   4 =   _____

ADVANCED SKILL QUESTIONS

    Fact and Opinion (2 items)   _____   x   4 =   _____

    Inferences (2 items)   _____   x   4 =   _____

    Purpose and Tone (3 items)   _____   x   4 =   _____

    Argument (2 items)   _____   x   4 =   _____

MAPPING (5 items)   _____   x   4 =   _____

TOTAL SCORE   =   _____%

Enter your total score into the **Reading Performance Chart: Ten Reading Selections** on the inside back cover.

6

Coping with Nervousness
Rudolph F. Verderber

Preview

Do you have trouble relaxing when you speak in front of a group? Do your legs tremble, does your heart pound, is your mouth dry? For many people, public speaking can be a nerve-racking experience. However, there are ways to deal with the nervousness. In this selection from his widely used college textbook *Communicate!* (Sixth Edition, Wadsworth), Rudolph F. Verderber provides information that may make your future speaking assignments less painful.

Words to Watch

virtually (2): almost
channel (3): direct
adrenaline (4): a hormone that stimulates and strengthens parts of the body
flabbergasted (5): amazed
eliciting (5): drawing out
psyching . . . up (9): preparing (oneself) psychologically
initial (10): first

1   Most people confess to extreme nervousness at even the thought of giving a speech. Yet you must learn to cope with nervousness because speaking is important. Through speaking, we gain the power to share what we are thinking with others. Each of us has vital information to share: we may have the data needed to solve a problem; we may have an idea for a procedure that will save money for our company or group; we may have insights that will influence

the way people see an issue. We can only imagine the tremendous loss to business, governmental, educational, professional, and fraternal groups because anxiety prevents people from speaking up.

2   Let's start with the assumption that you are indeed nervous—you may in fact be scared to death. Now what? Experience has proved that virtually° anyone can learn to cope with the fear of public speaking. Consider the following points:

3   *1. You are in good company.* Not only do most beginning speakers suffer anxiety at the thought of speaking in public, but many experienced speakers confess to nervousness when they speak as well. Now, you may think, "Don't give me that line—you can't tell me that [fill in the name of a good speaker you know] is nervous when speaking in public!" Ask the person. He or she will tell you. Even powerful speakers like Abraham Lincoln and Franklin D. Roosevelt were nervous before speaking. The difference in nervousness among people is a matter of degree. Some people tremble, perspire, and experience shortness of breath and increased heartbeat. As they go through their speech, they may be so preoccupied with themselves that they lose contact with the audience, jump back and forth from point to point, and on occasion forget what they had planned to say. Others, however, may get butterflies in their stomachs and feel weak in the knees—and still go on to deliver a strong speech. The secret is not to get rid of all of your feelings but to learn to channel° and control your nervousness.

2. Despite nervousness, you can make it through a speech. Very few   4
people are so bothered by anxiety that they are unable to proceed with the speech. You may not enjoy the experience—especially the first time—but you can do it. In fact, it would be detrimental if you were not nervous. Why? Because you must be a little more aroused than usual to do your best. A bit of nervousness gets the adrenaline° flowing—and that brings you to speaking readiness.

3. Your listeners aren't nearly as likely to recognize your fear as you might think. "The only thing we   5
have to fear," Franklin Roosevelt said, "is fear itself." Many speakers worry that others will notice how nervous they are—and that makes them even more self-conscious and nervous. The fact is that people, even speech instructors, will greatly underrate the amount of stage fright they believe a person has. Recently, a young woman reported that she broke out in hives before each speech. She was flabbergasted° when other students said to her, "You seem so calm when you speak." Try eliciting° feedback from your listeners after a speech. Once you realize that your audience does not perceive your nervousness to the degree that you imagine, you will remove one unnecessary source of anxiety.

4. The more experience you get in speaking, the better you become at coping with nervousness. As you   6
gain experience, you learn to think more about the audience and the message and less about yourself.

Moreover, you come to realize that audiences, your classmates especially, are very supportive, especially in informative speech situations. After all, most people are in the audience because they want to hear you. As time goes on, you will come to find that having a group of people listening to you alone is a very satisfying experience.

7   Now let's consider what you can do about your nervousness. Coping with nervousness begins during the preparation process and extends to the time you actually begin the speech.

8   The best way to control nervousness is to pick a topic you know something about and are interested in. Public speakers cannot allow themselves to be saddled with a topic they don't care about. An unsatisfactory topic lays the groundwork for a psychological mindset that almost guarantees nervousness at the time of the speech. By the same token, selecting a topic you are truly interested in will help you focus on what you want to communicate and so lay the groundwork for a satisfying speech experience.

9   A second key to controlling nervousness is to prepare adequately for your speech. If you feel in command of your material and delivery, you'll be far more confident. During the preparation period, you can also be "psyching yourself up°" for the speech. Even in your classroom speeches, if you have a suitable topic, and if you are well prepared, your audience will feel they profited from listening to you. Before you say, "Come on, who are you trying to kid!" think of lectures,

talks, and speeches you have heard. When the speaker seemed knowledgeable and conveyed enthusiasm, weren't you impressed? The fact is that some of the speeches you hear in class are likely to be among the best and most informative or moving speeches you are ever going to hear. Public speaking students learn to put time and effort into their speeches, and many classroom speeches turn out to be surprisingly interesting and valuable. If you work at your speech, you will probably sense that your class looks forward to listening to you.

10   Perhaps the most important time for coping with nervousness is shortly before you give your speech. Research indicates that it is during the period right before you walk up to give your speech and the time when you have your initial° contact with the audience that your fear is most likely to be at its greatest.

11   When speeches are being scheduled, you may be able to control when you speak. Are you better off "getting it over with," that is, being the first person to speak that day? If so, you may be able to volunteer to go first. But regardless of when you are scheduled to speak, try not to spend your time thinking about yourself or your speech. At the moment the class begins, you have done all you can to be prepared. This is the time to focus your mind on something else. Try to listen to each of the speeches that come before yours. Get involved with what each speaker is saying. When your turn comes, you will be far more relaxed than if you had spent the time worrying about your own speech.

12   As you walk to the speaker's stand, remind yourself that you have ideas you want to convey, that you are well prepared, and that your audience is going

to want to hear what you have to say. Even if you make mistakes, the audience will be focusing on your ideas and will profit from your speech.

13   When you reach the stand, pause a few seconds before you start and establish eye contact with the audience. Take a deep breath to help get your breathing in order. Try to move about a little during the first few sentences—sometimes, a few gestures or a step one way or another is enough to break some of the tension. Above all, concentrate on communicating with your audience—your goal is to share your ideas, not to give a performance.

BASIC SKILL QUESTIONS

Vocabulary in Context

1. In the excerpt below, the word *detrimental* means
   a. helpful.
   b. expensive.
   c. harmful.
   d. funny.

   "Despite nervousness, you can make it through a speech. . . . In fact, it would be detrimental if you were not nervous. Why? Because you must be a little more aroused than usual to do your best." (Paragraph 4)

2. In the excerpt below, the word *conveyed* means
   a. prevented.
   b. communicated.
   c. forgot.
   d. delayed.

   "When the speaker seemed knowledgeable and conveyed enthusiasm, weren't you impressed?" (Paragraph 9)

Central Point and Main Ideas

3. Which sentence best expresses the central point of the selection?
   a. Nearly everyone feels nervous about speaking in public.   Items *a, c,* and *d*
   b. It is possible to control the fear of public speaking.   are too narrow.
   c. You can control your nervousness about speaking by picking a topic that interests you.
   d. Even famous speakers report feeling nervous before giving speeches.

4. Which sentence best expresses the main idea of paragraph 3?
   a. Nearly everyone gets nervous before giving a speech, but good speakers are able to channel and control their nervousness.
   b. Franklin D. Roosevelt and Abraham Lincoln were nervous before speaking.
   c. Giving a speech can be a stressful experience.
   d. Speakers who tremble, perspire, and experience shortness of breath and increased heartbeat may lose contact with the audience.   Items *b, c,* and *d* are too narrow.

5. Which sentence best expresses the main idea of paragraphs 7–13?
   a. When preparing a speech, choose a topic you know something about and are interested in.
   b. You will feel far more confident about a speech if you prepare adequately for it.
   c.) There are various things you can do to cope with nervousness during the preparation for and beginning of a speech.
   d. According to research, it is just before you walk up to give your speech and the time of your first contact with the audience that your fear is likely to be at its greatest.   Items *a, b,* and *d* are too narrow.

Supporting Details

6. The supporting details in paragraphs 3–6 are
   a. reasons public speaking is important.
   b. suggestions for avoiding the fear of public speaking.
   c.) evidence that people learn to deal with the fear of public speaking.
   d. steps in the process of public speaking.   See paragraph 2.

7. Nervousness
   a. is rarely experienced by people who give speeches on a regular basis.
   b.) can actually help a speaker to do his or her best.   See paragraph 4.
   c. cannot be effectively controlled.
   d. always interferes with the effectiveness of a speech.

8. The audience
   a. is usually able to tell how nervous a speaker is.
   b. should never be allowed to make direct eye contact with the speaker.
   c.) usually underestimates the nervousness of a speaker.
   d. rarely is interested in classroom speeches.   See paragraph 5.

9. One way to control being nervous about a speech is to
   a. speak loudly.
   b.) prepare adequately.   See paragraph 9.
   c. avoid eye contact.
   d. all of the above.

Transitions

10. The sentence below expresses a relationship of
    a. addition.
    b. time.   How you feel is contrasted with what you can achieve.
    c. cause and effect.
    d.) contrast.

    "Despite nervousness, you can make it through a speech." (Paragraph 4)

11. The relationship of the second sentence below to the first is one of
    a. addition.
    b. an example.
    c. contrast.
    d. cause-effect.

    A second thing learned from experience is being added to a first one.

    "As you gain experience, you learn to think more about the audience and the message and less about yourself. Moreover, you come to realize that audiences, your classmates especially, are very supportive, especially in informative speech situations." (Paragraph 6)

Patterns of Organization

12. The main pattern of organization of paragraphs 3–6 is
    a. list of items.
    b. time order.
    c. contrast.
    d. definition and example.

    The paragraphs list points that prove that "anyone can learn to cope with the fear of public speaking."

13. The main pattern of organization of paragraphs 7–13 is
    a. time order.
    b. contrast.
    c. comparison.
    d. definition and example.

    These paragraphs present steps that take place "during the preparation process" and "the time you actually begin the speech."

ADVANCED SKILL QUESTIONS

Fact and Opinion

14. The sentence below is
    a. a fact.
    b. an opinion.
    c. both fact and opinion.

    While fear is subjective, it is real and can be studied factually.

    "Research indicates that it is during the period right before you walk up to give your speech and the time when you have your initial contact with the audience that your fear is most likely to be at its greatest." (Paragraph 10)

Inferences

15. The author suggests that
    a. thinking about your speech shortly before giving it is likely to make you more nervous.
    b. you should revise your speech up until the last possible moment.
    c. it is always best to try to be the first speaker of the day.
    d. with proper preparation, you will certainly not be nervous once your speech begins.

    See paragraph 11.

16. The author suggests that with practice, you
    a. can completely get over all fear of speaking in public.
    b. will find it is no longer so necessary to be in command of your speech material.
    c. will choose better and better topics for your speeches.
    d. will experience less fear.   See, for example, the end of paragraph 5 and the end of paragraph 11.
17. The author implies that
    a. it is possible to think about your speech too much.   See paragraph 11.
    b. everyone has worthwhile ideas to share in a speech.   See paragraph 1.
    c. making mistakes in a speech doesn't ruin it.   See paragraph 12.
    d. all of the above.

Purpose and Tone

18. The purpose of this reading is
    a. to inform.
    b. to persuade.   The author wishes to *persuade* us "to cope with nervousness because speaking is important" and to *inform* us about how to do so.
    c. both of the above.

19. The tone of this reading is
    a. optimistic and helpful.
    b. outspoken and critical.   The author stresses the positive aspects of speaking and the likelihood of success and provides encouraging advice.
    c. sympathetic and forgiving.
    d. excited and joyous.

Argument

20. One of the following statements is the point of the author's argument in paragraph 1. The other statements are support for that point. Circle the letter of the point of the argument.   Answers *b*, *c*, and *d* are reasons why speaking is important.
    a. Speaking is important.
    b. Speaking gives us the power to share our thoughts with others.
    c. Through speaking, we can provide the data needed to solve a problem.
    d. We may be able to share a money-saving idea for our company.

OUTLINING

Complete the outline by filling in the missing major and minor details. The missing items are listed in random order below the outline.

Central point: You can cope with the nervousness of public speaking.

  A. Introduction: Since speaking is important, it's important to learn to cope with nervousness.

B. *People can learn to cope with the fear of public speaking.*

1. Even good speakers get nervous; they just learn to channel and control their nervousness.
2. Nervousness won't stop you from completing a speech, and it will even help you.
3. Your nervousness during a speech won't show nearly as much as you might think it will.
4. The more experience you get in speaking, the better you become at coping with nervousness.

C. *There are various ways to cope with your nervousness about public speaking.*

1. Pick a topic you know something about and are interested in.
2. *Prepare adequately for your speech.*

3. Try to control your nervousness just before you walk up to give your speech.
   a. Try to schedule your speech at a comfortable time.
   b. Focus your mind on something other than your speech.
4. *Use coping methods for walking to the speaker's stand and just after.*

   a. As you walk to the speaker's stand, focus on your ideas and the fact that you're well prepared.
   b. When you reach the stand, do a few things to break some of the tension.
      1) Pause a few seconds and establish eye contact with the audience.
      2) Take a deep breath.
      3) Move about a little during your first few sentences.
      4) Concentrate on communicating with your audience.

Items Missing from the Outline

- There are various ways to cope with your nervousness about public speaking.
- Prepare adequately for your speech.
- Use coping methods for walking to the speaker's stand and just after.
- People can learn to cope with the fear of public speaking.

DISCUSSION QUESTIONS

1. What have your public speaking experiences been like? Have some speeches gone better than others? If so, what were the differences, and what do you think were the reasons for those differences? What did you find helpful in preparing and giving speeches?

2. Why do you think it could be helpful to speak on a topic you know a great deal about and are interested in? Can you think of any examples from the speeches you've given or heard?

3. You may need to give speeches in your classes, but do you think you will have to speak in public after you graduate from school? In what situations might you have to give a speech or even a presentation to a small group?

4. Obviously, Verderber feels that nervousness is no reason to avoid speaking in public. What other activities have you willingly done despite the fact that they made you nervous in some way? Was being nervous in these situations helpful in some ways? If so, how?

Check Your Performance   **COPING WITH NERVOUSNESS**

Activity	Number Right	Points	Score
BASIC SKILL QUESTIONS			
Vocabulary in Context (2 items)	_____	x 4 =	_____
Central Point and Main Ideas (3 items)	_____	x 4 =	_____
Supporting Details (4 items)	_____	x 4 =	_____
Transitions (2 items)	_____	x 4 =	_____
Patterns of Organization (2 items)	_____	x 4 =	_____
ADVANCED SKILL QUESTIONS			
Fact and Opinion (1 item)	_____	x 4 =	_____
Inferences (3 items)	_____	x 4 =	_____
Purpose and Tone (2 items)	_____	x 4 =	_____
Argument (1 item)	_____	x 4 =	_____
OUTLINING (4 items)	_____	x 5 =	_____

TOTAL SCORE = _____ %

Enter your total score into the **Reading Performance Chart: Ten Reading Selections** on the inside back cover.

7

Compliance Techniques: Getting People to Say Yes
Shelley E. Taylor, Letitia Anne Peplau, and David O. Sears

Preview

People who make a living selling products or ideas do not rely on mere chance as they make their pitch. They use time-proven techniques to convince buyers that they are getting a good deal. This selection from *Social Psychology*, Eighth Edition, reveals some widely used compliance techniques. See if you recognize any of them.

Words to Watch

compliance (1): going along with someone else's wishes
induce (2): persuade
explicitly (2): in a clear way
implicitly (2): in a way that is not obvious
replicated (4): duplicated
self-perception (5): how one views oneself
proposition (10): suggested plan
unscrupulous (10): without moral standards

1   Research has investigated the specific techniques that people use to gain compliance°. Robert Cialdini has studied car salesmen, con artists, and other professionals who earn a living by getting people to buy their products or go along with their schemes. He and other social psychology researchers have identified several important compliance techniques.

2 **The Foot-In-The-Door Technique.** One way of increasing compliance is to induce° a person to agree first to a small request. Once someone has agreed to the small action, he or she is more likely to agree to a larger request. This is the so-called foot-in-the-door technique. It is used explicitly° or implicitly° in many advertising campaigns. Advertisers often concentrate on getting consumers to do something connected with the product—even sending back a card saying that they do not want it. The advertisers apparently think that any act connected with the product increases the likelihood that the consumer will buy it in the future.

3 A classic study by Freedman and Fraser demonstrated this effect. Experimenters went from door to door and told homemakers they were working for the Committee for Safe Driving. They said they wanted the women's support for this campaign and asked them to sign a petition that was to be sent to the state's senators. The petition requested the senators to work for legislation to encourage safe driving. Almost all the women agreed to sign. Several weeks later, different experimenters contacted the same women and also other women who had not been approached before. At this time, all the women were asked to put in their front yards a large, unattractive sign that read "Drive Carefully."

4 The results were striking. Over 55 percent of the women who had previously endorsed the petition (a small request) also agreed to post the sign (a relatively large request). In contrast, less than 17 percent of the other women agreed to post the sign. Getting the women to agree to the initial small request tripled the amount of compliance to the large request. This effect has been replicated° in several studies.

5 Why this technique works is not entirely clear. One explanation is that people who agree to a small request get involved and committed to the issue itself, to the behavior they perform, or perhaps simply to the idea of taking some kind of action. Another explanation is based on self-perception° theory. The idea here is that in some ways the individual's self-image changes as a result of the initial act of compliance. In the safe-driving experiment, for example, a woman may have thought of herself as the kind of person who does not take social action, who does not sign petitions, who does not post signs, or, perhaps, who does not agree to things that are asked of her by someone at the door. Once she has agreed to the small request, which was actually difficult to refuse, she may have changed her perception of herself slightly. Once she has agreed to sign a petition, she may come to think of herself as the kind of person who does this sort of thing. Then, when the second request was made, she was more likely to comply than she would have been otherwise.

6 **The Door-In-The-Face Technique.** Sometimes a technique opposite to the foot-in-the-door also works. First asking for a very large request and then making a smaller request can increase compliance to the small request. This is sometimes called the door-in-the-face technique, since the first request is typically so outrageously large that people might be tempted to slam the door in the requester's face. In one study, subjects were asked to volunteer time for a good cause. Some were asked first to give a huge amount of time. When they refused, as almost all did, the experimenter immediately said then perhaps they might agree to a much smaller commitment of

time. Other subjects were asked only the smaller request, while a third group was given a choice between the two. The results were striking. In the small-request-only condition, 17 percent of subjects agreed. In the choice condition, 25 percent of subjects complied with the smaller request. But in the condition where subjects had first turned down a big request, 50 percent agreed to the smaller request.

7   This effect is familiar to anyone who has ever bargained about the price of a used car or been involved in negotiations between a labor union and management. The tactic is to ask for the moon and then settle for less. The more you ask for at first, the more you expect to end up with eventually. The idea is that when you reduce your demands, the other person thinks you are compromising and the amount seems smaller. In a compliance situation, such as asking for money for charity, the same might apply. Five dollars doesn't seem like so much when the organization initially asked for a hundred dollars.

8   Clearly, both the foot-in-the-door and the reverse tactic work at times, but we do not yet know when each of them will operate. Both seem to work best when the behavior involved is prosocial, that is, when the request is to give money or help a worthwhile cause. One difference seems to be that the door-in-the-face technique works when the smaller request follows the larger request immediately and is obviously connected. The foot-in-the-door technique works even when the two requests are seemingly unconnected.

9   **The Low-Ball Technique.** Consider how likely you would be to agree to the following requests. In one case, a researcher calls you on the phone and asks you to participate in an experiment

scheduled for 7:00 in the morning. In a second case, a researcher calls and asks you to participate in a study. Only after you initially agree to participate does the researcher inform you that the study will be scheduled at 7:00 a.m. When Robert Cialdini and his associates compared these two procedures, the found that the second approach was much more effective. When students were told from the outset that an experiment would be conducted early in the morning, only 25 percent agreed to participate and showed up on time. In contrast, using the second approach of initially concealing the time of the study, 55 percent of students agreed to the request and almost all of them actually showed up for the early morning appointment. Once having agreed to participate, few people backed out of their agreement when they were informed about the time of day.

10   This tactic, in which a person is asked to agree to something on the basis of incomplete information and is later told the full story, is called the low-ball technique. Essentially, the person is tricked into agreeing to a relatively attractive proposition°, only to discover later that the terms are actually different from those expected. This technique appears to work because once an individual has made an initial commitment to a course of action, he or she is reluctant to withdraw, even when the ground rules are changed. Although this technique can be effective (Burger & Petty, 1981), it is clearly deceptive. To protect consumers from unscrupulous° salespersons, laws have been enacted to make low-balling illegal for several industries, such as automobile dealerships.

11   Our discussion of the foot-in-the-door, door-in-the-face, and low-ball

techniques by no means exhausts the possible tactics people use to gain compliance. Research by Jerry Burger has begun to explore another strategy that he calls the **that's-not-all technique**. Consider this situation: A salesperson describes a new microwave oven to a potential customer and quotes a price. Then, while the customer is mulling over the decision, the salesperson adds, "But that's not all. Today only, we're having a special deal. If you buy the microwave now, we'll give you a five-piece set of microwave dishes at no additional cost." In actuality, the dishes always come with the oven, but by presenting the dishes as a "special deal" or something "just for you," the salesperson hopes to make the purchase even more attractive. The essence of this technique is to present a product at a high price, allow the customer to think about the price, and then improve the deal either by adding an additional product or by lowering the price.

In a series of seven experiments, Burger has demonstrated the potential effectiveness of the "that's-not-all" approach. In one illustrative study, experimenters held a psychology club bake sale on campus. At random, half the people who stopped at the table and asked about the cupcakes were told that they could buy a prepackaged set including one cupcake and two cookies for 75 cents. In this control condition, 40 percent of those who inquired actually purchased a cupcake. In the "that's-not-all condition," people who inquired were first told that the cupcakes were 75 cents each. A moment later, they were told that actually, they would get not only the cupcake but also 2 cookies for the 75-cent price. In this "that's-not-all" condition, 73 percent of people bought a cupcake, a substantially higher proportion than in the control condition.

12

BASIC SKILL QUESTIONS

Vocabulary in Context

1. In the sentence below, the word *endorsed* means
   a. rejected.
   b. asked for.
   (c.) supported.
   d. ignored.

   "Over 55 percent of the women who had previously endorsed the petition (a small request) also agreed to post the sign (a relatively large request)." (Paragraph 4)

2. In the excerpt below, the words *mulling over* mean
   a. regretting.
   b. paying for.
   c. agreeing to.
   (d.) thinking about.

   "A salesperson describes a new microwave oven to a potential customer and quotes a price. Then, while the customer is mulling over the decision, the salesperson adds, 'But that's not all. Today only, we're having a special deal.'" (Paragraph 11)

Central Point and Main Ideas

3. Which sentence best expresses the central point of the selection?
   a. Certain techniques are widely used to persuade consumers to buy a product or go along with a plan.
   b. The "foot in the door" technique relies on people's tendency to agree to a larger request after they have agreed to a small one.
   c. Anyone who has bargained to buy a car will recognize the "door in the face" technique.
   d. Social psychologists study why people are influenced by certain kinds of sales techniques.   Answers *b*, *c*, and *d* are too narrow.

4. Which sentence best expresses the main idea of paragraph 5?
   a. While it is not certain why the "foot in the door" technique works, there are some likely explanations.
   b. People adjust their actions based on changes in their self-perception.
   c. It is difficult to refuse a small, reasonable request.
   d. A woman may not have considered herself to be the sort of person who takes social action.   Answers *b*, *c*, and *d* are too narrow.

5. Which sentence best expresses the main idea of paragraph 7?
   a. The "door in the face" technique is commonly used when one bargains for a used car.   Answers *a*, *c*, and *d* are too narrow.
   b. When someone starts out making a large request and then replaces it with a smaller one, the second request seems reasonable by contrast.
   c. Compared with one hundred dollars, five dollars does not seem like much.
   d. People often begin negotiations by asking for more than they expect.

Supporting Details

6. The major supporting details of the reading are a series of
   a. questions.
   b. events.   See paragraph 1.
   c. techniques.
   d. steps.

7. One explanation given for why the foot-in-the-door technique works is that agreeing to a small task
   a. makes the person feel he or she has done enough.
   b. angers the person.
   c. improves a person's opinion of the requester.   See paragraph 5.
   d. changes the person's self-image.

Transitions

8. The relationship of the second sentence below to the first one is one of
   a. cause-effect.
   b. comparison.   The two events happened in sequence.
   c. an example.
   (d.) time.

> "Almost all the women agreed to sign. Several weeks later, different experimenters contacted the same women and also other women who had not been approached before." (Paragraph 3)

9. The relationship of the second sentence below to the first one is one of
   a. time.
   b. addition.   The degree of compliance in the first condition
   (c.) contrast.   contrasts with that in the second condition.
   d. comparison.

> "In the choice condition, 25 percent of subjects complied with the smaller request. But in the condition where subjects had first turned down a big request, 50 percent agreed to the smaller request." (Paragraph 6)

Patterns of Organization

10. Paragraph 5
    (a.) lists two explanations.   The explanations are introduced with
    b. describes two events.   the words "one explanation" and
    c. defines and illustrates a term.   "another explanation." The second
    d. compares and contrasts two events. explanation includes a detailed example.

11. The main pattern of organization of paragraph 6 is
    a. list of items.
    b. time order.   The door-in-the-face technique is
    (c.) definition and example. defined and then illustrated in the
    d. comparison.   context of a study.

12. The main pattern of organization of paragraph 8 is
    a. list of items.
    b. time order.   The foot-in-the-door and the door-in-the-face
    c. definition and example.   techniques are compared in the second sentence
    (d.) comparison and contrast.   and contrasted in the next two sentences.

ADVANCED SKILL QUESTIONS

Fact and Opinion

13. In the sentence below, the word that represents the authors' opinion is
    a. *researchers.*
    b. *several.*
    c. *important.*
    d. *techniques.*

    The word *important* places a value on something and thus represents an opinion.

    "He and other social psychology researchers have identified several important compliance techniques." (Paragraph 1)

14. The sentence below is
    a. all factual.
    b. all opinion.
    c. a mix of fact and opinion.

    While people might argue about what "unscrupulous salespersons" are, it is a fact that the laws have been passed for the reason stated.

    "To protect consumers from unscrupulous salespersons, laws have been enacted to make low-balling illegal for several industries, such as automobile dealerships." (Paragraph 10)

Inferences

15. We can infer from paragraph 3 that
    a. women are more likely to be concerned about safe driving than men.
    b. the experimenters were aggressive and pushy in their dealings with the homemakers.
    c. the "Safe Driving" signs were deliberately made unattractive.
    d. the researchers were truly employees of the Committee for Safe Driving.

16. We can conclude from paragraph 5 that
    a. experiments often reveal very little.
    b. even though an experiment proves something, that doesn't mean it is fully understood.
    c. human behavior is generally easy to explain.
    d. we will never know why the foot-in-the-door technique works.

17. We can conclude that the "that's-not-all" technique works because
    a. people like to buy things.
    b. microwave ovens are especially popular these days.
    c. people buy what they need or want.
    d. people like to feel that they are getting more for their money.

Comments: Item 15—Since the report characterizes the signs as unattractive, that feature must have been part of the study, and it conforms with the requirement that the second request should be something people would think twice about doing.

Item 16—See the first sentence of paragraph 5.

Item 17—See the end of paragraph 11.

Purpose and Tone

18. __F__ TRUE OR FALSE? The main purpose of this selection is to persuade people to stop using the techniques that are described. The authors suggest the techniques are widely used (paragraph 1) without indicating that they should not be.

19. The tone of the reading can be identified as
    a. upbeat and positive.
    b. scholarly and matter-of-fact.
    c. concerned and angry.
    d. forgiving and understanding.

    In general, the authors simply report on the relevant facts.

Argument

20. Which of the statements does *not* support the point of the argument?

    Point: There are ways to make it more likely that people will do what you want them to do.

    a. Experiments have shown that some compliance techniques work.
    b. Salespeople find that certain techniques work better than others.
    c. There is nothing wrong with trying to influence people.
    d. People are more likely to buy something if they are made to feel it's a great bargain.

SUMMARIZING   *Wording of answers may vary.*

Study notes on this reading might be made up of a summary of each compliance technique, including 1) a definition, 2) an example, and 3) an explanation of why the technique works. Complete the summary below by filling in the incomplete or missing items.

Compliance Techniques

1. Foot-in-the-door technique—getting a person to agree first to a small request so that he or she is more likely to agree to a larger one. This technique may work either because people become more committed or because they change their self-image. It works even when the requests appear unconnected.

   Example: Women were more likely to agree to put a large, unattractive "Drive Carefully" sign in their front yards if they had first signed a petition asking senators to work for legislation encouraging safe driving.

2. Door-in-the-face technique—first asking for a very large request and then *making a smaller request. The first request is so outrageously large that people might be tempted to slam the door in the requester's face.*

   This works when the smaller request follows the larger one immediately and is obviously connected to it.

Example: Study subjects were more likely to volunteer a small amount of time for a good cause if they were first asked _____ *to give a great*

deal of time   .

3. Low-ball technique— *asking a person to agree to something on the basis*

of incomplete information and then later telling the full story.   .

This may work because people are reluctant to withdraw after making a commitment.

Example: Students were more likely to take part in an experiment at 7 a.m. if they weren't told about the time until after agreeing to participate.

4. That's-not-all technique — presenting a product at a high price, allowing the customer to think about the price, and then improving the deal either by adding an additional product or by lowering the price.

Example: _____ *At a bake sale, customers were more likely to buy*

cupcakes for 75 cents if they were told they would also get two free

cookies.

DISCUSSION QUESTIONS

1. While reading this selection, did you recognize techniques that have been used to influence you to make a purchase or support someone's plan? How were the techniques used?

2. Which of the compliance techniques do you feel is most clearly deceptive and why?

3. The authors state that no one is really sure why the "foot in the door" technique is effective, but they offer two possible explanations. Do either of those explanations seem to you to adequately explain why the technique works? Can you think of an alternative explanation?

4. Imagine that you are in the business of selling home computers. Describe how you would use the foot-in-the-door technique, the door-in-the-face technique, and the low-ball technique to try to make a sale.

Check Your Performance   COMPLIANCE TECHNIQUES

Activity	Number Right	Points	Score
BASIC SKILL QUESTIONS			
Vocabulary in Context (2 items)	_____	x 4 =	_____
Central Point and Main Ideas (3 items)	_____	x 4 =	_____
Supporting Details (2 items)	_____	x 4 =	_____
Transitions (2 items)	_____	x 4 =	_____
Patterns of Organization (3 items)	_____	x 4 =	_____
ADVANCED SKILL QUESTIONS			
Fact and Opinion (2 items)	_____	x 4 =	_____
Inferences (3 items)	_____	x 4 =	_____
Purpose and Tone (2 items)	_____	x 4 =	_____
Argument (1 item)	_____	x 4 =	_____
SUMMARIZING (4 items)	_____	x 5 =	_____

TOTAL SCORE = _____%

Enter your total score into the **Reading Performance Chart: Ten Reading Selections** on the inside back cover.

8

Lizzie Borden
James Kirby Martin
and others

Preview

A prosperous businessman and his wife lay dead, murdered with an ax. Their unhappy daughter had the motive and opportunity to kill. Modern experts strongly believe that Lizzie Borden was guilty of her parents' murder. Yet she was swiftly found innocent. In this selection taken from the history textbook *America and Its People*, Second Edition, Lizzie's acquittal is examined in light of the social views of the late nineteenth century.

Words to Watch

maintained (1): claimed
alienated (3): set apart from
grisly (5): causing horror
preponderance (7): great amount
unanimous (7): agreed upon by everyone
affirmed (7): stated
preconceived (9): decided before knowing all the facts
docile (9): obedient
frivolous (9): silly

1   Andrew Borden had, as the old Scottish saying goes, short arms and long pockets. He was cheap, not because he had to be frugal but because he hated to spend money. He had dedicated his entire life to making and saving money, and tales of his unethical and parsimonious business behavior were legendary in his hometown of Fall River, Massachusetts. Local gossips maintained° that as an

undertaker he cut off the feet of corpses so that he could fit them into undersized coffins that he had purchased at a very good price. Andrew, however, was not interested in rumors or the opinions of other people; he was concerned with his own rising fortunes. By 1892 he had amassed over half a million dollars, and he controlled the Fall River Union Savings Bank as well as serving as the director of the Globe Yard Mill Company, the First National Bank, the Troy Cotton and Manufacturing Company, and the Merchants Manufacturing Company.

2 Andrew was rich, but he did not live like a wealthy man. Instead of living alongside the other prosperous Fall River citizens in the elite neighborhood known as The Hill, Andrew resided in an area near the business district called the flats. He liked to save time as well as money, and from the flats he could conveniently walk to work. For his daughters Lizzie and Emma, whose eyes and dreams focused on The Hill, life in the flats was an intolerable embarrassment. Their house was a grim, boxlike structure that lacked comfort and privacy. Since Andrew believed that running water on each floor was a wasteful luxury, the only washing facilities were a cold-water faucet in the kitchen and a laundry-room water tap in the cellar. Also in the cellar was the only toilet in the house. To make matters worse, the house was not connected to the Fall River gas main. Andrew preferred to use kerosene to light his house. Although it did not provide as good light or burn as cleanly as gas, it was less expensive. To save even more money, he and his family frequently sat in the dark.

3 The Borden home was far from happy. Lizzie and Emma, ages 32 and 42 in 1892, strongly disliked their stepmother, Abby, and resented Andrew's penny-pinching ways. Lizzie especially felt alienated° from the world around her. Although Fall River was the largest cotton-manufacturing town in America, it offered few opportunities for the unmarried daughter of a prosperous man. Society expected a woman of social position to marry, and while she waited for a proper suitor, her only respectable social outlets were church and community service. So Lizzie taught a Sunday school class and was active in the Women's Christian Temperance Union, the Ladies' Fruit and Flower Mission, and other organizations. She kept herself busy, but she was not happy.

4 In August, 1892, strange things started to happen in the Borden home. They began after Lizzie and Emma learned that Andrew had secretly changed his will. Abby became violently ill. In time so did the Bordens' maid Bridget Sullivan and Andrew himself. Abby told a neighborhood doctor that she had been poisoned, but Andrew refused to listen to her wild ideas. Shortly thereafter, Lizzie went shopping for prussic acid, a deadly poison she said she needed to clean her sealskin cape. When a Fall River druggist refused her request, she left the store in an agitated state. Later in the day, she told a friend that she feared an unknown enemy of her father's was after him. "I'm afraid somebody will do something," she said.

5 On August 4, 1892, Bridget awoke early and ill, but she still managed to prepare a large breakfast of johnnycakes, fresh-baked bread, ginger and oatmeal cookies and raisins, and some three-day-old mutton and hot mutton soup. After eating a hearty meal, Andrew left for work. Bridget also left to do some work outside. This left Abby and Lizzie in the

house alone. Then somebody did something very specific and very grisly°. As Abby was bent over making the bed in the guest room, someone moved into the room unobserved and killed her with an ax.

6   Andrew came home for lunch earlier than usual. He asked Lizzie where Abby was, and she said she did not know. Unconcerned, Andrew, who was not feeling well, lay down on the parlor sofa for a nap. He never awoke. Like Abby, he was slaughtered by someone with an ax. Lizzie "discovered" his body, still lying on the sofa. She called Bridget, who had taken the back stairs to her attic room. "Come down quick; father's dead; somebody came in and killed him."

7   Experts have examined and reexamined the crime, and most have reached the same conclusion: Lizzie killed her father and stepmother. In fact, Lizzie was tried for the gruesome murders. Despite a preponderance° of evidence, however, an all-male jury found her not guilty. Their verdict was unanimous° and was arrived at without debate or disagreement. A woman of Lizzie's social position, they affirmed°, simply could not have committed such a terrible crime.

Even before the trial began, newspaper and magazine writers had judged Lizzie innocent for the same reasons. As historian Kathryn Allamong Jacob, an expert on the case, noted, "Americans were certain that well-brought up daughters could not commit murder with a hatchet on sunny summer mornings." Criminal women, they believed, originated in the lower classes and even looked evil. They did not look like round-faced Lizzie, and did not belong to the Ladies' Fruit and Flower Mission.

Jurors and editorialists alike judged Lizzie according to their preconceived° notions of Victorian womanhood. They believed that such a woman was gentle, docile°, and physically frail, short on analytical ability but long on nurturing instincts. "Women," wrote an editorialist for *Scribner's*, "are merely large babies. They are shortsighted, frivolous°, and occupy an intermediate stage between children and men." Too uncoordinated and weak to accurately swing an ax and too gentle and unintelligent to coldly plan a double murder, women of Lizzie's background simply had to be innocent because of their basic innocence.

BASIC SKILL QUESTIONS

Vocabulary in Context

1. In the excerpt below, the word *parsimonious* means
   a. generous.
   b. lazy.
   c. stingy.
   d. deadly.

   ". . . tales of his unethical and parsimonious business behavior were legendary in his hometown . . . . Local gossips maintained that as an undertaker he cut off the feet of corpses so that he could fit them into undersized coffins that he had purchased at a very good price." (Paragraph 1)

2. In the excerpt below, the word *amassed* means
   a. spent.
   b. found.
   (c.) accumulated.
   d. donated.

> "By 1892 [Andrew Borden] had amassed over half a million dollars . . . . "
> (Paragraph 1)

Central Point and Main Ideas

3. Which sentence best expresses the central point of the selection?
   a. Andrew Borden's unpleasant personality and cheap ways probably led to his murder.
   b. The case of Lizzie Borden should be reopened and reexamined to determine if she was truly guilty.
   (c.) Despite much evidence of her guilt, Lizzie Borden was found innocent of murder because of society's beliefs about women of her social class.
   d. In the late 1800s, Americans assumed that middle-class women who were well brought up were silly people who could not possibly commit a murder. Answer *a* is incorrect; answer *b* is not addressed by the authors; answer *d* is too narrow.

4. The main idea of paragraph 2 is expressed in its
   (a.) first sentence.
   b. second sentence.   The rest of the paragraph illustrates the fact that
   c. third sentence.   Andrew "did not live like a wealthy man."
   d. last sentence.

5. Which sentence best expresses the main idea of paragraph 8?
   a. Lizzie had a round face and belonged to the Ladies' Fruit and Flower Mission.
   (b.) Americans couldn't believe a pleasant-looking, respectable woman like Lizzie could be a killer.
   c. Trials in the late 1800s were widely covered in newspapers and magazines.   Answer *c* is not stated; answers *a* and *d* are too narrow.
   d. Americans of Lizzie's day believed that killers looked evil.

Supporting Details

6. The supporting details of paragraph 2 are mainly about
   (a.) ways in which Andrew Borden saved money.
   b. Lizzie's and Emma's embarrassment with their home.
   c. the reason the Bordens often sat in the dark.
   d. the fact that the Bordens used kerosene rather than gas for light.

   The ways Borden saved money are the supporting details for the main idea. (See question 4.)

7. The odd occurrences in the Borden home began after
   a. Bridget Sullivan was hired to be the maid.
   b. Andrew Borden brought Abby home to be Lizzie and Emma's stepmother.
   c. Andrew Borden changed his will.   See paragraph 4.
   d. Lizzie joined the church's Fruit and Flower Mission.

8. When she tried to buy prussic acid, Lizzie told the druggist
   a. it was not his business why she needed it.
   b. that she needed it to poison rats.
   c. that Emma had asked her to buy it.   See paragraph 4.
   d. that she needed it to clean an article of clothing.

Transitions

9. The relationship between the two parts of the sentence below is one of
   a. cause and effect.
   b. contrast.
   c. time order.   The sentence contrasts two neighborhoods.
   d. addition.

   "Instead of living alongside the other prosperous Fall River citizens in the elite neighborhood known as The Hill, Andrew resided in an area near the business district called the flats." (Paragraph 2)

10. The relationship of the second sentence below to the first is one of
    a. time.
    b. contrast.   The first sentence presents the cause. The
    c. cause and effect.   second gives the effect.
    d. addition.

    "Society expected a woman of social position to marry, and while she waited for a proper suitor, her only respectable social outlets were church and community service. So Lizzie taught a Sunday school class and was active in the the Women's Christian Temperance Union, the Ladies' Fruit and Flower Mission, and other organizations." (Paragraph 3)

Patterns of Organization

11. Paragraph 2 is organized as a   The ways the Bordens saved
    a. series of events in the Borden household.   money are listed.
    b. list of ways in which the Bordens lived very thriftily.
    c. comparison and contrast between the members of the Borden household.
    d. definition of *wealthy* followed by examples.

12. The pattern of organization of paragraphs 4–6 is
   (a.) time order.
   b. list of items.
   c. comparison and contrast.
   d. definition and example.

   The author narrates events at the time of the murder in the order in which they occurred.

ADVANCED SKILL QUESTIONS

Fact and Opinion

13. The sentence below contains
   (a.) only facts.
   b. only opinions.
   c. a mixture of both fact and opinion.

   Everything in the sentence can be proved in historical records.

   "By 1892 he had amassed over half a million dollars, and he controlled the Fall River Union Savings Bank as well as serving as the director of the Globe Yard Mill Company, the First National Bank, the Troy Cotton and Manufacturing Company, and the Merchants Manufacturing Company." (Paragraph 1)

Inferences

14. We can infer from the mention of Andrew Borden's changing his will that
   a. he had decided to leave all of his money to his daughters.
   b. he was a lawyer.
   (c.) his new will was unfavorable to Lizzie.
   d. his new wife was not going to inherit any of his money.

   Lizzie apparently took action because the will was changed (see paragraph 4).

15. The authors imply that Bridget, Andrew, and Abby all became ill at about the same time because
   a. they became sick from living in the cold, dark house.
   b. they suffered from food poisoning as a result of eating three-day-old mutton.
   (c.) Lizzie poisoned them.
   d. Bridget poisoned them, but pretended to be ill herself to hide her actions.

   See paragraph 4.

16. Which of the following statements is a valid conclusion based on the information in paragraph 9?
   a. The editorialist for *Scribner's* expressed opinions that were unusual for the day.
   b. Lizzie Borden was an exceptionally unintelligent, gentle person.
   (c.) Men were thought to be more competent, mature, and intelligent than women.
   d. The ax used in the Borden murders was very heavy.

   See paragraph 9.

Purpose and Tone

17. The main purpose of this selection is to
    a. persuade the reader that society's views about women led to Lizzie Borden's being found innocent of two murders that she probably committed.
    b. inform the reader about the everyday life of a well-known nineteenth-century family and about a famous trial of the time.
    c. entertain the reader with a crime story.

18. In general, the authors' tone is
    a. sad and hopeless.
    b. objective and analytical.   The authors present facts and
    c. light and amusing.   reason out their meaning.
    d. bitterly critical.

Argument

19. Which statement does not support the following point?

    Point: Lizzie Borden was probably guilty.

    a. She had attempted to buy poison shortly before the killings.
    b. She was miserable living with her stingy father and disliked her stepmother.
    c. She was alone in the house with her parents when the killings occurred.
    d. She was active in church and community organizations.

20. One of the following statements is the point of an argument. The other statements support that point. Circle the letter of the point.
    a. The common belief that upper-class women were unable to swing an ax well was false.
    b. The jurors' reasoning in finding Lizzie Borden innocent was faulty.
    c. The jurors' idea that criminals looked a certain way was mistaken.
    d. The jurors' belief that women were too gentle and unintelligent to plan a murder was false.

Comments: Item 17—The authors show why they feel the jury was wrong.
         Item 19—Answer *d* is irrelevant to the point.
         Item 20—Statements *a*, *c*, and *d* are reasons for the conclusion in *b*.

SUMMARIZING

Circle the letter of the paragraph that best summarizes the reading "Lizzie Borden."

As you read the three choices, keep in mind that a good summary will include general statements that sum up the selection. It will cover the key elements of the reading. Some specific details may be included as well.

a. Lizzie Borden lived the respectable life expected of a woman of social position. One day she and her sister discovered that their father, Andrew, had secretly changed his will. Strange things then began to happen in the Borden household. First of all, their stepmother, Abby, became violently ill. After that, the Borden's maid, Bridget Sullivan, and Andrew himself became ill too. Then Lizzie went shopping for a deadly poison, prussic acid. She said she needed it to clean her sealskin cape. However, the local druggist refused to sell the poison to her. Lizzie later told a friend that she feared an enemy would do something to her father. On August 4, Lizzie was alone in the house with her stepmother. As Abby was making a bed in the guest room, someone came into the room unobserved and killed her with an ax. Later that day, Andrew came home for lunch and, feeling unwell, lay down on the parlor sofa and napped. He never woke up. Like Abby, he was axed to death. Although there is strong evidence that Lizzie was the murderer, she was found innocent in a trial.

(b.) Lizzie Borden lived the respectable life expected of unmarried women of her social class, but she wasn't happy. Although her father, Andrew, was rich, he was miserly, and the Borden home was grim. In addition, Lizzie disliked her stepmother, Abby. In 1892, she and her sister learned their father had changed his will. Soon after, Abby and then the maid and Andrew became very ill. After that, Lizzie tried unsuccessfully to buy a deadly poison. Then, on August 4, both Abby and Andrew were found axed to death. Lizzie was tried for the crimes. Although experts today conclude she was guilty, the jury found her innocent. Like others of their day, they believed that upper-class women were too gentle, weak, and stupid to plan and carry out a murder. Also, they believed that criminal women came from the lower classes and looked evil.

c. Andrew Borden was rich but miserly. The Borden home therefore lacked comforts. It had no running water on each floor, and the only toilet in the house was in the cellar. To save money, since kerosene was cheaper than gas, the house was not connected to the town gas main. And to save yet more money, the Bordens often sat in the dark. Furthermore, the house was in a neighborhood near the business district, not the elite neighborhood that his daughters, Lizzie and Emma, felt was equal to their social class. The sisters also disliked their stepmother, Abby. Women of the time were expected to marry, and while waiting for the proper man, to do volunteer work for the church and community. So Lizzie taught a Sunday school class and was active in such organizations as the Women's Christian Temperance Union and the Ladies' Fruit and Flower Mission. One day she discovered her father had changed his will; not longer after that, he and Abby were found axed to death.

DISCUSSION QUESTIONS

1. Based on the information in the reading, do you agree or disagree with the experts who say Lizzie was guilty? Explain your answer.

2. As you read this selection, what impression did you form of life in the Borden household? What particular details helped you form that opinion?

3. The authors imply that the story about Andrew Borden's cutting off the feet of corpses to make them fit undersized coffins was a rumor, not a proved fact. Why, then, do you think they include the story in this piece?

4. Do you believe that any of the notions about women that existed in Lizzie Borden's day are still at work in some ways today? Explain your answer.

Check Your Performance   LIZZIE BORDEN

Activity	Number Right	Points	Score
BASIC SKILL QUESTIONS			
Vocabulary in Context (2 items)	_____	x 4 =	_____
Central Point and Main Ideas (3 items)	_____	x 4 =	_____
Supporting Details (3 items)	_____	x 4 =	_____
Transitions (2 items)	_____	x 4 =	_____
Patterns of Organization (2 items)	_____	x 4 =	_____
ADVANCED SKILL QUESTIONS			
Fact and Opinion (1 item)	_____	x 4 =	_____
Inferences (3 items)	_____	x 4 =	_____
Purpose and Tone (2 items)	_____	x 4 =	_____
Argument (2 items)	_____	x 4 =	_____
SUMMARIZING (1 item)	_____	x 20 =	_____
		TOTAL SCORE =	_____%

Enter your total score into the **Reading Performance Chart: Ten Reading Selections** on the inside back cover.

9
Nonverbal Communication
Anthony F. Grasha

Preview

When we think of communication, we usually think of language. But a great deal of human communication takes place without speaking. When we are angry, we may make a fist. When we are happy, our faces give us away. The extent to which we reveal our feelings without words, however, goes much further than we are often aware of. In this excerpt from a college textbook titled *Practical Applications of Psychology*, Third Edition (Scott, Foresman/Little, Brown), Anthony F. Grasha provides an overview of just how much we really say without words.

Words to Watch

norms (2): normal standards
culprit (6): guilty one
manipulate (7): use
utterances (7): expressions
quivering (8): trembling

1   The way we dress, our mannerisms, how close we stand to people, eye contact, touching, and the ways we mark our personal spaces convey certain messages. *Such nonverbal behaviors communicate certain messages by themselves and also enhance the meaning of our verbal* *communications.* Pounding your fist on a table, for example, suggests anger without anything being spoken. Holding someone close to you conveys the message that you care. To say "I don't like you" with a loud voice or waving fists increases the intensity of the verbal message. Let us

examine the concepts of *personal space* and *body language* to gain additional insights into the nonverbal side of interpersonal communication.

NONVERBAL MESSAGES: THE USE OF PERSONAL SPACE

2   Edward Hall notes that we have personal spatial territories or zones that allow certain types of behaviors and communications. We allow only certain people to enter or events to occur within a zone. Let us look at how some nonverbal messages can be triggered by behaviors that violate the norms° of each zone. The four personal zones identified by Hall are as follows:

3   **1. Intimate distance.** This personal zone covers a range of distance from body contact to one foot. Relationships between a parent and child, lovers, and close friends occur within this zone. As a general rule, we allow only people we know and have some affection for to enter this zone. When people try to enter without our permission, they are strongly repelled by our telling them to stay away from us or by our pushing them away. Why do you think we allow a doctor to easily violate our intimate distance zone?

4   **2. Personal distance.** The spatial range covered by this zone extends from one to four feet. Activities like eating in a restaurant with two or three other people, sitting on chairs or on the floor in small groups at parties, or playing cards occur within this zone. Violations of the zone make people feel uneasy and act nervously. When you are eating at a restaurant, the amount of table space that is considered yours is usually divided equally by the number of people present. I can remember becoming angry and generally irritated when a friend of mine placed a plate and glass in my space. As we talked I was visibly irritated, but my anger had nothing to do with the topic we discussed. Has this ever happened to you?

5   **3. Social distance.** Four to twelve feet is the social distance zone. Business meetings, large formal dinners, and small classroom seminars occur within the boundaries of the social distance zone. Discussions concerning everyday topics like the weather, politics, or a best seller are considered acceptable. For a husband and wife to launch into a heated argument during a party in front of ten other people would violate the accepted norms for behavior in the social zone. This once happened at a formal party I attended. The nonverbal behaviors that resulted consisted of several people leaving the room, others looking angry or uncomfortable, and a few standing and watching quietly with an occasional upward glance and a rolling of their eyeballs. What would violate the social distance norms in a classroom?

6   **4. Public distance.** This zone includes the area beyond twelve feet. Addressing a crowd, watching a sports event, and sitting in a large lecture section are behaviors we engage in within this zone. As is true for the other zones, behaviors unacceptable for this zone can trigger nonverbal messages. At a recent World Series game a young male took his clothes off and ran around the outfield. Some watched with amusement on their faces, others looked away, and a few waved their fists at the culprit°. The respective messages were "That's funny," "I'm afraid or ashamed to look," and "How dare you interrupt the game." What would your reaction be in this situation?

NONVERBAL MESSAGES: THE USE OF BODY LANGUAGE

7   *Body language* refers to the various arm and hand gestures, facial expressions, tones of voice, postures, and body movements we use to convey certain messages. According to Erving Goffman, they are the things we "give off" when talking to other people. Goffman notes that our body language is generally difficult to manipulate° at will. Unlike our verbal utterances°, we have less conscious control over the specific body gestures or expressions we might make while talking. Unless we are acting on a stage or purposely trying to create a certain effect, they occur automatically without much thought on our part.

8   Michael Argyle notes that body language serves several functions for us. *It helps us to communicate certain emotions, attitudes, and preferences.* A hug by someone close to us lets us know we are appreciated. A friendly wave and smile as someone we know passes us lets us know we are recognized. A quivering° lip tells us that someone is upset. Each of us has become quite sensitive to the meaning of various body gestures and expressions. Robert Rosenthal has demonstrated that this sensitivity is rather remarkable. When shown films of people expressing various emotions, individuals were able to identify the emotion correctly 66 percent of the time even when each frame was exposed for one twenty-fourth of a second. *Body language also supports our verbal communications.* Vocal signals of timing, pitch, voice stress, and various gestures add meaning to our verbal utterances. Argyle suggests that we may speak with our vocal organs, but we converse with our whole body. *Body language helps to control our conversations.* It helps us to decide when it is time to stop talking, to interrupt the other person, and to know when to shift topics or elaborate on something because our listeners are bored, do not understand us, or are not paying attention.

BASIC SKILL QUESTIONS

Vocabulary in Context

1. In the excerpt below, the word *enhance* means
   a. replace.
   b. reinforce.
   c. contradict.
   d. delay.

   "The way we dress, our mannerisms . . . convey certain messages. Such nonverbal behaviors communicate certain messages by themselves and also enhance the meaning of our verbal communications." (Paragraph 1)

2. In the excerpt below, the word *repelled* means
   a. greeted.
   b. turned away.
   c. encouraged.
   d. ignored.

   Context clue: Being told "to stay away" would tend to turn someone away.

   "When people try to enter without our permission, they are strongly repelled by our telling them to stay away from us. . . ." (Paragraph 3)

Central Point and Main Ideas

3. Which sentence best expresses the central point of the selection?
   a. It is possible to express anger without words.   Incorrect.
   b. People communicate with each other in various ways.   Too broad.
   c. We can convey nonverbal messages and emphasize verbal messages through the use of personal space and body language.
   d. According to Michael Argyle, body language has several functions.
                                                                      Too narrow.

4. Which sentence best expresses the main idea of paragraph 7?
   a. We must plan our body language.   Contradicted in the paragraph.
   b. It is hard to control body language.   Too narrow.
   c. Actors use body language to create an effect.   Too narrow.
   d. *Body language* refers to the nonverbal ways we communicate, usually without conscious control.

5. The main idea of paragraph 8 is expressed in the
   a. first sentence.
   b. second sentence.
   c. next-to-last sentence.
   d. last sentence.

   The first sentence states that body language serves several functions, according to Argyle. The paragraph goes on to name and discuss three functions, highlighted by italics.

Supporting Details

6. According to Rosenthal's work, we
   a. frequently understand body language.
   b. rarely understand body language.
   c. always understand body language.
   d. never understand body language.

   See paragraph 8.

7. To support his central point, the author uses
   a. examples.   See paragraphs 3-6
   b. research.   See paragraph 8, for example.
   c. opinions of other experts.   The four categories of personal space, for instance,
   d. all of the above.   represent Hall's opinions on how to categorize personal space.

Comment: Item 3—The central point is clearly stated (and italicized) in paragraph 1.

8. Playing cards occurs within
   a. an intimate distance.
   b. a personal distance.
   c. a social distance.
   d. a public distance.

See paragraph 4.

9. The major supporting details of the reading are
   a. nonverbal messages and verbal messages.
   b. communicating well and communicating poorly.
   c. intimate distance and body language.
   d. communicating through personal space and through body language.

See the headings of the reading.

Transitions

10. The signal word at the beginning of the sentence below shows
    a. emphasis.
    b. comparison.
    c. contrast.
    d. time.

The sentence contrasts the control we have over "verbal utterances" and over body gestures and expressions.

"Unlike our verbal utterances, we have less conscious control over the specific body gestures or expressions we might make while talking." (Paragraph 7)

Patterns of Organization

11. The pattern of organization of paragraph 3 (as well as 4, 5, and 6) is
    a. time order.
    b. cause and effect.
    c. definition and example.
    d. list of items.

Each of these paragraphs begins with a boldfaced term which is then defined and illustrated.

12. On the whole, paragraph 8
    a. compares and contrasts body language and verbal expression.
    b. lists the functions of body language.
    c. defines body language and gives examples of it.
    d. uses time order to narrate an incident about body language.

See question 5.

ADVANCED SKILL QUESTIONS

Fact and Opinion

13. The sentence below is
    (a.) totally factual.
    b. only opinion.
    c. both fact and opinion.

    This information can be verified in records of Rosenthal's study.

    "When shown films of people expressing various emotions, individuals were able to identify the emotion correctly 66 percent of the time even when each frame was exposed for one twenty-fourth of a second." (Paragraph 8)

Inferences

14. __T__ TRUE OR FALSE? Just as body language generally occurs automatically, so does the use of personal space.

15. Goffman's ideas on body language (paragraph 7) imply that
    a. we usually are aware of our own body language.
    (b.) our body language might reveal emotions we wish to hide.
    c. we can never manipulate our body language.
    d. we should learn to manipulate our body language.

16. We can conclude from the reading and our own experience that body language
    (a.) communicates positive and negative messages of all sorts.
    b. is best at communicating friendly messages.
    c. communicates poorly.
    d. communicates rarely.

17. Two students reviewing together for a test would be working within
    a. an intimate distance.
    (b.) a personal distance.
    c. a social distance.
    d. a public distance.

    See paragraph 4.

Purpose and Tone

18. The author's primary purpose in this selection is to
    (a.) inform.
    b. persuade.
    c. entertain.

    The author is simply passing along information.

Comments: Item 14—Personal experience tells us that when people react to personal space in the ways Hall suggests, they are usually unaware of the issue of personal space.
Item 15—If our body language occurs "automatically without much thought on our part," we can conclude that we sometimes unknowingly move in ways that reveal our true feelings.

19. On the whole, the author's tone is
    a. humorous.
    (b.) objective.
    c. scornful.
    d. enthusiastic.

    The author presents the information in a straightforward, factual manner.

Argument

20. Circle the letter of the statement that is the point of the following argument. Note that two other statements support the point, and that one statement expresses another point.
    a. I became angry and generally irritated when a friend of mine placed a plate and glass in my space.
    b. As we talked I was visibly irritated, but my anger had nothing to do with the topic we discussed.
    c. Business meetings take place within the boundaries of the social distance zone.
    (d.) Violations of the personal zone make people feel uneasy and act nervously.

    Statement *c* is about the social distance zone, not the personal zone.

OUTLINING

Complete the following outline of "Nonverbal Communication" by using the information in the boldface headings, italics, and numbers in the selection. (Five items need to be added to the outline.)

Central point: Our use of personal space and body language communicates meaning and emphasizes verbal communication.

    A. *Nonverbal messages: the use of personal space* _____

        1. Intimate distance
        2. Personal distance
        3. *Social distance* _____
        4. *Public distance* _____

    B. Nonverbal messages: the use of body language
        1. Definition and explanation of body language
        2. Functions of body language
            a. *Helps communicate certain emotions, attitudes, and preferences* _____

            b. *Supports our verbal communications* _____
            c. Helps control our conversations

DISCUSSION QUESTIONS

1. What are your answers to the following questions from the selection? Why do you think the author included these questions?

   • Why do you think we allow a doctor to easily violate our intimate distance zone?

   • I can remember becoming angry and generally irritated when a friend of mine placed a plate and glass in my space.... Has this ever happened to you?

   • What would violate the social distance norms in a classroom?

2. This selection includes headings, italics, labels, and numbered items. How are these related to the author's purpose?

3. What are some examples of a dating or business situation in which someone's body language might contradict his or her verbal communication?

4. Give examples from your own experience of all four types of personal space.

Check Your Performance		**NONVERBAL COMMUNICATION**	
Activity	*Number Right*	*Points*	*Score*
BASIC SKILL QUESTIONS			
Vocabulary in Context (2 items)	_____	x 4 =	_____
Central Point and Main Ideas (3 items)	_____	x 4 =	_____
Supporting Details (4 items)	_____	x 4 =	_____
Transitions (1 item)	_____	x 4 =	_____
Patterns of Organization (2 items)	_____	x 4 =	_____
ADVANCED SKILL QUESTIONS			
Fact and Opinion (1 item)	_____	x 4 =	_____
Inferences (4 items)	_____	x 4 =	_____
Purpose and Tone (2 items)	_____	x 4 =	_____
Argument (1 item)	_____	x 4 =	_____
OUTLINING (5 items)	_____	x 4 =	_____
		TOTAL SCORE =	_____ %

Enter your total score into the **Reading Performance Chart: Ten Reading Selections** on the inside back cover.

10
Preindustrial Cities
Rodney Stark

Preview

"What was it like in London and Paris when they had only 40,000 to 50,000 residents and before they had factories or freeways, subways or suburbs?" asks Rodney Stark in his popular college textbook (*Sociology*, Fifth Edition, Wadsworth). If you think problems in big cities are modern "inventions," this excerpt from Stark's book may surprise you. In it, he discusses the uncleanliness, crowding, and crime that existed in "big" cities before machines and electricity changed society.

Words to Watch

densely (2): closely
virtually (5): for all practical purposes
ravaged (7): violently destroyed
trenches (8): ditches
strewn (9): scattered
radius (14): a line from the center of a circle to its edge
lurked (16): hid, ready to attack
incentive (18): motivation
vital (18): essential
innovations (19): things that are newly introduced
enticed (20): tempted
rampant (20): widespread
condoning (20): forgiving or overlooking
exalted (21): high
replenished (22): resupplied

1   Let us go back into history and examine what life was like in the famous cities of preindustrial times. What was it really like in ancient Athens and Rome? What was it like in London and Paris when they had only 40,000 to 50,000 residents and before they had factories or freeways, subways or suburbs?

PREINDUSTRIAL CITIES

2   Until very recently, cities were small, filthy, disease-ridden, densely° packed with people, and disorderly, and they were dark and very dangerous at night. If that description is unlike your image of Athens during the Golden Age of Greek civilization, that is because history so often leaves out the mud, manure, and misery.

3   Typically, preindustrial cities contained no more than 5,000 to 10,000 inhabitants. Large national capitals were usually smaller than 40,000 and rarely larger than 60,000. Few preindustrial cities, such as ancient Rome, grew as large as 500,000 and then only under special circumstances. Moreover, these cities rapidly shrank back to a much smaller size as slight changes in circumstance made it impossible to support them.

Limits on City Style

4   A major reason why cities remained small was poor transportation; food had to be brought to feed a city. With only animal and human power to bring it, however, food could not be transported very far. Therefore, cities were limited to the population that could be fed by farmers nearby. The few large cities of preindustrial times appeared only where food could be brought long distances by water transport. Ancient Rome, for example, was able to reach the size of present-day Denver (and only briefly) because it controlled the whole Mediterranean area. Surplus food from this vast region was shipped by sea to feed the city's masses.

5   However, as the power of the empire weakened, Rome's population declined as the sources of food supplies dwindled. By the ninth century, the sea-power of Islam had driven nearly all European shipping from the Mediterranean, and the cities of southern Europe, including Rome, were virtually° abandoned. In fact, Europe had practically no cities during the ninth and tenth centuries.

6   Disease also checked the size of cities. Even early in the twentieth century, cities had such high mortality rates that they required a large and constant influx of newcomers from the countryside just to maintain their populations. As recently as 1900, the death rate in English cities was 33 percent higher than that in rural areas (Davis, 1965). A major reason for the high mortality in cities was the high incidence of infectious diseases, which are spread by physical contact or by breathing in germs emitted by coughs and sneezes. Disease spreads much more slowly among less dense rural populations.

7   Disease in cities was also caused by filth, especially by the contamination of water and food. Kingsley Davis (1965) pointed out that even as late as the 1850s, London's water "came mainly from wells and rivers that drained cesspools, graveyards, and tidal areas. The city was regularly ravaged° by cholera."

8   Sewage treatment was unknown in preindustrial cities. Even sewers were uncommon and what sewers there were consisted of open trenches° running along the streets into which sewage, including human waste, was poured from buckets and chamber pots. Indeed, sewage was often poured out of second-story windows without any warning to pedestrians below.

9   Garbage was not collected and was strewn° everywhere. It was hailed as a

major step forward when cities began to keep a municipal herd of pigs, which were guided through the streets at night to eat the garbage dumped during the day. Of course, the pigs did considerable recycling as they went. Still, major cities in the eastern United States depended on the pigs for their sanitation services until the end of the nineteenth century.

10 Today we are greatly concerned about pollution, especially that produced by automobile exhausts and factories. But the car and the factory cannot match the horse and the home fireplace when it comes to pollution. It is estimated that in 1900 horses deposited 26 million pounds of manure and 10 million gallons of urine on the streets of New York City every week.

11 London's famous and deadly "fogs" of previous centuries were actually smogs caused by thousands of smoking home chimneys during atmospheric inversions, which trapped the polluted air. Indeed, the first known air-quality law was decreed in 1273 by England's King Edward I. It forbade the use of a particularly smoky coal. The poet Shelley wrote early in the nineteenth century that "Hell is a city much like London, a populous and smokey city." In 1911, coal smoke during an atmospheric inversion killed more than a thousand people in London, and this incident led to the coining of the word *smog*.

12 Pedestrians in preindustrial cities often held perfume-soaked handkerchiefs over their noses because the streets stank so. They kept alert for garbage and sewage droppings from above. They wore high boots because they had to wade through muck, manure, and garbage. And the people themselves were dirty because they seldom bathed. Not surprisingly, they died at a rapid rate.

13 Population density also contributed to the unhealthiness of preindustrial cities. People were packed closely together. As we saw in Chapter 13, whole families lived in one small room. The houses stood wall to wall, and few streets were more than ten to twelve feet wide.

14 Why was there such density when the population was so small? First of all, for most of its history, the city was also a fortress surrounded by massive walls for defense. Once the walls were up, the area of the city was fixed (at least until the walls were rebuilt), and if the population grew, people had to crowd ever closer. Even cities without walls were confined. Travel was by foot or by hoof. Cities did not spread beyond the radius° that could be covered by these slow means of transportation, and thus the city limit was usually no more than three miles from the center.

15 Second, preindustrial cities could not expand upward. Not until the nineteenth century, when structural steel and reinforced concrete were developed, could very tall structures be erected. Moreover, until elevators were invented, it was impractical to build very high. By expanding upward, people could have much greater living and working space in a building taking up no greater area at ground level. This could, of course, have meant that cities would become even more crowded at street level. They did not, however, because even modern high-rise cities have much more open space than did preindustrial cities, and, as we shall see, newer cities have expanded primarily outward rather than upward.

16 Preindustrial cities were not only dirty, disease-ridden, and dense but also dark and dangerous. Today we sometimes say people move to the city

because they are attracted by the bright lights, and we joke about small towns where they "roll up the sidewalks by 9 p.m." The preindustrial city had no sidewalks to roll up and no electricity to light up the night. If lighted at all, homes were badly and expensively illuminated by candles and oil lamps. Until the introduction of gas lamps in the nineteenth century, streets were not lighted at all. Out in the dark, dangerous people lurked°, waiting for victims. To venture forth at night in many of these cities was so dangerous that people did so only in groups accompanied by armed men bearing torches. Many people today fear to walk in cities at night. Still, it is much safer to do so now than it used to be.

Why Live in Such Cities?

17 Knowing what preindustrial cities were like, one must ask why anyone willingly lived there and why a large number of newcomers were attracted to cities each year from rural areas.

18 One reason was economic incentive°. Cities offered many people a chance to increase their incomes. For example, the development of an extensive division of labor, of occupational specialization, virtually required cities. Specialists must depend upon one another for the many goods and services they do not provide for themselves. Such exchanges are hard to manage when people live far apart. Thus skilled craftsmen, merchants, physicians, and the like gathered in cities. Indeed, cities are vital° to trade and commerce, and most early cities developed at intersections of major trade routes.

19 In addition to economic attractions, cities drew people because they offered the prospect of a more interesting and stimulating life. As Gideon Sjoberg (1965) noted, "new ideas and innovations° flowed into [cities] quite naturally," as travelers along the trade routes brought ideas as well as goods from afar. Moreover, simply by concentrating specialists in an area, cities stimulated innovation not just in technology but also in religion, philosophy, science, and the arts. The density of cities encouraged public performances, from plays and concerts to organized sporting events.

20 Cities undoubtedly also enticed° some to migrate from rural areas in pursuit of "vice." The earliest writing we have about cities includes complaints about rampant° wickedness and sin, and through the centuries cities have maintained the reputation for condoning° behavior that would not be tolerated in rural communities (Fischer, 1975). In part, this may be because from the beginning cities have been relatively anonymous places. Preindustrial cities may have been even more anonymous, given their size, than modern cities.

21 Consider that cities relied on large numbers of newcomers each year just to replace the population lost through mortality. As a result, cities tended to abound in people who were recent arrivals and who had not known one another previously. Before modern identification systems, many people in cities were not even who they claimed to be—runaway sons and daughters of peasants could claim more exalted° social origins. The possibility of escaping one's past and starting anew must have drawn many to the cities. But this also meant that cities then were even less integrated by long-standing interpersonal attachments than modern cities.

22   In any event, it was primarily adventuresome, single, young adults who constantly replenished° city populations. E. A. Wrigley (1969) has computed that in the years from 1650 to 1750, London needed eight thousand newcomers each year to maintain its population. The newcomers averaged twenty years of age, were unmarried, and came from farms. Most of these newcomers came from more than fifty miles away—at least a two-day trip at that time.

For all our complaints about modern   23 cities, industrialization did not ruin city life. Preindustrial cities were horrid. Yet for many young people on farms, the prospect of heading off to one of these miserable cities seemed far superior to a life of dull toil. Then as the Industrial Revolution began, the idea of going off to the city suddenly appealed not just to restless young people but also to whole families. Soon the countryside virtually emptied, as people flocked to town.

BASIC SKILL QUESTIONS

Vocabulary in Context

1. In the excerpt below, the word *checked* means
   a. encouraged.
   b. predicted.
   c. limited.
   d. increased.

   "A major reason why cities remained small was poor transportation. . . . Disease also checked the size of cities." (Paragraphs 4 and 6)

2. In the sentence below, the word *dwindled* means
   a. increased.
   b. decreased.
   c. remained the same.
   d. became less expensive.

   A synonym-like context clue.

   "Rome's population declined as the sources of food supplies dwindled." (Paragraph 5)

3. In the sentence below, the word *coining* means
   a. paying for.
   b. invention.
   c. denial.
   d. pronunciation.

   Context clue: New words are invented.

   "In 1911, coal smoke during an atmospheric inversion killed more than a thousand people in London, and this incident led to the coining of the word *smog*." (Paragraph 11)

Central Point and Main Ideas

4. Which sentence best expresses the central point of the selection?
    a. Poor transportation and fortress walls kept cities from becoming too large.
    (b.) Preindustrial cities had major disadvantages, but they still attracted people.
    c. Until structural steel, reinforced concrete and elevators were invented, it wasn't possible or practical to build high buildings.
    d. Life in earlier times was very different from life today.

5. The main idea of paragraph 6 is best expressed in its
    (a.) first sentence.
    b. second sentence.
    c. third sentence.
    d. fourth sentence.

6. Which sentence best expresses the main idea of paragraphs 17–21?
    a. Despite the great disadvantages of preindustrial cities, people were drawn to the cities for economic reasons.
    (b.) Despite the great disadvantages of preindustrial cities, people were drawn to the cities for several reasons.
    c. Preindistrial cities allowed people to escape their past and start anew.
    d. Our earliest knowledge of cities includes complaints about widespread vice, and cities have kept the reputation for allowing behavior that would not be tolerated in rural communities.   Paragraphs 18–21 discuss, in turn, each of the reasons.

Supporting Details

7. __T__ TRUE OR FALSE? According to the author, preindustrial cities, on the whole, were more crowded and dangerous than modern cities.
                                                                        See paragraphs 13 and 16.
8. The major supporting details of paragraphs 14 and 15 are
    a. 1) travel by foot or horse and 2) elevators.
    b. crowding of 1) preindustrial cities and 2) modern-day cities.
    (c.) the limits on city size caused by 1) city walls and 2) lack of construction technology.
    d. 1) cities with walls and 2) cities without walls.

Transitions

9. The relationship between the two sentences below is one of
    (a.) addition.
    b. time.   The second sentence gives another reason
    c. contrast.   for the small size of preindustrial cities.
    d. definition and example.

    "A major reason why cities remained small was poor transportation . . . .
    Disease also checked the size of cities." (Paragraphs 4 and 6)

Comment: Item 4—Answers *a* and *c* are too narrow. Answer *d* is too broad; it includes much more than just preindustrial city life.
Item 5—The rest of the paragraph discusses how and why disease affected the size of cities.

10. The relationship between the two sentences below is one of
    a. comparison.
    b. time.
    c.) cause and effect.
    d. example.

The cause: Many newcomers entered the cities each year.
The effect: Cities were filled with people who were strangers to each other.

"Consider that cities relied on large numbers of newcomers each year just to replace the population lost through mortality. As a result, cities tended to abound in people who were recent arrivals and who had not known one another previously." (Paragraph 21)

Patterns of Organization

11. The main pattern of organization of paragraph 4 is
    a. time order
    b. list of items.
    c.) cause and effect.
    d. definition and example.

The cause-effect signals are *reason, therefore, because.*

ADVANCED SKILL QUESTIONS

Fact and Opinion

12. Paragraph 6 is made up of
    a.) facts.
    b. opinions.
    c. both facts and opinions.

All the information in this paragraph can be verified in historical and medical publications.

Inferences

13. From paragraph 4, we can conclude that cities probably grew significantly larger after the invention of
    a. elevators.
    b.) trains.
    c. bicycles.
    d. antibiotics.

Trains enable food to be shipped to distant points.

14. The author implies that today's cities
    a. are as dirty as preindustrial cities were.
    b.) are better places to live than preindustrial cities.
    c. shouldn't have so many tall buildings.
    d. are very safe places at night.

See, for example, paragraphs 16 and 23.

15. From paragraph 11, we can deduce that the word *smog*
    a. comes from another language.
    b. is a shortening of a longer word.
    c. has no real meaning.
    d.) is a combination of the words *smoke* and *fog*.

The paragraph tells us that the "deadly *fogs*" in London were caused by "*smoking* home chimneys."

16. Reread paragraph 21; from that paragraph, we can conclude
    a. people's social class influenced how others treated them.
    b. it was easy in preindustrial times to check on people's pasts.
    c. both of the above.
    d. neither *a* nor *b*.

Statement *a* explains why people would claim "more exalted social origins."

Purpose and Tone

17. The author's main purpose is to
    a. inform readers of what life in preindustrial cities was like.
    b. persuade readers to appreciate the countryside.
    c. entertain readers with amusing details about preindustrial cities.

This purpose is suggested by the first sentence of the selection.

18. In paragraph 2, the author's tone is
    a. amused.
    b. disappointed.
    c. objective.
    d. critical.

The author uses negative words ("filthy," "disease-ridden") and then criticizes "history" for omitting "the mud, manure, and misery" of preindustrial cities.

Argument

19. To support the statement that "the car and the factory cannot match the horse and the home fireplace when it comes to pollution," the author provides in paragraphs 10 and 11
    a. facts about how cars and factories pollute.
    b. facts about how horses and home fireplaces pollute.
    c. both of the above.

20. Complete the following argument by adding a statement of support.

    Point: Preindustrial cities were not better than our cities.

    Support: Preindustrial cities had worse environmental pollution.

    Support: *Preindustrial cities were more crowded (or dangerous or disease-ridden).*

MAPPING

Complete the map of the selection by filling in the five missing major and minor details scrambled in the following list:

- Population density
- Opportunity to start a new life
- Disease limited size of city
- Reasons people were attracted to them
- Not being able to expand upward

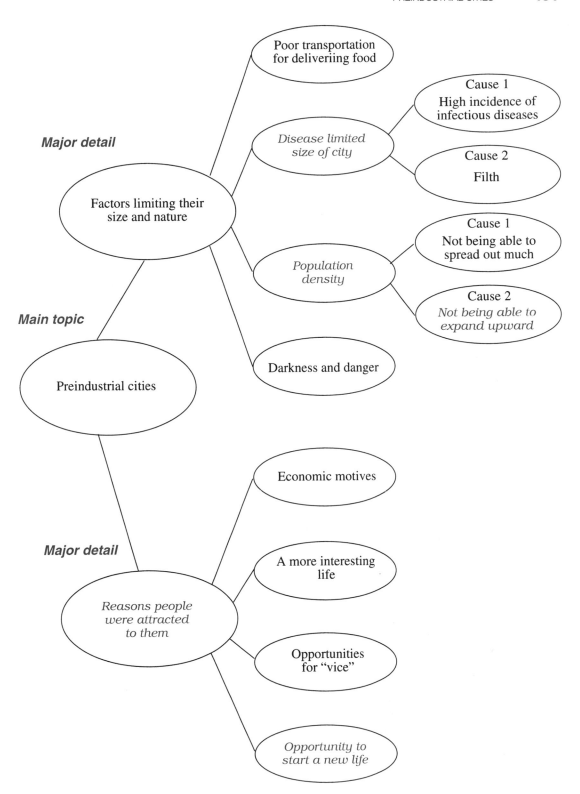

Major detail

Poor transportation
for deliveriing food

Disease limited
size of city

Cause 1
High incidence of
infectious diseases

Cause 2
Filth

Factors limiting their
size and nature

Population
density

Cause 1
Not being able to
spread out much

Cause 2
Not being able to
expand upward

Main topic

Darkness and danger

Preindustrial cities

Economic motives

A more interesting
life

Major detail

Reasons people
were attracted
to them

Opportunities
for "vice"

Opportunity to
start a new life

DISCUSSION QUESTIONS

1. If you had lived in preindustrial days, do you think you would have chosen to live in a city or in a rural area? Why?

2. What draws people to or keeps them in big cities today? Compare these reasons with those which attracted newcomers to preindustrial cities.

3. The radius of preindustrial cities was "usually no more than three miles from the center." What factors have allowed today's huge cities and their suburbs to exist?

4. According to the reading, preindustrial city dwellers had to protect themselves from the filth and crime in big cities. How are problems of city dwellers today the same or different?

Check Your Performance   **PREINDUSTRIAL CITIES**

Activity	Number Right	Points	Score
BASIC SKILL QUESTIONS			
Vocabulary in Context (3 items)	_____	x 4 =	_____
Central Point and Main Ideas (3 items)	_____	x 4 =	_____
Supporting Details (2 items)	_____	x 4 =	_____
Transitions (2 items)	_____	x 4 =	_____
Patterns of Organization (1 item)	_____	x 4 =	_____
ADVANCED SKILL QUESTIONS			
Fact and Opinion (1 item)	_____	x 4 =	_____
Inferences (4 items)	_____	x 4 =	_____
Purpose and Tone (2 items)	_____	x 4 =	_____
Argument (2 items)	_____	x 4 =	_____
MAPPING (5 items)	_____	x 4 =	_____

TOTAL SCORE = _____ %

Enter your total score into the **Reading Performance Chart: Ten Reading Selections** on the inside back cover.

Part III

FOR FURTHER STUDY

1
Reading for Pleasure and Power

I did little reading as a boy, with one notable exception: I loved comic books. In particular, I can remember reading comics at lunch time. Since I attended a grade school that was only several blocks away, I could walk home at noon. There I would drink chocolate milk and eat my favorite sandwich—baloney, mustard, and potato chips layered between two pieces of white bread. I would sit at the kitchen table with my two sisters, home from the same school, as well as my father, home for lunch from his job with a local insurance company. The four of us sat silently because we were all reading. My sisters and I read mostly Donald Duck, Scrooge McDuck, and Mickey Mouse comic books, while my father read *Reader's Digest, Life* magazine, or the morning newspaper. Coffee cup in hand, my mother hovered nearby, always a bit frustrated, I suspect. She was in the mood for conversation, but her family was too busy reading.

Even when I went on to high school, I was more likely to read a comic book than anything else. Each year my English teachers typically assigned two books for students to read and report on—books such as Sir Walter Scott's *Ivanhoe* and Charles Dickens's *A Tale of Two Cities*. I had no interest in reading such books, especially ones that seemed to be about, as I remember saying at the time, "old dead stuff." How then did I deal with these assignments? I was rescued by a series of comics called classic comic books, which were illustrated stories of famous novels. Classic comics helped me pass tests and do book reports. They also kept me from actually having to sit down and read a book—an activity that I never imagined could be a source of enjoyment.

What did give me pleasure was watching television. I developed a routine after school: get my homework done, do any household chores, eat dinner, and then spend the whole evening watching the tube.

Fortunately, something happened in the summer before my junior year that changed my life. The country was in the middle of a recession, so I was not able to get a job. I felt too old to spend the summer playing back-alley baseball with neighborhood buddies, and there was not enough on daytime TV (this was before cable) to hold my interest. Except for a once-a-week job of cutting my aunt's grass, I had nothing to do and felt restless and empty.

Then, sitting on my front porch one day in early June, I saw a public service message on the side of a bus that was rumbling down the street. I remember the exact words: "Open your mind—read a book." Such messages had always annoyed me. On general principle I never liked being told what I should know or what I should do. I also resented the implication that my mind was closed just because I didn't read books. I thought to myself, "Well, I'm not doing anything. I'm going to read a book just so I know for sure there's nothing there."

That afternoon I walked to the one bookstore in town, browsed around, and picked out a paperback book—*The Swiss Family Robinson*—about a family that had been shipwrecked on an island and had to find a way to survive until rescue came. I spent a couple of days reading the story. When I was done, I had to admit that I had enjoyed it and that I was proud of myself for actually having read an entire book. I also remembered the one other time in my life that reading had been fun. When I was about seven years old, my father had read me a spellbinding story by Rudyard Kipling called "Rikki-Tikki-Tavi." It described how a family pet called a mongoose saved a family living in India from a nest of deadly cobras.

In the perverse frame of mind that was typical of me at age 15, I thought to myself, "Dad and I just happened to pick out the two stories in the world that are actually interesting. Chances are there are no more left." But the more reasonable part of me wondered, "What if there are other books that wouldn't waste my time?"

I remembered that upstairs in my closet were some books that my aunt had once given me but I had never read. I selected one that I had heard of and that seemed to have some promise. It was *The Adventures of Tom Sawyer*, by Mark Twain, and it was a hardbound book now so old that its binding cracked when I opened it up. I began reading, and while the activities of Tom were interesting enough, it was his girlfriend Becky Thatcher who soon captured my complete attention. My adolescent heart raced when I thought of her, and for a while I thought about her night and day. For the first time in my life, I had fallen in love— incredibly enough, with a character in a book! The character of Becky helped show me what power a book can have.

Tom had a friend named Huck Finn, about whom Mark Twain had written another book. So when I finished Tom's story, I went to the library, got a library card, and checked out *The Adventures of Huckleberry Finn*. I figured this book might tell me more about Becky. As it turned out, it didn't, but by pure chance I wound up reading—without any teacher telling me to—a book that is arguably the greatest novel ever written by an American author.

If Becky had made my blood race, the story of Huck Finn and the trip that he and his friend Jim took on a raft down the Mississippi River caught me up in a different but equally compelling way. While I could not express what happened at the time, the book made me look at people in a way that I never did before. I saw a whole stage of characters who felt very human and whose stories seemed very real. Some of these characters were mean and stupid and cowardly and hateful, others were loyal and courageous and dignified and loving, and a few were a blend of good and bad. By the time I finished Huck's story, I knew that books could be a source of pleasure, and I sensed also that they could be a source of power—that they could help me learn important things about the world and the people around me. I was now hooked on books. By the end of the summer, I had read over twenty novels, and I have been reading ever since.

*   *   *

When students ask me today why they should read, I give the answer in two words: pleasure and power. First of all, reading can be great fun. One of the most magical experiences in life is to be caught up in the excitement and joy that reading can provide. Reading a book, I always feel a bit like Huck floating on a raft down the river, meeting fascinating people at every stop, sharing not only their adventures but even more wonderfully the secrets of their minds and their hearts. Unfortunately, many people never discover that magical river, so full of insight and of life; they never experience the joy of reading for its own sake.

Chances are that you have done little reading for pleasure in your life. You may be an unpracticed reader who has never gotten into the habit of regular reading. Perhaps you grew up in a home where a television set dominated the household, and there was little in the way of books or reading matter. Perhaps you got off to a bad start in reading class and never seemed to catch up. Or maybe you were eager to learn about reading when you began school but then soured on it. If you were given uninteresting and irrelevant material to read, rather than intriguing and exciting books, you may have decided (mistakenly) that reading in general cannot be an enjoyable experience for you.

But the truth is that reading can be enormously pleasurable. It can also be a source of power. Recently I was at a conference where a panel of first-year college students were asked, "If you could give just one bit of advice to high-school kids, what would it be?" One student answered, "I can answer that in one word: Read. Read everything you can. The more you read, the better off you're going to be." Up and down the panel, heads nodded. No one disagreed with this advice.

Here are some of the important rewards that the habit of regular reading can offer.

- Research has shown that frequent reading improves vocabulary, spelling, and reading speed and comprehension, as well as grammar and writing style. If you become a habitual reader, all of these language and thinking abilities develop almost automatically.

- Regular reading will increase your chances for job success. In today's world more than ever, jobs involve the processing of information, with words being the tools of our trade. Studies have found that the better your command of words, the more success you are likely to have. Nothing will give you a command of words like regular reading.

  There are hundreds of stories about people who went on to distinguished careers after developing the reading habit. One is the story of Ben Carson, who as a boy believed that he was "the dumbest kid" in his fifth-grade class. After he started reading two books a week, at his mother's insistence, his entire world changed. Within two years he had moved to the head of his class, and he was later to become Dr. Benjamin Carson, a world-famous neurosurgeon at Johns Hopkins University Hospital.

- Reading enlarges the mind and the heart. It frees us from the narrow confines of our own experience. Knowing how other people view important matters helps us decide what we ourselves think and feel. Reading also helps us connect with others and realize our shared humanity. We become less lonely as we share the common experiences, emotions, and thoughts that make us human. We grow more sympathetic and understanding because we realize that others are like us.

In a nutshell, regular reading can be a source of enormous pleasure and power. If you want that pleasure and power in your life, they are yours for the taking.

*   *   *

How, you might be wondering, does one become a regular reader? The key, startlingly simple as it might sound, is to do a great deal of reading. The truth of the matter is that reading is like any other skill. The more you practice, the better you get. In his book *The Power of Reading: Insights from the Research*, the reading scholar Stephen Krashen surveys an extensive number of studies and concludes that reading itself is the "way that we become good readers." The value of regular reading is a point about which common sense and research are in complete agreement.

The following suggestions will help you make reading a part of your life. Remember, though: The suggestions are only words on a page. *You* must decide to become a regular reader, and you must follow through on that decision. Only then will reading become a source of pleasure and power.

- Subscribe to a daily newspaper and read the sections that interest you. Keep in mind that it is not what you read that matters—for example, you should not feel obliged to read the editorial section if opinion columns are not your interest. What does matter is *the very fact that you read.* Feel perfectly free to read whatever you decide you want: the sports page, the fashion section, movie reviews, first-page stories—even the comics.

- Subscribe to one or more magazines. Browse in the magazine section of your library or a local bookstore; chances are you'll find some magazines that interest you. You may want to consider a weekly news magazine, such as *Newsweek* or *Time*; a weekly general-interest magazine such as *People*; or any number of special-interest monthly magazines such as *Glamour, Sports Illustrated, Essence*, or *Health and Fitness.*

    You'll find subscription cards within most magazines; and on many college bulletin boards, you'll see display cards offering a wide variety of magazines at discount rates for college students.

- Create a half hour or hour of reading in your daily schedule. That time might be during your lunch hour, or late afternoon before dinner, or the half hour or so before you turn off your light at night. Find a time that is possible for you and make reading then a habit. The result will be both recreation time and personal growth.

- Read aloud to children in your family, whether younger brothers or sisters or sons or daugthers or nephews or nieces. Alternatively, have a family reading time when you and the children take turns reading.

    Many books can be enjoyed by both adults and children. The children's librarian at your local library can provide some helpful leads. There are also many choices in the children's section at area bookstores. Large chains like Waldenbooks, Borders, and Barnes and Noble have staffs who specialize in helping customers select just the right book. An excellent mail order source of books is the Chinaberry Book Service, 2780 Via Orange Way, Suite B, Spring Valley, California 91978. Recommended books are grouped into five levels, from titles suitable for the very young to titles for adults. Many of the books are pictured, and each book is helpfully described. To get a catalog, you can call a toll-free number: 1-800-776-2242.

- Read books on your own. This is the most important step on the road to becoming a regular reader. Reading is most enjoyable when you get drawn into the special world created by a given book. You can travel in that world for hours, unmindful for a while of everyday concerns. In that timeless zone, you will come to experience the joy of reading. Too many people are addicted to smoking or drugs or television; you should try, instead, to get hooked on books.

What should you read? That's easy to answer. Select anything that interests you. That might be comic books, fantasies or science fiction, horror and mystery stories, romances, adventure and sports stories, biographies and autobiographies, or how-to books. To select a book, browse in a bookstore, library, or reading center. Find something you like and begin reading. If you stick to it and become a regular reader, you may find that you have done nothing less than change your life. I wish you success.

John Langan

DISCUSSION QUESTIONS

1. When you were growing up, what role did your family play in shaping your attitude about reading? Did anyone read to you as a child? Were you given interesting materials to read? Did the people around you read for pleasure, making you want to imitate them? Or was there little to read and just lots of TV to watch?

2. When you were growing up, what influence did school have in encouraging or discouraging you to read? Describe experiences in school that made you feel positive or negative about reading.

3. What do you think that parents and schools could do to make reading a source of pleasure for children? Suggest some specific ideas that would have worked for you as a child.

4. Think about your daily schedule. If you were to do regular reading, where in your day could you find time to relax for half an hour and just read? What do you think would be the benefits of becoming a regular reader?

An invitation . . .

To help you on your journey, Townsend Press is making the following offer. Tear out this page (or clip out the order form below), fill out the form, and mail it along with two dollars (to cover the cost of postage and shipping) to the address shown. (Please note that Townsend Press will not accept group orders. This book is available free only to individuals.) When you do that, you will be sent a free copy of *Everyday Heroes*, a book that tells the inspiring stories of twenty real-life men and women who had to overcome serious challenges to get into college and to stay there. Despite obstacles that included poverty, racism, abuse, neglect, illness, drugs, and violence, these extraordinary people found the strength to take strong, positive steps to better their lives. Along with *Everyday Heroes*, you will be sent a *reading list* that describes a number of books that many people have enjoyed.

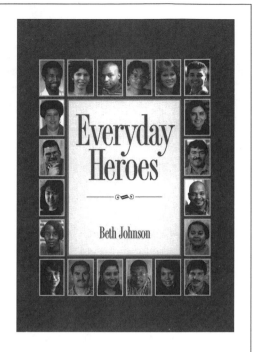

ORDER FORM

YES! Please send me a copy of *Everyday Heroes*. Enclosed is two dollars to cover the mailing and shipping of the book.

Please PRINT the following very clearly. It will be your shipping label.

Name _____

Address _____

City _____ *State* _____ *Zip* _____

MAIL TO: TP Book Center, 1038 Industrial Drive, West Berlin, NJ 08091.

2

Combined-Skills Tests

Following are twelve tests that cover the skills taught in Part I of this book. Each test consists of a short reading passage followed by questions on any of the following: vocabulary in context, main ideas, supporting details, relationships, fact and opinion, inferences, purpose and tone, and argument.

Note: In the comments on test items, the term "too narrow" describes a topic that is only a detail within the selection. "Too broad" describes an item that encompasses a great deal more than the topic of the selection.

COMBINED SKILLS: Test 1

After reading the passage, circle the letter of the best answer to each question.

¹Johnny Appleseed, one of the gentlest and most beloved of American folk heroes, was born in 1774 in Leominster, Massachusetts. ²His real name was John Chapman. ³Chapman's early life was full of misfortune. ⁴First, his father left home to fight in the Revolutionary War. ⁵Then John's mother and baby brother died before John's second birthday. ⁶However, John's fortunes improved when his father returned and remarried, and by the time John was in his teens, he had ten brothers and sisters.

⁷As a young man, John began traveling west on foot, stopping to clear land and plant the apple seeds he always carried with him. ⁸Settlers who followed John's path were delighted to find young apple orchards dotting the landscape.

⁹John was a friendly fellow who often stopped to visit with families along his way, entertaining them with stories of his travels. ¹⁰Tales of his exploits followed him through Pennsylvania, Ohio, and Indiana. ¹¹Many of the stories were true. ¹²For instance, John really did travel barefoot through the snow, lived on the friendliest of terms with Indian tribes, and refused to shoot any animal. ¹³Other tales about John, however, were exaggerations. ¹⁴Settlers said, for example, that he slept in the treetops and talked to the birds or that he had once been carried off by a giant eagle. ¹⁵Johnny Appleseed never stopped traveling until his death in Fort Wayne, Indiana, in 1845.

1. As used in sentence 6, the word *fortunes* means
   a. wealth.
   b. possessions.
   c. luck.
   d. health.

2. The details in sentences 4 and 5 support the point or points in
   a. sentence 1.
   b. sentence 2.
   c. sentence 3.
   d. sentence 6.

3. The relationship between sentences 3 and 6 is one of
   a. contrast.
   b. addition.
   c. cause and effect.
   d. comparison.

(Continues on next page)

4. We can conclude that Johnny Appleseed
   a. provided apples for numerous settlers.
   b. was quickly forgotten by the settlers.
   c. grew wealthy from selling his apple trees.
   d. left home because of problems with his family.

5. The passage suggests that Johnny Appleseed
   a. grew weary of traveling.
   b. had great respect for other people and animals.
   c. lived a very short but rich life.
   d. planted many trees other than apple trees.

6. Sentence 1 is a statement of
   a. fact.
   b. opinion.
   c. fact and opinion.

7. The tone of the passage is
   a. pessimistic.
   b. bitter and impassioned.
   c. amused and excited.
   d. straightforward with a touch of admiration.

8. Which is the most appropriate title for this selection?
   a. The Planting of American Apple Orchards
   b. Folk Heroes of America
   c. Settlers Recall Johnny Appleseed
   d. The Life and Legends of John Chapman

Comments: Item 2—Sentences 4 and 5 detail the misfortune mentioned in sentence 3.

Item 3—The contrast transition *however* signals a change in Chapman's fortunes.

Item 4—See sentence 8.

Item 5—See sentence 12.

Item 6—The part of the sentence between commas is opinion.

Item 7—The author's admiration comes through in the value words in sentence 1.

Item 8—Answer *a* is incorrect (while apple orchards are mentioned, the selection isn't about apple orchards in general). Answer *b* is too broad, and answer *c* is incorrect (the information isn't presented as being only the recollections of settlers).

COMBINED SKILLS: Test 2

After reading the passage, circle the letter of the best answer to each question.

¹Little League baseball in its present form should be abolished. ²For one thing, the pressure that children are put under to succeed may harm them more than help them. ³One mother discovered her son taking Maalox tablets from the medicine chest whenever a game approached. ⁴He explained that they helped relieve the stomach burn he would feel during the game. ⁵Other children have been found taking tranquilizers. ⁶Another drawback to today's Little League baseball is that some parents take the game too seriously and set a bad example for their children. ⁷Recently, a disillusioned coach said, "At our field, we put the bleachers way back from the dugout where the players are. ⁸That way, parents can't be hissing down advice to their children all the time and getting them upset." ⁹A final reason Little League should be abolished is that it doesn't offer enough success to most players. ¹⁰Instead, the game revolves around the more developed kids who are able to hit and throw the ball harder than the smaller children. ¹¹In one recent game, most of the batters were clearly afraid of the speed of the hardball, which was pitched by a boy bigger than many of the other players.

¹²A workable alternative to Little League hardball would be lob-pitch softball. ¹³The ball is pitched slowly and underhand, which offers a high level of success to kids without a high level of ability. ¹⁴Lob-pitch softball would get more children involved in the game, and help people remember that it is a game—not an adult arena where one is branded with success or failure.

1. In sentences 1 and 9, the word *abolished* means
   a. supported.
   b. eliminated.
   c. expanded.
   d. imitated.

2. According to the author, one advantage of lob-pitch softball is the
   a. weight of the ball.
   b. lesser degree of skill required.
   c. size of the field.
   d. age of the players.

3. The relationship of sentence 6 to the sentences that come before it is one of
   a. time.
   b. addition.
   c. contrast.
   d. comparison.

(Continues on next page)

465

4. Sentence 1 is a statement of
    a. fact.
    (b.) opinion.
    c. fact and opinion.

5. From the passage, you can conclude the author would agree with the idea that
    (a.) it's not whether you win or lose; it's how you play the game.
    b. competition in baseball helps prepare people for competition in life.
    c. children's games should imitate adults' games.
    d. sports should help children learn that there are winners and losers in life.

6. The author's main purpose is to
    a. inform.
    (b.) persuade.
    c. entertain.
    d. predict.

7. The main idea of paragraph 1 is best stated in
    (a.) sentence 1.
    b. sentence 2.
    c. sentence 9.
    d. sentence 11.

8. What is the most appropriate title for this selection?
    a. The Pressures on Today's Children
    b. Lob-Pitch Softball
    (c.) Let's Reform Little League
    d. Sportsmanship in Baseball

Comments: Item 2—See sentence 13.

Item 5—See sentence 14.

Item 6—Note the main idea in the next question.

Item 8—Answer *a* is too broad, and answers *b* and *c* are too narrow.

COMBINED SKILLS: Test 3

After reading the passage, circle the letter of the best answer to each question.

¹Most people dislike bats, and surely the most feared of all the species is the dreaded vampire bat. ²Vampires live up to their horror-story reputation as greedy and efficient stealers of blood.

³Depending upon its type, the vampire bat may prefer to dine on the blood of mammals (including humans) or birds. ⁴The bat begins its meal by circling above its usually sleeping target for several minutes, probably to allow heat-sensitive patches on its face to determine where best to bite. ⁵It then inflicts a small wound with its teeth, which are so razor-sharp as to make the incision virtually painless. ⁶The wound bleeds freely as long as the bat continues feeding, thanks to a substance in the bat's saliva that prevents clotting. ⁷As many as half a dozen of the bat's fellows may join it to feed from one wound.

⁸Vampire bats have such great appctitcs for blood that they may drink more than their own weight at one feeding, thus making it briefly impossible for them to fly. ⁹A single vampire drinks about twenty-five gallons of blood in its lifetime. ¹⁰Although vampire bats are sometimes responsible for the death of humans or animals, those deaths are not due to loss of blood. ¹¹Rather, the deaths are the result of rabies or other diseases spread by the bats.

1. In sentence 5, *incision* means
   a. heat-sensitive patch.
   b. cut.
   c. blood.
   d. saliva.

2. Sentences 10 and 11
   a. narrate events.
   b. define a term.
   c. compare two things.
   d. discuss a cause-effect relationship.

3. The main patterns of organization of the second paragraph are cause-effect and
   a. contrast.
   b. comparision.
   c. time order.
   d. definition and example.

(Continues on next page)

4. We can conclude that vampire bats use their heat-sensitive patches
   a. for personal temperature control.
   (b.) to find where blood is close to their victims' skin.
   c. to find sleeping victims.
   d. to find out which potential victims have the best blood.

5. The passage suggests that
   a. bats are usually solitary feeders.
   b. all vampire bats have rabies.
   c. vampire bats intend to kill their victims.
   (d.) vampire bats prefer victims that lie still.

6. The author's main purpose is to
   (a.) inform.
   b. persuade.
   c. entertain.
   d. predict.

7. On the whole, the tone of the passage is
   a. fearful.
   (b.) objective.
   c. disbelieving.
   d. playful.

8. Which is the most appropriate title for this passage?
   (a.) Vampire Bats' Feeding Habits
   b. Bats and Disease
   c. Bats in Social Groups
   d. How Bats Live

Comments: Item 1—*Incision* refers to the "wound" made by the bat's teech.

Item 2—Sentences 10 and 11 discuss the *reasons* people and animals sometimes die from the bite of vampire bats.

Item 4—Since the bat seeks blood, the heat-sensitive patch must help it find that blood.

Item 5—The passage says the bats' target is "usually sleeping."

Item 8—The passage is about only vampire bats, not all bats.

COMBINED SKILLS: Test 4

After reading the passage, circle the letter of the best answer to each question.

[1]The social psychologist Philip Zimbardo set out to test a theory that the anonymity of city life encourages crime. [2]He arranged to have automobiles abandoned in two different locations: New York City and Palo Alto, California, a medium-sized suburban community. [3]The cars' license plates were removed and their hoods were raised to signal that the autos were abandoned. [4]Then each car was secretly watched for sixty-four hours.

[5]The person assigned to watch the New York car did not have long to wait. [6]Within ten minutes the car received its first auto strippers—a father, mother, and eight-year-old son. [7]The mother appeared to be a lookout, while the son aided the father's search of the trunk, glove compartment, and motor. [8]He then handed his father the tools necessary to remove the battery and radiator. [9]Total time of destructive contact: seven minutes.

[10]This, however, was only the first "contact." [11]By the end of the sixty-four hours, the car had been vandalized twenty-four times, often by well-dressed, seemingly middle-class adults. [12]What remained when the experiment was over was a useless hunk of metal. [13]In contrast, the Palo Alto car was approached only once: when it started to rain, a passerby stopped to lower the hood.

[14]According to Zimbardo, the crucial factor in the different fates of the two cars was anonymity. [15]In a large city, where the chances of being recognized outside one's own neighborhood are extremely slim, even "upstanding citizens" can afford a temporary turn at thievery. [16]In a smaller community, on the other hand, the higher probability of being recognized and caught keeps people honest.

1. In sentence 14, *crucial* means
   a. least interesting.
   b. most important.
   c. most unlikely.
   d. most helpful.

2. According to the passage, Zimbardo's main purpose in doing the experiment was to
   a. illustrate a point.
   b. test a theory.
   c. catch thieves.
   d. teach honesty.

(Continues on next page)

3. The pattern of organization in sentences 5 through 9 is one of
   a. time order.
   b. list of items.
   c. comparison.
   d. contrast.

4. The relationship between sentences 15 and 16 is one of
   a. time.
   b. comparison.
   c. contrast.
   d. cause and effect.

5. Sentence 13 is a statement of
   a. fact.
   b. opinion.
   c. fact and opinion.

6. The passage suggests that
   a. people who vandalize cars always travel in groups.
   b. New Yorkers are more dishonest than people in most other big cities.
   c. social pressure promotes honesty.
   d. the car used in Palo Alto was probably in better condition than the car in New York City.

7. The tone of the passage can be described as mainly
   a. objective.
   b. doubtful.
   c. alarmed.
   d. scornful.

8. Which statement best states the main idea of the passage?
   a. Philip Zimbardo is a creative social psychologist.
   b. People are now more dishonest than ever.
   c. In big cities, ordinary people's chances of being recognized outside of their neighborhood are quite slim.
   d. Zimbardo's experiment suggests that the anonymity of city life encourages crime.

Comments: Item 2—See sentence 1.
           Item 6—See sentence 16.

COMBINED SKILLS: Test 5

After reading the passage, circle the letter of the best answer to each question.

¹We live in an era in which more women are entering formerly male-dominated professions, demanding equal pay for equal work, and generally rejecting the societal double standard which has held them back from reaching their full potential. ²Yet many women are still bound by old-fashioned and harmful ideas about sexuality. ³An epidemic of "date rapes" on college campuses is evidence that warped beliefs about sexuality are barriers that women—as well as men—need to break in order to achieve a full human partnership. ⁴As many as 25 percent of all college women may become victims of rape or attempted rape. ⁵Women at the beginning of their college careers are especially vulnerable to date rape. ⁶They may be living in coed dorms with men whom they assume they can trust. ⁷They are eager to appear cool, sophisticated, not paranoid or uptight. ⁸Most destructively of all, many women still subscribe at least subconsciously to the belief that they "owe" sexual favors to a man they date. ⁹After a sexual attack by a date, many women are racked with guilt rather than anger. ¹⁰Were they to blame, they ask themselves, because they drank too much? ¹¹Because they wore a short skirt? ¹²Similarly, men have grown up in a culture which suggests that once they have spent "good money" entertaining a date, they are owed sex in return.

1. In sentence 8, the words *subscribe . . . to* mean
   a. describe.
   b. agree with.
   c. ignore.
   d. argue with.

2. The relationship of sentence 2 to sentence 1 is one of
   a. addition.
   b. illustration.
   c. contrast.
   d. comparison.

3. The relationship of sentence 12 to sentences 9–11 is one of
   a. time.
   b. contrast.
   c. comparison.
   d. cause and effect.

(Continues on next page)

4. You can conclude that the author believes
   a. many men and women should change their attitudes about sexuality.
   b. attitudes about rights in the workplace have changed more than attitudes about sexuality.
   c. victims of date rape often feel responsible for having been attacked.
   (d.) all of the above.

5. The main purpose of this passage is to
   a. inform readers about interesting sexual attitudes.
   (b.) use facts to argue that sexual attitudes need improving.
   c. entertain readers with dramatic sexual images.
   d. predict the future of the American sex scene.

6. The author's tone can be described as
   a. sarcastic.
   b. optimistic.
   c. arrogant.
   (d.) concerned.

7. The point made in sentence 2 is best supported by
   a. sentence 1.
   b. sentence 4.
   (c.) sentence 8.
   d. sentence 12.

8. The main idea of the passage is that
   a. women are now close to reaching their full potential.
   (b.) societal attitudes toward sexuality are old-fashioned and harmful.
   c. colleges should provide better security in coed dorms.
   d. men's sexual attitudes are strongly in need of change.

Comments: Item 5—See sentences 2 and 3.

Item 7—The words "Most destructively of all . . . still subscribe . . . to the belief" in sentence 8 suggest that the belief is an old-fashioned and harmful one.

Item 8—See sentences 2 and 3.

COMBINED SKILLS: Test 6

After reading the passage, circle the letter of the best answer to each question.

¹The concept of adopting a child to raise as one's own is a relatively modern phenomenon. ²While there have always been instances of families taking in unrelated children to raise for a variety of reasons, most had more to do with helping the children of a dead or disabled relative or securing cheap labor than adding a new member to the family.

³A remarkable chapter in American history that began in 1853 helped to sow the seeds of modern adoption practices. ⁴The story began when Charles Loring Brace, a wealthy Connecticut man, visited New York City. ⁵He was appalled by the number of orphans and abandoned children he found living in the streets there. ⁶In response, Brace organized the Children's Aid Society, dedicated to finding loving homes for such children. ⁷Its method was to send trainloads of orphaned children into Western states, where community leaders would encourage friends and neighbors to adopt a child "to treat in every way as a member of the family."

⁸The Children's Aid Society was a remarkable success. ⁹By the time its program ended in 1929, "orphan trains" had carried almost 100,000 children to new homes. ¹⁰The orphans grew up to make solid contributions to their communities; many became respected farmers, while others went on to practice law or medicine. ¹¹One of the orphans became governor of North Dakota; another became governor of Alaska.

1. In sentence 5, the word *appalled* means
   a. annoyed.
   b. unmoved.
   c. excited.
   d. horrified.

2. The relationship between sentences 5 and 6 is one of
   a. cause and effect.
   b. addition.
   c. comparison.
   d. general idea and illustration.

3. Sentence 11 expresses
   a. fact.
   b. opinion.
   c. fact and opinion.

(Continues on next page)

4. The passage suggests that the success of the Children's Aid Society was due in part to
   a. the attractiveness of the children.
   (b.) the participation of leaders in the communities that the trains went through.
   c. the national reputation of Charles Loring Brace.
   d. none of the above.

5. The author's main purpose in writing this selection is to
   a. predict future adoption practices.
   (b.) inform readers about a significant chapter in American history.
   c. persuade readers to consider adopting orphans or abandoned children.
   d. entertain readers with stories of the "orphan train."

6. The author's tone in this passage is largely
   (a.) approving.
   b. critical.
   c. regretful.
   d. pessimistic.

7. The main idea of the third paragraph is stated in
   (a.) sentence 8.
   b. sentence 9.
   c. sentence 10.
   d. sentence 11.

8. Which sentence best states the main idea of the selection?
   a. Charles Loring Brace was appalled by the number of orphans and abandoned children he found living in the streets of New York City.
   b. Individuals can make a great impact on society, for both good and bad.
   (c.) Modern adoption practices began with the successful Children's Aid Society's orphan-trains program.
   d. The orphans placed by the Children's Aid Society made numerous worthwhile contributions to their communities.

Comments: Item 2—The *cause:* The horror of all the orphans and abandoned children living in the streets. The *effect:* Brace founded the Children's Aid Society.

Item 4—See sentence 7.

Item 6—See sentences 3, 8, and 10.

Item 8—Answers *a* and *d* are too narrow. Answer *b* is too broad.

COMBINED SKILLS: Test 7

After reading the passage, circle the letter of the best answer to each question.

[1]Perception is strongly influenced by attention. [2]Unfortunately, if you daydream during a lecture, little or nothing will reach your brain. [3]Attending is not always easy, so so you take notes and make conscious efforts to remain alert. [4]Did you notice an error in the previous sentence? [5]You probably were concentrating on the content and although your eyes saw the word *so* repeated, you ignored it. [6]Similarly, you were probably not focusing any attention on your thumb until you read this sentence. [7]You simply cannot attend to every stimulus around you, so only certain things are selected. [8]Have you ever driven down a highway with your gas needle nearing "empty"? [9]Chances are you become preoccupied with the location of gas stations. [10]Another day when your tank was full but your stomach was empty, the gas stations might have been overlooked, but every diner and restaurant would have caught your eye. [11]Attention is usually focused on needed things. [12]If you are hungry or thirsty right now, you might have a problem keeping your attention focused on the reading rather than on the refrigerator.

1. As used in sentence 3, the word *attending* means
   a. showing up.
   b. paying attention.
   c. taking care.
   d. waiting.

2. In sentence 9, the words *preoccupied with* mean
   a. fully interested in.
   b. forgetful about.
   c. expert in.
   d. confident about.

3. According to the author, we usually concentrate on
   a. what we are expected to pay attention to.
   b. random things.
   c. daydreaming.
   d. needed things.

4. The relationship between sentences 5 and 6 is one of
   a. time.
   b. contrast.
   c. comparison.
   d. general point and example.

(Continues on next page)

5. Sentence 12 discusses a
   a. series of events.
   b. contrast.
   c. comparison.
   (d.) cause and effect.

6. You might conclude from the paragraph that it would be a good idea to
   a. forget about taking notes in classes.
   (b.) avoid being hungry when you go to your classes.
   c. take a difficult class just before lunchtime.
   d. eat less.

7. What is the best title for this selection?
   a. Daydreaming
   b. Perception
   (c.) The Relationship Between Perception and Attention
   d. How Hunger Influences Attention

8. Which statement best expresses the main idea of the paragraph?
   a. You are unlikely to notice an error in writing if you are concentrating on its content.
   b. If you are hungry, you will focus on eating.
   c. Unfortunately, when students daydream during lectures, nothing will reach their brains.
   (d.) Perception is strongly influenced by attention, which is usually focused on needed things.

Comments: Item 3—See sentence 11.

Item 5—The *cause:* being hungry or thirsty; the possible *effect:* thinking about the refrigerator.

Item 7—Answers *a* and *d* are too narrow; answer *b* is too broad—the selection is about the relationship between perception and attention.

Item 8—Answers *a*, *b*, and *c* are too narrow.

COMBINED SKILLS: Test 8

After reading the passage, circle the letter of the best answer to each question.

^{1}In 1948, during the re-election campaign of Senator Claude Pepper of Florida, large numbers of leaflets with an unsigned message were circulated throughout the state just before election day. ^{2}The message was as follows:

^{3}Are you aware that Claude Pepper is known all over Washington as a shameless extrovert? ^{4}Not only that, but this man is reliably reported to practice nepotism with his sister-in-law, and he has a sister who was a thespian in wicked New York City. ^{5}Worst of all, it is an established fact that Mr. Pepper, before his marriage, habitually practiced celibacy.

^{6}In a literal sense, the statements were not false. ^{7}However, the words *extrovert* (a person who is active and expressive), *nepotism* (favoritism to relatives), *thespian* (an actor or actress) and *celibacy* (not being sexually active) were used in contexts that seemed threatening to people who did not know the meanings of these uncommon words.

^{8}A very clever and dishonest writer had purposely selected words that gave the impression that Senator Pepper was a very immoral person. ^{9}The effect was very damaging. ^{10}Senator Pepper was defeated at the polls by George Smathers, who denied that he was involved in this political "dirty trick." ^{11}However, the damage could not be undone.

1. In sentence 6, *literal* means
   a. based on imagination.
   b. marital.
   c. not understood.
   d. according to actual meanings of words.

2. The relationship of sentence 7 to sentence 6 is one of
   a. addition.
   b. cause and effect.
   c. comparison.
   d. contrast.

3. The pattern of organization of sentences 3 through 5 is
   a. time order.
   b. list of items.
   c. comparison-contrast.
   d. cause and effect.

(Continues on next page)

4. The passage
   a. defines and illustrates the term "dirty trick."
   b. lists a series of dirty tricks.
   c. compares and contrasts dirty tricks.
   (d.) explains a dirty trick and its effect.

5. The passage implies that Senator Pepper
   a. probably did not deserve to be elected.
   b. was in reality a very shy person who never practiced celibacy.
   (c.) may have lost the election because of a "dirty trick."
   d. had been an excellent senator.

6. You could conclude from the passage that
   (a.) the writer of the leaftlet assumed many readers would not know some uncommon words.
   b. Claude Pepper never showed favoritism to his sister-in-law nor had a sister who was an actress.
   c. the writer of the leaflet did not understand the psychology of the average voter.
   d. George Smathers was defeated in his next election.

7. The author of this passage would probably agree with which of the following statements?
   a. Honest political campaigns don't succeed.
   b. Political tricks have ruined Florida's politics.
   c. Senator Pepper should not have been a candidate for senator.
   (d.) When the truth is told deceitfully, it can do as much damage as a lie.

8. Which of the following statements best expresses the main idea of the passage?
   a. Dishonesty is a major problem in Florida's political campaigns.
   b. Florida's citizens are easily fooled.
   (c.) A "dirty trick" that twisted the truth affected the outcome of a political campaign.
   d. Claude Pepper should have run a better senatorial campaign.

Comments: Item 3—The sentences list accusations.

Item 5—See sentences 10 and 11.

Item 6—b. Since the leaflets made no truly outrageous accusations against Pepper, we have no reason to doubt their truth.
   c. Since Pepper was defeated, the leaflet writer's judgment was apparently proved correct.
   d. The passage gives no hints about Smathers's next election.

COMBINED SKILLS: Test 9

After reading the passage, circle the letter of the best answer to each question.

¹Mary was watching a mystery on television. ²The end of the movie was near, and she was totally engrossed. ³Then her baby started crying. ⁴She shouted at him to shut up. ⁵His response was intensified crying. ⁶Mary got angry and shook him. ⁷The baby cried even louder. ⁸In the meanwhile, the mystery's conclusion took place, and Mary missed it. ⁹Angrily, she slapped her son's face. ¹⁰In this situation, someone was pursuing a goal—seeing the end of a suspenseful television show. ¹¹But something happened to block the achievement of that goal. ¹²The person thus became frustrated, anger built up, and direct aggression occurred.

¹³Aggression is not always aimed at the original frustrator. ¹⁴For example, consider a businessman who had a hard day at the office. ¹⁵He was about to close a deal with a client when his boss clumsily interfered and lost the sale. ¹⁶On the way home in his car, the frustrated businessman blew his horn angrily at a car ahead when it didn't immediately pull away from a stoplight. ¹⁷As he entered his home, his dog jumped up on him, only to receive a quick kick. ¹⁸He then shouted at his wife during supper. ¹⁹All these aggressive behaviors are examples of displaced aggression. ²⁰Aggression against the person who caused the original frustration can often be harmful. ²¹In this case, assaulting or swearing at the boss could cost the businessman his job. ²²When the original frustrator has status and power over the frustrated person, aggression may be displaced onto a less threatening target, who may have nothing at all to do with the original frustration.

1. In sentence 2, the word *engrossed* means
   a. involved.
   b. disgusted.
   c. disappointed.
   d. bored.

2. The topic of the first paragraph is
   a. parent-child relationships.
   b. direct aggression.
   c. displaced aggression.
   d. suspense.

3. Aggression is more likely to be displaced if the original frustrator
   a. is a family member.
   b. has power over the frustrated person.
   c. is angry at the frustrated person.
   d. is unfair to the frustrated person.

(Continues on next page)

4. The relationship between sentences 11 and 12 is one of
   a definition and example.
   b. comparison.
   c. contrast.
   (d.) cause and effect.

5. The organizational pattern of each paragraph is
   a. a series of steps in a process.
   b. a contrast of events.
   (c.) illustration and explanation of a general concept.
   d. a comparison of two or more events.

6. The writer's main purpose in writing this selection is to
   a. predict how aggression influences relationships.
   (b.) inform readers about two types of aggression.
   c. persuade readers to be careful not to take out their aggression on the wrong people.
   d. entertain readers with dramatic anecdotes about aggressive behavior.

7. What is the best title for the selection?
   a. Family Relationships
   b. The Causes of Aggression
   (c.) Direct and Displaced Aggression
   d. Displaced Aggression

8. Which sentence best states the main idea of the selection?
   a. A great deal of frustration is aimed against family members.
   (b.) When frustration and anger build up, direct or displaced aggression may occur.
   c. Sometimes a frustrator may have a great deal more power or status than the person who is frustrated.
   d. Direct aggression is more satisfying than indirect aggression.

Comments: Item 2—See sentence 12.
Item 3—See sentence 22.
Item 6—The first paragraph explains and illustrates direct aggression; the second paragraph explains and illustrates displaced aggression.
Item 7—a. Family is mentioned only to illustrate the cause and types of aggression.
      b. The passage discusses both the cause of aggression and types of aggression.
      d. Too narrow; the passage discusses two types of aggression.

COMBINED SKILLS: Test 10

After reading the passage, circle the letter of the best answer to each question.

¹It would be a mistake to assume that primitive societies are mentally backward—unable to benefit from their environment or understand how to cope effectively with it. ²Given the general level of technology available, they do adapt to and manipulate their environment in a sophisticated and understanding manner. ³Countless examples can be cited to illustrate this point. ⁴Among some Eskimo groups, wolves are a menace—a dangerous environmental feature that must be dealt with. ⁵They could perhaps be hunted down and killed, but this involves danger as well as considerable expenditure in time and energy. ⁶So a simple yet clever device is employed. ⁷A sharp sliver of bone is curled into a springlike shape, and seal blubber is molded around it and permitted to freeze. ⁸This is then placed where it can be discovered by a hungry wolf, which, living up to its reputation, "wolfs it down." ⁹Later, as this "time bomb" is digested and the blubber disappears, the bone uncurls and its sharp ends pierce the stomach of the wolf, causing internal bleeding and death. ¹⁰This method, though harsh, is undeniably practical. ¹¹It is a simple yet fairly safe technique that involves an understanding of the environment as well as wolf psychology and habits.

1. As used in sentence 6, the word *employed* means
   a. hired.
   b. recognized.
   c. used.
   d. known.

2. The relationship between the two parts of sentence 5 is one of
   a. time.
   b. comparison.
   c. contrast.
   d. addition.

3. The author implies that among primitive societies, the Eskimos' cleverness is
   a. superior.
   b. typical.
   c. rare.
   d. inferior.

(Continues on next page)

4. The author implies that certain societies are considered "primitive" because of their
   a. attitude toward animals.
   b. level of technology.
   c. creative ability.
   d. understanding of their environment.

5. The author's attitude toward the Eskimos who created the weapon appears to be
   a. accusing.
   b. disgusted.
   c. objective.
   d. puzzled.

6. Which is an appropriate title for this selection?
   a. Mentally Backward Societies
   b. Dangerous Environmental Features
   c. Intelligence in Primitive Societies
   d. Land of the Eskimos

7. Which sentence best expresses the main idea of the passage?
   a. There are no greater challenges to a society than that of controlling the environment.
   b. Eskimos are able to control wolves.
   c. With increased technology, primitive societies should be able to cope even more effectively with their environment.
   d. Primitive societies can deal shrewdly and effectively with the demands of their environment.

8. The author supports the main idea with a
   a. list of several reasons.
   b. comparison of two things.
   c. contrast between two things.
   d. detailed example.

Comments: Item 3—The Eskimos' cleverness is used as an example of the point made in sentence 2.
Item 4—See sentences 1, 2, 10, and 11.
Item 7—a. Incorrect.
         b. Too narrow.
         c. Beside the point.

COMBINED SKILLS: Test 11

After reading the passage, circle the letter of the best answer to each question.

¹The Hawthorne experiment was conducted in the late 1920s and early 1930s. ²The management of Western Electric's Hawthorne plant, located near Chicago, wanted to find out if environmental factors, such as lighting, could affect workers' productivity and morale. ³A team of social scientists experimented with a small group of employees who were set apart from their coworkers. ⁴The environmental conditions of this group's work area were controlled, and the subjects themselves were closely observed. ⁵To the great surprise of the researchers, the productivity of these workers increased in response to any change in their environmental conditions. ⁶The rate of work increased even when the changes (such as as sharp decrease in the level of light in the workplace) seemed unlikely to have such an effect.

⁷It was concluded that the presence of the observers had caused the workers in the experimental group to feel special. ⁸As a result, the employees came to know and trust one another, and they developed a strong belief in the importance of their job. ⁹The researchers believed that this, not the changes in the work environment, accounted for the increased productivity.

¹⁰A later reanalysis of the study data challenged the Hawthorne conclusions on the grounds that the changes in patterns of human relations, considered so important by the original researchers, were never measured. ¹¹However, even if the original conclusions must be revised, they nonetheless raise a problem for social scientists: Research subjects who know they are being studied can change their behavior. ¹²Throughout the social sciences, this phenomenon has come to be called the Hawthorne effect.

1. In sentences 2 and 5, the word *productivity* means
   a. attendance.
   b. human relations.
   c. rate of work.
   d. health.

   "Rate of work" is used in sentence 6 as a "synonym" of productivity.

2. The pattern of organization of the second paragraph is
   a. list of items.
   b. time order.
   c. definition and example.
   d. cause and effect.

(Continues on next page)

3. The author implies that a sharp decrease in light increased workers' output because the workers
   a. experienced less eyestrain.   See paragraph 2.
   b. had to pay more attention to what they were doing.
   c. knew they were being observed, and this motivated them.
   d. in the experiment were paid more than other workers.

4. Employers might conclude from the Hawthorne experiment that they should
   a. keep plant lighting low.
   b. constantly change environmental conditions.   See paragraph 2.
   c. consistently let workers know that their work is important.
   d. keep social scientists away from their workers.

5. The Hawthorne experiment suggests that
   a. workers' attitudes are more important than their environment.
   b. social scientists are good workers.
   c. productivity in electric plants tends to be low.
   d. even those Hawthorne workers who were not in the experiment improved their productivity.

6. The Hawthorne effect is a problem for social scientists because
   a. the researchers did not measure the changes in human relations among workers.
   b. the results of a study will be questionable if the subjects were aware that they were being observed.
   c. the Hawthorne research was done too long ago, when working conditions were quite different.
   d. the group of employees who were studied was small.

7. The author's main purpose is to
   a. explain the Hawthorne effect.
   b. prove the importance of research.
   c. amuse with a surprising experiment.
   d. suggest ideas for future research.

8. Which sentence best expresses the main idea of the passage?
   a. The famous Hawthorne experiment took place in the late 1920s and early 1930s.
   b. The Hawthorne experiment took place because the management of an electric plant wanted to find out the impact of environmental factors on workers.
   c. An experiment revealed the fact, known as the Hawthorne effect, that research subjects may behave differently if they know they are being studied.
   d. A reanalysis of data from an experiment at an electric plant showed that the researchers were careless about how they conducted their study.

COMBINED SKILLS: Test 12

After reading the passage, circle the letter of the best answer to each question.

¹We all know deserts are dry places, but just what is meant by the term *dry*? ²That is, how much rain defines the boundary between humid and dry regions? ³Sometimes it is defined by a single rainfall figure, for example, twenty-five centimeters (ten inches) of precipitation per year. ⁴(*Rainfall* refers to the quantity of water that falls in the form of rain, snow, etc. in an area in a given amount of time.) ⁵However, the concept of dryness is a relative one that refers to any situation in which a water deficiency exists. ⁶Thus, climatologists define *dry climate* as one in which yearly precipitation is less than the potential loss of water by evaporation. ⁷Dryness then is related not only to total annual rainfall but also to evaporation. ⁸Evaporation, in turn, greatly depends upon temperature. ⁹As temperatures climb, potential evaporation also increases. ¹⁰Fifteen to twenty-five centimeters of precipitation can support forests in northern Scandinavia, where evaporation into the cool, humid air is slight and a surplus of water remains in the soil. ¹¹However, the same amount of rain falling on New Mexico supports only a sparse vegetative cover because evaporation into the hot, dry air is great. ¹²So clearly no specific amount of precipitation can serve as a universal boundary for dry climates.

1. In sentence 3, the word *precipitation* means
   a. weather conditions.
   b. humidity in the air.
   c. water that falls to the earth in any form.
   d. dry places.

2. Scientists who study weather consider a dry climate to be one in which
   a. ten inches of water fall each year.
   b. potential evaporation is greater than the rainfall.
   c. there is no rainfall at all.
   d. it gets very hot.

3. The higher the temperature,
   a. the greater the rainfall.
   b. the smaller the rainfall.
   c. the greater the potential evaporation.
   d. the smaller the potential evaporation.

4. In the discussion in the passage, temperature is
   a. a cause.
   b. an effect.

(Continues on next page)

5. The relationship between sentences 10 and 11 is one of
   a. time.
   b. comparison.
   (c.) contrast.
   d. cause and effect.

6. The main purpose of the passage is to
   (a.) explain.
   b. persuade.
   c. amuse.
   d. predict.

7. The author implies that one reason evaporation in northern Scandinavian forests is slight is that
   a. the rainfall is low there.
   b. there is no rainfall there.
   (c.) the air there is cool.
   d. a heavy ground cover prevents the moisure from evaporating.

8. Which sentence best expresses the main idea of the selection?
   a. The lower the temperature, the less the evaporation.
   (b.) A dry climate is one in which the rainfall is less than the potential evaporation, which depends on temperature.
   c. Evaporation in a northern forest is slight in comparison with the evaporation in a desert region like that of New Mexico.
   d. *Rainfall* is the amount of water that falls to earth as rain, snow, sleet, and hail.

Comments: Item 1—Sentence 4 suggests the meaning of "precipitation" as used in sentence 3.
           Item 2—See sentence 6.
           Item 3—See sentence 9.
           Item 7—See sentence 10.
           Item 8—a. Too narrow.
                 b. The first sentence suggests the point of the paragraph.
                 c. Too narrow.
                 d. Too narrow.

3
Propaganda

What do you think is the main difference between the following two evaluations of a city?

> The weather isn't bad in Philadelphia, if you don't mind a few months of winter. And the city has wonderful museums and restaurants. But the streets are often dirty there, and state and city taxes keep going up.

> Philadelphia is the place to live! Once you experience its pleasant climate, its museums, and restaurants, you'll agree with Phillies baseball star Ken Greyson when he says, "Home base for me is Philadelphia. Living here is a ball!"

Did you notice that the first evaluation is an attempt to be objective about Philadelphia? It mentions both positive and negative points so the reader will get a balanced picture of the city. The second approach, however, includes only positive points. It was not meant to provide a balanced, objective view of the city. Instead, it was designed to influence people to come and live in Philadelphia. When such biased information is methodically spread in order to promote or oppose a cause—whether the cause is a city, a political view, a product, or an organization—it is **propaganda**.

PROPAGANDA TECHNIQUES

Propaganda may use one or more common techniques for convincing people by appealing to their emotions. Recognizing these techniques will help you separate the substance of a message (if there is any) from its purely emotional appeal. If you are not aware of the propaganda devices, you may make decisions as a result of emotional manipulation. This chapter will introduce you to seven of the more common propaganda techniques:

- Bandwagon
- Testimonial

- Transfer
- Plain Folks
- Name Calling
- Glittering Generalities
- Card Stacking

Once you have learned these techniques, you will recognize one or more of them in just about every advertisement you encounter. Although many of the examples in this chapter and its tests are made up, they were inspired by real ads.

1 Bandwagon

Old-fashioned parades were usually led by a large wagon carrying a brass band. Therefore, to "jump on the bandwagon" means to join a parade, or to do what many others are doing. For example, we are often told to buy a product or vote for a political candidate because, in effect, "everybody else is doing it." An ad for a cereal may claim that "Sugar-O's Is Everybody's Favorite Breakfast." A political commercial may show people from all walks of life saying they will vote for candidate Fred Foghorn. The ads imply that if you don't jump on the bandwagon, the parade will pass you by.

Here are two examples of real TV ads that have used the **bandwagon** appeal:

> With appealing music in the background, flashing scenes show many people wearing the sponsor's jeans.

> On a beautiful day, almost everyone on the beach leaves in a hurry in order to attend the sponsor's sale.

➤ *Practice 1*

Circle the numbers of the two descriptions of ads that use the bandwagon appeal.

1. Famous actress Margo Lane explains that she loves to use a certain hair coloring.

2. Most of the people in a crowd at the ball game are drinking the sponsor's cola beverage.

3. A beautiful woman in a slinky red dress is shown driving the sponsor's car.

4. The tune of "God Bless America" is being played in the background as an announcer asks viewers to support the home baseball team by coming out to games.

5. An ad for a new movie shows people waiting to buy tickets in a line that extends halfway around the block.

2   Testimonial

Famous athletes often appear on television as spokespersons for all sorts of products, from soft drinks to automobiles. Movie and TV stars make commercials endorsing products and political issues. The idea behind this approach is that the testimony of famous people influences the television viewers who admire these people.

What consumers must remember is that famous people get paid to endorse products. In addition, these people are not necessarily experts about the products, or the political issues, they promote. This does not in itself mean that what they say is untrue. But realizing that celebrities receive money to recommend products that they may know little about should help consumers think twice about such messages.

Here are two examples of real ads that have used the appeal of **testimonials**:

A famous actor promotes a product intended to help people quit smoking.

A popular TV hostess and singer is the spokesperson for a cruise line.

➤ *Practice 2*

Circle the numbers of the two descriptions of ads that use a testimonial.

1. Numerous people crowd around the department store door, waiting for the store to open.

2. Famous actress Margo Lane explains that she loves to use a certain hair coloring.

3. A grandmother, serving a canned vegetable soup to her grandson, says, "This has all the simple, healthy, and delicious ingredients I use in my own vegetable soup."

4. A sports star praises the brand of basketball sneakers he is putting on.

5. An ad says, "We've got plenty of style and color at Sunny Styles, so come see how our fashions can bring out the rainbow in you."

3   Transfer

Ads that use the transfer technique associate a product with a symbol or image that people admire or love. The advertiser hopes that people's positive feelings for the symbol or image will transfer to the product. For example, calling an automobile "The All-American Car" appeals to would-be buyers' patriotism; the "All-American" image calls to mind all that is best in America. Or consider a real-life ad in which several nuns are surprised and impressed that the fresh-brewed coffee they think they are drinking is actually Folger's instant coffee. The qualities people associate with nuns—seeing them as honest, trustworthy, and highly selective in their worldly pleasures—are then associated with the product as well.

There is also a good deal of transfer value in good looks. Consumers **transfer** the positive feelings they have toward a sexy-looking person to the product being advertised. Many ads today use handsome men and beautiful women to pitch their products; more than ever, Madison Avenue seems convinced that "sex sells."

To summarize, the transfer technique depends upon the appeal value of two special categories:

1) admired or beloved symbols and images
2) sex appeal

Here are two examples from real ads that have used transfer:

An American eagle symbolizes the United States Post Office's Express Mail service.

A tanned blonde in a bikini is stretched out on the beach, holding in her hand a can of light beer.

➤ *Practice 3*

Circle the numbers of the two descriptions of ads that use the transfer approach.

1. An announcer claims that a competitor's tires don't last as long as the sponsor's tires do.

2. With the tune of "God Bless America" in the background, an announcer asks viewers to support the home baseball team by coming out to games.

3. A beautiful woman in a slinky red dress is shown driving the sponsor's car.

4. Several ordinary, friendly-looking young men in jeans buy the sponsor's beer.

5. "My opponent hasn't made up his mind about state taxes," says a candidate for mayor. "Obviously, he's too wishy-washy to be mayor."

4   Plain Folks

Some people distrust political candidates who are rich or well-educated. They feel that these candidates, if elected, will not be able to understand the problems of the average working person. Therefore, candidates often try to show they are just "plain folks" by referring in their speeches to how poor they were when they were growing up or how they had to work their way through school. They also pose for photographs wearing overalls or buying a hot dog from a curbside stand.

Likewise, the presidents of some companies appear in their own ads, trying to show that their giant enterprises are just family businesses. If a corporation can convince potential customers that it is run by people just like them, the customers are more likely to buy the corporation's product than if they felt the company was run by ruthless millionaire executives. In other words, people using the **plain-folks** approach tell their audience, "We are ordinary folks, just like you."

Yet another plain-folks approach is for a company to show us a product being used and enjoyed by everyday types of people—persons just like ourselves. (In contrast, the propaganda technique of testimonial features famous people. Also, while plain-folks ads feature individuals, bandwagon ads emphasize large numbers of people.)

Here are two examples of real ads that have used the appeal of plain folks:

> A president of a fast-food hamburger chain, dressed in shirtsleeves, carries a food tray to a small table in one of his restaurants, all the while pitching his burgers to the viewer.

> Average-looking American kids are shown at home trying and enjoying a cereal.

➣ *Practice 4*

Circle the numbers of the two descriptions of ads that use the plain-folks approach.

1. Two ordinary, friendly looking young men in jeans buy the sponsor's beer.

2. A famous baseball player wears the sponsor's jeans.

3. After seeing a play, a man leaves a theater with a big smile on his face. Then his chauffeur pulls up in a Cadillac to take him home.

4. "Drink our soda," says the announcer. "It's the real thing."

5. A grandmother, serving a canned vegetable soup to her grandson, says, "This has all the simple, healthy, and delicious ingredients I use in my own vegetable soup."

5 Name Calling

Name calling is the use of emotionally loaded language or negative comments to turn people against a rival product, candidate, or movement. An example of name calling would be a political candidate's labeling an opponent "uncaring," "radical," or "wimpy." Or a manufacturer may say or imply that a competing product is "full of chemicals," even though in reality everything is made up of chemicals of one kind or another.

Here are two examples of name calling taken from real life:

> In the early days of the "cold war" with the Soviet Union, in the 1950s, an exaggerated concern about communism in this country led to charges of un-Americanism against many people.

> A fast-food chain accused a competitor of selling a seaweed burger simply because the competitor used a seaweed extract to keep its burger moist.

➤ Practice 5

Circle the numbers of the two descriptions of ads that use name calling.

1. "Drink our soda," says the announcer. "It's the real thing."

2. "Brand X's spaghetti sauce tastes like the sauce that Mom used to make," says a man to his wife. "And you know what a lousy cook she was." Then he suggests trying the sponsor's brand.

3. An ad says, "We've got plenty of style and color at Sunny Styles, so come see how our fashions can bring out the rainbow in you."

4. "My opponent has lived in our state for only two years," says a candidate for state senator. "Let's not put an outsider into state office."

5. An ad for cigarettes shows a beautiful woman in a strapless gown smoking the sponsor's product and being admired by several handsome men.

6   Glittering Generalities

A **glittering generality** is an important-sounding but unspecific claim about some product, candidate, or cause. It cannot be proved true or false because no evidence is offered to support the claim. Such claims use general words that different people would define differently, such as "progress," "great," and "ultimate."

"Simply the best," an ad might say about a certain television set. But no specific evidence of any kind is offered to support such a generality. "Janet Mayer Has the Right Stuff! Vote for Mayer for Congress," a campaign slogan might claim. But what seems like "the right stuff" to her campaign manager might seem very wrong to you. The point is that the phrase sounds good but says nothing definite.

Here are two examples from real ads that use glittering generalities:

> A car ad claims, "It just feels right."

> A canned-food ad boasts of "nutrition that works."

➤ *Practice 6*

Circle the numbers of the two descriptions of ads that use glittering generalities.

1. "For a forward-looking government," says the announcer, "vote for Ed Dalton for governor."

2. A well-known astronaut says that he uses the sponsor's aspirin.

3. "Millions of satisfied customers can't all be wrong," says the announcer of an ad for grass seed.

4. "My opponent attends Alcoholics Anonymous meetings," says a candidate for city council. "Do you want him to represent you on the council?"

5. An ad says, "We've got plenty of style and color at Sunny Styles, so come see how our fashions can bring out the rainbow in you."

7   Card Stacking

Card stacking refers to stacking the cards in your favor and presenting only the facts and figures that are favorable to your particular side of the issue. It could also be called the "too-good-to-be-true technique" or the "omitted details technique."

In legal language, deliberately leaving out inconvenient facts is called "concealing evidence." In advertising, such evidence may be concealed in the interests of selling a product. For example, past advertisements for the drug Tylenol called it "the pain reliever hospitals use most," and this statement was perfectly true. What these advertisements failed to mention is that the manufacturer of Tylenol offered hospitals large discounts. Since other drug companies may not have offered similar discounts in the past, most hospital administrators chose to buy Tylenol. The advertising campaign depended on people's jumping to the conclusion, "Hospitals use more Tylenol than any other pain reliever. They must consider it the best drug of its kind available." In fact, other drugs with the same pain reliever as Tylenol might have worked just as well.

Read the following ad and then the list of omitted details below it. Then circle the letter of the missing detail you think the advertiser deliberately left out of its ad.

For only forty dollars, Credit Information Services will provide a copy of your credit report. Haven't you been wondering what information a potential lender gets when you apply for a loan? Now you will have all the information you desire for a single low yearly fee.

Missing details:
a. Each additional use of this service will cost only thirty-five dollars.
b. Credit Information Services already has 300,000 customers nationwide.
c. Federal law gives you the right to find out what is in your credit report—without charge.

If you chose *c*, you are right. If you know this detail, you are not likely to send forty dollars to Credit Information Services.

➤ *Practice 7*

Which missing details does the reader need to know in order to avoid being tricked? Circle the letter of the important detail that has been purposely omitted from each paragraph.

1. Not only is our new fruit punch delicious, but bottle for bottle, it costs less than the leading brand.
    a. The punch comes in assorted flavors.
    b. The punch is in a 6-ounce bottle; the leading brand is in an 8-ounce bottle.
    c. The punch includes a mixture of more fruit juices than the leading brand.

2. If your request for a loan has been turned down by your local bank, don't worry—no matter what your credit rating is like, we will lend you money.
    a. The lending company charges a far higher interest rate than banks.
    b. You can reach the lending company by calling a toll-free number.
    c. The lending company has been in business since 1976.

3. Congratulations! You have just won an all-expenses-paid three-night vacation to Atlantic City, New Jersey. You will dine at glamorous restaurants, enjoy stage shows, and swim in the beautiful Atlantic Ocean—all free. This free trip has been awarded to only a handful of selected winners in your area.
    a. The certificate for your free trip will arrive by registered mail within two weeks of your acceptance of this offer.
    b. You may stay at your choice of two casino hotels: Trump's Castle or Resorts International.
    c. You must pay $399 to join a travel club before you become eligible for your free trip.

➤ *Review Test 1*

To review what you've learned in this chapter, complete each of the following sentences about propaganda.

1. Propaganda is intended to *(inform, persuade)* _____ *persuade* _____ .

2. An important difference between a testimonial and a plain-folks appeal is that testimonials feature *(famous, ordinary)* _____ *famous* _____ people.

3. The *(transfer, plain-folks)* _____*transfer*_____ technique associates a product with symbols and images that people respect.

4. *(Glittering generalities, Card stacking)* _____*Glittering generalities*_____ is the technique of making dramatic but unspecific and unsupported claims.

5. The "omitted details technique" would be an appropriate alternative name for *(card stacking, transfer)* _____*Card stacking*_____.

➤ Review Test 2

In each pair of sentences below, the first sentence does **not** illustrate a propaganda technique, but the second one does. On the line, write the letter of the propaganda technique used in the **second** sentence.

___d___ 1. • Kiddy Kare is the largest day-care center in town.

 • Our competitor's day-care center is more concerned about profits than children.

  a. Bandwagon   c. Testimonial
  b. Transfer   d. Name calling

___a___ 2. • Sureguard sunglasses filter out harmful ultraviolet rays.

 • "I'm proud to wear Sureguard sunglasses," says actress Judy Winsor. "You'll love them too."

  a. Testimonial   c. Plain folks
  b. Transfer   d. Name calling

___a___ 3. • In a recent election poll, Margo Levy was ahead of the other candidate.

 • Add your vote to the landslide victory Margo Levy will win in next week's election.

  a. Bandwagon   c. Transfer
  b. Testimonial   d. Name calling

___d___ 4. • Twin Oaks is a residential development near Des Moines, Iowa.

 • There's nothing else quite like Twin Oaks, a great residential community where you will be proud to live.

  a. Bandwagon   c. Transfer
  b. Testimonial   d. Glittering generalities

_c_   5. • As a young man, candidate Alan Wilson had a variety of jobs working in a department store and in his family's TV station.

• As a young man, candidate Alan Wilson learned what it means to work hard by spending long hours lifting boxes and sweeping floors.

    a. Name calling   c. Plain folks
    b. Bandwagon   d. Glittering generalities

_c_   6. • A college degree opens up job doors.

• Comedian Bill Groff says, "A college degree opens up job doors."

    a. Glittering generalities   c. Testimonial
    b. Plain folks   d. Name calling

_b_   7. • I'm voting for Jones because he has had ten years of experience on the Senate's Committee on International Affairs.

• I'll bet my French poodle and German shepherd know more about foreign affairs than Smith does. My vote goes to Jones.

    a. Bandwagon   c. Transfer
    b. Name calling   d. Glittering generalities

_d_   8. • Markey's Used Cars will be open on the Fourth of July.

• A patriotic march plays, and a giant American flag waves over a used car lot. "Celebrate your freedom of choice on the Fourth of July!" says the announcer. "At Markey's, we'll honor the holiday by making some star-spangled deals."

    a. Testimonial   c. Bandwagon
    b. Name calling   d. Transfer

_a_   9. • The presidential candidate supports our country's farmers.

• The presidential candidate has her own small farm, so she knows the farmers' concerns.

    a. Plain folks   c. Glittering generalities
    b. Testimonial   d. Transfer

_a_ 10. • At Triple A Technical School, you can learn skills needed to become a plumber, mechanic, or electrician.

• Set the world on fire with skills you learn at Triple A Technical School!

    a. Glittering generalities   c. Bandwagon
    b. Name calling   d. Transfer

➤ *Review Test 3*

A. Each of the passages below illustrates a particular propaganda technique. On the line next to the passage, write the letter of the technique being used.

___b___ 1. The most beautiful hair this season has shape, style, and a luxuriant, natural feel. Leslie Langtree, the television actress whose lovely hair is her trademark, reveals that her secret is Flirt. "Flirt softens my hair and gives it great body," Leslie says. "Thanks to Flirt, my hair has never looked better."

a. Plain folks   c. Name calling
b. Testimonial   d. Bandwagon

___d___ 2. They say, "When life gives you lemons, make lemonade." But at Ace Autos, we say that if you paid $11,000 for a lemon at Wheelers' Car Dealers, you should demand your money back and come see us.

a. Glittering generalities   c. Testimonial
b. Transfer   d. Name calling

___c___ 3. Liberty Bell Airlines flies anywhere in this great land, from sea to shining sea. We proudly hail America's finest: Liberty Bell.

a. Plain folks   c. Transfer
b. Testimonial   d. Name calling

___c___ 4. Monroe Archer is a millionaire and the president of a large corporation, yet he has never lost touch with his small-town roots. Despite his power and fame, he still likes returning to his hometown to enjoy a summer band concert and a simple supper at Charley's Diner.

a. Name calling   c. Plain folks
b. Bandwagon   d. Testimonial

___c___ 5. "I wear Form Fit jeans—if I wear anything at all," whispers a shapely model in tight jeans and low-cut T-shirt.

a. Bandwagon   c. Transfer
b. Name calling   d. Glittering generalities

___b___ 6. Come one! Come all! Everybody's going to Linwood Furniture for the big eighth annual sale, a sale so big we rented a tent to hold the crowds.

a. Name calling   c. Transfer
b. Bandwagon   d. Testimonial

_a_   7. Cast your vote next Tuesday for Larry Lewis. This fine man has much to offer his community and his nation. As your representative, he pledges to do his best to improve conditions and to bring you closer to the fulfillment of your highest dreams.

    a. Glittering generalities   c. Bandwagon
    b. Transfer   d. Name calling

_d_   8. A small group comes onto a crowded beach carrying buckets of Deep Southern brand fried chicken. Other people nearby notice the group, leave, and come back with buckets of Deep Southern fried chicken. Soon everyone on the beach is either eating Deep Southern or going to get some.

    a. Glittering generalities   c. Transfer
    b. Name calling   d. Bandwagon

B. The following ads use card stacking—in some way, they are too good to be true. Circle the letter of the important detail that the advertiser has intentionally omitted.

9. Our new line of light cakes is made without any fats at all.
    a. The cakes come in six flavors.
    (b.) The cakes have the same number of calories as the company's cakes that aren't called "light."
    c. The cakes cost a little less than cakes that aren't called "light."

10. "As President," says a candidate, "I will do everything in my power to keep income taxes from rising."
    a. The candidate was governor of a large state for two terms.
    b. The candidate played basketball in college.
    (c.) The candidate is in favor of raising sales taxes.

Check Your Performance   **PROPAGANDA**

Activity	Number Right	Points	Score
Review Test 1 (5 items)	_____	x 4 =	_____
Review Test 2 (10 items)	_____	x 4 =	_____
Review Test 3 (10 items)	_____	x 4 =	_____
		TOTAL SCORE =	_____ %

PROPAGANDA: Test 1

In each pair of sentences below, the first sentence does not illustrate a propaganda technique, but the second one does. On the line, write the letter of the propaganda technique used in the **second** sentence.

___*a*___ 1. • Zesty Zip frozen fruit concentrate is made from five tropical fruits.

  • "I get each day off to a roaring start with Zesty Zip," says champion car-racer Miles Leonard.

  | | | A "champion |
  a. Testimonial | c. Bandwagon | car-racer" is a
  b. Plain folks | d. Name calling | celebrity.

___*d*___ 2. • Olsen Paint has rich color and lasts for years.

  • A man in painter's overalls is dipping his brush into a can of Olsen Paint. "Most of the week I'm president of Olsen Paint Company," he says. "On Saturdays, I'm a housepainter myself. So I know what people look for in a quality house paint."

  The company president is depicted as an ordinary guy.

  a. Transfer | c. Bandwagon
  b. Name calling | d. Plain folks

___*a*___ 3. • Frosty Diet Cola has no calories.

  • An attractive couple in bathing suits stop at a soda stand. "What are you drinking?" the man asks. "Frosty Diet Cola, of course," she answers as she slips her hand around his waist.

  The cola is associated with sex appeal.

  a. Transfer | c. Name calling
  b. Glittering generalities | d. Testimonial

___*b*___ 4. • We hope you'll find that Choco-Chip Cookies are the best you've ever tasted.

  • Try Choco-Chip Cookies—the cookies with goodness that doesn't quit.

  "Goodness that doesn't quit" is a significant-sounding but unspecific claim.

  a. Name calling | c. Testimonial
  b. Glittering generalities | d. Plain folks

___*c*___ 5. • Sea Fair cruises will be touring the Caribbean this summer.

  • Don't miss out on this cruise of a lifetime enjoyed by thousands of travelers. Ask your agent for details about Sea Fair's very popular tour of the Caribbean.

  The cruise's popularity is emphasized ("enjoyed by thousands," "very popular").

  a. Glittering generalities | c. Bandwagon
  b. Transfer | d. Name calling

(Continues on next page)

499

___c___ 6. • Come to Smith's Carpets' spring sale.

• We cannot tell a lie—we honor America's presidents with beauty and savings. Come to Cherry Tree Carpets to see the amazing quality and discounts at our Presidents' Day Sale.

     a. Bandwagon   c. Transfer
     b. Name calling   d. Plain folks

___a___ 7. • Wilson's Department Store carries clothing for men, women, and children.

• "I shop for my family's wardrobe at Wilson's Department Store. I want good values, not necessarily designer labels," says Anna Hendricks, bank clerk and homemaker.

     a. Plain folks   c. Transfer
     b. Testimonial   d. Glittering generalities

___d___ 8. • You can make a deal at Dave's Auto Dealership.

• Come early to Dave's Auto Dealership so you won't have to stand in line—because everyone knows you can make a deal with Dave and save.

     a. Name calling   c Testimonial
     b. Transfer   d. Bandwagon

___d___ 9. • West's Tall Men's Store sells well-tailored suits in all tall sizes.

• Buy your next suit at West's Tall Men's Store, and you'll be walking tall.

     a. Plain folks   c. Testimonial
     b. Transfer   d. Glittering generalities

___a___ 10. • We think Cheesy Pizza is delicious.

• Al's Pizza is like the thick cardboard we use to wrap take-home orders of Cheesy Pizza. Eat Cheesy Pizza if you're a pizza lover; eat Al's if you love cardboard.

     a. Name calling   c. Testimonial
     b. Glittering generalities   d. Plain folks

Comments: Item 6—The company associates itself with patriotism.

Item 7—The speaker is an ordinary person (a "bank clerk and homemaker").

Item 8—The sale's popularity is emphasized ("stand in line," "everyone knows").

Item 9—"And you'll be walking tall" sounds good but is unspecific.

Item 10—The ad makes negative comments about a rival.

PROPAGANDA: Test 2

A. Each of the passages below illustrates a particular propaganda technique. On the line next to the passage, write the letter of the main technique being used.

___d___ 1. "Out here in farm country I work hard and live simply," says a farmer. "I don't look for fancy, but I do require quality. That's why, for everyday down home toughness, I drive a Wellbilt pickup truck."

   a. Name calling   c. Bandwagon
   b. Testimonial   d. Plain folks

___b___ 2. The U. S. Heritage Committee has selected Bubble-O as the official soft drink of the Heritage Celebration to be held in the nation's capital this summer. Bubble-O: an important part of your heritage.

   a. Plain folks   c. Bandwagon
   b. Transfer   d. Name calling

___d___ 3. After six terms, the incumbent, Representative Snark, is part of the pampered Washington crowd, out of touch with the people who elected him. Vote for Loretta Reese!

   a. Testimonial   c. Transfer
   b. Glittering generalities   d. Name calling

___d___ 4. You can be part of the growing number of people who are saying "no" to drugs and "yes" to achievement. Be part of the crowd that makes a difference.

   a. Glittering generalities   c. Testimonial
   b. Name calling   d. Bandwagon

___b___ 5. A Pacekeeper minitruck is climbing a dirt road in the desert. "Pacekeeper," says the announcer. "The perfect vehicle to drive you into a new century."

   a. Plain folks   c. Bandwagon
   b. Glittering generalities   d. Name calling

___c___ 6. The best way to warm up on those cold winter days? Ask Olympic skier Terry Niles. "There's nothing like a good hot cup of Myer's Soup to take the chill off," says Terry. "Delicious Myer's makes me feel warm all over."

   a. Bandwagon   c. Testimonial
   b. Glittering generalities   d. Plain folks

(Continues on next page)

_a_   7. Rancher Bob Curren's casual manners and style are sure to bring a fresh spirit to the Senate. Aren't you ready for a down-to-earth senator?

    a. Plain folks   c. Glittering generalities
    b. Name calling   d. Transfer

_b_   8. An Arnold Autofocus camera is the camera of your dreams. This delightful camera will make all your photography a pleasure. You'll love your new Arnold Autofocus.

    a. Transfer   c. Bandwagon
    b. Glittering generalities   d. Name calling

B. The following ads involve card stacking—in some way, they are too good to be true. Circle the letter of the important detail that the advertiser has intentionally omitted.

9. Congratulations, Ms. Kerr! You are among the finalists for the Magazine Club's Ten Million Dollar Lottery.
    a. The ten million dollars will be split among several winners.
    b. There are several million other people who are also among the finalists.
    c. The company has sponsored lotteries for twenty years.

10. For only $25, Employment Education, Inc., will send you complete information on how to earn money stuffing envelopes at home.
    a. It is not difficult to stuff envelopes.
    b. The company also sells information on learning to type.
    c. Very few people are ever hired to stuff envelopes at home.

PROPAGANDA: Test 3

Read each of the ads below, and then circle the letter of the best answer to each question.

A.   ¹First America Bank offers a remarkable protection plan for lost or stolen credit cards. ²For only fifteen dollars, you can buy credit card protection that covers your losses up to $10,000. ³Isn't this impressive guarantee worth the small yearly fee? ⁴Losing a credit card naturally causes some anxiety, but First America's protection plan frees you from needless worry. ⁵We notify your credit card company, and we cover your losses, all for one astonishingly low fee. ⁶Remember, First America Bank is as sound as the country it serves so well.

1. Which propaganda technique is used in sentence 6?
   a. Plain folks
   (b.) Transfer
   c. Bandwagon
   d. Testimonial

2. Which of the following missing details has the advertiser intentionally omitted?
   (a.) Federal law limits a card owner's legal responsibility for lost or stolen credit cards to fifty dollars.
   b. The First America protection plan covers no more than twenty credit cards.
   c. A lost or stolen credit card should be reported within forty-eight hours.
   d. The bank offers its own Red, White, and Blue Bank Card to members in the plan.

B.   ¹"The Tri-County Regional Craft Festival is an event our family never misses," says Belinda Groffman, famous folk singer. ²"It's a weekend all of us look forward to all year," adds her singing partner and husband Bob. ³"Not only do we enjoy the best in crafts from all over the region, but the other activities are so much fun—from puppet shows to magicians and jugglers. ⁴This year, join the thousands of families who have already discovered how much fun they can have at the Tri-County Folk Festival."

3. Which is the main propaganda technique used in this ad?
   a. Plain folks
   b. Transfer
   c. Name calling
   (d.) Testimonial

4. Which words are a key to the main propaganda technique in the ad?
   a. "Regional Craft Festival"
   (b.) "Belinda Groffman, famous folk singer"
   c. "so much fun"
   d. "magicians and jugglers"

(Continues on next page)

5. Which is the main propaganda technique used in sentence 4?
   a. Name calling   c. Testimonial
   b. Bandwagon   d. Transfer

C. ¹Wouldn't a hot cup of coffee taste great right now? ²With a Dr. Zip coffee-maker, a fresh cup like the coffee Mom has always made for Dad will be ready in minutes. ³You can even set Dr. Zip's automatic timer to prepare a heavenly pot of coffee to greet you first thing in the morning. ⁴Dr. Zip has lots of convenient features, like the brew-strength lever that lets you decide how strong you want your coffee to be. ⁵And you can make as many as twelve cups of coffee at one time with a Dr. Zip coffeemaker. ⁶Follow the lead of Richie Martz, basketball's highest scorer this season, who says, "Every morning, I'm a beast until I get my first delicious cup of coffee from Dr. Zip."

6. Which propaganda device is used in sentence 2?
   a. Testimonial   c. Name calling
   b. Plain folks   d. Transfer

7. Which of the following is a glittering generality?
   a. "ready in minutes"   c. "automatic timer"
   b. "heavenly pot of coffee" d. "brew strength lever"

8. Which of the following details has the advertiser intentionally omitted?
   a. It takes only four minutes for coffee to brew in a Dr. Zip coffeemaker.
   b. The coffeemaker allows you to make as few as two cups at a time.
   c. The twelve cups made by the coffeemaker equal ten cups of other coffeemakers.
   d. The Dr. Zip company also makes its own brand of coffee.

D. Read the fictional ad below, and then circle the letter of the best answer to each question.

¹Get off of that sofa, thunderthighs! ²Drag your tired, shapeless body to Norman's Sporting Goods in time for our exercise bike and treadmill sale. ³Join the multitude of former slobs like yourself who are now fit, trim, and energetic, thanks to a regular program of exercise on one of our quality home workout machines. ⁴You can be like our customer James Woodall, a plumber, who says, "I shed forty pounds and cut my cholesterol level in half after purchasing one of Norman's affordable exercise bikes."

9. Which is the main propaganda technique used in sentence 3?
   a. Bandwagon   c. Transfer
   b. Glittering generalitires d. Testimonial

10. Which is the main propaganda technique used in sentence 4?
    a. Name calling   c. Plain folks
    b. Testimonial   d. Glittering generalities

PROPAGANDA: Test 4

Read each of the ads below, and then circle the letter of the best answer to each question.

A. ¹You are invited to join a new movement based on the belief that the cycle of losing and regaining weight is worse for people than maintaining a stable (yet plump) weight. ²Thousands of people are joining Roberta Rice, a champion of this splendid new cause, in the pledge, "I'll never diet again." ³True, Miss Rice weighs much more than the vain models whose thin, sickly thighs are displayed in fashion magazines. ⁴But she is attractive, self-confident, and delighted with her role in the new movement.

1. Which propaganda technique is used in sentence 2?
   a. Name calling   c. Bandwagon
   b. Transfer   d. Plain folks

2. Which propaganda technique is used in sentence 3?
   a. Bandwagon   c. Name calling
   b. Testimonial   d. Glittering generalities

B. At Build-Rite Furniture, we know that do-it-yourself is the traditional American way. Build-Rite carries a fantastic variety of exceptional home furnishings that await only your finishing touches. Just follow the simple instructions and, in no time, you've assembled a magnificent patio set or charming night table. Join the millions of Americans who take pleasure and pride in creating their own homes with Build-Rite Furniture, the right furniture to buy.

3. Which propaganda technique is used in the opening sentence?
   a. Testimonial   c. Glittering generalities
   b. Name calling   d. Transfer

4. Which fact has the advertiser intentionally omitted?
   a. Build-Rite's "do-it-yourself" furniture is cheaper than furniture assembled by a manufacturer.
   b. Build-Rite does not sell electronic equipment.
   c. Build-Rite's furniture does not come with the tools necessary for assembly.
   d. Build-Rite's furniture comes in a variety of woods and plastics.

5. Which of the following is **not** a glittering generality?
   a. "exceptional home furnishings"   c. "the right furniture to buy"
   b. "millions of Americans"   d. "magnificent patio set"

(Continues on next page)

C. Are you tired of big impersonal banks that treat you like a number? At HomeTown Savings and Loan Bank, you aren't a code in a giant computer somewhere. Here, you're a valued customer, a member of the community we're a part of. As lending officer Janet Morris says, "At HomeTown Savings Bank, I can assist my neighbors, people like me."

6. Which propaganda technique is used in the first sentence?
    a. Bandwagon   c. Transfer
    b. Name calling   d. Testimonial

7. Which propaganda technique is used in the last sentence?
    a. Transfer   c. Plain folks
    b. Name calling   d. Glittering generalities

D. Read the description below of an actual ad, and then circle the letter of the best answer to each question.

[1]Music plays as television viewers see a man, woman, and dog running through the rain, up some steps, and into a house. [2]The man sets down a grocery bag, the woman squeezes out her dripping shirt, and the dog shakes the rain off its coat. [3]A voice says, "In over half the homes in America, people come home to Kenmore appliances."

8. Which propaganda technique is used in the scenes described in sentences 1 and 2?
    a. Testimonial   c. Transfer
    b. Bandwagon   d. Plain folks

9. Which propaganda technique is used in sentence 3?
    a. Testimonial   c. Bandwagon
    b. Glittering generalities   d. Name calling

10. Which words are the key to the propaganda technique used in sentence 3?
    a. "over half the homes in America"
    b. "come home"
    c. "Kenmore appliances"

PROPAGANDA: Test 5

A. Below are descriptions of eight actual ads. On each line, write the letter of the main propaganda technique that applies to the ad.

a Bandwagon	**d** Plain folks
b Testimonial	**e** Name calling
c Transfer	**f** Glittering generalities

___c___ 1. An ad for Lever 2000 Bodywash shows a man caressing a woman. The text says, "Fresh, clean, soft skin. Your husband will love our bodywash, even if he doesn't use it."

___b___ 2. "I know how important training is to having a successful career," says Jackie Zeman, who plays a character on ABC TV's *General Hospital* in an ad for International Correspondence Schools.

___f___ 3. An ad for Heart Beauty System states that it is "the finest skin care system in the world."

___a___ 4. A Ford ad states, "More repeat buyers than anyone, domestic or import" and "The best-selling cars and trucks four years running."

___d___ 5. In an ad for Quaker Oatmeal, a cute girl holding a soccer ball smiles up at the camera. "She's got goals to shoot for," says the text. "Make sure she gets a good warm-up."

___e___ 6. "For moisturized skin even the leading bar doesn't touch," says an ad for Oil of Olay's soap and moisterizer product.

___c___ 7. For a "Presidents' Weekend" sale, a large picture of George Washington and red, white, and blue streaks accompany pictures of new Toyotas.

___d___ 8. In an ad for the Doubleday Book Club, there's a photo of a young woman identified as "Marylou 'Lulu' Johnsen, dental hygienist, wife, mother of two, and avid reader." Johnsen is quoted as saying, "Thanks, Doubleday, for all the terrific best sellers. I love to read after the kids are asleep."

(Continues on next page)

B. The following ads involve card stacking—in some way, they are too good to be true. Circle the letter of the important detail that the advertiser has intentionally omitted.

9. An ad for a shaving gel for women claimed, "New Soft Sense Moisturizing Shave Gel with Vitamin E." Circle the letter of the detail below that you think has been omitted.
   a. What the scent of the gel is like
   b. Whether or not vitamin E has been shown to moisturize well or benefit the skin in any other way
   c. The percentage of women who have decided not to shave their legs at all

10. A new roll of Bounty paper towels was hailed with the slogan "New! More Absorbent Than Ever." Circle the letter of the detail below that you think Bounty omitted.
    a. The new towels are 10 percent more absorbent than before.
    b. The new roll has fewer sheets of towels than before.
    c. The price has remained the same.

PROPAGANDA: Test 6

A. Below are descriptions of eight actual ads. On each line, write the letter of the main propaganda technique that applies to the ad.

a	Bandwagon	**d**	Plain folks
b	Testimonial	**e**	Name calling
c	Transfer	**f**	Glittering generalities

_b_ 1. Tennis star Michael Chang smiles at the camera and then looks over his Discover Card bill to see the good things he has bought with his credit card.

_d_ 2. An ad shows a grandmother before and after taking Tylenol: first she is suffering from aches and pains, and later she is able to play baseball with her young grandchildren.

_c_ 3. The top of a magazine ad reads, "Discover the Magic of the Green Valley Spa." Below that text is a large picture of a patient-looking angel with sunshine illuminating her wings.

_e_ 4. An ad reminds us to bring along our VISA card because "none of the ticket takers at Mountain Express take American Express."

_f_ 5. An ad picturing Harry Winston watches simply states, "The Ultimate Timepiece."

_a_ 6. Dozens of people are rushing to take advantage of a "Maaco madness" car-repair sale.

_b_ 7. Smiling broadly, actress Cindy Williams explains that she has gone down several sizes on a Jenny Craig diet.

_c_ 8. An ad for Pierre Cardin men's cologne shows a handsome young man in a tuxedo lifting a laughing young woman, blonde and attractive, up into the air. The woman is wearing a low-cut red evening dress and a necklace of large pearls.

(Continues on next page)

B. The following ads involve card stacking—in some way, they are too good to be true. Circle the letter of the important detail that the advertiser has intentionally omitted.

9. "The California Avocado. It's a rich source of vitamins and minerals—seventeen, to be exact. It also has lots of potassium. And it contains absolutely no cholesterol. So when it comes to adding nutrition to your daily routine, the delicious California Avocado is a natural."

   (a.) A California avocado is 90 percent fat.
   b. A California avocado has a small amount of sodium.
   c. Half of a California avocado provides a quarter of the Recommended Daily Allowance of vitamin C.

10. The Kellogg's Corn Pops box explains that an ounce of Corn Pops (once called Sugar Pops) contains less sugar than an apple, a banana, or two pancakes with syrup. What information has the advertiser intentionally omitted?

    a. Corn Pops contains less sugar than cola drinks.
    b. Corn Pops can be eaten out of the box like a snack.
    (c.) Many people eat more than an ounce of Corn Pops for breakfast.

4

More About Argument: Errors in Reasoning

Learning about some common errors in reasoning—also known as **fallacies**—will help you to spot weak points in arguments.

You have already learned about two common fallacies in Chapter 10, "Argument." One of those two fallacies is sometimes called **changing the subject**. In Chapter 10, this fallacy was described as irrelevant support. People who use this method of arguing try to divert the audience's attention from the true issue by presenting evidence that actually has nothing to do with the argument.

The second fallacy you worked on in Chapter 10 is sometimes called **hasty generalization**. This fallacy was referred to in that chapter as a point based on inadequate support. To be valid, a point must be based on an adequate amount of evidence. Someone who draws a conclusion on the basis of insufficient evidence is making a hasty generalization.

Below are some other common fallacies that will be explained in this chapter. Exercises throughout will give you practice in recognizing them.

Three Fallacies That Ignore the Issue

- Circular Reasoning
- Personal Attack
- Straw Man

Three Fallacies That Oversimplify the Issue

- False Cause
- False Comparison
- Either-Or

FALLACIES THAT IGNORE THE ISSUE

Circular Reasoning

Part of a point cannot reasonably be used as evidence to support it. The fallacy of including such illogical evidence is called **circular reasoning**; it is also known as **begging the question**. Here is a simple and obvious example of such reasoning: "Mr. Green is a great teacher because he is so wonderful at teaching." The supporting reason ("he is so wonderful at teaching") is really the same as the conclusion ("Mr. Green is a great teacher"). We still do not know why he is a great teacher. No real reasons have been given—the statement has merely been repeated.

Can you spot the circular reasoning in the following arguments?

1. Vitamins are healthful, for they improve your well-being.
2. Since people under 21 are too young to vote, the voting age shouldn't be lowered below age 21.
3. Abortion is an evil practice because it is so wrong.

Let's look more closely at these arguments:

1. The word *healthful*, which is used in the conclusion, conveys the same idea as well-being. We still don't know why vitamins are good for us.
2. The idea that people under 21 are too young to vote is both the conclusion and the reason of the argument. No real reason is given for why people under 21 are too young to vote.
3. The claim that abortion "is so wrong" simply restates the idea that it is an evil practice. No explanation is given for why abortion is evil or wrong.

In all these cases, the reasons merely repeat an important part of the conclusion. The careful reader wants to say, "Tell me something new. You are reasoning in circles. Give me supporting evidence, not a repetition."

➤ *Practice 1*

Circle the number of the one item in each group that contains an example of circular reasoning.

Group 1

1. Why support Ray O'Donnell's highway safety proposal? He's got the biggest collection of speeding tickets in the district.
2. The government should lower our taxes because taxes are entirely too high.
3. The people who are in favor of gun control are obviously not concerned about criminals taking control of this fine country.

Comment: Group 1—The statement that "taxes are entirely too high" means essentially the same as "the government should lower our taxes."

Group 2

1. Aretha Franklin is the best soul singer alive because her singing is so great.
2. A local association wants to establish a home in our neighborhood for retarded people. But the neighbors oppose the home; they say they don't want dangerous psychopaths roaming our streets.
3. Ms. Jones is an atheist and should not be hired as a math teacher.

Group 3

1. George wants the firm to hire more women and minorities. He doesn't seem to care how qualified our workers are.
2. I feel my salary should be higher because it is too low.
3. Councilman Hawkins is wholly unqualified to be elected mayor. He is a well-known homosexual.

Personal Attack

This fallacy often occurs in political debate. Here's an example:

> Senator Snerd's opinions on public housing are worthless. He can't even manage to hold his own household together, having married and divorced three times already.

Senator Snerd's family life may or may not reflect a weakness in his character, but it has nothing to do with the value of his opinions on public housing. **Personal attack** ignores the issue under discussion and concentrates instead on the character of the opponent.

Sometimes personal attacks take the form of accusing people of taking a stand only because it will benefit them personally. For instance, here's a personal attack on a congressman who is an outspoken member of the National Organization for Women (NOW): "He doesn't care about NOW. He supports it only in order to get more women to vote for him." This argument ignores the congressman's detailed defense of NOW as an organization that promotes equal rights for both men and women. The key to recognizing personal attack is that it always involves an opponent's personal life or character, rather than simply his or her public ideas.

Comments: Group 2—The statement that Franklin's "singing is so great" says almost the same thing as "Aretha Franklin is the best soul singer alive."

Group 3—The statement that one's salary "is too low" means the same as the statement that it "should be higher."

➤ *Practice 2*

Circle the number of the one item in each group that contains an example of personal attack.

Group 1

①. Why support Ray O'Donnell's highway safety proposal? He's got the biggest collection of speeding tickets in the district.
2. The government should lower our taxes because taxes are entirely too high.
3. The people who are in favor of gun control are obviously not concerned about criminals taking control of this fine country.

> The merit of O'Donnell's proposal has nothing to do with his speeding.

Group 2

1. Aretha Franklin is the best soul singer alive because her singing is so great.
2. A local association wants to establish a home in our neighborhood for retarded people. But the neighbors oppose the home; they say they don't want dangerous psychopaths roaming our streets.
③. Ms. Jones is an atheist and should not be hired as a math teacher.

> One's religious beliefs have nothing to do with his or her ability to teach math.

Group 3

1. George wants the firm to hire more women and minorities. He doesn't seem to care how qualified our workers are.
2. I feel my salary should be higher because it is too low.
③. Councilman Hawkins is wholly unqualified to be elected mayor. He is a well-known homosexual.

> One's sexual orientation is irrelevant to one's professional abilities.

Straw Man

An opponent made of straw can be defeated very easily. Sometimes, if one's real opponent is putting up too good a fight, it can be tempting to build a scarecrow and battle it instead. For example, take the following passage from a debate on the death penalty.

> Ms. Collins opposes capital punishment. But letting murderers out on the street to kill again is a crazy idea. If we did that, no one would be safe.

Ms. Collins, however, never advocated "letting murderers out on the street to kill again." In fact, she wants to keep them in jail for life rather than execute them. The **straw man** fallacy suggests that the opponent favors an obviously unpopular cause—when the opponent really doesn't support anything of the kind. Then that made-up position is opposed.

➤ *Practice 3*

Circle the number of the one item in each group that contains an example of straw man.

Group 1

1. Don't sign Elio's petition for longer library hours. He's never been better than a C student.
2. The government should lower our taxes because taxes are entirely too high.
3. The people who are in favor of gun control are obviously not concerned about criminals taking control of this fine country.

(circled: 3)

Group 2

People in favor of gun control don't believe that it will allow criminals to take control.

1. Your friends are a bad influence on you; after all, they encourage you to behave terribly.
2. A local association wants to establish a home in our neighborhood for retarded people. But the neighbors oppose the home; they say they don't want dangerous psychopaths roaming our streets.
3. Ms. Jones is an atheist and should not be hired as a math teacher.

(circled: 2)

Retarded people are not psychopaths.

Group 3

1. George wants the firm to hire more women and minorities. He doesn't seem to care how qualified our workers are.
2. I feel my salary should be higher because it is too low.
3. Of course Mel supports giving large malpractice awards to patients. As a lawyer specializing in malpractice, his only interest is in big fees.

(circled: 1)

George believes that many women and minority workers are qualified.

FALLACIES THAT OVERSIMPLIFY THE ISSUE

False Cause

You have probably heard someone say as a joke, "I know it's going to rain today because I just washed the car." The idea that someone can make it rain by washing a car is funny because the two events obviously have nothing to do with each other. However, with more complicated issues, it is easy to make the mistake known as the fallacy of **false cause**. The mistake is to assume that because event B *follows* event A, event B *was caused by* event A.

Cause-and-effect situations can be difficult to analyze, and people are often tempted to oversimplify them by focusing on one "cause" and ignoring other possible causes. To identify an argument using a false cause, look for alternative causes. Consider this argument:

The Macklin Company was more prosperous before Ms. Williams became president. Clearly, she is the cause of the decline.

(*Event A:* Ms. Williams became president.
Event B: The Macklin Company's earnings declined.)

However, Ms. Williams has been president for only a few months. What other possible causes could have been responsible for the decline? Perhaps the policies of the previous president are just now affecting the company. Perhaps the market for the company's product has changed. In any case, it's easy but dangerous to assume that just because A *came before* B, A *caused* B.

➤ Practice 4

Circle the number of the one item in each group that contains an example of false cause.

Group 1

①. I knew I shouldn't have taken the baby to the park today. Now he's got a cold.
2. While some people objected to the Vietnam war and didn't serve in the military, others were patriotic and did serve their country.
3. I don't know why you're so worried about my grades. Albert Einstein had lousy grades in high school, and he did all right.

Group 2

1. You'll either have to get a good job soon or face the fact that you'll never be successful.
②. After visiting Hal today, I came home with a headache. I must be allergic to his dog.
3. Of course the legalization of prostitution will work in America. It has worked in European countries, hasn't it?

Group 3

1. Young people must choose between a career that will help their fellow human beings and one that will earn them a decent living.
2. Chemicals have made wonderful synthetic fabrics possible, so what's wrong with using plenty of chemicals on our farms?
③. A month after the governor took office, my company fell on hard times, and I got fired. I'll certainly never vote for him again.

Comments: Groups 1 and 2—A single event is insufficient evidence for such generalizations.

Group 3—A complex economic event cannot be attributed to such a recent single event.

False Comparison

When the poet Robert Burns wrote, "My love is like a red, red rose," he meant that both the woman he loved and a rose are beautiful. In other ways—such as having green leaves and thorns, for example—his love did not resemble a rose at all. Comparisons are often a good way to clarify a point. But because two things are not alike in all respects, comparisons (sometimes called analogies) often make poor evidence for arguments. In the error in reasoning known as **false comparison**, the assumption is that two things are more alike than they really are. For example, read the following argument:

> It didn't hurt your grandfather in the old country to get to work without a car, and it won't hurt you either.

To judge whether or not this is a false comparison, consider how the two situations are alike and how they differ. They are similar in that both involve a young person's need to get to work. But the situations are different in that the grandfather didn't have to be at work an hour after his last class. In fact, he didn't go to school at all. In addition, his family didn't own a car he could use. The differences in this case are more important than the similarities, making it a false comparison.

➣ *Practice 5*

Circle the number of the one item in each group that contains an example of false comparison.

Group 1

1. I knew I shouldn't have taken the baby to the park today. Now he's got a cold.
2. While some people objected to the Vietnam war and didn't serve in the military, others were patriotic and did serve their country.
(3.) I don't know why you're so worried about my grades. Albert Einstein had lousy grades in high school, and he did all right.

Group 2

1. You'll either have to get a good job soon or face the fact that you'll never be successful.
2. After visiting Hal today, I came home with a headache. I must be allergic to his dog.
(3.) Of course the legalization of prostitution will work in America. It has worked in European countries, hasn't it?

Comments: Group 1—For most of us, a comparison with Albert Einstein is a false one.

Group 2—Different cultures may react differently to issues.

Group 3

1. Young people must choose between a career that will help their fellow human beings and one that will earn them a decent living.
2.) Chemicals have made wonderful synthetic fabrics possible, so what's wrong with using plenty of chemicals on our farms?
3. A month after the governor took office, my company fell on hard times, and I got fired. I'll certainly never vote for him again.

Either-Or

It is often wrong to assume that there are only two sides to a question. Offering only two choices when more actually exist is an **either-or** fallacy. For example, the statement "You are either with us or against us" assumes that there is no middle ground. Or consider the following:

> People opposed to unrestricted free speech are really in favor of censorship.

This argument ignores the fact that a person could believe in free speech as well as in laws that prohibit slander or that punish someone for falsely yelling "Fire!" in a crowded theater. Some issues have only two sides (Will you pass the course, or won't you?), but most have several.

➤ Practice 6

Circle the number of the item in each group that contains an example of the either-or fallacy.

Group 1

1. I knew I shouldn't have taken the baby to the park today. Now he's got a cold.
2.) While some people objected to the Vietnam war and didn't serve in the military, others were patriotic and did serve their country.
3. I don't know why you're so worried about my grades. Albert Einstein had lousy grades in high school, and he did all right.

Comment: Group 1—The speaker assumes that people who objected to the Vietnam war were not patriotic, but many who opposed the war did so on moral grounds and loved their country.

Group 2

1. You'll either have to get a good job soon or face the fact that you'll never be successful.
2. After visiting Hal today, I came home with a headache. I must be allergic to his dog.
3. Why can't I just quit school and go to work? Ken quit school and got a great job working at his dad's chain of restaurants.

Group 3

1. Young people must choose between a career that will help their fellow human beings and one that will earn them a decent living.
2. School prayer is a positive force in parochial schools, so why not try it in our public schools?
3. A month after the governor took office, my company fell on hard times, and I got fired. I'll certainly never vote for him again.

➤ Review Test 1

Answer each question with a **T** or an **F** (for *true* or *false*) or by circling the letter of the answer you choose.

1. ___T___ TRUE OR FALSE? The fallacy of personal attack ignores the true issue.

2. ___T___ TRUE OR FALSE? The fallacy of straw man got its name because an opponent made of straw would be easily defeated.

3. ___F___ TRUE OR FALSE? A false-cause argument assumes that there are only two sides to the issue.

4. To decide if a statement is a false comparison, you must consider how much two situations
   a. are alike.
   b. are different.
   c. both *a* and *b*.

5. In the either-or fallacy, the argument ignores the possibility of an additional
   a. cause for something happening.
   b. side to a question.
   c. comparison.

Comments: Group 2—There's more than one "schedule" for success.

Group 3—Some jobs, such as social worker or teacher, help others and also pay well.

➤ *Review Test 2*

A. In the space provided, write the letter of the fallacy contained in each argument. Choose from the three fallacies shown in the box below.

> **a** Circular reasoning *(a statement repeats itself rather than providing a real supporting reason to back up an argument)*
> **b** Personal attack
> **c** Straw man *(an argument is made by claiming an opponent holds an extreme position and then opposing that extreme position)*

_c_ 1. Supporters of state lotteries apparently don't think people should work hard for what they get. They believe it's better to get something for nothing.

_b_ 2. Earl will make a lousy class treasurer because he's just a conceited jerk.

_a_ 3. Pollution is wrong because it dirties the environment.

_c_ 4. Mr. Collins supports sex education in junior high school. Maybe he thinks it's okay for 13-year-olds to be having babies, but I don't agree.

_a_ 5. Watering new grass is important, since a lot of water is beneficial for new lawns.

B. In the space provided, write the letter of the fallacy contained in each argument. Choose from the three fallacies shown in the box below.

> **a** False cause *(the argument assumes that the order of events alone shows cause and effect)*
> **b** False comparison *(the argument assumes that two things being compared are more alike than they really are)*
> **c** Either-or *(the argument assumes that there are only two sides to a question)*

_a_ 6. Stay away from Mike's filthy dorm room. After the last time I went there to study, I actually got a rash.

_c_ 7. Did you tell the boss off, or did you act like a wimp again?

___b___ 8. There's a sign in the dorm lounge saying that excessive alcohol is dangerous. Well, so what? Too much mashed potato can be dangerous, too.

___c___ 9. Do you always tell the truth, or are you a liar?

___a___ 10. Last time there was an eclipse, the stock market went down. I'm going to sell all my stock before next week's eclipse takes place.

➤ *Review Test 3*

A. In the space provided, write the letter of the fallacy contained in each argument. Choose from the three fallacies shown in the box below.

> **a** Circular reasoning *(a statement repeats itself rather than providing a real supporting reason to back up an argument)*
> **b** Personal attack
> **c** Straw man *(an argument is made by claiming an opponent holds an extreme position and then opposing that extreme position)*

___b___ 1. Congressman Nagel's policy on welfare is nonsense. What do you expect from a man known to cheat on his wife?

___a___ 2. You can always trust an animal lover because people who like animals are more trustworthy than other people.

___c___ 3. The mayor wants to allow liquor stores in town. He may not mind having all those drug pushers around, but I certainly do.

___b___ 4. Who can take Jake Green's argument for raising the sales tax seriously? Judging by the age of his wardrobe and car, the man hasn't paid a sales tax himself in decades.

___a___ 5. Kim Lee is the best choice for city council because she's the best candidate.

B. In the space provided, write the letter of the fallacy contained in each argument. Choose from the three fallacies shown in the box below.

> **a** False cause *(the argument assumes that the order of events alone shows cause and effect)*
> **b** False comparison *(the argument assumes that two things being compared are more alike than they really are)*
> **c** Either-or *(the argument assumes that there are only two sides to a question)*

___a___ 6. I ate in the company cafeteria yesterday, and today I have the flu. That's the last time I'll eat there.

___c___ 7. There are only two types of citizens in this town: those who support building a new stadium and those who don't care about our town's future.

___b___ 8. Children are like flowers—you only have to feed them and let them have plenty of sunshine, and they'll grow up hardy and beautiful.

___a___ 9. I did well on the finals last semester after having Oreos for breakfast. I'd better remember to buy a bag of Oreos before this semester's finals begin.

___b___ 10. At the grocery, I pay only for what I want, so why should I have to pay taxes that go for welfare and other federal programs I don't support?

Check Your Performance   **MORE ABOUT ARGUMENT**

Activity	Number Right	Points	Score
Review Test 1 (5 items)	_____	x 4 =	_____
Review Test 2 (10 items)	_____	x 4 =	_____
Review Test 3 (10 items)	_____	x 4 =	_____
		TOTAL SCORE =	_____%

5
Writing Assignments

A BRIEF GUIDE TO EFFECTIVE WRITING

Here in a nutshell is what you need to do to write effectively.

Step 1: Explore Your Topic Through Informal Writing

To begin with, explore the topic that you want to write about or that you have been assigned to write about. You can examine your topic through **informal writing**, which usually means one of three things.

First, you can **freewrite** about your topic for at least ten minutes. In other words, for ten minutes write whatever comes into your head about your subject. Write without stopping and without worrying at all about spelling or grammar or the like. Simply get down on paper all the information about the topic that occurs to you.

A second thing you can do is to **make a list of ideas and details** that could go into your paper. Simply pile these items up, one after another, like a shopping list, without worrying about putting them in any special order. Try to accumulate as many details as you can think of.

A third way to explore your topic is to **write down a series of questions and answers** about it. Your questions can start with words like *what, why, how, when*, and *where*.

Getting your thoughts and ideas down on paper will help you think more about your topic. With some raw material to look at, you are now in a better position to decide on just how to proceed.

Step 2: Plan Your Paper with an Informal Outline

After exploring your topic, plan your paper using an informal outline. Do two things:

- **Decide on and write out the point of your paper.** It is often a good idea to begin your paragraph with this point, which is known as the topic sentence. If you are writing an essay of several paragraphs, you will probably want to include your main point somewhere in your first paragraph. In a paper of several paragraphs, the main point is called the central point, or thesis.
- **List the supporting reasons, examples, or other details that back up your point.** In many cases, you should have at least two or three items of support.

Step 3: Use Transitions

Once your outline is worked out, you will have a clear "road map" for writing your paper. As you write the early drafts of your paper, use **transitions** to introduce each of the separate supporting items (reasons, examples, or other details) you present to back up your point. For instance, you might introduce your first supporting item with the transitional words *first of all.* You might begin your second supporting item with words such as *another reason* or *another example.* And you might indicate your final supporting detail with such words as *last of all* or *a final reason.*

Step 4: Edit and Proofread Your Paper

After you have a solid draft, edit and proofread the paper. Ask yourself several questions to evaluate your paper:

1. Is the paper **unified**? Does all the material in the paper truly support of the opening point?
2. Is the paper **well supported**? Is there plenty of specific evidence to back the opening point?
3. Is the paper **clearly organized**? Does the material proceed in a way that makes sense? Do transitions help connect ideas?
4. Is the paper **well written**? When the paper is read aloud, do the sentences flow smoothly and clearly? Has the paper been checked carefully for grammar, punctuation, and spelling mistakes?

WRITING ASSIGNMENTS FOR THE TWENTY READINGS

Note: The discussion questions accompanying the twenty readings can also make good topics for writing. Some of the writing assignments here are based on them.

"Night Watch"

1. Imagine that you are the son of the old man in the story. The day after your father died, you arrived and heard the story of the other Marine who had been with him in his last hours. How do you think you would feel about the situation? Would you feel primarily grateful, sad, angry, regretful, confused, or something else? Write a paragraph that describes what you think your reaction might be. If your response would be a mix of several emotions, say so. Along with stating your feelings, tell why you feel as you do.

2. The young Marine stayed by the old man's bedside, he said, because "I figured he really needed me." Tell in a paragraph about a time you felt needed. Who was it who needed you, and in what way? How did you respond to that person? Did you feel able to give the person what he or she wanted from you? Was feeling needed a pleasant experience, or did it seem like a burden? Here's a sample topic sentence for this paragraph: "Once my older brother really needed my help, and it felt very good to be able to help him."

3. It's not uncommon to see people reach out to help their loved ones. But the final paragraph of this article states that "in a uniquely human way . . . there are people who care what happens to their fellow human beings"—in other words, they care about people to whom they have no particular obligation. Think of experiences you have had, or heard about, in which people went out of their way to assist someone they do not know well, if at all. Write an essay that tells the stories of two or three such incidents. You might conclude your essay by talking about what, if anything, the "givers" in such situations gain by their actions.

"Here's to Your Health"

1. Few people go through life without being exposed to the negative effects of alcohol. In a paragraph, describe an unpleasant or dangerous incident you have been aware of, or experienced yourself, in which alcohol played a part. Who was involved? What happened? In what way did alcohol contribute to the situation? How did the incident end?

2. The advertising and sale of cigarettes are topics of much debate. There are already some legal restrictions in place—cigarettes are not advertised on television, they are not to be sold to minors, and warning labels on cigarettes inform consumers of health risks associated with smoking. In your opinion, are such restrictions needed or helpful? Should more restrictions be imposed on the tobacco industry, or should cigarettes be advertised and sold like any other product? Write a paragraph that explains your opinions about how or if cigarettes should be regulated and why.

3. As this article shows, alcohol is advertised as something that makes people more successful, sexier, healthier, and happier. The abuse of alcohol, however, often has quite the opposite effect. Write an essay in which you describe what alcohol advertisements would look like if they showed the negative side of drinking. What images would you choose to include in such advertisements? You might organize your essay by addressing several of the positive "myths" about alcohol mentioned in the article and describing an ad that would contradict each myth.

"Child-Rearing Styles"

1. Near the end of the article, the author lists six recommendations to parents who want to raise "competent, socially responsible, independent children." Choose one of those six recommendations and write a paragraph that demonstrates how it was or was not practiced in your own home. Illustrate the paragraph with examples from your childhood. Conclude by stating how you were positively or negatively affected by those examples.

2. Reread the author's descriptions of three parenting style: authoritative, authoritarian, and permissive. Think of a parent you know who is a good example of one of those three styles. Then write a paragraph that describes how that person interacts with his or her child. Provide one or more examples that demonstrate the adult's approach to parenting. You might try using some dialogue to emphasize a point or two. In conclusion, comment on how you think the parent's style is affecting the child.

3. It is not uncommon to hear parents say of their children, "I don't understand—we raised them all just the same, and yet they've turned out so differently." Based on your own experience growing up and your observations of other families, write an essay that comments on several possible explanations for why siblings develop different—sometimes dramatically different—personalities. Provide vivid real-life examples to illustrate your points. A possible central point for this essay might be "Inherited personality, different parental treatment, and birth order account for many of the differences between siblings."

"Rowing the Bus"

1. Logan writes, "In each school, in each classroom, there is a George with a stricken face." Think of a person who filled the role of George in one of your classes. In a paragraph, describe why he or she was the target of teasing, and what form that teasing took. Include a description of your own thoughts and actions regarding the student who was teased.

2. Fearing that his life would be made miserable, the author decided to stop being friends with George. How do you feel about that decision? Do you think it was cruel? Understandable? Were there other options Logan might have tried? Write a paragraph in which you explain what you think of Logan's decision and why. Suggest at least one other way he could have acted, and tell what you think the consequences might have been.

3. In this essay, Logan provides many vivid descriptions of incidents in which bullies attack other students. Reread those descriptions and consider what they teach you about the nature of bullies and bullying. Then write an essay that supports the following main idea: "Evidence in 'Rowing the Bus' suggests that most bullies share certain characteristics." Mention two or three such characteristics and provide evidence from the essay that illustrates how they are present in acts of bullying. In your concluding paragraph, you might talk about what these characteristics tell us about bullies.

"Students in Shock"

1. Students face a good deal of pressure in their new environment, as this essay shows. But they are not the only ones susceptible to "shock." Anyone in a demanding new situation can experience depression, frustration, and hopelessness. For example, someone who is new to a job, to a neighborhood, to marriage, or to parenthood might experience his or her own brand of shock. Write a paragraph that explores the possible causes of shock in a person facing a specific situation. You may choose one of the situations listed here, or another that occurs to you. Suggest ways the person might reduce the pressure he or she feels.

2. When you experience stress, what helps you to relax? Write a paragraph that describes your own favorite stress-reduction technique. Is it exercising, talking with a friend, taking a bath, playing golf, punching a pillow? You might begin with a vivid description of how stress affects you, then contrast that with a description of how your favorite technique changes your mood. Explain in detail how you go about using the technique.

3. *Stress*, *anxiety*, *depression*, *burnout*—these words are common parts of our modern vocabulary. What do you think are some of the main sources of this widespread stress? Write an essay that describes several common causes of stress. You could use as your central point a sentence similar to this: "There are three common reasons why people today are so stressed out." For each cause of stress you mention, provide specific ways in which it affects people. Add interest to your essay by using examples from the lives of people you know or have observed.

"Communities and Cities"

1. What would you consider the pluses and minuses of living in a community like Mineville? Reread the description of life there and write a paragraph in which you state which aspects appeal to you and which do not. Realizing that people have different tastes, be sure to explain why you would like or dislike certain characteristics of small-town life.

2. In the place where you live, what is the general attitude about neighbors? Are they expected to know one another and be concerned with each other's affairs? Are they complete strangers? Is the relationship something in-between? Write a paragraph that explains how your neighbors do or don't interact. Provide specific examples of their behavior.

3. The selection states that the "subjection of the individual to continuous observation and control by the community" is a feature of small-town life that is lacking in a large city. How do you suppose the people in a small town are affected by the presence of such "observation and control"? How are city-dwellers affected by its absence? Write an essay that explains those effects, and in what ways you believe they could be either good or bad. Some effects you might consider discussing include the friendliness but loss of privacy in small towns and the possible loneliness but freedom in big cities.

"How People Rise—and Fall—to Expectations of Others"

1. Who in your life has shown that he or she has clear expectations for you? Were those expectations negative or positive? Write a paragraph that tells who that person was, how he or she demonstrated the expectations, and how you responded to them. Provide specific examples that illustrate the person's attitude toward you and how, if at all, the expectations influenced you.

2. Did you respond in the same way Sifford did to the announcement of the lockup teen dance? In what ways do you agree or disagree with his reaction? Does the idea of the dance concern you in any ways that Sifford did not mention? Write a paragraph that explains how you respond to the idea of the dance, and why.

3. Sifford contrasts two professional coaches, Mike Ditka and Whitey Herzog, and their differing expectations of their players. Think of two people you know — parents, teachers, coaches, bosses, friends — who have very different attitudes about life. Perhaps one seems to expect the best of every situation while the other expects the worst. Perhaps one is very trusting of others while the other is suspicious. Write an essay that contrasts these two people, showing how they communicate their attitudes. Provide specific examples of their behavior. Use contrast transitions (page 189) to make the differences clear to your readers. You might conclude by telling how these people's attitudes seem to affect their lives.

"I Became Her Target"

1. Think of a time when you felt like an outsider coming into a group. Perhaps you stood out because of your race, nationality, gender, language, or opinions, or simply because you were new. How did you feel at first—very uncomfortable, nervous, relaxed, angry? How did the group respond to you? As time went on, how did the situation change, for the better or for the worse? Write a paragraph that describes your experience.

2. Wilkins writes that, as a child, his opinions were based upon the opinions of his family and friends. Most children do accept their parents' ideas and ways of doing things as the right way, the normal way. As they get a little older, however, and are exposed to other ways of thinking and doing things, they may change their minds. Write a paragraph about a time when you began to question your family's opinions or way of life. What made you realize that you did not necessarily agree with your parents all of the time? Did you speak up about your opinions? Why or why not?

3. Who stands out in your mind as your most unforgettable—though not necessarily your favorite—teacher? Write an essay that explains who the teacher was. Demonstrate through vivid stories, examples, and dialogue, why he or she was so memorable. You might organize your essay around several incidents involving that teacher or around several of the teacher's characteristics. You might conclude by telling when and under what circumstances that teacher comes into your thoughts.

"Coping with Santa Claus"

1. As demonstrated in Ephron's essay, children often take satisfaction in telling other children about Santa Claus, the "facts of life," and other such mysteries. Think of a time when another child "set you straight" by passing on some surprising information. (The information may or may not have been

accurate.) Write a paragraph, serious or humorous, in which you describe the incident. What were you told, by whom, and how? How did you respond? Try to re-create your feelings during and after the conversation, and tell if it influenced you at all in the future.

2. Is it ever all right to lie? Julie's parents lied to her about Santa Claus for kindly reasons, but they did lie. Other people lie for a variety of reasons, some of them selfish and some not. It is common, for example, to lie in order to avoid hurting someone's feelings. Write a paragraph in which you explain when, if ever, you think it is acceptable to tell a lie. Provide specific examples—either from real life or from your imagination—to illustrate your point.

3. After Julie read "Santa's" note, Ephron and her husband were in the awkward position of having to confess what they had done. Think of a time when you needed to admit something you had done that you were embarrassed or ashamed about. Describe the incident in an essay. Tell the story as it happened, using time transitions (page 151) to make the sequence of events clear to your reader. At each stage of the story, describe what you were thinking about what you would or should do.

"In Praise of the F Word"

1. Has someone you know (or have you) received an F for a course? Write a paragraph describing what happened. What led to the poor performance? What effect did that experience have? Was failing a motivation to work harder? What were the effects, positive and negative, of receiving the failing grade?

2. This article concerns one way of motivating students—the threat of failure. Thinking back on your own classroom experience, what would you say are some other effective ways of motivating students to do their best? Write a paragraph that describes one other method teachers and instructors can use to motivate their students. Provide examples of times you have seen this method put into practice and how effective it seems to be.

3. Sherry believes that giving students F's when they deserve to fail would encourage them to take more responsibility for their performance. Most people agree that individuals truly overcome a problem only when they take responsibility for it, rather than expecting it to magically disappear or to be solved by someone else. In an essay, describe two or three people you know (you might be one) who have accepted responsibility for dealing with a difficult problem. The problems could be an unhappy marriage, an issue at work or school, or a crisis like substance abuse. How did the people demonstrate their willingness to take responsibility for their problems? What action did each take? How was the situation changed by what they did?

"The Yellow Ribbon"

1. Vingo's wife had to decide whether to forgive Vingo and welcome him back into her life. Think of a time when you had to decide whether or not to forgive someone. Write a paragraph that describes that situation. Begin by explaining who the other person was and what your relationship had been like. Then describe what he or she did to hurt or offend you and how you felt about what happened. Continue by explaining how you made the decision whether or not to forgive the person. End your paragraph by saying how you feel about your decision now.

2. In "The Yellow Ribbon," Hamill provides various clues to Vingo's character. His body language, his conversation with his fellow passengers, what he has to say about his past and his family, and his attitude as the bus nears his hometown all contribute to the readers' opinion of what kind of man he is. Write a paragraph that supports the following topic sentence: "Details in the story suggest that Vingo is a decent man who deserves the yellow ribbons." Find specific evidence in the story to back up that statement.

3. Vingo had to wait suspensefully to discover something important about his future. Most people have had the experience of waiting a long time (or what seemed like a long time) to find out something important. Such situations might have involved a job, pregnancy, romance, health, or school. Write an essay about a situation in which you (or someone you know) had to wait for something. Tell the story a little at a time, as Hamill does, in order to keep the reader in suspense until the end. Begin by explaining what was being waited for and why it was important. Continue by describing the wait and the emotions experienced as time went by. Use time transitions (see page 151) to help the reader follow your story. Finish by telling how the wait finally ended and how you (or the person you are writing about) felt once it was over.

"Urban Legends"

1. This article suggests that urban legends, Aesop's fables, and morality plays exist in order to teach us lessons. Familiar children's stories such as "Goldilocks and the Three Bears," "Little Red Riding Hood," and "Beauty and the Beast" could be seen as having a similar purpose. Write a paragraph in which you explain the lesson taught by one well-known children's story. You may select one of the stories mentioned, or another story.

2. Have you ever heard a story that you suspect may have been an urban legend? Write a paragraph in which you tell the story and then explain in what ways it seems similar to an urban legend. Refer to the reading to find common characteristics of urban legends that seem to apply to your story.

3. Johnson writes, "We haven't quite given up our need for scary stories." Write an essay in which you tell why, in your opinion, people get a thrill out of being frightened. Provide examples of two or three ways that people seek out scary experiences and what they gain from those experiences.

"Shame"

1. When have you, like Gregory, regretted the way you acted in a particular situation? Perhaps you didn't speak up when someone was being teased, or perhaps you spoke harshly to someone because you were in a bad mood. Write a paragraph that describes the situation and how you acted. Conclude by explaining why you feel you acted wrongly and what you wish you had done instead.

2. Teachers are powerful figures in the lives of children. At times, because of impatience, poor judgment, a misunderstanding, anger—or some other reason—a teacher may hurt a student's feelings. Write a paragraph about a situation you experienced (or observed) in which you believe a teacher acted inappropriately and made a student feel bad. Be sure to explain not only what the teacher did but also how the student was affected.

3. A dictionary defines a word by briefly explaining its meaning. In this article, Dick Gregory defines the word *shame* in a different manner. He describes two incidents in his life in which shame played a central part. Write an essay in which you define a powerful word by narrating one or more events. Some words to consider include "gratitude," "fear," "jealousy," "pride," "joy," "anger," "kindness," and "disappointment." Your central point might be stated something like this: "Two incidents that happened ten years apart taught me the real meaning of _____." Focus on those parts of the incidents that illustrate the meaning of the word. Your essay will be most powerful if you, like Gregory, include significant bits of description and dialogue.

"The Bystander Effect"

1. This article suggests that people act quite differently when they are alone and when they're in a group, or in public. Write a paragraph that contrasts your own behavior when you're alone and when you're in a specific public setting. Examples of public settings might be a party, football game, dance, family gathering, or workplace. The tone of your paragraph could be serious or humorous. Provide lively examples of your behavior to illustrate your points.

2. "The Bystander Effect" is filled with anecdotes of people who stood back when help was needed, preferring to wait for someone else to act. Think of an individual who has acted in the *opposite* way, someone who perceived a need

and quickly offered assistance. The situation might have involved an emergency like the ones mentioned in the article, or it might have concerned a more long-term need, such as an illness or a financial problem. Be specific in describing what the need was and how the individual reacted. Conclude by stating how the situation might have turned out if the individual had not helped.

3. Barkin defines "moral diffusion" as "the lessening of a sense of individual responsibility when someone is a member of a group." Drawing upon your own experience and knowledge of the world, write an essay that gives two examples of moral diffusion at work. For each example, describe what group is involved, how group members decline to take individual responsibility, and what happens as a result. Examples you might use include soldiers who commit war crimes and then say they were "just following orders," students who allow a classmate to be harassed because they don't want to get involved, or neighborhood people who let a park become overrun with trash because it's not their job to pick it up.

"Preview, Read, Write, Recite"

1. Have you ever discovered a technique that significantly improved your performance in something—studying, running, eating healthfully, communicating, saving money, getting housework done? Write a paragraph describing that technique in detail and how it has helped you do a better job. Include vivid examples that contrast your performance before and after discovering this technique. An example of a topic sentence for this paragraph is "By buying certain used items, I have managed to live well on my income and still save a little money each month."

2. Write a paragraph about an aspect of schoolwork that is particularly difficult for you, and one practical idea that might help ease the difficulty. For example, you might find it difficult to write fast enough to take notes during a lecture. A helpful idea might be to tape-record lectures and take notes from the recording. Be specific about why a particular part of schoolwork is a problem for you, and how that difficulty affects your work. Describe experiences from actual classes to illustrate your points.

3. The article explains in a clear, step-by-step manner, how to study effectively. Write an essay which gives similarly clear directions on how to do something. As you write, use time transitions—such as *first, then, later, next,* and *finally* (see page 151)—to make it easy for your reader to follow the steps. For your topic, you might choose a process that you are familiar with and good at yourself. Alternatively, you might have fun describing a step-by-step method for doing something poorly. Here are some possible topics to consider: how to study for a test, how to train a dog, how not to get a job, how to avoid housework.

"Coping with Nervousness"

1. What makes you nervous? What is something you occasionally—or often—need to do that makes your mouth go dry and your knees knock? Write a paragraph, in a serious or humorous vein, about a situation that makes you nervous and how you react to it. Some topics to consider include speaking in public, asking someone for a date, and applying for a job. Provide lots of vivid details so the reader can see and feel your nervousness.

2. Imagine that you were required to give a "how-to" speech on a process that you are very familiar with. What would you choose to talk about? Write a paragraph in which you state your topic, then give clear, step-by-step instructions on how to complete the process. Use time transitions (see page 151) to make your instructions easy to follow.

3. Verderber suggests that people who can master their nervousness, rather than allowing it to control them, will enjoy a sense of accomplishment. Think of a problem that you have faced and overcome. It might be a particular fear, like the one described in the article. Or you may have conquered a problem with a difficult person, overcome a bad habit, or figured out a solution to a problem in your life. Write an essay that explains, first, what problem existed and how it affected you; second, how you decided to deal with the problem; and finally, what happened as a result of your actions and how you felt about what you'd done.

"Compliance Techniques: Getting People to Say Yes"

1. Why do you think that compliance techniques are so often effective? What do they appeal to in the mind of the consumer that is lacking in the more straightforward approach of simply making a product available to those who want to buy it? Write a paragraph that explains a few reasons you think people are so easily influenced by compliance techniques.

2. Have you ever agreed to perform a service or to buy something and then later felt you had been persuaded by a clever, manipulative, or deceptive sales technique? Write a paragraph that describes the process that you and the seller engaged in. Use time transitions (page 151) to make the sequence of events clear to the reader. Explain how you believe you were manipulated into the agreement or purchase.

3. Think of a product you might want to sell or service you might want people to agree to perform. Write an essay that tells how you could accomplish your goal by using three of these four compliance techniques: the foot-in-the-door, the door-in-the-face, the low-ball, and the that's-not-all techniques.

Give a detailed explanation of the steps you would follow in each case. In conclusion, state which technique you believe would work best and why.

"Lizzie Borden"

1. Based on the information presented in the article, write a paragraph that supports one of the following main ideas: "I believe that Lizzie Borden was guilty of the murder of her parents" or "I think there is reason to doubt that Lizzie Borden killed her parents." Explain your thinking, backing up your opinions with evidence from the text.

2. Think of a time you were wrongly suspected of doing something bad. It might have involved anything from breaking a dish when you were a child to committing a crime. Write a paragraph describing that experience. Tell what you were suspected of and what (if any) evidence pointed to you. Were you able to prove you were innocent? How did you feel about being a target of suspicion?

3. The author suggests that a stereotype that existed in Lizzie's day had a very specific effect—that she was found innocent of murder because of it. What are some stereotypes that exist today? How are people of certain ethnic groups, genders, sexual preferences, or economic groups stereotyped? Write an essay in which you explain how you believe certain groups are stereotyped. What effects might occur because people believe those stereotypes?

"Nonverbal Communication"

1. Write a paragraph that describes a time when you were made uncomfortable by another person's nonverbal communication. Tell where the incident occurred, who else was there, and what the relationship was between you and the person whose communication disturbed you. Then describe specifically what the other person did that made you uncomfortable and how you responded. You may also want to refer to the article and describe what kind of personal space was violated by this person's behavior.

2. As you may know, the "personal space zones" described in the article are not the same worldwide. For example, people from some Middle Eastern countries are accustomed to standing close together as they talk, even if do not know one another well. Based on your reading of this article and your knowledge of human nature, how do you think a person from such a country might be perceived in America? How might an American visiting such a

country be viewed? Write a paragraph that describes how people from the two cultures might judge one another based on their nonverbal communication.

3. Think of some people you see often but do not know well—perhaps people like store owners, your mail carrier, school secretaries, a bus driver, or a new neighbor. Based upon their nonverbal communication, what do these people seem to be like? Write an essay in which you introduce each person and tell what impression you have formed of him or her. Be as specific and descriptive as possible as you tell about these people's nonverbal behavior and what it seems to say about them.

"Preindustrial Cities"

1. What do you think would most surprise someone from preindustrial London if he or she could visit a modern city today? Write a paragraph that tells about a few of the changes you think would be most striking to a visitor from preindustrial times. Draw from the article to describe conditions the preindustrial visitor would have been accustomed to, and then contrast those conditions with what the visitor would find today.

2. Are the problems of modern-day city-dwellers significantly different from or pretty much the same as those of people who lived in preindustrial cities? Write a paragraph that supports one of the following main ideas: "The problems of living in cities are basically the same today as in preindustrial times," or "People living in cities today have to deal with problems very different from those of preindustrial people." Use specific examples drawn from the reading and from your knowledge of modern-day city life.

3. What would you consider the biggest attractions of living in a city? What would draw you to live in a small town? What is there about the activities available, the quality of life, economic possibilities, or the like, that makes each attractive? Write an essay that spells out what, for you, would be the best points of city life and small-town life. Use vivid examples of what you could do, see, and experience only in a city, and equally lively examples of what life in a small town would offer. In your final paragraph, tell whether you would choose to live in the city or the town. Be sure to explain why you made the choice you did.

Limited Answer Key

An important note: To strengthen your reading skills, you must do more than simply find out which of your answers are right and which are wrong. You also need to figure out (with the help of this book, the teacher, or other students) *why* you missed the questions you did. By using each of your wrong answers as a learning opportunity, you will strengthen your understanding of the skills. You will also prepare yourself for the review and mastery tests in Part I and the reading comprehension questions in Part II, for which answers are not given here.

ANSWERS TO THE PRACTICES IN PART I

1 Vocabulary in Context

Practice 1

1. Examples: *the phones were constantly ringing, people were running back and forth, several offices were being painted;* b
2. Examples: *the TV is talking to them* and *others can steal their thoughts;* a
3. Examples: *"What sign are you?" "How do you like this place?" "You remind me of someone";* b
4. Examples: *gardening* and *long-distance bike riding;* a
5. Examples: *two heads* and *webbed toes;* c
6. Example: *a spoonful of rice and a few beans;* a
7. Examples: *financial help* and *free medical care;* c
8. Examples: *learning, reasoning, thinking,* and *language;* b
9. Examples: *folded arms* and *lack of eye contact;* a
10. Examples: *accepting a bribe from a customer* and *stealing from an employer;* c

Practice 2

1. embarrasses
2. examine
3. practical
4. begged
5. mercy killing
6. carried
7. opponents
8. arrival
9. customary
10. custom

Practice 3

1. Antonym: *great wealth;* c
2. Antonym: *long;* a
3. Antonym: *openly;* b
4. Antonym: *plainly;* b
5. Antonym: *active;* a
6. Antonym: *clear;* c
7. Antonym: *benefit;* b
8. Antonym: *increase in value;* b
9. Antonym: *careless;* c
10. Antonym: *weak;* c

Practice 4

1. c
2. b
3. a
4. b
5. c
6. a
7. c
8. b
9. c
10. b

2   Main Ideas

Practice 1

1. *Water clocks:* N
   Measuring time before clocks: T
   Ancient inventions: B

2. *Milk in TV ads:* N
   Food in TV ads: T
   Television: B

3. *Business problems:* B
   Using bingo: N
   Reducing absenteeism: T

4. *Human history:* B
   Early societies: T
   Hunting societies: N

Practice 2

Group 1

a. SD	c. T
b. SD	d. MI

Group 2

a. SD	c. SD
b. MI	d. T

Group 3

a. T	c. MI
b. SD	d. SD

Group 4

a. MI	c. T
b. SD	d. SD

Practice 3

1. *Topic:* c   *Main idea:* b
2. *Topic:* c   *Main idea:* a
3. *Topic:* a   *Main idea:* d
4. *Topic:* d   *Main idea:* b

Practice 4

1. 1	3. 1
2. 2	4. 2

Practice 5

1. 1	4. 1, 5
2. 4	5. 2
3. 2	

Practice 6

1. 2
2. 1

3   Supporting Details

Practice 1 (Wording of answers may vary)

1. *Main idea:* . . . discourage TV watching
   and encourage reading.
   1. Have only one TV set, and place it in
      the family room.
   2. Connect reading with eating.
   3. Don't put a TV set in a child's
      bedroom.

2. *Main idea:* . . . are transmitted to people
   in one of three ways:
   1. Direct transmission through bodily
      contact with an infected person
      a. Passing a cold along by a kiss
      b. Transmitting herpes through sexual
         contact
   2. Indirect transmission through air, dust,
      water, food, or anything else touched
      by an infected person
      a. Catching flu by drinking from a
         glass used by someone who has the
         flu
      b. Catching a cold by breathing air
         into which someone with a cold
         has sneezed
   3. Transmission by animals and insects
      a. Spread of yellow fever by
         mosquito bite
      b. Transmission of microbes to
         people by flies landing on food

Practice 2 (Wording of answers may vary)

1. Introduce yourself
   Refer to physical setting
   Ask a complimentary question
   Seek direct information

2. Adopt a written code of ethics
   Run values programs
   Screen potential employees for honesty
      Interviewer's questions
      Written "honesty" exam

Practice 3

1. c
2. b

Practice 4 (Examples may vary.)

1. . . . acting out of concern for another person, without expectation of reward.
   Ex.—A little girl shares half her modeling clay with two friends who say they do not have enough.

2. Passive listening—trying to make sense out of a speaker's remarks without being able to interact with the speaker
   Ex.—Students listen to an instructor's lecture without having the chance to ask questions.

4   Implied Main Ideas/Central Point

Practice 1

Group 1	Group 3
c	b

Group 2	Group 4
b	d

Practice 2

1. b   3. d
2. c   4. c

Practice 3 (Wording of answers may vary.)

1. People oppose capital punishment for different reasons.
2. There are benefits to watching television.
3. Many commonly held beliefs about sleepwalking are not true.
4. Being an only child is not as great a privilege as people think it is.

Practice 4

Central point: In fact, the days of a housewife in nineteenth-century America were spent in harsh physical labor.

Practice 5

Central point: In virtually every way imaginable, life is more difficult for poor people.

5   Relationships I

Practice 1 (Answers may vary.)

1. also   4. First of all
2. For one thing 5. Finally
3. In addition

Practice 2 (Answers may vary.)

1. After   4. before
2. Then   5. while
3. during

Practice 3 (Wording of answers may vary.)

A. Main idea heading: Reasons high schools should require uniforms
1. Saves money for both parents and children
2. Keeps students from having to spend time worrying about clothes
3. Makes divisions between rich and poor students less obvious

B. Main idea heading: . . . aging process
1. Our bodies simply wear out.
3. Our body chemistry loses its delicate balance.
4. Our bodies, with age, reject some of their own tissues.

Practice 4 (Wording of answers may vary.)

Main idea heading: The 1960s in America contained significant events.
1. 1963—the assassination of President Kennedy
2. 1965—urban riots in black ghettos
3. 1968—anti-war protests against the American presence in Vietnam

Practice 5 (Wording of answers may vary.)

Main idea heading: Steps to remembering your dreams
2. Put a pen and notebook near your bed.
3. Turn off alarm so you can wake up gradually.
4. Write down the dream immediately.

Practice 6

1. b   6. b
2. a   7. a
3. b   8. b
4. a   9. a
5. a   10. b

6   Relationships II

Practice 1 (Answers may vary.)
1. such as   4. For example
2. For instance   5. To illustrate
3. including

Practice 2
A. *boycott*; definition—1; example—2
B. *Shaping*; definition—1; example 1—2;
   example 2—10

Practice 3 (Answers may vary.)
1. Similarly   4. In a similar manner
2. like   5. Just as
3. in the same way

Practice 4 (Answers may vary.)
1. Although   4. in spite of
2. in contrast   5. However
3. but

Practice 5
A. Comparison: mysteries and science
   fiction
B. Contrast: federal government and
   journalists

Practice 6 (Answers may vary.)
1. Because   4. Consequently
2. as a result   5. therefore
3. Since

Practice 7
A. Meditation: cause
   Decrease or elimination of drug use:
   effect
   Cardiovascular improvements: effect
   Stress relief: effect

B. Daydreaming: effect
   Boring jobs: cause
   Deprivation: cause
   Discharge of hostile feelings: cause
   Way to plan for future: cause

Practice 8
1. c   6. b
2. b   7. c
3. a   8. a
4. c   9. c
5. a   10. b

7   Fact and Opinion

Practice 1
1. F   6. F
2. O   7. O
3. F   8. F
4. O   9. F
5. O   10. O

Practice 2
1. O   6. F
2. F   7. O
3. F+O   8. F
4. F+O   9. F+O
5. F   10. O

Practice 3
A. 1. F   B. 6. F
   2. F   7. F+O
   3. F+O   8. F+O
   4. F   9. F
   5. F+O   10. F+O

Practice 4
A. 1. O   B. 6. F
   2. F+O   7. F
   3. O   8. F
   4. F   9. F+O
   5. F   10. F+O

Practice 5
1. F   3. F
2. F+O   4. F+O

8   Inferences

Practice 1
1. c   3. c
2. d   4. d

Practice 2
A. 1. d   C. 9. c
   2. b   10. b
   3. a   11. c
   4. b   12. b
B. 5. c   D. 13. b
   6. b   14. a
   7. a   15. b
   8. c   16. b

Practice 3
A. 1, 4, 6
B. 1, 4, 6
C. 1, 3, 5
D. 1, 3, 6

Practice 4
1, 4, 5, 6, 9

9 Purpose and Tone

Practice 1
1. I   6. I
2. P   7. E
3. E   8. P
4. P   9. E
5. I   10. I

Practice 2
1. b
2. c
3. a

Practice 3
A. 1. admiring   B. 6. straightforward
2. sympathetic   7. sarcastic
3. critical   8. threatening
4. objective   9. self-pitying
5. ironic   10. sympathetic

Practice 4
1. h   4. f
2. d   5. g
3. e

Practice 5
1. b   4. a
2. a   5. b
3. b

10 Argument

Practice 1
1. a. S   7. a. P
  b. P   b. S
2. a. S   c. S
  b. P   d. S
3. a. S   8. a. S
  b. P   b. P
  c. S   c. S
4. a. S   9. a. S
  b. S   b. P
  c. P   c. S
5. a. P   10. a. S
  b. S   b. P
  c. S   c. S
6. a. S
  b. P
  c. S
  d. S

Practice 2
1. a, d, e   4. a, c, e
2. a, c, f   5. b, d, f
3. a, c, f

Practice 3
1. c
2. c

Practice 4
1. d
2. a

Practice 5
1. b
2. a

Practice 6
1. b
2. d

ANSWERS TO THE PRACTICES IN PART III

3   Propaganda

Practice 1
2, 5

Practice 2
2, 4

Practice 3
2, 3

Practice 4
1, 5

Practice 5
2, 4

Practice 6
1, 5

Practice 7
1. b
2. a
3. c

4   More About Argument

Practice 1
1. 2
2. 1
3. 2

Practice 2
1. 1
2. 3
3. 3

Practice 3
1. 3
2. 2
3. 1

Practice 4
1. 1
2. 2
3. 3

Practice 5
1. 3
2. 3
3. 2

Practice 6
1. 2
2. 1
3. 1

Acknowledgments

Barkin, Dorothy. "The Bystander Effect." Copyright © 1991 by Trend Publications. Reprinted by permission.

Barry, Dave. Selections on pages 292 and 318. Reprinted by permission.

Cosby, Bill. Selection on page 298. From *Love and Marriage*. Copyright © 1989 by Bill Cosby. Reprinted by permission of Doubleday, a division of Bantam, Doubleday, Dell Publishing Group, Inc.

Dunayer, Joan. "Here's to Your Health." Reprinted by permission.

Edwards, Gayle. "Preview, Read, Write, Recite." Reprinted by permission.

Ellerbee, Linda. Excerpt from *Move On*. Reprinted by permission of The Putnam Publishing Group. Copyright © 1991 by Linda Ellerbee.

Ephron, Delia. "Coping with Santa Claus," from *Funny Sauce* by Delia Ephron. Copyright © 1982, 1983, 1986 by Delia Ephron. Used by permission of Viking Penguin, a division of Penguin Books USA Inc.

Grasha, Anthony F. "Nonverbal Communication," from *Practical Applications of Psychology*, 3rd ed., pp. 248-250. Copyright © 1987 by Anthony F. Grasha. Reprinted by permission of Addison-Wesley Educational Publishers.

Gregory, Dick. "Shame," from *Nigger: An Autobiography*. Copyright © 1964 by Dick Gregory Enterprises, Inc. Used by permission of Dutton Signet, a division of Penguin Books USA Inc.

Hamill, Pete. "The Yellow Ribbon." Reprinted by permission.

Johnson, Beth. "Urban Legends." Reprinted by permission.

Kellmayer, John. "Students in Shock." Reprinted by permission.

Landers, Ann. "College Student Deplores the Drinking Around Her." Reprinted from the *Philadelphia Inquirer.*

Light, Donald, Suzanne Keller, and Craig Calhoun. "Communities and Cities," from *Sociology*, 5th ed. Copyright © 1989 by Alfred A. Knopf, Inc. Reprinted by permission of McGraw-Hill, Inc.

Logan, Paul. "Rowing the Bus." Reprinted by permission.

Martin, James Kirby, et. al. "Lizzie Borden," from *America and Its People*, 2nd ed. Copyright © 1993 by James Kirby Martin, Randy Roberts, Steven Mintz, Linda O. McMurry, and James H. Jones. Reprinted by permission of Addison-Wesley Educational Publishers.

Papalia, Diane E., and Sally Wendkos Olds. "How Parents' Child-Rearing Styles Affect Their Children," from *Psychology*, 2nd ed. Copyright © 1988 by McGraw-Hill, Inc. Reprinted by permission of McGraw-Hill, Inc.

Popkin, Roy. "Night Watch." Originally appeared in *The National Observer*. Reprinted by permission of Dow Jones & Company, Inc. Copyright © 1964 by Dow Jones & Company, Inc. All rights reserved worldwide. Also reprinted with permission from the September 1965 *Reader's Digest*.

Rhodes, Richard. Excerpt from *A Hole in the World*. Copyright © 1990 by Richard Rhodes. Published by Simon and Schuster.

Roberts, Paul. Excerpt from "How to Say Nothing in 500 Words." From *Understanding English* by Paul Roberts. Copyright © 1958 by Paul Roberts. Reprinted by permission of Addison-Wesley Educational Publishers.

Robinson, Edwin Arlington. "Richard Cory," from *The Children of the Night*. Published in New York by Charles Scribner's Sons, 1897.

Sandburg, Carl. "Grass," from *Cornhuskers*. Copyright © 1918 by Holt, Rinehart and Winston, Inc. and renewed 1946 by Carl Sandburg. Reprinted by permission of Harcourt Brace & Company.

Sherry, Mary. "In Praise of the F Word." Used with the permission of Mary Sherry.

Sifford, Darrell. "How People Rise and Fall." Reprinted by permission from *The Philadelphia Inquirer*.

Stark, Rodney. "Preindustrial Cities," from *Sociology*, 5th ed. Copyright © 1994 by Wadsworth, Inc. Reprinted by permission of the publisher.

Taylor, Shelley E., Letitia Anne Peplau, and David O. Sears. "Compliance Techniques," from *Social Psychology*, 8th ed. Copyright © 1994 by Prentice-Hall. Reprinted by permission of Prentice-Hall, Inc.

Verderber, Rudolph E. "Disclosing Feelings," from *Communicate!* 6th ed. Copyright © 1990 by Wadsworth, Inc. Reprinted by permission of the publisher.

Verderber, Rudolph E. "Presenting Your Speech," from *Communicate!* 6th ed. Copyright © 1990 by Wadsworth, Inc. Reprinted by permission of the publisher.

Wilkins, Roger. "I Became Her Target." Reprinted by permission.

Index